ADVANCED RACQUETBALL

STEVE BO KEELEY

Author of The Complete Book of Racquetball

ISBN-13: 978-1501072239

ISBN-10: 1501072234

This book was printed   in the United States of America.

First Edition

1 2 3 4 5 6 7 8 9 10

Keeley, Steve Bo
Advanced Racquetball —1st ed.

Published by Service Press

Cover photo of 'Smokin' Hogan' with permission from the Marty Hogan collection.

To order additional copies of this book contact:
Amazon.com or bokeely@hotmail.com

Andy Hawthorne forehand. (Freddy Ramirez)

DEDICATION

To the champions and those who dare - Match point ... Roll out!

Paola Longoria backhand. (Roby Partovich)

Testimonials

Keeley is the 'Holder' of all instructional titles. He sees angles and shots I never dreamed of. — *Marty Hogan, Six-Time World Champion*

Wonderful instruction- just like he played the game! — *Charlie Brumfield, King of Racquetball*

Keeley goes inside *Advanced Racquetball* to make learning it fast and fun. This is sensuous instruction. - *Brett Elkins, LA Racquetball, WOR Hall of Fame Committee*

Keeley is the best sport writer on racquetball, and will kindle an urge to old time attitude in the modern game. — *Cliff Swain, Six-Time World Champion*

Joe Sobek may have invented racquetball, but Keeley wrote it from day one. This book is an exceptional collection of articles for achieving players. — *Jim Spittle, early Pro*

Steve Keeley is one of the most accredited racquetball authors in the sport. His playing career, combined with his many years of instruction, give him a unique insight to all elements of the sport. I've enjoyed his clinics. - Jason Mannino, President, International Racquetball Tour

Reading this is like taking a fast step into the future for an aspiring player. — *Bo Champagne, Six State Champion, The 'Spirit of Racquetball'*

Keeley' s ability to seek and bring out the best in anything he writes on sport is unparalleled. He is one of the original grand masters of the game and unquestionably the greatest writer and historian. With this book, Steve has accomplished the impossible – A sequel to his best-selling *Complete Book of Racquetball* after forty years! — *Dave Fleetwood, Touring Pro*

Keeley taught me the backhand frisbee stroke and I love reading Keeley on racquetball. — *Hank Marcus, WOR Director*

Steve Bo Keeley is a gift to the game with either racquet or pen. He has already written the best-selling book on the sport, *The Complete Book of Racquetball*, and this *Advanced* sequel is another victory. — *Rick Frey PhD, Sport Psychologist*

The author is a champion of sport, an acute observer of racquetball, a historian and superb analyst of the game, who relates it better than anyone in the world.
— *Cathy Williams, Top Four Pro, Cofounder WPRO Tour*

Interesting and entertaining instruction, as always.   — *Doug Ganim, US Open Founder*

Steve Bo Keeley wrote the ultimate instructional The Complete Book of Racquetball and now the *Advanced Racquetball* with his drumbeat instruction is sure to mold future champions in international competition.
— *Charlie Garfinkle, 12 Hall of Fames, Touring Pro*

No one can compete at his level of writing the game. None surpassed his mind on the court. — *Jerry Hilecher, National Champion, Hall of Fame*

Steve has put his advanced teaching excitingly into a Tour de Force.
— *Rich Wagner, NRC Top 8*

This tome will become a doorstop on every exhibition court around the world for players to refer to during time-outs for instructions to win.   — *Passin' Through, Early Pro*

You've always been a great player and coach. I remember our matches and clinics together. — *Davey Bledsoe, World Champion 1977, Hall of Fame*

Keeley's writing is gifted and excellent.   — *Andrew Hollan, Sport Historian*

Steve Keeley has been the best teacher and writer of the game since we split matches throughout the Golden Era of racquetball.
— *Steve Serot, National Doubles Champion, National Junior Champ, Hall of Fame*

Yet I still recall how he held forth for an hour or so before a group of Vermont instructors on the dynamics of the grip. He had more faith in himself than the average movie hero, and he wrote his own script as he went along.
— *Art Shay, Official Olympic Photographer, Racquetball Hall of Fame*

Steve Keeley has helped my racquetball career going all the way back to when I first met him. After drubbing me in a first round match he gave me some court coverage advice that was simple, and really helped me back in the 21 point days. The advice? "You can get to more shots, you have to practice getting to more shots!" Since then his racquetball writings have influenced my teaching and coaching. The book, *The Complete Book of Racquetball*, still sits on my shelf, and I used it when I began teaching group lessons 35 years ago. His Mickey Mouse Theory is an example of simple advice that works. Before

7

I learned how to say "bounce, hit" courtesy to Tim Galway, I learned, "M-I-C-K-E-Y-M-O-U-S-E" as a mantra to repeat in my mind during tough matches, courtesy of Steve Keeley.
- *Jim Winterton, USA Team Coach, Hall of Fame 1999, USOC Coach of the year, 95, 99,03*

Ever since the *Complete Book of Racquetball* (1976) Steve 'Doc Bo' Keeley has written eloquent, humorous, and hugely informative articles and books on the techniques, strategies and development of racquetball. Anyone wishing to learn something about this fascinating sport will do well to get armed with this book.
  - *Bo Champagne, Six States & Multi-Regionals Champion, The 'Spirit of Racquetball'*

Here is a master author and player bringing out the topics of a very large span of instruction and history in our sport called racquetball. No one knows it better than the master himself. Bo is the racquetball fountain, where the old and the present come to drink for research, stories and documentaries written by this master.
– *Jeff Leon, South American RB Pioneer, 1989 World Masters Champion, 2013 World Golden Masters Champion, Mr. International Racquetball*

I thought the *Complete Book of Racquetball* was the best racquetball book ever written, but Keeley has surpassed the standard he set with it and his instructional and historical series he's written over the last ten years. The racquets, balls, and scoring system have all changed but forty years later Keeley is still the undisputed champ of racquetball authors!
– *Scott Hirsch, Founder Legends Pro Tour*

Bo Keeley's writing of the 'good ol' days' of racquetball has been inspiring. A wealth of information, especially the 'gory' details from knowing all the players.
  - *Debbie Tisinger-Moore, Indoor and Outdoor World Champion, Hall of Fame 2013*

Keeley's racquetball audience extends off the court into the many books and articles he's written over the decades, about the sport, about the players, and about 'life-after-21'. He appeals as much off as he did on the court to C players to the world champions. Three cheers for Keeley!!!   – *Judy Turlington, Women Early Pro*

Part of Keeley's ability to think 'outside the racquetball box' came from his unique approach to life. While he invented some of the early strategies and pioneered the shots of early racquetball, it was a simple extension of what he did off the court. Likewise, he could step into any court anywhere with any racquet, or hitting with a bleach bottle or book he always carried, and compete with a smile and a lesson for everyone.
  - *Mike Zeitman, 3-Time National Doubles Champion (with three different partners)*

SBK's enlightening, pleasurable, and in-depth communications revitalizes Racquetball memories for veterans and serves to inform subsequent generations of our heritage.
  – *Gordon Kelly, World Seniors Champion, 5 USRA Regional titles, MI Hall of Fame*

Steve Bo Keeley is simply the best writer on racquetball, period. He's Marty, Kane, and Sudsy. Other great players have taken a shot at writing how-to stories or personal accounts of memorable matches, but Keeley is a professional writer (and player) whose love of the game spans over 40. Whether you're a novice, a pro, or a fan, you can't do any better than Bo on Racquetball.   – *John Bramston, Memphis Sports Journalist*

He speaks from forty years of experience, and teaching, and writing. There are other racquetball grandmasters, but none so seasoned.   – *Cathy Luchetti, Player, Author*

Since day one, Steve Bo Keeley's tireless effort to put so much instruction, people and history together is fantastic. His personal connection to so much of these games provides insights as in no other sports.
   – *Eric Campbell, Age Groups Multi-National Champion in Racquetball & Paddleball*

Steve was a great pioneer for the sport. One of only a few that saw it all from the beginning and has kept track of the players, strokes and strategies from alpha to omega.
                    - *Doug Cohen, Pro in the Golden Era*

After our many years together, traveling on the early racquetball circuit, and stints of writing, I have read everything he's ever written. The *Advanced Book* is his greatest contribution to this sport I love.
          – *Jim Schatz, LA Pro and Coach, World Free Throw Champion Qualifier*

There were a couple better players through history, but Keeley's writing shines through.
                 – *Brad Kruger, Canadian National Three-Sport Champion*

In ten minutes you'll be absorbed. The rest is in the book.
                 – *Rodan Venice, Former Pro and Attorney*

Charlie Brumfield: King or Racquetball, 22-Time National and World Champion. (John Foust)

Contents

Strokes

13

Service

Shots

Tournament

Coaches, Camps, Lessons

Drills

21

Conditioning

Equipment

Personality

History

24

Michelle Key draws a bead on a ball at the 2013 WOR Summer Legends. (Mike Augustin)

Marty Hogan Foreword

I have known Steve Keeley for most of my life. Almost forty years ago I hopped in to the back of an old Cadillac and headed to the Racquetball Mecca of San Diego with Keeley. My life and my game has never been the same! During our time as transplant roommates, Keeley mentored me and I learned more about racquetball strategy, conditioning and how to win and behave on court from Keeley than I have from anyone else before or since.

San Diego was full of dozens of famous racquetball characters but no doubt Steve Keeley was the most interesting of them and not simply because he was one of the two best racquetball players in the world at that time. Keeley is truly brilliant, completely honest and a genuine free spirit who can play and teach racquetball in a way that is as easy to understand as it is effective.

Keeley's strategy as a racquetball player was advanced beyond any other. He was the first to incorporate a true offense and defense into the game. His defensive of perfecting the ceiling shot, the high-z and the around-the-world ball are still staples of today's game. His offensive strategy of ending every rally with any opportunity to hit a kill shot is the model today's top players use. Keeley was the only player of his generation able to put the ball away with the down-the-line, cross court, pinch or reverse pinch with his backhand or forehand from any place on the court. In many ways he had more influence on the modern game than any other player. I would rate Keeley as one of the five best racquetball players I ever played and as the best paddleball player I ever stepped on the court with.

Keeley's play was only exceeded by his unmatched ability to teach the game. He pioneered the racquetball camp concept and gave some of the best racquetball clinics throughout North and South America in the 70s and 80s. When Keeley returned to give clinics in conjunction with the Legends Tour a few years back, his lessons were as informative and well attended as ever. In addition to the thousands Keeley has taught directly and the thousands more they passed those lessons on to, he reached a couple hundred thousand other racquetball players with his best-selling book, *The Complete Book of Racquetball*. It was not only the best-selling racquetball book ever but the best written to date. I suspect only Keeley could and will top it with this sequel.

Marty Hogan
Six-time World Champion

Sudsy Monchik Introduction

I play a no-nonsense game, like a no-nonsense guy, and that's why I love *Advanced Racquetball*. We pros call the author "Doc Racquetball" because he cures your game. There's something for every player at every level, and the good doctor is in, so step up to your shots.

His assistants are the best I've faced on the court: Swain, Hogan, Ray, Gonzalez, Mannino, Brysman, the Pecks … and the current ones I'm set to face. Imagine a tournament of all the top stars from all the years playing and instructing under one cover – in your hands.

Play hard and have fun with this book!

Sudsy Monchik
Five-time World Champion

Cliff Swain Introduction

My first meeting with Doc Keeley was memorable. Sweat dripped on the Coral Springs Quadrangle Club locker room floor after beating pro Jason Mannino in a 2003 $10,000 winner-take-all challenge. I sat analyzing my game when an angular man in a Legends shirt appeared by my side. "The pivot of your game today is short-hopping the serve return," he kibitzed. In a second, he'd pricked the only flaw through six world titles. I practiced, and short-hopped to many more tournament wins. I think the kill is the coolest shot, and that was Keeley's big gun in beating every early national champion.

I would like to have played him. He wrote the best-selling *Complete Book of Racquetball* and coached around the world while promising an advanced book. Now, *Advanced Racquetball* draws upon an unmatched think tank to deliver new techniques and game-winning formulas. A rapid-sequence camera puts you inside the stars' minds and bodies. See you between the pages!

Cliff Swain
Six-time World Champion

Steve Bo Keeley Preface

Forty years ago, *The Complete Book of Racquetball* took the young sport by storm. 200,000 copies sold. The shots, serves and strategies became those of the Golden Era and beyond because, at the time, there were no other proper sources and coaches were few. The 'History' I wrote in the first chapter has become the history of the game as reported in nearly every subsequent publication.

Now, this sequel, *Advanced Racquetball* brings the players, coaches, fans and aficionados up to date with the newly evolved shots, serves, strategies, and my penchant for History perseveres. This book is entirely different from the first primer. This aims at advanced players to Pro level. It is larger, with more pictures and graphics. It is more anecdotal than the first, and you'll find many old and modern pros on the pages demonstrating their nuances.

I played professionally from the first pro stop in 1973 through 1980 as the ranked #2-4 most of the time, with a Canadian national singles title, hundreds of satellite championships, and six national singles paddleball championships. I was the first money

sponsored player, and had the first apparel contract with Converse, sporting dual colored 'Chucks' around the world. I established the game's first clinics and camps, and introduced the sport to Latin America with the first clinic tour. There are hundreds of published racquetball articles. My forte was, and is, teaching

With this background, I present *Advanced Racquetball.* It's divided into ten Parts: Strategy, Strokes, Service, Shots, Rally, Tournament, Coaches, Drills, Conditioning, Equipment, and progresses into the more anecdotal Personality and History.

This is an oversize book to read in any order you like. Skip around the longer articles, or to ones that suit your game. You'll encounter guest pieces by pros like Hogan, Swain,

Coach Winterton, Muehleisen, Brumfield, and others. You'll hear 'Pros Speak from the Box' from Sudsy, Robinson, Beltran, Rojas, Hawthorne, Pratt, Rajsich, Gudinas, Paraiso, Acosta, Cassino, Wachtel, Peck, Hilecher, Ellis, Gonzalez, Bledsoe, Ray and Hawkes. There are over 800 pages with 400 photos. This is the most complete book on advanced racquetball ever written.

Steve Bo Keeley
Miami
January 1, 2015

Strategy

Indoor or outdoor the strategy is serve and shoot. Ben Croft at 2011 WOR Nationals. (Mike Augustin)

The Big Game
Galvanized Racquetball

Keeley with John Foust

The racquetball Big Game is drive serve and shoot, which I call blitz racquetball. The first blitz player in 1974 when we were housemates betting mile runs on the outcome of his blitz vs. my conservative game- the 'year of the pivot' when Marty Hogan, ridiculed for his deep cannon stroke that tended to loosely fly all over the court- was Smokin' Hogan after he honed the powerful stroke and grew facial hair.

The reason Hogan was the Big Game firstborn is he was the first with the physical power and grace to allow it; the previous champs Bill Schmidtke, Bud Muehleisen, Charley Brumfield and I were tennis shod string beans who 'pushed' the ball around the court and a tediously effective strategy of waiting in prey for the opponent to error in 3-10 shot rallies, and then the final stroke.

Hogan was the first to *force* the error with booming drive serves, or his 142mph service return while the rest of us were clocked in the mid-70s at 110mph.

A cascade of factors enlivened the Big Game in the ensuing decade.

The mid-70s ball got so fast that we judged one acceptable if a ceiling shot didn't bounce over the back wall into the gallery and they started netting the upper decks. It was like substituting a hardball for a softball without moving back the outfield fence, and the result was the fans descended into the courts to imitate the pros blasting serves and shots.

The late 70s fitness craze spawned court clubs with the back racquetball courts filled with gym equipment, and bruisers strutted out the gyms and onto the racquetball courts to explode the Small Game.

In a blink, Power Racquetball of serve and shoot evolved new players and play.

The first Ektelon Contra big-head racquet in 1984 reinforced the power game, squatter players took to the courts, strokes abbreviated to rapid loops, and strong junior players started hitting the ball at 150mph.

It so happened that year the Big Game was locked in forever by a match rule change from 21-points to 15 per game, with an 11-point tiebreaker. This guaranteed national champs to eternity using a big head with serve and shoot strategy, to blitz anyone in streaks without fear of fatigue.

34

Racquetball as it was invented and intended by Joe Sobek in Connecticut, pioneered by Carl Loveday, Bud Muehleisen and Charley Brumfield at the Pacific Paddleball Association court, and developed at San Diego Mel Gorham's Mecca became a travesty in one season.

The sport shifted from aerobic to anaerobic.

The next alignment for the Big Game was the 1980's side glass and often front glass at tournament courts that guaranteed a seeded Blitzer need only breeze through the early rounds on solid wall back courts to make the semi's aquarium where his Big Game had a 5-point advantage in games to 15 points.

The One-Serve Rule of 1994 tried to divert the cavalier ace... or did it? The elite players overnight ciphered and experimented in the next tournament to discover that the attacking serves when they were not fatigued was the *only* winning strategy.

The axe was lengthened by a 1997 USRA rule change to allow the oversized frames to extend to 22" long.

What mutated sweaty chess to a blitz racquets? The associations and sponsors sped the sport to make it easier for youngsters, seniors and females to play the Big Game like pros. That is the racquetball evolution of ball and racquet, serve and return, forehand and backhand, player physique and psychology, and strategy in a nutshell.

How did the ousted pioneer champs react? All-night hashes at private courts across the country and shared at tournaments produced countless variations of new strokes, serves and strategies, but nothing jibed. The greatest old-timer, Brumfield, hung on for two years with warmed over gamesmanship and a new crack ace. The aging champs' bodies and personalities couldn't bear the Big Game and they curtsied off the courts to the new champs Mike Yellen, Dave Peck, Jerry Hilecher and Bret Harnett.

The first operant serve and shooter I met after Hogan was John Foust, who as a kid had multiple corrective leg surgeries and retains a gimp. His attacking strategy in a match at the Denver Sporting Club, home of early big tourneys, was such a shock that I would have lost at the peak of my career had not a patented backhand wallpaper serve eked a win. Foust wrote to me later to reciprocate for the wallpaper that he added to the arsenal, and to explain his Big Game. I realized he had sketched the perfect instruction that applies to the modern blitz of serve and shoot for all players:

> I had a foot in two racquetball worlds, so to speak. One was able-bodied that you're used to playing, and the other in a wheelchair. In the early 80s, the wheelchair game was coming on and though I was legally handicapped from polio in youth, I never dreamed of myself as that. I managed the Denver Sporting Club and was a consistent able-bodied winner in A division, and once won the 25+ Open Regional. Luke St. Onge, the USRA executive

director, asked me to play in the wheelchair division alongside my normal event, and I replied, 'I spent time in a wheel chair when young, and may again when I'm old, but I don't want to in-between.' However, Luke persevered.

It was bizarre going from the regular events where I was perceived as the 'good guy' with the game leg who beat most the field, to the wheelchair division where I was the 'villain' because after the match I could rise and walk with a limp from the chair. I grimaced before each match at having to approach another player to beg his chair. I was third and fourth ranked in the world from about '85-87 by virtue of my able-bodied racquet skills, but

De La Rosa plays the big game at the 2014 Tournament of Champions. (Mike Augustin)

always lost in the finals to one of the top two wheelchair champs (Chip Parmelly or Jim Leatherman) because of their familiarity with the chair- Understand that the chair is equipment, just like the glove, racquet and shoe.

After that, I entered only able bodies tournaments and walking into the court feeling as if I could win until proven otherwise. I practiced and taught myself how to kill the ball from everywhere. Defense wasn't my strong suit. The longer the ball was in play, the better chance I was going to lose the rally on a dope shot of which I simply could not get to. I relied on the drive serve to start the ball low into play to force the shooting game.

The blitzkrieg won the 1983 AARA regional championship in the 25+ division in going through three Open players to the finals. That was my biggest personal racquetball accomplishment- I beat three players who were very good. The closest I came after that to winning anything of substance was the Tournament of the America's in Santa Cruz, Bolivia in 1988. It was the first of five times I was part of the U.S. National Team. At that time, although not originally qualified as part of the team as a true player, I had the ability to score points for the team as a manager /photographer /low level coach. It was clear early on no one from the others teams were going to give me any credit- why should they? Not like anyone in Bolivia knew who I was, or had a resume to stand on. I completely understood. In the long run it worked to my advantage in getting to play. I made it to the semi's before getting beaten by a better player. The U.S. team was gracious enough to vote me to accept the Championship trophy.

Three parts to my game come to mind in any success I've had at racquetball. I felt I could serve with the best of them. That was my great equalizer and something I put a lot of effort into. I had the ball, I knew what I was going to do, and was a master of disguise about where. Drive serves were my forte. I used them on a first and second serve. It wasn't until later in my playing days I learned the value of a lob. I hated lobs.

In the event an opponent was able to retrieve my drive, I did the best I could to put it away quickly. If I couldn't serve 3-4 untouchable serves in a game I was toast. For the most part I did. My able-bodied style is to shoot the ball from everywhere, because the longer the rally the less chance I have to get to the opponent's shot because of my game leg. I practiced hundreds of hours shooting from every conceivable court position, and to drive serve to earn weak returns.

In the rally anticipation was key. Unlike a Hogan I didn't have all the tools necessary to play a complete game. I was good at the bait and switch. If focused in, I knew before my opponent what he was going to do. They would say, 'You're a lot faster than I thought,' a kind compliment but not true. I was quick in a short space. It appeared I was fast- smoke and mirrors.

My forehand was strong if I had time to set up. However, with a weak left leg, it was difficult to transfer weight. Hogan, as it appeared to me the visual learner, hit a lot of forehands off his back foot. I had no choice but to do the same and was comforted by the fact that's what he did well. On the other hand, a backhand was my natural shot with a stronger than normal right leg, I could step in, transfer weight, hit, and do what needed to be done. And, because of the situation, I moved to the backhand side much more easily. My backhand was something I visualized as being a lot more like it happened in the real world as opposed to my mental world where I was moving like everyone else. I think they call that dreaming.

Based on how Hogan whipped me, Foust had lectured me, and how fresh players came on strong with the Big Game in the late 1980's, I revamped my teaching style. The traditional instruction learned from Bud Muehleisen and expanded in *The Complete book of Racquetball* taught to aim for the bulls-eye, and later add increments of power. Now I teach first the power killshots from any position on the court, then the drive serve, and slowly hone into the target. The learning curve of blitz is just one year given a strong young body and daily hour's practice and another hour of game time. As the errors are dropped out of the attack, and greased by confidence, by year two a dedicated athlete may become an open player, and in another a pro.

The greatest upsets throughout racquetball history have been blitz serves and shootouts beginning in 1977 with Davy Bledsoe over Hogan, in 1983 Mike Yellen using the big head Contra over Hogan with his contract autograph model, and topples by Sudsy, Cliff Swain and King Kane all owed to the Big Game school.

Today the Big Game is the only game in town.

Give author John Foust a hand for the Big Game.

Scorecard Strategy

Brad Kruger

Two years before I had even thought of turning pro, an aging court warrior handed me a piece of advice. It was a note, scratched onto a napkin in ballpoint, and was barely legible. It read:

> *'Server: Shoot aggressively/retrieve conservatively –*
> *Receiver: Retrieve aggressively/shoot conservatively.'*

He promised that if I followed these rules, my game would improve four or five points … overnight.

Of course, I didn't believe him. Four or five points overnight? C'mon. I figured him for the type to be attracted to rooms with white walls, and maybe not just racquetball courts.

But anything scratched onto a napkin in ballpoint deserves a try. So I tried to prove him wrong. And I couldn't. By changing my personality between serving and receiving, my scores improved.

The key to his advice lies hidden in racquetball's scoring system. Amazingly, only a handful of players, and most of the pros, take advantage of it.

What the pros and that handful realize is that making mistakes when serving does not affect the score. Making mistakes when receiving not only affects the score, but hurts you.

By taking advantage of that knowledge, your game can improve immensely, like the aging court warrior promised, overnight.

Think of your average game to fifteen. How many shots do you skip in the receiver's position? A rough average is six, maybe seven shots. Well, that's half a game right there . . . given away! And the only reason your score stays close to your opponent's is that he has been making the same errors. Cut out those errors, and watch your scores improve!

In order to do it overnight, begin thinking of yourself as two different people as you play. And to understand why, you should know the secret behind racquetball's scoring card.

How the Score Is Affected Differently

Think of competitive racquetball as a race to 15 (put on your track shoes!). Whether pass shots are your specialty, or if you're a mean, lean killing machine, anything that raises your score closer to 15 is a friend; anything slowing it down is a foe. The first person to reach that far-off number wins.

Hall of Fame (1997) Executive Director and chief referee of the 1970s NRC tour Chuck Leve also developed the first racquetball ranking system for 'fair pro draws'. (US RB Museum)

As server, if you win a rally, you make a point. But if you lose the rally, you do not lose a point. You change positions and become the receiver, and the scorecard is not affected.

The receiver is affected oppositely. If he wins the rally, the score does not change. He only changes positions and becomes server. And if he loses the rally, his opponent gains a point.

On the scorecard, then, at best, the server has a positive effect on his scorecard; that is, he wins a point. At worst, he has a neutral effect on his scorecard.

The receiver, at best, however, has only a neutral effect on his score. At worst, he loses a point.

On the scorecard, the server has everything to gain and nothing to lose. The receiver has nothing to gain and everything to lose.

This means that assuming two different roles - a split personality as it were - will help make the most of your respective positions as server or receiver.

Role of the Server- *'Shoot Aggressively/Retrieve Conservatively'*

As server, you are never penalized on the scorecard, so you can afford to take chances. You can try low percentage shots, or zany pass shots, because if you miss, you lose nothing. If you hit your shots, you gain a point, and dramatic impact. Remember, you have everything to gain and nothing to lose. Lay siege to the court, rush everything and open fire.

This, of course, doesn't mean trying a pro special overhead-reverse-pinch-kill rollout from 39 feet when you're a novice-level player. It just means you can go for shots that are at the edge of your ability level.

Retrieve conservatively? It means your priority is offense, aggressively making the point winning shots. Since not reaching a ball before it bounces twice doesn't hurt your score, don't kill yourself to get it. You can afford to ease up. and not chase every ball until your legs drop off. Save your energy, you're going to need it as receiver.

Role of the Receiver - *'Retrieve Aggressively/Shoot Conservatively'*

In the receiver's position, no matter how well you play, the scorecard will not change for your benefit. You are in the neutral or negative position, with everything to lose, and nothing to gain but a positional change. If you lose this rally, your opponent is one point closer to the end of that race to 15.

As receiver, fortify your position and safeguard your score. Your racquetball radar system should be flashing 'defense, defense'.

Maria Jose Vargas shoots with the scorecard in 2013. (Mike Augustin)

Shoot more conservatively because you can't afford to make mistakes. Hit only the shots that have the highest chance of winning. One pro used to chant, 'I shall kill no ball before it's time'.

This doesn't mean go into a defensive shell, and hit only defensive shots. That's a fast way to get shell-shocked! Go for your aggressive shots within your ability level, but try these only when you are sure you can hit them. Otherwise, hit a safer pass or ceiling ball and wait until the time is right for your final blow. Pass when a kill is not easy, and go to the ceiling when a pass isn't easy.

Assume the role of the grappler, doing everything in your power to prevent a loss of rally. This means running hard. If your opponent's shot bounces twice before you return it to the front wall, he's a point closer to the end of the race, so retrieve every shot as if your life depended on it.

Even if the ball looks like it will bounce twice, chase after it. You'll surprise yourself. And if you're surprising yourself, how do you think your opponent will feel?

In essence, as receiver, force your opponent to earn his points. Don't give them away. Shoot conservatively and run down every ball you can.

(As a nice side benefit, larger and long term benefit on the scorecard comes from the wear and tear on your opponent. With only the idea of retrieve and 'keep the ball in play' in mind as receiver, you'll pick up many more shots than in previous matches. Most opponents search within their own game for an explanation, rather than credit your newfound speed. As a result, they try even harder to hit shots you cannot pick up, and make even more errors. That means more points for you!)

In Close Matches

In a close match, at around 14-14, the roles aren't as clearly defined. It is not unusual for the server to shift his playing role towards that of the receiver's.

At this time in a match, rallying a point is not the only important factor. Maintaining the position of server also becomes a priority. Nobody wants to throw that away. When the score is close, most servers will shoot a little less aggressively, and track down every ball possible.

But as server, it's your choice. You can try the tougher shots for the game winner, and missing doesn't cost you the match. Keep in mind, though, that a miss means a trip to the receiver's position . . . where the pressure gnaws at you.

An Advanced Tip

If you're an advanced player, feel confident to try zany shots, or shots that are out of character for your game ... being careful, though, to do this only when you are serving.

For example, when serving, a power player might try hitting a few touch shots; a ceiling ball master might try a few rollouts - just to keep the opponent on guard. Even if these alter-ego shots miss entirely, the message to the opponent is, 'Hey, my game is well rounded - I'll try anything.'

You'll keep him off balance, you'll make him pay attention for the rest of the match and, with luck, he'll be afraid to challenge your message. Trying the out-of-character shots when serving means you chance losing only position, not a point.

Practicing the Split-Personality Roles

As server you are the aggressive wolf, on the court to destroy your opponent with banzai-like attacks.

As the receiver, you are the enduring and elusive prey, doing everything in your power to survive long enough to become the server.

Two things help you in assuming these roles. One is a simple mental adjustment between rallies. Actually take a couple of seconds after every rally to review your position and remind yourself who you will be in the next rally.

The second thing is physical. Begin making yourself do five pushups at the end of every game for every ball you skipped in as receiver. In a big hurry, you'll notice how often you give away points, and in a bigger hurry, you'll cut down on them!

The biggest advantage in understanding the split-personality system comes when your opponent lacks the same understanding. Let him constantly make errors and give away points without even knowing it.

Then try to keep a straight face as he skips in points for you! He's practically sharpening the spikes on your track shoes for that race to 15.

(A version of this article appeared in National Racquetball / April 1987)

Pro David Horn at the 2014 Grand Slam Juarez Open. The better the athlete the more likely a scorecard strategy of kills when serving and a pass or ceiling on the service return. (Ken Fife)

Pros Speak from the Box
Vs. Power Player

First, determine if he's really a stronger power player. Most I can smack it out with. If not, slow the game down to break his power rhythm and establish a cadence of your own.
- Corey Brysman

I match power with power because that's the nature of my game, with this adjustment. A power player likes to groove, and upsets at something thrown into the mix, so I toss out a soft serve now and then.
- Cliff Swain

The key is getting the serve back. The serve is normally where the power player has the advantage. I plan on not hitting a weak return. The return can be a kill or pass or ceiling, so long as it isn't weak. Power players crumble if you can get them into a rally.
- Mike Ray

If the other guy has more power, pick the shots and returns where he has less. He will probably hate slow serves, the ceiling, and a slower pace of game, or anything that breaks his game rhythm.
– Dave Peck

Bring more pain, bring more heat, and make less mistakes.
- Sudsy

It's tough playing a hard hitter like Sudsy, Swain or Hogan but that's the job. Think about being at your home club and getting everything in order to put the pressure on them to miss their questionable percentage killshots.
- Ruben Gonzalez

I play against power like I play any player. Just find what works and exploit that weakness. The power player may not be able to handle a power game. Or, he/she may also not be able to handle a slow controlled game. It's my job to find out what works. Good racquet prep and focus on the ball are also important when playing a power player.
– Jackie Paraiso

Slow 'em down. I'll take my full nine seconds in the service box, raise my racquet to stall his serve, hit ceiling balls, and irritate him in some way to make hip pop his cork and fire the ball too soon. He's a 60rpm record that I put 45rpm.
- Jeff Leon

46

I'm an aggressive power player and know from experience that I like to hit soft serves to an opponent who doesn't like getting them, but they bore me to death. Anyone else should slow the pace of play starting with these lob serves. Fortunately, not many can battle it out with me on hard shots, so I don't have to think about that strategy often.

- Jim Spittle

The only way I've ever seen anyone beat someone like Hogan is by slowing the game down. It's like fighting a slugging George Foreman: You stay away from him until he gets bored or tired. *- Charlie Brumfield*

Kerri Wachtel slows the game, and then kills the first setup in a 2006 WPRO final. (Ken Fife)

If indeed the opponent is more powerful, move him into the most difficult positions for returns. This varies, but one sure bet against nearly anyone is to the deep, shoulder-high backhand. *- Marty Hogan*

I give them setups in deep court and play the percentages. I cover it, unless it's a rolloff, which isn't likely. This keeps the pressure on and they miss more and more with the fatigue of the match. So, I let them shoot themselves to death, like rope-a-dope.

- Alvaro Beltran

A power player blasts everything, so any setups you provide him should be in deep court where there's a greater chance for error in skipping the ball or leaving it up to cover. In fact, that's the Achilles heel of power, back there deep and shoulder high.. A control player, on the other hand, is more accurate from deep court because of more shot selection. Hence, a control player enjoys getting into a ceiling rally with a blaster.

- Derek Robinson

I use his/her power, adding a little more power.

– Susy Acosta

Personally, I play a power player with power.

– Davey Bledsoe

Really dig in on the service return and force them into my style of long rally games. Power players want things to end quickly and quite often they can tire with some extra movement combined with how hard they swing.   *– John Ellis*

Power player: Make him move, and don't let him set his feet. Get him off balance and return serve with passing shots. Z-serves work well too. Angles make it more challenging to hit it hard

- Charlie Pratt

Slow it down. I would resort to lob and half-lob serves and any type of ceiling games. But the slowdown is a way to force an offensive opportunity, and then I kill.

– Rich Wagner

I try to slow the game down, and maybe hit more lob serves.   *- Kerri Stoffregen Wachtel*

The primary change is a high hard Z-serve she/he can't 'T' off, and then play my regular game.

– Cheryl Gudinas

Make sure not to over-swing on balls and make sure to play center court a little deeper.

– Andy Hawthorne

I play a power player from behind the dashed line, with alert cue study of their often revelatory service motion, and I sport a little tighter grip, and a game plan to both neutralize their power with balls out of their wheelhouse, and constant changes in game tempo, with slow always the home I go back to give the power player a tough row to hoe.

– Ken Woodfin

48

Sword and Shield

Of the Early Racquetball Conquistadors

San Diego racquetball early royalty Bud Muehleisen and Charlie Brumfield used a noble offensive and defensive strategy in the beforehand days of racquetball jousts. Dr. Bud, AKA The White Knight, and Brumfield, The King of the Court and Holder of all Titles, employed the sword and shield technique to astonishing effect.

In the sword and shield, the forehand is the sword used to kill all setups and to administer the royal torturous tour of the court to those willing to run down shot after shot and die a slow death via racquet. By design, virtually all offense comes from forehand shots so to employ this regal game plan your forehand sword had better be sharp, and Muhl and Brum owned two of the sharpest.

The backhand is used as a shield originally to hit lob after lob on the paddleball court to protect against any attack and reverse court position. Over time, as the game switched from wooden paddles to strung racquets, the shield came in the form of a constant diet of deep ceiling shots, around the world balls and high Z shots to fend off even the best offense and to force the shooter to try to win the match from a dangerous 36-40 feet deep in the court.

How could they have won some 100 (!!) national and international championships between them when they only shot the ball from one side of the court? The game was slower and players with fast feet and quick minds had time to step around a backhand, set up and attempt a forehand from anywhere except within one thin foot of the backhand side wall. In addition, both players could attack offensively from a defensive position with two of the best overheads the sport has seen.

Was the shield ever used for offense? Yes, but rarely. The backhand was only used as an offensive weapon in front of the short line where it's a high percentage put away even for a less than stellar backhand stroke.

In addition to the classic Sword and Shield approach, top players in the early era of the game employed an offensive and defensive strategy to reach 21 points as fast as possible while trying to assure their opponents were kept off the score card. You would play conservative defensive oriented racquetball when your opponent was serving, never giving up a free or easy point on the race to 21. When you served and the worst case scenario was a side-out and a kill shot was rewarded with a point on the board, you'd play far more aggressively, trying to run off points on a flight to twenty plus one. Often times you'd save a favorite serve or shot you hadn't used just for the twenty first point, keeping it like an ace up the sleeve to be drawn only to end the match.

In today's fast, furious pro game, the offensive and defensive theories no longer apply as sharply to eleven point sprints powered by big racquets at over 170 MPH, but just might help you in your next club or tournament match and you could be King of your court.

Pro Kara Mazur doesn't need a backhand shield but returns a high backcourt shot to the ceiling in a 2006 WPRO event. (Ken Fife)

Importance of Sports Emotions Smoldering

Ken Woodfin

Sports emotions can range from satisfaction to exhilaration to inspiration or less favorably to frustration to anger to fear to panic, and emotions often change in just seconds when in training or competition.

The Sports Pyramid

Emotions is at the Top of the Sport Performance Pyramid with physical and mental the other two. Emotions dictate your ability to perform at a consistently high level under challenging conditions. Why do you want consistency from your emotions? As your emotions go, so goes your performance. The ideal: respond positively to challenges. How you master your emotions empowers you to use them as tools to perform better rather than as weapons to hurt your game.

Emotional Styles:

There are *seven emotional styles* among athletes: Bubbler, Actor Outer, Mr. Negative, Positive Thinker, Manipulator, Superior One, and THE GOAL, Grand Master. These are how athletes respond emotionally to their sport. Athletes with a certain style often react in a predictable way when they find themselves in a demanding situation. The emotional styles are defined as ...

The Bubbler

A Bubbler feels frustration AND anger build slowly. A Bubbler often appears in emotional control because negative emotions haven't surfaced, YET! The Bubbler keeps frustration and anger bottled up or in check when performing well and the competition is mostly going their way. If competition turns or they make a crucial error, a Bubbler may bubble and boil over and they implode and lose emotional control. Often, when not able to reestablish control, a Bubbler ends up sabotaging for themselves the competition or others (doubles partner, spectators, fans). Bummer. They self-destruct.

The Actor Outer

An Actor Outer feels anger and frustration strongly, but expresses those emotions immediately and openly. No internalizing here -heart on sleeve. Showing strong emotions relieves (or so they think). Emotions arise, are expressed, and then are released. By doing this an Actor Outer maintains a kind of emotional equilibrium in balance. Up to a point, the ongoing emotional vent helps his performance by increasing motivation and intensity and keeps emotions in check; they think. The Actor Outer lets negative emotions out, but do they really let them go? When competition turns, rage builds up until it finally engulfs and consumes and then controls them. At this point, emotions become enemies and performance deteriorates to losing a run of points or repeating unforced errors over and over and over. They self-explode. They're ugly to watch detonate. They act out.

The Mr. Negative

The Mr. Negative feels strong negative emotions. Most common emotions are despair and helplessness. Mr. Negative dwells often on negative experiences and dwells on his feelings. The Mr. Negative may pout. He looks miserable. Mr. Negative is very sensitive to highs and lows of competition and emotions tend to mirror these natural ups and downs of play. When performing well and winning, Mr. Negative is fine; but if he plays poorly and is losing "down" emotions emerge and hurt his performance. Mr. Negative often has an absorbing defeatist attitude and may give up under pressure. Many players and most Mr. Negatives have some brooding qualities, and those qualities can prevent their getting to the top of their sport, or station in life.

The Manipulator

The Manipulator is driven by emotions to become a puppeteer. Psychologically he targets his competitor, the referee, the crowd or all three. He tries through intimidation, confrontation, and gamesmanship to cleverly control the situation to do as he pleases. He raises the ire of his competitor. He may look to get the ref to do a make-up call for a prior that went against him. The Manipulator may decide to turn the crowd against him just to fire himself up. Or, he may get the crowd to cheer for him by showing off and belittling his competitor's mistakes. The fatal flaw for the Manipulator is that without the ability to be a puppeteer or "drama queen" he falls apart and shrinks down to true size when he is unable to pull the strings.

The Positive Thinker

An extremely common style is the Positive Thinker. He believes when there is no basis for belief. When the parachute doesn't open and the reserve chute fails to deploy, Positive Thinker still says, "So far so good". The Positive Thinker mindset is based on 'all things are doable', when he believes. Why is the Positive Thinker a winner at the State level but a loser at the National level? The state championships brim with Positive Thinkers who use positivism as their training wheels. Then they run into a wall of talent at the national level. They fall apart at the ultimate level because any amount of thinking positively that doesn't address reality evaporates.

The Superior One

The Superior One is seen by his competitors as believing he is all knowing. He's so vain he probably thinks this paragraph defines him. He is also bent on giving post-points lectures, detailing rules nuances, and explaining his reality. The Superior One must pontificate. If he's slips from the top, the superior one may vent his anger, play mad at the world, and direct wrath at his partner or competitor. The flaw in his crown comes in the

Paola Longoria with an ESP and bow but under it is she a Bubbler, Actor Outer, Ms Negative, Manipulator, Positive Thinker, Supreme One, or Grand Master? (2014 Juarez Open Ken Fife)

long run that he must continually correct and be correct to remain effective. If he is once wrong he loses the audience and there goes his grip. The Empower has no clothes.

The Grand Master

The Grand Master is the rarest of emotional styles. He seems to play sans emotion. He is all about executing his form and tactics. He seems to play *in the zone* or return back there on demand. He lets emotions ride through him that jolt most, and he continues with barely a grin or grimace all the way through match point. When losing or struggling, the Grand Master reinvests his energy into getting better. The Grand Master is unaffected by threat and negative emotions. Errors, a poor performance, and losing seem to slide off the Grand Master, as if he were made of Teflon. He owns the ability to NOT let pressure affect him. He is able to let go past mistakes and failure, like he has convenient short term memory loss. A Grand Master is a comeback king. He rarely shows his emotions, either negative or positive, and he maintains a consistent, calm, even demeanor, even during the BIG POINTS. He may be expressionless or don a cryptic Mona Lisa smile. This equanimity (calm, composure, and even temperedness) results in consistently high performances and positive reactions to the normal roller coaster ride of the game. Generally, the Grand Master is a winner or in worst case a happy, "I'm learning something", loser. He seems to learn, adapt, improve and *figure it out*. He usually reaches his potential and then he defines a NEW potential to shoot for.

What Is Your Style?

What emotional style best describes you? Think back to your competitions. What has owned you when it did not go as well as you would have liked (or as designed by you). And then, think of matches where you felt in total control, cool, energized, and confident. How did you respond emotionally? Were you a Bubbler, Actor Outer, Mr. Negative, Positive Thinker, Manipulator, Superior One, or Grand Master? It's likely that a pattern of emotional reaction will emerge in your sport that places you into one of the seven emotional styles.

Change Is Doable

Emotional styles are not so hard to change. Though some contend that you were born with a particular temperament, or in other words that we may be "hard-wired", if you define yourself and then practice a new 'self' then rewiring your emotion is possible. A real challenge but doable.

Step 1 & 2 To Emotional Control

Goal One: gain control of your emotional style (understand it). Now it will help rather than hurt your sports performance. Goal two: the more long-term goal is to alter your emotional style to one of the seven to naturally facilitate rather than interfere with your positive efforts.

Emotional Master or Victim?

Many believe they are the way they are. They feel they've little control over their emotions and nothing can be done to gain control. If emotions hurt them, they just accept it because they feel they can't do anything about it. They're emotional victims. Their emotions control them. Emotionally they hinder their ability to perform well and achieve their goals.

Become *Your* Emotional Master

Gain control of your emotions. Develop healthy and productive emotional habits. Emotions CAN facilitate your ability to perform and achieve your goals.

Pioneer holder of the most national and international titles'Dr. Bud Muehleisen and the modern holder Cliff Swain at the 2011 Fullerton Nationals, ask, 'Who has the biggest left swing ever?' (Roby Partovich)

Emotional Mastery

The process of emotional mastery: recognize negative emotional reactions. When starting to feel negative emotions, know what they are, for instance, frustration (argh!), anger (rrrr), despair (woe is me) or bagging it and mailing it in (oh, well). Then identify what situation is causing them. Then let them go or shrink um down to controllable size or feed off them and suck their energy and redirect them toward powerful good.

Review Comp

After competition, consider underlying causes. You might examine emotional baggage. If emotions are strong and present in other parts of your life, you might seek professional help. Focus on clearing emotional obstacles or hurdles. Understand emotional habits, how they may interfere with performance when less than constructive, and how to learn new emotional responses in sport and life.

Have Responses

Specify alternative emotional reactions to the situations that trigger negative emotions. For example, instead of yelling, "I am terrible," slap your thigh and say cooly, "Come on, Play better." Or, instead of screaming at the ref after a disputed call, turn and take several deep breaths. Positive emotional responses help you let go of past mistakes, motivate yourself to perform better next time, generate positive emotions giving you more confidence, and allowing you to focus on what will raise your level of performance.

Practice Emotional Mastery

Emotional mastery skills and positive reactions may not be easy at first because negative emotional habits are ingrained. Realize how difficult it is to change a bad technical habit. You practice technique over and over with a pro or an XK Feeder moving you about and testing your game. Then, with commitment, awareness, control, and practice you're feeling better and your performance improves with positive responses. Boost yourself. Believe. And you're giving your all. In time, retrain your emotions into positive emotional habits. Result: transition from being an emotional victim to an emotional master with tools to not only perform better, but be a whole lot happier. A Grand Master.

Pick 'n Scratch to Victory

There's a difficult and annoying player we call Mr. Pick 'n Scratch in all sport and business whom I'm certified to describe, but first a true story.

I just escaped Amazon cannibals in the heart of the Peru jungle in '00, and was medivaced by military helicopter to Iquitos, Peru, where I slid out the copter to stagger into a waterfront bar because a keeper, whom I'd never met, was a rare gringo and I needed someone to talk to.

"I was held captive by the Mayoruna Indians, and this is my first contact with civilization in weeks.'
'Have a beer.'
'I don't drink'
'Have a burger; I served Richard Nixon.'
'Look, I'm not any gringo off the streets. I'm a professional racquetball player and author…'
'And I'm from New York City, and played the hard outdoor handball courts for decades.'
'So what?' I yawned.
'All right,' barked the barkeep, 'Let's have a game here, a verbal match, and if you are what you say, the burger's on the house.'
'First serve…' he opened. 'Do you have a single teeny-weeny weakness in your game that I can pick and scratch incessantly?'
His boldness drew an honest repartee, "Sorry, there's not a single weakness."
"You're the winner!' he clapped my back. 'And welcome to Peter Gorman's Cold Beer Blues Bar.'

I've been a picker 'n scratcher since childhood in multiple sports and tasks, and claim it's blueprint to success for greenhorns to pros. Here's how to ferret a bidder's follies. Study his gait into the court, hands during warm-up, and preferable a previous match to identify three major weaknesses… to key later. As you surmise, figure ways to exploit each. Hence, you pick weaknesses before the game, and make him scratch them during the match.

The universal glitches of Pick n' Scratchers hatch counter-strategies in this **Pick 'n Scratch Chart**:

- *Weak backhand*… Counter with the drive serve, pass, and hone ceiling balls to it.
- *Slow reflexes*... Play a power game of low serves, hard kills and low passes.

Few in the world of racquetball can pick and scratch to victory like Janel Tisinger indoors, outdoors, in singles and doubles. In 2012, at 29, she is the first person, male or female, to win a Triple Crown at the WOR Championships in Hunting Beach, CA capturing the pro singles, womens doubles, and mixed doubles. (Mike Augustin)

- *Poor ceiling game*… Soft serve, and hit defensive ceiling service returns.
- *Inability to cover front court*… Kill and pinch.
- *Poor conditioning*… Test him in early game with extended rallies to determine if he can last an entire match.
- *Can't short-hop or volley*… Soft serve him.
- *Hot-headed, or has streaks*… Slow it down with ceiling returns, time-outs, and control pace of game.
- *Fails to watch the ball behind him*… Hit kills all day, or down-line passes.
- *Can't handle wall angles*… Try Z-serves, around-world and Z-shots.
- *Uses soft serves with no hard service*… Volley and half-volley the initial serves to ensure he never reemploys them.

- *Drive serves repetitively, with no second or soft serve*... Ceiling return his initial serves to test his ceiling game, which is usually suspect and yields set-ups.
- *'Chokes' in hairy moments*... Bring the heat into close scores by drive serving and forcing play.
- *Dives and flicks ball up*... Continue your kill attempts as the worst scenario is another set-up.
- *Wets the court*... How did that get in there?

This chart isn't inclusive. After identifying the imperfections, and exploitations, I like to enter the court and evaluate in the opening rallies if my pre-game analysis is accurate. The reasons: To quantify each flaw, to discover if the rival has a backup to cover his shortcomings (such as running around a weak backhand for a big forehand), and to gauge his early reaction to losing quick points in weak suits he must learn he holds.

One by one, I test the frailties, so by mid-game an overall strategic map unfolds. At this epiphany, relax, and decide either to pick and scratch him incessantly at one or more sore spots until it's all over, or to withhold and re-target the imperfections at crucial and game points.

Categorize the chart components for easy recount, in kind: Flaws in stroke, strategy, or general play. You may, as smart baseball pitchers, keep a journal of recurrent opponent defects with the player names in the left column, the 'picks' (flaws) in the right, and the 'scratches' in the middle.

Some of the top paddleball and racquetball pros had Achilles heels. Charley Brumfield dropped a few national titles with a fly-swatter backhand, and Marty Hogan's power game evaporated during a timeout after you sneaked a slow ball, or pricked the game ball with a needle from your sole. Champs Dave Peck, Mike Yellen, Steve Strandemo and Jason Mannino with superbly rounded games nonetheless went down lacking a specialty in a crux, like a crack ace or freak ball. The most seamless players I've met on the court are Mike Ray, Vic Niederhoffer and Cliff Swain, and, well, sometimes there's as fast a draw and you scratch your britches.

Practice like the pros your own weaknesses until there are none, and then practice your strengths to harden to tournament rigors. If you own a single stellar tool such as a booming serve or persistent ceiling game, then hammer it in early game to jump ahead, leave it, bring it back for big plays, and again for the final points to push the win.

Also, make a study of eclectic players from behind the glass or above the court, and ponder, *how would I pick and scratch him to victory?*

The first serve is struck! so begin gathering intelligence. Here, a master's experience shines, and you may earn it's no more difficult than to chew gum and swing, while watching.

There's no greater satisfaction in life than to meet and dismantle a superior athlete by funneling– shots to a-Keeley's heel. The next most stimulating thing is to watch a rival wither as he tests and finds no wise cracks in your game.

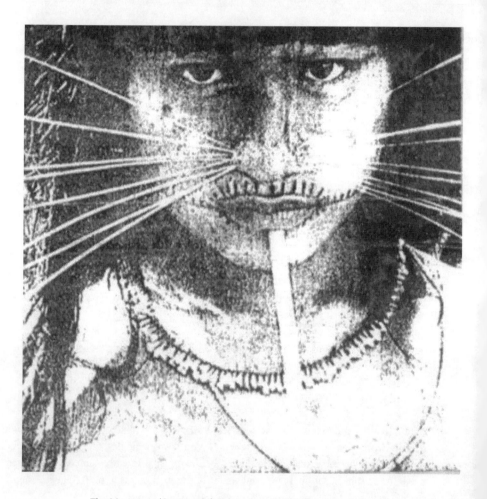

The Mayoruna 'Cat People' pick and scratch in the Amazon jungle.

Pros Speak from the Box

Vs. Control Player

This scenario of power (me) vs. control (him) is almost always the case, so I'm qualified in saying that you should be patient against someone like me and rely on me making mistakes. You've got to convert a battle of weapons to a mental battle, and must count on me beating myself on a given day. *- Cliff Swain*

Pick up the pace of the game, from the smack of the serve to the shots to the rally. The goal is to play at your best rhythm, so if the other guy plays to a slower beat, speed every facet until your tempo is reached, then hold it there. *- Corey Brysman*

I didn't run into this problem fortunately. There's much wisdom in what the other top pros intuitively grasp that the match is a court experiment where I'm the 'control', so to speak, and the outcome hinges on their performance rather than mine. *- Mike Ray*

Force the pace of the play against a control player like Ray, Keeley, or Gonzalez until the rhythm of their shot making breaks down. It's the exact opposite technique of reversing a power player. *- Charlie Brumfield*

Bring the pain, bring the heat, and don't make mistakes. *- Sudsy*

Kill the ball against the control player, then stuff the racquet in your gym bag and go home. *– Jim Spittle*

Control players usually have weak deep court games, so I give them setups there. *- Alvaro Beltran*

Control players don't use their serve as a weapon as far as 'heat' goes. So, it's important to return serve in such a way that the rally ensues rather than ending with your return. A top control player like Mannino baits you to make a low-percentage weak return because he knows he can't stay in once the rally begins. *- Derek Robinson*

Get into his mind and think a moment - what doesn't he want to see. He doesn't want to see the opposite of what he does. If you can answer the question 'What would he do to beat himself', and can do it then you've got a good chance to win. *- Ruben Gonzalez*

You have to find some way to get the good control player out of that mode. Try something he doesn't expect, like when an unknown comes out of nowhere and beats a top player with a personal specialty shot or a quirky strategy.   *- Jeff Leon*

Aggression in mind, Dan Fowler's serves and shots will thump a control player. (2006 Ken Fife)

I beat control with power.   *– Davey Bledsoe*

Try to bury the ball ASAP and over power them.   *– Dave Fleetwood*

Against control players: Be aggressive. Shoot the ball. Control center and be physical.
                                                                     - Charlie Pratt

Bring the gas mask. And unleash the power on them. — *Jose Rojas*

I do not change my strategy much against a control freak, just plan for longer rallies. Court positioning, shot selection, service, and service return stay about the same.
— *John Ellis*

I control a control or touch player with a faster paced game tempo, drive serves designed at all costs not to pop off the back wall, and I look for the fastest ball I Can Find!
— *Ken Woodfin*

It would depend on if they were a better control player than me. It's simple: With a better control player than me I force the offense. With a lesser control player I wait for the offensive opportunity a little longer. — *Rich Wagner*

Maintain control, literally, physically, as well as mentally. Don't rush the ball!
— *Jackie Paraiso*

First, learn to win rallies by passing people, not just rolling every ball. By learning good passing shots it keeps your opponent from generating solid offence. Serve the ball well, and take away their control with exceptional serves. — *Andy Hawthorne*

With control players, you have to be patient. I try not to be the first person to make a mistake. - *Kerri Stoffregen Wachtel*

Drive serves, and move my positioning up a little. — *Cheryl Gudinas*

Playing the Percentages
Shot Selection

A no-brainer offense with consistency is the goal of every intermediate to professional player from the instant he drops the ball to serve and to the conclusion of the rally. The strategy must work under heavy fatigue, at final point of the tiebreaker, and while tripping over a shoelace. This is a simple plan to ensure that every shot you take has a reason. With a little practice, the reason no longer needs be recalled for the body to default to the proper serve and shot. This strategy is called playing the percentages on shot selection where the base on the court where the player hits from dictates where the ball will go.

It is given that racquetball, like many other sports, is an offensive game. It follows that the winners are the most offensive players. The theory among the winners is that the one with the most consistent offensive shot selection strategy will step into the finals. The conclusion is that the champion is the player who 'plays the percentages' over and over to win the championship.

Question from the bleachers: One of the best pieces of advice at a clinic I've heard was about being purposeful on offense. After thinking about it, we could use more purpose.

Answer: Like most sports where aggressiveness is the key to winning, the player or team that comes out on top is determined by how many points you score. A racquetball game is about an hour long, putting pressure on each player to be productive. There are three aspects of scoring: shot selection, shot distribution, and percentage of successful tries. If there are 120 chances to score or achieve a sideout in a two-game match, and you shoot 75% successfully on each of these 'possessions', you will average 90 made points and sideouts per match. This is plenty to win, on mean, any match.

Based on this shooting percentage, it remains to define the spots on the floor from which these shots are taken (bases), what are the shot selections, the distribution or how often each should be hit, and a governing principle for offensive shot making.

1. **Where do these shots come from? (I mean, where on the floor you shoot them.)**

The floor has about twelve bases on the floor between the front and back walls from which shots are commonly taken. If there seems to be an overlap of squares where you stand, then like a checker on the board, consider yourself on the square you're most on. From each of these bases, whether a forehand or backhand, groundstroke or volley, on balance or off, and negating the position of the opponent as if he doesn't exist, you take the same shot over and over from each base.

Exactly - You may make up your own bases on the court with an overhead mind's eye view of the court, or look down on one from a gallery. The most common spots to take shots from are:

In front of the service box

Just behind the service box on both sides

Mid-distance between the short line and back wall

At the back wall

In addition, strong players have four spots within the service box to serve from

2. What kind of shot distribution – what percentage of the time should I shoot the ball from those spots?

Every time. Never a deviation from taking the same shot from the same base on the court. Even if the opponent 'catches' on. Racquetball is like many other sports that evolved the best strategy driven by the pressure of refining equipment. The original game used to be a defensive players' struggle. Then it became a sword-and-shield battle of protecting the backhand. The current game is serve and shoot and nothing else - using the Playing the Percentages plan on this page.

3. What is the offensive theory of play?

The guiding principal every time you set to stroke the ball on the court is the Offensive Theory of Play.

Given any shot anywhere on the court, the first thought is to kill the ball, the second thought is to drive the ball, and the third thought is to go to the ceiling or a different defensive shot.

4. What results should you see?

If you practice you will achieve consistency of the right spots from all the bases on the floor. The mistake I see at tournaments is 'aimless' offense where there is no consistent floor plan that dictates what shots to take from where. By having a map of the court in your head, or actual taped squares on the court, you may write and tape in the box the shot that should be taken every time. Handball great Paul Haber used to say, 'From every spot on the floor there is a right shot,' and by creating a flow chart on a court, or on paper, you will visualize Playing the Percentages.

Purpose is the most important in offensive racquetball. The player who drifts aimlessly about the court smacking the ball as hard as he can loses in the next bracket. The player who has a purpose in mind from every little square on the court goes far, and is not nervous before a tournament. It's as if it he already played the match.

He dropped the racquetball once and declared, 'I am the next National Champion.' He almost was, defeating Hogan in a Vegas tiebreaker. He went 56-3 against Gonzalez. I met him on a 2400 mile bicycle trip from San Diego to Michigan stopping off for the St. Louis 1975 National Singles and finishing 3rd ahead of Niederhoffer. The first time we saw each other on a court each was wearing different colored sneakers: He to demonstrate individuality, and I to promote Converse with a red and a blue Chucks. This is Victor Niederhoffer who went on to defeat some of the top pros in racquetball, before becoming the #1 commodities trader in USA for four consecutive years.

Pros Speak from the Box

Shot Selection

Shot selection is the navigation system in your game. It's crucial to know what direction you need to go to get to your destination of success. You may get there, but if you don't hit the correct shots it might take longer. A player who has good shot selection is working on keeping the opponent out of center court, forcing a set up or to give up a point.

– Jackie Paraiso

I base my shot selection on where the opponent is stands. If he's deep, I kill. If he's front and center, I down-line pass. If he's caught in a front corner, I cross-court pass. If he's tired, I pinch. *- Alvaro Beltran*

'The Big D 4-Box Shot Selection' answers the question. I'll describe the system. The court area forward of the foot fault line is off-limits for we don't play the game of racquetball there. Everything distant to the foot-fault line fall's within the Big D system, so we have a new court with a 'front wall' at the foot fault line, with the regular back and sidewalls. In the center of this draw a plus sign on the floor, so that the floor is divided into four equal squares. What I want you to do is find out where your opponent is standing – which box – and then hit the ball to the furthest box from him. For example, the boxes can be numbered clockwise circularly from the front-most left 1,2,3,4. If your opponent stands in box 1, then your shot goes to the furthest box away from him # 3.

- Derek Robinson

There's a best shot from every spot on the court, no matter where the other guy is standing. *– Jim Spittle*

I continually changed my shots to make it difficult for my opponents to guess what I was going to hit. I was always aware of hitting the easiest shot to win the point, but would sometimes go to a secondary shot to keep my opponent off balance. *– Jerry Hilecher*

Hit it where he ain't, and block him if you can't. *- Charlie Brumfield*

Take the most offensive shot whenever you can. *- Corey Brysman*

Serve and shoot. Serve and shoot. *- Cliff Swain*

Kills win the cup.

- *Sudsy*

You don't always have to hit the perfect shot, just the right shot.   - *Rhonda Rajsich*

Make the opponent move the greatest distance to the ball. That's the main secret to shot selection.

– *Cheryl Gudinas*

The shot selection on a dive is usually to kill and then wipe off the blood. (2014 Mike Augustin)

When your opponent is behind you, pinch. When your opponent is in front of you pass.

- *Kerri Stoffregen Wachtel*

The two most important factors in shot selection are where's your opponent, and what is the height, speed, angle of the ball.

– *Fran Davis*

Don't worry about hitting it too low and do not use the side walls very much.... Until it's time!

– *John Ellis*

Use the whole court or 4-corners or quad placements choosing shots intended to play keep-away from the competitor.

– *Ken Woodfin*

It is the most important aspect in the game.

– *Jose Rojas*

The moment you as a player can become conscious of what shot you want to hit, you are on your way to being a good player.

- *Charlie Pratt*

Chess and Sport

As a kid, our Idaho family home didn't get *The NY Times*, so my math-minded father one winter conjured a chessboard, set up little men like ants, and told me to move them as seemed logical by their stature. In one year I was beating him while reading funny books. He threw up his arms in disgust, and a week later Santa left *How to Win in the Chess Openings* by Al Horowitz under a pine tree in the living room.

Coach Bo Champagne carries a chess set from pro stop to stop and teach racquetball. (Legends)

Having spent an alarmingly chunk of the next year at the solitaire chess board, my mother encouraged me out to sports, and I undertook them with an onerous chess mind, flicking baseball pitches onto a canvas bull's-eye and football passes into a swinging bushel basket.

69

In winter, it was chess again, but also taking a shovel and rubber ball to the nearest vertical wall to remove the snow and bounce, bounce the ball for hours in practicing what I didn't quite know. The correct assumption was that solutions to problems I didn't know yet would crystallize, just like on the chessboard. If a theory sleeted in a blizzard, I retreated down the basement steps to the furnace room to bounce a basketball around pieces of coal that were the defense, and practiced it.

Anyone who wishes to learn how to play chess in sport may well become conversant in positions where the players are, were and will be. This is how chess guided me into sport, and especially racquet sports where I became a six-time national singles champion in paddleball and #2 ranked racquetball pro throughout the decade of the '70s.

Chess opened my eyes to a sequence of moves in sports, and to identify those action frames, lock on one, and alter the fate of play to championships.

(From the book Introduction of *Chess and Sport* by Steve Bo Keeley)

Pros Speak from the Box

General Strategy

Have all your strategies thought out before you enter the court. My way is to play consistently and let the other player make the mistakes is my technique. Thing about your mistakes on strokes, selection and strategy and eliminate them to let the points roll in.

- Mike Ray

Attack each ball until the motive of each rally is attack, and so the game goes.   *- Sudsy*

Serve hard, play offensively   *- Corey Brysman*

From the serve on, keep your opponent behind you whenever possible and the points will flow.   *– Marty Hogan*

My anticipation, fitness, and strong focus keep me in the game until I get a setup to hit my favorite kill, the pinch.   *- Alvaro Beltran*

If I'm the server in the rally, I attack everything to kill. As the receiver, I play conservatively to avoid skips unless there's an easy front court setup.   *- Ruben Gonzalez*

Find a general winning strategy that hurts everyone and requires little tinkering. Pick a weakness early in your opponent's bastion, and pick it apart but not to embarrass because then he has a will to rebel.   *- Victor Niederhoffer*

Go into a match with a strategy and a backup strategy for every aspect of the game. As the match progresses, don't flog a dead horse. If I'm shooting against a shooter and he's beating me, I alter my plan by soft serving, going the ceiling more, stalling and calling timeouts. Conversely, if I'm out-controlled by a control player, I pick up the pace with hard serves and returns. General strategy normally means examining either the height of shots or the pace of play, and these two are intermingled. Never change a winning game, which means stick with the working height of shots and pace of play… until the opponent devises to topple it, and then counter-adjust.   *- Jeff Leon*

There is no 'out-thinking' the opponent on the court. You're playing the percentages - the ball in the court - not your opponent. If the percentages aren't going your way, consider

71

playing stupid like him.   *- Charlie Brumfield*

Play the percentages. Base your strategy on your strengths first, then on your opponent's weaknesses.
                                                                      – Cheryl Gudinas

3 shot rallies: Serve return, Kill.
                                                                      – Andy Hawthorne

One of the principal and most ignored strategies is to volley the ball like Jansen Allen at the 2014 Kennex Tournament of Champions. Allen recently brought to pro racquetball a degree in Business, plus Championships in Intercollegiate Singles and Doubles, National Doubles, and National Mixed Doubles. (Mike Augustin)

Depends on the player, but overall I focus on my serve a lot.   — *Susy Acosta*

I play on the point. Once a point is over, my focus is what I have to do differently or the same to win the next point. The game is just an evolution of winning the next point through time. Win most of the points and you win the game, win most of the games and you win the match.   — *Jerry Hilecher*

Get a setup and put it away.   — *Rich Wagner*

Pound the lines.   — *Jose Rojas*

Hit the ball hard and make my opponent cover as much real estate as possible to retrieve my shots.   — *Brian Hawkes*

Make your opponent run the furthest distance to get to the ball.   — *Fran Davis*

My game strategy is to play smart and hard.   - *Charlie Pratt*

No unforced errors, and make sure to take smart shots and win the long rallies. I'm totally different now at 42 compared to my IRT days. After my first shoulder surgery and being down for 11 straight months, with only my left hand to play with, I realized that I can play so much smarter than I had. That situation, mixed with playing a little more squash, and my whole perspective on the game changed to not making mistakes and not worrying about power.   — *John Ellis*

My general strategy is to be in control of center court which is a few inches behind the encroachment line.   - *Kerri Stoffregen Wachtel*

My game strategy is to use my game plans, my style, and my temperament, conscious enough to be mindless or clinically proficient, as well as alert to learn what I need to change, and all the while ooze confidence, energy, and relaxation even if I'm just acting, until I believe it..   — *Ken Woodfin*

Old School Attrition
for Drunks, Zombies and Farm Implements

From the Bleacher: Your shot selection theory is a topic very near and dear to my heart. Thanks for putting it in clear terms that players should recognize patterns of play and be aggressive. I agree there are two ways to attack- All else is "D". It is serve and shoot. And not just server serves and receiver returns and then server shoots. It's server serves and receiver shoots anything he can touch.

The game today is pretty low %. And fast. Players do need a formula and bases or spots on the court to "T" off from, and realizing they're there (should) prompt them to shoot rote shots. Some post shot clearing is required to avoid hinders, collisions or retaliatory hinders.

The schism between the drive and the kill can become a chasm if the ball is higher, spinning, moving or the shooter is not. **However,** I teach that there's 3 angles nearly always from those 12 count bases for the 'thinking player'. Those angles are rare straight, crosscourt, and to the sidewall. The ball almost always 'wants' to go to one of those three angles based on its speed, spin and angle.

Answer: Remind me not to meet you in a dark alley of thought without a flashlight. Going to the court, you are presenting three angles from twelve bases, or sports, on the floor to take shots from. I am countering with two angles from each of the same. We are saying the same thing in two schools: modern fast and old school slow.

Your angles slice and dissect a player in the modern game. My two angles were a straight in kill and cross drive that put the opponent on a rack covering opposite directions. Let me give you a little 'old school' and you may decide to apply it to your modern game.

The reason I preach stark simplicity in strategy dates back to my own success with it in multiple championships with it in paddle and racquetball. Attrition had to be factored heavily into strategy unlike modern times. This changes everything. The rallies were twice as long, matches twice as long, 10x as many entrants and so twice as many matches per day, we played two divisions, the ball was slower and racquets relative pillows to require greater exertion. A player was on his feet all day long on Friday and Saturday working up to the finals.

The strategy I evolved from high school wrestling was the most aggressive to get on and off the court as quickly as possible to conserve energy for the hopeful finals. I was a 'pinner' on the court who killed or less often drove every shot, to exert only about 1/5 the calories as those chipmunks in the court wheels.

74

The fittest racquetball player ever, according to the USAR, is Bret Harnett here in the 2013 3-WallBall World Outdoor Championship in Las Vegas. Brett nearly ruled the roost in the 1980s sustaining a Top 4 ranking. The US Olympic Committee created a series of fitness tests (strength, speed, endurance) that was given to the athletes of all sports who attended the elite camps at the USOC. Over 500 top athletes from all over the country tested and Brett was #1! The USOC stated he would rank high among any Olympic athletes. (Mike Augustin)

The 12 bases I shot from were lifted from a childhood superhero comic book in which the Mortals vs. Immortals from another dimension who leaped the rim as if earth was zero gravity. The Mortal coach told his boys in a chalkboard talk a week before the match, these are the X's on the court, go and practice shots from them until you rarely miss, and then in the galactic championship go to the x's on the court (don't worry, I'll see that they're there), and put the ball through the hoop. In school I practiced basketball in a barn and put pebbles down for x's like the winning team.

From all this comes here to me the bottom line of what used to be racquetball, and it's still true though to a lesser degree today. Any strategy MUST be predicated on being able to execute it while 'in the tank', cramped, mind blown by a gamesmen, sliding on a wet spot, or psyched out at the final point. The strategy had to be simple enough that a zombie of the dead could execute it, because that's what one felt like beginning the middle of the second game. We were indestructible 'farm implements' from the Midwest but in playing each other the match always toiled down to *who could hit the shots when the tiredest*.

Swain ate splinters for this win over Ruben Gonzalez at the 1984 Montreal Open. (Murray Diner)

The Offensive Theory

Add Five Points to Your Game in Ten Minutes

Let's keep it simple, let's keep it short.

Aggressive play is the rule to winning rackets, and expressly in racquetball where the equipment has evolved to allow the fastest Big Game on earth... if you play it that way. The Big Game is serve and shoot with 140-180 mph shots.

Long before the Big Game hit the scene I devised and used the Offensive Theory to win multiple national paddleball and racquetball titles. The only thing that has changed over the decades is that the theory has gotten stronger.

Take a notebook and pencil to watch a top pro match and jot in five columns how the points or side outs are won: Kill, pass, error, ace, and other. That is the precise order of winning shots in an elite game, and those are the elements of the Offensive Theory.

The Offensive Theory for advanced players is: Given any shot anywhere on the court, the first thought is to kill the ball, the second thought is to drive the ball, and the third thought is to go to the ceiling.

That gets you leaning in the right direction. When do you know when to make a drive instead of a kill, or a ceiling in lieu of a drive?

It's pretty simple. If the ball is presented below the waist then kill; if it's waist to chest high then pass; and if it's above the chest go ceiling. Stated another way, every shot that can be killed should be killed, any shot that can't be killed should be driven past, and any shot that cannot be driven should be knocked to the ceiling.

Put the Offensive Theory to test. In your next practice match take the most offensive shots possible on every setup and watch the point spread grow against opponents. They will start to 'cheat' toward the killshots but it doesn't matter. The equipment is too strong to favor the defensive player.

A good killshot producer will trounce a decent killshot coverer at the Open level every time. If the pair continues to practice together the point spread will grow wider until the shooter advances into the pros and the defender stagnates in the lower ranks.

The intent of the theory is an aggressive *attitude* that translates into a sequence of offensive shots during tournament play. It is not that every ball should be an attempted kill. The idea is to play offensively at every opportunity. Among top ranked players

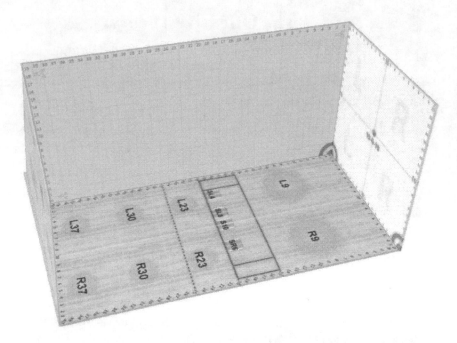

12 Base shot selection virtual court by Xia Yang. The shot depends on the court position where the floor is divided into twelve general bases: left and right side, and the # of feet from the front wall. With this simple strategy, the opponent is negated and the shots and serves are chosen by the base. For example, from deep left court (L-37) the common shots are a straight-in kill, pinch kill, splat kill, down-line pass, cross-court pass and wide-V drive, or ceiling ball. (Xia Yang)

since the fast ball advent in '73 and then the oversized racquet in '84 the only victory path is the one of broken balls from drive serves, kills, and drives.

The offensive theory doesn't distinguish between server and returner. Arguably the server should play more offensively and the receiver more defensively, however if you have an aggressive instinct and stroke, then the suggestion is to use them equally while serving and returning.

The secret of the offensive theory is that it relaxes because it is simple, it is constant through all match variables, and it is a slim theme to practice.

Practice. Try the Spray Practice of giving yourself setups off the front wall at random all over the court- soft taps, ceiling setups, volleys and off the back wall. As the ball arrives in the hitting zone administer the most offensive shot: if it is below the waist kill; if it is below the chest drive; and if it is above the chest ceiling. You may count shots to 500, or just stay on the court in constant motion for a good workout in thirty minutes.

The Volley Drill hitting shots before a floor bounce is the best training for aggression. Count another 50 volleys from the short line to back wall or stay on the court another 30 minutes.

After one month, or in my case one year, your instinct will be to kill, step up, volley, and drive hard.

If you are an intermediate player who has achieved by a defensive campaign of control shots and scrambling coverage, congratulations- it's time to shift gears into the Open. The rule of individual sport is that beginners win more with defense, intermediates have great battles with like-talented offensive players, and advanced players win on the offense.

The Offensive Theory could also be called the Kill-Pass-Ceiling mantra that even in the worst of times of pressure or fatigue transforms into graceful execution.

The Offensive Theory is the elixir.

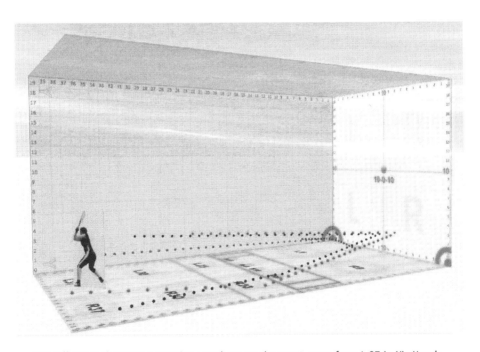

The Offensive Theory is aggressive anywhere on the court, even from L-37 in Xia Yang's virtual court. The shooter's notion should be the most offensive shot, a straight in kill; next a pinch kill; third a splat kill; and last a down-line, cross-court or wide-V drive. Advanced players rarely hit another shot from this base. (Xia Yang)

Southpaws, Mirrors and You

Left-handers comprise about 10% of the total population, but I think they account for a greater proportion of the better participants in all sports. The reason is that athletes hone their skills and strategies against the most available fodder, righties. In racquetball, there are some things you should know, that a southpaw intuits in his mirror world of playing against right-handers, to gain back the edge. Sit back and prepare yourself: This article contains both tips and related quirks.

Certain serves and shots work better against lefties. Your down-line drive serve to the backhand becomes a deathblow to the southpaw receiver. I use one spot about six feet from the right side wall to hit a medley of three drive serves off the same stroke motion for deception. The first is a drive right along the wall to his backhand, the second is a drive-Z right, and the third is a drive left that surprises him provided it doesn't come off the back wall before the second bounce. These are really the only serves you need in a serious game against a left-hander, and the usual variation is 50% drive right, 30% Z-right, and 20% drive left, though you can tinker with the recipe.

If you find him scrambling more for one of the serves, raise that ratio. If you fault the first serve, use the Z or lob for the second, unless you're particularly confident about the drives. A final note is that the Z-serve, especially well into the intermediate skill level, is tailor-made for use against a lefty (and vice-versa) because it's simple to strike, allows large margin of error, and gives additional angle due to the extra reach and positioning within the service box nearer the right side wall. Practice until you can hit 9-of-10 Z's perfectly. Vary the Z's velocities and heights to prevent the opposition from forming a rhythm or volleying the return.

Return of service against a southpaw enters a new dimension since your more naturally strong cross-court backhand now pulls the shot hard to his weaker and shorter reaching backhand. (The backhand stretches about a foot less out, or up, than the forehand because it must reach across the body.) The ceiling, pass or cross court kill all work, though fundamental service return strategy advises you to be able to hit the ceiling shot well before progressing to the pass before learning the kill.

In the rally likewise, you can direct cross-court passes with greater margin of error, as long as the ball doesn't rebound off the back wall. When a lefty begins to 'cheat' to cover your cross-court passes and kills, keep him honest with a kill to the other front corner (straight-in or pinch). Cross-court ceiling returns and ceiling rallies are also usually easier than down-line. Try for a spin on the inside of your hit ball that causes it on reflections off the ceiling, front wall and floor to angle straight toward the back wall rather than hop into a side wall. The best way to improve passes and ceilings for use against future left-handers is to drill at perpetual cross-court passes, or ceilings, or mixing the two, against a lefty.

Southpaws, as mentioned, generally come with the foregoing tips already parcel to their game plans due to a past of playing the 'mirror game' against right handers. In course, it will help righties to understand how to better play lefties by imitating the serves, returns and shots that they use against you! I once went against a lefty who lost point after point against my Z-serve to his backhand. Finally, he turned and smiled at me from the service box, and hit the same Z to my backhand, and I was compelled to display the definitive return, a volley. I couldn't serve him another Z for the entire match.

My expertise in writing this article is as a developing ambidextrous player. For the past year I've played primarily southpaw due to an arm injury, and in earlier years entered tournaments right-handed in pros and left handed in opens. I hope to see other aspirants at the first Ambidextrous Championship, whenever that may be.

Why play lefty? Obviously, upon reverting to your dominant hand, you'll start beating lefties more handily, plus there are other benefits: 1) You teach yourself to be a teacher by having to learn strokes from scratch. 2) You're able to pick up more informal games in tapping a new pool of lesser players for competition. 3) Rallies are up to three times as long for speedier, better workouts. 4) It's a fun challenge! 5) Monumental insights to your normal strokes pop up during the learning process.

World Champion lefty Mike Ray.

6) You can alternate hands in successive games to last longer on the court. 7) It's backup if you injure the main arm during a match. 8) You can enter more events in a tournament. 9) It's a way to continue to play while resting chronic inflammation in the dominant elbow or shoulder. Swing away, southpaw!

I was said to have the game's best slow-ball backhand, and when I finally started to believe it, I attributed it to writing extensive longhand throughout life. The backhand movement of the pencil across the paper repeats tens-of-thousands of strokes and lines, using the same fine motor and visual components as the racquet stroke. The first thing I did after deciding to become ambidextrous was to switch to writing mirror image, right to

The devastating southpaw of the 1080s Bret Harnett. Serve and shoot and dive – the predecessor of modern racquetball in circa 1982. (US RB Museum)

left, to more quickly gain a lefty backhand. The next move was to turn books upside down so that the print flows right-to-left as Arabic, Chinese or Hebrew, and I've read the last 300 books in this fashion. It trains the eyes to become 'ambi-visual' in tracking print, ergo balls, from right to left. This aids the right-hander's backhand stroke, since 80% of serves and shots on the court travel in that direction. Our daily world is seeing so much print flowing from left to right, that you should never again explain away your cheesy backhand with bogus excuses until you've learned to track the ball better from right to left. That can be the solution to your next tournament win. Next, I wrote 1000 pages of an autobiography Catman Keeley: The Adventures of a Lifetime on an upside down monitor, like the one I'm looking at now.

Least you think there is something odd about any of this, I wish to advance that Leonardo da Vinci kept journal notes in mirror writing that his peers called 'secret code' to prevent theft of ideas. I rather think he just wanted to balance aspects of his life. Da Vince was many grand things, and foremost an anatomist who must have understood the premise for visual balance from his dissections. Mammalian eyeballs removed from their sockets are as ping-pong balls with muscle attachments about the sphere causing it to turn and twist, plus a colored iris made of muscle, and a lens with muscle attachments for accommodation of vision. Seeing is as much lifting weights as curls and presses. If you read only in the conventional direction of left to right, the eyes become muscularly unbalanced and will trace moving objects such as balls weakly from right to left.

The other profits from reading and writing backwards include greater stamina (in turning the book at 30-minute intervals from upside down to right side up), relief from eye, neck and back strain due to prolonged reading or writing, writing class notes that no one will want to borrow, coding, and reading the newspaper simultaneously from across the table with your mate.

There's sufficient ado over left-right brain dichotomy to make Leonardo roll over in his grave, however the classic Drawing on the Right Side of the Brain is worthwhile. I once offered to teach (where I was also coaching racquetball with the methods) a college course on The Art and Science of Mirror Reading and Writing but was thwarted by the dean, so I may write a serious book with the same title in mirror print that comes with a mirror bookmark for transition. I presently sub-teach middle and high school, and write assignments on the black boards in mirror image, causing the girls to use their compact mirrors to read to the rest of the class until they're all fluent in a week. Wonderfully, most middle-school students turn books upside down and read immediately, high school females typically do the same, but males stumble over words. Male athletes are more persistent at the task in believing that it helps them see a baseball, basketball, etc. better. The principal summoned me to his office once to ask why so many students about campus were observed reading their texts upside down. I explained the benefits of the

The two times to focus are on the serve and stroke. Javier Moreno in 2010. (Mike Augustin)

habit for sports to the chief, an ex-boxer and wrestler, who asked for a personal lesson on mirror writing.

I'm a proud self-taught dyslexic who often sees 'tixe' and doesn't know where to go. An eerie thing happened one stormy night a few years ago while reading in a coffin lined with electric blankets to make a comfortable bed. I was teaching myself with an optical-quality mirror to read Lewis Carroll's Through the Looking Glass and came upon the passage of 'Twiddle-Dee and Twiddle-Dum' that's written in actual mirror image! I bolted straight up and shut out the light.

Am I right? There are many tips and related quirks in this essay to combat the plague of left-handers, while paradoxically encouraging you to become one. By now, it's evident that playing lefty is a new frontier that many will realize, that writing mirror image is a first step in that direction, and further that reading upside down aids visual tracking. Now the best southpaws march in.

The All-Time Top Ten Lefties:

1. **Cliff Swain** – Six-time world champion.
2. **Kane Waselenchuk** – The most successful heir to Swain, and some argue his better.
3. **Mike Ray** - World Champion, smooth and consistent, with the best overhead.
4. **Bud Muehleisen** – The first world champion, and great all-racquets athlete.
5. **Bret Harnett** – Two-time Pro Player of the Year, and hit almost as big as Swain.
6. **Steve Serot** – Power southpaw in the days of slow balls, who finished #2 to Brumfield.
7. **Craig McCoy** – A top pioneer pro with stylish and smooth strokes, similar to Mike Ray.
8. **Bruce Christensen** - His lefty power serve took out Brumfield at one pro national.
10. **Mike Guidry** - A top singles and doubles competitor for over a decade.

Even the Best Have Weaknesses to Exploit

In today's superfast shoot, shoot, shoot game it seems that even the top players in the world have a philosophy of playing the ball, not their opponent. They have practiced for hours all their shots repeatedly and play what can be called 'situational racquetball'. They select shots exclusively based on where the ball bounces in the court paying little attention to how that shot plays into the strengths or weakness of the opponent. While this brand of racquetball has advantages and clearly has a place in your repertoire, it's not the only strategy to play and in some cases is not the best.

When I was a young player of all sports there was a sports comic book in which a superhero team visited the home court of a super-villains with a nefarious referee and little chance of winning- sounds like old time racquetball- until one of the good guys instructed his teammates to stop at certain X´s around the court and take the same shots repeatedly. This is where I learned situational strategy.

If you encounter an opponent you've never played before in a league match or tournament, and you've heard no scouting report, and observe no weaknesses during his warm-up, then situational racquetball of playing the ball and not your adversary is definitely the way to start the match. As the games progress and you pick up a flaw or tendency in the your opponent´s game, you can switch to a modified strategy of taking your best shots, while looking to expose your rival´s weakness, and take advantage of his tendencies and patterns. Then in the course of the match the shot selection technique often evolves entirely to picking the challenger's weaknesses like an old scab while avoiding his strengths.

Do all contestants have at least one weakness? The answer is yes, in that there is the weakest link in any chain. But it's not always that easy to spot and exploit it. For a decade in the 70´s I played the best of the best and the best of the rest in the world of racquetball and virtually all had weaknesses. This is how at one time or another I was able to beat all of the national champs of an era. They were stellar, better and quicker and greater stamina athletes than I, but in fact most had more than one weakness. I was able to spot and catalogue flaws like a baseball pitcher knows the areas to pitch to of all the power hitters in the majors. In virtually every good to great player I ever played there was either a chink in the armor or weakest link in the chain, and you can learn to spot and exploit them too. It´s usually worth three points in an eleven point game and five in a fifteen pointer to target a flaw. Can you afford to give those points away? If your name is not Kane Waselenchuk, the answer is probably no.

One of the most feared and revered champions of the 1970's was Bill Schmidtke. He was feared for his unmatched forehand kill shot and revered as not only a two-time national

Who will bring down the King? (Poster by Mike Augustin)

only titles Brum didn't win were taken by Schmidtke who won the 1971 and 1974 IRA National Championships with Brum and the rest of the top players in the draw. Bill's ability to relax and play well on big points was legendary, and his endurance to run hard and play all day was amazing

I had the honor of drawing the defending national champion Schmidtke in the first round of the first National Invitational Championship in 1971. While I was the new National Paddleball Champion, my experience with strung racquets was a few months paling next to Bill who had been a finalist in 1968 at the first ever National Strung Paddle Rackets Tournament- that's what it was called way back then. I noticed immediately that Bill's backhand posed no offensive threat, and that even though he never missed a forehand he struggled with my backhand down the line ceiling shots, pass drives and kill shots. I could beat Bill on all levels as long as I kept the ball along the left side wall and away from the vaunted forehand. I turned the 40′x20′ court to 40′x1′ isolating the entire match along the left side wall. While it required control and concentration exposing Schmidtke's vulnerability led to a 21-8, 21-4 victory over the multiple national champ. I would continue with that same strategy for the rest of my career against Bill beating him nineteen out of twenty games, only losing a 21-20 tiebreaker coming off mononucleosis that I still can't remember a point of to this day. Even the great Schmidtke could be neutralized by recurrently exposing his weakness.

In the next round, which was the quarters of the sixteen man Invitational, I played New York State Champion Charlie Garfinkle. Never having played each other before we each entered the match with the same situational shots of hitting forehands kills into the forehand corner and backhand kills into the backhand corner, and when in question drive or ceiling to the other guy's backhand. This played right in to my sweet spot as I had the best backhand killshot and the second best backhand ceiling game after, Charlie Brumfield. My backhand was stronger than my forehand, which was highly unusual in the early 70s. The Great Gar's forehand was solid as oak but his backhand didn't hold up as I picked at it like a woodpecker until I won the first game 21-1, an unheard of score against a star player. Yet Gar was also a keen strategist and reversed the second game with his never-before-seen patented Garfinkle Serve to my forehand. (A shoulder height Z medium paced serve that would bounce a foot behind the short line, strike the right side wall and die in the right rear corner.) By keeping the ball away from my trusty backhand he turned the direction of the match and won the second game 21-18. I regrouped in game three, stepped up and cut off the Garfinkle Serve with a forehand volley (before the short hop service return rule) and was able to expose his backhand again in game three for a competitive 21-12 tiebreaker to move to the semis.

As an aside and in the gallery that day Carl Loveday who begat Bud Muehleisen who begat Charlie Brumfield together developed most of the shots of pioneer racquetball. However, as Brum is apt to say, 'Even a blind squirrel finds an acorn', and against Gar I had invented the definitive fly return that sealed his doom on the tournament circuit as other players picked it up, which is too bad because I really liked him.

After losing in the semis to my often nemesis, Charlie Brumfield with Brums Bleacher Bums hoisting signs that said and singing, 'Brum #1, God #2, Keeley #3′, I had to play teenage phenom Steve Serot in the third place match. At the age of fifteen Serot already had the best combination of a power backhand, power forehand and unmatched diving and court coverage of any player on the hardwood. To make matters worse, he was a lefty. Thankfully even Serot had one Achilles heel. He hadn't yet developed the ceiling game that Brumfield and I had mastered and some say invented. While Serot was the most dangerous player in the world from the front wall to thirty-five feet back, I managed with consistent ceiling shots mixed with a few Around the World and high Z balls that he also had not seen, to keep Steve 36′ or deeper throughout the match. From there even young 'Splinter Chest' couldn't dive and retrieve my kill shots. By finding his single flaw chest high in deep court I was able to take the match 21-11, 21-11 against the player who turned out to be my toughest opponent and best rival for a decade.

The most flawless female player in history may have been leapin' Peggy Steding. (Legends)

Even the best players over the years have had some part of their game that left them exposed or at least neutralized their strengths.

Cliff Swain, the player I consider the best ever, and Mike Ray his southpaw rival dominated in the early and mid-90s but shared the same weakness. Ray is well over six feet tall, thin and had long arms and legs. While Swain was an inch or so under six feet, he had the wingspan of a player much taller, allowing him like Ray to get to balls that seemed to be well out reach. Both players liked to camp out at center court just behind the short line. This position was exploitable. Marty Hogan and Sudsy Monchik were more successful against Swain and Ray than any other players in history because they attacked that little known defect. Both Cliff and Mike who could cover the whole 20 foot width of the court in a bound were vulnerable against a hard ball hit just to the right of their bodies. Instead of hitting away from the two storks, Marty and Sudsy pounded body shots causing the lefties to flick the ball back with their backhands because even with perfect swing preparation their front court position and long arms left them open to the direct attack. Swain and Ray conquered all challengers for an era except Hogan and Monchik who discovered their little known weakness.

Marty and Sudsy shared a common vulnerability as well, but it took nerves of steel to expose it. Marty hit the ball over 140 MPH with a small racquet and Sudsy hit it well over 180 MPH with the big racquet, and the pair were the two hardest hitters of their generation. Both owned explosive power off the backhand and forehand wings but both players were prone to making infrequent mistakes with their ultra-powerful forehands. On the professional level this is a foible. So, if you overcame the fear of their pace and kept the ball deep to the forehand both Hogan and Monchik would eventually yield a ball slightly up, or skip a few forehands and hand you the game if you worked hard. Most players avoided their thunderous power and hit the ball to their powerful backhands that were more consistent, and of course most players lost that way.

Ruben Gonzalez and Jason Mannino both haled from Staten Island and are two of the fastest players to play the game and two of the best front court players you'll ever see. The only way to neutralize these two diving machines is to keep them deep in the back court while you take center court position. While keeping them deep is no cake walk to victory, letting them stay in the front court is their walk in the park. You must force them into the improbable odds of beating you from 36′ to 40′ deep. In the early years of the slow ball before these guys were born to the court, I did it with the ceiling shot, high Z and Around the World ball. Later in the 80′s squash legend Victor Niederhoffer kept Ruben deep in the back with precise wide angle and down the rail passes. And in the 90′s Sudsy beat both Ruben and Jason with crushing cross-court power passes to either side. No matter how you do it, you had better keep the two New Yorkers really deep or sign the ball′s death warrant.

We just dissected the vulnerabilities of ten of the best players in the history of the sport. With keen observation and a refined strategy, you too can expose the weakness in anybody's game.

Strategy: A Smorgasbord

The right strategy must come to mind in the worst scenario –
losing, tired, hometown ref, and nowhere else to turn but inside.

1. Always change a losing game; never change a winning game.
2. Always have a plan going into a match, and a backup plan.
3. Always have a surprise to pull out all the stops.
4. Reconnoiter your opponent before the match for his strengths and weaknesses.
5. Have a general strategy against all power players, and another against all control players.
6. Analyze every match – how would you play it differently next time.
7. Keep a log of your strategies, and of the opponents.
8. Always have a customized strategy against each opponent, if possible.
9. Call a timeout when you skip two straight shots, or the opponent runs three points.
10. Keep a coach in the crowd for a second opinion.
11. Have an offensive second serve, such as the jam or Z.
12. Save your upset serve, for example a crack ace, for game winning points.
13. Have a no-fail strategy that kicks in in the worst case scenario.
14. Define your strengths and weaknesses between tournaments, and drill the latter.
15. Set a goal, and time increments to achieve it.
16. Resist the norm – The way to the top is almost always a way no one else has tried.
17. Don't share your personal original strategies during your competitive career.
18. Find one edge against an opponent, or the field, and repeat it over and over.
19. Make your backhand as strong as your forehand.
20. Know the counters to all your strategies.
21. If an opponent throws something at you during a match that you can't handle, hit the same at him next point to know how to respond.
22. Use a slow game pace against a rabbit, and a fast pace against a sloth.
23. Always volley the ball when possible.
24. Always take the most aggressive shot possible during a rally.
25. Be able to hit five perfect consecutive ceiling balls as a fallback.

26. Match your physical attributes with your strategies, for example condition, age, grace. Elephant tusks cannot grow out of a dog's mouth.

27. Pick an overall strategy that is fun to play.

28. Strategy evolves on the sweaty hardwood, not in ivory towers, so think as you play practice matches.

29. Agree with your partner to pause after each game to dissect each other's play.

Champs like Sudsy and Rocky are open mouth about strategies if you ask. 2000 US Open. (Ed Arias)

30. Ask every instructor or pro you meet for his best secret strategy.

31. Ask better players to critique your strategies.

32. The best place to glean tidbits is by watching good players, or at a pro stop.

33. Unclutter the Clutter. Stop the mechanism. Have a sure-fire mantra or method to calm down instantly.

34. Develop a 'Muehleisen's Rheostat' at will of being able to crank up or down your intensity of play by 10%.

35. Fight first and save thoughts of victory for later.

36. The highest form of generalship is to conquer the gamesman by a stratagem.

37. At the beginner level a defensive strategy wins, but at an advanced level the most

offensive strategy always wins.

38. Have one strategy for a slow ball and another for a fast ball.

39. The best general strategy is serve and shoot.

40. Go to the ceiling if the rival runs a string of points.

41. Go for the jugular with aces and cracks when you have momentum.

42. The shot to practice the most is the kill, because it's the only stepping stone.

43. The serve to practice the most is the drive, as it's the most forceful in an aggressive game.

44. Save your best strategy for the ripest time - pick the flower when it is ready to be picked.

45. When you go up to the mountain often, you will eventually encounter the tiger, so be ready.

46. During a reconnoiter find a tiny edge. A tiny is the best soldier that quickly becomes an army.

47. Strategy is about setting yourself apart from the competition: it's a matter of being different at what you do.

48. Always have a backup service strategy.

49. The greatest tactic is to be able to execute at the worst times.

50. To win by strategy is no less the role of a general.

51. Practice the weakest link in the chain of each of your last performances.

52. Have a short term goal and a long term goal at all times.

53. Use glass to your advantage with serves and shot selection.

54. Shot selection is the most common trait of a win, and flaw of a lose.

55. Have pre-designed strategies for every game style.

56. The greatest strategy is to commit no mental or physical errors in a match.

57. If you're losing a match, is it because your strategy is failing or because of faulty execution of strategy?

58. Use a new strategy a hundred times in practice before taking it to a tournament.

59. When in doubt grab the bull by the horns.

60. Nothing is more beautiful in sport than a well-conceived plan that's executed flawlessly against a superior opponent for a win.

61. Study strategy over the years to achieve the spirit of the warrior.

Strokes

Cliff Swain practices what he preaches: ESP at a Virginia Pro Stop. (Ken Fife)

Early Swing Preparation

Swain, Sudsy, Kane Have ESP

The best modern racquetball players I have seen are Cliff Swain, King Kane and Sudsy. If only, I thought, I could find a common denominator of their strokes then I might also become a king.

The first thing that struck me is that they are the hardest hitting players.

The next step was their stroke analysis by getting on the court with Swain, then Sudsy, and closely examining Kane, to spot the shared factor. It was Early Swing Preparation.

ESP is the one thing that separates them from all others for velocity, accuracy and accumulating world titles.

Historically, they have the Earliest Swing Preparation I've ever seen and the ESP that make them winners almost every time except when they play each other. Racquetball is a game on inches and a game of milliseconds. Extremely tiny margins separate the very best from all the rest at the top. Cliff and Sudsy both would get their rackets up and ready for the next shot as their opponent was preparing to contact his shot. By the time the opposing player hit the ball these two ESP champions already had the racquet up, cocked and ready for the forehand or backhand stroke.

I think this preparation allows them to hit almost every shot with maximum power because they're ready to rip before they even get to the ball. In addition, it allows them to skip the step of getting the racket up and swing ready when getting to the ball.

It's not all about Early Swing Preparation but also where to cock the racquet at the top of the backswing. Each of the three champs keeps his backswing extremely low relative to the other top players.

Hence, the two commonalities of the hardest hitting, greatest racquetball players in history are: ESP and a flat, low cocked backswing. The early preparation provides the power, and the flat backswing ensures a level swing through the ball and level follow through to kill at the bottom board.

In the decades prior to this sort of Early Swing Preparation it wasn't really necessary. Rackets were smaller and much less advanced, balls were slower, and a player with quick feet and a sharp mind had plenty of time to get to the ball and set up his swing. The first ten National Champions all started by playing racquetball's slower sister-sport paddleball,

Bow forehand with ESP by Xia Yang in the 2012 Houston finals. (Xia Yang)

before picking up strung rackets and not one of them ran around the court with a racket high in the air.

The big head racquet is the impetus for the ESP swing, that were never available to the pioneer players.

My estimate is Swain, Sudsy and Kane hit the ball with the oversized racquet at 175 MPH. A great champ like Jason Mannino at just over 150 MPH, and so much faster than Marty Hogan with a small racket at a clocked 142 MPH in 1975. Even at 53 years old in 2111, Hogan hits about 160 MPH off both wings with a big racket.

96

Were they the three fastest players on tour? Was their court coverage keeping them in front of all others? No, it takes watching only one tournament to realize Jason Mannino is the fastest and keenest player on tour and covers the court better than anyone since the days of Brumfield and Serot.

Since the Hogan reign of the 70s through 80s, for one decade from 1993 to 2002 Cliff Swain and Sudsy Monchik dominated the sport to such an extent that that they won ten World Professional Championships. Then King Kane stepped in to take nearly every event to date. It almost seems mandatory to have ESP to win a single IRT pro event.

Early Swing Preparation. (US RB Museum)

97

Flipbook Forehand

Kimi Ferina (by Ken Fife)

Pros Speak from the Box

Forehand Grip

I teach the grip I use which is had by sliding the palm along the face to the handle and grasping with not too tense a handshake so that when the racquet's brought down into the potential contact zone the face is slightly closed to the front wall. My thought is the further down you can hold the racquet without losing control, the more power due to increased leverage. The purpose of the proper grip is to hit the ball flat and powerful.

- Cliff Swan

I use a traditional grip with the V of the thumb and forefinger over the top center handle surface.   *- Alvaro Beltran*

Paola's closed grip extends the elbow on contact at the 2014 Ektelon Nationals. (Mike Augustin)

I over-rotate the handle more than most hitters to close the racquet face. My pinkie barely touches the end of the grip.   *- Derek Robinson*

I turn the handle a quarter-turn between the forehand and backhand.   *- Corey Brysman*

The forehand grip I use is revolves around the handle to close the face of the racquet before the swing starts. This for me causes when the extension of the arm is full at the point of contact the racquet to be square and come through flat on the ball.   – *Dave Peck*

I grip lower and with the racquet turned over more than most people. Exactly, my little finger is nearly off the bottom of the handle so the butt's in the palm. The top face gets tilted toward the front wall a couple inches from upright. This modern low grip seems more natural to provide a flatter, stronger hit.   - *Sudsy*

I teach the standard grip of sliding the palm along the racquet face to the handle in a handshake with the V of the forehand and thumb over the middle of the top handle surface. When they become great players, then they can do a little switch moving the V one way or the other to close or open the face, but in the early stages the advantage lies in the standard grip. Now, in the years preceding Sudsy and then popularized by the 'man' himself, players began holding the handle low with the little finger off the butt and essentially only three fingers and thumb grasped. These tend to be the players with high velocity serve-and-shoot games, and true enough. It gives a longer racquet for more leverage.   - *Jeff Leon*

I use a 'slide-down grip by putting the palm on the face and sliding down to the handle, then grasping with the V formed by the thumb and forefinger over the center of the top handle surface. It feels strong like a handshake.
- *Marty Hogan*

I was one of the few players who, like Hogan, didn't change my grip from forehand to backhand. Players who choke down on the racquet are going for power, but control was my goal.
- *Mike Ray*

I believe the forehand grip in the modern game should be more westernized, which is to say that because of the speed of the game the racquet should be flattened out in the contact position by turning the hand (if you're right handed) around the handle a quarter-turn to the right from the handshake position. The face closes and flattens to the front wall, ready to hit. In the old days, we used a continental grip that's more toward the backhand side because there was more time for the grip change.   *- Charlie Brumfield*

I watched the grip change evolve popularly from the classic standard of holding the racquet with the butt-in-heel of hand of players like Keeley and Brumfield, to Hogan and the power generation who slid down a bit, to the modern players many of whom like Swain, Doyle and Sudsy climbed to the top by holding the butt in the palm of the hand. Who know where it will go next? The latter 'power grip' players all tilt the face of the racquet downward (top of racquet tilts an extra inch at the front wall) for a 'closed racquet' and they consistently get a flat, strong contact with a whipping forehand stroke.
                                                                                              - Jim Spittle

It is the same grip like I am shaking someone's hand.   *- Kerri Stoffregen Wachtel*

It is a normal forehand grip that similar to how you half a baseball b at with your primary hand.   *— Andy Hawthorne*

My forehand grip is just like my grip on a baseball bat. It's natural and feels great on the racquet.   *— John Ellis*

It was the traditional trigger grip and it came totally natural perhaps from my baseball background.   *— Davey Bledsoe*

Sliding my palm down the strings and on to the handle places my hand in my medium to low "handshake" grip.   *— Ken Woodfin*

103

Gripping action at the 2013 3-WallBall World Outdoor Championships. (Mike Augustin)

Jessica Parrilla's grip at the 2013 3-WallBall World Championships in Las Vegas. (Mike Augustin)

Pros Speak from the Box

Forehand

The most important thing on improving the forehand is racquet preparation. You don't hear it spoken often in racquetball but in tennis they talk about it all the time. The racquet should be up and waiting as the ball approaches, like a baseball player with the bat up, never down. In racquetball, players hold the racquet down, never up, and the ball's coming twice as fast as the baseball. I look like a praying mantis prancing about the court with the racquet up and ready, and I think there should be more like us.- *Cliff Swain*

The beginner should start in the court on the forehand side without a racquet and throw the ball sidearm down the forehand side. That's your sidearm kill stroke. After a few minutes practice, slide the racquet into your hand and use the same swing. Drill every day for a month with and without and with a racquet. The sidearm motion opposed to a three-quarter or underhand also ensures horizontal accuracy, pleasant since the target strip for kills is horizontal across the front wall. In later development, the shots are lowered to kills and velocity is added. The fly-kill follows. With learning, if they miss a shot they have to do push-ups or sit-ups. I recommend getting success with the forehand in the first month before thinking about the backhand.   *– Jeff Leon*

I teach a baseball batter swing with the legs spread and the smooth, perfect swing. Move forward to meet the ball and catch the opponent with his guard down. Strive for consistently solid hits.   *- Ruben Gonzalez*

I use a bigger back swing than most, and come over the outside top of the ball for a naturally powerful stroke with lots of top-outside spin.   *- Alvaro Beltran*

The stroke is hit according to the way you set for it. Think of a major league baseball hitter being prepared at the plate, stepping into the pitch, and swinging for a homerun. You never see a homerun hitter stepping across the plate, but straight into the coming ball.   *- Derek Robinson*

I emphasize extending the arm as the swing approaches the ball contact so that at the hit the arm is fully extended. The full length gives a longer radius of torque for greater head speed hence faster ball velocity.   *– Dave Peck*

My personal stroke is somewhat compact and close to the body like a muffled explosion.

How do I hit my backhand? Possibly better than anyone else in the history of the game. My teaching method is sound fundamentals, compact, very flat, and quick. Sound fundamentals means a high, deep back swing, turn the hips, come through the ball very flat with a controlled aggression on a lengthened arm, the weight transfers to the front foot, and follow through so your racquet points to the back wall. *— Sudsy*

Make sure the stroke is flat just before, during and after contact. *- Corey Brysman*

A perfectly fluid horizontal bow by Robert Sostre at a 2014 WOR event. (Stephen Fitzsimons)

Watch the ball, set up, and keep the racquet head level. The feeling is that I can handle anything, and the ball always makes the front wall. Keeping the head level means having the handle parallel to the floor rather than dipped, so that if you're a little behind the ball it goes side wall to front wall, and if you're a bit ahead it goes across the court. Again, everything makes the front wall. *- Mike Ray*

The forehand is the point getter, so try for a winner on any easy setup. Even if you miss,

th of torque for greater head speed be weak and the rally becomes one offensive opportunity after another.   — *Marty Hogan*

My stroke technique is moving into the ball with a closed stance. Whereas today's players open their stance with a short power stroke, mine is full body movement into the ball with a closed stance. This keeps my options open of down-line, pinches and cross-courts. I feel the closed stance gives greater consistency and deception. With a proper motion and point of contact, the opponent stays frozen longer and success percentages go up.   — *Jerry Hilecher*

Open stance, closed face, with a level follow through by Rocky at a WOR final. (Mike Augustin)

I believe the ball has to be hit either at the place where it's easiest to kill, or at the place where it's easiest to block the opponent so that you can hit to the open court. My winning preference has been to hit the ball where my body can protect the shot. Even if I don't roll the shot, the opponent is shielded out. Since the opponent can't re-kill, it's a 100% ploy.   — *Charlie Brumfield*

The forehand for most players is the center of the game, and that's been my case. Step forward into the ball, even if you're jammed take a quick-step, and complete the swing. All of our 'big forehands' use this body momentum transferred to the ball. The modern big hitters talk about their faces being square to the front wall on the hit as the most important aspect of their forehands, but let's think about this. Actually the racquet face due to the grip begins, as most have said, closed to the front wall during and just up to the contact. Then the pros pronate, or turn the wrist over quickly, to close the face of the racquet for the hit. This contact lasts longer than most think, a few inches in terms of space due to the elasticity of the ball and strings. Here's the kicker, on why the modern hitters use a closed face but talk about flat hits. Nearly every shot coming at you has topspin, and the closed racquet counters this to hit the flat, spin-less, powerful shot.

- Jim Spittle

The three important tips on the strokes are: 1) Hit 'em as early as you can in their trajectory back to you, preferably on the fly or half-volley. Rather than let the ball drop to give your opponent leisure time, take the shot higher up to force him to react in an enfeebled way. 2) Use a continuous swing from the backswing to the follow through rather than segmented jerks that cause power shortage. 3) Hit with abandon. In many challenges in life you can't grind but must be bold. As they say in Vegas, 'If you're going to gamble, gamble.' *- Victor Niederhoffer*

Take a complete backswing and "salute" the racquet to your head. Keep the elbow up and level to the floor. *– Davey Bledsoe*

Hit it flat. Elbow in on downswing and the slap the ball. *– Susy Acosta*

Stay low, hit flat. *- Rhonda Rajsich*

Flat and level. Think a baseball swing. *– Fran Davis*

Do not feel the need to over swing. Stay down on the forehand, especially on your back leg as you come through the ball. Same for the backhand too. *– John Ellis*

Use your hips and keep your weight behind the ball when you make contact. *– Andy Hawthorne*

Attempt to add a little top on impact. *– Dave Fleetwood*

Make it feel like you are throwing a side arm pitch in baseball. *– Jose Rojas*

I want to always swing level. I pretend I am hitting the ball off a glass coffee table and I don't want to break the glass. *- Kerri Stoffregen Wachtel*

Go skim some flat stones on a glass water surface and you'll lead with your elbow, lead with the inside edge of your palm (racquet butt to target), and then begin on court what becomes the twirl of your forearm that marries up with the roll of your wrist to turn your forearm and palm inward, as you wave the racquet strings through the ball, as after the strings face toward ground into first a target pointing and then curving around you follow-through up to below your off shoulder. *– Ken Woodfin*

The bow forehand follow through is as level as it was drawn. Greg Lewerenz at the 2014 WOR Belle Isle Outdoor Longwall National Championships. (Greg Lewerenz)

Success on both sides takes lots of practice, timing, leg strength, and patience. Patience in letting the ball drop and fall into your hitting zone. *– Charlie Pratt*

Flipbook Forehand

Rhonda Rajsich (by Ken Fife)

A Horizontal bow raised with the elbow, arm and racquet face in a high plane off the Pacific Ocean at the Huntington Beach 2012 WOR Championships. (Mike Augustin)

Flipbook Forehand

Rich Benderoth (by Ken Fife)

Pros Speak from the Box
Backhand Grip

I adjust from a forehand to backhand grip by rotating my index finger knuckle two-tenths of a turn on the handle in the direction away from the front wall (while facing the right side wall for a lefty backhand.)
- Cliff Swain

Still low on the racquet handle per the forehand grip, I change drastically to the backhand to close the face more than most players.
- Sudsy

I use the conventional grip, slightly closed from the forehand grip.
- Alvaro Beltran

I use the more revolved grip to close the racquet face before the swing starts. The closed face that begins the swing squares to parallel to the front wall with full arm extension. At the instant of contact the strings are parallel to the front wall to cause the ball to fly solid and straight. Once more for clarity: The more closed face actually becomes flat to the front wall due to the full extension of the hitting arm at the point of contact.
– Dave Peck

Whereas my forehand grip was over-rotated to close the face, my backhand is phenomenally over-rotated to close the face more. Hence, there's a high degree of rotation change between my forehand and backhand. Rotating the racquet on the backhand to my extreme is much harder and longer to master, but once that happens then I believe it's a stronger stroke. We all stand on the heads of the giants of the game that preceded us, and I like to think that one day I'll be remembered for my innovation of the greatly over-rotated backhand grip that leads to a stroke with more of a chopping wood than traditional wrist snap. I learned it from hitting two-fisted backhands when young, and kept the same grip without the second hand on the backhand swing as I got older. The edges it provides are a quicker setup time and more power, plus a larger hitting zone that includes not just waist high shots as earlier, but shoulder high kills as well.
- Derek Robinson

The modern game of speed demands a backhand grip like Sudsy or Peck where they turn the racquet from the handshake position over to the left (for right handers). This closes the face to the front wall to keep the ball from flying up and coming off the back wall, which is the main correction among amateur players.
- Charlie Brumfield

Backhand grip close up by Brian Pineda at a WOR Championship. (Mike Augustin)

Solicit expert advice at least once if one of your strokes is weak, so you don't practice a bad habit for years. For the backhand, it's almost always the grip's fault.   *- Jim Spittle*

Your grip on forehand and backhand should be the same, and very close to perpendicular to the ground.   *- Charlie Pratt*

I was one of the first pros to not change grips from the forehand to backhand, and I feel this gives me a quicker racquet preparation and 20% more backhand power by closing the face and allowing a deeper contact zone. This no-change backhand presents an 'open' or slightly tilted back face that angles the ball up, but I compensate with a strong wrist movement to bring the racquet face parallel to the front wall for solid hits. I can contact at mid-line or toward the rear foot with a level handle and flat face. The no-change grip makes even more sense in the modern game where you can put a hard shot right at a player who gets hand-cuffed between grips.   - *Marty Hogan*

No difference in backhand or forehand grip; you want to hold the racquet where you have a good wrist snap with no restrictions on the follow through off both wings.

— Rich Wagner

De La Rosa in a gripping dive at the 2014 Pro Kennex Tournament of Champions. (Mike Augustin)

I rotate grip about 45 degrees from the forehand grip. It feels comfortable and that is where I have had the most success.   *– Andy Hawthorne*

I definitely change my grip and believe players that want to excel need to have not just one backhand grip, but several depending on the shot from that side. A backhand ceiling ball is a different grip then a pass or the dink shot.   *– John Ellis*

Everything changes and now the backhand grip has morphed to place the hand behind the handle for more support and stability to be able to swing faster. The index finger knuckle goes on top, the palm diagonally riding the edge between the top plane and back slant, the routine trigger grip spacing between pointer and big finger, and the belief you can shoot hard, even high-to-low, and, as needed, with reckless abandon or delicate, feather touch.
                                                                        – Ken Woodfin

The BH grip should be the same as your drawing a sword from underneath your opposite armpit.   *- Kerri Stoffregen Wachtel*

For BH your index finger knuckle has to be over the top part of the grip.   *– Jose Rojas*

My BH grip is very similar to the FH, not much change but turning the wrist on my BH stroke. A 14 -year old recently told me to use Paola's grip from now on so I can kill it... so I told him to call me in ten years and tell me how that's working for him and let me know if he has 8 national open titles with that grip. Ha ha!   *– Cheryl Gudinas*

The Bow Backhand

with Dave Peck

The secret meeting

I was thrown for a loop in 2003 when my former nemesis, World Champ, and Legend Dave Peck whispered for a quiet meeting in a back room of the Coral Springs Quadrangle Club where I was an advisor to the Legends Pro Tour. We sat on a hard bench as he explained, 'I heard you were looking for racquetball secrets, so here's mine. It's the Bow Stroke.' Later, in 2011, Coach Jim Winterton claimed the Bow Draw is the basis of all modern stroke instruction, 'though it's misunderstood by many.' This tutorial describes the stroke straight from Dave Peck's demonstration and description in that closed door meeting.

This article focuses on the backhand because, up to this moment, it's the flaw of most advanced players' repertoire.

The Soul of the Bow

The essence of the Bow backhand is the racquet is drawn back early in the swing so the hitter looks like an archer about to release an arrow. The position is statuesque, fairly rigid, and corks up marvelous power. The player may pursue the ball on the court with the racquet fixed in this position, or he may begin the draw after planting for the swing. The better method to start, and that is used by many of the current (2014) pros, is to draw the bow while scooting around the court.

The Details of the Bow

'This is the first time I've told the aspects to anyone,' revealed Dave, and then he began to cry a little. He is a big man, a 185-pound wrestling champion and fullback at University of Texas before pro racquetball, and so I was moved to listen. The aspects are:

- The grip ideally should be a severe Eastern grip so there is no excess wrist movement.
- The elbow should be out, like throwing a Frisbee.
- You get power from a counter rotation to a rotation - so the first body torque is away from the ball, not into the ball.
- You also get power from height and depth of the backswing.
- The archer's elbow is the key with the arm lying in a horizontal plane to the floor.

- The trajectory should take an out and around plane - imagine a hula hoop placed around one's waist - that is the trajectory.
- The follow through should be level - the ball will go where your follow through goes.
- The power comes from the back - not the front.
- Thus out and around with the motion, not up and down.

Dave finished, 'I just want everyone to know that Dr., Bud Muehleisen taught me what I know about the game, and then I practiced very hard.'

The developer and refiner of the Bow Stroke, Dr. Bud Muehleisen with 70 national and international titles and World Champ Dave Peck. (Chelsea George for the 2003 Legends.)

Implement the Bow

Usually, an experienced player adds only the elbow crook to his current stroke to make the power Bow work. The elbow and arm lie in a plane like a floating plate parallel to and between the ceiling and floor. The drawn Bow power works for both the backhand and forehand. It is practiced the same way as other strokes by the repetition of drop and kill, set up and kill, and assorted practices with partners.

It is a kill stroke with superb horizontal accuracy (at the sacrifice of vertical accuracy) since the front wall target for nearly every racquetball shot is a horizontal bar across the

Jose Rojas running bow backhand at the 2011 WOR Championships. (Mike Augustin)

125

front wall extending from the floor up to about 6" high. You may envision an open 6" window from side wall to side wall across the front wall and attempt to put the ball through the window.

It's more important to aim the shot and control where it's going, rather than blast it hard. Today's game seems to demand velocity since the ball's fast and the racquets are weapons. However, without accuracy the shots are sloppy and the game's a loser. Ferocious power tempered by control describes Dave Peck's drawn Bow strokes that won the 1982 Ektelon championship and #1 Player in the World, breaking Hogan's winning streak, and forming the model for the modern strokes.

When the Drawn Bow Power Strokes Came About

Coach Jim Winterton describes, 'I remember passionate arguments about mechanics and Dave was part of a group of people in the 90s when he worked for Ektelon arguing out in Colorado Spring with amateurs who did not grasp his concept. AMPRO, the professional teaching organization, finally adopted an 'out and around' stroke mechanics theory circa the mid-90s when they formally adopted the Blow mechanics. I asked him, 'How did you learn this stroke?' His reply was, 'Trial and error.' Dave Peck revolutionized the game by changing stroke mechanics, which my competition is still struggling with. I use Dave as a resource, often; without Dave, Winterton does not exist - at least in the way I do now!'

The Next Champ to Draw the Bow

Cliff Swain was a natural phenom who learned on the 60-foot three wall courts at The L in South Boston. This was AKA The Graveyard of Champions where Cliff became a diamond in the rough. Then Dave Peck polished Cliff's strokes and strategy for the classical ESP Bowed forehand, backhand and serves.

And after Swain, came King Kane and the rest of the rest who may be identified in the pictures in this book using the Bow strokes. The reason is Dave Peck's Bow and Arrow draws the backswing to level the release with power and horizontal accuracy.

Why the Bow Works

The bowed elbow on the crank puts everything in a horizontal plane to provide horizontal accuracy across the front wall. All killshots require horizontal accuracy. It's as simple as that. With the Bow stroke if you 'release early' by hitting the ball too soon on the stroke it's still a flat kill deflected to the left; or if you 'release late' by hitting the ball too soon it's still a rollout deflected to the right.

The Bow is also a natural Early Swing Preparation for some players who choose it to be – you may chase the ball around the court with the Bow drawn like in the archer battles in *Lord of the Rings.*

The big Bow Forehand by Charlie Pratt at the 2011 Las Vegas Outdoor Nationals. (WOR)

Cross Train with Archery

It's obvious, isn't it? Early racquetball professionals cross trained their backhand with golf. The Bow backhand may be bettered by taking up archery. There are also weight machines that imitate the draw Bow action.

Photo Opportunity

This is one motion that may be learned straight from the still photos in this book since the elbow cock is pronounced, and frozen, during the stroke like a stop frame action. You may even make the drawn Bow your Early Swing Preparation for the backhand. There are many photogenic examples of modern pros using the draw backhand clustered around this article, and a couple of flip card sequences with the other backhand articles.

A Bow backswing also works on the forehand, and service, as viewed in the other photos.

The Bow backhand is a panacea, the most significant development in stroke work since Marty Hogan introduced Power Racquetball, and now racquetball thanks Dave Peck and his mentor Bud Muehleisen.

The point to remember is the Bow increases backhand kill accuracy while reducing errors by placing the hitting arm in a horizontal plane that is the same as the horizontal stripe target across the front wall. It's hard to miss with the Bow, which is why nearly every modern pro uses it in one form or another.

Daniel De La Rosa backhand with an extended elbow on contact at the 2014 Pro Kennex Tournament of Champions. De La Rosa broke onto the IRT in 2008 at the ripe age of 16 after being Introduced to the game by his parents at the tender age of five years old. (Mike Augustin)

Dane Elkins strokes a bowed backhand which make him the junior to watch in 2014. Here in the 2014 Ektelon nationals he won dual divisions in the 14 and 18 years. The bowed elbow on the crank puts everything in a horizontal plane to provide horizontal accuracy across the front wall. All killshots require horizontal accuracy. 2014 was a decent year for his bowed backhand. He made the USA indoor and outdoor team, won an outdoor world junior title, two junior Olympic titles, and the two at Ektelon's nationals. (West Coast RB Museum)

Flipbook Backhand

Rhonda Rajsich (by Ken Fife)

Balls, Body and Swing

An Evolutionary Article

Sports equipment evolves the player...movement... and final strategy.

In the beginning, 1971, the racquetball was mush, and the strokes slow to push it around the old courts in winning rallies. The pros, like me, were string beans wielding tiny racquets..

Then in the 80s, the ball quickened and the strokes changed to power, with deeper contact and a bullwhip crack.

In the 90s, the pace of play was frightfully heightened by the superball with big-head racquets, crisper strokes, and squat players.

There have been three epochs. The early, lanky champs with push strokes were Bill Schmidtke, Bud Muehleisen, and Charley Brumfield. The intermediary fireplugs with power swings on a relatively fast ball were Mike Yellen, Dave Peck and Marty Hogan. The current bulldog elite are Sudsy Monchik, Jason Mannino and the better of the rest who explode on shots like weightlifters at a bar. The power serve increasingly dominates over time, and the rally length and millisecond to ponder between shots decrease in proportion to ball speed.

The ball begot the stroke begot the player, and that's the history of racquetball. And, likely, any sport, military or industry evolves with equipment.

What can you do about this trend to improve your game? My play girdles all the game eras, so these solutions are from observations of ball, racquet and champ body developments, and matching my molasses stroke against the diverge of three swings of the 'Big Three' players in successive eras- Marty Hogan, Sudsy Monchik and Cliff Swain.

Each champ adapted with a stroke to meet the speedier ball, yet with commonalities. These shared elements are: 1) Fast set-up on the shot; 2) Quick swing, tending from linear toward circular; 3) Deep contact to allow the speeding ball; 4) Stroke power for ball velocity; 5) A closed racquet face to counteract the approaching topspin ball scooting along the hardwood.

The three model strokes by yesterday's and today's 'Big Three' players embrace all these requisites, with a gripping consistency near the butt low on the handle. This gives leverage a la holding a hammer handle bottom, 'closes' the racquet face to off-set an oncoming topspin, and allows a deeper contact where the face automatically squares to meet the ball.

Alvaro making his 21st IRT pro final in 2012 with a postcard bow backhand. (Mike Augustin)

The trade-off of power boost for loss of accuracy is no longer debatable: the name of the new game is power, not bulls eye. To the contrary, I first honed accuracy as a novice, and gradually increased power, as portrayed in a daily practice Heads Up! drill with the Michigan State University hockey, wrestling and football teams. One player sat with his back against the front wall facing the service line, as the other dropped and killed the shot to a halo region around his head. The idea was to simulate tournament pressure and not blink. Eventually someone got bonked and the roles were reversed.

Now look at the three almighty unalike strokes of the Big Three, and match the salient points of quick set-up, quick swing, deep contact and power. These stroke variations in biological evolution (don't blink) are called adaptive radiation, so let's briefly look at each.

Marty Hogan's young stroke was ridiculed by the era's masters as an awkward use of raw power, even as they ate crow. Hogan's fulfills the requirements for a modern stroke by using a pendulum swing that contacts the ball deeper heretofore than anyone. 'The pendulum starts way up, 'as high as I can reach on the back swing,' he says. The mechanics are the more an arc uplift of, say, a clock pendulum, the greater the swing power. Marty boosts this force by supinating (laying back so the palm is up) the wrist at the top of the forehand, and pronating (flexing the wrist approximately the opposite direction) at the top of the backhand back swing. It allows a very deep hitting zone -an extreme off the rear foot- that translates into a split-second extra set-up time with a stronger report. At his level, shades make the difference in brilliance.

Sudsy Monchik takes a new swing that, like predecessor Hogan, engendered a new crop of strokes across the country. 'Compact, close to the body and explosive, like a bull tossing its head,' he describes his swing. The grip for his forehand and backhand, as noted, is low on the handle with an extremely closed face. The swing is best described as classical explosive with precise timing. The odd thing is Sudsy may run the court in a crouched position as if in a horizontal mine shaft, chasing and hitting faster than most uprights.

Cliff Swain's success with a dissimilar stroke relies on early racquet preparation. His teaching clinic preamble and conclusion is, 'I hate to harp, but get your racquet up and back early'. Cliff is a praying mantis on the court, stalking prey, ball, and leaping to score. Where Hogan gains a precious instant with a deep contact, and Sudsy by scampering in a squat, Swain has already made a back swing- low, wrist cocked- like a gunslinger who replies without flinch, 'That was my draw, do you want to see it again?'

When the smoke clears on equipment, stroke and body type evolution, adaptive radiation is the driving force. This is the process in which one species gives rise to multiple species that exploit different niches, in a relatively short period of time. The changing ball has produced new anatomical champs exploiting forced new strategies.

Who's responsible for the speeded ball? The answer is the reason baseball prevailed over softball, sponge ping-pong paddles won out, and basketballs are highly pressurized. The ball manufacturers ultimately control a sport's evolution, racket makers fall in step... and it's all due to public capability and culpability The manufacturers hype action in sport to convince participants it's more fun, pressurized balls wear out and break sooner, and a fast game is easier for beginners, youngsters, elderly, and particularly ladies whom the males follow buying more balls.

The tendency in recent decades in all sports is away from analysis toward frenzy. The process is rapid and ongoing. My fellow animals, swing with the champs, and win!

Mexican professional André Parrilla forehand with deep contact and a flat swing through the contact zone at the 2014 Juarez Open. (Ken Fife)

Point of Contact

A Swing through History

While many racquetball books will try to teach you how like the pros to prepare the racket early, emulate the mechanical stroke, and even copy the grimaces of top players, most miss one very important point. They miss the contact point.

Almost every great shot throughout history has been struck by every great player at different points of contact in the downswing. The point of contact is three-dimensional, and has the aspects of a baseball suspended in mid-air:

- **Depth** in the swing from in the back of the rear foot to in front of the lead foot.

- **Distance** out from the body from on the navel to extended racquet's length.

- **Height** from close to the floor to overhead.

You can't hit the splat like Hogan or Kane while contacting the ball in front of you no matter how many years you practice, and so on with the pinch, wide angle pass, and every other shot and serve. However, a brief review of the points of contacts of some of the greatest shots ever and their artists will provide starting points.

The most amazing contact point is the reputed 'best shot in history' that I saw repeated consistently over the years until all-racquet champ Vic Niederhoffer *three-wall boasted* at 20-20 to beat a young Marty Hogan in the tiebreaker at the !1975 NRC National Championships in Las Vegas. This is normally a dangerous shot even when relaxed. Niederhoffer let a 140 MPH Hogan photon pass his body before calmly exacting the three wall-boast that because of the deep contact hit directly into the side wall next to him, then zoomed to the opposite side wall less than a foot from the front wall, and died as soon as it touched the front to bring the house down.

The next deepest contact point and probably the most famous overall in racquetball is the Marty Hogan *splat*. Hogan with a pendulum swing and fierce body torque would contact the ball so deep in the stroke it was slightly behind the rear foot when he snapped his wrist to explode on it. This shot prior to1975 nationals had never been hit with the early wooden, metal or fiberglass rackets used at that time strung with 25-30 pounds of pressure. Hogan was able to execute it at any tension with equal power with his backhand or forehand, and from any height or position on the court making him almost impossible to beat. The perceived sound is like a water balloon bursting on the front wall, with about as much rebound. The Hogan splat caught on in the mid-80s when the technology of graphite oversized racquets that now weigh less than the 18" models, and faster balls, allowed virtually any tournament player to hit the shot, but always deep in the swing.

Davey Bledsoe, who defeated Hogan to win The 1977 NRC Nationals, had a forehand *pinch shot* that didn't miss, as I stood shaking my head fifty times in the previous round before he advanced to Hogan. Davey from Knoxville, TN fondly taunted, 'You can't beat

A famous photo of the remarkable Hogan power serve with mid-line contact. (Art Shay)

139

my peench shot!' and in 1977 he was right. Bledsoe contacted the ball just barely behind the rear foot and with great velocity, killing pinch after peench all the way to beating the best of the rest and then the best of the best.

Two-time National Champion Bill Schmidtke had the best down the line forehand *straight-in kill* I ever witnessed up close, and World Champ Dave Peck had one of the best straight-in backhand kills in the day. Both players contacted the ball out from their navels and followed thru smoothly hitting perfect down the line kills. Schmidtke contacted the ball below his knees per the 70s style, and Peck anywhere from ankle to chest in the mid-80s faster game. But the depth of contact was consistently out from the navel.

Steve Serot's power lefty cross court backhand kill and Sudsy Monchik's equally devastating righty cross court kill are executed by contacting the ball slightly out in front of your lead foot and exploding on it. Serot used more wrist snap, while Sudsy applied more body torque.

The wide angle passes perfected by Charley Brumfield, Mike Yellen and Jason Mannino all are contacted even further in front of the body than the cross court shot forcing the ball to take a more extreme angle and hit the opposite side wall after passing your opponent. This is an easy and effective shot but it's a safe bet that you can't hit it effectively without contacting the ball in front of you.

My favorite shot with a forehand on the backhand side or a backhand on the forehand side is the *reverse pinch* which is contacted even further out in front than the wide angle pass, It's also aimed lower. To hit the reverse pinch you must make contact well in front of your lead foot and drive it low into the near side wall before it trickles off the front.

Moving from shots to the serve, one of the things that makes Cliff Swain's serves so difficult to return is the camouflage of his down the line, cross court, z-serve, and jam serve using only the slightest difference in where he contacts the ball. Swain contacts the down the line out from the navel, the cross court a bit out in front of him, the jam serve a little more out in front than the cross court, and the Z a little further in front of that. So why can't you look at the contact points and see what Swain is going to serve? The problem is his motion is so fast and the ball is struck so flat and low and is travelling at 180 MPH that if you even mildly misjudge you just gave up an ace. So, the serves of Swain adhere to the shot contacts throughout history- from deep to out front- only from the receiver's viewpoint each is eclipsed by Swains body and the contact point of all four serves is identical. Even if you could peek around or see through him all the contact points appear in a straight line.

That's a quick swing through the points of contact in racquetball history.

Pros Speak from the Box
Why My Backhand Works

For many years I met upcoming players around the country who used my backhand and hadn't seemed to develop it independently. Turns out they learned it from someone from someone else who had seen me in a tournament or book. It spread like a good joke. The stroke sacrifices about 15% control for a 25% power boost, and you'll see the winners use it wherever the ball's lively.   *- Marty Hogan*

Where the forehand metaphor is the quick baseball second-base sidearm throw to first for the double play, the backhand has a parallel in the sidearm Frisbee throw. I teach a young player the backhand the same as the forehand, through drills. I give them progressively more difficult setups: Soft setup off front wall; front wall sidewall, ceiling; back wall; volley. All these initial shots that may take days are straight in, not touching the sidewall, skipping nor coming off the back wall. Mistakes are corrected with push-ups and more drills, while success earns lavish praise.   *- Jeff Leon*

Iron grip, tough focus, and the drawn bow for a Rocky Carson killer backhand. (Mike Augustin)

The backhand is a motion less often used off the court, especially for a lefty who usually handwrites with a 'forehand' across the page, so it takes more practice to develop and typically is the big step into Open play. The biggest mistake I see in city after city is poor racquet preparation. Have it up and ready as soon as you anticipate the ball going to one side or the other. Early racquet preparation gives you that extra split second for excellent timing on the hit. I visualize and try to make the ball leap off and leave the strings immediately for crisp shots. The follow through is fairly level as a natural result of the level early racquet preparation.

- Cliff Swain

Early racquet preparation, and get the racquet to behind the back of the body. Turn away from the ball so you can hit with power into the side wall nearest you. This trick of practicing hitting into the side wall corrects the basic error of trying to gain backhand power by hitting cross-court and typically to the opponent's forehand

- Charlie Brumfield

Take the racquet back far enough on the backswing to force the body to coil up, because it'll uncoil powerfully on the downswing.   *- Corey Brysman*

Skimming or tossing a frisbee is very similar to the backhand stroke. As you coil the frisbee disk back, you then toss the disk with a potentially explosive forearm and wrist snap to project the frisbee disk accurately, even over great distances.   *– Ken Woodfin*

It's a mirror image of the forehand, with the same mechanics. Watch the ball, setup, and maintain a level racquet. If these mechanics are in place and you hit the sweet spot, bam! Practice to eliminate the common swing error. I generate power on the backhand and forehand with the wrist rotation. A lot of players now use the chop, but wrist rotation like the strongman bending a bar. The arms rotate the wrist -pronation followed by supination for the backhand, and vice versa for the forehand. This wristy motion takes the racquet over the top and outside of the ball. The English language isn't precise for the strokes. In racquetball, pronate on the backhand. This means turning the palm face down and bending the wrist at the top of the backswing, and supination is to bring the palm face up and then toward the front wall on the downswing. On the forehand, the palm on the upswing turn to the ceiling followed by the downswing with the palm flexing and turning down. If you can figure out this natural wrist rotation, you'll tap as strong a power source as legs and hip coil.

- Mike Ray

Turn the hips and torso, uncoil hard, hit flat and aggressively, and follow through. I might mention the backhand overhead splat shot to demonstrate that if I can hit it with repeated power and accuracy then you should be able to hit anything less with power and accuracy.   *- Sudsy*

My major contribution to racquetball has been the backhand, and there are a number of intermingled factors. I contact the ball deep in the stroke, allowing for no grip change from the forehand and for a high, deep backswing. I rotate my forearm and wrist at the peak allowing for a great shoulder and hip torque, and come down like a pendulum –

boom with a flat face – and the follow through goes up like a pendulum. Consider the maximum speed of a swinging arc and add the wrist snap at there at the bottom.

– Jim Spittle

There was a spell after coming from the big forehand outdoor games when I concentrated heavily on my backhand, and I recommend that anyone with a weaker backhand do the same. Now both sides are strong, with the advantage of the practiced backhand intensity.

- Ruben Gonzalez

Backhand grip with a raised bow and eye on the ball by Craig 'Clubber' Lane. (Mike Augustin)

It's flat, consistent, and powerful. *– Jose Rojas*

I hit it as flat as I can. *– Susy Acosta*

I feel I can hit it flat or with cut spin. It's easier on my shoulder to hit as well.

– John Ellis

I hit it hard and accurate. I feel I have decent angles and know what shots I hit well on that side of the court.   *– Andy Hawthorne*

My backhand works because it's built for speed, versatility, shot making, spin imparting, angle creating, sure commitment to flow, and my backhand stroke keeps evolving and staying sharp through practice, watching others innovate, and adding shots and concepts, like the swoop through of the racquet head to arm arrow with the in-sync forearm/wrist roll is da bomb!   *– Ken Woodfin*

I am ambidextrous, so it feels very natural to me. The motion is like hitting an opposite hand forehand.   *- Rhonda Rajsich*

Precise prep and lots of practice. It's always been my favorite side.   *– Cheryl Gudinas*

Angela Grisar's backhand works because of an ESP bow and hustle, with Kerri Wachtel in the rear at the 2006 WPRO final. (Ken Fife)

Beach Ball Pinpoint

Down-line vs. Cross-court Shots

This point of contact tip aims at players who want to better choose down-line vs. cross-court pass or kill. The answer to this riddle lies within the Beach Ball contact zone (covered in another tip) that floats around the court with you. Recall that the beach ball goads you to dash around the court until the racquetball drops into this ideal contact space for the strong hit.

A deep stroke contact means hitting the ball more posterior (toward the rear foot) than usual, at the body mid-line or further back to the rear foot. A forward stroke contact is hitting more anterior (toward the front foot) than normal, at or ahead of the front foot. Remember that 'normal' in our individualistic sport is a loose term where each fresh champion does something that was formerly aberrant and becomes the rule after he takes reign. I'm not going to sit here and tell you that you must hit the ball at a certain spot, but simply that most players find it easier to observe the contact guidelines in this piece. In light of the beach ball analogy, if you make a forward contact by hitting the racquetball within the front of the beach ball, the shot goes easily cross-court or to a reverse pinch. If you hit deep in the stroke by maneuvering the racquetball ball into rear of the beach ball, then the ball naturally travels down the line.

Nowadays, with a big racquet and speedy balls, I 'pinpoint' the contact spot as an orange within the beach ball that sits straight out from the mid-line to the lead knee (after the step forward into the swing), and about mid-shin high. Personally, the 4' beach ball itself that floats out from my body is the 'point' for me. Recall that your own beach ball grows larger with game maturity for greater stroke latitude, and it's certainly a relief and saves time from running around the court.

Perspective is a delightful examination. Marty Hogan talks about clouting the racquetball at different horizontal levels on the court, as if the ankle plane is the same as the ear plane for killshots. 'My goal as a young player was to smash winners from anywhere (any vertical level) on the court.' My jaw dropped to my calf when I heard this, for I'd always thought of hitting around the court in terms of distance from the front wall: When I was in front court I shot the ball, when in mid-court I hit kills and passes, when in deep-court I hit kills and ceilings. Sudsy Monchik transcends both of us, "I attack and kill the ball within every cubic inch of space on the court that I can reach.'

So you see, there are more dimensions to stroke than just depth, and this article is hors d'oeuvres. Nothing's been said about the contact distance from the body, yet it's an adjunct to depth. I admonish you to enlarge your beach ball contact zone over the months

145

by exploring hits in an ever-expanding radius from center. The maximum distance you can contact the ball from your body is with the arm and racquet out-stretched, say a surprising 4', and the closest is teed-up on your navel.

Here's an advanced angle off the same tip. You can eventually learn to deceive your covering opponent by choosing a deceptive point of contact. Usually this means hitting a cross-court shot deep in the stroke and a down-line shot forward in the swing. It's a more difficult stroke, and the tradeoff is barring the player from anticipating your shot. Hogan hit the racquetball scene with a bang in the 70s when I was near the top, and I'll squeal the reason for his instant success that the other pros and he probably didn't realize. Hogan was the first player ever to contact the ball deep in the stroke at mid-line or further back, while the rest of us pushed the ball around the court off the front foot. He hit straight-ins, pinches, reverse pinches, and cross-courts from the same posterior contact that made covering the court against him ticklish. In the 80s, with the advent of a livelier ball that aided further the odd stroke, Hogan's deep contact became the standard as it is today at the Junior nationals and in everyday play across the country.

This same deception is carried nicely to the drive serve, where you can fake the receiver out of his jock or bra by mixing the deep or forward contacts with cross-court and down-line serves. The explanation is that it's a natural to use a deep contact to hit a down-line drive, and to employ a forward contact for a cross-court drive, and these I suggest to beginners. However, advanced players may reverse the contact spots for fudge. I use still a different tactic of striking exactly the same contact point for all my bag of hard serves. That is, I serve drive left, drive right and hard Z-serve at the same contact and with similar motion. Any greater deception, I get confused.

Balance everything you ever hear about strokes and contact with the 'interface imperative' (Reviewed in 'Horizontal Fences and Telephone Poles'.), that really what happens on the stroke is seen within a microcosm of the swing when the ball's on the strings for a couple inches/quarter-second. In this short span, the player willfully can flick the wrist, rotate the torso, or loosen/tighten the grip to drastically alter the spin, swing, shot course, and fate of the match.

You've learned so far to explore the outer limits of your personal beach ball to expand it. There's always an orange core at the center that is the gun sight of the stroke. Draw!

Fences and Telephone Poles

In Sports with Striking Implements

My early pro career was playing hard for tournament T-shirts and trophies, plus perfection. The attitude hasn't changed over the increasing prize-money years, except I'm grateful not to hitchhike around the nation to senior tournaments.

Have my patience from these early excursions where, one sunny Nebraska day, I learned the granddaddy secret of all racquet sports and others using a stinking implement-horizontal fences and vertical telephone poles.

Gym bag in hand, and thumbing rides with the other, I peered at a rock pile alongside the road, and then up-and-down at a telephone pole behind a rail fence. I dropped everything to throw rocks with a mind's eye on sport. The basic throwing motions were sidearm, overhand, underhand, ¾ overhand and ¾ underhand. The conclusion was the most accurate, by far, for the telephone pole, was the overhand throw. Bam, Bam BAM the rocks struck the post.

Gathering more rocks, I eyed the horizontal fence rail. The sidearm throw produced a huge correlation with smash, Smash, SMASH.

Even with the off-left hand, the overhand pounded the vertical, and the sidearm the horizontal. Take a moment to ponder, why, and what are the targets in tennis, squash, racquetball, badminton, baseball, football throw, soccer, even golf or a martial arts blow?

My expertise is racquetball and paddleball, where the horizontal and vertical targets are for killshots and down-line passes, respectively. Each target lies in a narrow horizontal (and vertical) plane that spreads from point of contact on the racquet forward.

In these sports, a 1´-high stripe or tape is applied to the front wall from sidewall-to-sidewall, like a squash tin, except with a different strategy. The real or imaginary 'tin' resounds from a killshot with a bang!. The most noise is generated on the forehand sidearm swings like a baseball bat, and on backhands like a Frisbee throw.

The down-line pass, oppositely, requires vertical accuracy to insure it within an upright alley along either sidewall. This shot is the second only to the killer in a racquetball arsenal, yet discover for yourself with anything you wish to hit, fling, pass or kick that vertical accuracy is honed with an overhand (or underhand softball pitch) action.
Winning is all about increasing your margin of stroke error.

Horizontqal swings with handles parallel to the floor at the 2014 Juarez Grand Slam with the eventual winner Alejandro Landa hitting at the top and David Horn in bottom photo. (Ken Fife)

A quick analog shows the work: A right-handed baseball batter swings at a fastball, and then at a change-up, that angle in sequence down the right and left sidelines. The batter's bat was 'late' on the first pitch (behind the ball), and 'early' on the second (ahead of the ball). You may also see this in every other racket sport, especially the zealous tennis vertical overhead early into the net.

However, in racquetball for horizontal kills, it really doesn't matter if you're late or early in the contact zone, because whether the ball angles right or left off the racquet is immaterial. It still hits the target tin. The advent of the speedy ball in many racket sports met with a deeper, crisper strike with a flattened face to allow nanoseconds extra set-up time, and using a lower grip to square the face with the front wall. Take a side swing for greater stroke forgiveness on kills, or tennis shots that brush the net, or squash nicks just over the tin.

Similarly, the margin of error for racquetball pass shots, tennis line serves and squash rail shots is better a looping vertical stroke that, if struck late or early, simply lifts higher or lower to hit the vertical target.

Now, think of activities where an edge goes with selecting a three-quarter motion for *dual* horizontal and vertical accuracies. Examples are throwing a baseball to first base, archery, and avoiding an eagle in the pilot's seat.

Edges repeated thousands of times spell a winning tide.

Now, leap to an understanding that the 'moment' of contact is a miniature unfolding of the full stroke. This small, time-measureable scenario of strings-on-ball recapitulates the larger stroke. The more proficient the player, the greater insight and longer the moment *seems*, yet all are assured the 'travel' of racket-on-sphere is longer and farther than you suspect.

Ergo, the interface is influential, I propose, more so than the stroke.

Having swung everything from my *Complete Book of Racquetball*, bleach bottle, 4'' mini-racket, and Converse shoe against Miss World, the premise is that the touted ideal stroke in any sport shrinks in import to the ensuing moment of contact. Precision is born during travel.

Instant replay: Run a mind's movie of the strings-on-ball during, say, a travel of half-second and two inches. Stop action: This few frames sequence determines the destiny in of the flying projectile. The more 'elastic' the moment, the fewer frames, and more difficult to control.

If during the interface the swing is level, despite being late or early, then horizontal accuracy propels the ball; or, if during travel the racquet angles up-to-down, or vice-versa, then vertical is mastered.

Years later, I presented the concept at a Florida clinic and asked the group why it was so that sidearms make better kills and vertical strokes better alley passes. A 12-year-old piped, "Because the contact stripes are in the same planes as the target stripes." There is no more succinct an explanation.

I made it to the Colorado racquetball tourney, and beyond hitched and hoboed to hundreds more, all the while tossing stones, swatting flies, and ducking a few, that engineered a decade win streak after the original thrown rock.

Every racquet except one on the court is carried in a horizontal, parallel to the floor angle, because doubles racquetball is a killshot sport demanding horizontal 'fence' targets. Mejía-Gutiérrez over Cardona-Partner in final at the 2014 Juarez Open. (Ken Fife)

The Box Theory

Shoot the Corners

Baseball has the home run, golf the hole-in-one, bowling the strike, and racquetball has the killshot. Rolling the ball off the front wall within inches of the floor is the name of the game. With an arsenal of killshots one makes the jump from A to Open player, and with a killshot consistency of 80% you may expect to enter the pros. This tutorial deals with killshot placement and strategy, but excludes 'splats' and focuses on straight-in and pinch kills.

Where and How to Kill

It is assumed that the player is satisfied with his killshot stroke and is ready to add a sophistication to the offense. Before introducing the box theory, one strategic point must be made, understood, and practiced to become a habit. The strategy divides the court in half between the side walls, and states that most (about 80%) of forehand kills struck from the forehand side of the court should be hit into the forehand corner, and most backhand kills into the backhand corner. Repeating, most forehand set ups, whether from a weak serve, short ceiling ball, poor pass, or off the back wall should be hit to the near front corner.

Why? Proper killshot placement is exhibited by nationally ranked pros and this is proof enough. Beyond that It is simply the percentage play. The reasons are:

· The shortest distance from the forehand set up on the forehand side of the court to the front wall is a line from the set point to the forehand corner, and likewise for backhand setups.

· The natural side-spin English imparted to the ball by the racquet face tends to cause the ball to neatly "wrap" or run around the comer for a pinch.

· A mishit kill that errs on the high side that would normally be covered by the opposition becomes a '100% shot' because the opponent is
blocked visually and physically from getting to the ball. (The worst that can happen is a hinder call as long as you make a small attempt to get out of the way.)

The third reason above has won more national titles than any all the other shots and serves combined. With an open stance like a bowlegged gunslinger, a long backswing and follow through encompassing a large space, the human obstacle eclipses the rival and is difficult to circumnavigate to get at the ball.

Now that the player is convinced of the proper placement of most forehand kills on the forehand side and backhands on the backhand side, the next question is- should the kill be straight in or a pinch? The large answer is that it normally does not matter which initial wall the ball hits, as long as it is low enough. A flat backswing and follow through generally ensures the bottom board on kills.

Jake Bredenbeck with a big, flat, sweeping forehand over David Horn at 2014 Juarez. (Ken Fife)

However, the small answer is that a straight-in kill is the higher percentage when the opponent is standing between you and the center line of the court. And, a pinch is the more obvious when he is positioned between you and the side wall. In each case the ball if hit a tad high carries away from his reach for a winner.

It is enough to aim low for the crotch intersection of the front and side walls 1-6" from the floor. However, if you feel more comfortable shooting for a certain wall first, then go for it. Racquetball is 50% feeling comfortable to take the next shot.

You may also 'splat' or 'boast' kill the ball from deep court, but that is outside the realm of the Box Theory.

The Box

And now to the Box Theory of racquetball. It's a visual trick. Walk into a court and gaze at the right front corner. Soon, if you want it, a little box will appears. The only important thing is the size. Let's say it's a one foot cube. It's the target of everything that's been said about killshot strategy.

The idea is to knock the box to smithereens with the killshot. I used to teach accuracy first and gradually add power; but the better technique now is nearly full speed and hone in on the target.

So the box is the target like a dart board or soccer goal. If you smoke the ball above, below (skip) or to either side then you miss, but if you hit the box no opponent can get it. It's actually OK to err a bit to either side and a flat swing ensures this horizontal accuracy for winners.

The Box Theory works as explained by the analogy of the archery target. If you stand 39 feet from the front wall with a racquet and ball or a bow and arrow and try to hit a quarter taped in the kill zone the experiment is doomed to failure as the shots spray wide of the target. However, if you tape the quarter inside a paper plate most of the shots strike close or on the nose. It's a visualization trick.

Practice to Make Perfect

The transmission of knowledge to performance requires practice. When one practices alone he can concentrate on one specific shot or strategy without the interruption of others. The solitaire player also hits about four times as many shots in a given time as with another. The following six drills guarantee an understanding of what a great gift is in the Box.

Preliminary Exercises:
   · Drop and kill. Drop the ball and attempt to kill it. Do this exercise from three positions on the court along the forehand side wall starting at the short line, deeper, and then from the back wall. Hit the box. (The drill is the same along the left side wall for backhands.)
   · Set up and kill. Give yourself an easy rebound set-up off the front wall and try to kill it. From the three positions on the court.
   · Back wall kill. Toss the ball into the back wall and kill after the first bounce off the floor.
   · Back wall set up and kill. Stand just behind the short line and give yourself a set up off the back wall, as might occur during a game. Gallop back, set, and kill into the proper corner. Aim for the box.

Advanced Exercises:
   · Ceiling set up and kill. Hit yourself a ceiling ball that falls short of the back wall and shoot through the box.
   · Fly kill. The last shot to be mastered in racquetball. From the three positions on the court, rebound the ball off the front wall and strike it in mid-air before a floor bounce. This is the ultimate Box Theory drill.

   As the killshots improve shrink the box until it is the size of a cigarette box.

You may place cans instead of a box in the front corners as the targets. Or, unsmoked cigarette packs. (US RB Museum)

Pros Speak from the Box

Kill Stroke

Practice your regular forehand and backhand strokes – quick and compact – to kill the ball away from the opponent. Every champion has ridden the killshot to victory, while everyone else has fallen aside.

- Sudsy

Cliff Swain reaches to kill at Hollywood, FL outdoors vs. Jim Spittle. (Legends)

Let the ball drop. My method is based on getting the feet set, looking at the ball, and swinging level. If you let the ball drop to your ankle and swing through the contact zone flat, the ball will go into the front ankle high.

- Mike Ray

Contact the ball low in your stance with a spot in your mind where on the front wall it's going to hit. That's the launch and target. At the beginning stage look at the spot on the front wall, then with experience know where in the court it is with hardly a glance. I'm

156

most comfortable with a straight-in kill, or a pinch close to the front wall. Picking one of these depends on court position, opponent position, my body stance, and the ball spin during setup.   - *Corey Brysman*

Your kill stroke mechanics are the same as the drive serve, so have one to know the other. Step forward always, contact low and follow through.   *– Jim Spittle*

Kerri Wachtel over Kristen Walsh with a flat follow through at a 2006 WPRO pro event. (Ken Fife)

The best advice for the absolute kill is to take the ball at calf height. Back up and wait for it to drop as low as possible. The highest percentage of flat rolloffs come from a level stroke just off the ground with a line of trajectory nearest parallel to the floor. Some of the greatest shooters in history I could have sworn hit the ball on the upswing of the second bounce off the ground. Now, my personal method was an emphasis of blocking the opponent from getting at the shot in open court, which necessitated sometimes charging forward to take the ball higher and get in position.   *- Charlie Brumfield*

Rocky Carson forehand from an open stance in 2005. (Ken Fife)

I teach the regular sidearm strokes of the second baseman throwing to first on a doubles play that guarantees sufficient accuracy and power for killshots. However, sometimes with certain players I try the pendulum swing that's defined as going from up to down to up, looking like a U when viewed from the side. The racquet face is open on downswing, at contact it's flat (parallel to the front wall) and level (handle parallel to the floor), and follows through with either an open or close face. Start by learning the sidearm stroke, then try the pendulum.   *- Jeff Leon*

On both strokes, the best shot is the kill, and for me the secret to killing the ball is to let it drop very low to the floor before contacting.   *- Alvaro Beltran*

On the splat, step into side wall as opposed to stepping into the front wall. This turns the key that unlocks the otherwise difficult splat. Besides more power and proper angle, the step toward the side wall cues the coverer to cover down-line away from front and center where the ball actually ends up.   - *Derek Robinson*

Stay down on the ball and make sure to watch the ball as long as possible. Don't let your eyes fade on the ball, but really see it.   – *John Ellis*

Stay flat and aim low.   – *Jose Rojas*

My kill stroke was to keep the racquet flat and just off the floor by bending my back leg all the way to the floor.   – *Brian Hawkes*

Get low, and work on leg strength to bend.   – *Cheryl Gudinas*

Get low, swing flat, 90% of the time DTL.   – *Dave Fleetwood*

Swing flat and bend from the knees not the waist. When killing balls make contact extremely low.   – *Andy Hawthorne*

Try not to kill anything above your waist. Take those balls to the ceiling since it could be a low percentage shot. I try to kill all my balls between my knees and hips.
                                                                                      -*Kerri Stoffregen Wachtel*

The theory was to let the ball drop as low as possible, and that would help you hit the ball lower. But if the ball's on you fast, there's no model stroke or height. You can kill it from any position, upright in an open stance jammed to the naval. A kill's a kill.
                                                                                                        – *Rich Wagner*

The killshot stroke may be struck from high-to-low or low-to-low, with low contact preferred because it eliminates the need for a downward shot angle. Getting wound up, moving in, turning the knees, hips, core, and shoulders before releasing the upper body catapult that snaps the whip of your arm and wrist, which propels the ball. And always following-through fully on targetward at first, then around in front of you and beyond to guarantee accuracy and a well-weighted ball struck with grace.   – *Ken Woodfin*

Bow backhand by Craig 'Clubber' Lane at the 2013 WOR Las Vegas Championships. (Mike Augustin)

The New Millennia *Top* Backhand

Ken Woodfin

*The New Millennia *Top* Backhand plus some from start to finish.*

• **Building backhand muscles**

- Frisbee toss, a backhand (BH) motion -

First, for fun, let's build some muscle memory skimming a frisbee. Skimming or tossing a frisbee is very similar to the backhand stroke. As you coil the frisbee disk back, you then toss the disk with a potentially explosive forearm and wrist snap to project the frisbee disk accurately, even over great distances.

a. How to skim a frisbee

Frisbee in hand, stand in the front court, your partner in the back. Lightly hold the disk thumb on top, fingers beneath. So the disk will be on what is your backhand side, turn sideways to face the sidewall as you turn your shoulders. In doing this, draw the frisbee back to slightly below your off shoulder. Feel the stretch of your arm back into a curved, "bow-shaped", > 90 degree angled position at the elbow. Skim the disk toward your partner and notice your side-to-side wrist pop and your release point directly toward your partner's hands. Ok, that's a backhand sensation. That's what a backhand *feels* like.

- Bunt drill, a racquet face feel builder -

Second, grab your racquet, a ball, and go up into the front court. Face the front wall about equidistant from each sidewall standing on the first line called the service line. Assume <your> backhand grip and shield your body by holding the racquet out in front of you about waist high, strings facing the front wall and pointing your racquet head at your backhand sidewall. Bounce the ball out front with your off hand so you may contact the ball about knee high. Bend your knees and bunt the ball straight in toward a target low on the front wall. As the ball travels toward the front wall, if necessary, begin taking little steps to adjust your position so you'll be directly behind the ball as it takes its first bounce. After the bounce, bunt the ball again into another low front wall target or what is called the "low board". Rollouts, or balls that hit right at the bottom of the front wall and floor simultaneously, are the aims. Balls that touch the floor between you and the front wall are skips, not good, but they give you valuable feedback on your racquet face control.

- Bunt control -

You may slope or bevel the racquet face to adjust to field higher or lower balls. For a higher ball, sloping the racquet face downward or so the top edge of the racquet is tipped forward produces a high-to-low trajectory and possible topspin or overspin. For lower balls, sloping the face up so the top edge is tipped back produces backspin or under spin to be able to carry the ball to the front wall when contacting the ball from below. Keep the drill going to work on watching the ball and controlling it on your strings. The bunt drills helps you learn to control spins, ball height, your racquet face, and your eyes on impact with the ball.

- Muscle build and control

What these drills have taught you is how your backhand muscles feel skimming a disk and how to control your racquet face. The backswing and commitment of the wrist release is trained by the frisbee skim. When bunting the ball, if you find it a challenge to control the ball with your grip, you might consider trying a different grip designed specifically for the backhand.

• Intro -

A new backhand dominates the racquetball game in the 21st century. Let's jump into the New Millennia *Top* Backhand. It comes with a new grip, new backswing arm position, new power stance, emphasized arm reach, and new or newly described forearm/wrist action. Of course *you* get to decide on which parts you want to fold into your own game. There's no cookie cutter RB backhand stroke. Being aware of your game, breaking it down and building it back even better, is how to keep your game fresh and grow with the sport.

• Format of Material -

In advance, I apologize for repetitions and the lavish detail. The format is to break down complete concepts and give context that looks ahead to the next stage, as well as conceptually at the whole technique. The intent is to leave fewer open questions, like: "what comes next?" Here's a big picture hint: it's Back and then Thru. Sans pics for this version, I provide the imagery in descriptions and I depend on your visualization skills, and we'll collaborate to give you insight into the skills. Suggestion: Digest a little bit at a time. Stand up and try the skills. Use a mirror. Build your stroke in increments. You *can* do it. Your backhand should be almost as explosive as your forehand and it should produce any shot you can imagine from chest high to rollouts all over the front wall or passing angles galore.

• A paradigm-shift

Sport technique has a wonderful way of evolving and getter better. The New Millennia *Top* backhand does it all better in a very, very different way. There are many facets of

162

the backhand that have changed. Let's start with the new grip. You may use any grip you want and still use many of the other new techniques. One aspect to consider is whether your grip allows you have the range to shoot high-to-low, and with power, which is now required to be successful in today's highly aggressive game style.

Bow backhand with a counter balance arm at the 2014 WOR Nationals. (Stephen Fitzsimons)

163

• *Top* edge knuckle location -

Your stroke starts with your connection with your racquet, your grip. The new over-the-top or *Top* grip is simply paradigm-shifting.

a. Knuckle on top -The index finger knuckle NOW rests on the topmost, flat edge of the handle. *Where on top is your choice, middle, front, back (or almost over the back going toward a western tennis grip)* - more to come on where edgewise in a sec.

b. V on back - The V formed by your forefinger and thumb hugs the flat edge furthest from contact.

c. Spin free grip (in your hand) - The inside of the thumb knuckle locks down the lowest beveled edge furthest from contact preventing the handle from spinning in your hand at contact.

• Knuckle on top, where? -

Placing your knuckle on the middle, front, or back of the top edge (or even the top bevel furthest from contact, for the Western grip) is your choice. Hand (knuckle) placement on the handle produces different responses to impromptu changes in impact point. For example, a delicately side-spun ball low into a corner can veer away from your briefly stranded competitor. And, since your competitor generally feeds off of pace, touch and placement may work better at times instead of always blasting the ball. Some players use several grips for any one stroke based on contact height, unplanned changes in contact depth, spin desired, or their position in the court and all for the shot they envision. Some players stick to one grip and they use control of the racquet face to create angles and spins. It's all personal and it takes on-court practice and then testing under match conditions to find your favorite grip (or grips) and stroke *arcs* for each situation. More on *arcs* to come later. Moral: use a grip *you* can use to rip, spin, and create.

• Where is the handle in your palm?

Another part of the grip change is that the handle lays *across* the bottom of your fingers and top of your palm V down through the middle of your palm. This angle increases the strength of your grip and thus your power over the racquet and, by extension, the ball.

• Grip pressure -

Grip down as lightly as you can without letting the racquet go at contact. One image that may help you is to squeeze on the racquet handle like you're holding on to a live bird. Too hard, hurt bird. When you over-squeeze, your muscles shut down, your

Bow backhand with body twist by Michelle Key at the 2014 WOR Nationals. (Stephen Fitzsimons)

joints won't flow as smoothly or easily, and you may end up muscling the ball and under-hitting no matter how hard you may try. Grip lightly.

• Versatility -

The New Millennia or *Top* backhand grip produces greatly versatile and adaptive results for a range of contact points from low to very high (shoulder high) and a horizontal (and vertical) array of targets, with bottom board its top priority. The *Top* backhand encourages topspin by allowing a high-to-low, over-the-top, flowing stroke production. The *Top* grip possesses great power potential by allowing a loose wrist and a full flowing body action. The *Top* also allows low-to-low, flat racquet face contact. The *Top* permits sidespin for manifold sidewall targets, generating front wall hugging outcomes. The *Top* also provides outside-in spin for crosscourt "V" passes, WAP's and the more avant-garde front wall/sidewall low board targets seen today from crosscourt angles or even down the line aimed for front wall/sidewall crackouts.

• **How do you grip?** -

Before we begin to breakdown the stroke, it's worthwhile to discuss *how* to spread your hand on the handle.

• **"Trigger" grip** -

By placing a finger's width distance between your forefinger and your 2nd finger on the handle, the trigger grip spreads your hand more evenly over the entire handle. Spreading your hand serves a valuable relaxation purpose. Loosening your hold frees up your wrist for a more supple snap action.

• **Grip Sensations** -

Some players pump their hand on the handle as they settle upon and <feel> their grip for ^that^ particular shot. Some players start in a trigger grip and then, as they squeeze down slightly at contact, they may slide their index finger down closer to their 2nd finger just as they snap through the ball. You may have your own little trick or idiosyncrasy. First and foremost, sport a good backhand grip that fuels your own repeatable, reliable, fearless, and broad-ranged backhand stroke.

• **Basics** -

These next few bullets cover the basics of the *Top* backhand. They contain assumptions and observations that will help once we dig deeper into the details of the stroke from Back to Thru contact, and beyond.

• **Spatial relationship** -

Plan your movement to the ball to end up behind and to the side of the ball. That spacing allows you to *move into and through the ball* to create contact. When your selected contact, or the ball's court position or speed dictates contact that is high, shorten up your stance. Still strive to get within an arm's length of the ball, behind it slightly, and gear yourself to move into the ball to make contact out in front of the suggested stroking shoulder (or your midline or at *your* selected impact). The new grip actually places the impact point a little further out front than its predecessor, the Eastern backhand's grip, whose impact was even or just slightly in front or *off the shoulder*.

• **Contact point disguise** -

Flow your racquet head through the same contact point during a game to create deception. Very little change in *your* impact point is disguise. Allow your contact point control to produce various angles, spins and combinations of those. To execute a waist high, routine ball shot into a high-to-low bottom board target, drop the ball low on your racquet face. A near corner pinch may have BOTH inside-out and over the top action to produce the spiraling, double spin shot. The contact point on the sweet spot will be both lower AND slightly further out to generate that combo. The intent here is to open your mind to let your talent create shots. Be aware that way out in front contact raises a red flag that you're going crosscourt (or reversing). Instead, draw the ball in on your strings contacting the outside of the ball and then flow your racquet head unreadable to produce the crosscourt angle you visualize that your competitor can't anticipate.

Doubles Landa-Longoria over Keller-Carrasco at the 2014 Juarez Open. (Ken Fife)

• 45 to body image -

An image to retain is that at contact, from the belly button on down to your ankle bone, the stroking arm ideally hangs or dangles down below your shoulder at about 45 degree angle out away from your stroking shoulder in relation to the line of your shoulder to waist or your torso.

• Wave-like, arc stroke image -

The arm to body angle changes and increases to turn out to be MUCH greater than 90 degrees for above bellybutton contact. As you get closer to chest and shoulder height, you must arc up OVER the ball with the racquet head above your hand at contact. Up higher you will produce a more wave-like, circular, over-the-top motion. That arc motion *will be* a stroke you perfect and perform with experimentation and error correction. The *Top* grip (or the Western grip) helps you achieve the wave-like motion by allowing you to close your racquet face, on command.

• **Timing Image -**

As the ball approaches your contact zone, coil your shoulders as you turn sideways (face sidewall) and reach back behind you with your *bow-shaped* racquet arm up above contact height in a menacing pose. You're ready to pounce on the ball in your new contact range from shoulder high all the way down to ankle bone low.

• **The *Top* racquet work -**

Since the *Top* grip (or Western grip) and *Top* BH mechanics are new, a description of the racquet work to prep, forward stroke and after to follow-through will really help. Primarily, we'll focus heavily on the new methods and nuances of the *Top* backhand. The BH basics will be covered, too, as we work from beginning to end on the stroke. Some of the new methods promote unique techniques that are effective. Being new, they're still not chiseled in stone, or need they be done only one way. These are the suggested ways to do the *Top* BH as seen on the pro tour and used by open and inventive players taking the game into a new era of power and burgeoning versatility.

• **Advanced recon -**

First, let's start right before contact. That's where you wanna go to produce your most compact, time-pressed backswing. Your Thru impact stage is THE result you seek after you've backswung and now begun your forward stroke motion to and thru impact. That final impact stage of the forward stroke is critical to achieve strings to ball, solid contact and produce the *Magic* of the *Top* backhand. This is where it is suggested you begin, and then build your stroke from *here*.

- **Forearm and wrist roll -**

The final impact stage *magic* takes place from forearm rear back or spring load thru wrist snap. For context, as your elbow drives forward, your forearm gets to a point where it flattens out and subtly wraps back around you; the arm and hand then coil palm down. As your contact point is chosen, the forearm then starts out. As the butt to target interim point is passed, the forearm *twirls*. The arm begins to arrow, with forearm twirl allowing the wrist side-to-side release to flow freely into wrist roll through a blur of ball impact and well beyond to a partial palm up finish.

168

• Breakdown -

Now the full breakdown of the "Top" backhand. This outline covers the basics and hits on the BIG *Top* backhand Keys, as well as to emphasize areas of innovation and nuance biomechanics that permit greater efficiency in the new *Top* backhand stroke.

• Basic stroke requirements -

... good grip (*know* your racquet face) and then ...

(1) Fine tuned feet-work to get to the ball

(2) Space to swing

(3) Set back foot, shoulder turn and draw racquet back (BACK)

(4) Move into the ball

(5) Reach to stroke at preferably low contact without hesitation or putting on the brakes (stroking like riding a wave with contact on the wave)

(6) Follow-through, improving flow of whole body stroke and releasing all backswing energy (THRU)

(7) Recover regaining your balance

(8) Move to clear and cover in case the rally were to continue ...

• Starts and *almost* pauses in sequential order -

It's like you are an animatronic brought to life, with body levers connected by sequential, timed maneuvers that start and then pass on to the next part that actually escalates or builds progressively into a BIG climactic forceful ending wrist snap and follow-through. It's doable. With practice, build your series of motions a sequence at a time, to flow through the ball.

• Stroke Key thoughts -

Move your feet. Get behind the ball. Well use your time to best prepare. Watch the ball, with BOTH eyes. Pivot away from the ball. Turn back into the ball. Focus most on the ball in your impact point. Those aren't just reminders. They're Stroke Keys to review as you practice or reminders as you play. PICK ONE KEY or one stage as you stroke to drill, or should things go less than perfectly for you in live play.

Kara Mazur bow and torque with a raised racquet prep at a 2006 WPRO event. (Ken Fife)

However, if you get in the "zone" and you're feeling it, stroke without thinking other than on shot selection.

• Phase 1 - BACK

1. Match follow-through to Backswing -

First, always have a backswing! Second, match your follow-through to your backswing's size, tempo, and consistently purposed trajectory or swing arc. There it is! Be committed. Prep to stroke and flow completely through the ball.

a. Good Posture -

Turn and face your backhand sidewall. Keep a little hip flex. Although being too bent over both puts strain on your turning action for your required Back (coil) and your encouraged Thru (forward, around and through). Use good posture.

2. Set the back of your stance as you turn -

As you set your back foot as your push off leg, TURN YOUR SHOULDERS. Your back foot sets everything up that comes after it. Even if you find yourself landing in a jump stop, come down behind the ball, emphasize shoulder turn, and build your weight on your rear foot. Even if you're in an open stance, set on the back foot of your open stance as you shoulder turns.

a. Step in the bucket -

Even when you land in a jump stop or when you finish your flick, shuffle steps into stroking position, focus on setting the *back* foot of your stance. Again, it drives everything ahead of it. Even for an open stance stroke, the back foot rules. A concept that may help is to *Step in the bucket* behind and to the side the ball (arm distance away) and you'll be ready to flow with your lower body into the ball.

3. Turn BOTH shoulders -

The back or off-shoulder should turn too, as part of connecting both shoulders, turning them together throughout, as they coil and de-coil fully. Your shoulders will work together throughout your stroke. Your wind up flows up thru your knees, through your body and finishes in your shoulders and arm, as the ball approaches you from in front or as it's about to pass you coming off the back wall. It all depends on the time the ball gives you (or you've taken). At the end of your prep shoulder coil, a natural result sees the front shoulder ever so slightly lower than the back shoulder.

a. Wind up Prep -

Your *move* back winds you up like a top. An image that may help is what you see an ice skater do at the end of their spinning jump. As they land, the spin continues as they continue to wind up. A skater allows their momentum to continue to twirl them after landing. They continue to spin using the natural force of their turning and momentum. Spoiler alert: skaters draw in their arms, like your off-arm folds in against you to speed up your spin kick starting your thru stroke.

4. LOOKing AHEAD Image: *Be* the Banana -

Picture a huge banana laying out on the court at your feet (or a small banana for high contact). Then, *dance the banana*, stem in. Take a stride into every stroke and make the stride into your stance look like the banana facing you on the floor. Stride slightly towards the sidewall, and land pulling in toward you. That inwards pull best capitalizes on the centripetal (toward center) force from your legs and adds weight to your stroke. If the banana stem were pointed out, your weight and momentum would flow out away from you to under power and imbalance your stroke.

a. Time short: tuck front shoulder -

If time were to be short, coil or tuck your front shoulder inwards and draw your racquet across your body. This is the quick-draw stroke, but it's far better than prepping with a wet noodle!

b. Quick-draw draw back -

If you have just a little bit of time for a quick-draw stroke, you still have time to draw your racquet arm across your body so the racquet is (pushed) on the other side of your body near your off-shoulder. This gets your racquet back lightening fast and it coils your stroking shoulder to get ready, even if you are robbed of time to completely coil both shoulders. Then, jumping ahead in the story, to stroke draw the sword from a scabbard on your back hip, pull the blade across your body and slash thru the ball. This beats a punch volleys or <bunts> almost every time. Just be able to do them, bunts or volleys, too!

5. Draw racquet back -

As part of the end of a less pressured shoulder turn, draw the racquet across your body behind your back shoulder as if someone were stretching you back by tugging on your hand all the way to shoulder high.

6. Arms work as one unit -

To ensure you draw the racquet arm back fully, time permitting, take both arms back together, as one unit, with the back shoulder wind up, too. It should be in autopilot that the off-arm goes back UNDER your racquet arm, guiding it back. A key is to keep the arms slightly separated to avoid contacting the off hand in the Thru impact stage of the stroke. Also, avoid the tendency to hold the frame with the off hand and prevent either a full backswing or a <when should I let go?> timing thought for the forward swing. Forecast Hint: the off-hand actually precedes the racquet hand in the first stage of the Thru into the forward stroke (it folds in, like a skater).

7. Weight shift -

Your shoulders coil has the potential to coil your whole body from knee turn, to hip twist, to core crunch. Another beneficial result is weight shifts to your back foot. That's all good. Let your weight build to the tune of about 60% back for setups. Prep more compactly for quick reaction balls when little time is available to build your weight back. As you're setting your back foot and ALWAYS TURNING YOUR SHOULDERS, your weight will build on your back foot, running, open stancing, jump stopping, or banana'ing in.

Jack Huczek tight bow backhand kill at a 2005 IRT pro stop. (Ken Fife)

8. Image: Weight your shots –

When you can, shift your weight back to prepare, and then you have more to press back and move toward your front foot, as you transfer your weight and rotate powerfully through the unsuspecting ball. Put weight into your shots.

a. *Top* BH range Hint: Take a stand -

Even when you're backing up, take a stand and push back into the court. Your greater range of contact points allows you to (realize and react) go back forward! Attack the ball at a higher height. Hold your position. Trust your front foot will land. Push off to go forward and stroke usually a pass and definitely a best *shaped* shot available. You will land. Practice this and it'll become *your* skill.

9. Best case prep: back to target -

For a backhand back corner setup, Xia Yang, my student, notes pro players face the back wall with their whole chest in preparation to stroke. Now THAT is full body coil! Coil so that your back and both shoulders face the target in full prep. Then, as you forward stroke, you'll be really ready to uncoil your whole upper body effortlessly, monstrously into and through the ball. Also, when you chose disguise, look deceptively like you're gonna blast the ball. Then you have the option to dial down into a smooth stroke, while consistently keeping up your racquet head speed.

10. *Top* Stroke Prep Key: "Bow-shaped" Arm -

Unlike the 90 degree angle at the elbow for forehands or old-school backhands, draw your arm back in a more curved, *bow-shaped* position. The angle is held out further at the elbow to about 110 degrees. To picture this, think of how the bow of a bow and arrow looks. The reason for the increased angle at the elbow is to make sure your elbow is ready to flow more forward, *out* AND around into the contact zone instead of all down and over the top. The *bow* allows you to reach back further to smite the ball. Bending the elbow 90 degrees is discouraged because it produces TOO much over the top action translating into skips or yips. Yips are crowding the ball or under hitting. Keep the elbow bent until right before impact. Flex your elbow until your arm almost straightens. Kinetic hint: when you can feel your upper arm (bicep) flex a tad, your arm's in a *bow*. Vision ahead: as the forearm twirls and then the wrist begins to snap, the arms extend, too.

11. High hand -

At full backswing, draw the racquet arm hand back and up to above back shoulder high. That's streeetched.

12. Keep your hand back -

Once you draw back your hand, keep your hand back, even as your elbow slides forward, until you're ready to reach out to make contact.

13. Measured prep, Bigger IS Better! -

A consistently deep backswing translates into obviously plenty of power. As mentioned earlier, *BIGGER* prep also provides unreadability through disguise. You want your stroke to sometimes appear bigger than it may actually turn out to be. Your deception creates disguise and, as a result, maybe deeper court positioning by your competitor. Or your apparent power potential may cause your competitor to drift TOO early, anticipating they <must> move to cover an obvious opening. Can you say, wrong foot? When there's enough time and you've racquet prepped to change your shot and conceal your intention to take advantage, it's a very welcome peripheral sight to pick up your competitor drifting out of the corner of your eye. Then just, "Hit um where they ain't!" - Casey Stengel, baseball manager great.

a. Take your space -

If you take a shorter backstroke, the competitor knows you have less stored energy and you'll probably hit more softly. If you look like you've only got enough to bunt, the competitor may think to actually squeeze YOU down into less court, as he or she moves in front, dis'ing your potentially smaller follow-through. So, go as big as you can with your backswing and take *your* space. Your stroke rhythm and racquet speed will still be consistent, even when you dial it down for an off-speed, shaped low board shot or a controlled pass intended to strand your competitor.

b. Tactical tip: Semi-circle the ball -

Looping back or taking a semi-circle approach into the ball carves out more space and more valuable court for you, as well as building momentum to stroke. Don't lose track of your prize, seeing the ball the whole time. You can freeze your competitor in jail on a sidewall when you curve in to appear to take a swing volley and then you drop back and give him or her, at best, just time to step off the wall for a leap over your well seen ball you'll roll out. Losing track of the ball and being <boxed out> is on you!

14. *Top* Stroke Prep Key: Loaded for bear, Elbow coil -

This is mustard for your *top* move back, and it does load you for bear. As you reach back, you may feel your forearm and upper arm coil in very slightly up toward your chest at the end of your racquet prep. This tuck in of your forearm or waggle in up against your chest builds up even more arm spring to use in your forward stroke. This forearm coil sensation is still available and may be sought after in a quick-draw when you time is shrunken for you to get the racquet waaaaay back. For time

175

A classic bow backhand by Jansen Allen at the 2012 WOR Championship. (Mike Augustin)

sensitive situations, you still have time to tuck your shoulder, and draw the racquet across your body. Optionally you may coil BOTH your wrist (hinge) AND forearm to prepare to stroke compactly, though still explosively.

15. Wrist cock; hinge is enough -

The *Top* backhand is simpler and requires fewer moving parts. Other than a slight wrist hinge at the very top of your backswing, no extra wrist prep is required. Just draw the wrist back toward your forearm and you're good to go. This natural move at the end of your full shoulder coil and drawing your racquet back hinges your wrist by the natural motion of tugging your index finger knuckle back toward your forearm.

16. *Top* backhand wrist Coil, on autopilot -

For more stored energy, many <still> coil their wrist when they pull their palm in toward the inside of their forearm and their racquet face parallels the back wall. An assurance may help with your peace of mind that <you need not coil>. You need only stay relaxed and let nature take its course. No matter how you hold or prep your wrist, as part of the forward stroke, your wrist WILL cock plenty, as you commit to rip the *Top* backhand. As part of the thru stroke, after elbow drive around, you forearm *rears back* to wrist cock, and then you flow on to forearm twirl and wrist snap (side-to-side to roll).

• Phase 2 ... THRU ... BACK, and now THRU ...

Now you're ready for the forward stroke ... an image to keep in mind as you complete your backswing is to flow immediately into your forward stroke without hesitation or interruption. Make your Thru a hitch-free transition from Back to a continuous Thru. *Your* cat sense has told you where you're gonna make your stand and stroke. Use your natural rhythm and personal tempo to stroke in one continuous flowing motion, back and, now, thru ... when you can just about reach out and pluck the ball out of midair, you should be finishing your racquet draw back.

1. Mindset: Progressively forward -

Allow your stroke to build up from the floor. Turning all at once takes away the sum of the forces of moving side-to-side and the cumulative turning effect of your legs, hips, core, shoulders, and that of reaching your arm out and turning your wrist. Allowed to collaborate, those 3 forces (sideways, turn, reach to turn) power your complete stroke to a balanced peak, and your contact is consistently solid.

a. Lower Body Thru -

You're now ready to *move* forward ... The ball is closing in on you (or best yet you're closing in on the ball!).

2. Image: Ground up -

An image that connects you to the floor is to stroke *from the ground up*. The ground powers your high backswing and now your forward stroke by how your feet work together. For higher contact, a narrow stroking stance provides balance and a

Mauro Rojas (Cousin of Jose and Markie) hits a horizontal bow backhand in 2014. (Mike Augustin)

high center of gravity. Even when you land in a jump stop, weight the back foot and *see* yourself *move forward* ... For low balls, bend you knees, stride into the ball and keep your chest up ...

178

3. Practice good "Feet-work" –

When you're running and stroking, the forces you generate are naturally lessened mostly due to your balance being less stable and your feet being unable to turn and weight your shot as much. Yet, with practice, you can get your body sideways, as you virtually stop yourself to stroke with a quiet, level head and equally level, practiced stroke. It's often said that, "My timing was off". Extra needed time may be created with active feet and body control.

a. It's all in the timing -

It's a matter of timing when moving. Suggestion: delay ever so slightly as you approach a ball to stroke. DON'T RUN THROUGH YOUR SHOT. You're better off pausing to swing volley (or punch volley or short hop) so you can keep your head still and your stroke more on level. Then you see THE main target, the ball, better and you swing more on balance, smoothly and, as you visualize, accurately.

4. How to move forward -

To move forward think of it as riding, with one foot then the other, a seesaw - with an extra added *see* at the end. You *see* forward (step) on the seesaw. Immediately you *saw* or press back on the board. That saw sets you free to go fully forward. And you *see* forward, building your move on to (and across) your front foot to stroke the ball.

a. Image: *Banana in approach* -

Remember the banana image to help you assume a partially closed, weighted stance. Step on an imaginary banana to achieve a closed stance. Your back foot started on the big end. Now step banana stem in with your front foot. Stepping on the pointed-in stem pulls your weight more in toward you for added centripetal (moving toward your center) force.

5. Image: Half a sneaker closer to the sidewall stance -

Suggestion: Building your stroke from the bottom up, you're able to turn most efficiently with your knees and hips in a slightly closed, about a 22.5 degree stance or half the old 45. The stance to build your backhand stroke from the bottom up and turn most efficiently with your knees and hips is a slender, closed stance. Neither a difficult to balance, parallel, nor a hip blocked, overly closed stance provide the same freedom of movement or full range of shot options. Practice yourself assuming different stances and see which one lets YOUR knees, hips and core (back) turn most fluidly. You may find a half a sneaker closer to the sidewall is 'just right'. Also, with a slightly closed stance, you look to the competitor, "DTL", but you can hit the ball anywhere.

a. Image: Slightly closed stance -

Reminder: again, a 45 degree, closed stance prevents your hips from being optimally involved and it could tweak your lower back in a 45.

b. No golfing allowed -

A parallel or feet equidistant from the sidewall stance leaves you off balance and maybe tempted to lock up your front knee for support causing you to push back and <hit off your back foot>. A golfer's stance can also tweak your front knee, as it battles to absorb the side-to-side wrenching action without the help of your hips turning to spread out more of the force. Instead, it's upper body working against versus with your lower body. Bad possibly for both your knees and your blocked off lower back. You don't have cleats or a driver. Stagger your stance.

6. Image: Stance fuels bend -

Looking ahead, at the end of your move into your half a sneaker front foot stance, ideally both feet point slightly forward and down along the sidewall. Your knees bend and point easily over your toes. Both knees finish turned (bent close to 90 degrees for very low balls) accepting your move forward. And you end up balanced and ready to recover (shift back and move) should your competitor stab and make a get! Now how do you get to this ideal position?

7. Image: Take the roller coaster down -

You have (own) the final upper body piece of the puzzle embedded in your mind's eye (the drawn back forearm then twirls to wrist snap). Let's get DOWN there champing at the bit to stroke the ball. How? Do It with bent knees, a subtle side-to-side shift or drift of your pelvis, hips afirin' (poppin and turnin) and knees driving. It's imagery filled to picture yourself riding a roller-coaster sitting sideways, as you move down AND turn from side-to-side, to create a full, lower body stroke.

8. Image: Upper and lower at same time -

At the same time as you push off your back foot driving your back knee forward, fold in your off-hand to your side (heel of hand to bottom rib). Your off-hand and back foot combine together into action your dual upper and lower body engines. Just in case you're confused, yes, you have already stepped forward, and, like a baseball hitter striding in, that step didn't necessarily commit you to turn. Instead, by working your hips against your front leg pressing with your back leg and folding in your hand, THAT is when you commit and your upper body accelerates into action. Your power core catapults your shoulders around until they whip your arm through to full leverage and stinging, crack-of-the-whip wrist snap to flow thru the ball and (always) way beyond contact. Now let's fill in the blanks.

9. Now, HOW? Image: Tread out on thin ice -

For waist high to below knee high, step as if you're feeling out on thin ice for terra firma or firm footing. Tread carefully ahead of you because you want to step, hold your weight back, and THEN transfer your weight forward progressively or a little bit at a time. Your goal is to build from back to front and then finish bottom to top in a full-body stroke.

a. Step(s) to stance: Glide stride forward -

Again, take a low gliding stride onto that ice into a pillow soft, *heel-toe* landing. That's the "see" of the see-saw.

b. Anchor -

Your front foot will anchor you and your knees will drive in concert with your hips pop and against that accepting, *bracing* front leg.

c. Feeling: Springy stance -

Even if you happen to jump stop to stroke and the contact were to be high, keep your stance springy, even when it's narrow. And still focus on working your feet, from back to front.

10. Image: Save some for later -

For low balls (ALL balls) stride forward, but hold something back. For ankle bone high balls get down low with a low gliding, reaching stride. For high balls, still move forward, while holding something back in reserve.

11. Work your feet -

Looking ahead - You'll finish the stride by rolling over the length of your front foot, and push hard off your back foot just as you're about to get your shoulder behind your selected impact zone.

12. Push back to go Forward -

Once you've taken a glide stride forward, push back just a little with the plant foot to engage the back knee. The *push* forward -actually- begins from front to back. The push back powers your feet to work together to propel your weight forward into your stroke. Once you've *rocked back* (or *sawed* back in the seesaw), drive your back knee out and use your "power-base" to turn your whole body into the stroke with all you've got or all you've prepared in your backswing. That's the "saw" part of the see-*saw*-see, the *push*.

13. Hip drift frees -

The move back releases your hips that immediately are set free to first drift side-to-side. Then, as you push forward, flip your back hip, as your front hip resists and your trunk begins to spiral force upwards toward that racquet ...

14. Press *down* -

It's easiest to push forward by pressing down on your back foot. You pivot slightly off the inside of your back foot pad. You may lift your back heel off the ground a little and pivot on the ball and front-side-most part of your back foot to power the push. Pushing off the inside of your foot will do. Locking off or pointing the foot backwards is less desirable because it discourages your lower body turning. The press down and push off ignites the second *see* of the see-saw-*see*. You're moving forward on to the board.

a. "Squish the bug" -

The ultimate in baseball hitter's terms, "squish the bug", sees you grind into the ground and pivot on the ball of your back foot. Squishing whirls your back heel around behind you in an exaggerated fashion. The dual foot action moves your feet and powers the full body rotation going on above ground. You don't HAVE TO squish the bug, but you should at least scare <him>!

b. Keep knees flexed -

2013 Summer Legend Rhonda Rajsich. (Mike Augustin)

Be aware that unbending your front knee too early or straightening your leg throughout can translate into hitting off the back leg. Keep both knees flexed.

15. Torso Torque -

Ground up in summary: From the ground up, the idea is you stride forward, rock back to release your hips and then you push off your back foot. That initial forward movement

183

starts your lower body engine and your stroke builds from the ground up. It builds up through your knees with the push back. Then your hips turn *you* up through your power-packed core. The upper, upper body follows suit as it too turns quickly launching into the ball following your torso torque. Ideally the lower body turn releases the upper body into action, up through your waist, through your chest and on to catapult your spinning shoulders. You crunch and torque your front side obliques to slingshot your shoulders that fling your arm, like a wet towel being whipped and just as fast and stinging.

16. Takeaway image: Sit down into your stroke -

Think of it as sitting down into your strokes to get your upper body close to a torso's length above even ankle bone low contact. For high-to-low, narrow stance, lean back as if resting on an imaginary stool. Then pivot your lower body that rotates your middle. The torso turn engaged by your hip pop catapults your shoulders around to momentarily pause a smidgen behind contact ... then ...

• UPPER BODY THRU STAGE -

Commit to swing *out* ... hit your power accelerator ... Hypothetically which comes first, the chicken or the egg, the lower body or the upper body? Observation: they go thru together.

1. Shoulder exchange -

Up through your body the de-coil progresses and, as the hips tug it, the big triangle formed by your shoulders and waist turns thru as you unconsciously, subtly raise your front shoulder and drop your back shoulder. That shoulder exchange action was THE stroke key of THE greatest squash player of all time, Hashim Kahn; so it MUST be true! Your shoulders lead, then delay, as your elbow catches up to whip into *overdrive*.

2. Keep your elbow loose -

Avoid straightening your arm too early to stiff arm and <muscle> the ball.

3. *Top* Stroke Prep Key: Rounded elbow drive -

Your elbow drives *around*, as your shoulders turn. As the shoulder delays or is put on pause right before contact, the upper arm turns at the shoulder joint. The elbow drives forward to get to point where it pauses and that stop action whip your elbow into *over-drive*. The elbow flows out and around to get to a point where it sets up your forearm to begin its final approach. The *Top*'s more curved arc elbow drive has replaced the more down, over the top motion.

184

Michelle Key cross-over step to a backhand like a dancer at a WOR event. (Mike Augustin)

a. Elbow drive drill -

In a clinic back in the 80s Ruben Gonzalez showed us an elbow *catching* drill that helped me learn how to drive my elbow.

b. Catch your bow -

Start with elbow back and ideally up a tad, as if you're about ready to stroke down and thru. Place your off-hand at the ready to catch your driving elbow with your fingers right before you're about reach to make snap cracking contact. You actually catch your elbow at THE "interim" point right when the racquet butt faces your target. Remember your *impact* point is <there> off your shoulder (or where *you* choose to make consistent contact). Of course, the faster you drive your elbow down and around toward contact, the more racquet head speed at contact.

c. *Top* BH practice: Play catch -

Practice catching your elbow with your off-hand. You'll see that you drive your still bent elbow in a diagonal path down and around in a curved path. Catch your elbow right as your arm enters the *slot* or just even with your shoulder when it reaches the front of your torso. The slot is the long, flat portion of the Thru. This drill trains you to drive your elbow hard toward your contact zone. It teaches you a determined, committed elbow drive, and it helps you increase your elbow and, by extension, your racquet head speed, as well.

4. Elbow spin -

As your elbow (and shoulder) briefly *pauses* inches behind contact, your forearm rears back and flattens out to its spring-loaded position. To reach to contact, spin at the elbow joint, as the forearm is set-a-twirl to flow out and reach to almost full arm extension.

5. Wrist loads -

After the forearm rears back and levels out, the wrist cocks naturally. Instinctively (subconsciously) you flare or draw your forearm back behind you. This rear back action with your forearm develops more stored inertia for the long, flat extension stage of the forward stroke. The wrist cocks or hinges or spring loads naturally as the forearm rears back and you're about to enter the *slot*.

a. Baseball crossover technique -

Wrapping your forearm back around you in a laid back position is very similar to how baseball hitters now drop their bats from up high to down about shoulder height, when they extend the bat back behind them, before swooping it around and THRU their strike-zone.

6. The Slot -

As the forearm gets in its laid back position, your arm enters the *slot*. Get ready for the straight line stage of the stroke. The longer the flat portion of your stroke, the more power produced AND control managed. This has been termed "swinging on a table". The only addition to the on the table concept is that the hand dangles down ever so slightly to free the wrist to roll. This dangle is for belly high or lower balls. You would see sparks fly were you swinging across a metal top table as the heads dips in mid table at impact. *Note that for higher balls, the head of the racquet will rise to wrist height or even higher for chest to shoulder high contact.

7. Butt to target -

The racquet butt to target interim phase precedes the final *roll* phase of the complete impact stage. If the impact stage wanders on you, go back to butt to target and let 'er rip! From butt to target, <try> not to rear back. When I show this to a player, he'll often rear back to get more oomph into the ball. No need. You've oomphed up the stroke before this, and now the arm needs only roll and straighten.

8. *Top* key: delayed wrist -

The *Top* BH slot includes keeping the wrist hinged, as long as possible, before reaching to make contact. As mentioned before, the rearing back or laying back of the forearm cocks or hinges the wrist just a little, just enough for you. Let your wrist cock and keep it hinged until right before contact. If you find yourself unhinging your wrist early, see if your whole arm may be straightening too early, too, disallowing it to be the true whip IT can be.

9. Racquet head below –

Again, you're prepping for the racquet head to drop a little below the wrist for balls below bellybutton level for optimal, fluid wrist motion from wrist load (forearm rear back and hinge) to snap and roll ... Above bellybutton contact the motion is more wave-like and over the top, as the racquet head will rise above the wrist to compensate. With the *Top* grip (or Western grip) that high contact is immensely doable.

• ROCK AND ROLL STAGE ... when *MAGIC* happens!

1. How to ensure good contact -

Contact is based on riveting your eyes upon the ball AT impact so that you make the contact you want to produce the shot you visualize. Fixate closely on the ball at your impact point. The motion's a blur. So is the ball. However, the better you focus and *see* the blur, the better your contact and the better your shot. The tip here is to shift your eyes to impact versus riding the ball in all the way in to contact. Your hand eye coordination picks contact and your eyes confirm that contact by finding the ball in the impact zone with your racquet face AND your eyes.

2. Commit: Rock and Roll! -

Timing: You ROCK your weight forward. Right before you reach for contact, about when the butt of your racquet faces the target and your shoulder pauses behind contact, your forearm ROLLS at the elbow and whirls out and around. Right before full reach ROLL the wrist or perhaps most vividly tumble and whip your wrist thru and beyond contact.

3. Twirl to extend powerfully -

As you reach the butt to target turning path, your forearm will then initiate its twirl, and, as the arm almost arrows, then your wrist will flow thru contact. Your ultimate goal is to make your contact *zone* a long, flat, powerful, across the gashed table one. Now here's what seems preternatural in its speed and success ...

a. Twirl Magic -

This is when the shoulder making its final push forward and your resisting core translates, at lightening speed, into your arm ripping through, like a bull whip cracking. Set a-twirl, it 1-2-3: (1) your upper arm turns at the shoulder; (2) your forearm turns at the elbow; and (3) your hand turns at the wrist and they all finish twirling explosively together peaking right as your arm extends to full reach at speeds unseen by the naked eye. Your forearm twirl or roll precedes and accelerates your wrist snap, as your arm AND wrist roll from palm down toward "PALM UP" through a potentially fierce, explosive, flowing contact zone and a full, wide-arced, energy releasing, free flowing follow-through.

- b. Upper and Lower arm spin fast! -

The upper turns at the shoulder and THEN the forearm will twirl at the elbow so fast, again, you would barely see it before the wrist unhinges, even faster! - *Feel* it versus looking for it. Develop it. Practice it. It'll become habit.

4. *Top* BH key: arm straightens, as racquet head trails -

At contact your shoulder, arm, hand, index finger knuckle form a straight line. The angle of the racquet face places it just bit behind that straight line at impact. If the head were along the same shoulder to knuckle line, your grip would be weaker and your stroke less potent.

a. Image: You're a Samurai warrior -

You command the racquet head like a Samurai swordsman wields his sword. A Samurai's strongest cut is with his blade just trailing his wrist. That further explains and confirms using the Top or Western grips to *power* your stroke.

5. Proprioception - the ball acts as your stimulus -

188

Low-to-low the racquet faces parallels the front wall. The racquet face closes (or the ball drops on your strings) the higher you determine to make ball contact. That's due to the position and movement of your racquet face that you possess thru good technique and practice both on and off court (visualizing).

Doreen Fowler cross-over backhand at a 2006 WPRO tournament. (Ken Fife)

6. Reaching crescendos forces -

The cumulative effect of all the forces is greater than their sum into your relaxed, whip-like wrist roll right as your arm straightens to make sure, stinging contact.

a. Sum of forces greater than each alone -

The forces that peak and pass on greater force to one another are (1) side-to-side (lateral step), (2) turning (angular body rotation), either reaching for (3a) inside-out, or (3b) outside-in (reaching for inside-out = centrifugal - moving away from center force or reaching for outside-in = centripetal - moving toward center force), and (4) finally snapping your wrist (angular wrist roll). Sum and progressively add all of the forces together and you multiply their individual contributions.

7. No brakes allowed -

Stopping the wrist is unnecessary and may be injurious. Let the natural turning over of your forearm continue up your arm and allow your wrist to flow to and thru contact and on around you. The BH's wrist roll is not quite as accentuated as the forehand wrist roll, but allowing the strings point slightly down after contact increases racquet speed and avoids stopping your wrist, smothering the ball and dumping your shot.

8. Roll on -

As Ted Williams, the last .400 baseball hitter in baseball put it, "wrist roll is only halfway done at contact". The wrist will move side-to-side and it's already tumbling over as your forearm, knuckles and racquet face roll to face forward and then even more over thru and after contact. A complete palm up finish won't be necessary and it could cause too much over the top action. Just letting go is plenty. Forcing your wrist "over the top" is unnecessary. Stopping your wrist may be possibly injurious and kinda silly. Let your wrist and your arm go out and around naturally, fully unhindered. Release the energy stored up in your preparation backswing.

9. Trust your instincts -

A key concept is realizing *you* have cat-like instincts. Your hand-eye coordination naturally slopes your racquet face slightly downward or you drop the ball ever so slightly on your racquet face to shoot high-to-low (or medium-to-low = waist to shin). Either that closing or dropping action produces slight topspin action on the ball and an angled ball path down to your lower target on the front wall. Theoretically your sweet-spot control allows you to drop the ball down below the exact middle of the sweet spot on your strings. High speed film bears that out. Accepting either concept, sloping the face or your cat-senses dropping the ball on your strings produces the high-to-low action and residual, favorable topspin. Either angling the racquet face or dropping the ball on your strings, or both, avoids the much dreaded high contact to high target, straight in straight out, back-wall setup situation; unless you wanna run um forward!

a. Drill your new skill -

Let yourself shoot high-to-low and create topspin. Getting ahead of myself drilling wise, start at the butt to target stage at 22 feet back and dop-n-hit a topspin pass about waist level. Successful? Shoot taking the ball lower, with same, impact stage prep. Success? Take your backswing back higher.

b. *Feel* your contact -

You *feel* how to make contact to place the racquet on your sweet spot or angle your racquet face. When you've done it before, you can repeat the magic. When it was lucky, thank your lucky stars. Although don't necessarily try to catch lightning in a bottle again. Get on the practice court and learn how to do magic consistently.

• FINAL STAGE, THE FOLLOW THRU – now you're ready ...

1. Finish pointing the head target-wards -

Allow your body turning action to continue. Your racquet and body finally reveal the ball's direction by pointing at their target after contact. After briefly, unconsciously pointing the head of your racquet target-wards your shoulder and your arm keep turning around in front of you until...

2. Point behind -

You complete the follow-through stage with a low sweeping arc of the racquet around to extend the racquet head back behind you at pretty much the same height as contact. Your competitor is supposed to honor the space to complete your full, injury eliminating (for you, respect from them) follow-thru.

3. Free flow follow-thru -

Your racquet follow-thru, strings slightly to floor continues on unimpeded, low, and fully around you as much as 270 degrees or more of arc for a full backhand stroke.

4. Finish fully, recover fairly -

Like the tennis saying, "Call um close, call um fair", where you make fair calls on close serves, gets, and *your* skips. Your follow-thru should be long and flowing or at least never swing-interruptus. But when you're through with your stroke, ALWAYS *clear and cover* to finish fully and recover fairly to give your competitor a direct line to the ball, a chance to see of the ball rather than just a glimpse, and a full swing, too.

a. Hit-n-Move "away" -

In simple terms, stroke and finish your stroke, and then move, even if it's to go get the ball to serve! If you hit it high (pass), move forward and angle away from your competitor's anticipated covering lane. If you hit low (kill), drop back diagonally away from their covering run. As a general rule, move away from their straight line run to get and hit. Continue your cover run to circle to the best spot your shot has left you in center court. Hint: don't hide the ball. Sleep well at night.

5. How to recover -

Push back from your plant, front foot, rebalance yourself, and dash expectantly to clear first and cover always ...

• Phase 3: DRILLING

Extra little tidbits that'll help build your confidence in your BH thru practice.

1. Start with medium balls -

Big step backhand by Jose Rojas at the 2014 Pro Kennex Tournament of champions. He has placed in the Top 4 every season since 2011. (Mike Augustin)

Practice taking medium balls (bellybutton) first. And progress on up to chest high, focusing on working your feet properly in a narrow stance. When your feet are doing their thing (pushing back and pressing forward to allow knee drive, hip pop and rolling across your front foot) and your contact feels consistent off your front shoulder (or where you feel it's right for you), begin taking the ball at lower heights, with a reaching, lunging stride. Be ready to stride, push back, press forward, and pivot off your back foot. The abridged version: step, set, lean in and stroke.

a. High and wide -

For very high contact, the stance may be just a little bit wider than shoulder's width. The height of the backswing or your stretch up, even to on your toes, will be higher to accommodate the higher contact point. Keep your knees flexed. If you sense you have to straighten your legs to make contact, maybe you better go to the ceiling or go overhead because the stroke you're about to produce is no longer really a <groundstroke>.

2. Topspin easy -

Topspin is typically a very positive result of the *Top* BH because the ball drops on your racquet face for contact from above ankle bone high. Topspin causes the ball to stay lower coming off the front-wall by producing overspin that makes the ball dive down. The competitor must contend with either digging low spinning kills or chasing down dropping, curved path passes.

3. Splat friendly -

Along with its ability to generate high-to-low target results, the *Top* BH stroke is tailor-made for splats. High-to-low mechanics capitalize on a high contact height for what once would have been relegated to be either a ceiling ball or run-around-the-backhand desperate forehands or overheads. Splats also use both that ability to topspin in combination often with inside-out sidespin to cause a front wall hugging result. Situation: If your competitor is camped on the line and the ball is dropping invitingly toward the sidewall, don't hold up, splat!

4. *Top* Backhand Serve Tip -

Use your backhand to hit drive serves, drive Z's, and jams to work on your stroke in practice and even at tournament matches. Practice your backhand serves and open up your serving arsenal to include more challenges for the receiver. When you stroke backhands the spin you put on the ball may be altogether different. Try topspin drives. Perfect drive Z's standing way over on your forehand side into that front corner, hiding the ball very temporarily. In singles, hit backhand drive serves down your forehand side once or twice a game to maybe generate a mistake or wrong foot the receiver for an ace or weak return. Also, recall this is your *Top* backhand. Hit some extremely powerful ones down your backhand line. Also, cut the ball or stroke inside-out slightly for crackouts along your backhand wall. Even balls coming out of the rear corner may react differently, perhaps hugging the sidewall instead of popping out of the corner for a set up pinch drill for your receiver. Lefty forehand spin is what you're imparting. Make the receiver react, while you keep your *Top* backhand warm.

5. *Top* Backhand ceiling ball -

Sporting the *Top* grip a ceiling is very doable. The racquet face can be positioned easily for a slice ceiling or the newer *power* ceiling. (The power ceiling has a deeper ceiling target, more pace and less spin). Copying the forehand ceiling technique, the *Top* backhand ceiling allows you to point the racquet head up (and sloping back) when preparing and when making contact. Were you to find yourself going back in a time capsule pointing your racquet head diagonally up at the sidewall to shoot your ceiling, when the ball is shoulder high or lower, it's *Top* time to use your wave-like, over-the-top stroke and be more aggressive with your shot making. One deterrent to being conservative that should factor into your decision to be more assertive with a high-to-low stroke is that many players are short hopping ceilings when they see their competitor's telegraphed defensive position and they know he or she has yet to unveil their hidden high-to-low, *Top* backhand skills.

The 'G-Man' Dave Golman level handle backhand at the 2014 WOR Nationals. (Mike Augustin)

Pros Speak from the Box

Power Source

I coil and uncoil big-time on the strokes, so the main power source is the hips and legs.

- Sudsy

Power comes from first bowing the arm in early racquet preparation. Second, the hips rotate on the setup to uncoil forcefully on the swing. The goal of bowing and coiling is to uncork at once with full elbow extension on the ball. Leverage, not brute force, makes the ball go faster and straight. *—Dave Peck*

Legs and wrist. Spring and snap.

- Jeff Leon

As with any sport, your core is the key to the power you will have in your shots.

— Jackie Paraiso

It's a combination of legs, upper body, arm and wrist, in that order of building power on the swing. *— Alvaro Beltran*

The source in deep court for me is separating the feet for a base of leg-and-hip leverage. In front court, it's a fast, strong wristy hit while charging the ball for a quick winner.

- Ruben Gonzalez

The pendulum swing is the key to my backhand power. I start with the racquet way up on the backswing, and remember the higher you can get it the larger the 'power arc'. Force, whatever the source, demands body control or else the swing 'blows apart' and the ball's flailed. My explosive stroke developed alongside an increasing racquet control resulting in less loss of accuracy. Anyone can accomplish this with body kinesis awareness as you strengthen the legs, arms, shoulders and wrist. *- Marty Hogan*

As in golf, the main source of power varies from player to player depending on body build. I was heavy-legged and hipped so used my lower body to generate torque for ball impetus. People with large hands and forearms, and quick wrists can use more of a forearm stroke. Examine your body type and imitate the power source of a pro of similar build. *- Charlie Brumfield*

There are five sources of power on the stroke, and their synergy creates an effortless

195

nuclear explosion. The five are: torque and un-torgue of lower body, coil and uncoil of upper body, bow early swing preparation, flat wristy contact, and a full follow though. That adds up to five, and when timed correctly they add up to 10.   – Jim *Spittle*

All the power should come from the legs and core muscles.   *– Andy Hawthorne*

Core Strength, Hips and Shoulders, and good Footwork to set up precisely. Without feet, it's impossible.   *– Cheryl Gudinas*

The power source on back wall shots is torque of legs and shoulders. Dan Fowler, 2006. (Ken Fife)

The power source for a stroke is the interwoven, in-sync twirl, as the arm arrows by spinning at the elbow and is joined by the wrist rolling to SNAP together, and, like a wave crashing over, as you time placing the racquet face to shape this shot, as you roll your hand and racquet face through the ball peaking your balanced, full-body knee and hip turn friendly and fueled, poetry in motion, uniquely you stroke.   *– Ken Woodfin*

Hip - wrist motion.   *- Kerri Stoffregen Wachtel*

Staying balanced and torque from the body creates power.   *– Jose Rojas*

I think powerful legs really turning hard into the swing with good arm and wrist timing on contact.   *– Rich Wagner*

Timing.   *– Dave Fleetwood*

Power source comes from good form, leg power, core, and a durable, flexible shoulder.
                                                          - Charlie Pratt

For me it's my ass and upper legs. I can feel my strength and balance in those areas when I want to hit the ball hard.   *– John Ellis*

The reverse weight shift utilizing the larger muscles of the legs and back. The summer before I beat Marty Hogan to win the Nationals I water skied every day on the Colorado River with Bud Leach and got my legs into the best condition of my career for my biggest upset.   *– Davey Bledsoe*

Backhand (BH) History

... Past grips and the strokes they power-ed ...

Ken Woodfin

These are insights into the past, most prominent BH in history, and to another one that was perhaps THE most powerful backhand. This explains the old-school backhand strokes and how their grips and mechanics fueled present day strokes. From the past we have learned better ways.

1. Eastern backhand pretzel logic -

The first backhand, the Eastern grip-based stroke overlapped (came before and was used after) the "power" backhand. This section covers the Eastern backhand's (evolved) technique. Then, the first "power" backhand will be touched upon. These two BH's set the foundation for the New Millennia backhand.

• The Eastern Grip -

One grip has survived the entire history of racquetball. It predates our sport. The Eastern grip is still taught and is in use today. The Eastern BH grip originated from other racquet sports. It's easy to learn. For the Eastern BH grip, the V of thumb and forefinger aims down the bottom line of the upper, back beveled edge of the handle. And the racquet hand index finger knuckle rests on the topmost, front beveled edge. The handle goes down through the meat of the palm.

A) Eastern backhand qualities included:

1) *Low contact -*

The Eastern BH grip was tailor-made for very low contact (knee down to 2 balls high; remember: smaller racquet heads). It also allowed for medium ball contact (below waist high). Some under spin would often be applied to balls in the higher range of its strike zone.

2) *Educated wrist" for high contact –*

As practitioners using a forehand grip to stroke backhands MUST always do, Eastern BH grippers must adjust the face of their racquet to flatten their strings when making medium

198

Racquetball Legend and Hall of Fame Bret Harnett hits his signature bow backhand in his hometown Las Vegas at the 2013 Nationals. (Mike Augustin)

to high contact. They would *educate* their wrist to make it just right or flat for contact. Again, often a slice or cut action would be required, with an Eastern grip, when the ball got to about waist high or higher. Slice generally means softer contact and potentially slower, floating, more coverable shots.

199

2. **Eastern BH stroke technique** -

A) *Unique preparation* -

Worth noting was the Eastern BH's singular preparation. How the prep was done was the reason for the Eastern BH's good, low contact and only decent pop generated. Although the Eastern BH did outdo the previous backhands hit using only forehand grips and often out front stabbing contact. As an Eastern BH player would raise his or her racquet, he or she would coil their 90 degree bent racquet arm HIGH above the front stroking shoulder. The backswing culminated in a pose that looked very much like a scorpion, its stinger, er I mean racquet, curled high over the back.

B) *Eastern backhand wrist prep(s)* -

• Menacing wrist, too -

Often the wrist wound up so that the racquet head tipped slightly forward, in an even *more* scorpion-like, threatening stinger raised. The knuckles drew back toward the top of the forehand. The wrist and arm combo created a contorted *pretzel* ready to spring into action in the forceful forward stroke.

• **Wrist <Coil>** -

Some players would twist their wrist so that, at full stretch back, the side of the strings designated to make ball contact would completely face the back wall. To twist their wrist, the player would pull their palm in toward the inside of their forearm to <coil> their wrist exaggeratedly. The coil would require more and well-timed wrist uncoil in the bottom of the forward stroke.

C) *Eastern Thru* -

- *To forward stroke ...*

To produce the forward stroke, lots of front shoulder action prompted elbow drive and then lots of delicately timed wrist action. The start of the shoulder arc, a scooping arc motion or shoulder joint spin was the catalyst for the arm *whip*. The arm action was violent and fast. From the spring loaded arm and wrist position, the wrist drew a big, elongated letter "C" down to contact. Both the wrist AND elbow curved and drove down. At the bottom, the forearm whipped down toward arm extension, and then the wrist did not so much snap as pop, as the wrist flicked in a brief, controlled side-to-side abbreviated motion. The fully engaged shoulder continued to flow as low crowding contact ensued. The conventional wisdom of Eastern BH teachers and their practitioners was that the wrist was only to travel halfway forward and then keep pace with the shoulder, as the strings faced the target on through a brief, shocking follow-through. Again, the wrist punch was to finish (stop) and then join in on the shoulder-centric stroke that incorporated the upper body triangle (shoulders/waist) in a gravity assisted shoulder drop. The racquet head, pointed at the sidewall and then whipped through a short, vibration filled contact zone. The Eastern BH contact provided a cracking sound, but not near the sonic boom one heard from the forehand then or the bombastic noise produced by newer backhand techniques today.

Michelle Key cross-over to a backhand covers enormous lateral court in 2012. (Mike Augustin)

- Evolution of the Eastern BH body turn –

As the shoulder and core became a more central focus of both the prep and concurrent re-turn and downwards flow, the shoulders were even *more* depended upon as THE power source. Players would turn their backs to the front wall to prepare. Then, to swing forward, they would turn their shoulders around and through a still violent, though short follow-through.

D) *Contact Analysis* -

For low contact, the Eastern grip produced a very flat racquet face and consistent low-to-low results. It's just on high balls where the Eastern grip was left wanting. The risk is that when contacted high and hard without slice, the high-to-high shot could become a fat, juicy, flyer off the back wall. Also, the Eastern BH doesn't promote either topspin or reckless abandon stroking.

E) *Eastern on line follow-through* -

Impact was followed by a follow-through on toward the target line with very little arc around behind the player, although some raising up of the racquet head at the end of the follow-through was present.

F) *Putting on the brakes* -

Strangely the commonly accepted practice by many STILL is to pop and only halfway snap the wrist either to turn in convert with the shoulder or to hold the strings on target.

3. **Lessons Learned from Eastern BH -**

To learn from what happened before 3 things jump out about the Eastern backhand that have changed. (1) The Eastern grip has evolved into more versatile grips that allow for broader range of contact heights. (2) It was learned that the racquet arm could be drawn across the body and stretched back beyond 90 degrees to add much more oomph to your stroke by actually adding *more* straight line force than even the Eastern stroke had sought. Also the contact zone could be further out from the body developing more leverage, less crowding of the ball, less under hitting, and less of a possibility of coming over top and skipping the ball. (3) The wrist blocking was unnecessary, and letting it go releases more forearm action, more potential power, more shot options, and less wear and tear on the wrist, elbow or shoulder. Moral: let it flow!

4. **At its apex ...**

The Eastern BH was used throughout the late the 70s, 80s and 90s. It was pretty much completely shelved on the Pro tour and in topflight Open play by the beginning of the new century. However, the Eastern grip and the stopped wrist is still used and taught today, even with the new, stronger grips of today and the new, much deeper backhand preparation taking over at the Open and Pro level in the The New Millennia.

Grip and Stroke #2 -

1. The Marty Hogan All-purpose grip and power backhand -

Marty Hogan is recognized as one of the all-time great "power" players. Marty's reported all-purpose grip was used at one time to power both his forehand and backhand strokes. His "pendulum" swing arc revolutionized the game back in the late 70s and throughout the 80s.

2. Power grip -

According to his book, *Hogan's Power Racquetball*, Marty set the V formed by his thumb and forefinger on the upper edge of the top left bevel of the 8-edged grip. The knuckle of his index finger rested along the bottom of the upper front, beveled edge. This is the "Continental" grip still widely used in Tennis today to serve and volley because it is a powerful, flexible, wristy grip that allows you to either serve flat (hard without spin) or with lots of cut or spin to make the ball either jump out or into the court depending on your string direction at contact. And, when net rushing and holding the racquet high and out in front, using the Continental grip, a player can knife penetrating volleys, with plenty of safety margin over the net. Oh, that's a big hint. The Continental promotes cutting or knifing or slicing navel high to shoulder high balls. Also, as a disclaimer, Marty may've gravitated to a different grips for higher contact as his career progressed. His wrist strength and adaptiveness *are* extraordinary.

A) *"Reverse supination"* -

Marty used his grip to contact the ball very deep in his stance. And he used "reverse supination". Supination is palm up and reverse means coil his wrist in toward the thumb on the backswing. Marty estimated his wrist provided 60% of his power and 40% came from his body.

3. Some keys to Marty's power stroke included:

A) *The pendulum* -

Hogan would meet the ball on the down swing of a long arc he would swing through with the racquet swooping down from above his head to about shin high. His arc was like a pendulum where the top was his full stretch backswing and the bottom was where the racquet head pointed downwards at almost floor level. Given time Marty would use his off-hand wrist to stretch his racquet arm wrist up extremely high to prep. The bottom of

The Marty Hogan backhand that brought power to the game in the 1980s. (By Art Shay)

his stroke was explosive racquet head contact with the ball taken slightly deeper than his stroking shoulder.

B) *Another power factor: closed face* -

Here is yet another contributor to "how" Marty creates such explosive contact:

De La Rosa 2013 high backhand. (Mike Augustin)

- Top -

As his book says, "...the racquet is in a slightly closed position at contact, which transmits tremendous power and, for him, excellent control." It speaks of it elsewhere in the text, and, in a nutshell, Marty closed his racquet face as he topspined the ball. You can also top the ball with other grips, too.

4. Limiting grip - High contact skills a must -

The drawback with Hogan's one-grip grip is that it was designed for primarily extremely low contact for kills (or volleys and overheads). Although patience and low contact is always highly prized, today's fast paced game demands greater variety and being able to adjust because now, aggressive, HIGH CONTACT IS WHERE IT'S AT!

Model Player – Not Model Stroke

with Bo Champagne

Let's begin with individuality. There are no exact championship motions for everyone. Ax-wielding Abraham Lincoln has the first and last word on strokes, 'You can please some of the people all of the time, and all of the people some of the time, but you cannot please all of the people all of the time.'

There are no model strokes, only model players.

The more you watch racquetball- especially the pros- the more you come to realize that no two players strike the ball exactly alike. The conclusion should be that there is no single correct way to hit a racquetball. You will limit yourself unless examining the history of Model Strokes from day one to present.

In the beginning, 1949, Joe Sobek invented racquetball, called Paddle Rackets, with a sawed off tennis racket in a winter handball court, and the handful of players used a stiff wrist **Tennis Stroke** for a control game of passes, kills and lobs.

The **Handball Swing** supplanted and was superior to the tennis allowing a low contact and wristy underhand or three-quarter underhand for an attacking game, and this remained the style throughout the '50s.

By the end of the '60s the **Paddle Racket Stroke** per the sport name prevailed using a more sidearm pitch, contact off the lead foot, and natural follow-through. The first national champs Bill Schultz, whom I watched, and Bill Schmidtke, whom I played often, offered two of the best forehands and worst backhands the game has known for national champs. This 'sword and shield' was typical of the era and there were few ceiling shots.

The **San Diego Stroke** from 1969-'71 was pioneered by Carl Loveday, Bud Muehleisen and Charley Brumfield, all cross-over champs from badminton and paddleball, that improved on the old Paddle Racket Stroke with the first studied and controlled swing that became the standard. The stroke they taught themselves on the first ever private Pacific Paddleball Association court was dissected frame-by-frame and puttered with each. Muehleisen taught me to teach in clinics to transfer to the ball two raw sources of energy: the weight transfer from rear to front foot, and the wrist snap. He demonstrated each, and in synergy, by hitting initial shots with only the weight transfer at 50mph, only the wrist snap at 30mph, and combined them for 90mph.

The Vertical Bow forehand with a flat contact by Krystal Ackermann at a 2010 WPRO event may be the stroke for you. (Mike Augustin)

207

The Michigan Stroke evolved parallel to the San Diego one, and was dubbed the 'farm implement stroke' to honor the state inventors and champions, and describes a powerful plowed flat and tireless action with an abbreviated backswing that geared at the back with a wrist cock, short down stroke, with enhanced wrist snap for in-spin. This is the stroke I used with one secret tinker to win multiple paddleball and racquetball championships. Finding myself on crutches one month after an accident, I took one into the court and learned to kill the ball from everywhere on the court from an absolute upright position. The contact was between the knee cast and chest to defy the sacred principal of contacting killshots as low and close to the floor as possible. I threw away the crutches and retained that trademark upright disguise of kills that appeared off the racquet as passes. The Michigan Stroke overwhelmed the San Diego classic because as the ball livened in the early '70s it offered a quicker set with the shortened backswing, and a faster downswing to rewind for the next shot.

The **St. Louis Stroke** at once replaced the Michigan in the hands of a mid-west contingent who invaded San Diego from 1971-4. The spearhead was 15-year old Steve Serot who made the semi's of the inaugural 1971 National Singles Invitational that was the first true national tournament because all the top players participated via previously unheard of comped plane fares. The free-wheeling swings of Serot, then Marty Hogan, Jerry Hilecher, Ben Colton, Jerry Zuckerman and a few others who played summers at the St. Louis JCC before relocating in San Diego, put the first bang in the game. Their look-alike strokes surpassed all previous with a wider arc backswing and follow-through, strong wrist snap, and for the first time pounded rather than pushed the ball. These were the first players to hit the ball in the 120mph range as clocked on radar.

The stage was set in '74 for the most unorthodox and influential **Marty Hogan Power Stroke** that was so superior in a deep contact, with an amplified force via body coil albeit less accuracy, that it engendered Power Racquetball and no instruction could sell during the remainder of the decade without the phrase. The reform beside a deep contact was a shift from the pioneer weight transfer from rear to front foot, to instead a body coil like a golfer, and in fact the analogy of a golf swing was applied to the backhand. Yet a key element was missing. Marty and I were housemates and competitors that allowed a study that technically he didn't know how he hit what no one else could. It was finally exacted as a 'bullwhip crack' like a towel snap that may double head-speed at the instant of contact. In the end, *everyone* hit it.

The Hogan stroke prevailed through 1983 when the incumbent champs with new big head racquets and often one-grip forehand and backhand started a **Fairgrounds' Hammer Swing.** By tournament osmosis nearly every pro tweaked Hogan's power swing of deep coil and contact to a compact version for more swing control to hit the target. This stroke was the utility through the mid-90s.

The **Bow-and-Arrow Stroke** was first seen in the mid-90s that is utilized by many present elite. It was perfectly described by Dave Peck who credits Bud Muehleisen to almost come full circle in the history. Peck draws the hitting arm back as if drawing an arrow in a bow, the arm is parallel with the floor, it rests a split second at the top with a crooked elbow, descending with a short loop to pound the ball very hard and accurately. The beauty is an absolute flat backswing to ensure with a tiny loop a mirror downswing that propels the ball accuracy to a bottom board across the front wall. If the ball is hit too early, it's a flat rollout to the left corner for a righty, and if it's hit late it's a flat rollout to the right. If ever there is a model power stroke to start a beginning player with fast progress in strength and accuracy, this is it. That's why it's the sport standard.

Metaphorically then, the model racquetball stroke has gone from a tennis swing, to roundhouse handball, baseball pitch, farm implement, push broom, wristy flyswatter, fairgrounds' hammer, bullwhip, to bow-and-arrow… and who knows what's next?

The point is that the Model Stroke throughout history is a symbiosis of strokes. It depends on the equipment, and in part on the player's physiotype and personality. I would say to stand on the shoulders of the champs one-at-a-time who designed the Model Stroke for an epoch that hundreds of thousands copied, and create your own.

The champions through history have been the innovators. (Mike Augustin)

A Backhand Arrives

I started paddleball at Michigan State University, switched to handball, and then when rumors of a professional tour and the first racquet arrived in 1970 at MSU, racquetball was the only game.

I had never hit a single anything before enrolling at Michigan State. The first time I walked into the Intramural Building a pivotal mentor swayed me. I heard the crack of ball on wood and looked down into those concrete pits and saw a purple ball - my specialty - any kind of ball. They had zoomed at me in the past in all sizes and shapes on house lawns, corner lots, the streets or parks.

The player down on the Challenge Court wore sunglasses under the bright ceiling lights. He carried a dozen purple balls around and around the court in a motorcycle helmet. Leaning in and watching, someone in the gallery complimented that he was Al Moradian, blinded by his own brilliance, the perennial campus champion. After watching him drop-and-hit, drop-and-hit for a few months, and with quite a bit of practice, one year later I stepped into his tennis shoes as the perennial paddleball champion.

The reason is I earned a backhand that Al didn't own. After watching him on the challenge court, I rented from the sports cage a flimsy plastic paddle that flexed like a flyswatter… and practiced. Paddleball suited me because one could sequester in a downstairs court for hours and hit balls, and the shots came back without chasing them off the four walls. Moreover, I discovered that the amount of initial practice directly related to improvement, and flattened out but was effectual. My theory of sports is to practice the weakness, not the strength, and to let the field try to secret their imperfections with various strategies.

Beside practice, the backhand arrived for two other reasons. I took class notes in longhand, as computers were nonexistent, and the flow of the pen across the page from left to right was cross-training. And, I became arm strong and ambidextrous from rectal palpations of hundreds of cows to determine their states of estrus.

I became the Intramural champion at paddleball, racquetball and handball, and in doubles in all three sports. They gave an official green MSU windbreaker for every championship, and in a couple of years I had a closetful. The year after racquetball arrived, the house I was living in burned down and the jackets melted. This was fortunate because studies in Veterinary school were getting tough, and because I never wore jackets even in winter, but bartered them for dates with the Michigan farm girls. Now with a backhand, books, and no girls, my grades and game improved.

210

After graduation, I took a west turn out of university for the west coast and became one of the first pro players, and the first with racquet and apparel contracts. I simultaneously entered and won satellite pro events right-handed and open division left-handed.

The primary reason was a backhand that became the Golden Era of Racquetball's best, according to the fans and magazines. It enabled me, whereas it was the flaw of nearly every player at universities and YMCA's across the country, and, because of racquetball, at private clubs in the court club boom.

A very well-known and historical racquetball item but rare, the wooden Joe Sobek racquet. It was created in the 1960's and was named the Joe Sobek Official Paddle Racket. This was one of the first racquets many former pro players owned, and the one I played with after the flimsy plastic 'flyswatter' in 1967. The weapon provided new offensive thrust and accuracy because despite the cumbersome appearance it was finely balanced and strung. Now it is fondly dubbed

'The Club'. (US RB Museum)

211

Pros Speak from the Box

Velocity vs. Accuracy

I have a personal mixture of power and accuracy. You have to have both weights to tip the scale, and you can vary the ratio to personal perfection.   *- Sudsy*

Accuracy has the upper hand 90% of the time, so think accurately before thinking speed.
- Corey Brysman

I favor control, with by-product power. It's like in golf where the smooth stroke has innate mechanical power. There's nothing overt about it, no rippling muscles or grunts, just mechanical advantage.   *- Mike Ray*

It's the same as in pitching. Good location is better than speed, but speed and location is better than location.   *- Charlie Brumfield*

I'm a high energy player who likes to put additional pace on the ball, so I use the pendulum swings with deep contacts to gain substantial power while giving up some accuracy. Trace the history of the ball from slow to lively and there's a parallel advance of the strokes from pushing the ball to cracking the whip.   *- Marty Hogan*

I'm an accurate as opposed to big hitter, but for most players it's a closer mix of accuracy and velocity.   *- Ruben Gonzalez*

It's more important to aim the shot and control where it's going, rather than blast it hard. Hard is good; however, without accuracy the shots are sloppy and the game's a loser.
– Dave Peck

At the beginning level, I think it's all about setting up and hitting the same stroke time after time until it's second nature. I would like to see a student of mine set up for every shot the same way and hit with the same velocity and accuracy every time. His stroke in terms of velocity and accuracy becomes grooved like a record. Every beginner has a slightly different swing like fingerprints, but he should leave them all over the court. Now, narrowing the answer to velocity vs. accuracy, I teach with more emphasis on velocity and a smaller degree of accuracy. Accuracy comes naturally with drilling. Later on, the advanced player takes pace off the ball depending on the shot.   *- Derek Robinson*

Speed first. I used to teach stroke accuracy and slowly increase speed. Now I teach hit hard with good stroke mechanics at about 70% maximum effort, and over time hone the target. You must eventually hit the target. *- Jim Spittle*

The beginner thinks about solid contact, then as he progresses drills on solid shots down the line. Just strive for success in meeting the ball and getting it straight ahead to the front wall. Later, lower the shot hard on the front wall, gradually increasing the mix of velocity and accuracy. Don't fall into the common trap of blasting the ball as hard as you can in hopes that something good will happen, because it's very self-limiting. Young players should emphasize accuracy, because as they get older and stronger the power comes naturally, and now you've got a good player coming up. *- Jeff Leon*

Unfortunately it's a defect of the game that power has the big upper hand over accuracy. It's unpleasant and belittling to just belt the ball and play a guy who belts the ball. It would be a great sport for the masses if the rallies were slowed and extended by some means. *- Victor Niederhoffer*

It took a while to figure this out, but power really has very little to do with racquetball at all levels except the very highest. It definitely helps as a top 5 pro. *– John Ellis*

Both are necessary for ultimate effectiveness at the top levels of play. *- Rhonda Rajsich*

Both are important in racquetball. Velocity makes it so accuracy might not have to be as precise. Again, both are essential at the pro level. *– Andy Hawthorne*

I would prefer to have accuracy but I think I have more velocity. *– Susy Acosta*

The harder you swing, the more difficult it is to accurately place the ball. There's a fine line. *– Jose Rojas*

It is much better to be accurate than powerful. But both is great. *- Charlie Pratt*

High velocity and very accurate. *– Dave Fleetwood*

Velocity never hurts but accuracy is key. *– Davey Bledsoe*

Placement rules, and pace assists. So, when practicing control the ball to place the ball and then add pace to rob time from your opponent. *– Ken Woodfin*

Rich Bendercroft coils lower body for power and face concentrates for accuracy. (2006 Ken Fife)

Two Kinds of Bows

You have just studied nearly 100 photos of forehand and backhand strokes, and perhaps noticed one glaring difference. Almost all are either horizontal bow or vertical bow strokes. The horizontal has the early swing preparation or backswing with the arm, elbow and sometimes the racquet in a horizontal plane with the floor. The vertical bow has the racquet arm raised upright so the arm, elbow and often racquet lie in a plane perpendicular to the floor. The horizontal bow is superior since it 'forces' a flat stroke through the contact zone as if sweeping glasses off a table. The result is killshot after killshot across the front wall target in a thin stripe from the floor up to 6 inches. This is also the easier stroke to learn with the fastest results for the most killshot, and for the least skips or risers. (Yet, some players use a vertical bow when the ball is chest high or if they want a little vertical accuracy for a pass.)

Experiment with both types of bows. Once you favor one, practice until it becomes automatic.

Below are examples of pros hitting shots with each of the two bows.

HORIZONTAL BOWS

Horizontal Bow Backhand at the 2014 Juarez Open Doubles. (Ken Fife)

215

Horizontal Bow Forehand by Rocky Carson at the 2012 WOR Championships. He has placed in the Top 3 indoors for each of the last seven seasons, and finished in the Top 8 for each of the last fourteen seasons. (Mike Augustin)

Horizontal Bow Backhand at the 2014 Grand Slam Juarez Open by Paola. (Ken Fife)

VERTICAL BOWS

Vertical bow forehand by Alejandro Cardona at the 2014 Juarez Open. (Ken Fife)

Vertical Bow Backhand at the 2013 WOR Championships by Craig Lane. (Mike Augustin)

Vertical Bow Forehand by Paola Longoria at the 2014 Juarez Open. (Ken Fife)

219

Spin Made Simple

This is simply about spin.

There may be a dozen talented athletes including a couple of regional champs and your club pro who can beat you for the city championship, only because they know the spin of the racquetball. Pro players, whether knowingly or unknowingly, put the right amount of spin on each serve and shot, whether it's a kill, pass or ceiling ball.

Four Quarters

Did you know that the racquetball is divided into Four Quarters? (There may be more divisions, depending upon your mood, but let's keep it simple.) The quarters are:

1. top-right
2. bottom-right
3. top-left and
4. bottom-left

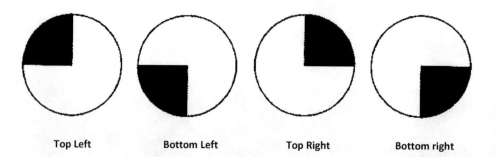

| Top Left | Bottom Left | Top Right | Bottom right |

Which quarter of the ball do *you* hit on your forehand kill? Your backhand down-the-line? Ceiling ball? If your response is that either you don't know or that you hit the same part of the ball on all serves and shots, then you are losing an edge every time the ball comes off your racquet strings. You are making spin an affair of luck rather than a control factor.

Why not learn to control the spin and get that edge the pros do. When Cliff Swain kills a forehand, spin causes the ball to recoil flat off the front wall and slide along the floor rather than to pop it up. When Marty Hogan hits a backhand down-the-line pass, spin causes the ball to wallpaper along the left side wall all the way to deep court. When

Kane hits a splat the spin helps make the bed sheet tearing sound and die off the front wall.

Controlling spin on your shots is often a matter of hitting one of the quarters of the ball. The next logical question is which quarter to hit on which shot. Experiment: First, pick a shot, any shot. Let's say you decided to test spins on your backhand ceiling ball.

Position yourself in the left rear corner of the court. Drop and hit a ceiling shot with your normal stroke, only contact the bottom-left quarter of the ball with your racquet face. Repeat this a half-dozen times or until you get a feel for the way the ball comes off the strings (power, solidity of hit). Also observe what the ball does after it hits the ceiling, hits the front wall, and then which way it bounces when it hits the floor. You usually want backhand down-the-line ceiling balls to hit the floor and hop toward the center of the court. (Diagram 1 below.) The result is a nice wallpaper shot which runs along the left side wall en route to the back wall and is difficult to return. This shot can only be returned with another backhand ceiling ball.

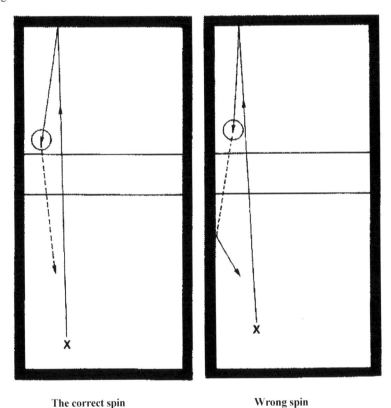

The correct spin   Wrong spin

221

Now that you've knocked six or so ceiling balls on the bottom-left quarter of the ball, hit another half-dozen on the bottom-right quadrant. The results probably won't be as pleasing. Experiment by hitting each of the four quarters until you are satisfied with the best spin. Then move on to the next shot.

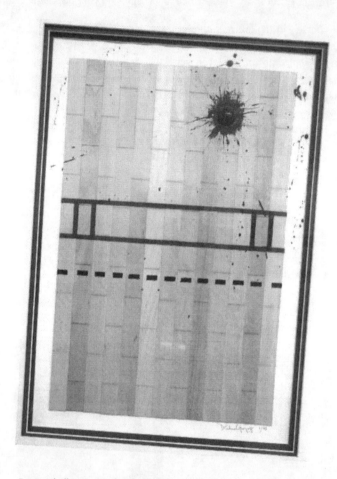

Racquetball Art spins the viewer's frame of reference. (Ruben Gonzalez)

Other shots to try the same Four Quarter spin drill on are:

1. Straight-in kills
2. Pinch and splat kills
3. Down-the-line pass
4. Drive serve cross-court

5. Drive serve down-the-line
6. Z-serve

Now continue to your other favorite shots.

Finished? Write the best spin for each shot and serve in a racquetball diary because the sun hasn't set.

Four Halves

The advanced information is that it's arbitrary to divide the ball into four quarters. There are at least two other common methods of dividing the ball up into hitting areas. One arrangement is the Four Halves. They are:

1. top half
2. bottom half
3. inside half and
4. outside half

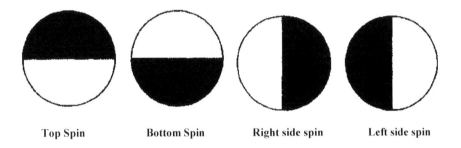

| **Top Spin** | **Bottom Spin** | **Right side spin** | **Left side spin** |

Experiment with your various shots hitting a particular *half* of the ball to learn its effect on the way the ball leaves the strings, reflects off the front wall, floor, side wall, and even off the opponent's racquet.

The Four Halves method allows defining of some common terms like Out spin (hitting the outside half of the ball), as opposed to in spin (hilting the inside half), plus Top spin and Bottom spin.

Clock Division

Besides the Four Quarters and the Four Halves approaches to ball spin, you may conceive a more detailed technique to visualize the contact surfaces of the ball. This is the Clock Division where there are 12 striking surfaces. The zones correspond to the numbers on the face of a clock.

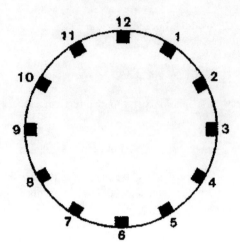

Try the o'clock method to produce different spins. For example, what happens when you hit a cross-court forehand kill, striking the ball at two o'clock? At seven o'clock? At eleven o'clock? Experiment with the clock method for other shots and serves too. It's just a matter of picking the right time to hit the spin.

Conclusion

Surprise. There is such a wealth of material on spin in the practice court you'll be as busy as a bee for some time. Proper spin gives you a distinct edge. You might not think that the ball twirling a bit this way or that on a shot is such a big deal but it is. And consider that if you have the right spin on each and every serve and shot, then all of those little twirly advantages sum to a wide winning margin. If you learn the best spins for each occasion you will beat your former self sans that knowledge by seven points in each fifteen point game.

Pros Speak from the Box

Spin

I apply some sidespin on pinches, and topspin on the drive serve to keep the ball low to the ground and sliding on the bounce.   *- Ruben* Gonzalez

The kill stroke for a pinch Is like skipping a rock on a still pool. Envision having a rock in your hand and with a sidearm motion 'throw' it with sidespin into the side wall which makes it slide low and quick to the front wall. Leaving that, there may be more to spin than meets the eye, which is to say that gyroscopic effect may play in. Look at Sudsy hit the ball with not a sidearm but a downward pendulum swing from the back swing, yet the ball goes into the front wall on a level with an over-spin that causes it to rebound and hug the floor.   *- Jeff Leon*

Most my shots are flat except as a by-product of the follow-through. I put purposeful topspin on the drive serve to make it skid on the floor.   *- Sudsy*

I don't purposely put spin on a shot, but often there's some as a natural result of the stroke. Some players find a sidespin useful on the pinch to make it zing off the side to front wall. This sidespin can come from the racquet, from the side wall due to the angle of inflection, or both.   *- Marty Hogan*

I don't use spin at all. In serious games, I try to hit all my balls flat.   *- Corey Brysman*

In general, I don't use much premeditated spin, however there are certain exception shots. There's side-spin on pinch shots.   *– Dave Peck*

I hit the ball level and flat, except in a few instances like the ceiling ball slice to make it carry into deep court. The splat is a different time where a sidespin off the side wall (not necessarily off the racquet) causes the ball to shoot off the front wall toward the other court side. Remember you can create spin off the strings or the walls.   *- Mike Ray*

I hit balls flat, without spin. I don't know the physics of why, but most player's forehands hit this way hook initially then go in straight. This is best viewed from sitting at a level with the ball behind back wall glass while someone else is playing. Once in a while, I put a little cut on my lefty drive serve to the righty's backhand to make the ball slide along the wall.   *- Cliff Swain*

I always use spin on the ball. In squash most spins are side or slice, but on the bigger court of racquetball I believe nearly every shot should be hit with some kind of top (spin) to impart originating power and a faster spin rebound off the front wall. Remembering the wall reverses the spin, the ball comes back with back (spin) to slide along the floor.

- Victor Niederhoffer

Spin has preoccupied me for thousands of hours to say that those who think their balls don't spin, have never put a paint spot on it to watch the travel to the front wall.. There is a right spin for each shot to enhance it, make it pop off the strings, grab or reflect off the front wall, scoot or hop on the floor, and do obstinate things on the opponent's strings.

– Jim Spittle

Sometimes, depending on when it is called for.   *- Rhonda Rajsich*

I use spin for the forehand side-spin pinch shot in the right corner.   *– Davey Bledsoe*

All the time, mostly on my backhand shots and serves.   *– John Ellis*

Besides trying to generate spin on Z-serves, I try to hit the ball as flat as possible without putting any spin on it.   *– Andy Hawthorne*

I use spin to shoot crosscourt by contacting the outside of the ball and flowing crosscourt, or I swing from inside to out creating in-spin that turns the ball into the target wall, as spin rules, to curve shots or keep the competitor off balance.   *– Ken Woodfin*

Primary spin is top as it helps me paint the wall down the line.   *– Dave Fleetwood*

Sometimes, I don't really like to spin.   *– Jose Rojas*

Spins: Birds Do It, Bees Do It

Kids, send the grownups out of the court. This is something they should have learned a long time ago. Spin separates the men and women from the boys and girls. This is an egghead article, but spin's useful on every shot. Let's first look at the basics.

One of the first pros to come over the top-outside of the ball was pro Rich Wagner. (US RB Mus.)

227

There are three possible axes about which a sphere like the racquetball can rotate. Think of them as skewers through an orange:

1. Vertical, or spinning about an axis that runs from the center bottom to top of the ball.
2. Horizontal, or for our purpose, an axis that goes through the ball's center from sidewall to sidewall.
3. Front-to-back, or an axis that runs through the center ball from front wall to back wall. Of course, there are various blends of these basic three axes, but let's keep it simple.

Realizing the three axes, the ball may rotate in one of two directions around each, giving a total of possible six spins. These are:

1. For the vertical axis – in-spin or out-spin. In-spin is where the ball's inside-front edge leads the twirl. That is, for the righty forehand, in-spin when viewed from the top goes clockwise. Out-spin rotates in the opposite direction.
2. For the horizontal axis – topspin or bottom spin (also called under-spin). Top-spin is where the top-front edge of the ball leads the twirl, and bottom-spin goes in the reverse direction.
3. For the front-to-back axis –outside corkscrew or an inside corkscrew. The ball rotates as if looking at the south end of a chicken on a rotisserie spit. An outside corkscrew for the righty forehand when viewed from behind is clockwise, and the inside corkscrew is counterclockwise.

If you're new to this game, stick with the basic six for a while. If you're eager after the six, continue to assay combinations of these, per the specific shot chart below, or others. For example, an out-spin combined with a top-spin produces an out-top spin that's useful on the cross-court drive serve.

We've defined 'interface' in a different article as the miniature frame of space/time when the ball's on the strings. This may last for a couple inches, or in terms of time, a split-second. The interface is where the ball takes the spin. Understand also that the ball has spin coming into the racquet, and it will pick up slight English in the 'wind' to the front wall. Yet, spin is best studied at the interface. Traditionalists will further argue that back swing, follow-through and chewing gum affect spin, but I think the focus should be on the interface per the tip 'Fences and Telephone Poles'.

There's an interesting trade-off of velocity and spin that, I believe, leads many players to conceive they hit the ball hard because they hit it flat and spin-less. The idea is that an X

Paola Longoria's imitable forehand at the 2013 US Open in Minneapolis. (Roby Partovich)

given force can be imparted to the ball as either spin or forward velocity. There are as many arguments against as for this. For example, I think a spinning ball 'cuts' through the air to reduce residence hence boost speed, and I know that a rotating top or sphere has greater stability due to angular momentum. Nonetheless, the general safe assumption is that spin takes some pace off ball while gaining control since it stays on the strings longer. I relish it. The delayed release off the face also allows the foe to commit to the wrong direction before you commit the shot. In contrast, the hardest hitter to date (180 mph clocked, about twice as fast as a baseball fastball), Cliff Swain, tries to get the ball off the strings as quickly as possible for greater boom and less reaction time by the opponent.

229

Early in stroke training, one must mix accuracy into the salad with spin and velocity. My thought is that the more spin to a degree, the more accuracy. The more excessive velocity, the less accuracy. My advice is to experiment systematically with spin, velocity and accuracy to arrive at your personal best, and keep the counsel of master Bud Muehleisen, 'When you take just 10% off the ball through a slightly less intense swing, you'll avoid over-hitting and change the complexion of the match; and when you add just 10% speed to the ball through slightly increased intensity on the setup, you can quicken the pace and turn the match.' A little goes a long ways in the trilogy trade-offs of spin, velocity and accuracy.

The most telling change in racquetball teaching methods since I invented many day one has been the turnabout in stroke focus from accuracy to power. From the 70s to mid-eighties, my instruction was to hit the ball with control and accuracy at a front wall bulls-eye, then add increments of velocity over time. From the mid-80s to present, the beginner is probably rightly taught to hit initially with raw power into the front wall, and gradually hone in on the bulls-eye. The adjustment, certainly, is a reflection of the equipment. If you've got a big gun and a high-caliber bullet - why not shoot it, and later install accuracy slowly. I don't like the game's status-quo, but have coped, as has my teaching style. Let's jump back to spins in a big way.

Shot and Spin Chart- Examples of spin on specific shots

1. Down-line pass or killshots – Out-spin. Top-spin or bottom-spin works on passes but lacks the requisite horizontal accuracy for kills. Outside corkscrew provides an effective 'wallpaper' down-line pass, but is contraindicated for kills.

2. 'Feathered' ceiling shots – A bottom-spin from a full-overhand stroke that 'feathers' the bottom backside of the ball causes it to carry deeper in the court and along the sidewall alleys.

3. Down-line drive serve – Topspin, or bottom spin. The former keeps the ball low off the front wall and floor. An outside corkscrew is good for a softer drive or lob.

4. To lower drive serves – Topspin, when the shot's hit hard.

5. Cross-court drive serve – A blend of top and out-spin imparted by coming over the top-outside of the ball. An outside corkscrew works for a less-powerful serve.

6. Straight-in kills – I like out-spin with a fast ball, and in-spin with a slow one, but other players succeed with different blends.

7. Pinch kills – In-spin causes the ball favorably to hurry without dropping along the side to front walls.

8. Down-line pass – Out-spin, outside corkscrew, top-spin or bottom-spin.

9. Cross-court pass – Out-spin or outside corkscrew. (Note that in-spin on a down-line or cross- court pass is normally disastrous in causing the ball to hop into rather slide along the near side wall.)

10. Overhead pass – Topspin is preferred, though a mix of top and out-spin works.

11. Overhead kill – ¾ overhand stroke with a natural top and out-spin is usual.

12. Duck wings over a pond - (Read notes below.) In-spin, or out-spin.

13. Toy top gyroscopic effect - (Read notes below.) In-spin, or out-spin.

14. Mid-court overhead rise (Described in 'The Rise and Fall of Your Game'.) – ¾ overhand stroke with a spin mix of top and out-spin.

Players even at the pro level avow, 'I hit the ball 'flat'!', or without spin. I think otherwise, and you'll decide only by watching us through a glass-walled court. When one of their tours comes to your neighborhood, reserve a spot on the carpet outside the back or side glass wall. Crouch low so the eyes are at a level with the mean killshot racquet contact, about a foot off the floor. From the sidewall glass, look for the ball rises and falls en route to the front wall due to spin; and from the back glass, look for curves side-to-side due to spin. One day the manufacturers will mold a 'Zebra', 'Neapolitan', or 'Dalmatian' ball to aid spin observation. You can paint your own balls back at home with a spray can, typewriter correction fluid, or magic marker to delve into spins.

I'll touch lightly on the esoteric topic of harnessing the cosmos via spin to advantage on the court. Of the many, I like three paths:

1. *Ball curve due to 'wind' on the lead edge.* This in-flight push against the ball's leading surface causes it to curve, hop or dip. It's analogous to the baseball or ping-pong ball swerves, but is too tricky here to state whether the racquetball acts as a non-textured ping-pong, or a seamed baseball, or both.

2. *Duck wings over a pond surface.* This is favorable little hop of the killed ball (I think not imagined) near the floor just before the front wall which helps prevent skips. If you misshape the ball on impact, and spin it in flight to build pressure underneath, it should 'hover' rather than touch when nearing the floor. When a duck takes off from a still lake with wings flapping and feet touching the water

for a distance, the duck stays low to the surface for building air pressure between the wings and water.

3. *Toy top gyroscopic effect.* This is a vertical hop, or drop, of the ball within the realm of gravity that has no bearing on air. It can happen in a space bound court as long as you know the direction of the pull of gravity. If you've ever seen a toy top climb a string, the possible effect on the racquetball is easier to swallow. In summary, you can combine the above three agents to put bizarre stuff on the ball.

Kerri Wachtel over Angela Grisar with a tight bow in a 2006 WPRO final. (Ken Fife)

I started in paddleball, and switched to racquetball with little change in stroke for many years. In racquetball mid-career. I adjusted my stroke to suit the equipment 'advances'. Paddleball uses a wood paddle and slower ball that can be misshaped and spun to buffet against the win to produce in-flight hooks and jumps. This is harnessing the air pressure. A sidearm in-spin stroke levered greatest rotational speed to attack the air, plus provided a gyroscopic Frisbee rise near the front wall to help prevent skips. When I transitioned within racquetball, I found that the faster speed somewhat negated the air effect on the ball, so I learned to use out-spin to enjoy the gyroscopic toy top effect from gravity rather than air.

That isn't to say that you can't use a racquetball in-spin stroke for similar fruit, but in racquetball I prefer the fringe benefits of out-spin (or a combination out and top-spin) that include: A faster swing, deeper contact in the stance, less interface time, ability to 'crack the whip' on the stroke, and down-line serves and shots that run the alleys. This has been a motivational paragraph for you to try everything you can think of; as I have.

Let's take a visionary quest to answer exactly where on the court spins most affect the ball in play. Following these spots helps you to spin, stabilize and curve your own balls auspiciously and often, until the day you arrive as a spin-master and everyone calls you 'Lucky' over and over. I'll list the typical places with little comment: 1) Off the strings – This is where the ball rotation is fastest for the most vigor against air and gravity. 2) In flight to the front wall – The ball can alter course due to a change in air pressure at the surfaces. Try to have the ball curve away from the opponent, and/or away from the near sidewall. 3) Within the final three feet of the front wall – this is sticky to explain, but try to bend the flight path to keep the ball from slipping, and to control the angle of incidence into the front wall. 4) Reflection off front wall - Consider that the front wall 'hits' the ball back at you, hence is a big racquet. The angle of reflection should be away from the opponent, while more importantly sliding along the side alley if hit down-line, or clinging low if hit cross-court. 5) In flight from the front wall – Certainly the returning ball's path, albeit traveling slower, is affected by the air, and the idea is to continue the ball's swerve as in the previous #4 so that it slides along the sidewall, stays low to the floor, and keeps distant from the opponent's reaching racquet. 6) Floor bounce – This overlooked intersection is where the ball scoot low to prevent it coming off the back wall, and should either hop away from the rival's racquet or more generally along a sidewall alley. 7) Finally, as handball players know, you can impart a lasting spin that makes the opponent's stroke awkward. Superior players have hop served the ball into my jockstrap until i conceded the point.

I acknowledge the head shakes in the reading audience, and the wonder at what's coming next. All I can say, is that the foregoing points are true, because I've seen various players utilize each of the listed seven spots, and one player whom I'll introduce shortly as Mr. Q.E.D, that used at least five of them every rally. In the meantime, if the preceding paragraph is 'Quite Easily Done' by you on the court, please drop a line for a one-way ticket here to coach me.

Let's take a tour of today's spin-master:. The most recognizable is Marty Hogan whose fantastic sidespins (in-spins and out-spins) earn flat kills and wall-hugging passes. Cliff Swain uses an expert top and out-side combo on cross-court kills and service cross-court aces with such consistency that one suspect he's aware of what makes spin work. Sudsy

Monchik has a grand gyration spin on his backhand that some deem the best stroke in the game. Jason Mannino just won five straight pro stops using predominantly soft serves with a gathering angular momentum at the ball's bottom to keep them low and difficult to short-hop. Dave Peck has a wicked array of twirls that strand competitors with the ball always just out of reach. Ruben Gonzalez has the best mid-court overhead pass on the rise, one of the sports more difficult shots, by applying a snappy three-quarter pitcher's motion. Mike Ray claims that spin varies with balls and courts, so he comes early to practice shots with spins to know what to use in an upcoming match. As for me, one summer I spent 30 days at 10 hours a day on and off the court studying just spin, and those notes of twenty years ago fill a barrel.

To me, the only player in history to fully understand and employ spin at top-level racquetball is Vic Niederhoffer. He played in over 10,000 refereed racquet matches, so spin comes naturally. His inaugural racquetball win over a young Marty Hogan with a third game 20-20 'super-pinch' that hit both sidewalls and rolled out on the front for match point has been called 'the most memorable shot in history'. I still play midnight 'Moth Ball' with Victor on his outdoor, ceiling-less, four-wall court set deep in the Connecticut woods whose lights attract thousands of moths and we chase shots with closed mouths. I owe so much of my English fluency to being frustrated by his. His racquet seems a wand that customizes shots for each court situation.

Once in frustration, I picked up another missed ball to palpate to learn something. The sphere was oddly warm, misshapen like an egg, with hard dimples, and spun in my hand as to give a blister. I fell in love with spin that night while holding it. Niederhoffer spooked all the pro players for a year while on circuit, despite an inability to kill the ball. The blessing in witnessing or knowing that such a spin-master exists is that it gives everyone a confidence of what's possible and a standard to shoot for.

A racquetballer's goal is to find, love, and marry one stroke with just one or two spins for all of your shots and serves. You'll feel like you can conquer the world. There is more than one proper stroke, which is to say there is not a universal spouse. From the Hall of Fame we see five stroke choices:

1. Cliff Swain's controlled blasts hinge on racquet preparation.
2. Sudsy Monchik explodes with strokes close to the body.
3. Marty Hogan's power smashes utilize a raised racquet and pendulum swing.
4. Mike Ray offers the paragon control strokes with level swings and hits.
5. The 'Smarty Stroke' is a composite built from the assets of the four other strokes for the 'ideal' swings. One stroke, one spin.

In a wrap, these four champions with diverse strokes and spins have won 21 total world championships, one for every point of the game.

Marty Hogan was the first to contact the ball at midline per this pic, or even off his rear foot. It necessitated a closed grip (nearly a one-grip system with the forehand) so the racquet was square on contact so deep in the stance. The deep contact and closed grip produced the first bullwhip snap in history. The bullwhip stroke is demonstrated at YouTube https://www.youtube.com/watch?v=meA_U-bVmqg using the real thing. It's the same towel snap used in the boys lockerroom at the kids´ privates in fun that causes double the head speed at contact than the old push stroke. Everyone preceding Hogan - Muehleisen, Brumfield, Schmidtke, Lawrence, Keeley, and the other champs - had used the push tennis strokes off both wings. And then, all the champs following Hogan used the whip. The new Hogan power stroke was ushered in by the fast ball. That's how equipment singularly evolves a sport.

Service

Dillon Silver drops and serves at the 2010 WOR Championships. (Janel Tisinger)

Drive the Swain Way

Cliff Swain called me from a new Porsche won with tournament purses to talk about his drive.

'This advice is intended for those of you who have a little extra "horse power" in your stroke.' If you're driving a Porsche or Ferrari, and your opponents a Chevy or Ford, why not use that additional power to leave 'em standing still. The court is your track and you should make it a quick race.'

Flashy Swain won more tournaments than anyone in professional racquetball history by wheeling his awesome power into drive serves and power kills. It's safe to point out he uses only the bottom eighteen-inches of the wall (except for occasional pit stops to the ceiling).

Cliff just drives past opponent after opponent in a blur at 180MPH. He's not a big guy...

'If you've got a fast car, why drive slowly?' he asks.

The dual Swain model is as simple as it is powerful:

1. Drive Serves - Hit each as hard and low as possible without losing swing control. 'I practice the serves alone as if in a tournament court.' Use the following variation: 50% drives to the backhand, 25% drives to forehand, 20% drive-Z's to the backhand, and 5% jam serves. If an opponent really struggles with any one of these, hit it again and again.

2. Power Kills – 'Practice until you can shoot almost everything.' Your first choice is down-the-line, as the quickest way to any point is a straight line... and it's a race. Your second choice is cross-court, when they lean to cover the line. If you see the opponent pause behind the five-foot line to deal with your power kills, use the pinch kill. If you see the opponent belly up towards the service line to deal with your low shots, go around with a wide-angle power pass. If he soft serves you, return a volley or short-hop kill to leave him at the starting line. If you ever miss two kills in a row, take a pit stop on the ceiling, and then get back on track.

The Swain Plan is simple, and deadly. It helps to be able to hit 180MPH, but 130 will do.

'Just drive, Drive, DRIVE!'

Sharon Jackson employs a very closed grip forehand at the 2013 Christmas Classic. (Mike Augustin)

Hesitation Serve: The Killer

A presently rare, and therefore useful, service strategy is a pause near the top or during the downswing.

This hesitation serve is unlike any other and with distinct advantages. There is a pause between the start of the downswing and the ball contact. It is like a hardly perceptible stammer, or a slight hitch in a horse's gait. In that split-second, a decision is made to adjust the flight of the ball relative to the lean of the receiver. The basis of the decision is the old sport adage, 'Hit it where he ain't'.

Learning the hesitation serve is easy with a quick read of this article and practice of 1000 shots on the court. Then you will understand its success comes from the *receiver*. In The serve gains three smaller advantages that quickly will be discussed before getting to the fourth and heart of hesitation.

The pause in the stroke provides:

A) The body weight shifts to lower in the legs (lower center of gravity) to increase stroke power.

B) By crouching the ball becomes screened from the receiver's eyes.

C) The returner physically vacillates in his tennis shoes with uncertainty.

D) He is also caught in a quandary of building suspense throughout the match.

Looking at these individually, in the first effect the short pause in the stroke automatically lowers the body weight to the legs, in the model of a lifter hefting a barbell overhead with a Clean and Jerk. At the pause in the clean, or uplift, the knees are bent to provide better spring to the legs. In the second effect, by the weight lowering into a slight crouch the ball becomes eclipsed from the receiver's eyes by the greater 'balling' of the server's body. An analogy is trying to see the sun with the moon in the way, a solar eclipse. And the third effect is that the returner must rise and ready on his toes to quickly shift weight depending on if the ball is hit to his right or left. This is fatiguing, and becomes irritating in a three game set.

Now to address the major effect brought about by the hesitation serve… quandary. This is a psychological upset. During the short stutter, the returner falls into a trap of indecision. An internal dialogue of uncertainty occurs, don't you think. The receiver must ignore the stutter serve, which is difficult, or fall into a trap of doubt. It creates a quick freeze and a wait-and-see attitude. This will be ameliorated and wear off in a fairly short time... after the rally is over!

For all four reasons, a short delay in the server's downswing increases the receiver's relation to risk. It is said that on the hardwood plains of hesitation bleach the bones of countless losers who, at the dawn of decision, stood to wait, and waiting watched the crack ace.

In baseball pitching it's the same. When you hesitate on the throwing motion, the receiver is forced to do the same, and you become his driver. The hesitation, like a fastball, works best on low, hard serves including the drives to both side and the Z.

The game is like a dance, and one must know when to move and when not to. When you pause on the serve, the receiver is thrown out of step with the ball coming out of reach or at his face. You make one error, you pause, waiver, stumble and lose the edge on the return. Colonel Tom Parker of Elvis fame said, 'Either operate from a position of advantage, or do not operate.' This advantage repeated dozens of times per game fetches points that lead to championships. This is called a specialty champion who has one difficult-to-see ploy that is his game lever.

The first player ever in racquetball to use the hesitation serve was Dr. Bud Muehleisen, winner of the first 1969 IRA Nationals and in the ensuing three decades 70 more national and international titles. Bud was a patient dentist, and patient were his opponents focusing on the pause at the top of his backswing. Because the ball was slower then, it was more of a stutter than a stammer, but with the same effect. I had the bright idea to study it from the gallery a hundred times, and surmised two extremely important things. First, his opponent was gung ho, and it is interesting to watch a Type A go nuts in a staccato tempo in the full course of two games. Second, and more important for our upcoming match, I learned what I believe is the ONLY secret to beating the hesitation serve. You may not expect to watch the downstroke with its hitch and stay focused. Instead, during the downswing you must watch something near him- the 'E' in the Ektelon on the back of his shirt, or a spot on the wall, and then, at the contact viewing the racquet and ball again. It is like leaving one frame out of a video and not missing a thing… except the debilitating pause.

Cliff Swain has one of the best hesitation serves the sport has seen, and it's because he has a set of eyes that can focus on so much at once. He learned it in his first year at Providence State and months later captured his first big pro win. He described to me, "I think the hesitation at the top of the swing is the best, most consistent and most powerful." Swain used ESP (Early Swing Preparation) in holding the racquet high in the backswing while following the ball around the court. In the case of the serve, the only difference is that the forehand is more stationary, with a step into the ball. Where most players use a smooth, rhythmic backswing and downswing to strike the serve, Swain has a hesitation at the topswing that allows him while watching the ball to also observe the opponent's position and lean. For Swain, the first pro win due to the hesitation serve lost him the ensuing Regionals when he was disqualified for having accepted money as a professional.

Predecessor pro Jim Spittle had success on the 1980's pro tour as the ball livened to allow his big serve to come to bear hideously on his opponents. Unfortunately, Jim had no backhand to augment his ace serves and kill forehands, or he would have been seen in the winner's circle with Hogan, Mike Yellen, Dave Peck, Jerry Hilecher, Davey Bledsoe, Bret Harnett, Ruben Gonzalez and Ed Andrews.

242

Sometimes you meet an unknown player in a remote court with a narrow specialty that makes him a virtuoso. You have just met two. Swain had the specialty hesitation on his serve (and strokes!) with a balanced game to be one of the greatest. The only difference between Cliff and Jim is that the latter couldn't hit a backhand into a dumpster from ten paces. This is all the more reason to focus on his hesitation serve that enlivened his pro career. Once he demonstrated and explained the mechanics around his attorney instead of a referee in his Memphis office.

"Your down-the-line drive serve is used in combination with a cross court serve that is effective because of a hesitation in the swing before striking. For me, this 'hitch' is on the downswing is a split second before contact. In that frame of a split second, you look at both the ball and the receiver's position. At his position and his lean in anticipation of the serve going down-the-line or cross-court. The hesitation allows me to adjust the angle and point of contact to direct it away from the returner's commitment. 'It's all about first intent,' piped the lawyer ducking a swing, and he is right. The receiver must commit and cannot recover before the server decides which of the two sides of the court to serve the ball. The decision is made during the hesitation."

For Swain, the pause and choice is made at the top of the downswing; and for Spittle it's at mid-swing before ball contact. Which is better? I don't know, and it probably depends on the physiotype of the server. In both cases, the receiver is left holding his jock.

This is called the big game, of a booming serve for an ace or weak return. Everyone these days is familiar with the style, but few take the step of adding a hesitation for a quantum improvement.

The key of the hesitation allows you multiple serve options, and often gets your opponent to commit prematurely. You look, he moves, and during the downswing from the pause near the top of the swing you serve away from the notion of his lean. If the receiver is leaning toward the cross-court serve, the pause enables you to serve down the line. But, if he is leaning toward down the line, you can hit it cross court.

When one considers how many serves are hit to game point, and that the modern quick ball makes the service the most important part of any strong player's offense (the second essential is a killshot), it makes winning sense to spend more time practicing it than any other shots. In tennis there is the parallel of practicing the 'big serve' over and over until there is enough muscle memory that the motion becomes natural, fluid, unconscious, and independent of fatigue or psyching out.

The bottom line is that if you had an exact racquetball twin with whom you played a game to a draw using identical shots and strategies, the first one to add the hesitation to his service would gain a five point advantage. He who hesitates is won.

Drive Service Pictorial

Paola Longoria at the 2013 US Open (by Roby Partovich)

Pros Speak from the Box

Serve Strategy

Being a southpaw, I have two spots in the service box for the drive serve. The first spot is on the left side 4-5 feet from the sidewall so it goes to the righty's backhand with my body screening the ball. The drive right has the most angle from this spot, the hard Z left picks up maximum spin from here, and the jam serve left works well. The second spot in the service box is on the right 4-5 feet from the sidewall but uses only two serves, a drive right down the line that's partially screened, and a wide angle drive left that's hit with a little topspin to make the ball slide on the floor to the backhand. These sum six serves, with an infrequent lob, provide the requisite variety, deception, angle and power to keep the receiver off balance throughout the match. What more do you need except strong kills to put away the weak returns?

- Cliff Swain

There's wisdom in another baseball analogy. Service isn't about striking everyone out, but in making them hit grounders and pop flies. My goal is to have either one or three-shot rallies. Ideally, my serve will be an ace, or force the weak return for a kill. That's all there is to it. My most favorite spot in the service box is on the far right to 'shade' that drive down the right line. From here also, with the same driving stroke for deception, I hit the cross-court and jam to the left. I'm standing to serve as close to the 3-foot screen zone rule plane as possible.

- Derek Robinson

My goal with the lob wallpaper to the forehand and lob nick to the backhand is to get a weak return anywhere on the court so I can put it away the next shot. When I'm serving, my ideal rallies last three shots, and if I put one after the other successfully, I believe I can beat anyone.

- Alvaro Beltran

Try putting the ball into play that can't be re-killed. If you master a variety of serves, hitting the ball where you want it to go, you'll go far in the game. I never tried to win off the serve but rather get a defensive return because I thought that because of my court presence during the rally, if I could initiate one then I'd win the point.

- Charlie Brumfield

If I can get the ball into play under the one-serve rule without a strong return, then I figure I can beat anyone in a rally the majority of the time. If I can keep the match close, then I figure I can power serve the last few points with greater concentration to win.

- Marty Hogan

My service strategy is to "Find what works and then exploit my opponent's weaknesses." Use the entire service box. One day your best serves may not work against someone, and maybe a serve you never thought would work will be the winning serve. The more variety you have the better chances you will find what works. Once you find the key serve, continue to use it. I always teach my students that it's like going into war: "The more arsenal you have going into each battle, the better chances you will have to win the war."

— Jackie Paraiso

The serve is a good time to control the momentum of play if you wish. A drive serve begets a fast game, a lob a slower game. Slow a fast game with a lob serve, and vice versa. Take more or less time in the service box to stall or speed the opponent's mind. Mix the serves to keep him always off-balance. If the player misses a serve, dish it right up again and again until it feels like he's getting the hang of the return.   *- Mike Ray*

Service and return becomes a cat-and-mouse game. The receiver tires to read if the server will hit hard or soft, and the server tries to disguise this. The best way to cloak service level is by crouching a bit on your lob motion to hide the ball itself and to feign a low serve.

- Ruben Gonzalez

The most important and ignored part of the game is the serve. It's the one time when a player is in total control by dropping the ball exactly where you want it in center court, and hit it exactly where you want it while your opponent has to stand at the back wall guessing. You can make the serve become 50% of your overall game if you think about all this every time before you drop the ball.

— Jim Spittle

There's service variety, deception and syncopation. The last is 'setting up' the receiver for ensuing serves. I open a match serving the first 3-4 to his forehand (maybe a drive, Z and jam), so now he's plumped for the next deceptive sudden drives left. Therefore, in the first ten points I've used variety to ferret his weak returns, and pick them apart the rest of the match and his life.

- Jeff Leon

When you need a point or two at a crucial moment, go with the serve that's been working best. Hence your 'best' serve varies from game to game, and you should be able to hit them all.

- Sudsy

Whatever stroke you use for a down-the-line or cross-court past the outstretched racquet, never let the ball come off the back wall or it becomes futile.   *- Victor Niederhoffer*

Drive serve to keep the pressure on the opponent.

— Jose Rojas

My service strategy is simple – hit the drive serve.   *– Susy Acosta*

Service strategy is to get them off balance by being unreadable and unpredictable.
                                                                        - Charlie Pratt

To hit a serve well enough that it is a 3-shot rally.   *- Kerri Stoffregen Wachtel*

Get a weak return while using the least amount of energy to serve.   *– John Ellis*

Dictate a specific return so that I may end the rally on the 3rd shot.   *– Dave Fleetwood*

Keep the service to his weaker side and out of kill range.   *– Davey Bledsoe*

My service strategy is to attack the receiver's vulnerable spots on the court in the back corners, the cracks along the sidewalls, and at them with an arsenal of serves boasting changes in speed, spin, angle and delivery timing all from numerous positions in the 14' foot box. Yes, stay inside the lines to make the receiver cover both of the back corners for each serve, even in doubles. Finally, attack a glaring weakness and don't get bored or show too much compassion.   *– Ken Woodfin*

Force a weak return by creating variety … an ace is a BONUS.   *– Fran Davis*

Make opponents move feet as much as possible when returning. Keep them guessing.
                                                                        – Andy Hawthorne

Go with what works. Don't change a winning serve until they prove you need to.
                                                                        – Cheryl Gudinas

Crack Ace Serve

It's Easier Than You Think

by Brad Kruger *with Keeley*

The 1970's famous 'Carl Loveday Crack Ace' as taught to Charley Brumfield hitting a crack ace consistency ratio of 8:10 earned a place with Brumfield's retirement and four National Singles Titles to racquetball's Folklore Locker, which is nice... Except this service weapon holds for anybody willing to take the time to master it instant points.

The crack ace serve, should you still be on unsure grounds, is the only serve that is officially 'good', yet never really puts the ball into play. It rebounds off the front wall, and squeezes into the crack between the sidewall and floor just behind the short line... rolling out from the wall without a bounce.

*It is the Ego Crusher, a serve that screams at opponents, 'You're powerless! You're going **down!!**'*

If It's So Easy, Why Isn't Anybody Hitting It?

'Luck is the residue of Design.' -Breach Rickley

The crack ace, itself, is not so difficult. It is the conventional approach that makes it so tough. Since game one, about 40 years ago, through to today, racquetballers have struggled to crack the crack ace formula ... but they've always attempted it from the middle of the service zone.

This practice dates back to the days of the more primitive equipment- sawed off tennis racquets and balls so slow they must have been straight from Fido's mouth when serving strategy was more conservative: Put the ball into play, pray for a weak return, and maintain a strong positional advantage near center court at all costs. Serving from the middle of the service box enabled the server to both remain near center court and hit deceptive drive serves to either rear corner. More often than not, attempts at the crack ace missed, bouncing up as set ups. Rather than experiment and search for the perfect formula, most players abandoned hope.

'If at first you don't succeed, try...' gave in to the more concrete results of conservative serving.

'The trick is not to let yourself be hypnotized by traditional and present solutions, but to see the whole wide manifold of possibilities, to generalize the problem, to scan the whole field with all the possible dimensions and degrees of freedom and then pick the best possibility.' I tore that shred of wisdom from a ten-year-old magazine in a dentist's waiting room. It seemed to make a lot of sense. Watch films, review the right ways of the legends, the wrong ways of others. Embrace the pros, dispose of the cons, if you will, and see what you end up with.

No two pros, no matter how similar their game styles, have the same service motion. The following generalities, however, indicate what the composition of a good crack ace is:

· Begin the service motion with your heels on the service line three feet from and parallel to the side wall.

· Use a 'two-step' walking serve motion'.

· Make contact with the ball six feet from the sidewall.

· Contact the ball within eight inches of the floor.

· Aim at a target point on the front wall four feet from the sidewall.

· Angle is more important than power or deception.

· Move to center court immediately.

Which all looks fine and well, listed behind bullets on paper ... but how does one bring about the crack ace on the court? The bulk of this article explains the whys and what forces of this service approach succeeds where others fail. The bullets are broken down one-by-one, as follows.

Begin the Service Motion with your Heels on the Service Line Three Feet from and Parallel to the Side Wall

When the ball is served from the middle of the service zone, the chances of an effectively hit crack serve are minimized. The wide angle the serve carries into the sidewall, forces a wide angle coming out. The ball flings off the sidewall, usually bouncing knee-high into center court- a set-up for the receiver.

Use the 'Two-Step' Walking Serve Motion

The 'two-step' walking serve is the best service motion to hit the crack ace consistently. With both feet together and heels on the three foot tape, the server begins his motion by

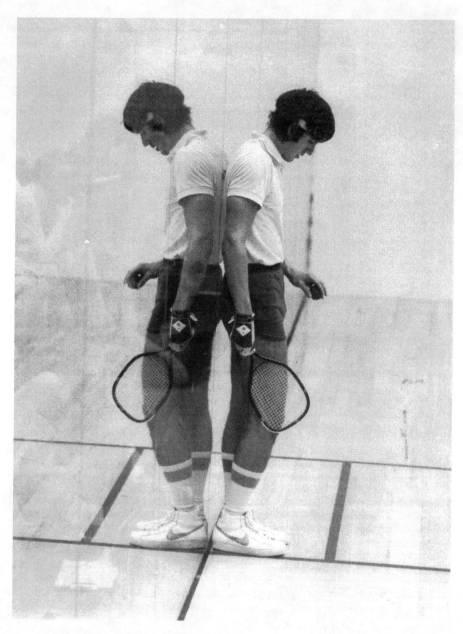

Jerry Hilecher mirrors the legal screen serve that he invented. The rules altered to try to ban it and, over the years, he adapted by moving this way or that in the service box. By the time the fast balls and short (15 point) games rolled around for the Big Game of Serve and Shoot, Jerry was ready. He won the 1976 World Championship, and no one saw it coming. (US RB Museum)

252

stepping first with his right foot, bouncing the ball into the target region (six feet from the left wall), and then launching the left foot toward the point of contact zone.

Make Contact with the Ball Six Feet from the Sidewall

The point of contact made with the ball is the single most important element in hitting a consistent crack ace serve. Make contact with the ball about six feet away from the left side wall. Moving near the sidewall:

(1) Reduces the target options for error on the front wall. Instead of aiming at half the front wall, you now have only to aim about four feet off the left wall.

(2) It eliminates the momentum riding the ball as it travels into the side wall. With contact close to the sidewall, the ball's flight will be on more of a parallel plane with the side wall- less acute. The ball will have more of a tendency to slide into the crack.

(3) Continues to allow the other service options (i.e. z-serve, cross-court drive, etc.).

Angle Is more Important than Power or Deception

One of the few players to master the crack ace, former touring pro Steve Mondry knew how important the angle was. Before each match, he would actually 'walk off' his serve ..• and mark the spots with small strips of masking tape.

Hitting the proper angle is more important than anything else. Hit the crack ace at about 65 to 70 percent of your power and you'll hit crack after crack. Save the photon power for your rallies. The harder you attempt to hit the serve, the less likely it is to slide into the crack. The blasting serve has more force, and often pops out high from the crack. That's not the only problem. The strong momentum from a hard hit crack ace attempt propels the ball faster and farther into deep court, and consequently closer to your opponent. Also, the more effort you put into your power stroke, the greater the chance that you will miscue at the point of contact with the ball.

Deception is always a plus in racquetball. In general, however, the more effort you exert in disguising your serve, the less concentration you will generate toward its success. Properly hit, the crack ace leaves opponents dazed and confused, even if they fully anticipate it. Remember- accuracy is more important than power. Hit crisply at the proper angle, and you will hit crack after crack, ace after ace.

Contact the Ball within Eight Inches of the Floor

The ball must be contacted low, within about eight inches of the floor. Ultimately, the serve should travel toward the front wall at a low angle and close to parallel to the floor. By minimizing the serve's upward angle, you minimize the angle as it rebounds. If the serve is struck higher in its bounce, it will bounce higher when it hits the floor behind the short line.

Aim at a Target Point on the Front Wall Four Feet from the Sidewall

Where, exactly, should the ball contact the front wall? Basic geometry rules here. Try to mentally calculate the angles. Go onto the court and walk it off. Your hitting point is six feet from the side wall and you want your serve to rebound into the crack just behind the short line. The point to be aimed at on the front wall, then, is four feet from the left side wall. Moving close to the side wall greatly reduces the target area on the front wall. When starting at center court, you have roughly half of the front wall to aim at. But, in moving to the sidewall, the area on the front wall is much smaller, roughly one-quarter of the front wall.

If there is a problem with accuracy, adjust only the target point on the front wall. Do not adjust your point of contact with the ball. Six feet from the sidewall serves as your anchor for consistent results. Hit these two marks- your point of ball contact and the target point on the front wall- and you are on your way to a consistent crack ace. If the front wall target feels restrictive, aim for a point on the front wall directly in line with your left shoulder upon contact with the ball.

Move to Center Court Immediately

Drive your hitting shoulder into the ball, and upon contact move quickly to center court The successful ace serve passes closely to the server but is .into a strong playing position a legal eclipse as the ball passes between the point of contact and is suddenly glaringly visible to the opponent. It is not a screen serve. That is not to say a screen will never be called, but it is a legal screen.

A missed crack ace attempt will usually roll down the wall for a strong drive serve, or pop out at a strange angle far in front of the receiver-s racquet. The effect is either a crack ace or weak return.

You stand at the threshold of a crack serve ace with your heels on the line and envisioning the next moves: Use the' two-step 'walking service motion, contact the ball six feet from the side wall and within eight inches of the floor, aim at a target point on the front wall four feet from the sidewall, and angle is more important than power or deception. The rulebook allows ten seconds for this, and in addition to driving the opponent crazy, enjoy each and every one of them. Crack an ace!

Jam Serve Up Tight

A jam serve is a low drive that hits the side wall on the fly near the service box and reflects quickly with the proper spin into the receivers feet, handcuffs him, or into his body. The one risk is that if it's hit too high it wraps off the back wall for an easy set up for the opponent. The jam is not bread and butter but instead a treat to catch the opponent off balance by making use of a difficult angle and unfrequented play space.

The jam serve is virtually the same as the low drive serve from any of your favorite positions in the service box. The only differences are the angle of the ball, a 6" higher contact on the front wall, and it's always hit very hard. For a wider angle toward the side wall, move the ball approximately 12 inches left or right of where you hit your normal drive to the back corner. The ball must contact the side wall on the fly, angling toward the receiver in such a way as to hit the floor at his feet, jamming his hands, or on the fly into his body.

The jam is an excellent mix after you have hit a few drives to the back corner and your opponent is getting a jump on the serve. Additionally, it works against a slow footed receiver, or when your opponent is flat footed or off balance in the receiving position.

Practice as you do the drives, either with a bucket of balls alone, or with a partner who wants to practice his service return repetitively without keeping score. Score your success on how many times out of ten repetitions you hit an effective jam serve: 0-5 you need more practice; 5-7 don't use it in a tournament; 8-10 you got the jam.

I was around when the jam serve was developed and first seen in the Golden Era mid-70s when Charlie Brumfield emerged from a catacomb sabbatical with Carl Loveday in the San Diego PPA court with the new jam. It was effective for a short while on the circuit. Why the short success? I read once in an early edition of *Ripley's Believe It or Not* that if you whisper a secret at midnight in a graveyard then by sunrise everyone in the world knows it. It's a lesson in propagation, and within one season by simple observation and imitation the jam spread across the country … and its counter. Why don't you see the counter often? Because it requires very quick hands, eyes and feet.

The sure-fire return of the jam serve is to read the server's motion to know it's coming, and step up and put forward momentum into the ball and either volley or short hop the return to the front or the server's body. The server ends up jammed or hurt and will never hit another at you.

Rocky Carson craftily serves to Jack Huczek. A favorite spot to stand is a few feet from the right side wall to serve a drive right, that this receiver must shade to his right to see, or a drive left, Z right, or a jam left. Service is all about where the server stands. (2011 Michael Williams)

Tips on the jam serve:

- Slam it hard.

- Aim for the receiver's feet or body.

- Keep it low to not wrap around off the back wall.

- Use it suddenly in the middle of a game or after a string of drive serves.

- Top side spin off the strings usually reverses off the side wall to bottom side spin and swiftly at the opponent.

- If the receiver volleys or short hops the jam, give it up.

- It's more effective with the one-serve rule because there's no chance of a short serve.

- Use it as an offensive second serve with the two-serve rule.

- It's operational against a flat-footed, tired or opponent who stands near the back wall.

- It's a fine doubles serve to split a lefty-righty team between their backhands.

- The jam serve requires little practice if you own a strong drive.

Get good quick at hitting and returning the jam serve by going into the court with one partner and one ball. One person hits the serve repeatedly while the other returns it. Stop. If the serve was successful, the server shouts, 'Jam!', and if you return it well yell, 'Jelly!' Whoever's ahead when the nut wagon pulls up wins.

Drive Service Pictorial

Ben Croft at the 2013 US Open (by Roby Partovich)

Pros Speak from the Box

Favorite Serve

The drive serve is the beginning of my offense. The four important aspects are variety, deception, angle and power, just like a good baseball pitcher. You can use repeated drive serves are your best pitch by mixing these. Since it's a strength move once-a-minute for up to an hour match, it requires outside weight training. Since the one serve rule, it requires practice for confidence. Throw in an occasional soft serve to keep him off balance. My game pivots around service, aces, and weak returns.   *- Cliff Swain*

Marty Hogan's favorite drive serve with a drawn bow to the receiver's backhand. (Art Shay)

The low drive to the backhand is my favorite over the years because I've practiced to perfect it so long that it gives me a good feeling to hit it right, as well as get a weak return.   *- Corey Brysman*

The most important part of the game at the pro level is the serve. How important? I'd say 60%. That's why the next month is dedicated to working on the drive serve. I keep a sheet on the things I'm working on now, and to work on in the future. That way I don't miss a part of my game. The next thing to practice is the drive serve, where I hope to come on the court and hit a hundred drive serves every other day until it becomes so natural I can do them in a tournament in a close match when tired. My best serves right now are the lob nick to the backhand and wallpaper lob to the forehand. These generate a return to deep court that I can kill with my big pinch.   - *Alvaro Beltran*

Drive serves to both sides, crack serves, and high lobs for variety. I like to stand in the center of the box for most serves, using deception from there.   - *Sudsy*

The jam is my specialty serve. It's part of and does a great job of hiding itself within my other drive serves. I use it to 'strike out' the receiver per a baseball analogy of the pitcher jamming the hitter with inside pitches, then strike him out with an outside corner pitch. Actually, the two serves – jam and drive down-line to either side – complement each other. You can hit drives down either side to set up the jam, or vice versa. The key for me to hitting the jam is to have the ball come low and hard off the side wall, land at the receiver's feet, and ricochet quickly off the back wall and toward the opposite side wall. If your opponent is fumble-footed or clumsy-handed in any way, the jam's a breeze.
                                                                   - *Derek Robinson*

Once I got a power stroke, the rest of my game was enhanced including the serve. When I wanted a point I hit a hard drive serve to the backhand, and when I wanted a string then I hit a sequence of drives to both sides that were hard to read. This all switched with the one-serve rule where I now soft serve to get the ball into play without error, but it still makes sense in a do-or-die situation – down 10-8 in the tiebreaker – to bring back the power serves. This is one reason I'm known for getting into and winning close matches.
                                                                      - *Marty Hogan*

My favorite in 'two-serve' is a right side down-line drive at 120 mph that cracks behind the short line. I love that serve because it progressively closes in on a shorter crack...shorter crack...ace! If the serve's short, I lob the second to the deep backhand to keep him off-balance for the next right side attack. This plan is impractical with the '1-serve', where I put the ball safely into play with a lob intent on winning the rally.
                                                                    - *Ruben Gonzalez*

A mix of low hard serves from the same spot in the box using deception and visual screening with no serve ever coming off the back wall. The recipe is usually 5 down-line drives to one cross-court drive to one Z. You may use a continual pattern and few players will figure it out. My 'big serve' is the drive to either side with a Z to the right thrown in, all off deceptive motion. For each, I like to stand just to the right of center, drop the ball in front and step forward for weight transfer. This position and height of the ball drop

'I hit a hundred drive serves every other day.' - Alvaro Beltran. (Ed Arias)

helps shield the intent from the opponent. A contact inches off the floor gives a natural three-quarter spin over the top-outside that keeps the serve low and scooting on the bounce. Put your extra effort of bending, stretching to drop, stepping far, and hitting low while thinking deception and you may take your play to the next level.   *– Jim Spittle*

I teach an effective formula: 2-spots in the box, and 5-serves from each spot. The first spot is on the right side just in from the doubles partner line, where your five serves are a drive right, Z right, drive left, 'jam left, and a lob left. The second spot is mirrored about 6-feet from the left sidewall where you hit the serves recalled from the right with the exception that the lob still goes left (to a righty). That's a total of ten serves, all you'll need to raise to A, Open, and then Pro level.   *- Jeff Leon*

I like to be moving on the serve rather than stationary. I find that when I hit it sharply with a lengthy follow through there's greater explosion off the front wall. The serve is too much a part of the game, and the rally too little, and historically when this happens in racquet sports everyone suffers from the fans down to the players. The one-serve rule has come to aid and other regulatory changes are required.   *- Victor Niederhoffer*

My favorite has varied with the times. I won the nationals during the two-serve era with a hard drive to the backhand. Most of us winning players went right at the line right at the crack…for the pure winner. With the coming of the one-serve, we started using low lobs and Z-serves. The crack ace for me involves more aim than speed, with a deceptive arsenal of slices to vary what the receiver sees coming at him. Every serve can't crack out, you know.   *- Mike Ray*

I love the Jam/Z Serve in doubles because there are so many variables to it. And, there is nothing more satisfying then acing a person to the forehand side!   *– Jackie Paraiso*

I prefer the lobs and half-lobs (garbage serve) to get the ball safely into play without a mistake, then to win the rally. When forced to go for an ace at a crucial moment, it was a left crack drive serve just behind the service box.   *- Charlie Brumfield*

My early years, before racquetball hit the St. Louis JCC courts, were spent at handball, and in fact I placed third in the national 18-and-unders around '69. I believe my racquetball serve started out with my motion in handball: Walk into the ball somewhat horizontally, and use body movement to generate power and deceptiveness. I would start a few feet from the left wall, and walk across the box making contact a third of the way to the right wall. I then drove the ball to either side without giving a clue which direction it would go. Balls to the right picked up a hop and slide along the right wall, and balls to the left would be aimed to die in the back left corner. The receiver was visually screened. The key was deception and angles, with the power part secondary. This serve became extremely effective paving a world championship.   *- Jerry Hilecher*

Any drive serve.   *– Jose Rojas*

My favorite serve would be the drive serve to the right side of the court.

– Andy Hawthorne

Hard-Z left to the backhand.   *– Cheryl Gudinas*

Hard-Z to the backhand.   *- Cristina Amaya Cassino*

263

My favorite serve is the Jam served from off center so I'm out of the way with the ball ricocheting off the selected sidewall aimed at the hip on the receiver's racquet side, and the jam can fly off the back wall and die on the sidewall eliciting a racquet tensile strength testing return right up against the sidewall.   *– Ken Woodfin*

High lob that barely goes over the line. It's my experience that not many players can effectively return this serve consistently.   *– John Ellis*

Backhand half-lob.   *– Rhonda Rajsich*

Horizontal bow stroke suspended over a drive serve at the 2011 3-Wall Nationals. (Mike Augustin)

Serves and Strings

Why not attach an imaginary string to the ball next time you enter the service box? In this way, you judge the important angle the ball takes from launch on strings to the front wall plaster. Have someone watch your strings from a prospective crouched near a sidewall in front of the service box. Then trade positions to analyze his strings.

Let's look at the angle possibilities:

1. The string is level. That is, the racquet and front wall contacts are at equal height. This is the conventional ideal, I believe, and the zero angle (parallel to the floor) that is practiced by most of the top pro drive servers. Obviously, the ball must be hit with effort to zing and level over the short line.

2. The string level angles up from racquet contact to front wall. This may or may not be an error, and examine it as the latter if your drive serve trajectories continually carry off the back wall for plum setups. Flatten the string rather than take steam off the ball to correct this cardinal sin.

3. The string angles down from the racquet face to the front wall. Curiously, this was the preferred technique of the early, softer ball racquetball pioneer servers, but I deem it deleterious to the modern power serve where the lively ball because of the angles carries off the back wall. Summary: Try to flatten your serves to near parallel to, while lowering the string closer to, the floor.

Spin? Yes, and most pros say they utilize a topspin to keep their hard serves low to the front wall, and to make them scoot lower after the floor bounce - all in pursuit of hitting it harder without coming off the back wall. That said, some other players find that either an 'outside' or, seemingly contradictorily, an 'inside' spin causes the ball to run favorably straight down-the-line rather than bounce into a sidewall. Remember always that it's better to have a stock drive serve (and a standard down-line pass shot) that 'wall-papers' along the alleys without touching the sidewalls. This principle of drive serving is of secondary in import only to keeping the ball off the back wall. Summary: Experiment with different spins to keep your drives both low and parallel to the sidewall.

I've always thought that the perfect drive serve, as hit best historically by Cliff Swain, is remarkably low and hard off the racquet and front wall, touches the floor just beyond the short line, skids low along the hardwood, and travels straight back without touching the side or back wall before two bounces. This statement is the most important tip any pro player will read. I'd be remiss to overlook the 'controlled' drive serve as utilized by world champs Mike Ray and Ruben Gonzalez. Each has a similar deceptive bag of

Drive service is all about angles. Attach a mental string from the racquet hit spot to the front wall to the short line to drive the ball low to the receiver. (US RB Museum)

service tricks that rely more on placement than power, so anything you read in this article about 'power' serves also can be performed with an accurate, controlled swing that doesn't break Mach 1. "I love the 20 mph crack ace," quips Gonzalez. "I target the crack on either side just beyond the short line, then next crack serve closer to the short line…" Likewise, I've watch Mike Ray methodically dismantle pros with medium-speed, targeted drive serves left and right. However, when push comes to shove, boys, my analysis is the harder hitting drive server has the upper hand.

Body type comes into play on the serve, but is too often an excuse from bending in hard service. Fat people and pregnant women who can't bend over know what to do. Tall, string-bean bodies must flex at all joints to get down on the ball, and should utilize the full service box without foot-faulting. There are various approaches, as in bowling, but remember that within the service box you can slant your approach toward a sidewall for more step space. The service stroke is usually the same as your forehand stroke with weight transfer from rear to front foot to impart force to the ball, as in hitting a baseball. Since there's time to think and move, get real low for the stroke. Some players find that by dropping the ball more in front, near and close to the front foot, it eclipses from the receiver's vision until crossing the short line. This is normally a perfectly legal serve, and forces the receiver to uncomfortably adjust his stance for a clear view. In the middle of a heated match, that's like trying to move the world.

Pause a second in the service box before each drive serve to reflect the sweet scenario. This is the one time of the game when you're in the most control, ball in hand in center court, with the opponent out of position. Now strike the game's best serve - the drive. Please avoid the sin of hitting a drive that takes a floor bounce and comes off the back wall, because it negates the server's aforementioned sweet advantages. Better to short-serve the first and take a 'safe' second serve such as a Z-serve, than to hit your first drive off the back wall. I've never seen a hard drive bounce three times on the floor before reaching the back wall, but it's a worthy image to convince all that your drives can bounce two times before kissing the back wall.

I recently watched two of the sport's eminent power servers, Marty Hogan and Cliff Swain, play to a tiebreaker that was decided when Swain sneaked a few more 180 mph drive serves into the corners. Importantly, these were controlled swings and never flails. I assumed a ground level view to verify that Cliff contacts the serve about 10" off the floor, and Marty about 14". Swain's imaginary string from racquet to front wall contact may actually dip downward and then hop slightly during front wall reflection due to a topspin, with the net effect that the string going away from the front wall is level and at the same height of the racquet contact. Hogan's out-spin and in-spin serves were also close to level going into and from the front wall, but without the jump on the front plaster. The one-serve rule that the Legends tournaments mandate can pave the future of a better racquetball history. The game with two-serves at top levels has been and is tedious and annoying. One-serve happily partially negates the impact of this written article, yet at the end of the day the Legends finalists are still the big drive servers.

An effective training technique used the South American teams' coach Jeff Leon is to place a spare racquet on the hardwood just beyond the short line as the drive serve target that players must hit once before retiring for the day. It's akin to a basketball player's fate to sink a certain number of free throws before heading for the showers. I use the variation of putting down a strip of masking tape three feet behind and parallel to the short line. This makes solo practice of the serve more fun, but can also be used as a guideline with a partner. Score a point for yourself each time the drive touches within this three foot target strip, and subtract a point each time it goes short or long of the strip. Subtract two points if the serve carries off the back wall before two bounces. Time how long each day it takes to reach 10-points, and stencil the resultant graph on your tournament T-shirt.

I have such faith in the drive serve that a strong server, which I'm not, need have no other in his service repertoire. National championships have been won where the only serve for an entire game was the drive to the backhand, so you see that deception is out the window when one owns a particularly potent weapon. Yet, the recommendation is to build a service arsenal around the basic drive serve. I 'formula' my hard serves in an ever-repeating cycle of about three drives to the backhand, one drive to the forehand, three drives to the backhand, one Z-serve to the backhand… repeat the sequence throughout the match. It's unlikely anyone will guess the system unless you write about it.

Some tidbits: For a second serve, I like either a hard Z-serve to the backhand, a 'garbage' (low lob), or a low lob. If my foe has a 'big game' of forehand serve and booming forehand shots to shield a weak backhand, then I limit the serves to his forehand, except perhaps on match point to rub it in. If the rival is a power player who loathes the ceiling game, I experiment early on with soft serves to disturb his rhythm. If he stands too deep to receive, or puffs after a hard rally, or is psychological suspect at critical points, I go for crack aces just over the short line. I've had to eat these cracks myself, and find them as distasteful as the next player.

I recommend picking two favorite spots from which to serve within the service box. For righties vs. righties, these are usually: 1) about six feet from the left side wall, or as close as you can get to the 'legal screen line' without breaking its plane, and 2) about six feet from the right side wall, where similarly you can mix in legal screen drive serves down the right line. Mark the two spots with a tape X or bubblegum. The idea is to get comfortable with 3-5 serves from each of these two locations, to build a winning service formula, and to blend deception into a complete service attack. I truly dislike playing against another who uses these techniques.

If you try your full service repertoire in the initial points of a match, by mid- game you know which serves work best, so it's nice and impolite to withhold and serve them at the final two points of game one. Same with game two.

But it all begins and ends with strings and serves and angles, and making sure your hard drives bounce twice before touching the back wall. My California desert property borders a bombing range where the evening show is helicopters firing large-caliber bullets at dozens-of-rounds-per-second as best seen from a lawn chair atop my trailer three miles from the target. Every tenth round is a tracer that streams like a mile-long bright string across the sky, so I know when the bullets drift too close to head for my other underground trailer. It's as loud as Charlie Brumfield and as rapid-firing as Cliff Swain.

Dillon Silver puts a string on a drive at the 2013 3-WB World Championships. (Mike Augustin)

269

Service Tip from the Tomb of an Unknown Receiver

Sometimes you meet an unknown player in a remote court with a narrow specialty that makes him a virtuoso. This hot tip comes from Scott Hops who has a pro drive serve and high Open forehand with a poor backhand.

'You're down-line drive serve used in combination with a cross-court serve has one nuance for success on the cross-court. Hesitate a split second in mid-stroke before you hit the cross-court. This allows the receiver to commit a step in the wrong direction (down-the-line), it lets the ball drop lower which ultimately prevents it from rebounding off the back wall, and as the ball drops lower it's also contacted deeper in the stroke to deceptively cue the opponent to the down-line drive. He's caught holding his jock.'

This limited arsenal wins 80% of Scott's points on aces and killed weak returns against players at all levels. It's called the Big Game of a booming serve and follow-up cannonball forehand, and the only way around it is to isolate his backhand.

This classy bow stroke serve by Davey Bledsoe drove him to a 1977 World Title. (Art Shay)

270

Legal Screen Serve Short Course

Within the Top Four players in the world, #1 usually has the best legal screen serve.

There's one spot in the service box on the right near the side wall to stand, an exact spot depending on the height and stroke of the server, and the height the stance of the receiver, and legally drive the ball right or left so it's at least partially eclipsed from the receiver's eyes. From this spot there are three serves: the drive down the right wall, a drive left, and a Z right. Each must be off the same motion so the receiver can't or has a very hard time guessing which it will be. Remember he can't see the served ball being hit either. The other variables that figure in are where the server cradles the ball, drops it, and contacts it.

Then the second legal screen serve spot in the service box (the player should have both) is slightly to the right of center in the box. This forces the receiver to pick either to be eclipsed from seeing the drive left, or he must move way to his left that opens the drive serve right. From this spot the server may also serve the Z left but that's minimal as you reach the top pros.

If you draw a straight line between where the ball is cradled and the receiver's eyes, and another straight line from where the serve is struck and the receiver's eyes, these are guides to the optimal situation where the receiver is least able to see the struck ball and the most visually screened as the ball passes the server's body.

As the server, you are trying to block the receiver's vision of your serve as *the ball flies toward the front wall.* The objective is to hide the entire serve until the ball rebounds off the front wall, and better until the ball reaches the front service line. The receiver's line of vision, then, is of utmost concern. When hitting the serve, determine exactly what his line of vision is to the front wall, and then block it. The receiver will not see the ball until it has hit the front wall and rebounded at least a few feet. Ultimately, the receiver shouldn't sight the ball until it is very near the short line. The receiver has even less time to react.

Returning The Legal Screen Serve. Improve your chances of returning this serve by confusing the server's ability to judge your angle of vision of the ball's flight toward the front wall. The server is trying to block your vision of the ball as it travels toward the front wall. You must constantly change your line of vision to his serve. Ifs easier than you think. First, cut down the angle that you'll have to cover on any serve aimed at a rear corner, by moving forward about eight feet from the back wall. Now you'll have only a step or two to move toward the ball (instead of three or four from your regular position). Crouch low. Shift your weight to one leg and peer around his body to the visible alley.

Drive Service Pictorial

Rhonda Rajsich at the 2013 US Open (by Roby Partovich)

273

Drive Serve: How to Practice

With all the pictures, verbal instruction is hardly needed. However in studying them you will discover these factors:

5 Quick Tips

1. For the drive serve, the primary serve of advanced racquetball, a lower crouch is required. Hit the ball with knees deeply bent and bowed at the waist. This lowers ball contact.

2. The crouch also adds spring to the legs for better drive on the ball.

3. Cradle and release the ball from a lower altitude, out and away from the body.

4. Stand in a position so the receiver is screened from seeing the ball at contact.

5. Hitting the ball lower keeps it off the back wall. Really, the only mistake you can make is to have it come off the back wall.

How to practice

Alone: Take a basket of balls into the court and hit drive serves for an hour.

Alone with a coach: Serve and the other person catches the ball and tosses it back. The coach is the basket.

With a partner: Player A hits ten minutes of drives to Player B who makes any serve return he wants. The rally ends without a third shot. Then the server and receiver exchange places for ten minutes more, and so on for an hour.

Scoring Your Drive Serves

This is the most important, whichever drill above you choose. Score a point for yourself if the ball goes past the short line and doesn't come off the back wall. And, subtract a point when the ball fails this. Then, at the end of the hour tally your points. In this way, you may determine progress day to day.

A Ridiculous Hoax that Works

Pretend the back wall is poisonous paper and every time the ball comes off it before a second bounce the paper collapses on the server.

Better, every time the serve is short or off the back wall do five pushups.

Pro Goal

Consider yourself a pro if you can serve 20 drives without a short or the ball touching the back wall before the second bounce.

A legal foot on the line by Eric Leach serving to Ben Croft at the St. Louis pro stop in 2011. The USAR Rulebook that Rule 3.9(a) therein addresses the server's foot being either totally or partially over the Service Line. Meanwhile, Croft must guard the right alley where he's legally screened, as well as the left side drive which is a farther distance. Even this stop action photo doesn't reveal which side Leach will serve to. (Michael Williams)

276

Serve Return: General Advanced

The springboard of service return is all returns should follow the offensive theory of play. Always make the most attacking shot possible:

1. If the serve is a setup kill return.
2. If it can't be killed hit a drive.
3. If neither is possible go to the ceiling.

The impulse while standing aggressively in the receiving position is to kill the return.

If you want to slow down play, have skipped in a couple returns, or the opponent has run a thread of points, then go to the ceiling for three consecutive service returns.

The service returner at an advanced level must be comfortable hitting a perfect five ceiling rally.

Lower level players will have more success with a prevailing notion of going to the ceiling on his return. Then, as the beginner progresses, he must discard this urge and think kill.

The pros are grandmasters at both the kill and the ceiling.

Volley a soft serve whenever possible. This startles the receiver, is the shorter distance to the front wall, and is forgiving for a mishit shot. The volley return is a kill or drive. Watch the legal line, but test the ref early on to know if he enforces it. If he does, short-hop the serve. This is the deepest pocket secret of service returns.

Always volley or short hop if possible the server's first Z serve. This requires reading his motion, and committing *after* he does. If you guess right, there are no worries of another Z for the rest of the game. Drill the return into the front wall or his body.

Expect a jam serve for the server's second, and anticipate it during his motion edging forward so the body momentum advances while striking the ball. You can't return a jam on the volley while backpedalling. The receiver wins the 'intent war' of who may commit last because the server must look down first at the serving ball.

Experiment with standing a step closer to the short line than is comfortable to become effective. In practice, drill closer and closer to the short line as your reflexes get faster and faster.

Mannino receives service from Sudsy. (John Foust)

Whenever the server stands upright in a relaxed form to serve, edge up to volley the lob or garbage return.

Against lobs. It is easier, much easier, than you think to volley a lob scraping the side wall at shoulder height – *if* you develop the eye. Practice a thousand shots a week with a partner who agrees to lob serve, you volley the return, then play stops, and another lob comes. In general, strike the lob *before* it glances into the side wall rather than after. The *only* time to bounce the lob serve is if it comes off the back wall, in which case kill the return.

278

Vs. the screen serve. Complain the first time the server hits a screen. Have memorized the rule to quote to the ref.

Vs. crack ace. Stand closer to the service line to dissuade it, and to make the server uncomfortable trying it.

Really the *only* threatening thing a receiver may expect is strong camouflage from one position in the service box of a drive left, or right, or Z. That is the history of racquetball championships decided in a crystal ball. If you can't read a champion's service motion to anticipate his blazing mix of drives to either side and Z, then he will march through you.

There are two ways to conquer a Kane or Swain with their deceptions:

1. Watch him from the bleachers hit the serve over and over a thousand times to know which he is going to hit *before* he strikes it.
2. Find a practice partner who has the best serves and practice your returns only, without continuation of the rally.

The faster the ball, or the stronger the server, the more you have to concentrate on your service position, stance, demeanor, and inclination.

Position. Stand in center court just off from the back wall and watch the server closely as if on a date. What's his motion, crouch, do his feet go differently, or his wrist on certain serves? These 'tells' forecast which height, side, and what type of serve is coming. Most servers put 90% to your backhand, so as he begins the motion and a tick after he commits to the serve type, shift slightly to your left for inertia. Now, if he's a crack server, as he moves but before he commits move two feet forward to upset him, then back up to your original spot just before he hits.

Position of the receiver has a range rather than spot. You're within it somewhere center or slightly to the side walls, and one to six feet from the back wall. The pro (who sees mostly drive serves) stands in the middle and about three feet off the back wall. If the ball's slower, move slightly forward. If the serves are a barrage of drives stand a foot deeper, and if serves come soft a foot up for a head start to charge the volley.

Stance. Choose from a few:

1. Swain is like a gorilla awaiting charge, legs fairly wide, arms swinging side to side, and eyes narrowed on the server.
2. Sudsy is like a wind-up doll at full tension before the switch is flicked on. His stance may be different each time, but always intense.
3. Mannino assumes more of a squash players ready stance with feet evenly spread, on his toes, and racquet slightly up in front at the midline.

279

4. Hogan is like Sleepy of the seven dwarfs, often resting hands on knees, feet more closely spaced, head up and very watchful.

Know when to commit. As the server winds up, there is a split-second on his downswing when you sense the server has mentally delivered the serve and may *not* change his mind. In this split-second make your move, usually a charge to one side. Most feet-work against the drive after the initial charge is lateral. Study YouTube videos of the pros to verify it.

The basic strategy for the advanced player *up to* the pros is to regain the front court. Some opponents respond more weakly to a ceiling ball, pass or kill, however the intent is to get the server out of front-and-center. Take it over because that's where most points are scored. However, the pros is a different ball game. Their intent follows the offensive theory of play to try to kill any setup. This too gets the server out of center court quickly.

You have to be in motion as he serves and moving forward as the ball comes at you. Meet it head on with your best shot. Beginners can try the 'quick-step' from tennis where you're on your toes, or shifting weight from foot to foot, and jump from this to greet the ball.

Think in terms of coach Jeff Leon's service return 'rebuttal'. Just as a salesman has a rebuttal for every line from his client. There are a finite number of serves, and for each the best possible reply for you. Having the complete script and rebuttal list in mind allows you to relax whenever he serves.

When in doubt. If you're uncertain, tired, or an intermediate player, returns should be defensive against hard serves, and against the lob the choice is ceiling or volley/short-hop. You can drive servers bonkers by never deviating from these rules.

The fastest, most efficient way to become a great serve returner is with the buddy drill of returning hundreds of serves per day, sans the rally. He hits serves, you hit returns.

Finally, if an opponent opens with a serve that's hurting you, when you get the serve back go ahead and hit the same to him to hurt him or see the ideal return.

Stand aggressively to receive, and your correct shots will follow.

Debbie Tisinger awaits service at the 2011 Nationals. (Janel Tisinger)

Pros Speak from the Box
Serve Return

That first shot return is extremely important, so ya better be focused on that ball. There is a lot that goes into reading where your opponent is serving. Analyzing everything on your opponent from head to toe will make your service return successful. Everything from your opponent's eyes to where their foot steps gives you a hint to what serve is coming and which side it's going to.
— Jackie Paraiso

Stay balanced on both feet while awaiting the serve, slightly on the toes, with knees bent ready to push off in any direction. Think offensive on the serve return, and adjust to a more conservative return as needed.
- Corey Brysman

I stand very close to the back wall, not on the toes of my feet but ready to spring any direction.
- Alvaro Beltran

I'm like a cheetah low and ready to attack a human arm length from the back wall. The goal of any return I is to force a weak shot that I'll eat up.
- Sudsy

I stand to receive about three feet off the back wall and right in the middle, neutrally balanced on the two balls of the feet, concentrating more left-to-right than up-and-back, while musing that if the serve has the slightest flaw then I'm going to bash it for a kill or pass. I have success against control players like Mannino who utilize soft serves by knocking out their service. This is done by mixing the returns - charging to volley one time, and hanging back to go to the ceiling the next. Once you upset the rhythm of the soft server, it's your game. But a power server using drives and Z's pretty much forces your hand, depending on the accuracy of the serve. A weak serve deserves a strong return, usually a kill. A strong serve can be put to the ceiling to get the rally going in a neutral manner.
- Derek Robinson

You have to be in motion as he serves and moving forward as the ball comes at you. Meet it head on with your best shot. Beginners can try the 'quick-step' on return from tennis where you're on your toes and jump from this to greet the ball. Nothing stops the otherwise irritating criss-cross (Z) serve faster than volleying the ball down his gullet. All lobs should be volleyed or short-hopped rather than allowed to the back wall.
- Victor Niederhoffer

The one-serve rule revolutionized service return in that now soft serves began crossing the short line and we became proficient at the definitive returns of volley and short-hop. At a top level of play, you had to fly-kill or short-hop kill a lob straight on or after a wall nick, otherwise the other guy would clobber you. That's the situation today. I've tried different methods of weight shift while watching the server windup, but for me it's best to remain ready while relatively stationary, then react upon knowing where the ball will be.   *- Mike Ray*

I stand in center court one big step off the back wall, physically and mentally shifting. I study the server's movement initially to determine by the height of contact if he's going to drive or lob, then I read his body language and racquet inclination to gauge to which side it'll go. I'm in motion to the spot after he takes his eyes off me and hits. My general mindset at that point is to smash a weak serve with a roll-off or low pass, or to flick a strong serve to the ceiling because I don't mind a rally. Serve and return is a two-man poker game with sweat dropping.   *- Marty Hogan*

Jason Mannino's head is in a sweet spot for the service return. (Freddy Ramirez)

Think in terms of 'service return rebuttal', just as a salesman has a rebuttal for every line on his script. There are a finite number of serves, and for each 1-2 proper replies. For instance, when I'm lobbed, the definitive return is the volley (or short-hop), but the other possibilities are the floor bounce in deep court that demands a ceiling return, or the carry off the back wall for a straight-in kill. Having the complete script and rebuttal list in mind allows you to relax whenever he serves. Also, If an opponent opens with a serve that's hurting you, when you get the serve back go ahead and hit the same to him to hurt him as well and likely see the ideal return.

- Jeff Leon

I stand two feet off the back wall midway in the center anticipating that 90% of the shots are going to my backhand. I'm a small guy and can look between the legs of the server to see what he's going to hit, then move in that direction. If the serve's soft, I fly or short-hop. My aim is to return without a skip ball, then win the point in the rally.

Gonzalez

Put your opponent in the back of the court - 39' back … the furthest.

– Fran Davis

My basic strategy is to regain the front court, and the shot varies. Some opponents respond more weakly to a ceiling ball, pass, or kill, however the intent is to get the server out of front-and-center and take it over because that's where the most points are scored.

- Jim Spittle

The biggest error on serve return is trying to do too much with the ball. The object is to get into the rally without losing it right there. Most players are too aggressive for their ability level, have not thought out how to move their opponent out of center court position with a minimum amount of risk, and thus are prone to having a number of points run against them. I might shoot an occasional serve return, but if it fails then I'll go to the ceiling on the next return so there's not a run. The court position on serve return is perhaps the most unexplored area. Almost everyone has a preferred spot on the court, which I don't think should be the case. I believe you should start deep in the court and as the player serves, break off the motion to keep the server queasy about where you're going to intercept the ball. The average player must be able to hit the ball on the way in at the front wall, which no one does.

- Charlie Brumfield

Square up, racquet up, then DTL!!

– Cheryl Gudinas

The goal on service return is to take back control of the rally. Try to be as offensive as possible.

– Andy Hawthorne

Return the serve to get your opponent out of center court.

- Kerri Stoffregen Wachtel

Remember that the object is to regain the "V" just behind the service area in the middle of the court leaning to the side of the ball.

– Davey Bledsoe

Unless I can attack the serve with confidence, I'm willing to hit a good ceiling ball and get into a rally.

– John Ellis

Serve return is the hardest part of the game. So it takes lots of practice.   *- Charlie Pratt*

Keep the ball alive. Don't try to do a lot with a good serve.   *– Susy Acosta*

The goal is to push my opponent back or kill the ball when the opportunity arises.
   – Jose Rojas

Get low enough to see the ball hit the front wall, then rise up, take a little hop into a split-step, cross-over, study the ball come up off the bounce, and either take the ball out in front of your bod or dance with it when it's coming out a back corner. In either case, as you move visualize and select the best shot available, as GO-FOR-IT.   *– Ken Woodfin*

Jessica Parrilla service return at the 2014 New Jersey Open. (Mike Augustin)

How to Volley Return the Z-Serve

I like to think there's a best return for every single serve, and this is true of the cantankerous Z.

Since the Z is in every advanced player's arsenal, and is a frequent first serve in 1-serve rule, and second serve in 2-serve rule, every advance player should practice this definitive return.

It's a pretty easy return because it's a mental rather than physical adjustment in your game. You practice for one hour to program your mind to step up and volley (or short hop), and it's good for life.

Rush and volley or short-hop the ball. The surprise of the charge knocks the server out of the box. He'll never be comfortable serving another Z, and you may relax never having to receive another. You have destroyed his favorite first or second serve.

Charge and volley his *very first* Z-serve. He'll probably wait a few serves and try one again; but if you volley it too, he'll resign himself to another service. Many Open matches are won or lost on this little pivot.

Who commits first? You are advantaged and the server disadvantaged in preparation for your volley (or short hop) of his Z-serves. The reason is because he must watch the ball and front wall target. The arrangement is like the baseball pitcher who must commit at last to watch the batter, and in this instant the runner at first may steal second base. The server can't see you creep up for the volley (or short hop).

Early prep. Get your racquet up early, move forward, and smote the ball hard to negate the angle and spin. The server has almost zero time to clear the service box and see your return, and – after you warn him once – don't worry about hitting him with the ball. Warn him once, make sure the ref understands, and then hit him. It's a winner both ways: a point on the unexpected return or an avoidable hinder. (For kids, beginners, and hip replacements, of course, take a little more time to patiently explain the facts surrounding the volley return, so that you'll keep a cool court mate.)

Read the Z-serve. You anticipate a Z-serve by his lowered crouch, greater body tension for a hard serve, often looking up at the target, and his motion toward the front wall target. You may have to study the racquet angle at the last instant, but you can nearly always read a Z-serve on the Open and Pro levels. The better the server camouflages the Z, the less time you'll have to step up to volley, but you can do it.

What shot? Hit a hard kill to the near corner or a drive down-the-line or cross-court. The shot need not be precise, just pounded.

Important: Some Z-serve cannot be volleyed without infringing on the legal serve return line. Overcome this by short hopping the return. Every Z-serve may be short hopped without breaking the legal return plane. There are four things to remember about short hopping the Z-serve:

1. Every Z-serve may be returned without breaking the legal return plane.
2. It is an extremely difficult shot to learn, perhaps the hardest of all racquetball.
3. It's the most exacting and effective serve return of the Z.
4. A smart server will never serve you another Z after you volley one.

The volley of the Z is called an antidote. There is nothing the server can do to combat it, and he will never serve another to you. For this reason, the first time he serves you a Z in practice or a tournament, reply with the volley or short-hop.

Many pro top pro matches boil down to the short hop return of the Z. It is generally the *last* shot any pro masters. When he does, he's immediately boosted up the ranks. *(See the 'Cliff Swain Introduction' of this book.)*

Short hop tips are:

1. Be on your toes to move up as the server drops the ball.
2. He must commit to the Z before you react by charging it, so the deck is stacked in your favor.
3. During his downswing his attention is on the ball and cannot see you moving up to volley or short hop.
4. Stroke the ball confidently, smoothly, and hard.
5. The kill or drive return need not be exact since the server is confused, out of position, backing up, and afraid of being hit with the ball.

Practice the shot with a buddy or ball machine. They hit you a Z-serve over and over for 30 minutes (to both sides, but primarily to the backhand), and you volley kill or drive the ball down the near wall. You will be moving forward while striking the shot, and hit it hard to overcome the spin. If the buddy is in the way, doesn't have time to clear, hold up in practice, but in a tournament warn him the first time, and then there's no other choice than to drill him in the kidney with the ball. Some servers accept only consequences to their favorite point winners.

You may also practice the short hop alone on the court, as I have for hundreds of hours in as many courts across the country, by standing on the court alone. Start in center court at the short line and tap yourself a setup off the front wall that reflects in front of your feet, step up and short hop it. After a dozen shots, move back to the 5-foot line and do the same. Then 5-feet deeper in the court, and so on to the back wall. You may also position to practice the short hop *anywhere* on the court. The hardest return in racquetball, and thus the one to practice the most, is the short hop in deep court on the backhand wall.

Many happy returns.

The bow forehand arms the stroke for volleys of the serve return or any shots during a rally. Dan Fowler unleashes one at a 2006 pro stop. (Ken Fife)

Pros Speak from the Box

Short Hop

It's a mandatory, especially on the service return of lob, and requires even more impeccable timing than the volley, so you must practice the short-hop endlessly.

- Cliff Swain

Move forward as if to volley the ball and if you happen to short hop it for the point, move faster forward next time. Be encouraged that it gets easier as you get quicker.   *- Sudsy*

It's almost like playing baseball in that you really have to focus on the ball and where you think it will hit the ground before the quick pickup close to the floor on the rise. I've found that if you go to short-hop the lob serve, it's most common use, get to the dotted line as fast as you can and wait then you'll have more success than trying to time the arrival of your feet at the same time as the ball.   *- Jeff Leon*

Footwork in going to the ball is important. Start early and swing with confidence.

- Corey Brysman

I'm not a short-hopper because I get to the volley, and advise others to do the same. The single time for the short-hop is on service return because you penetrate the 5-foot plane for the surprise.   *- Ruben Gonzalez*

It's easier with the big, modern racquet with some practice. The drill I used was to follow the ball until just after the second bounce, or hit it at the start of the first rise off the floor. Learn to short-hop the ball and you've a built-in weapon for serve return of anything soft.

- Charlie Brumfield

It's a difficult attack that's worth practicing.   *- Marty Hogan*

It's the final key shot that baptizes a top Open into the Pros.   *– Jim Spittle*

Shots

Paola Longoria watches the ball, with ESP and body torque at the 2014 Juarez Open. (Ken Fife)

Kill-Pass

This is your intended kill that somehow rises a few inches for a pass winner. It doesn't matter why it rises, the fact that it either rolls off for a winner, or elevates to pass the opponent is what you're aiming for.

The method is to *always* try for the kill. Like shooting a gun, the projectile ascends a tiny bit en route to the target. Don't try for a pass to hit this shot; it won't work.

The great value of this ruse is that it hits winner after winner with little chance for error. It is hard to skip the ball knowing it will either flat roll out or go for a pass a few inches high. You might be surprised that many champions never try to flat kill the ball but always expect the ball to be either a kill or a naturally rising pass.

The gallery often believes the pass was the intent, but it was a planned kill.

We're talking about the difference between a flat rollout and one that rebounds less than eight inches high off the front wall for a pass. Hence the margin of error on the ball striking the front wall is from 0-8" up from the floor. So, you may relax on the stroke and aim for a stripe 0-8" across the front wall above the hardwood.

Mike Yellen had the best kill-pass in the history of the game, explained in 'Ode to the One-foot Pass', with five end of season #1 finishes and dominated the 80s. And, I am the only player who consistently beat handball great Paul Haber in hands vs. racquet exhibitions throughout the golden era 70s because the sole shot I used, stroke after stroke, was the kill-pass. Otherwise, Haber beat other top pros Steve Strandemo while wearing a walking cast on one foot, and downed Hall of Fame Steve Serot giving him 10 points a game in best two of three to 21, and defeated Bud Muehleisen hands vs. racquet in the *Sports Illustrated* big money match.

In reflection, the kill-pass is a shot intended as a kill but rises for a low drive, either down-line or cross-court. Try the following experiment to determine if the kill-pass may replace both your original kill and pass shots: Play one game against an equal opponent where you strike a kill-pass at every opportunity. Then play a second game where you stroke your regular kills and passes. This one hour experiment may downshift the complexity of your strokes, simplify the game strategy, reduce errors to nil, and crank you one rank up the ladder. This shot alone with a strong drive serve enables an A player to become Open, or an Open player a Pro almost overnight!

Pros Speak from the Box

Back Wall

Back wall shots are relatively easy if you follow the basics of good footwork, watch the ball, and a level swing. There's plenty of time to set up, there's no distraction by the opponent, and the shot is usually a kill or pass. It's an easier shot than the ceiling ball that comes up short in deep court, so think to score a point on that shot or the ensuring setup.

- Mike Ray

Get back behind the ball, and follow it out. Of the two regular methods of flow vs. plant-and-swing, the latter fails miserable. Then there's the opportunity when the opponent's over-hit ceiling shot comes off the back wall that handcuff some players. Overcome it by looking early at where the ball will appear off the back wall. Couple the anticipation with rapid footwork and quick stroke preparation, then go offensive. If you can make sure every time you go to the back wall is an offensive opportunity for you, it prevents the other player from manhandling you during the rally. *- Charlie Brumfield*

Get to where the ball will be for the hit even as it goes to and comes off the wall, then everything else will fall into place. Handle ceiling balls off the back wall in the same way, with good footwork, and anticipate a sharper angle off the wall by moving the feet even quicker and closer to the wall.. *- Corey Brysman*

Get behind the ball (between it and the back wall), get real low, and drive though. The over-hit ceiling ball that carries off the back wall is tough for most players, but you can learn to pummel it as I do so that he'll never want to hit it to you again. *- Sudsy*

The best tip you'll ever get for back wall play is to learn to hit the shot straight down the line. The hitter's inclination and the opponent's anticipation is cross-court, so picture a vertical rank straight back along the near side wall. Keep the ball low in this rank with a kill or drive. The first article I ever read by Keeley said, "The first player who learns to hit a consistent down-line wallpaper shot will dominate the game," and that's what happened. *- Marty Hogan*

The instant you see the ball's going to the back wall, race there to set up. The common error is to hesitate and flick off the back wall. *- Ruben Gonzalez*

Move while watching the ball to the back wall, then position yourself while still moving to let it get out in front of you so that it's closer to the front wall than your body. Then contact low for a kill or wide-angle pass. *- Jeff Leon*

To return the ceiling off the back wall get *real* close to the back wall and stay low to kill it. *- Alvaro Beltran*

Susy Acosta of Mexico takes a ceiling ball off back wall with ESP and focus. (Roby Partovich)

The glitch for some players on moving to take the opponent's ceiling shot that rebounds off the back wall is that he doesn't plant his rear foot close enough to that back wall to allow room to step forward into the stroke. It's as simple as that: stick your rear thigh against the back wall, bend low, and step into the swing. The shot return is usually a kill since the ball's struck so low and with the opponent often stationed in deep court from his last shot. The straight-in kill is desirable, but the pinch or splat likely because you're compelled to contact the ball so deep. *– Derek Robinson*

Back Wall Pictorial

Samantha Salas (by Ken Fife)

Hogan's Volley

'The game's up in the air', according to Marty Hogan. 'The one vital shot to fly is the volley.'

I agree, and add it's a mental adjustment from your long habit of floor bouncing the ball before the hit. Break it with Hogan's drill, and you're on your way.

Personal progress is best examined in terms of identical twins, or clones. If two clones vie with the only variable that Mr. X has no volley and Mr. V volleys at every opportunity, V will trounce the rival. Think of yourself as one of a clone pair as you read this tip.

This article won't belabor the landslide odds that favor you, the *vollier,* but recall in brief the benefits: 1) You surprise the opponent, 2) You often takes a position for the hit in front of him to visually and physically screen his play on your shot, 3) You control the rally pace, 4) The volley is always a shorter shot than letting the ball bounce, and 5) If the volley is a return of the foe's lob serve, he'll be twitchy about soft serving again. The usually volley shot for an advanced player is the kill, though a pass is feasible. The better your volley gets, the more you lower the shot. Also, the intended kill often has a force and spin that causes it to rise a tad to go for a pass winner, and a point's a point.

Marty Hogan, one of the strongest volliers in history, describes his early experience as if it were a first date: 'Taking the volley as a young player made such a dramatic difference in my shot selection, power game, and control of pace of play. I always volleyed the ball in tournaments, and the root of success was in my solo drills.'

The young Hogan didn't practice the drop-and-bounce or set-up with a bounce drills that grab the focus of 99% of other beginners including this author. Instead, he practiced fly-kills down the sidewall alleys. 'Every day I entered the court and stood on the forehand side on the red line of the service box. I gave myself ten setups off the front wall and tried to fly-kill straight-in. As soon as I could hit ten shots with about 80% accuracy, I allowed myself to go to a second spot, deeper in the court on the red short line. There I stood and gave myself setups until there was 80% accuracy on ten hits. Then I progressed - like baseball or basketball 'work-up' - around the court: The third 'work-up' spot was ¾ of the way back on the forehand side until there was 80% proficiency, then I stood near the back wall until I got the same. That completed the forehand straight-in volley kills, and then I went to the backhand side on the red service box line and did the same thing all the way to the back wall.'

It took him an hour in the initial practice days to achieve the work-up, if indeed he reached the final spot on the backhand side near the back wall at all. However, he persevered over the months until he could do the full work-up in twenty minutes.

There are four key elements in his routine: 1) Volley the ball, 2) Kill the volley 3) Kill straight–in rather than pinch or cross-court, and 4) Increase the increment of difficulty by working your way around the court only after you've mastered 80% at a given spot.

'The universal tendency is to pull the ball cross-court, and this is all wrong in racquetball offense because the shorter distance is straight-in, and your body screens the opponent when the ball goes straight-in,' says Hogan. 'The other important thing to remember is that 80% of all game shots are taken close to one of the side walls rather than toward the middle of the court.'

Miss Volley, Laurel Fenton

The Hogan Volley Drill for straight-in kills paved the way to six world titles.

Pros Speak from the Box

Volley

Commit. The key is to commit. The potential volley 'hangs' in the air a moment during which time you have a choice: Commit to the volley is correct. *- Derek Robinson*

Because the ball's moving fast within a shorter travel distance, watch keenly as it comes. Learn through drilling to move fluidly to, and swing smoothly at, the ball.

- Corey Brysman

Charge the ball, what are you waiting for. Go to it, attack! *- Sudsy*

It's the most underused surprise in the rally. I hope my peers don't read this.

- Marty Hogan

I brought a great fly-kill from one-wall where you have to chase the ball if it goes over your head. Move up fast and fly-kill. The quick volley makes even a great opponent run and dive all over the floor while you waltz to the music. *- Ruben Gonzalez*

There's nothing quite like watching someone dominate play by stepping up to fly-kill every opportunity, and the consistent volley player owns a 5-point advantage per game. It appears he's in a better world, especially if you're caught on the court with him. The last question answered in racquetball will be, why don't others, including pros, copy? Take it right there, and don't bounce it or allow it to the back wall. *- Jeff Leon*

It's absolutely crucial to take the ball out of the air whenever possible. The stroke should begin with early racquet preparation and almost caricature footwork, like the cartoon figure stepping off the cliff and moving his feet real fast, only on the court you go places. I practice the fly-kill tons to this day. *- Cliff Swain*

Always volley when you think you can, running forward to meet the ball rather than bounce or let it pass to the back wall. *- Victor Niederhoffer*

I fly-kill the ball by letting the power of the ball reflect on a blocked racquet to propel it accurately at the front wall. The guiding motion off the properly inclined strings into the target area that's shielded by your body from the opponent makes a winner. If your fly

299

kills go too high, you're probably swinging to hard and should try a blocked stroke.

- Charlie Brumfield

Work on your quickness and balance outside the court with explosive exercises, then practice it on the court with the racquet and ball to volley.   *- Alvaro Beltran*

Yes!   *– Susy Acosta*

Yes, it keeps pressure on the opponent.   *- Rhonda Rajsich*

Very, it puts more pressure on your opponent.   *– Jose Rojas*

Definitely, and being only 5'5" helps to stay down on the ball.   *– John Ellis*

Short hops and volleys are useful, but do not attempt if you have not practiced.

- Charlie Pratt

The volley is fine for those who can do it. It's not for everyone. It takes form, quickness and focus to hit effectively. It keeps your opponent on her/his toes, and maintains your center court, if used properly.   *– Jackie Paraiso*

Yes, if you can hit it, it is a great weapon. The timing just takes practice.   *– Rich Wagner*

The volley can be a punch, flick or full swing when intercepting a ball out of midair. The more peculiar short-hop requires very close positioning, a slightly hooded or closed racquet face set right behind the bouncing ball, a smooth, short follow-through, intense ball focus and a felt low target.   *– Ken Woodfin*

The volley catches my opponent off guard and I'm that much closer to controlling center court. I also short-hop all over the court.   *- Kerri Stoffregen Wachtel*

The volley and short-hop are very useful, although I didn't start using them until 2000, per Tom Travers suggestion.   *– Cheryl Gudinas*

Yes. By cutting balls off mid-air, and staying aggressive, you can catch your opponent out of center court and control a rally.   *– Andy Hawthorne*

Outdoor and indoor pro Ben Croft volleys at the 2013 3-WallBall Championships. He has finished in the Top 8 indoors every season since 2007. (Mike Augustin)

The Overhead Killshot!

Loveday and the Evolution and lost Art

with Marty Hogan

Almost forty years ago I found myself in double trouble in a doubles final. Our opponents were at the time the #1 player in the world, Charlie Brumfield and his legendary coach, Carl Loveday. They were two of the best strategist in the game. My partner was a green teenager I was mentoring for the summer in San Diego in his first Open or Pro level final. The youngster's name was the to-be legend Marty Hogan.

Marty thought that Loveday with a pot belly and smelling of cigar smoke was a bit past his prime, and he picked on the old guy. He tried to engage Carl in a *mano-a-mano* right side ceiling challenge by hitting one ceiling ball after the other to Loveday, while Brumfield and I twiddled thumbs watching with amusement on the left sideline. Carl returned some perfect forehand ceilings hugging the right side wall, and the others he flat out killed with an odd shot of the era… a perfect overhead kill in the right corner.

One after another the world badminton champ Loveday rolled out overheads.

In no time, we were down six points and griping. Marty the kid still couldn't believe Grandpa Loveday was taking him apart on the right side. ''Timeout!'' I yelled. Loveday exited for puffs on a cigar, as I explained to Marty that Carl could drop those overheads in the corner like a bird all day long. Instead, I told him, crush the ball hard and cross court so I could get into position and take control of the game, despite my perennial nemesis national champ Brumfield.

By blocking the overhead, we closed the gap and took the match in a close win. Marty won his first Open/Pro level title but not before learning the lesson of the Loveday overhead kill.

Carl later taught the same lesson to his two most famous students, Bud Muelheisen and Charlie Brumfield, and I copied from them. Both could execute the overhead kill as well as Loveday and used it to win more national titles than I can count. My personal variation was a shot only a few including one-time national champ Davey Bledsoe could execute offensively called a backhand reverse overhead pinch, which I could kill eight out of ten on even a slightly short ceiling ball.

The overhead kill became a staple in 1970's pro racquetball. Brumfield's overhead was the best of all the top pros. Hogan and I in singles matches against the bearded machine used to watch it like a movie, mouth agape and all the gallery had to do was throw in popcorn, as he blew open our games with an offense from a defensive position by putting

302

Vertical bow for the overhead by Daniel De LaRosa at the 2012 US Open. (Mike Augustin)

away a less than perfectly hit ceiling ball with a nearly perfect overhead kill shot in *either* corner.

In the 1980's, the overhead remained a big weapon and the two best belonged to two of the best players, the now matured Marty Hogan and world champ Dave Peck. Marty would hit an overhead tomahawk chop reverse pinch with his forehand in to the left corner and after hitting the side then front wall it would roll out to the right. Dave, a student of Loveday and Muehleisen, used the overhead kill pinch to both corners and mixed in the overhead pass for deception as well as the masters did years before.

Perhaps the greatest overhead ever hit was by Muehleisen in a doubles game at the Pacific Paddleball Association where I was his left side antagonist. He wound up on a short ceiling shot like the tennis champ he had been, and smashed the ball that exploded in mid-air into two halves, and each rolled off in the respective front corners.

The 1990's saw the overhead employed by the game's very best very effectively. Cliff Swain, who'd learned the overhead from Peck, who'd learned it from Muehleisen, who'd learned it from Loveday, would kill, pinch or splat his overhead as part of an all-out attack. Mike Ray, a tall lean lefty with a build and overhead to match that of Dr. Bud, mixed in his extremely consistent overhead kills with a variety of offensive and defensive shots as part of the true all around power/control game. I played Ray once in the autumn of my career and stood shaking my head like a rake as the balls dropped like leaves in the front corners.

When I started following the top pros again nine years ago in '03, I noticed they were fast, athletic and hit virtually every shot with these big racquets. But even Sudsy Monchik and Kane Waselenchuck who were the two best offensive players in the sport didn't use the overhead in their repertoire. I deduced that the bigger racquets and balls traveling over 180 miles per hour would leave anything but an absolutely perfectly hit overhead as a set up for a Jason Mannino diving re-kill.

Like most sports, racquetball has evolved into a totally different game with new strategic shots than it was forty years ago, and I've accepted that, but I'll always miss the days of wooden and metal racquets strung less than twenty pounds, playing without gloves, 21-point games and the overhead kill!

Michelle Key overhead at the 2013 WOR Championships in Huntington Beach. (Mike Augustin)

Pros Speak from the Box

Overhead

Use the overhead at an unexpected time, and disguise it until the last moment. Surprise is necessary because nobody has the ability to hit the overhead kill repeatedly with the other person looking for it. The only players to use the overhead as a standard weapon have been Bud Muehleisen and Mike Ray whom I assume inherited it from the tennis serve.

- Charlie Brumfield

My strong forehand overhead evolved because of a high backhand weakness. Most players take a shoulder high, deep backhand and splat it, but I run around the ball with my southpaw and hit a forehand overhead. Others say it's become a lethal part of my game. The shot selection is targeted at either a winner, or as often a weak return. The choices are a down-right line pinch, drive to the left side, or a forehand reverse splat in the left corner that I must credit to an unnamed Texas guru.   *- Mike Ray*

The majority of my shots are offensive, so I don't back down from a ceiling shot that comes over my head. I shoot or drive it right back.   *- Sudsy*

Mine is an unorthodox 1-wall technique of letting the ball drop to shoulder high and hitting a hard drive to open court. This is easier than the normal overhead hit higher, and results in an opponent's poor position and weak return.   *- Ruben Gonzalez*

I smash an overhead pass when my opponent cheats toward the front wall to cover my previous kills, or when he's got a solid court position that I want to regain.

- Marty Hogan

I use it mostly to return a soft-Z serve or ceiling ball to the forehand. The ball is head high or above, there's plenty of time, and the direction can be down-line or cross-court. I tend to go down-line more and use my body as a legal barrier to the opponent chasing the pass. The overhead splat is less used since it's harder to hit, but figures in the mix of things to keep the guy restless.   *- Derek Robinson*

Eye contact and a strong follow-through (to bring the ball down) are the points usually missed.   *- Corey Brysman*

The stroke is strikingly the same as the tennis serve, and put steam on it for any shot selection while making sure it doesn't come off the back wall. If a player has a strong overhead kill to a front corner, I advise him to keep hitting it despite the lower percentage for most. That said, if there's room in the court behind you, it's better to back up, let the ball drop and go with the regular kill stroke below the knees.   *- Jeff Leon*

Don't try it too much. Just go to the ceiling.   *– Jose Rojas*

The overhead is a last resort shot for me. - I'd rather go to the ceiling if I am hitting the ball from that height.   *- Kerri Stoffregen Wachtel*

I don't really use the OH.   *– Cheryl Gudinas*

An overhead is an advanced shot. By hitting an overhead you are trying to force a set-up, not really looking to kill the ball right away.   *– Andy Hawthorne*

The Orange Juice Club of Chicago played every early mornings for decades. (Art Shay)

Chain to Championship

Corey Brysman

If you're an aspiring or current pro (other skill levels should return to this tip after jumping ranks), here's the neatest thing since sliced bread for your game. The way to championships is a chain of three repeating links, like three Christmas tree light colors winding in tri-series to the top.

These are truly the only significant links in the chain used at top-world play:

1.   The drive serve. You need no other, though a backup arsenal is advised.

2.   The ceiling shot. This is the standard and sole defensive weapon to use whenever there's no opportunity to hit the third link, as follows.

3.   The killshot. Absurd as it sounds, the top pros use only this offensive shot, with a sprinkling of 'kill-passes' (A pass whose primary intent was a kill).

A picture of recent world championships emerges of elite combat, and potentially of yours, that includes drive serves, ceilings, and kills.

Convince yourself of this surprising reality the next time you play by hitting only the 'big three' for one whole game. (Your opponent can agree to hit only the same, or you can blitz him.) How does the play and outcome compare to your usual methods? Can you foresee that this simple strategy will improve your lot on the court?

This chain of the three shots provides a path, or pull, for progress to the top if you're willing to practice. The jolly thing is that you really have only three shots to practice in your routine. However, the grumble that I don't want to hear is that you have to practice the weak links initially until they become as the stronger ones; after that you're allowed to drill them all equally.

Doesn't it make sense to build a chain? For most, this means at first hitting thousands of drive serves, kills, and ceilings. Since Open level or better players already have substantial kills, for them it's just drives and ceilings. True, these two shots are less fun because killing is so cool, but I predict failure with any other method, so steel up.

The third link in the Chain to Championship is the killshot. Jake Bredenbeck readies to kill one with early swing prep and a drawn bow against David Horn at the 2014 Juarez Open. (Ken Fife)

Pros Speak from the Box

Kill Strategy

The time to kill is anytime there's a setup. The station of the opponent is secondary to the prime need to put the ball hand and low on the front wall.   *- Corey Brysman*

90% of my shots are offensive to maintain an overall aggressive game style.   Given an isolated situation - say a shoulder high set-up in deep court on either side – a defensive shot is normally called for, but no way am I going to slow the pace of the rally, game and our minds by hitting anything but an offensive shot.   *- Sudsy*

For setups on the forehand side, if your opponent is between you and the near side wall then pinch or cross-court kill; but if he's to the open court side of you then kill straight in. Same strategy on the backhand side, and it's all to give greater margin of error on the shots.   *- Ruben Gonzalez*

Anytime you have a setup in front court, kill it. Anytime your opponent is behind you, kill it. Kill shots off the back wall or in deep court until you miss two in a row, and then hit a wide-angle pass. In general, kill to the open court away from him. If he's between you and the sidewall, think pinch. If you're between him and the sidewall go straight in.   *- Jeff Leon*

I try to stick to the general rule of pinch when in front court, especially if the opponent is near a side wall. Given that, the higher level of play up to the pros, the less likely it is to win a point hit from deeper court with a pinch because they're so quick to cover. So, I use more straight-ins as the players get better.   *- Cliff Swain*

My specialty is the pinch kill. Try to hit the side wall very close to the front wall because then the opponent cannot hear the ball on the side wall so early. Listening is a surprising aid in court coverage.   *- Alvaro Beltran*

My bread-and-butter shot is a forehand pinch, though I could always kill down the line with either stroke. I had to get out of squash and a squash strategy in racquetball because it developed a sound passing game that 'won the rally but lost the point'. Pros dive and re-kill passes, so kill the ball at every opportunity. I think out before a match if I want to

Feel Smashin! (US RB Museum)

hit the majority of kills for either stroke either straight in or pinch. If your swing is flat, an intended straight-in may pinch, or vice versa depending on if you connect early or late in the stroke, and you grin all the way to the service box because it's a result of your practiced level swing.
- Mike Ray

Every shot among good players should be hit with the thought of precluding the rally.
- Victor Niederhoffer

To kill the ball as far as I can from the other player.
- Cristina Amaya Cassino

Take the right shot that moves the opponent the greatest distance. If you kill it, it's icing on the cake.
– Cheryl Gudinas

I played a scorecard killshot strategy: Went for the kill as much as possible on my serve, and hit the higher percentage shots when my opponent was serving.
– Brian Hawkes

I play the percentages ... kill when your opponent is behind you.
– Fran Davis

Serve, return, kill. That's 3 shot rallies all day.
– Andy Hawthorne

My killshot strategy is to initially look to shoot every ball I field. My priority is to let every ball drop as low as I possibly can, with quick little adjustment steps, looping on-time, and not too early prep behind my uniform. It's disguised impact point and smooth, swooping, shot making stroke imagined before I shoot and visualized throughout my stroke, and even including a clearance plan after impact. The ball goes where it wants to go to die.
– Ken Woodfin

I didn't have a killshot strategy. My objective was to hit a shot good enough to win the point. If my opponent was quick and could get to shots then I would lower my percentages and go for a lower shot. If he was slower and if I didn't have to go for bottom boards I would not lose points by skipping shots in. I realized that winning involved playing with percentages.
– Jerry Hilecher

Well, everyone wants to kill the ball, right? If it's working then use it. If it's not, then it's most likely a skip shot. And, if I'm off a little, I can't afford a point against me. So, I will either raise the ball a little or go for the higher percentage drive, or go to the ceiling. When I am skipping the ball too much I will focus on just making the front wall, forcing my opponent to miss or set me up, regrouping, and then shooting the next shot.
– Jackie Paraiso

Bittersweet Dispatch

Allow me to hang my credential on the court door. My sole arsenal is the killshot. My national standing in the Golden Era was #2-8 in beating all the national champs at one time or another… with just the kill.

This record is arresting in reflection because my serves lacked luster, court coverage was slothful, and passes were poor; however, these were overcome by a no-miss kills and strong ceiling that out-lasted opponents for a setup to kill the ball.

This article is a license for you also to kill.

The small print in this advice is it's for advanced players only. You must already possess solid strokes, serves, volleys, short hops, ceiling game, and a sound playing minds.

Since pro racquetball started in the early '70s, a horizontal plane could be lowered like a 20' X 40' false ceiling onto the world championship court so it hovers about three-feet above the floor. This 'ceiling' allows only the protrusion of the players upper bodies and ceiling shots, while all the other shots, serves and returns fly low and hard beneath the plane. This, of course, is a dramatization to impress upon you the value of the kill at skilled levels, and to underline its practice requirement. If you flesh out the following killshot tips with strong drive serves and a patient ceiling game, my feeling is you will peak sooner as a player.

The first step to killing the ball, of course, is the stroke; the second is to practice the stroke a thousand times before using it in a game; then play a hundred games before using it in a tournament; and finally, steel the swing over many seasons until it's like an automatic gun. That's all I want to say here about the stroke that's fully addressed in other articles, for the aim of this essay is theory.

Killshot strategy includes:

1. Time to kill,
2. Placement of shot,
3. Deception of stroke, and
4. Use against particular game styles.

The time to kill for an advanced player is anytime the ball is presented at waist level or below when you can plant your feet somewhere on the court. With progress over the months, you begin to successfully entertain more errant kill shots that are shoulder high while you're off balance. I, and some peers, eventually reached a grade that reminds me of the special watch that some used to wear into cantinas so that when someone asked, 'What time is it?' the wearer pressed a button that made the piece flash, 'Time to go to bed!' It's always time to kill, if you're able.

Steve Keeley had the best rollouts of the Golden Era, said his nemesis Charlie Brumfield. (Legends)

Here are some general notes on the time to kill: 1) Kill when you're in front court with your opponent behind you, 2) Fly-kill volleys, 3) Shoot deep court set-ups off the opponent's short ceiling balls, and 4) Roll-out most back wall shots. In addition, there's the familiar scenario of two exhausted players in the third game of a protracted battle,

314

where the false analysis is that both players are so dog-tired that if one can make the other run after just one more pass then surely he'll win the point and eventual game. My refreshing premise is that the dude who makes the killshots in the final moments wins, because it's as tiring to stretch to cover his kill as a pass, and all the more discouraging if it's irretrievable.

There's a special time not to kill, even for this purist, and that's when you miss three kill attempts in a row. Call a time out to block the opponent's psychological run, and begin the next rally anew with some ceiling shots. There's a parallel story of being so nervous at a tournament kick-off match that your hands shake overly for accurate kills, so you hit a few ceiling shots off the bat to even out, and then resume with a full-force assault. I've been through this, and however have concluded the contrary, that it's better to suffer missed kill attempts (unless it's three-in-a-row) in the baptismal tournaments in order to gird yourself for future crucial moments when, from past habit, your hands will steady and you can kill with the devil breathing down your shirt.

Players talk about bad days, and allow me to relate the only bad game in thirty years. It was an early-history pro stop in Milwaukee with the stands full of jeering spectators rooting for their home boys, serious cow milkers and farmers as were my roots, when suddenly I lost my grip on the court. In game one, my unflagging killshots inexplicably sank for skips or rose for passes – never rolled out - as I turned crimson trying to figure it out. I lost that first game, and slumped outside the court wading through my gym bag for a towel. My fingers wet with something slimy that was a shampoo bottle whose lid had loosened. I felt my racquet handle that was like snot on a doorknob, and breathed a sigh of relief. I cleaned the handle, entered the court, and killed nearly every setup to victory, escaping also by a planned route from the scrappy fans.

As important as the time to kill is where to hit killshots. This map is of my own construction, where the shot placement depends frankly on the opponent's court position. If you're in front of him, then always try to kill the ball into the near corner. If your behind him on the court, then similarly aim for the near front corner as follows: When he's between you and the side wall then pinch kill, but when you're between him and the side wall then hit a straight-in kill. The reason is compelling: If you miss-hit the shot a little high, then the ball rebounds away from him for greater margin of error on the shot, while all the while your body shields him visually and physically from getting at the ball.

It's called a '100% ploy' because your kill (provided it doesn't skip) must go either for a winner or a hinder. If every rally ends in a 100% ploy, the rival doesn't score a point in the game.

315

Kara Mazur's bittersweet smile before a killshot at a 2006 WPRO event. (Ken Fife)

Another basic rule of kill is to hit to the open court, which means to direct the killshot away from the opponent. If he stands way on the right side then you kill to the left front wall, and vice versa. An odd trivia is that the standard shot selection used to be to strike a pass to the open court, but this article hints throughout that the kill has pretty much replaced the pass. Most passes now are fluky arisen kills, and a point is a point.

As for stroke deception, my experience is that it doesn't matter if your adversary knows that or where you're going to kill the ball, so long as you kill it accurately. A convincing anecdote is detailed in the tip 'Wanted: Two Feared Killers' where I recall a match in which I predicted all the shots in the pre-game handshake, essentially providing a script to the opponent, and won.

There's one more amusing story about how I lifted my contact zone to raise my level of play. In the 70s, there was an elite knot hitters who perpetually vied in the semi-finals and finals across the country, and I grasped that only a nuance separated the best from the rest. What could that edge be? That and serendipity were soon defined after a wrestling injury put me on crutches for a stint. I broke doctor's orders and went into the court to practice nightly with a crutch under one arm and a racquet in the other hand. After a few days, I could balance without crutches but couldn't bend, and this was the crossroads of Killshot Keeley. I learned in the next week to hit balls off balance, and more importantly to contact the shots much higher than the traditional ankle-to-knee. Turn the watch forward a few months, and it's time to kill! In the first tournament, I was alarmed and amazed at how easily I dispatched of my previous peers by now contacting killshots waist to should high. I realized that the universal tendency was for the coverers to hang back because of the raised contact in anticipation of a pass, and that's where I launch most killshots to this day. It's not a recommendation for the everyday player.

Few also will agree, but that led to the 'Floating beach ball theory' for the contact zone. As stated, the conventional hitting spot for kills is ankle-to-waist high, but I discovered that with a little ball spin (like a toy top gyroscopically up-righting), some air pressure under the ball (like duck wings taking off from the surface of a pond), and the grand deception of contacting the ball high in the stroke, a superior kill zone is exposed that can be represented as a beach ball. The Floating beach ball is the imaginary contact area that moves around with you in the court, the space in which you attempt to allow the ball to drop for the hit. Greenhorns start with a small beach ball out from their shins, and progress to a 4-foot diameter. You can see the larger balls on the better players as they approach and size their capacity to kill. In sum, run quickly during the rally about the court to maneuver the ball into the beach ball to hit.

Ode to the One-Foot Pass

The varnish reveals all.

Another element was brought to the surface in a study years ago. It determined that the majority of nationally ranked racquetball players were able to effectively kill only 2-of-10 shots from 38-feet (discounting back wall shots,). Let's not peck vigorously at this statistic, but rather extract some basic tips for your game.

A kill in the research was described as a hard shot that takes its first bounce before the front line of the service box. Ergo, the four court areas where the varnish vanishes are: Where the ball bounces in front of the service box, within the box from service scuffs, at the prime center court real estate for coverage (See the tip 'Court Coverage'), and in deep court especially on the backhand side at 38 feet, about two feet from the back wall. This article is about the varnish disappearing at the last spot.

Five-time world champion Mike Yellen was the first pro to aim and successfully launch one-foot after one-foot pass with the full intent at that one-foot target and reflection along the sidewalls. His game sounded like a staccato drumbeat. Note that you may think I've called the one-foot pass in other tips the 'kill-pass' shot, but that's not so. The kill-pass is an expected kill that rises inexplicably for a fortuitous low pass. However, Yellen's, and hopefully your, one-foot passes are pre-meditated with murderous intent.

Canadian national champ, Brad Kruger, who trained under guru Carl Loveday and teamed with Charley Brumfield in doubles, initially noticed Mike Yellen's winning proficiency at the one-foot pass. In fact, he took a hard lesson from that tourney all the way home, and in ensuing matches tried what he calls 'The Yellen Experiment'. 'I couldn't hit the one-foot passes quite as well as Mike, but I was determined to learn since, like him, I had no special lightning in my feet nor racquet as other players, but I could run and hit smartly all day. In the first tournament experiment, I promised myself to hit no kills, nothing but one-foot passes for offense and ceiling balls for defense. Like Yellen, I continued to drum passes a foot high on the front wall, in turn driving the opponent again and again to rear court. Certainly he got to shots in the initial rallies that brought the gallery to its feet, but as he and the varnish wore out his gets got slower and the tally reversed.'

You may find in trying yourself The Yellen Experiment that after ten minutes during which you're behind in score, the rival suddenly begins to wither. He walks slowly from and to the service box, he misses front court opportunities, his time-outs get used up, and in such ragged condition he misses back wall shots where the varnish grows thinner. You win in a long two or three games! The summation is that pass shots aren't as spectacular as the kills and splats, but they lead to rapid attrition, often so subtly that the opponent can't even pin it down to turn it around.

In earlier racquetball times, the pro tournament matches were three games to 21, with up to six matches per day if one chose to play two events. It was at such a tourney at the Chicago Circle Campus that I unleashed my own punishing brand of the experiment against the era's indomitable 4-time world champion Charlie Brumfield. It was a known fact that if you could get Charlie so tired he could no longer open his jaw, you'd win. I entered the hot, summer court in the building where there was no air-conditioning and felt fit and confident with a game plan. I'd cramp his ass and it would work its way to his mouth, for the win.

5-time National Champion Mike Yellen was a master of the one-foot pass revolving around a center court position vs. Marty Hogan. (US RB Museum)

Need I detail the drawn rallies and sweat pooling on the floor for an hour-and-half? In the third game, Brumfield suddenly wheeled to the referee, who happened to be the tournament director and USRA second-in-command, for it would be a significant outcome on an important day with the Chicago mayor having thrown out the game ball, and shouted oddly through a clenched jaw, "Injeery Time-out, Ruf!' 'What did you say, Champ?' answered the ref, but alas Charlie had exited the court limping. I stayed on court arguing the technicalities of the injury time-out rule that long ago I'd memorized, along with other murky passages from the official rules.

It dawned on me that the fodder was escaping, so I hurried outside the court door into the catacomb that housed the university courts and began explore myriad concrete passageways for Brumfield. In doing so, I myself began to cramp and get lost. We both made it back to the court about 30 minutes later, and all I can report is that he won the all-time cramp match on pure guts.

Something died in me for racquetball that day of the thousand one-foot passes, and I never used it again. I expect they've re-varnished the court but, if not, you can go there to learn a lesson from it. I'll save you the trip because you might get lost: Per the opening study in this article, not even a top pro hitting from 38 feet and off-balance after a moving one-foot pass is going to be able to kill the ball. You needn't even hit all one-foot passes to wear the varnish there - vary them with wall-scraping ceiling shots to the same corner. That's where the vast amount of action is!

Coach Jeff Leon advises some of the better running players of his Pan American teams to open a match with 3-5 hard passing rallies to see what the opponent's made of. If he starts to peter, keep up the passes. If he appears not to tire, nonetheless that hard ten minute run will stay in his legs and be remembered in a third game when he starts to wobble and think fuzzily. What if the table is turned: Can you run hard the first three rallies or all first game, and still win? How do you counter the ruse? That's foodstuff for another tip.

The pass-kill is an ignored winning shot. Hard and fit running players will like it. Intermediate skill tournament players get good success with it. Anyone spotting a portly upcoming opponent should initiate The Yellen Experiment as a weight loss plan. The slower the ball, the better the one-pass plan, by the reverse logic that the opponent has more difficulty shooting the repeating returns. Mike Yellen, Brad Kruger, and others have demonstrated this powerful tool in the big game.

Stand where others have before you, and win!

(Thanks to Mike Yellen and Brad Kruger*)*

320

Wanted: Two Feared Killers

Advanced players should be on the lookout for the two most wanted shots in all the game: The front court set-up and the back wall set-up. Kill them. These set-up brothers must be dealt with severely. Their impact is so important it sways hundreds of thousands of matches daily across the nation.

The front court set-up is a ripe opportunity because the killshot target is so close (the near front corner), while the opponent is so far behind you in the court. The back wall setup is juicy since there's time to think and swing, with the ball already moving at the target (usually to the near front corner).

The shots are easy to practice alone by dropping-and-killing from either side of the service box for the front court kills, hitting straight-in or pinching. The general beginners' rule is to develop a straight-in kill initially, and the overall intermediates' strategy is to kill straight-in when you're between the opponent and near side wall, and to pinch when he's between you and the side wall.

For back wall kills, drop onto the floor-back wall to practice alone, and the straight-in kill is usually superior because if the ball is miss-hit slightly high, it should run along the alley for a down-line pass. Many a pro has hit such a pinpoint pass while aiming for a kill, and strutted for the service box with the gallery none the wiser. The pinch off the back wall is used when the rival is trapped against the near sidewall, and the same shot is a better part of the doubles arsenal.

Advanced players also should heed these two killer shots, and here's a supporting anecdote. At a Chicago pro stop once, I knew after watching my upcoming opponent hit a few warm-up shots that I was going to beat him about 21-10 each game. However, he seemed to be a pro hunter,, so I offered after the coin toss, "Look, I'm not condescending but I noticed during your warm-up that your killshot strokes are good but the placement needs improvement. I promise you that every setup I get on the forehand side of the court is going to be killed into the forehand front corner, and every setup on the backhand side goes into the backhand corner. I won't hit any passes, and the only other shot I'll use is a ceiling ball on shoulder-high shot in deep court. As for the kills, whenever I'm stationed between you and the near side wall, it'll be straight-in, and wherever you're between me and the side wall it'll be a pinch.' I guess I delivered it with such devotion that he just nodded dumbly, and it took but few shots in the first game to find I was a player of my word. I skipped some balls, but took the shots. By the second game, he began camping in the proper front corners, but I'd exactly called every shot before the match and won about 21-10, 21-15.

WANTED

REWARD $$$$$$

The reward on the current WPRO tour is high.

Besides killshot placement, this story addresses a question I labored over in prior years: Should one kill the logical corner despite an opponent's anticipation. Shot making has the upper hand of anticipation.

The kill strokes are your usual forehand and backhand swings, which are the subject of another lesson where the side arm swing is encouraged for horizontal accuracy low and across the front wall. It's like the pitching sidearm for the forehand, or baseball hitting (or

322

Frisbee throwing) for the backhand. Most players have the greatest success in contacting the ball between ankle and waist high with some degree of sidespin, either inside spin or outside spin of the ball.

Advanced players may experiment with a hitting zone above this, and it's a nice knack for charging the serve or volleying. You may want to think of the contact zone for the swing as a fat 4' diameter 'floating beach ball' that travels about the court as you move – just out from your thighs. Don't use your stomach as the enlarged zone. The imaginary beach ball is the space into which you let the ball drop for the big hit. All the 'big hitters' from Hogan to Swain to Sudsy have contacted the ball above the knees when it hasn't been possible or polite to let it drop lower. I developed the beach ball theory while on crutches, unable to bend due to knee surgery but nonetheless wanting to practice kills. In fact, later on I raised the beach ball to Adam's apple height and caught my opponents for years lounging as I took higher setups for serious kills.

So, here's something to shoot for: As your skill progresses, add more kill shots from deeper in the court and higher above the waist. The ultimate goal is to be able to consistently and accurately kill the ball from every square inch of the hardwood from floor level to neck high. It's done every day by the pros and Legends.

The reward for killing these two varmints is looking more like twenty-one every day.

Pros Speak from the Box

Ceiling

People get tired of hearing me say 'early racquet preparation' but that's the only way, and it's true on the ceiling ball. Everyone has the ability to take the racquet back early while pursuing the ball.

- Cliff Swain

Hit the lights, which are usually about five feet off the front wall. With a lively ball that I'm accustomed to using, a stiff wrist and/or locked elbow may provide adequate power plus increased control in getting the ball to carry just deep and accurately enough.

- Derek Robinson

There's usually a set of lights just before the spot you should hit on the ceiling, and if not just aim very close to the front wall. A natural backspin will take the ball to the front wall, floor and into deep court. Decide on a body, or a wristy, or a combination stroke, and under-hit rather than over-hit to keep the ball off the back wall. Direct the shots to either the right rear or left rear corner, but not to the center where it gives the opponent an overhead opportunity. Even skilled advanced players must patiently embrace the ceiling because if you can keep it up there, sooner than later... I 'give' a promising player a corner in the deep forehand court for one hour a day to hit nothing but ceiling balls and count. When he messes up, he has to start the count over. Then each day after the forehand, he went to the deep backhand quadrant to hit and count another timed hour. Later in matches, it's easy to hit 5-7 ceilings in a row that opponents can't outlast, and once you finally give a promising player a setup the ball rolls out.   *- Jeff Leon*

Let the spin bring the ball back after the ceiling and front wall bounce, rather than try to power the ball. I use a slice to accomplish this. I contact the ball shoulder high, at a nearly maximum distance from the body, and with a level swing that slices the ball. during a ceiling ball rally for the eventual setup, then kill.   - Mike Ray

It's the depth that the shot carries that's important, more than which side. Don't over-swing so the ball comes off the back wall, nor under-swing so it comes up short. So, the ceiling rally becomes a matter of staying within these limits until the other guy over-swings or under-swings, and you try to put the shot away.   *- Alvaro Beltran*

Hit the ball hard enough to carry deep but not hard enough to come off the back wall. Better the ceiling ball come up short for a more difficult because they're so quick to

324

cover wall.   *- Marty Hogan*

I can't give a tip on ceiling balls because I play so offensively that my lack of a ceiling game is worthy of imitation.   *— Sudsy*

Nice slice to the ceiling at the 2014 Pro Kennex Tournament of Champions. (Mike Augustin)

The ceiling ball requires patience, and the only way to develop it is by doing it. You have to hit at least hundred ceiling shots per practice session, striving to hit ten in a row to know that you'll get the first setup off a ceiling ball rally in a match. If you can outwait and outperform the opponent in ceiling play, you can relax during much of the game. There are different methods for keeping the ball up-and-down the wall or cross-court at will, and these will develop during the sessions. My ceiling game irritated opponents because the shots grabbed the side wall all the way to the back wall, accomplished by turning my back on the play (toward the left rear corner for a righty), then swiveling into the ball and hitting it square. Down the line it goes. *- Charlie Brumfield*

The modern ceiling is a safety net for desperation shots. Concentrate on not over-hitting the ball so it stays off the back wall. *- Ruben Gonzalez*

Ceiling can be your best friend in tight situations. Don't neglect it. *– Susy Acosta*

This is the most important aspect of one's game if they want to move up levels. Master the length of the ceiling ball and then add the angles. *– John Ellis*

A good ceiling game takes practice. *- Charlie Pratt*

Drop it in the back 4-feet corner region without it coming off the back wall. *– Dave Fleetwood*

You've got to have a tight ceiling game where you carve soft ones up to the first row of lights to bounce and pillow drop them 2-feet from the floor on the back wall. Or, you may power them up to behind the first row of lights to make the ball fly deeper, faster, meaner. *– Ken Woodfin*

For the ceiling return, it's better to hit a shorter ceiling ball vs. letting it come off the back wall. *– Jose Rojas*

The ceiling ball is a great way to restart a rally. I've won many a match playing a boring game with lots of ceilings. But I have the victories. *– Cheryl Gudinas*

The ceiling game can be very effective against certain people, especially at the lower levels. As a player gets better, he or she should learn to be a little more offensive and use the ceiling balls as a backup. *– Andy Hawthorne*

It is a great defensive shot because it gets your opponent out of center court. But, you have to be willing to get in a ceiling rally and be patient. *- Kerri Stoffregen Wachtel*

Be patient. *- Rhonda Rajsich*

A lifesaver. *- Cristina Amaya Cassino*

Paola ceiling in doubles Longoria-Laude over Keller-Carrasco at the 2014 Juarez Open. (ken Fife)

Invention of the Ceiling Shot

with Charlie Brumfield and Randy Stafford

When you saw those first ceiling balls in history come out of the blue at the 1971 Louisville Invitational Doubles Tournament, it didn't start with me but with Charlie Brumfield.

We had just spent the previous summer together at Michigan State after he had handed me my first racquet as a racquetball player. It is hard to believe now, but the racquetball in 1971 was so slow that the standard defensive shot was a lob. Charlie, a few weeks before the Louisville tournament, suddenly stopped a defensive lob drill with me, walked to the left side wall, and suggested, 'Try this.' He hit a ceiling ball. Astonished, I knew this shot would boost my game since I could 'feather' backspin the ball like a handball to carry after the floor bounce deep into the back court. It was the perfect defensive tool.

However, hitting the racquetball ceiling required tremendous effort, anaerobic, and after just four shots the arm felt like lead. The fifth shot erred, and gave the opponent a pumpkin, for the coup de grace kill. Since I was physically stronger than Brum I probably had the best ceiling game and by its virtue was theoretically the best player in the country for one week.

Certainly, prophet Brumfield never revealed anything unless he was going to get something in return, and I showed him the 'feather' backspin. Yet, he frowned and went into cloister.

After a week's practice on a closed court, he emerged with the ceiling shot added to his repertoire. It was a defensive shot that would become the shield in his Sword (forehand) and Shield strategy to become the most successful player of pioneer racquetball through the 1970s. He had added an uncharacteristic body torque like a distance golf driver for backswing power, and a stiff arm like a tennis player to impart a touch of outside spin to run the ball along the left wall to back court. It was the first 'wallpaper shot' and nearly nonreturnable.

And NOW Brumfield had a backhand shield to go with the unrivaled forehand to ride out an unprecedented 57 tournament win streak. He developed the best ceiling game the world has seen, and probably will ever see, because the modern fast ball extinguishes ceiling rallies.

Jimmy Lowe to the ceiling at the 2014 US Open. His matches are referred to as the "Jimmy Lowe Show" for the entertaining value he brings to the courts! His achievements: USAR Hall of Fame – 2014, 13 U.S. Open Championships, 22 National Singles Championships, 19 National Doubles Championships, 6 time winner of Bud Muehleisen Male Age Group Athlete: 1999, 2004, 2005, 2008, 2010, 2012, 6 time Armed Forces Champion. (Ken Fife)

329

A typical ceiling rally in the early 70s Golden Era of racquetball was three shots, and it was very, very, very easy to predict who would win a title match. It was whoever could hit the most continuous perfect ceiling shots. By 1973, all of the top 16 players had mimicked and could hit two perfect ceiling shots; I could hit four; but Brumfield could string together about eight in a row. His body torque and stiff arm stroke became the standard through four National Singles Titles owed mostly to the ceiling. That's how the ceiling ball started, to my knowledge, and was propagated up and down the court walls around the country.

The first time I saw you (Keeley) was in 1971 at the Top 16 Louisville Invitational Doubles. You were on the court hitting ceiling balls, the first time I had ever seen that shot before. I played with a guy named Jim Thoni and he had never seen one either. Anyway, it was a great way to meet everybody. I remember they gave us all a jock with our initials on the front of it, but Charley Brumfield got one that was tiny with his initials. Did this have anything to do with ceiling balls?   - Randy Stafford

The first time I saw a ceiling ball (other than just an inadvertent miss-hit) was in the 1969 National Tourney in St. Louis. The striker of the shot was Mike Zeitman. He used it in his quarter-final match against Chuck Hanna. Later, I learned that the hard ball handball players used it occasionally, and that one player, Paul Haber, had made a science of the ceiling. He had the 'feather touch' as well as the off-hand fist to the ceiling. After watching Haber, I commenced my effort to incorporate the ceiling in as my principal defensive shot. This was in the summer of '71 when I stayed with Steve Keeley in Lansing, MI. I hit a thousand a day while Keeley was attending veterinary school in the mornings, and then I would play him using the ceiling ball system in the afternoon. Keeley did not like the ceiling game particularly as he felt it took the excitement out of the rally, not to mention as a shooter he preferred my defensive shot to be somewhere other than 'wall paper' at 39 feet. As the ball sped up in the '73 season, I converted my game back to the passing method as my ceiling ball did not reliably stay short of the back wall. Also, I had signed with Leach and the ceiling ball sticking to the wall was not easy to hit with a fiberglass instrument, which was less firm at the edges of contact.
- Charley Brumfield

Ceiling Pictorial

Kara Mazur at the 2006 WPRO (by Ken Fife)

Ceiling and Drills

Many players shake their heads up and down in agreement that they became Open after they made the ceiling their friend. It gave them a place to go when tired, to slow the pace, to control a power player, and to break a run of skips or an opponent's hot streak, to cool their jets under pressure, and for a pause to think. Most importantly it gave them a steady reply to the drive serve. Now in the Open, they have the same arsenal of shots as the A's, plus the ceiling ball.

Being skilled at the ceiling means you can hit five excellent ones in a row, that don't come up short, off the back wall, off the side wall, and with a spin that keeps them in track along the backhand (left) side wall. For left handers, it would be a cross-court five that do the same thing.

Each ceiling shot drops in an imaginary 4x4x4' box in the left rear corner. The only viable option for the rival is to go back up to the ceiling, and if he's unable to hit five excellent ones in a row like you, he's dead meat.

There's no universal ceiling stroke. What's important takes place in the instant ball-string interface at contact. Hence you will see pros hit perfect ceiling balls off a variety of strokes with the constant same spin. Experiment, but most players succeed at the ceiling who put a bottom-outside spin on the ball. This is the lower-outside-rear quadrant, at about eight o'clock.

A couple other tips are to have the feet pointing at the side wall while starting the swing, transfer the weight forward during the stroke, and use a fairly rigid hitting arm, and stiff wrist. But remember, the most important part of the stroke is when the ball touches the strings for the right spin. Let the spin bring the ball back after the ceiling and front wall bounce, rather than try to power the ball.

You may practice the ceiling alone or with a partner. A machine has more stamina than a partner, so it's a viable option.

1. **Launch Pad Ceiling Drill.** Draw a chalk or tape line on the floor of the left rear corner that's eight feet square. This is your launch pad. Hit continuous ceiling shots to yourself for 30 minutes or until you can hit at least five in a row without leaving the pad. Better players can clock the shots to see if you can hit for 30 seconds without stepping off the pad.

335

2. **Drive Serve Ceiling Drill.** Since the primary use of the ceiling shot, besides a reply to a ceiling ball, is to return a drive serve, this drill practices it and requires a mate. He hits drive serves for fifteen minutes to anywhere on the court, and you put each up to the ceiling. The ball is then caught, and the server repeats.

3. **Touch Line Ceiling Drill.** This conditions the shot and the body. Both players start with one foot touching the 5-foot line as a base. As one player hits a ceiling shot to the left rear corner, his partner races back and returns with a ceiling ball to the same corner. The latter dashes to touch the 5-foot line with his shoe or racquet, and then back to the launch pad to continue the ceiling rally. It's touch and hit, touch and hit. You may keep score.

4. **Cross-Curt Ceiling Practice.** Not to forget lefties or the possibility of hitting to a weak forehand or weaker doubles player, the cross-court drill begins by placing two players in the opposite rear corners on their 8' square launch pads. Alternate cross-court shots to see who can hit the most ceiling balls into the pad area.

5. **Alternate Corners Race Drill.** This is the same as #4 except the players are required to exchange pads after each shot by running to the opposite rear corner.

6. **Solo Cross-Court Drill.** This is the same as #4 except you are alone. Hit a cross-court shot from the left pad, sprint to the right to hit the next, and so on.

7. **Corridor Game.** 90% of the play in Open and above takes place in the backhand corridor along the left wall for two righties. The playable surface in this drill is the rank from front to back wall within 12' of the left side wall, and may be marked with tape. It is as though the rest of the court has disappeared. It's a regular game but the serve, return, rally, and footsteps must all fall within it.

8. **Continental Divide Drill.** The classic intent of the ceiling shot is to clear the rival out of center court and to the back wall, and then to out-rally him up there until he mishits a shot for a kill setup. The other constant use of the ceiling ball is as a retort to a sharp drive serve. Remember, however, that if an oncoming ball can be shot to kill, kill it! This drill teaches that. In any of the above drills, throw in one variant to establish the Continental Divide: If a ceiling ball arrives that you can hit below your waist, shoot it. If the ball is above the waist, go up to the ceiling. If the ball is exactly waist high, it's your call. With practice, you can win many tournaments with just these two shots and the discerning when to hit each: kill and ceiling.

Take a moment after these drills to reflect on how well you did, your breakthroughs, what can and needs to change, and keep a progress chart of your ceiling game.

Jo Shattuck returns a ceiling shot in deep court that allows time to draw her bow. (John Foust)

Here Come the Around-World and Z-Balls

In 1971, after Charlie Brumfield and I 'invented' the ceiling ball and were the first as far as I know to use it as a defensive tool at the Top 16 Louisville Invitational, we quickly felt in the new ceiling an attrition rally that threw us into late tourney rounds with sore arms. Even the 'strongmen' of racquetball Mike Zeitman, Ken Porco and Myron Roderick couldn't keep it up. The shot did not propagate at the Big Four annual events-National Singles and Doubles, and National Invitational Singles and Doubles- until by '72 Brumfield would perfect, employ, be faintly copied, and was the sole player ever to earn consistent points off ceiling 'aces'. I know because my ceiling game was the second best.

Three strikes with the 18'' racquets on that dead old '71 ball way up to the ceiling left us looking to the lights for a shot to replace it, and the working lob, as the front line of defense from 30 feet. A strong answer from deep court to neutralize rallies would guarantee a season of trophies.

The first was a crazy Around-the-World ball that we would yell to MSU freshmen fodder, 'Chase it around the world!' and they did. Singles players raced each angle of the ball in a circle like a hamster in a wheel until it fell to the spot they had started. Doubles players collided in mid-court, spit epitaphs and called time-out. I developed a solo practice in a sans-gallery court cloaked from Brumfield of alternating forehand and backhand continuous Around World balls until the shot was 95% effective, and then never hit it again until the final points of the Big Four events to conserve the potency, as Brumfield was doing unbeknown to me with the first crack ace serve.

The even nuttier shot that we developed within a week after the Around World was the Z. We had never seen it before as competing National Paddleball champs, nor in my three years in handball, and I believe it was new to him with a racquet when... One day he miss-hit an Around World into the front wall high in the right corner, and the ball angled sharply across and off the left side wall to strike me in the body for a point. He shrugged making me think it had been intentional. We then came to discover that it took terrific effort within a small square footage behind the short line to blast the new Z, but beyond that it was simple for me to secret to practice for thirty minutes to master. It's likely that in hundreds of university and YMCA courts across the country the same serendipity and experiments were taking place, but Charley and I had never seen it One of us named the Around-the World, but not the Z that seemed to have derived a few years later from Charles Garfinkel's innovation called the Z-serve.

338

The epidemiology of the Around Wall and Z Ball are interesting as the two were new 'diseases" to other players until we 'inoculated' them in tournaments. I must take credit because Brumfield was busy perfecting and winning off the ceiling, and the Around-World and Z became my pathogens to foster. I applied them sparingly at crucial points in the Big Four events, and withheld them from Brumfield because he was Doctor Racquetball quick with the counter. For one season in '72 the Around World and Z allowed me to dominate the field except for my nemesis who had my number with gamesmanship. I used the Around-World ball to become the first racquetball player to defeat the great Paul Haber in mano vs. racquet using a handball that broke Haber's ceiling attack.

The '73 season with the first ever pro stop rolled around and now every top 16 player was 'infected' by the Around World and Z shots that had propagated to every court in the USA. Seemingly no one had the 'pill' to stop it. Yet I had squirreled the cure for one year, and unleash it to stay #2 for another season. The only counter against the Around World is to volley the ball before it bounces, and the volley honestly was the only shot I practiced tens of thousands of times for one year until I could kill the ball from any angle everywhere on the court. By '74 the volley return of the Around Wall, service return and rallies became the standard. I owe the Around World and Z, and their counters, for the two best seasons of my career in racquetball's 70s Golden Era.

An interesting thing happened late in 1973 that changed the history of these three early shots- ceiling, Around World and Z. In the short span of a few months, the ball livened to annihilate Doctor Brumfield's and my pathogens, and were hardly seen again.

Paola makes layered cake of a volley around-world at the 2013 Christmas Classic. (Mike Augustin)

Pros Speak from the Box

Specialty Shot

My bread-and-butter is the fly-kill to either corner.   *- Ruben Gonzalez*

The backhand pinch and splat kills. I make a splat by pointing the ball at the side wall a little further back than the regular pinch to let it flatten out so that it ricochets obliquely off the front wall toward mid-front court.   *- Corey Brysman*

If you have a natural specialty shot – for me the surprisingly accurate overhead reverse splat – consider a couple strategies. Use that shot early on repeatedly to win points until the opponent adjusts, then use his change of court position to open up your other shots. Or, save that specialty shot until near the end of a game or match to win a couple big points.   *- Mike Ray*

I play a high class low percentage style game, and the lesson here is that any specialty shot you have that works – don't listen to anyone who says you can't do it and more.

- Sudsy

Watch better players and modeling after their strong specialty shots. For example, each of the pros for three decades, I know from having seen and played in their tournaments and pickup games, has a specialty shot that most of the other pros can0t do. That doesn't mean that you or I can't imitate them. I'd peg these specialty shots: Hogan for the backhand, Sudsy for stroke power, Swain for the drive serve, Gonzalez for the fly kill, Mike Ray the overhead, Dave Peck for the bow backswing, Keeley the cool, and Corey Brysman for fitness.   *- Jim Spittle*

Wherever I've played, I have the nickname of 'screen serve Jeff' but accept it as a grudging compliment. The most important moments of the match are hearing your rep, and remembering it every time you enter the service box to select a serve. I stand on the right side legally in from the screen line per the rule and nonetheless ruthlessly blocking the receiver's view of the ball, as I cradle it and begin the motion. Then, the ball passes to and from the front wall at such an angle to eclipse - line up the ball, my body and the receiver's eyes –his view. The stroke is a body motion sliding left with the wrist out and away right to contact ahead and lace high, so the receiver can't see or read the ball until it passes the service line. If you practice this odd movement hundreds of time, you get a sense of the opponent's frustration on the legal screen serve right, and surprise him off the same motion with a drive serve left a couple times. Now I've got him off balance, and hit a right-Z from the same spot and motion. Now I've got him off-balance and thinking, and can mix the three serves successfully for the rest of the match. *- Jeff Leon*

The point winner of my game is the pinch kill. It makes the other player go the full length of the court to reach the ball, on glass it's hard to see, and the pinch allows a deeper contact in the stroke. Part of the reason for my success with it is a natural top-outside spin that, when the ball initially strikes the side wall near the front wall, the spin is in the direction of the ball's travel to the front wall. So is like a rocket booster to ensure hard contacts with no skips. After a while in a game, the repeated pinches that take the opponent into the far front and middle court open up the whole sidewall alley for down-line passes. It's a perfect combination. *- Alvaro Beltran*

Rhonda Rajsich is keen to kill the ball whenever it enters a kill zone from ankles to waist indoors or outdoors. 2014 WOR World Championships. (Stephen Fitzsimons)

Forehand splat from my knees. *— Andy Hawthorne*

Right corner pinch with topspin. *— Davey Bledsoe*

Then it was a mock nine pass shot, but now it's my ceiling ball and backhand spinning half drive serve! Oh to get old!!!
— John Ellis

Specialty shot is forehand cross court.
- Charlie Pratt

FH DTL. Actually forehand and backhand kill straight-in unless the opponent was well behind me, and then it was a pinch where my body could shield a miss if i did not flatten the pinch. If my straight-in kill didn't flatten then it automatically became a power pass forcing the opponent to run thru me and hopefully the furthest distance.
— Dave Fleetwood

DTL kill over and over and over.
— Cheryl Gudinas

I love ripping backhands.
— Jose Rojas

Forehand pinch.
- Kerri Stoffregen Wachtel

Forehand pinch.
- Cristina Amaya Cassino

My specialty shot is the trickling splat I hit when the ball and I intersect close to a sidewall. As I glance the ball off the wall at multiple heights with English causing the ball to spin in to the sidewall and then come super low off of the middle of the front wall, spinning wildly away from the desperate competitor.
— Ken Woodfin

Rally

Chris 'The Giant' Crowther and Tony Carson joust for center court. Chris has finished in the Top 8 every year since the 2009 season. (Freddy Ramirez)

Court Coverage

with Dave Peck

The elements of coverage are where to stand, the stance, watching the opponent's swing, predicting the shot, and moving toward it.

Now the details.

Where to Stand

Hover around the five-foot line during the rally when the other guy is taking the shot behind you. If he's up front, then prepare a bit closer to the service line.

Stance

I teach to await the shot in a diagonal stance with the feet staggered rather than both on the five-foot line.

Watching

Besides position, mental anticipation is key. This requires studying him swing by turning the head a tad. If only a glimpse, you may predict his shot before the opponent knows where it's going.

Predicting

When he takes the ball in his power hitting zone, start to edge forward with the swing to cover the kill. If he takes it higher than the power zone, then relax a hair and prepare for the pass or kill. If he contacts behind the three-dimensional power zone, be ready for a side wall front wall. But if it's in front of the zone, it's going cross-court. You only know what the opponent is doing by, while standing near the five-foot line, you glance back over your shoulder to observe.

Practice Coverage

You can practice court coverage like any other aspect of the game. If you drill it alone, then it's like shadow boxing using an imaginary opponent, and the scene unrolls like a play. It's even more beneficial to drill with a partner who wants to practice his shot selection and deception on the strokes.

Start with the idea that there are a finite number of shots including forehand and backhand off the back wall, deep court set-ups off ceiling balls, front court volleys, and more. Once you've made a list of the common shots, you have also made a list of all the situations which the covering player must learn. For instance, for the forehand off the back wall, the designated 'hitter' is given the set-up and the 'coverer' awaits his shot properly in center court. As the hitter makes the shot, the coverer retrieves it, and the rally ends after these two shots, to be repeated until the cows come home. Note that the hitter tries different shots using different deceptions to provide the coverer with the gauntlet of coverage predictions.

Doubles Coverage

A word on doubles as relates to court coverage. The best racquetball court coverers are former squash players and doubles racquetball players. Squash is cross-training specifically for coverage. Racquetball doubles is better than singles to develop your singles coverage. Everything is up front, and fast.

Dives

Whether you dive or not, the essence of court coverage it to re-kill the ball rather than to keep it in play.

Dave Peck ousts Marty Hogan from center court and the 1982 World Championship. (Legends)

345

Pros Speak from the Box

Court Coverage

I think of myself as a blanket able to get to and cover every inch of the court, and this makes me move like a herd of gazelle in the wild.

- Sudsy

Center court is somewhere between the short line and 5'-line. That's where you'll stand ready and looking over your shoulder at the shooting player. Let him commit before you move, then go in for the shot. If you practice being quick in this way, then you always have the upper hand during the rally.

- Alvaro Beltran

The single mental frame that describes today's play that was nonexistent ten years ago is diving and while in mid-air three feet above the floor taking a full swing to hit a 170 mph return.

- Derek Robinson

Own the middle! It's a 6' by 6' box that starts on the dotted line and back.   *- Fran Davis*

I'm a taller, lanky player and take advantage of reach by being in position as the opponent sets up. Coverage boils down to whether or not you're in court position – be there and you have the greatest opportunity to get the most balls. I stay balanced on both feet at the dotted (five-foot) line as the opponent sets up, observe him, and like a baseball pitcher have a catalogue of the specific batter's favorite shots. As the opponent makes contact, I begin my reaction in the anticipated direction.

- Mike Ray

Opinions vary on coverage, and I try to get quickly as he chases my shot to the dotted (5-foot) line in center court because I want to control that court. Now, if he's in center court and it's my shot, I hit a nice ceiling ball or pass to get him out of there and regain it. Look at the ball all the time to predict what'll happen next. The opponent setting up in deep court is a walking bag of clues and favorite shots, who's easy to read once you learn how. I'm moving to cover his broadcast favorite shot even as he swings, or he'll think twice and be forced into another shot he's not comfortable with.

- Jeff Leon

Back off a moment and speculate about the nature of racquetball as it's played at top levels today. One (15-point) game is a sequence of, say, eighty 20-second bursts of effort spaced by 20-second rests. Game over. Specificity of training off court insists you train similarly, not with distance running or long Stairmaster or treadmill, but rather with the short interval speed-work that hurts to do, hurts to think about, and the only time you

346

appreciate it is when you run circles around your opponent on the racquetball court. In truth, that's the secret to any advantage I have covering on the court.   *- Cliff Swain*

Figure options, then guess. As the opponent sets up for the shot and you set for the cover, funnel the possibilities through your mind to anticipate the top three. Choose the most likely and move there. It's an intelligent guessing game that isn't 100% accurate, but the news is that if you guess right and his shot still wins, it upsets his future shot selection.   *- Marty Hogan*

I'm a physical player, and a large specimen, the goliath on tour. I have an aggressive will that makes me even larger than size on the court, like posturing for attack. Racquetball, remember, is a physical game.   *- Derek Robinson*

Study chess to learn court coverage, because each is mental anticipation. When I crouch in center court to watch the opponent take the shot, I think what are the two options he's considering. If I know general shot selection as well as his personal preferences, then I'll be able to lean in both directions of his next move. Sometimes you know his shot before he does by thinking as he does, but faster, then just before he hits you jump back into your own thoughts and move. Sometimes you have to dive. After years on outdoor courts, diving indoors is like falling on a pillow.   *- Ruben Gonzalez*

I was the most voracious coverer in the game. If the guy has a setup in deep left court, the objective is to maximize his inclination to hit cross-court. This takes away the stock down-line and pinch kills. So, I come into his line of view as he winds up effectively blocking him visually and mentally from taking the relaxed shot, and forcing a cross-court. Then I sling-shot my body from the down-line target back and right for the eventual cross-court, thus making myself look fast and telepathic. When I go in on the ball, I'm thinking the opposite.   *- Charlie Brumfield*

The urgent part is moving forward that's a trait of most squash players to put you a step ahead to front court where most points are scored.   *- Victor Niederhoffer*

I've always considered myself clumsy, and am confused when others say I cover well. Physically, I try to be on my toes leaning forward to jump lightly at the projected shot. Mentally, I study the opponent and his racquet during the downswing, too often know where his shot is going before he does. The game at top levels is so much lateral movement that it helps to think of both feet parallel to the two side walls, with only a slight stagger toward the side the ball's on. Study the opponent out the corners of the eyes or with a slight turn of the head. Then, just before the hit when he can no longer look up at you, take your best guess, and zoom in on the ball. After you learn the coverage basics of positioning, stance, watching, anticipation and motion, the best tip is to take away the opponent's best opportunity. This means giving him sufficient room to make the customary shot from that position while physically blocking his body or swing from taking more court space than he deserves, as well as knowing his pet shot and blocking it from there.. Leave him just enough open court to take his least desirable shot. You may further irritate by 'cheating' toward the prime target with a body feint as he takes the swing. Know and be able to quote the rulebook on hinders and avoidables in this instance. This all makes him edgy throughout the match..   – Jim Spittle

Stay low. I try to carry my center of gravity around the court lower than my opponent's.
                                                                                    – *Susy Acosta*

Court coverage requires a low center of gravity and staying in center court.- *Charlie Pratt*

The "V" behind the service box is the control point in any rally. Always capture it before your next shot.   – *Davey Bledsoe*

I see too many players fighting to maintain the "X" on center court when I believe that isn't always the best way to cover a shot. Center court isn't just the "X" in the center, but encompassing a larger area in the court. As your opponent moves around the court, you move within that area to cover the shot.   – *Jackie Paraiso*

Don't worry too much about the front of the court, just do not get passed.   – *John Ellis*

A good court coverer dives at times. Next, he knows to dive and kill rather than flip the ball up. 2013 action at the 3-Wall Ball World Outdoor Championships in Las Vegas. (Mike Augustin)

Play deeper. If they roll a splat in your face it doesn't matter how far up you are, it'll be tough to retrieve.   – *Jose Rojas*

Let front court go a little bit and play center court behind the receiver's line. Most balls that bounce twice in front of service box are retrievable anyway, so cover the rest of the court as well as possible.   – *Andy Hawthorne*

Your opponent is going to hit a killshot every now and again. Let them have the 3 or 4 feet near the front wall. You want to cover everything else which should be getable. That is why "center court" isn't exactly in the center of the court.   - *Kerri Stoffregen Wachtel*

Court coverage is the best available sharing of center court, with grit, hustle, and choreographed feet-work for covers from center court, when retreating out of the box, while returning serve, and when you hit and clear.   – *Ken Woodfin*

You must train off the court to cover on the court effectively. The person who covers the court best isn't usually the person who runs the best 50 yard dash. Shorter dashes preceded by anticipation.   – *Cheryl Gudinas*

The biggest thing in anticipation and court coverage is your focus the instant your opponent is hitting the ball. At this time: Stand at center court, watch him make contact, and do the little 'bunny hop'. The bunny hop is based on Newton's Law of Motion that an object at rest will remain at rest, and an object in motion will... cover the court.
- *Brian Hawkes*

Some players are very fast, but I think court coverage is more anticipatory. Move just after the hitter looks away and before he hits the ball to be there on time. – *Rich Wagner*

You work on the basics for a year and then at some point you just feel it.
- *Cristina Amaya Cassino*

Who is the best diver in history? Jay Jones, 6th ranked pro and Hollywood stuntman, takes the cake with racquet in hand at a Las Vegas grand opening in the Golden Era. (US RB Museum)

Court Position

by Marty Hogan

There is a sweet spot in the center of your strings and there is one on the court. A spot I'd suggest to players at all levels because that's the heart of the action.

I'm going to get right to the point- the ideal court position in today's fast game is just behind the five foot line. If you do nothing but go back to just behind the five foot line every time after you strike the ball, your game is bound to improve.

I've experimented over the years, and the evolving racquet and ball have moved the sweet court position from hither in the past to the just behind the five foot line,. When the racquets were smaller- about 18''- the game was slower with a ball that kill shots carried just a head butt off the front wall, and ceiling shots that hardly made the back wall. We pros had to cover more territory but had more time to do it. We tried everything from playing at the short line to standing thirty feet back like Keeley with his irritating ceiling game. Forget that in the modern game- right now go to just behind the five foot line.

Balls today stay up and there in the sweet spot you are close enough in to get anything but a perfect kill that you couldn't get no matter where you were positioned.

It's also strong to be as close to the center of the court as possible but it's not as important these days as staying the right distance between the front and back walls. Remember a racquetball court is only twenty feet wide and it's forty feet long, twice the distance to cover from front to back.

Why not play closer to the front wall? The problem with getting in closer than the five foot line is racquetballs travel at you 135 MPH to150 MPH depending who you are playing, and at this speed you need to be more than fifteen feet back to handle the pace.

Cliff Swain, one of the greatest sticks ever to play simply wouldn't adapt his court position as the big racket came into vogue. This gave me a winning edge as I'd catch Cliff in front of the short line three or four times during a game and be able to jam him. Every time I caught him out of the corner of my eye in what I consider No Man's Land, I'd hit a 100% power drive at him just to his right, so it 'bodied' him- He'd be forced to flick it back setting me up for points I usually won. Considering our typical match was 11-9 or 11-10 in the tiebreaker, court position was the single reason I was able to beat Swain the majority of the times we played in the mid and late 80s, as good as he was.

If court position could beat Cliff Swain, believe it can beat you. Cliff still won most of his matches and got away with his court position flaws because he had the best serve in the history of racquetball, with great strokes, and was a southpaw.

Cliff is certainly not the only player with some court position issues. When I watch pro matches today court position is one of the first things I look at. It amazes how many players will stay at the short line after getting overpowered or passed time and again. In tennis, if you can't handle a big serve then you take a step or two back to return, but this doesn't seem to be happening in racquetball. It's not always that your opponent has the best pass shots in the world, it's just you are playing too close.

You can also play too far back. If you notice you are getting burned by the soft stuff or by pinch after pinch, the odds are you are playing too far back. You want to be behind the five foot line, but just behind it. If you are thirty feet deep you will get beaten up front.

In one of the last competitive matches I played on The Legends Tour in 2005, I went up against Woody Clouse in the Boston finals. I had watched Woody win a squeaker over Ruben Gonzalez in the semis hitting the ball and moving as well as anyone, but he was hanging too far back and Ruben made almost all his points in the front court. When we played the final a few hours later I concentrated on one thing only- getting to the sweet spot in center court just behind the five foot line after every shot. Woody positioned behind me most of the first game and was forced to shoot around and run around me to cover, besides being visually screened from front court. As well he was shooting, I won 15-9 in the first on court position, plus a sally of splats. In game two, Woody decided to overcompensate by playing up in front of the short line. He'd made an adjustment but it wasn't the right one. I ripped passes cross court and down both lines to an even easier 15-3 victory. Court position instead of shots won 20 of the thirty points in that final, but it will never happen again if Woody reads this.

The good news is now that you know where to be, You'll camp out just behind the five foot line near center court and you may not win every time but you won't get beaten on court position.

Pepper the Court to Cover

Court coverage takes place after you hit the ball … and before you hit the next shot. Some players base their games around blanketing opponent's shots and, the incumbent IRT champ Jason Mannino, has such comprehensive coverage it buffalo others from shooting the ball. Yet even he was not the best court coverer ever and, respectfully, he may benefit from the Pepper Drill.

The best court coverers I ever saw were Charlie Brumfield and Victor Niederhoffer, and they couldn't dive into a swimming pool much less the hardwood. Yet they fantastically retrieved shots that the rest of us couldn't touch with a three-foot racquet. The one time in 35 years I saw Brumfield dive was at a recent Portland tournament where he landed on a knee so virgin that blood spurt in all directions, as he screamed, 'Finally, the stigmata!'

There are three kinds of great court coverers: 1) One uses primarily his mind to anticipate, 2) Another uses mainly his body, 3) The best uses both mind and body to all cover shots. Daniel De La Rosa dives at the 2014 Pro x Kennex Tournament of Champions. (Mike Augustin)

As for Niederhoffer, once I hit a fine rollout at game point with him planted in deep court, as instantly he disappeared and reappeared at the front wall to reach the ball and bank his head for match point.

Simply, the great coverers are above diving. These two characters- I've lived with both-strike with peculiarities that may invite us into the secret rooms of coverage. Each is fairly non-athletic looking and would never be picked out of a lineup of the most feared coverers. Both are leg-strong, hand-and-eye quick, fluent in body language, and literal geniuses off the court. Of these traits, let's examine body language, then hand-and-eye quickness as the easiest for improvement.

The player setting up for a shot displays clues and tells of his next hit, much like in poker or dancing. Sometime you, the *coverer*, will know the shot he'll make before he does. Body language includes in approximate order of importance: 1) The racquet face angle of the player taking the hit. 2) The most logical shot from the spot he shoots from. 3) His shot selection history from that spot, as observed before or during this particular match. 4) Which direction his front foot points. 5) Where his eyes and 'mind's eye peek. 6) His general muscle tension, where more intense indicates a more offensive shot. 7) The height of ball contact (higher is likely a pass instead of a kill). 8) The depth of stroke contact (deeper toward the rear foot tells a down-the-line or pinch, while a far forward contact is cross-court. 9) Reading 'intent', which is guessing what the other player is thinking, and so on.

Any strong coverer possesses these traits, consciously or unconsciously, while Brumfield and Niederhoffer were flush in all. As an anecdotal sidelight, I was rightly called the 3-toed sloth, which is the slowest land mammal, yet covered as well as any except the two aforementioned players. You can practice reading body language as I did in many places: From the court gallery as others play, on-court during your games, at the airport, a Laundromat, etc. It's no secret that I learned the nuances as a veterinarian to prevent getting bitten, scratched or kicked, and from attending a bar for exactly one hour nightly for ten years– never drinking, just studying peoples' movements and thoughts.

Body language is a big chunk of court coverage, but this article's thrust is three Pepper Drills that you've probably not faced. Each shall enhance your hand, foot and eye quickness while training you to rekilling the ball. This article is dedicated to their three originators, respectively, of Cliff Swain, Charlie Brumfield and the Idaho Falls Russets.

Pepper Drill #1. Swain practices a unique drill that others can imitate whereby he plays a game against himself as if the shots are a real tournament. It's hard to find that kind of competition. Briefly, he hits himself a great kill or pass, then returns with an equally tough kill or pass, and continues until the rally ends. I'm told by his former teammate Scott Hirsch, "Cliff comes out of the court dripping sweat after just 20 minutes with a carnivorous look in his eye."

354

Pepper Drill #2. An equally arduous routine was set by Brumfield in which, for an equal amount of time without rest, he plays a continuous solo rally disregarding the number of bounces the ball takes and extending fully after every shot. "I believe that thrusting after the ball in practice tunes the body for tournament rigors, so that by the third game the rival is either so far behind or so depressed at seeing my constant effort that he throws in the towel."

Cheryl Gudinas commands center court as Doreen Fowler struggles to go around at a 2006 WPRO stop. Cheryl's motto is "Sweat more in Preparation, Bleed less in Battle." (Ken Fife)

Pepper Drill #3. Enter and stand on the court with your back near either of the sidewalls, perhaps pretending that it's Brumfield or Niederhoffer looking over your shoulder. Knock the ball hard and low into the opposite side wall and rekill it repeatedly in a continuous rally. The ball should stay below a horizontal plane of three-feet above the floor at all times. It's ok if the ball bounces twice before your rekill it. This shrunken 'field' quickens your reflexes, and you'll make gains on those other fellows looking over your shoulder.

That brings us to an anecdote of the Idaho Falls Russets, a semi-pro baseball farm team where I as a youth sneaked around the sideline fence to watch the warm-up 'pepper' drill. A batter on a grassy area repeatedly knocked ground balls to an awaiting fielder scooping them up from a scant 5-yards. There was a line of such batters and fielders stretched to my small eyes' horizon, and balls whizzing between them. This was my first experience with sports excellence, an image that's helped me in many arenas right along to this tip.

The third pepper drill may also be done with another person, as in volleyball spike drills, where one player stands with his back against a wall and the other stands against the opposite wall, then they tap grounders back and forth like the Russets. You walk out perspiring with a fresh view of the ball.

Diving is the most exciting but overrated aspect of coverage, so let's quickly get it out of the way. Sometimes it's necessary to fling forward or sideways to reach out to cover an opponent's shot. The two best divers ever are 'Cannonball' Jason Mannino and an early player 'Superman Steve Serot'. Fans flock from around the country to witness the acrobatics of these top divers. Each owns a personal launch, but the standard in-flight patterns are an extension of the body and limbs, a mid-air wristy blast of the ball, initial 'one-wheel landing on the heel of the non-racquet hand, and second-wheel landing on the opposite elbow. The best divers don't belly flop, but absorb shock and push right back up with the knees. It's like not seeing the fastest draw in the west as you feel the slug and look up to see his gun holstered; and in our sport the ball zooms at you and the diver seemingly hasn't left his feet. I used a lamentable diving method that ended in a slow cartwheel that once left me actually stuck upside down in a handstand in a rear corner, as the opponent's next shot came back at me. I swung and landed on my nose.

That's small compared to a Chicago gymnast at satellite pro stops with dives with graceful tumbles and handsprings. He also hit me in the right eye on one tumble and detached a retina. Top Legend Ruben Gonzalez grew up on the outdoor 1-wall and 3-wall courts of Spanish Harlem, and claims, 'After ten years on concrete, diving into 4-walld is like falling on a pillow.' Any diver must remember, as Gonzalez showing his treads to the back wall gallery, to kill to end the rally, rather than flick the ball up.

Hence one player should never dive twice in the same rally.

Two adept coverers still in the game who haven't been addressed are 6-time world champ Marty Hogan and 5-time world champ Sudsy Monchik. Hogan in his best years was a sluggish coverer, but didn't need to because of raw power. However, Marty (my former housemate and nemesis) a few years ago started playing squash and in later years is dramatically faster up front.

Sudsy recently took residence at the Florida Quad Club where I slept for three months on a mattress in the furnace room between games. On the court I felt like the Tin Woodsman next to his blurring figure. He also talks a good game, "I crouch like a big cat awaiting the shot, spring like a herd of gazelles, and cover the field like a blanket." Also, the only female national champ who could carpet the entire court with gets was another squash champ named Heather McKay. This is irrefutable cross-training advice to the serious racquetball player.

Court coverage is the last frontier of strong players... and Pepper is the vehicle.

The basic difference in court coverage, outdoor or indoor, from the older game in the 1979s is the smaller racquets and slower ball allowed the coverer to take an staggered stance toward the front wall for back-to-front action. However, the current game is more lateral movement and the coverer takes a more open stance with both feet nearly even to the front wall. Outdoor National Doubles Champions Charlie Brumfield hits against Steve Serot for the Singles Championship at Orange Coast College, CA. (US RB Museum)

357

Pros Speak from the Box

Tip to Beginners

In your first and next play times on the court, just try for solid contact and try to make the rallies last a long time. When you hit a couple of square shots you feel good, and things happen quickly from that point on. After the initial outings, you'll enter one of the best eras of your game in that the rallies last a long time and you run like a squirrel to work up a great sweat. Gradually over the first month your eyes and reflexes improve, your strokes get stronger, and there comes a moment when you realize you're hooked on a new sport. Now more fun begins in delving into stroke perfection through endless practice, shot variation and the world of strategies. It's a good idea somewhere about this time to take a couple lessons not only to ease any growing pains, but to ensure no bad habits pass from your court childhood into adolescence. Branch out from your usual practice partners to play in club leagues and one day, in about a year, you might get an itch to enter your first tournament. That's where the championship bug may bite, but continue through your career to strive for self-perfection, to be the best you can be.

- Jeff Leon

The forehand comes naturally, but develop your backhand to have a balanced game.

- Marty Hogan

Play hard and have fun!

- Sudsy

Develop your strokes initially by practicing alone, and watch top players' mechanics, and ask for their instruction.

- Corey Brysman

Get lessons immediately, and take a peek at one of my teaching or playing videos. Drill the fundamentals that a coach or book will provide.

- Cliff Swain

I can't stress basics enough: watch the ball, get set up, and swing level. That wins the rallies because other beginning players make mistakes.

- Mike Ray

Once you learn your strokes, it starts to get fun. That's the time to examine two new areas of study: Court positioning and shot selection. The former allows you to get to shots, and the latter to make them so your opponent can't.

- Derek Robinson

Practice the strokes where the force goes from the legs to hips to shoulders down the arm

358

to the contact. Imitate a baseball hitter. *- Ruben Gonzalez*

Don't think it strange to hit thousands of balls a week and chart them. *-Charlie Brumfield*

Three pointers: Learn the strokes. Know how to position properly in the rally. Practice.
- Dave Peck

Get an early stroke lesson to ensure you practice right. If there's no 'swing doctors' or you can't afford one, watch the best players around. Once you feel good on both sides of the ball, the game is a joy. *- Jim Spittle*

Keep a piggybank next to your gym bag and relate how you fill both with coins and dreams. Francis Galton had four fundamental business principles that I've applied to sports: Persistence, health, organization and a modicum of ability. *- Victor Niederhoffer*

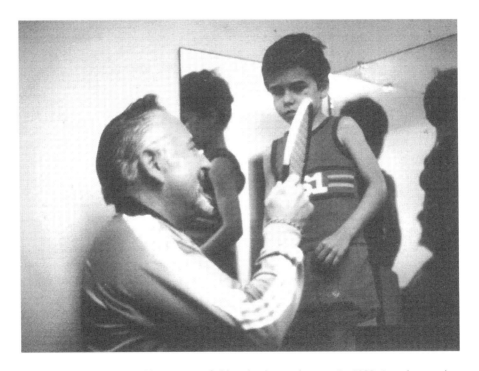

Carl Loveday tutored Muehleisen, Brumfield and other early pros. In 1982, Loveday coaches grandson Kirk Loveday at the 2nd Annual Christmas Junior Classic in Torrance, CA. (US RB Museum)

Deep in the Volley

The goal is to beseech volley so often that you must prove the author wrong. This is your racquet's heavyweight, underused shot.

Become twice the volleyer by combining some of the volley drills like *Hogan's Volley* (see other tip) with once-a-week cross-training trips to the squash court and outdoor courts (1-wall or 3-wall) . The latter are open in city parks, beaches, at colleges and high schools.

Traditionally, racquetball great volleyers are squash or outdoor crossovers. In squash, the mid-air kill is constant because the slower ball otherwise passes overhead to die at the back wall. Likewise, in outdoor racquetball or paddleball, the incentive to volley is greater because there is no back wall.

The reasons to volley in our indoor 4-wall game are identified in other tips, except one miserable excuse: 'Volleying leaves me weak from the effort." I hear. However, the greater incentive to progress to volley is gained fitness from striding up, and smashing the ball on the fly.

Sport training techniques include increased speed, weight or repetitions. Volleying the ball combines two of these- more speed (footwork, eye and racquet), plus more 'weight' to the ball (force = mass X acceleration, where the ball has higher force before a softening bounce on the floor). So the old lam, 'Volley makes me tired,' sidesteps the corollary that the opponent is not allowed to rest against a volleyer, and it's *he* who becomes weaker!.

These weekly trips to the squash and outdoor courts will benefit players of all skill levels up to the pros. Marty Hogan became one of the all-time great volleyers via the *Hogan Volley* detailed elsewhere; Cliff Swain bagged six world titles by training off-season on South Boston's three- wall courts;. Sudsy Monchik, five-time national champ, is a great volleyer from in-court practice and squash training; and the greatest volleyer in racquetball history, Vic Niederhoffer jumps in the squash court whenever possible. (Remember that every time the ball in outdoor racquetball or squash goes over the head, the volley opportunity replaces the back wall setup.) These experiences will teach you to recognize these setups, and take advantage.

Within a matter of weeks, I guarantee you will add an aggressive instinct to your game that will give your competitors fits, and you'll have made a happy author.

New World Outdoor Champ Rocky Carson volleys the ball with a rushed stroke to control center court and catch the opponent off guard at the 2014 WOR Championships. (Mike Augustin)

Volley the AW and Z

The Around-Wall and Z ball tie some advanced players in knots, and this trick unties them overnight.

The two shots are effective only because of the angle and spin which are unlike any other shot during the rally. Extinguish both of these by returning the balls on the fly. It's a mental rather than physical adjustment.

Here's the easy return:
1. The instant you see an AW or Z come off the opponent's racquet, retreat to a position in deep court a little left of the midline where you anticipate the shot will be volleyed at waist to chest height.
2. Step into the ball coming off the side wall and smash it hard in midair to overcome the spin. You must make the volley advancing forward, not backpedaling.
3. The return is a kill to the near left corner or drive down the left wall.

The sweetness of the volley is any return you make is forgiving – you may mishit and still the shot is successful nearly every time. There are three reasons for this success of the volleyed AW and Z:
1. The unorthodox return startles the opponent. He doesn't have time for footwork and can't see the volley directly behind him.
2. The volley is a shorter shot than the option of bouncing the ball to the back wall.
3. The return whizzes past the rival's ear, and he remembers it.

You make the mental adjustment from bouncing the AW and Z balls with one session of practice that requires a buddy. For thirty minutes, he strikes AW balls and you volley the return for a kill or drive. Then, he hits Z balls from behind the service line and you make the same returns. Both of you should start the drills standing in the coverage area near the 5-foot line and center court. The volley return is like riding a bike: Some players get it in minutes, and others in an hour, but in all cases, since it's a mental correction, it's remembered for life.

The next time an AW or Z ball comes at you, you will step up and powder it in midair.

Pros Speak from the Box

Z-Ball and Around World

Rarely used when no other offensive shot or a ceiling ball is possible. *- Corey Brysman*

It's a rare shot in good play because it comes down for a setup for anyone who can kill.
- Mike Ray

There's no place in my game for these shots. *- Marty Hogan*

Think ahead to better offensive play where you don't have to use these shots. *- Sudsy*

You recall we invented and used the Z-ball early on when the ball was slower and would die at the back wall with the rival tied in knots. The around-wall and z-ball have no place beyond the beginning levels of modern racquetball, but the around-wall is particularly effective in hybrid ball using a paddle and racquetball. *- Charlie Brumfield*

Infrequently you can hit one of these shots off a ceiling ball, however they're not the strong part of defensive that resides in ceiling play. *- Jeff Leon*

These were used in the old days, but anytime the ball comes across the middle now, it's cut off. *- Cliff Swain*

Volley the Z and around wall and you will never see another from the same opponent.
- Jim Spittle

363

Focus

Q: *Should I watch the ball or the target?*

A: Since the sport is kills on glass at advanced levels, this explains it, but the same focus applies to all shots...In the early days of racquetball the court walls were white, the balls black and there was great contrast. I watched **BOTH** the ball and the corner I was going to kill into. There was about 50-50 focus on each item.

This focus can be **'one picture'** in the eyes of both the ball and corner; or it may be a quickly alternating frame by frame of the ball, then corner...

I used primarily the method of seeing both ball and target simultaneously - the 'big picture' but staring only at two objects.

It should be noted that most of the Power players, unlike me, focused mostly on the **ball** during the stroke. They may have caught a glimpse of the corner during the downstroke, but as the racquet closed on the ball their attention was entirely on ball. Hence, they had more focus for the power, and less for accuracy.

Then, over time, glass courts came into play. The new green or blue balls were camouflaged against it. There was probably a political decision for the ball color instead of basic black as a difficult to see sphere promoted the harder hitting champions. When the court walls went **all glass**, even the front like an aquarium, I had difficulty seeing the corner and ball in one picture. The ball was lost in the glass, and the corner was lost in the glare. I had to switch techniques to focus on the ball, while hardly perceiving the corner.

The best is to think outside the box: try everything.

Jason Mannino dives watching the ball and target with little regard to the floor. (Mike Williams)

Pros Speak from the Box

What to Watch

Look at Paola watch the action behind her. (Roby Partovich)

Always look at the ball. Never lose sight of it. Watch it when your opponent is setting up instead of watching him. Sleep with your eyes open on it. *- Sudsy*

I look at the whole ball, usually out of the corner of my eye because that's what's

366

possible when it's moving fast. I focus fully on the whole ball during service or when it slows down like on a ceiling ball set-up. The rest of the time because of ball velocity it's more a 'feel-vision' of watching actual frames of the ball when possible, and inserting anticipatory frames in between.   *- Corey Brysman*

Teach your eyes to go to the ball by watching it even off the court. I used to be 'hungry' for the ball after watching it like a cat off the court. The body follows the eyes around the court. Nothing intrudes if you watch the ball.   *- Mike Ray*

Everybody watches the ball (except one) in the Men's Doubles final of Mejía-Gutiérrez over Cardona-Partner at the 2014 Juarez Open. (Ken Fife)

Don't join many players in the bad habit of looking at the front wall during the rally or you'll end up looking like an idiot. The thing to watch is the ball. When it's ahead of you that's easy, but when it goes in deep court just swivel your head with eye guards in place and watch as the opponent sets up for his shot. Of course, you'll be able to see him and his racquet too but the main focus is on the ball. You'll see it come off the strings, disappear and reappear on the front wall toward which you're already moving. *- Jeff Leon*

Don't hit the ball until your eyes can focus on the label.   *- Charlie Brumfield*

I think that watching the ball is overrated amid all the aspects of the strokes, and especially as an excuse for a missed shot that I attribute to poor racquet skills or concentration. If you carry a general concentration throughout a match, you'll watch the ball without a problem.

- Cliff Swain

On a solid wall court you may look at the ball and target, plus the opponent, while taking the stroke. On glass, however, the primary if only focus is on the ball with a 'sense' of where the other two stand.

- Jim Spittle

Watch the BALL the BALL the BALL and based on height, power and angle you line your body up accordingly. As you are doing that, peripherally watch your opponent so you know the shot to hit.

- Fran Davis

A good rule of thumb is never to take your eye off the ball or after the shot. I liked the way Hogan watched the ball closely after his shot, like a pro basketball player following up in case of a rare miss. During service return, watch the ball cradled in the hand, dropped, and hit to get it. I watch the whole ball rather than a seam or logo.

- Victor Niederhoffer

Watching the ball is key, even to contact. Your peripheral vision will take care of knowing where your opponent is standing as well as where you are on the court.

– Brian Hawkes

Many pros on the follow through watch the spot where the ball was hit at contact. Alejandro Landa over Javier Moreno.at the 2014 Juarez Open. (Ken Fife)

Aim

Q: Aim. Should I aim at an exact target or a general one?

A: Most players don't think about it, but if their subconscious spoke it would say that they were aiming at an exact target. It's better to think about it, and then choose: Do I aim at an exact or a general target.

One of the keys of my game was to aim not for the bulls eye but instead at the ring around it. A larger space. I learned from darts that when I fired one in an exacting manner, there was a hesitation or tremble sometimes, and the dart went astray. Likewise in racquetball, especially on close-game rallies.

I came up with a model in racquetball after darts called the **Box Target**. In this, an actual or imagery box about 1' square (depending on skill level) is placed in the front corner that you are shooting a kill into. I discovered consistency. Aiming at the box took the ball into the center of it.

When golfers aim for a hole in one it's with the green in mind.

David Horn aims and shoots at the 2014 Grand Slam Juarez Open. (Ken Fife)

When to Call 'T.O.'

- The first law of inertia is after your skip two shots in a row, call a time out.

- The second law of inertia is after dropping three quick points, whether due to your poor shots or an opponent's streak, call a timeout.

Nobody can break these laws without the universe frowning.

There are two reasons for calling 'T.O.' in each of the above cases: You break the opponent's confidence, and, you regain your own rhythm.

There are few players in history who disallowed themselves timeouts. I called about one T.O. per season for ten years of pro play. Peggy Steding came to me once after ten years at the top of the Women's Pro tour and winked, saying, "I'm the oldest lady on tour, and I've never called a timeout in my life."

How about you?' When the inertia of the game is going against you, by all means call T.O. Or, when the tide of play is with the opponent, shout 'T.O'.

Wallpaper
Remembering the Shot

A significant event in the rise of my left-hand in court sports occurred in the far flung Niederhoffer mansion in the Connecticut woods where I lived during the golden summer of '95 with the owner, and perhaps best all-around racquet player of the 20th century.

He knows and possesses the key to racquetball, squash, tennis and paddleball called the 'wallpaper ball' on both forehand and backhand. This shot is a plaster-clinging, down-the-line pass, lob, kill or serve from strings to front wall, and reflects likewise sliding along the side wall. It chews up more opponents' rackets and paddles than the rest

Jake Bredenbeck is wallpaper in Men's Singles vs. David Horn at the 2014 Juarez Open. (Ken Fife)

combined. I watched Victor Niederhoffer effortlessly strike the ball thousands of times in practice, and against me, on his in-house courts and thought, if I can just nail this shot I'll phoenix my multiple-racket careers.

The manor outdoor 4-wall racquetball court with glass back wall, killshot-blown leaves in front corners and night lights, was ceiling-less. With little else to do outside the trading room and famous library, my nightly racquet sessions extended into the wee hours. Once, I practiced the wallpaper ball from sunset till sunrise, as the day traders trudged up the spiral stair to shout encouragement before trading commodities.

Another time, I drilled barefoot so long on the concrete court floor that the callousness wore off and soles leaked blood from the court into house that was a hit with the licking dog, but not wife.

Night practice sessions were an entomologist's delight! The bright court lights attracted thousands of moths of dozens of species from the deep, dark woods surrounding the court. They fluttered audibly and darted visual hinders each self-rally, and hundreds finally settled on the floor and wall galleries. Mothball is the most telling footwork drill since boxers chased a chicken down a blind alley. Shots are held in mid-swing to prevent racquet and body lets, and you dash closed-mouthed to stop choking.

In the end, after a month working out the bugs, the wallpaper shot became mine. Why? The ball spin, shape off the strings and front wall, center of gravity, spin axis, angular momentum, and wind resistance synergize to propel it straight down-the-line, and on reflection kiss the side wall from front to back. The shot looks like a moving nose along a clown flat face to an opponent.

The wallpaper shot is a blood trade secret; however, knowing that it *can* be hit is half the battle. The rest is analysis of every blend of the above-named factors. Practice each permutation until the key unlocks the secret.

The Rise and Fall of Your Game

I want to reveal a tip about *your* game, and your opponent's, though we've never met. The rise and fall of success depends on it.

Through twenty years and a dozen national championships in racquet spots, I occasionally heard the masters speak of hitting the ball on the 'rise or fall', but was too wet behind the ears to ask the meaning. I screwed up my courage one day and was told by an all-racquet champ, 'Racquetball players across the board hit the ball on the fall, a grave deficiency. If they started to hit the ball on the rise like tennis and squash players, their games would gain ground.' Hitting on the rise means that after the ball takes a floor bounce there's an opportunity to strike it: 1) On its rise from the floor, 2 At its zenith, or 3) On its fall from zenith. As the Dude said, most racquetball players back up and wait until zenith or after the ball begins to plummet before making the hit.

However, stronger players learn to hit the more difficult but advantageous shot as it springs from the floor. The exact point of contact on the rise can be next to the floor (for example, inches up for a short-hop lob service return, or up to nose-high (on an overhead taken on the rise).

The profits from hitting on the rise are: 1) In cutting off the ball you shortened the distance of the shot to the front wall, hence are closer to center court position – often in front of the rival. 2) The opponent is surprised by the play, and disallowed from rest during that portion of the rally. 3) Most strategic, the foe is a step deeper away from center court himself because of smaller time for your setup. The summation of these advantages is that you'll pick up about five extra points per 21-point game. Also, the competition will be more uncomfortable and tired against your aggressive style for the ensuing games.

The specific times to think about hitting on the rise are on: 1) Lob serve short-hop returns, 2) Any half-volley during the rally, and 3) Mid-court overheads. The final situation is a revelation in our game where about once every three rallies a ball, for example off an opponent's pass shot or flicked-up return, comes to you head high just behind the service box. Picture your opponent standing at your side or just behind, as you step forward and contact the ball on the rise at waist-to head high and pummel it low into a front corner for a winner or surprise pass. Review the assets of the rise-shot in the previous paragraph and understand that none of these would have happened had you not stepped up: Your adversary is stuck behind you, he can't see the ball, he's startled and annoyed, he must jump out of his shoes for a retrieval, he'll probably lose the point, and he's got to think twice about hitting the same shot to you again in the future.

374

I loathe playing guys who hit on the rise because it makes me work so hard. One of my mentors, Bud Muehleisen was the first to use it winning more national titles than anyone on record. In those days, like everyone else, I didn't have a clue that one could hit the ball either on the rise, at the zenith, or on the fall; I just smashed it to my false thrill. By the late-70s, squash and tennis players invaded our sport and though I observed they used the half-volley and short-court overheads, I never put a finger on the rise. In the 80s, with the livening of the ball, power players like Dave Peck, Mike Yellen, Marty Hogan and others began smashing on the rise for winners as blind squirrels find acorns. Still, I hadn't spoken with the Dude and didn't understand at all.

Cliff Swain's patented ESP vs. Ruben Gonzales hustle at the 1984 Montreal Open. (Murray Diner)

375

Nowadays, you see the best rise hitters ever in Ruben Gonzalez, Dave Ray and Cliff Swain.

The best clue I can offer to getting used to taking the ball on the rise is to command yourself to move forward instead of backward in a situation (paragraph 4 above) where a rise-shot is possible. As Sudsy Monchik, another expert asserts, 'I step up, attack, and kill everything before the opponent has a chance to blink.'

The shot to make off the riser is what I call a 'kill-pass', with emphasis on kill. I like to aim low for a front corner, for a straight-in or pinch kill. Since the ball has undue topspin from the rise, this English is continued off the front wall and floor bounce to cause the shot to squirt along a sidewall alley out reach.

The stroke is a normal forehand or backhand except that the ball is hit as it goes up from the floor to the ceiling, rather than down after the apex. The height of contact is anywhere from ankle to overhead. The rising ball has topspin that some players reflect successfully off their racquets with continuing topspin toward the front wall, as mentioned. However, recall from the article 'Horizontal Fences and Telephone Poles' that topspin provides vertical accuracy only within an alley from front to back wall, so you may want to add a flavor of horizontal accuracy that's gotten with a side-spin stroke. Personally, I find that a combination of both topspin and sidespin (a sum ¾ overhand spin, like a ¾ arm pitch) is the proper blend to hit on the rise all day. Experiment, and scratch in blood on the back of your hand, "The only error on hitting the riser is to have the ball come off the back wall before two bounces.'

Ceiling shots that come up short of the back wall would seem but are not likely candidates for hitting on the rise, as you'll ascertain by attempting it - though it's possible. Years ago, Joel Scheimbaum invented the freaky front court short-hop return of the ceiling ball that gave others fits. He cuts short ceiling rallies by sneaking forward of the service box, as one focused on his own next ceiling hit, and short-hops the ball with a stiff-wrist inches up from the floor and a few feet from the front wall. It's kooky, but easy because the malcontent is stranded unaware in deep court.

Be forewarned that the riser is challenging to learn because of the sudden racquet-to-eye reflex against the quickly springing ball. Drills include whatever you can come up with, and you can use mine: 1) Practice the regular half-volley by giving yourself a soft set-up off the front wall to short-hop it deep the service box. 2) Have a comrade lob serve you, and return a short-hop on the rise. 3) Bounce the ball anywhere on the court and hit it on the rise rather than after the zenith. 4) Stand six feet from a sidewall anywhere on the court and toss the ball directly into it, then half-volley the shot into the front wall. 5) The best drill specifically for the short-court overhead is to stand deep of the service box and tap yourself a ball about mid-height into the front wall that reflects lazily to bounce

376

between the short and 5-foot lines. Charge as the ball approaches, and smote it on the rise chest-to-head high with the suggested ¾ overhand swing.

Your reward for these drills will be a high-caliber addition to your shot arsenal, the ability to quicken the pace of play at will, a definitive return of any soft service, and an irritation to anyone who languishes in back court.

Ben Croft hits the ball on the rise from an open stance with thumb in fist for balance as most use the tongue in cheek. (Freddy Ramirez)

377

The Dude who must be credited for this article is squash, tennis and racquetball champ Victor Niederhoffer who explained during one of our nightly outdoor Moth Ball sessions. 'Racquetball players across the country hit the ball on the fall, a grave deficiency...' That's when I began formulating theories and shots about hitting on the rise.

The begged closure is, 'Why throughout history have racquetball players among the court sport ignored hitting the ball on the rise?' The answer is seen from a sidewall view of the ball's trajectory after it comes off the front wall. A softer, higher shot such as a lob serve or easy pass bounces up from the ground at an angle that's more vertical than the angle during the fall after the apex. It's easier to hit a ball that approaches more horizontally than vertically.

Álvaro Beltran hits the ball on the rise with a perfect bow forehand from an open stance. (2005 Ken Fife)

Ten Top Tips for Advanced Juniors (And Their Parents)

Brett Elkins

Racquetball may be the best sport in the world for Juniors since they get to play together in the same court right next to their Junior opponents. For this reason, Juniors usually end up becoming the closest of friends for life. More importantly, they learn together to be honest and play fair. As the coach and Director of the Los Angeles Juniors for ten years I've also made hundreds of little friends for life, and learned from them their best 10 tips for advanced Juniors that they'd like passed along as quick as a King Kane serve.

1. Always put yourself out there and never worry that you are not great yet - you will be great soon enough if you set your mind to it.

2. Next, the secret to playing better is to play better players, and then ask every better player you know for advice. You decide - You can mirror your game after players who are better than you.

3. A fun quote is 'The more you lose the better you get.' Loses are stepping stones to championships because you get to sit and analyze after a loss what went wrong, to correct it, practice it, and do better the next time. My son Cody, 10, had lost 65 sanctioned Junior matches in a row by the young age of 8 and because he learned this lesson well and loved the game and wanted to improve, he's finally winning by appreciating his many losses.

4. Step right from practice games into tournaments. Playing lots of games won't help improve your game much unless it's proven in tournaments.

5. The top Juniors always practice on their game alone religiously drilling the same shot over and over again and playing much less than they practice. The three primary things for advanced Juniors to drill alone are drive serves, killshots and ceiling balls. It's easier than you think: You should hit at least 50 drive serves, and then 50 forehand kills, 50 backhands, and then 50 ceiling balls. If you really want to get good fast step up and volley in mid-air shots all over the court with both wings for 15 minutes.

6. Play in adult divisions at tournaments whenever possible to get used to the pace. Girl Juniors should play with the boys if allowed. Play in as many divisions as you can since the more you play the better you get. Try to play in two or more tournaments a month no matter what level you are. Some of my Juniors have played in hundreds of tournaments

since starting as young as age 5 when they could barely hit the ball. You should see them now!

7. The biggest mistake in racquetball at young advanced levels is not having a professional level coach. Get a professional coach and take lessons weekly. Make sure your backhand is right-on early on so it becomes a habit and you become great. If there is no coach or money for one, a fast way to get better is to keep asking better players for help - ask questions and don't feel silly. Then ask, 'Will you work with me for 10 minutes?' Later, that great player may decide to mentor you.

8. Doubles. Plays doubles with friends five times a week. Nothing like racquetball doubles increase hand, eye and feet speed up front for singles.

9. Here's a tip from almost the top for Junior players and their parents. If you have top grades and play racquetball at the annual Jr. Olympic Nationals, you will have an opportunity to get a full ride (or at least admission) into a top Ivy League college. All a racquetball Junior basically has to do is play at one Nationals and 'place', which is almost a certain outcome since so few Juniors go to this event. Unlike other sports, like volleyball or soccer, where you have to qualify to play Jr. Olympic Nationals, in racquetball only about 150 Juniors aged 6-18 typically play. Show up, place, and you win a scholarship. There are about 18 total divisions since two are for multi-bounce for younger players, there's boys and girls, singles and doubles, and mixed doubles. It's almost a certainty every Junior entrant will win a scholarship or admission, if his or her grades are also good. Be a big fish in a small pond and go get a major national experience and an education.

10. Of course, if items 1-9 fail above, remember to always have FUN and stop playing when it becomes a chore. You will be back when you miss it. There is nothing else like racquetball and nothing better than seeing little grown-up friends at tournaments these days that beat me. We have a bond and it's because of Junior racquetball.

Pros Speak from the Box

Tip to Juniors

Have fun. Avoid too much regiment at an early age. If what you're doing on the court feels fun, you're on the right track.
- Mike Ray

Be positive on the court. Be competitive. Be gracious.
- Corey Brysman

Get comfortable on the court as if it were your home. Learn where the ball will stop after it descends. That's where the junior learns to play. Then, find something to follow in the form of a lesson from a coach or an image from watching a pro. Youth assimilates by imitation what's nearly impossible to teach an adult.
- Charlie Brumfield

I've worked hard to remain a kid, so a tip is easy. Play lots of sports for the fun of it, and then pick the ones you want to specialize in and practice. I never drank or smoked, just did athletics.
- Marty Hogan

Play hard and have fun!
- Sudsy

Take a lesson, a camp, or watch someone good to avoid early bad habits. It's all about enjoyment, so if when something else creeps in, step back.
- Ruben Gonzalez

Play hard, eat well, sleep plenty, go to school, and have a good time whatever you do.
- Alvaro Beltran

Once you've got good strokes, there are two areas where you're going to score most of your points as a junior: the serve and back wall. These are the two times when your developing swings and reflexes have the opportunity to hit the ball strong. The third place to play aggressively with a kill or pass is in front court because the front wall's so close and opponent's so far away. Oh, juniors from the day I played until present pick at each other's' backhands. Be the first in your court to have a stronger backhand than forehand by practicing it more.
– Jim Spittle

First, learn your good stroke mechanics for the forehand and backhand. Second, gradually come to understand all the aspects of the game including the serve, return, offensive and defensive play, positioning, and so on. Third, there's a thing called 'muscle memory' where if you practice alone the strokes that you've learned, then when you get in a game those muscles will automatically react as you've trained them to hit the shots well.

- Dave Peck

Your most important drill is the volley, and everything comes easily after that shot.

- Victor Niederhoffer

Watch ball, early swing prep, and bow backswing by a 2014 WOR Summer Legend. (Mike Augustin)

A coach, anyone else who practices or this book can give you enough drills until your first championship. The wide angle-V is an underrated, beautiful shot as an alternate to

382

deep court kills off the ceiling and back wall setups. From a position on the right side, hit the ball hard on the front wall just left of center, it ricochets to the left side wall just above the service doubles box, then scoots around the opponent and kicks to the right rear corner where it originated without coming off the back wall. The wide-V requires less accuracy than a kill, it goes to the weaker backhand, the coverer is annoyed at having to break and chase, and may you get many weak returns that are easier to kill than your original back wall or ceiling setup. Juniors want to play, but if you want to excel in racquetball you must practice alone. *- Jeff Leon*

Make this part of your career on the court the best, so that you'll one day look back and marvel at what a blast it was. Compete in as many leagues and tournaments as you can. When you grow up, try to keep that feeling of being a kid. *- Cliff Swain*

Keep it fun, keep learning and practicing, and be grateful for your opportunities. *- Rhonda Rajsich*

Have fun and get good exercise playing one of the greatest, most fun games there still is. If you are a competitive person, play in leagues and tournaments. If you are really good, take the game as high and as far as you can. *– Rich Wagner*

The 2011 Fullerton, CA National Juniors. (Bonnie Rejaei)

Play as much as you can and try to play as many different players as you can. Having fun is extremely important. Don't give up.
— *Jose Rojas*

Put in the hours of repetitive drills and cross-train. Don't expect it to come too easily!
— *Davey Bledsoe*

Be in better condition than anyone else. Surround yourself with only positive people. Learn to manage your mind.
— *Cheryl Gudinas*

Learn the physical training: weights, footwork, and conditioning. Learn the value of hard work. Train like an athlete and don't leave anything out of your training. You need everything to be the best you can, and the game becomes more fun when you are physically ready.
- *Charlie Pratt*

Really work hard on learning where the ball is going to go at all times. That means playing a lot of RB while you're young. But, play other sports too as the athleticism from other sports will roll over into one's RB game.
— *John Ellis*

Do not skip service return.
— *Dave Fleetwood*

Juniors, get out there and have fun, play, learn, stroke build, stock your serve arsenal, develop an array of shot making options, be tactical, be fair, respect players of all levels, get help from a coach or mentor or several and be open to any and all advice, but learn what with a grain of salt means. Get stronger, fitter, better at breath control, and able to play with energy, confidence, calm, composure, and endurance to withstand a hard played, long match, a big onslaught of points, a grueling rally or a tough, emotionally tiring match.
— *Ken Woodfin*

Drilling gets you better faster and have fun with the sport.
— *Andy Hawthorne*

Have fun and get your friends involved. Kids tend to play sports that their friends are playing.
- *Kerri Stoffregen Wachtel*

Enjoy the game every second.
- *Cristina Amaya Cassino*

Slow Feet, Fast Mind? – Drill!

Think of this as a fast shoe for your feet. I feel black-and-white and red all over in writing it because my nickname 'Three-toe Sloth', the slowest land mammal, still stings. I'm going to declare what I've learned from the trauma and its redress.

Many players self-berate 'Move your feet!' yet don't, and I'm sure it's a correctable, neuro-muscular factor rather than that you're a Frankenstein. Indeed, the mind says,

Cheryl Gudinas drilled for hundreds of hours to move quickly to an open stance forehand. (2006 (Ken Fife)

385

'Yes, you can move with alacrity', but the feet seem distant and unable to grasp the command. The solution is here. Re-design the mind with the following thoughts, and shoehorn the feet with these simple practice drills.

The key is: *Immediately move after you hit!* As the batter moves off the crack of the bat, jump in the court right after your swing. It'll be excessive and odd in the learning period, but smoother thereafter.

Then, as you and the ball approach on the court, exaggerate your footwork a la Mohammed Ali's 'Float like a bee' jig where he scissored his feet in a blur before a punch to befuddle the foe. This comical footwork, akin to the Roadrunner treading air after stepping off a cliff, pays dividends down the road. Now, as the ball and you close for the actual contact, it's important for your future fleet feet to intensify your setup effort. Bud Muehleisen once expressed, "Adding just 10% intensity to your setup or shot can turn your game around.'

The service return is a ripe time to adjust your intensity that can carry over to enhanced footwork, movement and shot success during the rally. Some pros stand still but ready to receive, while others do a tennis shimmy to generate instant inertia (that may or may not be in the right direction). The best advice is to try both techniques, and remember that even the pros who stand rather than shift while awaiting serve are on their toes and internally 'moving' in anticipation.

Now for the brain food, the drills which I've tailor-made for you and me. Let's scamper through them:

1) Alternate cross-court passes. This and the rest of the drills, save the last two, are performed alone. Start on one side of deep court and hit a cross-court pass to the other side, dashing to hit a pass back to the original side, etc.

2) Alley passes with enhanced footwork. Hit continuous passes up-and-down the forehand alley with some exaggerated footwork such as hopping, scissoring or a jumping jack between shots. Remember your setup intensity. Do the same on the backhand alley.

3) Alternate ceiling and overhead in middle court. Stand in the middle of deep court and give yourself a ceiling setup that comes back to middle. Use exaggerated footwork as above between shots and return with an overhead pass straight down the middle, then continue to alternate ceilings and passes.

4) Cross-court continuous ceiling rally. This is frolic and a boon to the ceiling game. As implied, carry on a cross-court rally with yourself.

5) Solo ceiling rally with red line touch. A tough drill guaranteed to develop fitness and agile footwork. Start near the back wall on one side and hit a ceiling shot down the alley, sprinting to touch the red 5'-line with your foot, and returning to deep court in time for the second ceiling shot, etc. With proficiency, touch the service box line between shots.

6) Scissor legs between ceiling balls. Scissor your legs once, or hop twice, between shots of a perpetual ceiling rally with yourself down the alleys.

7) Solo match allowing multiple-bounces. This is also called the 'Charlie Brumfield thrust drill' in which you kill every ball on the court in a continuous rally that can't end

because it ignores skips and allows multiple bounces. It's the most perfect workout in the shortest time I've ever practiced.

8) The 'Moving Game' with a partner. I'm the proud inventor of this sweaty diversion in which you must move your feet even between points and during timeouts, or a point is subtracted from your score.

9) Squash racquetball with a partner. Tape, or imagine, or bring in a piece of wood to act as a squash 'tin' horizontally across the bottom couple feet of the front wall. All shots must strike above the tin, or the rally is lost. Up the ante by disallowing the ceiling, if you wish.

What fun and fast feet lay ahead!

A parting tip to take from the courts is ankle-weights. I'm a proponent because in considering the three ways to elicit a training effect: Increased speed, higher reps, or more resistance (weight), my belief is that the legs of the conditioned athlete can benefit predominantly from increased weight. Ankle weights come in 5 or 10-pound pairs (i.e. 2.5 or 5 lb. per leg) from sports stores and are the cheapest training investment you'll ever make at about $25 a pair. They strap around the ankles and can be worn at work, play, to bed, during workouts, and if you really want to feel an effect while on the bicycle. Wear them over thick layers of socks or high-tops or boots to prevent chafing. Use a light pair at first, and for playing sports, to avoid injury. If there's ever knee soreness, back down the weight or rest from the devices. Every few months for the past ten years, I've opened a letter or Email to the effect, 'I started wearing ankle weights, and my life changed.' They're a pleasant burden you soon grow accustomed to which succeed phenomenally by forcing into use the smaller leg muscles as well as the tendon attachments to the bones that normally default to the larger muscles. That's my theory, anyway. I had no difficulty in coming back after my 20-year Rip Van Winkle 'sleep' to racquetball while traveling the world because there was rarely a moment except in showers and sleeping that I didn't wear the weights. One year, I got stranded in the winter Andes mountains without a jacket, and it had been so many days that I forgot they were on and could have died walking out, and you'd not like that in this article.

Another quirk worth emulating for speedy feet is backward walking, for which folks write similar testimonials. Take stairs and hills backward to save the knees and work the hamstrings, and to bring your mind to a new awareness. World-class sprinters have begun to train by running backwards to prevent hamstring cramps. I walk backwards with ankle weights around my remote desert property, and one evening backward walked a dirt road for a mile with my eyes closed, knowing when to turn to my trailer by the crickets' call in the wash. I've backed into a cactus only a few times.

The benefits I've gleaned on the racquetball court from the information and drills in this article are looking less stumblebum as I get to more balls, and on leaving the club I prance. Now, step on.

Another strong open stance hitter is Kristen Walsh at a 2006 WPRO pro stop. (Ken Fife)

Cross Step vs Shuffle Hop

A **back cross step** is placing one foot behind and lateral to the other in order to move laterally and backward after the ball, for example in covering a pass shot.

A **front cross step** is the same thing only one foot crosses in front of the other to gain a new position closer to the front wall, for example in covering a killshot.

A **shuffle and hop** is old school. It is the same sort of movement as either of the above, only more lightly on the feet with the body center of gravity higher. It is inferior for the modern fast game for many reasons given below.

WHY REINVENT YOUR WHEELS?

The support from many sports is**:**

- Before they dug blocks in the dirt for **sprints** (now they make them) they outlawed cross overs from standing starts in shorter sprints... out of the blocks runners cross over anyway.

- Another proof is: Drop step came from **basketball**. It's to go behind you. It's a pivot or cross over.

- Another model is: If you've ever been in a **dark alley** the baddest guys cross step to cut the distance.

- **Boxers** cross step to cut corners.

- **Chickens** cross step when running for or away from something.

- Modern **racquetball** players cross over after cross over because the sport is interval sprints.

- The two best **coverers** in history were Niederhoffer and Brumfield who used crisscross steps without peers.

- In a ten-second clip of any top ranked racquetball **pro** you may see eight cross overs and only one shuffle step in which the shuffle loses a split second.

In any sport where distance must be covered quickly the cross over is superior.

390

"Feet-work" for Racquetball Court Movement

Ken Woodfin

How you move on the court greatly affects how you play because ultimately when you aren't there you can't create your competitor's despair.

First, here are movement suggestions for your feet, or "feet-work", and how to build these skills. Second, we'll progress to tactical feet-work and how using certain feet-work skills will raise your game in specific match situations.

I. Feet-work Skills

• Stay Active

Keep your feet alive. And begin from the middle! Here we start with simple principles and then we cover other effective and innovative movement skills.

- Keep moving

When you close in on a ball, take small adjustment steps as you read the ball. Keep your feet light and moving so you may adapt to the bounce of the ball. Play the ball instead of allowing it to play you. Think of it as when your feet stop moving your brain may stop, too! So keep your feet alive, your mind open, and then react and stay active right up until you can just about reach out and pluck the ball out of the midair. Then set your back foot, wind up as you walk into your shot and stroke confidently.

- Go Middle

After you stroke the ball make it *your* tendency consistently to move middle. Even in a slower paced rally, like a nick lob game or ceiling ball exchange, simply *take a walk* back middle. That walk gets you in prime coverage position. When you stay on the fringes of the court, such as against the back wall, up against a sidewall, or locked in the service box after serving, you leave yourself way out of position. Take a more proactive, tactical approach and seek control of the middle. From the middle you may move where you see the ball going or you may move to allow the required straight and crosscourt shots owed your competitor. Now let's explore faster ways to move about the court and always return to the middle.

• Athletic Body Position

Front leg cross-over to a forehand by Rocky at the 2012 WOR Championship.. (Mike Augustin)

How tall are you? Play a little bit shorter than your full height. Why? Know that as soon as you stand up too tall, you have to drop down to move, burning up your moving time. Also, when you bend down too low, you first have to rise up a little to move most efficiently. Slightly bend at the waist. Flex your knees and ankles. That slight body coil spring-loads your whole frame to be ready to move about the court more easily and smoothly.

• Be "ambi-footress" - Start on Either Foot

Choose to avoid being, for instance, just right footed, like you may be right-handed or right eye dominant. Learn to start out equally well off either foot and you'll be able to move about the court even more efficiently and quickly. You can teach yourself to be "ambi-footress". Place your heels flat up against the back wall. Step off aggressively with one foot. Sprint off the wall for a short distance. Return. Switch to the other foot. This exercise is done for two reasons. One, by learning to take shorts sprints off the wall, you train yourself to eliminate a possible false step backwards, while you step off strongly with the lead foot to begin your sprint. That forward only move makes you faster because you don't start going forward by first going backwards. Two, by switching feet and drilling with both, you teach yourself to step out equally well with either foot as you move about the court. That duality makes you a more versatile, efficient mover and harder to back into a corner.

• How to Shuffle Step

Most players are very familiar with the shuttle step as a form of court movement. Here is a short primer: Start near back wall facing either sidewall. Drop down a little height-wise and slide step sideways away from the wall using the foot furthest from the wall. To complete a shuffle step, slide the trail foot sideways, bringing it up next to the first landing foot before you continue your sideways shuffle.

• Power Down to Stop Shuffle Step

As you reach the service line or first line, put on the brakes by bending your lead knee and then flex your trail knee to lower your body. This knee work gracefully stops your forward momentum. The braking move lowers you center of gravity. Bending your knees uses their natural shock absorption to slow down your body when moving about the court. The ability to stop puts you in better, lower position to: (1) perform a balance stroke, or; (2) "freeze" to cover as your competitor strokes, or; (3) bolt to take off in another direction. How do you *bolt* best?

• Why Use Crossover Steps?

393

The crossover step gobbles up ground from the get-go. To teach yourself to crossover, again do the shuffle step from the back wall toward the service line. When you approach the first line, again put on the brakes by bending the outside leg and then flex the trailing leg. The control method first: As soon as you stop, push off the lead, outside leg and step off in the opposite direction with the trailing leg, the one furthest from the line. Take off in a sprint towards the back wall and slow down well before you reach the wall. That's the SLOW way! Now let's learn the faster, crossover way.

US Open Doubles champ Janel Tisinger stretches for a rekill. (Debra Tisinger Moore)

- Crossover As You Learn

To incorporate the crossover, repeat what you did before by shuffling to the service line. This time, when you get to first line, bend that outside, lead knee, then inside, trail knee, brake, and push back as you pivot off both feet (on the pads behind the toes). Then stay extra low as you turn your hips and shoulders and crossover aggressively with the outside, trail leg. Make it a big crossover step. Drive your arms, even pumping with the one holding your racquet, as you dash your very best to the back court. This big

394

crossover step simply makes you faster. The crossover step works for several court coverage situations, such as ...

- Dash Forward

When you're stuck in the back court or right up against the back wall and you can see the competitor placing a low kill in the front court or when you see a high ball about to fly way off the back wall, use your jets to dash forward. How: First step crossover into a low, arm pumping all out sprint. Stay low and run quietly or avoid stomping. On the way decide which shot you should hit? Take off running with the ball making sure the ball is away from you. If the ball is flying off the back wall, keep it in the corner of your eye to avoid it running up your back. Use the racquet in your hand and pump both arms to run to where you think you can intersect with the ball while letting it drop extra loooooow.

- Play Keep-away vs Always Drop Shooting

Front court rundown shot tip: get up sideways to the ball and selectively use soft drop shots against a rapidly closing competitor. Be ready to snap off an angled pass toward the least covered back corner. Only when the competitor checks up and backs off to camp on your pass should you hit a soft, disguised dropper.

• Just Jump

An advanced form of the shuffle step is a flick of the feet into a small leap or jump. The jump is used to begin your move or jump to a stop. The player jumps back, sideways or forwards off both feet at the same time. The jump is used to instantaneously adjust your positioning to: (1) clear for your competitor; (2) approach the ball, or; (3) start your run. The landing of the jump is ideally soft and springy, ready for more movement. Still lots of little adjustment steps remain to get in the best position to cover or to flow into a ball that's still reacting to walls or spin. Both an analogy and a metaphor may help explain the ease of the jump and the importance of still moving after landing.

- Leap to Start Analogy

Watch basketball players standing along the free throw lane. After a made fee throw the players do a little rising up leap to get their engine running before they head down court to switch ends. That leap on court can be a little more plyometric or a rapid leap to move over some distance. Learn to emulate a b-ball player by getting yourself in motion.

- Mighty Mouse Swoosh Metaphor

Oftentimes players land like Mighty Mouse just even with the ball as if to say, "Here I am to save the day!" But really Might Mouse has lots more still to do. Landing a little behind contact allows for momentum to be built up in the post landings stroke. Coiling back and then stepping into the ball or at least moving forward into the ball is best done with little adjustment steps, then weight back and through, and timed body prep and uncoil.

• Split Step Potential

A technique well known in tennis is the split step. In serve and volley tennis, as the server approaches the net, at the "t" formed by the center line and the back line of both service boxes, the net rusher spreads his feet to a two-footed, paused landing type hop versus coming to complete stop. He reads the situation and then takes off toward the angle where he sees or *expects* the ball to be. The same principle of using a split-step may be applied to racquetball, too.

Fernando Ríos lateral leg lunge to a forehand vs. David Horn at the 2014 Juarez Open. (Ken Fife)

- Block the Reverse

- Split-Step Tactical Cover

After stroking a deep pass or ceiling ball, dash forward to the dashed line. Step on the line with one foot, and spread your feet to a balanced, on your toes, split-step ready position. Partially face the competitor and read his shot. Get ready to take off toward any one of the 4 quadrants (4 corners). Adjust. If your competitor must retreat to a back corner, you may split-step again to angle off and partially face the competitor.

Move and split-step ON the imaginary diagonal line between the ball in deep court and the opposite front corner. On the diagonal you have a good view of the competitor, while you face the front corner on that side of the court. You get to legally block the reverse by the competitor when you get there before he can set up to shoot. On the diagonal you're ready to cover first the down the line, then the front court, then the crosscourt, and always a ball back through the middle. If instead you were to just face the front wall, widest DTL balls may be just tantalizingly out of your reach.

• Crisscross, a Football and Basketball Feet-work Staple

When you move sideways along the sidewall and you can see the shuffle step is just not gonna cut it and you need to get further, faster, the crossover step with the trail foot BEHIND your lead foot, the "crisscross" gets you there on balance, quickly. As you crisscross, the foot that's being crisscrossed acts as the post. That post foot is your temporary balance point supporting you until the other shoe lands. The crisscrossing foot lands just past the posting foot. Then the posting foot flashes ahead to complete the crisscross. Crisscrossing is sort of a skipping maneuver behind your back. The object of moving about the court is to go as efficiently as possible. The crisscross allows you more options when you need to move sideways lickity-split. As an example, many top flight players serve and then crisscross with their lead or plant foot behind their trail or back foot as they retreat out of the box. It's all about the way to most quickly move and clear the box to cover the receiver's options by being a "littler" further back. A crisscross is much faster than the shuffle step out of the box. A full crossover step commits you more toward the side where you crossover leaving you more vulnerable to the crosscourt return angle. So the crisscross-over is often the crossover of choice to escape the box. The crisscross is an example of a transition to tactical feet-work. Now let's look at more tactical feet-work examples.

II. Tactical Feet-work

• Banana In Approach

Ideally stroke the ball from a light, springy, slightly closed stance, with your front, plant foot half a sneaker closer to the sidewall than the back, push off foot. The partially closed stance allows you to turn your body into a forehand or backhand. How do you get into that ideal stance off BOTH wings? Once you've moved behind and to the side of the ball so that it's about an arm's distance away, you're ready to take on the *banana in approach*. Set the big end of your imaginary banana as the back of your stance. It'll be the push off leg. Then step in with a curved stride with your plant, front foot. This is the "banana in approach", stem in. Stem in means your weight pulls "in" toward the stem or in toward your body. This flow of force and body weight in toward your center gets your legs involved. Force then works up through your hips, turning your torso and finally catapulting your upper body as it synergistically connects to your lower body for greater summed forces.

• Jab and Cross

When the serve is not rocketed into a corner, use the time to jab step with the foot closer to the ball. Then crossover with the trail foot to both close your stance and apply better force and weight into your return. The crossover offers the best balance, while ideally allowing you the receiver to take the ball out in front or ahead of your stroking shoulder.

• Crossover Lunge For Photon Serves

When you pick up a super-fast "photon" serve as it rebounds off the front wall or worse case, as it rockets by the server, crossover with the far leg and lunge low. Be purely focused and doggedly determined to get the ball back to the front wall. Know that you may make contact BEFORE your lunging leg lands, but fear not; you WILL land! The crossover step also serves to coil your shoulders and your racquet naturally flares back with them. Use that natural prep and look to go down the line with your ROS or even DTL to the ceiling to push the competitor sideways and back. Know the main object is to get the ball back to the front wall. The secondary objective is to get the competitor out of the middle. Even a crosscourt pass or ceiling may work because the server will many times be moving your way pursuing the flight of his serve and blanketing the line which is the most dangerous return. Often making good string contact will be enough because you may use the server's power against him to bunt the ball away from him before he may react.

• 2-step Serve Footwork

Paint the edges of the very back line of the box with your sneakers. The foot that will be the plant, lead foot in serving stance starts ahead of the other. The feet are slightly apart and you're in a slight crouch or balanced bend while not squatting down. The racquet is out in front of you in a threatening position. The ball in your offhand resting against, let's say the grip of the racquet. Step up with the back foot toward the front foot. Land inside the front foot and just behind it with both sets of toes pointed at the sidewall.

*Rec: as you step up, draw your racquet back and use and your other arm like a tightrope walker holding his balancing bar.

- Immediately crossover with the front foot toward the front of the box, even landing with the arch of your foot on the front line. Then work your plant leg against your push leg to power your drive serve.

Womens Singles Quarters Sharon Jackson over Carla Munoz Montesineros 2014 Juarez. (Ken Fife)

• Get Out of the Box

AFTER you serve and complete your full follow-through your next step is to get out of the box. When you stay in the box you make yourself vulnerable to the pass you can't reach or the ceiling you can't short-hop. Sure you're closer to the attempted kill, but "he", the receiver *sees* you and his pass may rocket by you. So clearing the box, even by just a step, improves your chances considerably.

- How to Get Out of the Box

The way to get out of the box is to first regain your balance. Most of your weight is ideally on your front foot after you serve or stroke. So backshift your weight from your front to your back foot. Take a crossover step with your front foot toward the middle and partially spin toward the ball to flow out of "no mans' land" in the service zone. Only

399

body spin enough to get a view of the receiver over your shoulder. For protection use your racquet head to look through your strings as you cover your head.

- Retreat with a Crossover or Crisscross

The crossover step is the fastest way to retreat out of the service box. The crossover step may be in front of your back foot or it may be a crisscross-over behind your back foot, which will be covered later. The main point is to avoid a stretch back step with your back, trail foot. A step with your back foot spreads you out, slows you down, exposes you to a loss of balance and an inability to quickly reverse your field should you need to dash back into the front court for a possible low return. Pivot on your back foot and crossover. After the first "crossover" step do another crossover to cover ground even faster. You may shuffle, side-to-side to flow back for serves you read the receiver will return way back in deep court. However, compared to the crossover, the shuffle is in slow motion, as you retreat out of the service box.

- Practice Getting Out of the Box

As part of practicing your serves, practice the crossover (or crisscross-over) step to get into center court. The ultimate objective is to straddle the dashed line with both feet. At a minimum, make your goal to touch the dashed line with your back foot. ALWAYS BLOCK REVERSE pinch angle. From there you can cover most all ROS's. Finish by angling off and face the sidewall in the front court and be ready to blanket the line, your primary and most vulnerable cover.

- Crisscross Retreat After Serve, How?

One use of the crisscross is to clear the box after you serve. Serve, shift your weight back, pivot off both feet, and then crisscross with the front foot behind the back foot to initiate your slide quickly into center court, occluding the reverse pinch return as you do.

• **Skip for Back Wall Setups**

Skip with your feet to move back and then off the back wall for back wall setups. Actually it's a double skip because first you skip back behind the ball, and then you skip out to get into optimal position to shoot a winner or forcing shot. "Skipping" gets you back behind the ball to read its rhythm (timing, arc and pace). And then skipping out gets you in position to shoot. Skipping beats moving to a spot, planting, and hoping you've magically predicted where you might make contact. The skip maneuver is a little hop and then a sideways step. To skip you elevate, land softly and then you step that way. Skip back behind where you sense you will make contact. Then skip out "with" the ball to react to its curved, readable path. As the ball passes your stroking shoulder, shoot!

400

• Feet-work Covers when Toeing the Diagonal

Here's how to cover the receiver's returns when toeing the imaginary diagonal line between the ball and the opposite front corner. Toe the line and pick up cues on where the competitor may be shooting.

Cross-over step to cover lateral court quickly at the 2012 WOR Championship. (Mike Augustin)

- Primary Cover: the Line

The Down the Line (DTL) is so dangerous because it's both the shortest shot to the front wall and the sidewall might fight you for the ball! To cover the DTL, pre-program your feet-work to cover it. Learn and drill your feet just like you do your strokes. Here is how to cover the line:

- Lunge and Optimize for Toughest DTL's

Worse case, for low bullets, you may attempt a crossover lunge. Pick your intercept point for lower ones by lunging forward into the front quadrant along the DTL side. Or lunge backwards into the back quadrant for high or super fast DTL's. It is easier to intercept the ball going diagonally backwards versus going straight at the sidewall. Going directly to the wall is the least advantageous option because your perception of the ball will be at its worst. Going backwards buys you time to better see the ball. The ball also slows down a little for you. And you have a little more time to prep your racquet.

- Two-Foot DTL Cover

A more ideal situation is when you have time to step twice, first with what will be the back foot of your stance, and then to crossover with your front foot to finalize your stance. For low, trackable balls, ideally the two-step move is diagonally forward intending to meet the ball out in front. For higher, manageable balls, a diagonal two-step move backwards buys you time and provides you a better view of the situation that includes: competitor coverage, shot options based on ball speed, angle, spin, and more time to select your intercept location. The backwards diagonal may be with either foot. The object is to get to the ball, prepare as best you can and shoot the best shot available.

- DTL Risk Cover

From the diagonal starting line sometimes you may appear to create time by stepping out and attacking the oncoming ball. You feel the return is going DTL. You move diagonally forward because you read it's going DTL. You jab step and crossover and you have laser focus on the ball. If you make good contact and a good shot, you act like it was routine, a walk in the park. If you miss or you were fooled by the competitor's shot, at least the competitor has to factor into future rallies that you do anticipate and take chances.

• Crosscourt Shots Cover

When you position yourself on the diagonal, you may also cover, through observation, flow, and controlled feet-work, shots that happen behind you into crosscourt angles, too. Through observing the ball going crosscourt you may flow to cover the wider angled shots. Here's how:

402

Ronda Rajsich stalks a forehand with a near leg lunge and prepared bow in 2006. (Ken Fife)

- Crosscourt Cover

Your feet-work allows you to *drop step* into the 2 quadrants behind you to cover crosscourt shots. With the front most foot, drop step forward for observed low balls. Or, drop step diagonally back behind you to adapt to observed higher passing shots. The follow-on step after the drop step is a crossover step to cover the quadrant under attack. Pursuit, hustle, and efficient feet-work allow you to make a balanced attack on a crosscourt ball. Note that it is your observer dynamics that allow you to react to the ball in offensive or defensive situations. Keep track of your positioning in past matches and especially the current match to allow you to adapt best. Observe and react to be the best cover player you can be in each rally. With proper motivation and practiced feet-work, you may track the ball down and respond with your best-shot-available (BSA).

• Drop Step to Counter Ball Off Sidewall

The bugaboo of many players is a ball coming off a sidewall. At times it may be due to ball read or really more accurately ball misread. Or, it could be due to the distress caused by that one time when the lob or the Z looked like it was gonna come off the sidewall fat and juicy, but instead it zipped into the back corner only to squirt out right along the sidewall; the dreaded wall paper shot. Traumatic. So a player suffers feet-work lockup, even when the ball is clearly coming off the sidewall as a setup. I call those physics gone wild gutter balls. Let 'um go. Play what you see. Give yourself space. Drop step back with your back foot to back up and get behind the ball. This little move opens up your shot selections to almost anything you may want. Often your competitor may hug the line so an inside-out DTL pass may need to be shaped like a cursive *i* to curve your pass around him. The crosscourt pass may appear to be about to pop them. Take your shot. The main point is you buy yourself room and time by backing up with your back foot first. You get a much improved view of the court, what's covered, and your best shot options. You may then step in with your front foot and stroke the ball assertively and solidly toward your extra time bought to decide a target.

• Escape the Trap in Ceiling Ball Rallies

When stroking a DTL ceiling ball from a rear corner make it a point of emphasis to follow your shot to the front wall and, as you approach the dashed line, make a beeline to the middle. The point is to avoid the tendency to retreat along the back wall. Should you retreat, you risk being backed into the opposite, rear corner, while your competitor selects how to put the ball away catty cornered into the opposite front quadrant. Use your follow-through and weight forward stroking to boost your run along the wall. Step onto your front foot, as you rise up to your ceiling, and flow forward. After contact make a crossover step with your back foot. Hug the sidewall until you almost get to the dashed line and then shuffle or, for more speed, crossover into cover positioning on the diagonal. Granted you must give room to your competitor to take a straight line to the ball. Although, don't allow the trap to be fully set by using your own assertive, forward flowing strokes and escaping feet-work. When you do get trapped (it will happen), go far enough to clear their stroke and then quickly circle around your competitor to get back into the middle. When trapped you still might beat the competitor to block the reverse, and you still might pressure the diagonal quadrant you've left open. The key point is to avoid the trap whenever possible by following your ceiling to the front wall.

• Running Strokes

At times you only have time to step to the side with the front foot and stroke. Step and focus on staying balanced and keep your weight under control. You can step, stroke, and THEN allow your momentum to carry you into a follow on step with the back foot

404

landing further toward the sidewall. Land with your back foot (after contact) and then push back with that foot into the court. Then move off the sidewall and back toward the middle.

David Horn over Fernando Ríos in a duck walk at the 2014 Juarez Open. (Ken Fife)

• Open stance feet-work

Sideways facing strokes offer better balance, form, and generally more and better shot opportunities. Although, there are many times in rallies when you may be unable to turn to face the sidewall to stroke. You find your feet are left facing the front wall, glued to the floor or, due to the ball's pace, you are rushed and robbed of time to turn and face the sidewall. It's okay. Make lemonade out of the lemons you've been dealt. Here's the feet-work to stroke from an open stance:

- Open Stance, How to Do It

First, pick a side or which stroke you're going to use. Then, as always, turn your shoulders. That upper body turn allows your weight to build up on what will be the back foot of your stance. Your front foot aids in the push back. Keep your knees bent and your eyes riveted on your ball. As the ball is about to reach your racquet shoulder contact

405

zone, push back toward your resisting front leg. That push off begins to turn your knees and hips to build toward making contact with the ball off (in front of) your racquet shoulder to shoot toward your chosen wall target. Often a crosscourt target is the easiest and most makeable. Emulate a very common tennis player tactic by using lots of body rotation for angular or turning force. With deeper contact and a little more patience, an inside-out shot is doable. For example, an open stance, inside-out forehand from the backhand side of the court may be turned into a crosscourt forcing or winning pass or a near corner pinch winner into the opposite front corner.

- Open Stance Stroke Drilling

Like your regular sideways facing strokes, practice your open stance strokes and you'll be ready when the *opportunity* opens up. Choose which side you want to practice your open stance stroke. Face the front wall. Place your feet so that they're spread a little wider than shoulder's width. What will be the front foot of your open stance should be ahead of you slightly and the back foot should be about even with your upper body. With your non racquet hand, bounce the ball a little bit in front of you and off to the side. Place backspin on the ball so it feeds back toward you. As the ball draws toward your contact zone near your racquet arm's shoulder, turn your shoulders and load up your back foot. Keep your knees bent. To stroke, push off the back foot toward your bracing front foot. Practice a crosscourt shot first because it's easiest to control and easiest to power with your body rotation. Then work on deeper contact and inside-out strokes. A backspin ball that backs you up or pushes you sideways simulates a ball that forces you to retreat into an inside-out, open stance stroke situation.

- Drill Feeding Yourself Open Stance

As soon as you have begun to master the drop-n-hit situations, expand to facing the front wall from center court and flick yourself open stance situation balls. Flick balls off the front wall directly toward you or balls coming off the sidewall to practice more game-like conditions. Of course, even in the midst of this open stance specific drill, when you see you have plenty of time, turn and face the sidewall, get behind the ball, and stroke facing sideways to keep that good habit. However, when confronted with open stance situations in games, this drilling will prepare you to be better than just defensive, and ideally successful with your open stance shot selections and shot making.

Ken Woodfin is a former NASA information specialist with twenty-three years in teaching racquetball since 1980. He was in PARI and AmPro professional racquetball, and was a pro instructor and eventually became a clinician, trainer of trainers. He also is a certified personal trainer. In the pros, Ken once played against Mike Yellen in an 80s Texas pro event, where after their match Ken and Mike collaborated a diagonal theory that was written up in a Racquetball Illustrated *tutorial. Following that, many of Kens other articles were printed there and in other publications. He played Marty Hogan too, in the late 70s in Philadelphia, and Marty gave him too big a lead, but they immediately played a second game and Marty was a tad bit more focused.*

Ken still plays age division tournaments and coaches constantly, and writes. His philosophy is that a lot of details of knowing what you're doing, or everything you can about your art, is priceless. Self-introspection is invaluable. He teaches anyone to hold a thought in mind while "chewing gum" during a rally. Like asking a player, "Do you breathe out when you stroke?", it may be hard to convince some to focus on it or accept innovation, even when it'll raise their game. The intent of his reader-friendly writing is to make the topic visual and complete. In this article on Feet-work he thoroughly breaks down and provides drills for an important subject that previously has been left unaddressed or poorly explained in racquetball literature. - Steve Bo Keeley

Paola Longoria over Ximena González with some fancy footwork and a flat, level swing in center court at the 2014 Juarez Open. (Ken Fife)

Doubles: A Survival Manual

by Brad Kruger

Doubles. The word alone is like fingernails on a chalkboard for some. For others, however, it's a dream come true: a chance to scan through the catalog of racquetball skills and pick whatever you are missing.

A court codger, for example, aged with experience, but lacking mobility, can regain lost youth by choosing a thoroughbred as a partner. Or a one-armed bandit with only a forehand can pick a partner with a reverse affliction. Apart, these players are incomplete. But together, as a team with a precise modus operandi, they can defeat a team of even the most accomplished singles players.

How? Synergy, in a word. By merging their individually limited resources, the two players grow into a stronger unified force. They learn each other's moves and patterns of play. They know exactly where, when and how their partner will react in any situation.

What follows is a condensed doubles survival manual, a nutshell analysis of the innermost secrets of doubles, aimed at minimizing the confusion and indecision between players and maximizing two players' abilities as a team.

Choosing a Partner

As mentioned earlier, you should look for your alter ego. Not someone whose game is a clone of your own. That's about as sensible as a football team of punters. Look for someone with every racquetball skill you never developed. The trick is to round out your strengths. Eliminate your weaknesses.

Now that you've imported this labor-saving device, there is only one problem ... how do you work the damned thing? It does, after all, have a mind of its own. Thus, the ability to communicate should be high on your list for a partner. All the skills in the world are great, but they aren't worth a cup of coffee if you can't function as a team.

Together, you must devise a schematic, a concrete modus operandi, as it were, on how to position yourselves to maximize each other's strengths. Indecision is the major problem blocking successful teamwork. It can never be eliminated, but it can be significantly reduced. Which player is to take which shot? The first step.is to divide the court into zones-of-coverage which maximize each player's strengths, while minimizing his or her weaknesses.

Once done, each player's responsibilities must be discussed and defined. The term *teamwork* has been largely misunderstood. It projects the image of each player covering up for his partner whenever a difficult shot is hit. Nothing would be more defeating. If one player is constantly worried about his partner, he won't be focusing 100 percent on his own responsibilities.

No, the court should be divided to maximize strengths and minimize indecision between players. Each player must be made responsible for any shot that enters his coverage zone. There is little need for backup from either partner. In fact, if you move into your partner's territory, you will be disrupting the entire system – not to mention chancing a head-on collision.

US Open Doubles champion Janel Tisinger rekills from center court. (Debra Tisinger Moore)

Zones-of-Coverage

Of course, as in any sport, the chalkboard has been stained white from various theories on how to best apportion the court. In the following, we'll cover the most conventional methods - side-by-side {righty-righty), side-by-side (letty rights) and the "I" formation - saving anything more complex for locker room banter. Having done that, we'll wrap up this thumbnail manuscript with some suggestions about how to best handle center court, serves and general strategy.

Side-by-Side

Side-by-Side *(for two right handed players)* is the most common system used in doubles. In this formation, the left side player is responsible for covering any shot that enters the left quarter of the front court or the left two-thirds of the back court. Any other area is the right sider's responsibility.

The left side player – The person playing the left side should naturally be the stronger of the two; that is, he should have the strongest backhand. Not only does he have more court to cover, but he must hit all of the backhand shots that travel down the left wall. Endurance and a good backhand - these are the basic requirements.

The right side player – Because he generally plays a little farther up in the front court than his partner, he must decide quickly whether to hit a shot or leave it for his partner. He should, therefore, be the quicker of the two players. It's no wonder that he is considered the gardener. With fast hands, quick feet and lightning quick reactions, it is his job to dig up any of the opponent's kill shot attempts. Also, the right sider will seldom hit a backhand.

His position cannot be overemphasized. He must plant himself *on top* of the imaginary line that divides the court lengthwise, primed for action. From here – and only here - can the right sider maximize his strength and hit almost every shot in his zone with his forehand. Any more to the right, and his opponents' shots would pelt his midriff, forcing him to use his backhand. Clearly, he would not be maximizing the strength of his forehand. But doesn't this central position leave the entire right alley open for an opponent's pass shot?

Well, it certainly *looks* wide open. But it's really a play called "baiting the trap". The alley looks open, and is tempting enough for the opposing team to try to sneak a pass shot by. Privy to their intentions, however, the right sider is ready to pounce on this ball and put it away.

As you can see, just because the right side player gives up the backhand, his job isn't easier. He must always be alert, perched for attack whenever the opportunity arises, yet he must contain himself with the thought that if he leaves the shot, his partner may have a better opportunity.

The Grey Areas - The grey area is where indecision runs wild. It is the undefined area where zones-of-coverage overlap. To consolidate the strengths of the team, the left-side player should take all shots along this line of play. In an attempt to reduce confusion further, whenever a grey area arises, the left sider should yell "mine!" or "yours!" clearly, delegating responsibility for the shot.

410

Why the left sider? His deeper position grants him a few extra milliseconds to evaluate the rally and decide which player should take which shots. It's not a lot of time, but usually enough. The commands should be short and to the point. Obviously, there is seldom time to ramble off a sentence or two. If the right sider disagrees, he should quickly reply with his own command, again keeping it short and to the point. The left sider should comply. Time for discussion has run out.

Side-by-Side *(for left hander and right hander)* is probably the strongest team combination for effective doubles. The advantage is that there is no wall played by a backhand. Both players can use forehands to scrape the "wallpaper" balls off the sidewalls.

Most left-right teams use the side-by-side formation, with a slight modification. The court must be divided straight down the center of the court, with *both* players positioned on the dividing line, primed to cover the sidewall alleys .In this way both players are maximizing their forehands. Remember: consolidate your strengths.

Fast feet up front come from doubles. Men's Doubles Final Mejía-Gutiérrez over Cardona-Partner at the 2014 Juarez Open. (Ken Fife)

As you can see, there is a large grey area right down the center of the court - an area where both backhands are exposed. Before the game, decide who is responsible for the majority of these shots. The strongest backhand is elected.

"I" Formation

The "I" formation has one player positioned on the short line and the other about five feet from the back wall, with zones-of-coverage divided by the short line. The front court player is responsible for covering the entire front court. He is usually the quicker of the two, a good retriever with quick hands and feet and reactions. The back court player requires power, accuracy and control of shot.

The "I" formation is seldom used these days, mainly because it does little to reduce indecision. Quite the opposite, really. Because a player doesn't have eyes in the back of his head, it is difficult for him to decide whether to take a shot or leave it for his partner. He doesn't even know where his partner is. And speaking of eyes, the back court player is often screened by his own partner. And let's not forget the two major weaknesses:

(1) Two backhands are exposed on the left wall, and
(2) Almost every ball travels between each players' coverage zone, making decisions about responsibility difficult.

Center Court

Hugging a side wall or hiding in a corner is a natural' tendency. Intimidated by the social pressures (i.e. kicking, biting, gouging, etc.) that come from four people in a space for two, primal fight-or-flight kicks in. The best solution is obviously ... *panic!*

Actually, there is no defined area where you must stand. The proper place to stand comes from understanding doubles' strategy and rules of play. Naturally, you want to stand very close to just behind the short line. Ninety percent of all shots come within a quick step of this area, and you can hit your most accurate shots from here. The problem is, the opposing team wants this area too.

There's not a lot of room. Who gets the space? The answer comes in stretching the singles rules to a doubles definition. When one team is hitting a shot, the opposing team should be allowed a clear path to retrieve it. It's that simple.

How much room must you make? A clear path - just enough room for your opponents to retrieve the ball. Don't worry. It's not as much room as you're thinking. In most cases, a half step is usually sufficient. Which is little enough, and it still allows you to maintain center court positioning.

412

The Serve

The doubles serve has the same aim as in singles: to ace or obtain a weak return from your opponents. Try to expose and exploit a weakness of the opposing team. Concentrate all forces on the weakness. In doubles, this often means bombarding the weaker player with all the serves. But not always.

When both opponents are equal in ability, you must search for each individual's weakness. For example, if both receiving players have weak backhands, hit the serve to the rear left corner. If the receivers both have weak forehands, hit the serve down the center of the court or to the right rear corner. Obviously, playing a lefty-righty team, the serve should travel down center court. Recognize and expose any apparent weakness on the opposing team.

There is one serve - the "jam & fly" - that continues to baffle even the best doubles players. After a few of these, it is said, the player on the receiving end is never quite the same. The server strikes the ball from a wide angle on the court. The crisply-hit serve strikes the front wall in the center and rebounds off the side wall, which it contacts about two feet above the short line. It doesn't take its first bounce until it is about five feet from the back wall, between the opposing players. Then it ricochets off the back wall into the sidewall, plunging to a quick death.

The receiver usually waits too long, not returning the ball until after its first bounce. Then, of course, he's in trouble. As the ball caroms off the back wall toward the sidewall, the player is forced to turn with the ball. Otherwise, he loses sight of it. At this point he is in trouble ... caught in the clutches of "the death spin".

Basic Strategy

Two quick things about strategy. The more you understand it, the more comfortable you will be with three other people on the court, and more safety conscious as well. Also, the more you know about your intentions, the less you'll feel haunted by the evils of indecision. In singles, matches are won by exposing an opponent's weakness until he gives in. The same holds true in doubles. While it may not be the nicest prospect, doubles matches are won by bombarding the weaker player of the opposing team (aka "the weakness") with as many shots as possible. Barring that, expose and exploit individual weaknesses, as with the serve.

If both players are equal in ability, then you must concentrate on playing basic racquetball doubles strategy, attempting to freeze one of the players. To do this, try to move one of the players to an extreme position inside his coverage zone. Once done, hit the next shot again into his coverage zone, but to a point too extreme for him to retrieve.

For example, you can move one player into a deep corner and follow up with a kill shot into the front corner of his coverage zone. I know, it looks easier on paper than in actual practice but you'll get the hang of it quickly.

Here are a few more guidelines

Hit the kill shot, and all shots for that matter, at photon pace. Even a miss-hit ball missed at torpedo speed will be difficult for opponents to handle. A softly hit kill shot, on the other hand, takes longer to bounce twice, and gives the opposition a few extra milliseconds to move in and return the ball.

Hit a lot of pass shots and hit them hard. They reduce the do-or-die pressure of a kill shot, and they also cross over the opponents' lines of responsibility, exposing grey areas of indecision. And, of course, as in singles, the pass shot drives an opponent deep into the rear court, where it is difficult for anyone to be accurate.

Racquetball's 01' Faithful, the ceiling ball, is a great way to slow down the rally and open up center court for comfortable occupation. Also, in order to win off a ceiling ball, the opposition must be pinpoint accurate. Thus, the ceiling ball seriously limits their shot options as well.

Here's an advanced tip: Whenever possible, hit the ball on the fly, before the first bounce. The ball will be moving before the opposition has had time to react and regain position. They will have little time to communicate and will be forced to hit indecisively, off balance.

Conclusion

This thumbnail summary is meant as a guide, not a bible. Let's face it, the fast pace of doubles makes it pretty tough to consult this article during the fury of a rally.

The thing to remember, above all else, is safety, which comes from a command of the game. Second to that, you should do everything possible to keep returning the ball to the front wall before it bounces twice. All the techniques, strategies, pills and magic elixirs are useless if you fail in this one regard. Hopefully, this article has defined the techniques to maximize team strengths to get you closer to that end.

(A version of this article appeared in *National Racquetball* / March 1987)

Doubles Trouble

Q: *There's a repeating occurrence in doubles when a shooting player is off to one side in deep court, and his partner and opposing side player joust for position in front court to cover the shot. It becomes elbows and kicks, whereas I try to explain to them that front court positioning should be a beautiful dance. The players of the covering team not shooting take front court, and after they make their return they give ground to the opponents to cover their hit. It's an exchange of position. It's about being fair. Instead, a battle ensues for position in front of the service box. How do I teach how to waltz on that prime real estate? I'm tired of being blocked myself when I have the right of way.*

A: What you describe is exactly the crux of doubles. It's the one strategic focus that wins or loses the games. It's been argued for ages because there's a 'fair' and a 'winning' way to do it. If I understand correctly what you're saying, the situation that occurs over and over per rally is:

> One player of the shooting team takes a deep court shot that brings to prominence the position of the shooter's partner and his side's opponent. The 'fair' way is for you're the front player of the shooting team to give his side rival an opportunity to cover your shot. The 'winning' way, however, is for the shooting team front player to physically or visually (and partially or completely) block his side rival from covering the shot up front.

In the Golden era doubles pro football players took to the court wearing mouth guards and sweats. The sweats were to enlarge the legs and absorb winning shots.

It is an unarguable given that the rules and ref cannot control the situation.

So, what pans out is that either all players are fair and the beautiful 'dance' that you describe ensues, or one player is so intent on winning that he blocks the front rival that is such an advantage that it certainly wins the game... unless the other players adjust and begin blocking. Then the dance becomes a wrestling joust in front court. There's a beauty to that too, but it's called hardball.

There is no other answer except to start playing the game with the 'fair dance', encourage it among the other three players, and then if they reject it by blocking then let be the bigger, stronger, faster and nastier team dominate the front line. Sooner or later, like an NFL line, the defense and offense come to a silent agreement over a bit of blood and bruises of just how far to press their advantage, or a pecking order is established.

The foregoing has been for tournament play. However, for practice simply explain before the game or after the first bump what you've described that the partner of the shooter and

415

his side rival circle around each other giving the person whose partner is not shooting the ball the opportunity to cover the front court. As each shot progresses, one player steps in front, then the other player steps up. They go around rather than through each other and one gives the other room to circle. To orchestrate this you may have to stand the four players on the court without the ball and walk through a dozen times before it 'takes'.

The Siamese twin team of Strupp-Rassenti were the dominant team to beat in Canada in the early 80s. This photo of Heather and Dena was taken at Club 230 at the 1983 Canadian National Doubles that she won. (Courtesy Dena Rassenti)

Tournament

Rob Hoff and Rocky Carson after their comeback victory in the 2013 WOR Doubles Final. (Augustin)

Muehleisen's Rheostat

Bud Muehleisen won a record 69 national and world championship titles. I once went in his attic and found stacks of trophy plates removed (the cups donated to kids' charities), and a thick scrapbook that opened with a clipping, 'Birdy Basher Bud Muehleisen wins Navy championship'.

However, what caught my attention was a certificate for #1 standing in his university dentistry clinic. I asked, how, and what's the relationship to sport?

Dr. Bud gazed down through spectacles and said, 'Players can learn a lot about their games, and lives, by examining personal intensity on the set-up and swing.

'The most important place for a personal rheostat is on the swing. Strokes aren't knee-jerk reactions that turn on or off. Slide the action along an intensity from low to high. Try two things: Increase swing force just 10% on a few shots, and see what happens. Then, lower swing force by 10%, and think about it. The adjustment one way or the other should prove beneficial.'

You may tinker with stroke intensity on the whole, or by dissecting the many variables: A change in overall body tension, a sharpening mental focus, altering the body coil or wrist snap, step into the ball, and so forth. Work on the variables one-at-a-time.

Yet, the normal method in a tournament match is to adjust the stroke rheostat remotely by psyching up or down a tad (start with a 10% change). The body will follow suit with a resultant smoothing out of swing. This corrects the three most hideous errors in crucial rallies- over-hitting, under-hitting or fainting away.

It accordingly zeros in on three court personalities: the *Good*, *Bad* and *Ugly*:

- The *Good* jovial lazy bones slaloms between hits for fear of stepping on his opponent's toes and upsetting karma. There have been *Good* champions in all sports from Mike Ray in racquetball to boxing's great Joe Lewis.

- The *Bad* player is so wound up by the coin toss that he doesn't wind down until match point. He operates at such high intensity the match becomes an attrition of energies. Sudsy Monchik's patented strategy to 'turn up the heat' from first serve increasing to last, won an unprecedented 50 pro tournaments.

- The *Ugly*, like big-time wrestlers, employ ostensibly whacko rheostats to turn each sporting moment to unpredictability. People do not want to be near you when you act crazy.

Muehleisen famous forehand with the Ektelon 'Dr. Bud'' autograph. (1972, age 40, Muehleisen)

If you're not already a champ, how can Muehleisen's Rheostat carry these racquet personalities to greater success? What are the defenses?

The *Good* should take an intensity supplement on shot setups, that trickles to other areas of the court. It yields instant results for languid players who shift just one higher gear on setup, swing, mental attitude, and court scramble. Curiously, it produces a style displayed

419

by legendary Cliff Swain gliding about the court until planting for the swing, and he lightly jerks to focus.

The *Bad* should maintain his excellent high intensity throughout the match, except regulate it down (10%) on the swing to avoid over-hitting. Slowing the swing a tad relaxes the body a lot.

The Ugly is a tough crack, but I'll clue you that champs like Hulk Hogan and Charlie Brumfield own fine control over their irregular rheostats to orchestrate show to victory. You may enhance personal nuttiness by playing for bets, against gorillas, or simulations of tournament pressure.

The defenses against each of the three are reversing their rheostats. Turn on the heat with drive serves, harder shots, and body contact against the dopey *Good* player to shake his strategies. Turn down the intensity against the *Bad* competitor who hates a slow game of lob serves, ceiling shots and timeouts. Finally, ignore the antics of the *Ugly* who, given a driving, extended three-game match, melts in the back corner like the Wicked Witch of the West.

Dr. Bud's Rheostat worked for me.

Physical vs. Mental Errors

It's tournament time in Racquetown, USA. where ten courts arranged in two rows with a gallery plank above and between them is about to bust open with first serve. The left row hosts the beginner through Open divisions, and the right is strictly pros and racquetball Legends. Soon, we'll take a comparative squint at their physical vs. mental errors, and intentions.

The first two terms are my inventions, but intentions have been with us since the first Neanderthal raised a club for advantage.

Physical errors occur when you miss a shot due to a bad footwork, poor swing, or anything not having to do with a mistake in shot selection. Players make physical errors all the time, and it's no big deal, they say. It's true that a corrective lesson, plus practice, insure a diminishing chance of repeating physical errors.

On the other hand, mental errors are faulty brainwork, usually in shot selection. You should have taken a specific shot from a certain court position, but for some reason did not. These errors may be corrected instantly by an assertion of will, even inside tournament pressure. However, unnoticed or uncorrected mental slights become losing habits.

Let's stage the two types of errors before we look in on the action at Racquetown.

Physical errors:

1. You take a forehand back wall shot and miss a killshot because you were tired. This was the ideal shot but it skipped, hence a physical error.

2. Your step up to volley your opponent's lob serve, but your return zooms off the back wall for a plum setup. The analysis is that you made the proper return attempt, but missed, perhaps because it's a difficult shot.

3. You plant to kill a mid-court shot, a logical thought, and miss it because you forget to step into the ball. You call timeout and sequester in the corner to practice stepping into the ball for a minute, and resume with confidence that you've corrected a physical error. Get the idea?

Paola Longoria! wins the 2014 Paola Longoria Grand Slam Tournament in Mexico for her 137th consecutive match victory using strong strokes, strategies, and few mental errors. (Mike Augustin)

Mental errors:

1. You gaze in front court at an oncoming ball with your opponent behind you, and hit a pass. This is a mental slight, *whether or not* the pass wins the point. The correct shot in front of the rival should have been a killshot.

422

2. A ball lofts softly off the front wall that may be volleyed with one step forward, or floor-bounced three steps backward. You choose the later, committing what Ben Franklin called an erratum, a failure in your systematic shot selection. Always step up to volley whenever possible.

3. It's match point serve as you pause inside the service box to gather courage for a surprise serve to his forehand. At the last instant in the service motion, you psyche out and lift the ball for a safer Z-serve that scores an ace. Nonetheless, this is a mental error, so keep your victory speech short.

At the lower skill level, every rally is fraught with physical and mental errors, and the general rule is the first player to correct them via lessons and practice advances to a higher division. He'll still make a few correctable physical errors in progressing on to the pros, where the rule is no physical errors. It's all mental.

\what can you do right now from an armchair to discipline physical and mental errors? Order the mind to be content after a lost rally using perfect shot selection, since a physical flaw has been unearthed to practice.

Also, swear to reinforce regret after poor shot selection wins a rally, since its repetition loses ensuing volleys. Unrecognized mental errors become physical habits over time that takes long practice cures. Worse, mental errors explained away because of won points pave a path to an irrational life.

Physical vs. mental errors is about delayed gratification. Try a game where you and your opponent agree after each rally to pause five seconds to reflect on each other's mistakes. Identify the physical and the mental ones. Watch them diminish until the play advances to intentions, talked about shortly.

Physical, and especially mental errors, steamroll from inside to off the court, and into your future. A single erratum now may domino to knock out of a lifetime deal anywhere. This is why it's important after a match to sit down with a Gatorade and pencil, and analyze your repeating physical and mental errors. List the physical ones in a column on a sheet of paper, with a remedy practice drill next to each. List the mental ones in a second column, and next to it a vow or trick not to do it again. Some methods to clear up the mental error column are mantras, mental rehearsal of the right shots, and practicing correct shot selection with a partner who agrees to end the rally, and thus a point against, the first player to use incorrect shot selection.

It becomes apparent that for any given shot the permutations are:

1. No physical or mental error

423

2. Physical + mental error

3. Physical error only, or 4) Mental error only. Charting these helps open door #1 to victory.

What's more important in the overall game: physical or mental errors? Rookies who conquer physical errors such as a poor grip or slow backswing go on to win. Yet, as the skill level heightens with fewer physical errors, mental play keys in. He who commits fewer mental faults then wins.

Strive for errorless games with stick-and-carrot tricks. The most common beginner folly of protecting a weak backhand by running 'around' it for a forehand, or by hitting the ball with into the back wall, is quickly fixed by racquetball's premier early coach, Jeff Leon. For each mental error, the player must drop to the hardwood and do ten pushups. He concurrently praises positive actions.

Intermediate players may place a small pot in a rear court corner, next to a roll of nickels. The house rules are: 1) When you make a physical error, put a nickel in the pot. 2) For every mental slip put in three nickels. 3) Take a nickel out for every point scored. Now, can you get to 21 points before losing all your change to the pot? Want to bet?

Almost flawless Cliff Swain in 2013. (Augustin)

I threw carrots and sticks at myself on the court for years hinged on an updated list on my locker of physical and mental errors, till the career autumn as uncovered balls began bouncing twice beyond my reach. Frankly, toward the end, it was easier to store errors in mind as there were so few. Often a rally, game and match- but never a full tournament- passed with zero physical and mental errors.

One lesson from the chart was there is absolutely no such thing as an 'off day' that millions of sportsmen across America fondly lament. Once you peak in a sport, where no further physical training beyond maintenance is required, and the strategies are understood to eschew mental slips, you may *not* perform badly. What the people are describing as bad days are unrecognized or uncorrected physical and mental errors.

I carried that hypothesis into a ruinous first game at a Madison Pro stop. Nervy Ken Wong had burst into the pro ranks as the first successful Chinese player who used an inscrutable service motion to lob or drive. He stood like a statue in the service box and looked long up into the lights, tossed the ball nearly to the ceiling, and struck a perfect lob or drive serve with one deceptive swing. I couldn't do anything right against him, and the gallery hooted Chinese hex. I exited the court after the first game loss, just not grasping why shots went crooked. I reached into my gym bag for water only to feel slime- a bottle of Prell shampoo had broken coating the racquet grip with soap. I grabbed a spare racquet with a dry grip and re-entered the court for a showdown win. Some mistakes are committed before one enters the court and need to be corrected to take the streaks out.

My peak performance among about 1000 tournament matches was against Mr. Racquetball Marty Hogan at his peak on the front wall-glass exhibition of the Denver Courthouse. In the first game, I made no physical and no mental errors in a state of high difficulty due to the glass and, behind, a sea of bobbing heads screaming 'Hogan!' mixed with Marty's invisible power serves. The ball disappeared into someone's mouth, and suddenly was upon me. After losing the first game, in the second I made one physical and no mental errors. I lost my best match ever- the one that on any other day would have beaten myself-. 21-20, 21-19. I kept my chin up as my opponent was physically and mentally tortured.

It's a ball-buster to run around the court against an unerring human machine. He is the 'control' in the sport experiment, and you are the variable. His game is unchanging, so how you stack up depends entirely on *your* play. These champs are called Walls, and are invaluable to lose to, or win against, since they identify your mistakes.

My favorite brainy quote from the Racquetball Legends as their 2003 historian and psychologist, is from Mike Ray, the Andy of Mayberry with a racquet. He gets things done, and quietly. He beautifully describes playing one game against himself, and another against the opponent, simultaneously. 'When I'm on the court I have a strategy that I know if I execute well and the opponent doesn't do anything special, then I'll win. I just hit my shots, repeating the situations I've been in a thousand times before, so surprises are rare in a year. I ignore the score and let the ref keep it because it has no bearing on my shot selection. Often, my opponent walks off the court and I'm left holding the ball, until the ref yells, 'You just won the tournament!''

Now let's look in on the play in progress at Racquetown. Glance up-and-down the courts of beginners on the left, and pros on the right, and tally the number of physical vs. mental errors per rally per player. Among the 'C' players, each makes both errors on nearly every shot, so the games are long, sweaty rallies. (Racquetball survived early growing pains because of this.) At the 'B' level, see about half as many mistakes. At the 'A' level, the physical errors are ironed out but mental errors abound each second. In the Open division, we see only one physical error by each competitor per 4-shot rally, but two mental ones.

Examine your game from all angles for physical and mental errors. Bill Sell at the National Doubles, circa 1987. (John Foust)

Then turn around and peek into the pro courts. A player only loses a rally who makes an error in shot selection that the rival invariably rekills. Most pros, except one in an epoch, make one mental error every two rallies.

Leave Racquetown knowing there's room for betterment through awareness and practice.

The professional level of anything is all about intentions. Locke said, 'Intention is when the mind, with great earnestness, and of choice, fixes its view on any idea.' In sport, you study the opponent's face, hands, gait and grace to quietly determine how he will act the

426

next split-second. What is his design? How soon does the scheme dawn on him, and how long before he physically reaches a point of no return and executes it? Observing these signs is to predict *first* intent, and make a counter even as, or before, he moves.

The opponent, of course, is looking you up and down the same. Hence, second intent evolves during first; a counter to a counter.

Intention is stretching the mind toward an object, and with practice you will anticipate a competitor's actions before he does. I learned the most about intentions in 3500 straight non-drinking nights in bars studying drunks, along miles of speechless dog and cat kennels, and trails of survival around the globe.

How far intentions reach is problematic: 1st... 5th... in chess predicting ten moves ahead blindfolded. Keep grounded that second intention is reference to signs, properties, guesses and relations among first intentions. Sequentially, third intent is established during second, and so on. Then decide how far you can or want to go.

Most people use intention sequences all the time, without realizing it. Let's look at a model of sport intentions to apply to business, dating and walking under dim streetlamps. Fencing intentions are described by the *tactical wheel* that teaches that each tactic will defeat the one before it, and be defeated by the one following. The fence, racquet rally, business negotiation, courtroom unfolding, early romance, political race or street brawl is an endless game of Rock/Paper/Scissors revolving around guessed intents by the players. (Rock breaks scissors, scissors cut paper, paper covers rock, and so forth.)

By assuming the opponent's attack while planning yours, you make a choice what move to use in the bout. That's first intent.

When you study the other's first intent in order to plan yours, you assume he is doing the same, and may alter your next move in what is called second intent. If your foe also notes your second intent, it progresses to third, and so on.

Intention doesn't play a large role in boilerplate sport and business, but it's the wild West throughout history for world beaters like Charley Brumfield, Amarillo Slim, Henry Kissinger, Thomas Jefferson and Perry Mason.

In other words, if one of them presents scissors, you can choose rock, and if you guess he or she will choose scissors again, you may assume he's picked something else for the next round, and so forth, perpetually altering your tactics.

In fencing, the first attack is certainly false, making the opponent perform a parry-riposte, while the real attack is a timed stroke against the opponent's riposte. In boxing, the first lesson from the horsehair mat is left jab, right- cross and Palooka's uppercut through a hole. Gunslingers at nineteen paces rely on multiple intent to shoot accurately first.

The problem with hitting on first intent, which is a euphemism for a 'model stroke', is that it's easily anticipated and countered. I favor second intent *only*, feeling that to journey farther into third intent against superior intellects that I'm accustomed to squaring off with, is suicidal.

This was the sweat-lesson, evening after evening for two hours, in the upstairs dungeon Michigan State University racquetball courts. No one could see me. I descended every couple of months to bash around in an intramural or fraternity contest, got clipped, and trudged up the steps again. Then one evening I thought of intention, without knowing the word. The next decade of championships in paddleball and racquetball relied on the exclusive stroke strategy of secondary intent. In setting up to swing, I always stepped, looked and angled the downswing (till the instant of ball contact) in precisely the *opposite* direction the ball was going.

For example, every right-hand killshot to the right-front corner began with a step into the ball cross-court, looking left, and striking the ball waist high. The technique runs tearfully counter to standards, but I wanted to better that, and so build strong first intent into the stroke to fool opponents. My killshot to the right front corner looked like the model stroke of a cross-court drive to deep left. The white lie, forehand and backhand, repeated millions of times in exhibitions and tournaments in a dozen countries without, I believe, anyone reckoning it.

The problem with third intention, and beyond, is that a mental state and stroke built on too many camouflages breaks down with physical exhaustion. Keep it simple, I reminded myself, and win, until *all I could do* for years is hit second intent shots even after knocked semi-conscious by a ball. In the more poised competitions of baseball and attorney work, you may safely extend into fourth or fifth echelons, reading the opponent's body language and 'mind' to establish his chain of intentions, and evolve your counters.

There's no riddle a computer poker, Jeopardy, or as once I was interviewed by a psychiatrist program, cannot solve. Cold hardware, given the proper juice and circuits, surpasses human. However, bloodless machines move pitifully in tennis shoes, and will never beat a racket player.

So, who are the best of the short line of court sport thinkers in history who committed the least physical *and* mental errors, hence the strongest 'intentors'? The list embarrasses since, I believe, built into every cerebral champion is a physiological shortcoming that *trained* his mind. Starting at the bottom, for racquetball:

428

- Ruben Gonzalez
- Bud Muehleisen
- Paul Lawrence
- Peggy Steding
- Mike Ray
- Steve Strandemo
- Mike Yellen
- Jason Mannino
- Charlie Brumfield
- And…

The greatest cerebral player is probably Victor Niederhoffer, who for decades plopped around squash, tennis, paddle and racquetball courts more noisily than I. We met to warm up on a St. Louis court at the 1973 national racquetball tournament, each wearing different colored sneakers. He in a black and a white, and I one red and a black. We eyed each other across the service box with first, second… I don't remember how many intentions. I was playing on a sprained ankle with a Converse Chuck on the hurt right, and a low-cut left. I asked myself, 'What does this guy know that I don't?' We've basically been inseparable ever since. There have been countless matches in multiple sports, evenly split, except I always walked away with an intent headache.

Niederhoffer and I entered a NYC squash court just before New Year's 2011 for a hybrid game using a racquetball and he a child's tennis racquet against my wood paddle. He's loosed up over the years, a hip replacement pops, but it's still hard to force his hand by intent. He won a tiebreaker to 11-points, but that night I left the court feeling pretty good for once.

1975 IRA National Singles Champion, 1975 Canadian National Singles Champion Wayne Bowes was steady while rival Linsey Myers was inspired at the 1976 Canadian Nationals. (Murray Diner)

Pros Speak from the Box

Pre-Tournament

The champion material is in you. If you have to work to psych up then it's a problem. Make a decision if you want excel.

- Sudsy

It depends on the personality and the mood of the day. I listen to music, from jazz to easy to hard rock.

- Corey Brysman

I'll tell you how to produce a winner. Want to do the best you can, and to be the best.

- Marty Hogan

I have a pre-match routine of treadmill work, stretching, and hitting drills. I always run ten minutes on the treadmill 45 minutes prior to a practice or tournament match to get warmed and loosened up. It works great for me.

- Derek Robinson

Before a tournament:
* I practice daily, even if I don't think I need to. It's good for my confidence level.
* Get at least 7 hours of sleep the week going into it; that's the toughest for me.
* Eat well, no sugar or breads.
* Practice visualizing.
* Keep the stressors low around me - my husband helps out with this. Yeah, Michael!

– Jackie Paraiso

In the hour preceding the match, I stretch, always take a shower, and keep to myself.

- Alvaro Beltran

Kids, don't put the pressure on yourself in a tournament. Take a deep breath instead. Intermediates, mental rehearse. I just spent fifteen minutes on my gym bag with my eyes closed picturing the shots for the upcoming match. Watch me hit all those shots between little deep breaths in the match.

- Ruben Gonzalez

Make a game plan and relax.

- Mike Ray

When I step into a tournament site, I like to know that I've prepared physically, that I have foreknowledge of the draw and have specific plans for serves and shots, and that I'm rested and relaxed.

- Cliff Swain

430

Having a proven game plan is so relaxing that I fall asleep before important matches. For others, to stop pre-tournament jitters try different tricks, find one that works, and use it. But always have a game plan, and a backup.   *– Jim Spittle*

The stunning clue is not that Rhonda's head is about to hit the ceiling but that her racquet is up in early swing preparation for the shot by Kim Ferina at a 2013 WPRO stop. (Mike Augustin)

Preparing in the hours before a tournament is an individual thing. Some psych up and others down. You can practice your shots, mentally rehearse, seek solitude, plan strategy and counter-strategy, sleep, cook in a sauna, or listen to 'Rocky'. If I ever had jitters so bad my hands would shake, I'd hit the first 4-5 shots hard to the ceiling and wait for things to even out. All players put on their shorts the same exact way, but they prepare for tournaments in a private way I can't tell you about.   *- Jeff Leon*

I stretch out in the Jacuzzi or sauna to loosen the muscles and alert the mind of an upcoming shift into high gear. The second part of the preparation is coming up with a game plan that maximizes my strengths, avoids my weaker areas, while doing just the opposite to the opponent's strengths and weaknesses.   *- Dave Peck*

I guess I never lost a match I should have won. I was focused and calm and prepared by absenting myself from the site and players until the game ball was thrown. Certainly between games have your equipment ready in an isolated spot to avoid mingling, and get back on the court with the boost of a couple minute rest. I had that funny thing that I used to do where I'd wear a sock on my right hand so no one would shake it. I wasn't a king or prince who they say that by the time they reviewed a troupe or group they were so energy-less from shaking hands and so forth they couldn't move, but I usually went to the later tournament rounds and had I taken the victory bows and gone into the locker room the same thing would have happened.   *- Victor Niederhoffer*

The best way to prepare for a tournament is to develop pressure in practice sessions. The way I did it isn't recommended, but I had people hit me in the back with the ball when I missed a set-up during the two weeks prior to a tournament. This was called 'butts up'. It might work better to force a habit change while increasing fitness by substituting dropping down for push-ups after each miss. The built-up punishment makes the tournament court less a pressure cooker.   *- Charlie Brumfield*

I prepare for an event by not drinking alcohol, hydrating, eating well, practicing almost every day, but not too much. Nothing that makes my body hurt. Yoga is always good too. It is good to work on the things that need work. Or, things you might need if you play a certain player.   *- Charlie Pratt*

I like to focus on service and service return. I usually get a partner to serve me balls over and over and play rally scoring games.   *– Andy Hawthorne*

From day 1 of recognizing the schedule and seeing the program ahead, I pick up the intensity in my play, in my off court training, in my preparation for the division entered, including the type of court, ball, match format, and the expected competition level, with arranged matches and terrorizing my sparring partners.   *– Ken Woodfin*

Mentally visualize match before I walk on the court - serves, serve returns, etc.
                  – Dave Fleetwood

Late in my career I spent much more effort in preparation, and part of that included mental exercises like meditation, visualization, and guided imagery.   – *Brian Hawkes*

I play a little more, and work out less a few days before the tournament. I also like to get in a day before it starts to get used to the courts and practice.   - *Kerri Stoffregen Wachtel*

Never play competitive 3 days before a big tournament. You need to condition at a lower level and get your mind off the game.   – *Davey Bledsoe*

Eat and rest well.   – *Susy Acosta*

I would be in the best shape possible for the tournament but a couple of days before, just hit by myself to maintain timing. Hitting before a tournament by myself added confidence as I would work on shots and certainly not stop until I felt that I was hitting great.   – *Jerry Hilecher*

I try to not think about racquetball at all and not worry about anyone's expectations. I just play and stay focused.   – *Jose Rojas*

The Live Five Mental Mind Jive

Coach Jim Winterton

One of the most common sense questions I get at every season opener is, 'I'm having a hard time transferring good technique and skills from practice to competition, especially at tournaments. What advice might help me correct this?

I remember one year at the nationals- I am talking with one of the greatest players of all time, and I told that player the same thing- I was having trouble playing under pressure of tournaments and I never used to have that problem. Something was pointed out that should have been so obvious. I had become head coach of the USA team. Naturally people wanted to see how good this old coach was to all these great players. I perceived I had to be on my 'a' game when someone was watching, which is impossible to do. Once I figured it was impossible, I began to play more relaxed.

Now let's transfer my lesson to you. If your practice is not transferring to game results it could be a number of things. The most obvious is technique; many times players get a 'rep' for choking, when actually it is a technique problem. All the mental imagery cannot help you if a game technique such as a nuance of stroke, serve or shot selection needs to improve because it crumples under pressure.

Assuming you have good technique, is it *nerves*? If so, are you warming up correctly? Are you a slow starter? Or are you like I was, trying to play perfectly? Here are a few strategies I have used, and found all of them to work at different times at a 30-plus year career of amateur and age division level racquetball even under hard stares.

Since Racquetball is all about process and not the outcome let's focus on the process by using a group of feedback techniques I like to call, 'The live five mental mind jive!'

1. Play the ball and not the opponent.

2. Play small games to five- when it is over, win or lose, go to another game to 5. (Some players use three points.)

3. Employ a small mantra to get the score (external) out of your mind. Say to yourself 'bounce' when the ball bounces on the floor, and say 'hit' when you hit the ball. (From *The Inner Game of Tennis* by Tim Galway.)

4. Another mantra I have used is to repeat in your mind during crucial spots: M-i-c-k-e-y-m-o-u-s-e--. This tip I blatantly stole from another great player, Steve Keeley, author of the first racquetball book I ever saw, *The Complete Book of Racquetball*.

434

This little trick frees your mind so you are not thinking of outcome; and thus focuses on process.

5. Now the last thing to remember is to practice these techniques; whichever one(s) you choose. Get into your practice match and simulate tournament pressure and practice the imagery and mind freeing techniques above ... and be there!

Angela Grisar's big forehand with level follow through at a 2006-WPRO final. (Ken Fife)

435

The Art of Reconnoiter

Nearly everyone has a flaw that like a rock in a tumbler breaks down after a few tumbles around the court. I recall few players in any sport who didn't have one little thing to examine and exploit. In my own sport of racquetball, historically everyone in the top ten has one chink in their armor.

You just play hard, wait for it to happen, and it does.

The solution is how to reconnoiter a player in sport to discover a-Keeley's tendon. I was a dominant force in racquetball for a decade in the 1970's whose inertia was halted only by stalling and other tricks of gamesmanship. With this all-around eye I could quickly evaluate an upcoming rival to select his flaws in a one minute screen, or even none at all!

Inside the master's mind while reconnoitering is Charlie Brumfield in the Golden Era. (Art Shay)

The most important point of reconnoiter is known to few. There are two types of weaknesses - BP and AP, Before and After Pressure.

1. Before pressure is in the first game when he's fresh physically and mentally in his peak performance. This is an important study in vivo or on video to know how to roll with his early blows.

2. MORE importantly at the PRO level of any sport is scouting when the rival is compromised. Watch him when he is tired, under the gun of game point, or psyched out.

The courts, fields and stadiums are full of the top hundred best when they are fresh, but only one in one hundred of them executes in the final points as well as he did the first ones to become the champion. So, you may scout and beat 99 out of 100 future contestants by studying him in the initial as well as last points of a match.

Every sport has its typical weaknesses that are the ones to look for first in the BP and AP investigation. In racquetball or tennis it's the backhand; in boxing the blind spot; in baseball the first baseman and catcher; for swimmers the dive off the blocks and turns; to fencers the shortest chain parry to a thrust; and among team sports the weakest player. Every sport by definition has its most difficult aspect, and for every participant that is usually the most exploitable.

Sometimes you meet a player who has had the sense from the first day of his career to practice the weakest link in the conventional chain until it becomes his strongest. Then most opponents are fooled. However, with a slightly longer inspection of such a champion the thinnest spot in his overall game is found and shredded. The only players in the fifty year history of racquetball who had zero weaknesses in a truly rounded game were World Champions Mike Yellen, and then Dave Peck, followed by Mike Ray and Jason Mannino, and finally in the superball game by Cliff Swain and Kane. Having no chinks, they could only be defeated by a similar player on a good day. I played in tournaments or practice all but Mannino and Kane, and found only one solution. That was to have an equal well-rounded game and be at least 1% more consistent on each shot. This edge repeated 1000 times in every rally of a match slowly adds up to a sure win.

Examples of Specific Champions

Charlie Garfinkle's backhand fell to 95% when he tired in the pressure cooker. **Victor Niederhoffer** always could hit every shot under any kind of condition, but like **Mike Yellen** you just had to beat him on every front with consistency. **Charlie Brumfield** was unbeatable unless you could tape his mouth shut and stop manipulation of the ref, and then he became a dream instead of a nightmare. **Bud Muehleisen** mule was a curiosity with no backhand on the first or last point, and yet possessed every other tool in the game box that no other player on record has had. You just kept asking him to produce the missing tool.

Dave Bledsoe was inconsistent and if you become a 'wall' he beat himself, but anyone else could lose to him. **Steve Serot** was difficult except for a psych artist like Brumfield who played the ugly game. **Steve Strandemo** was not a gifted athlete, and so was 10% behind everyone else on every shot of the rally, but compensated with hustle. **Ruben Gonzalez** was a perfect player who could only be beaten by a lethal sword like **Marty Hogan's** backhand. Hogan couldn't be touched except with a slow ball, and then he couldn't rock and roll. **Jerry Hilecher** had zero backhand, so in the early chess-like play could be steered around the court. **Sudsy Monchik** like **Jason Mannino** had to be fought toe to toe on each point with steadiness, or be flattened by one swift armament such as **Cliff Swain's** serve.

Examples of Other Sports

On a lower level of play just outside the champion's circle, for racquet sports if you know a player's sports background you'll know how to play him nearly every time. You just read his resume on the program, and it's a done deal in the following manner. *Squash* players like Garfinkle, Niederhoffer and Heather McKay could beat everybody at the top who forgot to capitalize on the universal weakness of squash players repeated to the ceiling. It's the same to a lesser extent with **tennis** players who cannot hit a ceiling shot, but he will know the volley better than you. A *football* player has a meaty forehand and a backhand he thinks is great! but it breaks down quickly because the hand musculature wasn't developed in youth for the backhand grip. *Golfers* like Strandemo and Dr. Bud are tougher coming from that sport with all the grip skills, strokes, hand-to-eye and patience but are defeated by making them pull out their weakest 'club' in racquet sports. An expert *board games* opponent such as bridge or poker never has the time to develop physically to reach the very top. A *race car* driver can't focus for long in a slow drive defensive game. And *Don Juans* lose their knees after a long rally.

A final tip of reconnoiter is always to look for a physical crack in his game, and never for a psychological one. Jimmy Conners, Yogi Berra behind the plate, Walter Samuel in soccer, Sam Huff of football, and Charlie Brumfield all had to work very hard to keep a mental catalog of how to irritate their opponents, and remain clear headed throughout a matchup to know when to implement it.

If you study the art of reconnoiter long enough there is a point where the student 'senses' that he can knock off a top player. That sense is his subconscious telling him to think deeply for the technique. Then, if he studies the art a bit longer, there is a transformation and the method will come to mind. It doesn't ensure a victory, but it's a big lead.

There are thousands of players out there waiting to beat you at your own game whom you will meet, one at a time, throughout a career. The free spirit advances with a lamp of investigation and surveys the ground he'll occupy. You may spot a scout by his confident stride and whistle on the way into the court. In his mind, the game is already played and won.

Reconnoiter comes naturally to an outdoor and indoor champion like Janel Tisinger, hitting here at the 2013 WOR Championships. (Mike Augustin)

How the Average Joe can Become a Pro

Dave Fleetwood #5

You gotta knock off a superstar to become a pro overnight. It's been that way since day one with Steve Keeley, Marty Hogan, Mike Yellen, Jerry Hilecher, Cliff Swain... And I on occasion beat some of them to break into the top ten with a best #5 rating. Once you're in, it's self-perpetuating. You get the better draws and reputation until you become a bad season dropout, which happens as quickly as yesterday.

No one I know of has bothered to explain how to come through as a dark horse.

You have to be a serve and shooter, as I was. Commence with an aggressive serve and hopefully result in an ace or poor return. As soon as the window opens, shoot it. The odds are that you will become a flash in the pan and knock off a superhero to get the recognition you deserve for figuring out the strategy. Then it's a coast for a while with the cream of the crop.

I was a pure serve and shooter, and an aggressive rally player who unfortunately did not always practice what I taught. I've always had a natural athleticism which is a blessing and a curse. As a blessing I could win many matches as I was simply better, but as a curse I thought I could simply walk on a court and win because I was David Fleetwood....a fatal flaw in my thought process. You strive past the winner's tape and not become complacent. Then you can play with the pros picking up their tricks and become another King Kane on the lookout for the washouts like me.

But I was there, and know how it is as no one else, because I was also 'not there'. Following a national ranking, I got teaching gigs wherever I wanted. I taught camps, clinics and exhibitions where I would focus on the basics. I emphasized the only real difference between a Pro and Am... the pro executes the basics more consistently.

The Basics

· The first basic is the **Serve**. This is the one time when you are in total control, select where you stand, and execute a specific serve that dictates the opponent's return allowing you to control the point. The serve is not **a** means of start the rally but a way to end it. I always had an ace in front of my mind on the motion, and in the back a weak return.

· **Return** – Simple. If the ball is below the waist with time to shoot, make the play. If it's above the waist, hit the ceiling.

440

·	**Unforced Errors** is the strategy after the serve-and-shoot. The rally should have ended during the service or return, but if not I played errorless ball. Twiddle the thumbs until the first opportunity to shoot, and kill the rally. There were no miracle shots in my repertoire, so the percentages were 2 of 3 in my favor of leveling the playing field during the rally.

·	**Home court Position.** I pound home the middle position and racquet preparation. Position in a location that eliminates many of the intruder's shots but allowing them several options without an avoidable called. I crowded the porch.

·	**Drill with Intensity** – none of the long hour nibbling at life like there's nothing else to do. I prepared against my idols by drilling in 45 minutes what took them 1.5 hours.

It's really a simple game...as they say keep it simple stupid.

The Author's National Racquetball Club (NRC) Profile in 1979: 'David Fleetwood Memphis, TN 4-22-57 Right handed, second year on tour, sponsored by Ektelon. A young serve and shooter who has come out of the pack to rank #5 going into the Nationals. Superb second half of season led by vastly improved backhand. Quickness and natural ability should lead to a great future with forehand shooting providing the base of repertoire.'

Dave was also Rookie of the Year for International Professional Racquetball Renovation (IPRR) in 1977, the year Elvis died. Fleetwood had been a member of the mid-70s 'Elvis and the Memphis Racquetball Mafia' who played racquetball and football with Elvis.

David gave everyone on tour a scare at one match or another. He was never a Bledsoe, Brumfield or Yellen, but you don't make it to number 5 without having some good events and years. For this consistency the aspiring player may identify with his strategies and methods in trying to knock off the superstars.

'I started to play racquetball in 1974 where there were about 50,000 players. Racquetball was on the verge of a sport expansion like no other. I, like the next 10,000,000 players, immediately became hooked and as a kid I could not wait to receive my IRA Magazine. I loved the game and I could not wait to read what the superstars were doing. It was my dream to make the tour and simply be on the court with these guys I've been reading about. I started to attempt to qualify for events, which I did, and typically I was a sacrificial goat for one of the top four. I had reached the mountain top and gave all of them a scare up there. I had achieved my goal!'

– Dave Fleetwood

Built like a roadrunner, David Horn is the quickest, most agile pro on tour taking a front cross-over step to rekill a ball that is already on the racquet at the 2014 Juarez Open. (Ken Fife)

442

Pros Speak from the Box

Tips to Pros

Two tips for pros: Practice alone, and play top competition. Take that experience to tournaments. If there's no competition in your area, play two-on-one or opposite handed.

- Ruben Gonzalez

You can't substitute tournament play. You gotta play tournaments to play better in tournaments. Teaching pros must remember there are two mindsets: the teaching and the playing approaches. I used to get them confused at times. *- Mike Ray*

You can't practice too much for me. *- Corey Brysman*

Find someone who can help you get to the next level. Perhaps you've surpassed the local competition, and that's where you'll stagnate (unless you're a tenacious solo practitioner) unless you can find a mentor or brain trust. Once you've found that help – a person, camp, the right book or video – commit. Commit to reaching the stars. What I say comes from personal experience. Thank you, Dr. Bud Muehleisen. *– Dave Peck*

You have to practice everything to earn a rounded game without flaws. When you have a single flaw, your pro opponent will discover it and pick on it to win, and everyone will copy them. . But if you have nothing but strengths, you can outlast and pick him apart.

- Alvaro Beltran

I think the number one mistake from the armatures to the pros is not getting back far enough in setting for a shot that you can step into it. I teach to back up so you can move forward to greet the ball with more body inertia in your swing. Play as many pro events as possible, because nothing else will move you farther and faster along the path to becoming a pro. *- Derek Robinson*

Keep working hard, don't give up, and your day in the sun will come. You get out of it what you put into it. Work your behind off training for the event and then you can enjoy playing it! *– Jackie Paraiso*

The biggest need among the pros is to analyze the percentages of their actions. Nearly all of them are so caught up in hitting the great shots that they can on occasion hit that they overuse this greatness. They should consider developing what used to be called in tennis

443

a 'ground game', and a backup strategy.   - Charlie Brumfield

Aspiring pros should look in the mirror at two things: physical condition, and elimination of all weaknesses. The big boys are so equally matched that the edge at the end is who was in better shape, and played with the fewest flaws.   *- Marty Hogan*

Five-time World Champion and color commentator Sudsy reflects in the sound studio that he played hard and had fun! (Michael Williams)

Pause a moment in the service box to consider this is the one time you're in total control and the opponent is not. Make the service 60% of your game strategy by making a point or forcing a weak return every time, even in 'one-serve'.   *- Jim Spittle*

The on-court attitude is something the pros should work hard on. You're setting examples of life patterns for the youth any anyone who watches. You-re considered 'experts' therefore worthy of emulation. Imagine being surrounded by a world of young 'yous'.   *- Jeff Leon*

There's some co-court bickering that can be stopped if you cultivate your own garden and don't worry about your opponent.   *- Victor Niederhoffer*

444

Try to play as hard and have as much fun as me.   - *Sudsy*

Be excellent in all areas of your life - not just racquetball. As you get better, you are more of an influence to others, especially those younger than you. Be a positive influence by treating others well, and appreciate what you have - don't expect anything.
– Brian Hawkes

You win tournaments during the week with preparation. The matches are just tests
– Andy Hawthorne

Have a professional mindset where you get up and go to work, learn the tools of your trade, constantly tweak and improve, carry yourself like a champion, build a physique maximizing your potential, and keep a book on your competitors. In tournaments call your skips, two-bounce gets and avoidables on yourself, and be unsurprised when others don't. Add something new to your game every three months and especially be better after your summer and winter breaks, and have a plan for your workouts, multiple plans for your matches, plans for your practice sessions and arranged matches, and record progress and regress in that notebook. And finally, aspiring pro, give something back by teaching both good and enthused players, as well as do some writing or video training to share your ideas and seek to understand others and their perspectives, inspirations, motivations and belief systems.   *– Ken Woodfin*

Never stop gaining experience.   - *Rhonda Rajsich*

No matter how good a person is in any sport, the time frame for greatness is a short window. Take the game as seriously as you can and make the most of what, for me, was an amazing opportunity which I will never forget.   *– Rich Wagner*

Improve your traveling skills. It is tough battling the elements on the road. Different courts, weather, food, beds, airplanes, etc. Find a routine that works for you and stick to it, no matter where you are. Book your travel early and have everything planned out in advance. Control the things you can control.   - *Charlie Pratt*

Enjoy your journey - You are doing what you love and making a living at it.*– Fran Davis*

Enjoy the travel. I have been to so many amazing places al l because I play racquetball.
- *Kerri Stoffregen Wachtel*

Take care of your body in a very serious way. That will be the difference of years to your career.   *– John Ellis*

Be kind to the little man. "Friendship first…competition second" – Chinese Ping Pong Team.
— *Davey Bledsoe*

Alejandro Landa s-t-r-e-t-c-h forehand at the 2014 Juarez Open. (Ken Fife)

Latin America is taking over the world of racquetball. The pros trickle up from a solid playing mass to occupy six of the Top Eight World positions. The Johnny Appleseed of Latin racquetball for 40 years has been Jeff Leon. He was teaching racquetball on a Panama City squash court to a handful of players and soldiers in 1984 when there were only about 300 players in all of Central and South America. Every Latin has been taught by Leon since he trained the early champions who were emulated by the hundreds of thousands, and now he teaches the teachers and coaches in Central and South America. The Darien Gap should be renamed the Isthmus of Leon, for his influence on the current game is greater than Hogan, Swain, Kane and all the rest of the world champs and coaches rolled into one. In this photo Alejandro Landa defeats Javier Moreno at the 2014 Grand Slam Juarez Open. (Ken Fife)

Listen to your coaches.
— *Susy Acosta*

Stay humble. Respect everyone.
— *Cheryl Gudinas*

The Traits to become #1

1. Genetic gift without which no one gets to a competitive #1.

2. Inclination and time to practice long hours.

3. An organized, analytical chess playing mind.

4. A strong coach or role model is helpful but not necessary.

5. The patience to walk away from drugs, alcohol, romance and secondary influences.

6. A weak peer competition helps but isn't always available.

7. The secret to being #1 in a strong field is an edge, a tiny advantage repeated over and over, to make everyone else below #1.

Who's #1? (Art Shay)

447

Pros Speak from the Box

The Reason for My Success

I have a strong athletic presence on the court from an all-around sports background. I'm fiercely competitive and think just enough on the court to help my physical skills.

- Cliff Swain

Racquetball is fun, and that led to practice and that made me a winner.   *- Marty Hogan*

Solid strokes within a sound pre-game strategy.   *- Mike Ray*

I'm his worst nightmare on the court.   *- Sudsy*

My competitiveness from an ongoing on-court sibling rivalry with my brother made me focused and level-headed in later pro matches.   *- Corey Brysman*

I truly love the game, and work very hard at it. I started at four years old playing strictly indoor.   *- Alvaro Beltran*

I've ridden a will to win through my career, and my backhand has been there.

- Derek Robinson

Court presence, and the ability to convince the opponent that I can impose my will on him.   *- Charlie Brumfield*

The competition, the thrill of competing, the competition… for years.   *- Ruben Gonzalez*

Dedication, hard work, passion and commitment …a DRIVE to be the best.

– Fran Davis

I don't have a magic coaching wand, and the players I coach have to drill the lessons I teach. The more you practice the better you become.   *- Jeff Leon*

I play and practice for self-perfection, and winning is a by-product. To be the best that I can be... that is the question.   *– Jim Spittle*

The thrust of business and sports is to produce products that the average person can buy, and I came from snob's game of squash and found racquetball an invigorating replacement. The first shirts that were produced were cotton for the workers in the textile factory, not silk. You might say whatever success I gained was at the expense of the stick and temptation of the carrot.   - Victor Niederhoffer

The 'first' National Racket Ball Champion Bill Schultz (left) defeated Bill Schmidtke at the 1968 first National Rackets Tournament at the Milwaukee Jewish Community Center. (US RB Museum)

Racquetball's Elusive Triple Crown

Keeley with Jim Spittle

Many tried, a few came close, but only two players wore the Racquetball Triple Crown.

The goal of the top competitors in the early days of the sport was to one day become 'the Holder of All Titles'- no player had never won national racquetball singles, paddleball singles, and outdoor racquetball singles championships..

Similar accomplishments in other sports have turned athletes into legends such as Secretariat winning at various distances on all three different racetracks, or Rod Laver winning four majors on three surfaces in one year to capture The Grand Slam of Tennis. In no sport has this mastery of all competitions been tougher than in racquetball.

Charlie Brumfield was the first to achieve this herculean racquets-paddle feat and still proudly answers to his nickname, 'The Holder'.

Brumfield alone is the only player ever to hold a career Triple Crown in *both* singles and doubles. He first captured the 1968 and 1969 Paddleball National Doubles titles with partner Dr. Bud Muehleisen, and added the 1969 and 1970 Paddleball National Singles Titles. He won his first official IRA National Singles Championship in 1972 and first official IRA National Doubles Championship in 1973 teamed with Steve Serot. Brumfield later added four more National IRA and NRC Singles Championships and two more National Doubles Championships on the indoor racquetball courts. To complete his Triple Crown, The Holder won the singles titles at the 1974 and 1975 Outdoor Racquetball Nationals, and doubles in 1974 teaming with trusted partner Muehleisen. Brumfield would never again play the outdoor events leaving him undefeated under the sun, and the holder of career Triple Crowns in both singles and doubles and a second Triple Crown in singles- an accomplishment unlikely ever to be matched.

Marty Hogan was Brumfield's polar opposite on the court with one exception: they ferociously always seemed to find a way to win. Brumfield looked at racquetball as a physical game of chess where his racquet carried out strategic moves he learned from Grand Masters Carl Loveday and Bud Muelheisen to put opponents in Checkmate.

Hogan approached racquetball as a game of checkers where his unparalleled athletic ability and power allowed him to jump over every player on the board until he was King.

The mismatch styles earned the same results.

Hogan dominated as Brumfield had before him. After a 1977-78 season with nineteen out of twenty event wins and National Championships on both the NRC and IPRO Tours, Hogan set his eyes on the only title he didn't have, the Triple Crown.

From October of 1978 until December of 1979 Hogan appeared unbeatable. He went over a year without losing a single match while playing four versions of the game. In the process Hogan won his second consecutive NRC Pro National Championship,, and then went outdoors and beat all the top three-wallers to win the 1979 Outdoor Nationals. The final leg of the journey took him into unfamiliar territory. In order to win the third jewel of the crown Hogan would have to beat the best using the heavy paddles, slow balls and long rallies that are part of the Paddleball Nationals.

Hogan showed up in Ann Arbor, Michigan without the prerequisite experience and yet with athletic prowess, superb conditioning and sheer determination won his first Paddleball National Championship to earn the only single season Triple Crown in the history of the sport. I remember because he edged me out of what would have been my sixth National Singles and eighth overall Paddleball National Championship.

The only Triple Crown Winners in history reunite at the 2013 US Open: Marty Hogan and Charlie Brumfield. (Roby Partovich)

The Mythical Racquetball G.O.A.T.

Few historians of any sport endure long enough to actually see in live action the legendary competitors they write about. Having started my racquetball journey well over forty years ago, when Leach and Ektelon were California backyard industries pumping out a racquet a day, when the handfuls of players at YMCA's strewn across the USA used wood clunkers in but two national tournaments per year that we hitchhiked to and lived on hospitality room grub and couches to try to win a T-shirt and little cup… in the sport of racquetball that is just over fifty years old, I can honestly say I have seen all the greatest players play with my own four eyes.

That doesn't mean with certainty that I can pick out the greatest of them all. The problem in making this determination is an inconvenient truth that the fifty year old game has evolved so much over the last four decades that it's next to impossible to compare one era to the next.

The racquets have grown to double head size, much lighter and better made. The strings are strung with 400% more tension than when I hit the court. The doubly faster ball moves like a hummingbird instead of a sponge, the scoring system today is different with shorter games, and many rules changes have obliterated early strategies and given rise to new ones. The sport was and is called racquetball but the greatest players throughout the four eras really played different games.

What I can objectively deliver is a comparison of the very best, and the best of the rest, of each era… and maybe you can decide who was the *greatest* of them all.

We can divide racquetball in to four distinct eras since the first national tournament in 1968. Each with its own version of the game, personalities, strategies, equipment, rules, and one great champion. The *Pioneers* competed from the first National event until the mid-seventies. The players of the *Golden Era* vied from the mid-seventies through the eighties. The *Modern Era* of the sport consisted of the nineties to the mid-two thousands. The *Current Era* is the last five years through the present 2013.

We will examine the champion and top ten contenders of each era of racquetball. Of course, some long-lived players crossed eras, but I have listed each in the era he most identified with, and no player is listed in more than one era for this exercise. Once we journey through racquetball history and its best competitors, you will have as much information as any authority on the sport to form an opinion on who is the Greatest of All Time. It will be an informed opinion based on decades of history, and I believe your truth is your truth and you're entitled to it.

The Pioneer Era

Still Smokin' after all these years! 2003 in Miami. (Legends)

The pioneers of championship racquetball were more often described as Docs than Jocks! We played sweaty chess, a slow strategic contests won by the smarter player and not the best athlete. We played with an extremely slow ball with wood frame and new-fangled

453

medal racquets strung at less than fifteen pounds tension in two out of three games to twenty-one point marathons. The ball only moved 90mph and typical rallies went six or eight shots before a point ended. How accurate was the Doc moniker? Well, five of the top ten of the era and numerous contenders just off the list had Doctoral level degrees in medicine, dentistry, law, psychology, and in my case veterinary medicine.

The hands down Champion of the Pioneer Era was Charlie Brumfield. Bill Schmidtke's forehand was slightly better than Charlie's, my backhand was superior, Steve Serot ran circles around the bearded wonder, and in a nutshell Brum wasn't especially graceful. However, the one thing he did as much as the rest of us combined was to win. Charlie Brumfield was the most intelligent, determined competitor in the history of our sport, and would and did do anything and everything to win. He invented the Sword and Shield method of play to protect a weak backhand, the donkey kick to clear central court, the crack ace with Carl Loveday's, ushered in the ceiling and around the wall balls, utilized referee bullying, crowd management and sending soiled doves to upcoming finalists' rooms at the midnight hour. Charlie was known as The Holder of All Titles which was accurate. He won multiple IRA National Singles and Doubles Championships, multiple National Invitational titles in doubles and singles, and when pro tournaments rolled around in 1973 three Pro National titles on tour, and a pair of Outdoor National singles and doubles championships. He beat all of the best in the biggest competitions of our era including a twenty consecutive tournaments streak. That's saying something among the Docs.

Just behind him, the Top Ten Contenders of the Pioneer Era in no particular order: Bud Muehleisen, Bill Schultz, Bill Schmidtke, Craig Finger, Paul Lawrence, Steve Keeley, Steve Serot, Mike Zeitman, Steve Strandemo and Ron Rubenstein.

The Golden Era

The Golden Era was aptly named at the highest point in the history of our sport. The game was evolving in the Golden State California and burgeoning across the nation with the first pure racquetball court clubs, female tournaments, the first pro tours, and Hollywood stepped into the courts. Many of the top players sported in imitation my golden afro and mismatched colorful Chuck's tennis shoes. The game was being played by as many as fifteen million players worldwide. A couple of top professionals made as much as a million dollars in endorsements in one year, *Sports Illustrated* covered tournaments, and some events were nationally televised during prime viewing hours.

The Golden Era game was played with racquets the same head size as the original sticks but much lighter, strung with more tension, and hitting a much faster ball. A plethora of new manufacturers jumped into the sport, and larger racquets were introduced toward the end of the era. The Golden Era game saw shorter rallies with balls blazing at 130mph where the Docs, having little time to think, were supplanted by the pure Jocks. An accurate term was coined that sticks to this moment- Power Racquetball! You see, the new equipment, bulldog player physiotypes and erupting mentalities spawned new strategies and rules. The 21-point games switched to 15-points, the 11-point tiebreaker added, the screen serve was invented and combat by a side wall server line, ceiling shots became vague memories, and legions of thrilled fans urged 'Serve and shoot!' to break the front wall bottom board.

The Champion of the Golden Era, Marty Hogan, was the best athlete of the day and in my opinion the best natural athlete to ever hold reins on the sport. A physical dynamo sporting a golden afro and using the same and sometimes inferior old equipment, he regularly smacked the ball 20mph faster than the next biggest hitter. He hit shots at such speeds as never before that two new ones evolved- the jam serve and splat kill. Marty's unprecedented pendulum power swing smashed with equal power backhands and forehands. His drive serve was the most potent and copied weapon of the day. Hogan was number one of fifteen million players and a dominant personality with the most endorsement contracts in history. He won the Leach NRC Nationals five consecutive times when it was the biggest event in racquetball, plus more total events per annum than any other player for ten consecutive years. At his peak, Hogan went over a year without losing a single match in singles, doubles and outdoors. He even took the paddleball Nationals from me, the reputed legend of wood, to prove he was the second Holder of All Titles and the best of the era.

Just short of him, the Top Ten Contenders of the Golden Era in no specific order were: Mike Yellen, Dave Peck, Jerry Hilecher, Davey Bledsoe, Bret Harnett, Rich Wagner, Craig McCoy, Gregg Peck, Ruben Gonzalez and Ed Andrews.

The Modern Era

The Modern Era was played with big racquets that were both light and powerful, almost identical to the ones used today. The Tarzan players with driving type A personalities vied in three out of five games to eleven with the fast Pro Penn Green ball and a new one serve rule to elongate the serve and shoot rallies. Most of the top players of the Modern Era started in junior competitions during the Golden Era, and many were the offspring of noteworthy racquetball players. The second generation players with their super-sized racquets took the game to a new level with 170mph shots the norm in a pro contest. The swing of the era became less pendulum and flatter with extreme body torque and explosive contact. The fast furious pace demanded early swing preparation using fast twitch fibers and mesmeric alertness. The US Open replaced the Leach Pro Nationals as the gala event of the year.

Passing the Torch – Marty Hogan to Cliff Swain: The King is dead, long live the King! In the Hogan era Marty achieved a 6th and final #1 World ranking in 1989 beating Swain in Oregon and in St. Louis… Both 11-10 tiebreakers! Now Hogan passes the royal racquet to Swain who in the Cliff era wins the first next season of six #1 World rankings. (Photo after the Oregon tourney of Marty Hogan. Hogan center, Swain right.) (Marty Hogan collection)

The Champion of the Modern Era was Cliff Swain who to me resembled a praying mantis stalking and blowing the ball to kingdom come. Swain was a jock like Hogan with less bulk and a half-step quicker, with a fierce will like pioneer Brumfield. In addition to sharing these sports traits of the earlier champions, he was a lefty with a serve that was eclipsed by an eyeblink. Television cameras couldn't follow the ball, much less the service returner. Cliff introduced the flat back-swing, and early swing preparation that is popular today. He won more professional titles than any other player in history, and was the number one ranked player for six years in a testy competitive era. Swain never went a single year without losing a match as Hogan had, and never won twenty in a row like Brumfield, but he was equally impressive in reigning for nearly twenty years from 1985 to 2005 at or near the top of the sport.

The Top Ten Contenders of the Modern Era again not listed in any particular order were: Sudsy Monchik, Jason Mannino, John Ellis, Mike Ray, Drew Kachtik, Andy Roberts, Jack Huczek, Mike Guidry, Tim Doyle and Tim Sweeney.

The Current Era

The Current Era is played almost exactly like the Modern with a couple of improvements. The racquets are still big and getting better every year. The ball frequently travels over 175mph, matches are still the best three of five game. The new Purple Pro ball is a tad slower than the Green of the Modern Era, and the two serves allowed in the original game have replaced the one serve rule. In addition, line judges in big matches watch the serve line and the overall officiating is improved. Jason Mannino, a champion of his own right from the Modern Era, now heads the IRT, and the pro stops have gone international including Canada, Mexico and all over South America.

The Champion of the Current Era is Kane Waselenchuck. Kane is a lefty with a power serve, flat back-swing and early swing prep, and a crushing competitiveness. At the same time he pleases the juniors with trick shots on his knees and behind the back. He seems capable of doing anything on a racquetball court except losing. Kane has lost only once in the last five years, before recently retiring after a match injury. He is by far the most dominant champion within one era in history, and the gap between him and everyone else is vast.

The Current Top Ten Contenders in order after Kane are: Rocky Carson, Álvaro Beltran, Jose Rojas, Chris Crowther, Shane Vanderson, Ben Croft, Tony Carson, Javier Moreno and Charlie Pratt.

Four Eras and Four Champions

So, among the four eras and champs who is the best? Ask yourself: Who holds the mythical Crown of the Greatest of All Time? A simple query may give you the answer to the mystery of the GOAT. Would Kane be just as dominant and rack up undefeated seasons with a prime Cliff Swain, Marty Hogan and Charlie Brumfield? If you believe the answer is yes, then you've answered the question and Kane is clearly the greatest. If you believe the answer is no, the debate is open and your opinion is probably stronger and more informed than ever.

The next G.O.A.T. may be Latin. Dan De La Rosa 2014 Tournament of Champions (Mike Augustin)

Honesty, Cheating and Gamesmanship

Three Game Styles

There are three game styles: honesty, cheating, and gamesmanship. I was too ignorant to cheat in the racquetball and paddleball pros, and tried eight times in winning seven national singles championships during the sports' golden decade of the 1970's... in retaliation to like. The formula was if a rival cheated the first time, let it slide as an oversight; the second time politely point it out; and the third time cheat back or trim his the earlobe with the next shot.

There are three approaches into the court or any sport or business. The traditional was play hard and the best man wins. The second method is win at all costs, tantamount to a war. There isn't necessarily anything wrong with an anything goes contest, however it groups you with birds of the feather. The third is the most fascinating and irritating, gamesmanship. This is bantering and bending the rules, manipulating the ref and hypnotizing the crowd to gain an edge on the court.

The best gamesman in racquetball history was my nemesis Charlie Brumfield, a genius attorney who applies his techniques in the court of law and routinely gets thrown out by judges for quoting Perry Mason or must stand behind a screen before the jury box. The problem is there were no judges as racquetball referees, and hoarse traders earned a point for each cheat and shenanigan until a straight player gave away 10-points in each 21-point game.

There are a hundred tricks. Intentional long servers control the game pace and double the length of matches- the better delayers loft the serve out of reach to the back wall for a long 'fault', and it rolls to the front corner to be fetched at an amble. You squeeze or wet the ball before serving to make it knuckle and slide. A sweating receiver lingers in one spot until a pool forms, and the next time serves into it. Physical intimidation in blocking opponents or the ball, striking him with the racquet, ball, elbow, or in combination agitates. The 'donkey kick' was in vogue where a player jumped and kicked backward into the foe's midsection to propel himself to front court. Before a national doubles championship an ex-professional football player approached to wish me well, and quickly slammed my head against the wall. He tried to wish himself well in the match but it didn't work.

The best strategy against a Yankee operator, given a spineless referee and a conscience not to fight him, is stoicism. A strong stoic cuts the gamesman's edge by 70%. The breathing room opens an opportunity to run him with superior shots until he may no longer talk. There has never been a dumb gamesman.

459

Sooner or later the luck of the draw brings on the cruelest strategist and you get fan support. They heckle the clown to fair play, or threaten him during timeouts. There's no need for that. An opinionated girl in the San Diego gallery once sat through the glass in the left rear corner and flashed her underwear every time Charlie Brumfield went for my passes.

The 'referee in the sky' is to distinguish honesty, cheating and gamesmanship. (Legends)

I used to quantify wheeler-dealer moves. When Brumfield threw his racquet cover into the court to hit his opponent's racquet, it was worth the first point. When handball best Paul Haber entered the court wearing boxing gloves and pounded the glass perimeter as the fans outside ducked reflexively, it earned the first game. When Muhammad Ali leaned against the rope and gasped expletives it won the heavyweight crown.

Heads meet at the 2006 WPRO final: Kerri Wachtel vs. Angela Grisar. (Ken Fife)

Pros Speak from the Box

Handle the Psyche

When you opponent gets in your face, stand there and look at him like a used car.
– Jim Spittle

I don't let distractions bother me, and nothing else comes to mind.   *- Alvaro Beltran*

My preference is to just play. I don't get baited into conversations. Strive to get to a level where your game does the talking.   *- Corey Brysman*

It's good! I like to play at a high arousal level, pissed off describes it, so when the other guy tries to psych me only, it properly psyches me up.   *- Derek Robinson*

Bore him to death with a wall of consistency. I don't engage in the verbal 'punk trash' because it takes two to tango and I never provided a partner.   *- Mike Ray*

Nobody's going to psyche me out. I've been on the courts for forty years.
- Ruben Gonzalez

I believe the relationship I have with my Lord and Saviour, Jesus Christ, is what has helped me mentally in my career. I know that He is ultimately in control. I focus on "bringing it and playing my best" and pray that it's His will that I leave the last server on the court.   *– Jackie Paraiso*

It isn't likely to occur.   *- Charlie Brumfield*

There are simple ways to handle the psych artist. You can throw the same psych techniques back in his face, you can remain stoic and wait for him to wither, and if need be a forearm shiver delivers a point.   *– Dave Peck*

Enter the court with a game plan you're convinced succeeds, and execute. - Realize when the other guy starts to try to think for you, he's in trouble.   *- Marty Hogan*

I'm a nice enough guy, but on the court I like to shove it down their throats. Beat 'em, crush 'em, make 'em cry and never want to play me again. When someone like me

462

enters the court at the same time, it's a shoot-out and may the best man remain standing for the applause.   - *Sudsy*

I focus on the job I've rehearsed and done so many times on the court that it's nearly impossible for anyone to distract me. If I'm serious, I pay no attention to him or anything he says or anything else. If he claims my grandma wears black hi-tops or hits me with the ball on purpose, then I try to keep that out of my mind because if I get angry and try respond with grandma's techniques or revert to football tactics, I've not only lessened my likelihood of winning that game but also have to walk off the court ready to practice more focus drills for future tournaments. When I see one of my players start to fume, I tell him to call timeout, exit the court, and I talk him down.   - *Jeff Leon*

One of the first things you learn at racquetball tournaments that when someone does something ridiculous or bad to you the he simply hurt you by doing something bad, but if lose your energy by coming back at him then you're hurt twice, and if you *think* about what he did then he's hurt you three times. So, at an early stage of a match that promises to be caustic, cut your losses short and just stop arguing and become a stoic.
                                                                     - *Victor Niederhoffer*

I disengaged from anyone who likes to talk a lot, like pushing in the clutch. - *Cliff Swain*

No issues there, I feel I can still beat anyone on any giving day, including Kane. Probably wouldn't happen, but I believe it could so my confidence is constant.   – *John Ellis*

If you are so good, nobody can dent that.   – *Rich Wagner*

My psyche is like a butterfly, most often floating and then sometimes it's like my tummies full of butterflies, but what I know is what I can do, what I want to do, and that only I can control my spirit, my calm, my fire, my chi, my aura, and my mind or my mindlessness.   – *Ken Woodfin*

Handle psyche the same way as concentration: Breathing!   – *Jose Rojas*

The psyche: Always a battle between positive and negative energy. The more positive, the better.   - *Charlie Pratt*

I didn't have problems blocking outside influences. Most people felt that I was continually trying to psyche out my opponents - the reality is that I didn't have to try as typically they worried so much about it that they just brought it upon themselves. Another aspect of this is that I rarely felt pressure. Knowing that pressure is self-inflicted and controllable, I realized that I was in control of my emotions and rarely

allowed pressure to enter into my cognizance. I was focused on my intent to win the point.
— Jerry Hilecher

I try to stay as calm as possible. No highs and no lows in emotion.   *— Andy Hawthorne*

I was rarely aware of the opponent's presence. I experienced the Zen of Racquetball many times just like the book "The Zen of Motorcycles" - Be one with the game.
— Davey Bledsoe

I stay calm (as calm as possible).
— Susy Acosta

It really doesn't bother me. I know at the end of the day, I am going home to a job, family, and friends. If an opponent has to try to psyche you out, so be it. It rolls off my back.   *- Kerri Stoffregen Wachtel*

I use people's antics as fuel.
— Cheryl Gudinas

Electrified! Bill 'Radiation Man' Gotlib in the winner's circle at a 70s MI tournament. (US RB Mus.)

The First Racquetball National Final!

This picture was taken just before the final match started between Brumfield (20yrs.) and Dr. Bud (37yrs.) at the 1969 1st Open Racquetball Singles Championships in St. Louis at the JCC. Note that Brumfield is using the Joe Sobek 'Wooden Clunker' and Dr. Bud used the Dayton Steele Racket which was double strung with wire strings. Note also that in that day, the ball was so dead that a ceiling ball was impossible to execute. Hence the rallies were lengthy and the games were best of 3 to 21 points.

Each player sands about 6'-even and brought multiple racquet accolades going into the racquetball finals. Dr. Bud held championships in paddleball, badminton and tennis, while Brumfield won them in paddleball and outdoor pink ball handball. Muehleisen captured this final but Brumfield, 17 years his junior, went on to dominate with three national singles titles through the 1970's.

The St. Louis JCC court in this picture is a cornerstone in history as the breeding ground of the St. Louis power hitters Marty Hogan, Steve Serot, Jerry Hilecher, Jerry Zuckerman, Doug Cohn, Ben Koltun and others who took over after Mule and Brum left the sport. The particular court is of further historical significance as it was converted into a storage closet and library after the racquetball boom played out in the 90s. Look at all those racquet scuff marks and paint chips on the walls! Then in 2003 the Legends Pro Racquetball Tour paid to refurbish the court to hold their season's Legends finale, the biggest event in their history. The players in that tournament included most of the forenamed only a step slower and longer in the tooth, making for sensational competition. And so racquetball came full circle to the St. Louis JCC court.

1969 photo at the St. Louis JCC taken just prior to the 1st National Open Singles Final. Charlie Brumfield (age 21) with a Sport Craft 'Wooden Clunker Racquet' and Dr. Bud (age 37.5 and the winner) with a 'Dayton Steele Double Wire Strung Racquet' .... and away they go in the first 'Racquetball championship'. (Bud Muehleisen collection)

Who's Who of the Early Champions

Today, fifty years after the first National Racquetball Champion was crowned, and as ridiculous as it sounds, who was it?

When was it?

Where?

This is the first Who's Who of the sport's initial national champions.

Bill Schultz - Won the first ever National Gut Strung Paddle Rackets Tournament in 1968 defeating Bill Schmidtke in the final.

Bud Muehleisen – Won the first IRA National Championship in 1969 beating Charlie Brumfield in the final

Craig Finger - Won the second IRA National Championship in 1970 defeating Charlie Brumfield in the final.

Charlie Brumfield – Won the first IRA National Invitational Tournament in 1971 ousting Bud Muehleisen in the final. He won the 1972 and 1973 IRA National Open titles.

Bill Schmidtke - Won the 1971 IRA National Championship defeating Craig Finger in the final. He won the 1974 IRA National title defeating Steve Serot in the final.

Steve Serot – Won the first NRC Professional Racquetball Tournament in 1973 beating Bill Schmidtke in final.

Mike Zeitman – Won the first IRA National Doubles title in 1969 with Hyman. He also won the 1971 IRA National Doubles title and National Invitational Doubles Championship with Ken Porco. He won the 1975 NRC Pro National Doubles Championship with Davey Bledsoe.

I played them all and beat them all at one time or another, and from that perspective offer my assessment of my peers from the early racquetball days. All won one or more of the early national titles. It's impossible to answer who's the best. Craig Finger got the better of Charlie Brumfield on most days with a racquet or a paddle by psychoanalyzing Brumfield during rallies. Bill Schmidtke beat Brum to plumpness in the big matches by sending him big boxes of Whitman's Sampler Chocolates the night before the final. However, Brum won more tournaments than both of them put together. Contrarily, I beat both Schmidtke and Finger almost every time but didn't win a single national title. So the best of the best is mythical depending on the equipment over the years. However, one clear thing emerges from the list.

Who is the first racquetball champ? There are three, and it's just that the sport went under different names in the Pioneer days. Bill Schultz is the first national champion but because of the nomenclature has been ignored by the Racquetball Hall of Fame. Bud Muehleisen won the first IRA national championship and is in H of F. Craig Finger won the second IRA nationals but is ignored by the H of F. Steve Serot won the first pro NRC (National Racquetball Club) racquetball tournament and one year ago was inducted into H of F. Mike Zeitman has won numerous national titles to date but is not in the H of F.

National champs like Schultz, Finger and Zeitman being overlooked by the racquetball Hall of Fame is like the baseball Hall of Fame ignoring early greats before it was named baseball.

Those are the first seven national champions of racquetball.

2011 National Paddleball Doubles at San Diego, still California Dreamin'. (Mike Augustin)

468

Shared Championship Phenomenon
Paddleball in Racquetball

The winners of first ten National Racquetball Tournaments all started as paddleball players.

- 1968 Bill Schultz Wisconsin Paddleball Player

- 1969 Bud Muehleisen San Diego Paddleball Player

- 1970 Craig Finger Michigan Paddleball player

- 1971 Bill Schmidtke Wisconsin Paddleball Player

- 1972 Charley Brumfield San Diego Paddleball Player

- 1973 Brumfield

- 1974 Schmidtke

- 1975 Brumfield

- 1976 Brumfield

- 1977 Davey Bledsoe Knoxville Paddleball Player

Also, the first two professional National Racquetball Runners-up started in paddleball.

- 1973 Steve Serot St. Louis Paddleball Player

- 1974 Steve Keeley Michigan Paddleball Player

The conclusion is that not only was paddleball racquetball's older 'ugly sister', but that if one starts, or at least cross-trains at paddleball, the championship racquetball courts draw nearer.

The reasons are the slower paddleball game lays a physical and mental foundation for the faster sport. In the same manner one crawls before walking, paddleball builds strong muscles and reasoning powers so that ten years down the line in a racquetball tiebreaker the muscles respond and the mind brings to action the right tactics.

Hogan was the first player to not learn with wood and reverse from racquetball to paddleball to win national titles in 1979 and 1987 without dropping a game.

A torrid marriage of racquetball and paddleball took place in 2003 with the first ever Hybrid Racquetball Tour featuring the paddleball champs and racquetball legends on the same court hitting for money. I was co-inventor in a long-shot wish to find common ground between a sport that is too slow for the masses and another too fast for its own good. The matrimonial rule was using wood paddles and a racquetball. Every former national paddleball champ had his way paid to coast to coast stops in determining that the Hybrid Game winners were the top racquet champs but from third place down the paddle champs had depth. Both parties preferred their pure sports and after one season the tour disbanded.

Here are the lists of National Racquetball Champions followed by National Paddleball Champions.

Bill Schmidtke, 2-time IRA Professional champ. The game's elder statesman from Apple Valley, Minnesota.

Dual champion Bill Schmidtke early 70s poster.

National Racquetball Singles Champions

* Indicates NRC National Champion

1973-74

1) Charlie Brumfield
2) Steve Serot
3) Steve Keeley
4) Bill Schmidtke
5) Steve Strandemo
6) Jerry Hilecher
7) Ron Rubenstein
8) Mike Zeitman
9) Dan Alder

10) Bill Dunn

1974-75

1) Charlie Brumfield*
2) Steve Keeley
3) Steve Strandemo
4) Steve Serot
5) Jerry Hilecher
6) Craig McCoy
7) Bill Schmidtke

470

8) Rich Wagner
9) Ron Rubenstein
10) Mike Zeitman

1975-76

1) Charlie Brumfield*
2) Marty Hogan
3) Steve Keeley
4) Steve Strandemo
5) Steve Serot
6) Jerry Hilecher
7) Rich Wagner
8) Mike Zeitman
9) Davey Bledsoe
10) Craig McCoy

1976-77

1) Marty Hogan
2) Davey Bledsoe*
3) Charlie Brumfield
4) Jerry Hilecher
5) Rich Wagner
6) Craig McCoy
7) Steve Serot
8) Steve Strandemo
9) Steve Keeley
10) Ben Koltun

1977-78

1) Marty Hogan*
2) Charlie Brumfield
3) Steve Serot
4) Rich Wagner
5) Craig McCoy
6) Davey Bledsoe
7) Ben Koltun
8) Jerry Hilecher
9) Jay Jones
10) Steve Keeley

1978-79

1) Marty Hogan*
2) Jerry Hilecher
3) Mike Yellen

4) Rich Wagner
5) Steve Strandemo
6) Craig McCoy
7) Charlie Brumfield
8) Dave Fleetwood
9) Davey Bledsoe
10) Dave Peck

1979-80

1) Marty Hogan*
2) Mike Yellen
3) Dave Peck
4) Jerry Hilecher
5) Don Thomas
6) Steve Strandemo
7) Ben Koltun
8) Charlie Brumfield
9) Doug Cohen
10) Larry Meyers

1980-81

1) Marty Hogan*
2) Dave Peck
3) Mike Yellen
4) Craig McCoy
5) Jerry Hilecher
6) Don Thomas
7) Rich Wagner
8) Steve Strandemo
9) Bret Harnett
10) Scott Hawkins

1981-82

1) Dave Peck
2) Marty Hogan*
3) Bret Harnett
4) Jerry Hilecher
5) Mike Yellen
6) Rich Wagner
7) Craig McCoy
8) Don Thomas
9) Gregg Peck
10) John Egg

National Paddleball Singles Champions

Year	Tournament Site	NPA Open Singles Champion	Champion's Hometown
1962	Madison, WI	Paul Nelson	Madison, WI
1962	Madison, WI	Paul Nelson	Madison, WI
1963	Madison, WI	Bill Schultz	Madsion, WI
1964	Flint, MI	Paul Nelson	Madison, WI
1965	Ann Arbor, MI	Moby Benedict	Ann Arbor, MI
1966	E. Lansing, MI	Bud Muehleisen	San Diego, CA
1967	Bloomington, IN	Paul Lawrence	Ann Arbor, MI
1968	Minneapolis, MN	Bud Muehleisen	San Diego, CA
1969	Ames, IA	Charlie Brumfield	San Diego, CA
1970	Fargo, ND	Charlie Brumfield	San Diego, CA
1971	Flint, MI	Steve Keeley	E. Lansing, MI

Year	Tournament Site	NPA Open Singles Champion	Champion's Hometown
1972	Knoxville, TN	Dan McLaughlin	Ann Arbor, MI
1973	Eau Claire, WI	Steve Keeley	E. Lansing, MI
1974	Ann Arbor, MI	Steve Keeley	E. Lansing, MI
1975	Livonia, MI	Dan McLaughlin	Ann Arbor, MI
1976	Adrian, MI	Steve Keeley	San Diego, CA
1977	E. Lansing, MI	Steve Keeley	San Diego, CA
1978	Ann Arbor, MI	R. P. Valenciano	Flint, MI
1979	Ann Arbor, MI	Marty Hogan	San Diego, CA
1980	Lansing, MI	Dick Jury	Haslett, MI

Year	Tournament Site	NPA Open Singles Champion	Champion's Hometown
1981	Ann Arbor, MI	Steve Wilson	Flint, MI
1982	Lansing, MI	Larry Fox	Ann Arbor, MI
1983	Ypsilanti, MI	Steve Wilson	Flint, MI
1984	Lansing, MI	Steve Wilson	Flint, MI
1985	Saginaw, MI	Steve Wilson	Flint, MI
1986	Davison, MI	Mark Kozub	Livonia, MI
1987	Ann Arbor, MI	Marty Hogan	St. Louis, MO
1988	Davison, MI	Andy Kasalo	Calumet City, IL
1989	Ann Arbor, MI	Mike Wisniewski	Bay City, MI
1990	Davison, MI	Mark Kozub	Livonia, MI
1991	Saginaw, MI	Mike Wisniewski	Bay City, MI
1992	Midland, MI	Andy Kasalo	Kalamazoo, MI
1993	E. Lansing, MI	Mike Wisniewski	Bay City, MI
1994	Pontiac, MI	Mike Wisniewski	Bay City, MI
1995	Eau Claire, WI	Mark Piechowiak	Bay City, MI
1996	Midland, MI	Mike Wisniewski	Bay City, MI
1997	Midland, MI	Bob Groya	Bay City, MI
1998	Midland, MI	Mike Wisniewski	Bay City, MI

1999	Pontiac, MI	Andy Mitchell	Kalamazoo, MI
2000	Ann Arbor, MI	Andy Mitchell	Kalamazoo, MI
2001	Kalamazoo, MI	Andy Mitchell	Kalamazoo, MI
2002	Livonia, MI	Mike Wisniewski	Bay City, MI
2003	Midland, MI	Mike Wisniewski	Bay City, MI
2004	Ann Arbor, MI	Kelly Gelhaus	Riverside, CA
2005	Ann Arbor, MI	Kelly Gelhaus	Riverside, CA
2006	San Diego, CA	Chris Crowther	Riverside, CA
2007	E. Lansing, MI	Kelly Gelhaus	Riverside, CA
2008	San Diego, CA	Aaron Embry	San Diego, CA
2009	Ann Arbor, MI	Cesar Carrillo	Memphis, TN
2010	San Diego, CA	Mike Wisniewski	Bay City, MI

The most successful modern dual player is pro racquetball's Chris 'The Giant' Crowther who is also the 2006 National Singles Paddleball Champion. (Legends)

473

The First Ten Money Winners in Pro Racquetball

(In sanctioned pro stops of the NRC or IPRO)

Who won the big money? In the first pro stops it is surprising that the first two money winners were young Steve Serot and Steve Bo Keeley in 1973 at the sport's inaugural pro stops. In the chart below, of course, many of the winners took multiple purses but this lists the first event won by each of the first ten players to win a sanctioned event.

The first pro tour was launched by National Racquetball Club (NRC) in 1973. Prior to that event we played for tournament T-shirts and trophies, hitchhiking, busing, freighting and carpooling across the country to the Big Four annual tournaments: National Singles, National Doubles, National Singles Invitational and National Doubles invitational.

The first prizes were about $1000 to the winner, $500 runner-up, and $250 third.

Serot used his purse to get his first St. Louis date with a top girl who worked the JCC cage and became his wife. I bought a '74 Chevy van and drove players to tournaments, including Fillmore Hare, a 7' stuffed rabbit riding shotgun with an invisible fish line attached to his hand to wave down fans to fill the bleachers. And, Charlie Brumfield bought a new luxury Cadillac Seville and took his father around the block.

As a side note in history, the most pivotal unofficial pro event was the 1971 National Singles Invitational at Mel Gorham's Sports Center in San Diego that for the first time brought all the top players together. There was no prize money, however our plane fares were comped and Bud Leach, who was pressing the sport's first fiberglass racquets under his car wheels in a garage, handed each player a new Bandido fresh off the press with $20 bills wrapped around the handles. There were bathing beauties, and the tournament set the tenor and seeds for future racquetball, and many future champions were produced.

Here are the first money winners:

1. Steve Serot def Bill Schmidtke in Houston, TX - September 1973 NRC Houston ProAm

2. Steve Keeley def Charlie Brumfield in Long Beach, CA - October 1973 NRC Long Beach ProAm

3. Charlie Brumfield def Steve Serot in Milwaukee, WI - March 1974 NRC Milwaukee Open

4. Steve Strandemo def Jerry Hilecher in Memphis, TN - December 1974 IRA/IPRO Tanner ProAm

474

The first big money was in the sport's first international clinic tour though Latin America where, here in Bolivia with a two-feet stack of Bolivian currency worth US$250, he is apprehended by the police for trying to exchange it on the black market to buy a meal. (1984 Chelsea George)

5. Marty Hogan def Steve Keeley in Burlington, VT - October 1975 NRC New England ProAm

6. Rich Wagner def Bill Schmidtke in Buffalo, NY - May 1976 NRC Buffalo Open

7. Jerry Hilecher def Steve Strandemo in Chattanooga, TN - May 1976 IRA/IPRO Nationals

8. Davey Bledsoe def Charlie Brumfield in Memphis, TN - December 1976 IRA/IPRO Tanner ProAm

9. Dave Peck def Davey Bledsoe in Memphis, TN - December 1979 NRC Tanner Coca Cola classic

10. Mike Yellen def Marty Hogan in Beverly, MA - April 1980 NRC Seamco Classic

Who makes the big money now? Rocky Carson in center court at the 2014 Pro Kennex Tournament of Champions (Mike Augustin)

476

From towel boy to millionaire, Marty Hogan shouts his mating call, 'I am the Greatest!' (Legends)

Smokin' Hogan Wins First Pro Stop

Marty Hogan inserted 'Smokin' into his name at his first pro win in 1975 at Burlington.

Going into the finals he had never made a previous pro quarters and was unknown but had an easy knack with people. In an instant the gallery shifted attention from me to Hogan.

He slapped off a dozen jumping jacks making clown faces out the aquarium glass at the howling spectators. He popped off a dozen push-ups over the short line. He sprinted to the right front, left front, left back and right back corners leaping in the air and screaming, 'Win!'

The gallery drummed feet and clapped hands as he marked his territory… except for quarter-final victim national champ Charlie Brumfield, and semi-final victim #2 seed Steve Serot. He had thrashed Brumfield, squeaked by Serot, and now eased by me in the finals to launch power racquetball and a blazing career.

Hogan turned professional with this win and went on to become the first millionaire in the history of racquetball. Hogan was so dominant that he lost only four matches in three years during his prime. He lost only one match in 1977, two matches in 1978, and one match in 1979. His greatest season was 1979; not only did he win the Pro Racquetball Nationals, but he also won the Outdoor Racquetball Nationals and the Paddleball Nationals for the Triple Crown. Hogan was 6-Time World Racquetball Champion.

Pros Speak from the Box
Memorable Moment

My first pro win as a teen in Burlington, Vt. where I came outa nowhere to beat my three idols: Brumfield, Serot and Keeley. I got my mother on the phone and screamed "I made it, Ma!" From then on, I was a confident player and became a millionaire. -*Marty Hogan*

I won the 2000 World Championships in Mexico, my breakthrough and a good day in

Latin America. Nobody had heard of me, I came out of little Tijuana, and in fact was on the balance between going into racquetball seriously or quitting. Suddenly, I struck gold and sponsors came knocking, and I chose Adidas and E-Force. I still thank every day by working hard that I get travel and money for playing what I love.   *- Alvaro Beltran*

Oh wow! I have so many memorable moments. I don't think I could sum it up in one moment. Here are some moments I cherish the most:
   * Making the US Team for the first time in 1990. I believe I was down 10-1 in the tie-breaker and worked my way back to win 11-10. This was the beginning of my 20+ years on the US Team.
   * Winning my first Gold Medal at the World Championships in 1990. Playing and winning with a team was very rewarding.
   * Winning the first Gold Medal with my twin sister, Joy. It was always fun winning with her. I loved standing on the podium, right hand across my heart, looking over at her and singing the National Anthem together-a special and a great honor.
   * When I was inducted into the Racquetball Hall of Fame. I was honored to receive the pinnacle award of my career.   *– Jackie Paraiso*

The match-winning shot at the 1994 U.S. Olympic Festival to win the gold. That put me on the US. National team to win three Pan American Game medals, two World championships, and spending almost three years traveling the world on the US team. Wilson picked me up and we started the Big D Road Show of clinic tours in this country. That's been some life change from that one shot, but much prior work went into making it.   *- Derek Robinson*

My two most memorable moments are separated by 7 days. The first was 1981, when Charlie Drake was handing me a first place check for winning the first pro stop of the 1981 "Invitational" pro tour that I competed in as an "Amateur" due to being excluded from the Top 8 invited players even though I was ranked number 2 at the time. The 2nd happened 7 days later, when I beat Hogan, and Yellen in the finals, becoming the # 1 Player in the World, and Charlie Drake's assistant coming up to me and saying that they decided to now accept me into the tour.   *– Jerry Hilecher*

My peak experience was when I won the 1982 Ektelon championship and became #1 player in the world. Before that, the most memorable was in the early 70s going head to head with Dr. Bud Muehleisen on the San Diego PPA single court. That court was haunted by the first racquetball legends. Dr. Bud took me apart the first game and put me back together the second. I went outside on the steps and cried. Then I practiced, and became the World Champion.   *– Dave Peck*

At the 1988 nationals I beat Yellen in the semis for #1 ranking, and Eagan in the finals for the championship all in one weekend.   *- Ruben Gonzalez*

My peak moments were whenever I played a great historical competitor like Ruben Gonzalez. I wanted them to play their best so I would know how I measured up to myself. The top competition brought out the self-awareness that I craved. — *Jim Spittle*

It doesn't matter which nationals it was. The ball in a specifically important match was too slow despite my suggestions to Keeley and the ref to change to a respectable one, and play continued. I swung on the final shot and the ball disappeared. We exited the court and noticed the ball wedged in the crotch of my racquet, causing me to win the tournament, and later suggest to our sponsors to liven up our balls or string the crotches.

- Charlie Brumfield

My racquetball breakthrough was as a freshman at Providence college in '85, when I went to my first pro tour in Tulsa. I was a nobody who beat Learner, Hilecher, Harnett, Price and Oiver. I was elated, and won $6,000, enough to pay for the apartment for three years. The big win was called a flash in the pan, and that I was just a big server who'd won a single event on a glass front wall. Three months later, at the Ektelon nationals in Anaheim, I beat a tough draw Hawks, Ray, Hogan, and both Pecks to win. For the first time, the observers gave me credit. In those two tournaments, and to this day, I go in not thinking about the event, but about each opponent in turn. *- Cliff Swain*

The 21st point in the 3rd game of the 1977 National Professional Championships…Left fist to the air! — *Davey Bledsoe*

Winning the World Championships in Ireland 2008 after getting attacked and having reconstructive surgery. *- Rhonda Rajsich*

When you have enough fun moments, it's hard to pick just one. I appreciate my wins over Cliff and Suds in the same tourney more than any other events. But the reality is the sport has provided me with some fun moments in my life, and picking one is impossible. — *John Ellis*

Winning 2013 Kansas City stop. Beat Kane and Rocky. — *Jose Rojas*

My three best moments: Winning the Pan Am Gold in 1999 on little sleep over five days, and after being down 8-10; winning Pan Am Bronze on a torn meniscus; and my first World Championship in 2000, down 4-9, and winning 11-10. — *Cheryl Gudinas*

There are a number of times I've been down in the tiebreaker, gained the serve, and come back to win by forgetting the score and focusing on one point at a time. Those are my best memories of the game. *- Corey Brysman*

Absolutely, in 2005 after winning the World Outdoor Championships - my kids (and some of our friends' kids came running out and gave me a big group hug. – *Brian Hawkes*

Cliff Swain turns pro this instant with his first paycheck at the 1984 Montreal Open. (M. Diner)

Making the US team for the first time at the nationals, and later that same day I got engaged to my wife.   – *Andy Hawthorne*

The most memorable is the day I moved to San Diego from New Jersey to go to play ball. I rode my bike to Mel Gorham's where all the pros played, and Steve Keeley was there. My jaw dropped at seeing and then talking to a racquetball hero. Then he played a game with me! I was an 18 year old kid who just arrived in Heaven.   – *Rich Wagner*

When Two Hall of Famers Collide

by "Dr.Bud" Muehleisen

Let me set the scene a little bit......'back in the day', when Racquetball sported some 12 million players in the United States alone, and you could hardly find an empty court to play on, there emerged two of the finest women Racquetball players the game has ever known. At that time, 'The Women's Pro Racquetball Tour' was firmly established and it's fans were increasing as the 'Tour' made its way around the country.

Lynn Adams hailed from Southern California and got her early start by playing in Outdoor Tournaments, where she quickly became a dominate force. Following that success, she had little trouble converting to the Indoor Game by winning numerous National titles in the Amateur ranks before she made the transition into the Professional Game. As I recall, her 1st real Pro title was winning the 1st Professional National Mixed Doubles Title, pairing with yours truly. In the finals that year, we defeated the then reigning Pro Singles Champions in the Men's & Women's Divisions, namely Shannon Wright and Dave Peck.

Heather McKay was from Australia, and she burst onto the scene heralded as the 'World's Greatest Woman Squash player,' which included 7 World titles among her many laurels. Heather was a superbly conditioned athlete when she took up Racquetball. She entered the game with an intimidating athletic history and proceeded to play Racquetball like she played Squash.   Initially, her ground strokes were either up and down the line or crosscourt with the ball dying at the back wall.   That was probably from all her the years of playing Squash, which utilizes a 'tell-board' at the front wall. Playing as just described, Heather's game controlled the front court and her opponents had never really witnessed that type of offense utilizing such ball control. Thereby, they found themselves almost always being at the back wall while seemingly to be on the defensive. Also, it took no time at all for Heather to develop accurate pinch shots and low kill shots to the front wall which then made her even stronger as a player.

Lynn and Heather were equal in speed and quickness, including reflexes. Heather once asked me to show her how to hit flat overheads off the ceiling ball and she quickly picked it up like the pro she was. When Heather join the Pro game, she literally dominated the field, including Lynn most of the time, especially in their early matches. Heather also gave up a few years in age to her younger opponents.

I also recall the many times Lynn had spent developing her game, as she would drive her little Volkswagen, each week, 200 hundred miles round trip to San Diego for her lessons. Lynn was an exceptional student and a dedicated worker as well as a fierce

483

Lynn Adams was the #1 Women's Player in the World 1981, 84, 85, 86, 87, 88, 90; eight-time Player of the Year 1982–88, 1990; with six pro tour season titles 1982–1983, 85–88; and seven overall Championships 1982–83, 85–88, 90. She won 325 of her 369 professional matches for a .887 win percentage in a tough field including a slightly older Shannon Wright, and motherly Heather McKay against whom the mutual career 24-24 win-loss record is celebrated. (Art Shay)

competitor. Gradually in time, her serves became more effective in all departments as well as her getting over the intimidation factor that Heather had over most of the field.

Also, it should be pointed out here that Heather never beat herself. You, had to beat Heather in order to emerge the winner. Again, while Heather played almost errorless

This photo was snapped in 1980 when Heather McKay, at the age of 39 and with one year of racquetball experience, won the first of five Canadian National Singles titles. She wasted no time becoming the best women's racquetball player in the world. The others were overwhelmed, as the championships piled on. Before returning to Australia in 1985, the Australian born Canadian national amassed nine National titles McKay is considered by many to be the greatest racquetball player in history, and definitely the greatest squash player ever, and possibly Australia's top sportswoman. In racquetball, she won the American Amateur Racquetball Championship once (1979), the American Professional Racquetball Championship three times (1980, 82, 83), and the Canadian Racquetball Championship five times (1980 and 82–85). She was inducted into the USA Racquetball Hall of Fame in 1997. (*Murray Diner*)

ball, her opponents could never quite figure her out how she was maintaining such excellent control of the front court position. So, they would try almost anything in an attempt to derail her. In doing so, their own games quickly went out the window as they became even more frustrated.

As time progressed, Lynn fully realized the challenges that lay ahead of her if she was going to become number 1 in the women's pro division. Full of determination, she took on the task to become the accomplished player that she knew it would take to overcome her polished opponent. Diligently, she pursued perfection in honing her many skills.

Eventually, as her defensive game and over all control of the ball became more consistent, it was accompanied by her offensive skills increasing greatly in their percentage of execution. Therefore, as the pendulum began to swing, Lynn's percentages took over and eventually Heather led by only one match at 11-10. I don't believe anyone ever realized that including myself. Actually, that number of matches has been documented.

Then, as time would have it, their matches came to a rather abrupt halt as Heather opted into retirement to return to her Homeland in Australia. How fitting, that that record is left standing there for all time, as some of the finest matches between two of the greatest women players who ever took to the court. The game of Racquetball can be well proud to have been able to have showcased their outstanding talents. I know that I will not soon forget one of Racquetball's greatest confrontations!

Respectfully submitted, "Dr. Bud"

Outdoor action at the 2013-3-WallBall World Outdoor Championships. (Mike Augustin)

486

Sport, Politics and the Catalina Tour

The Olympics just opened in London, while I sit in a jungle in Peru and think about the spectacle of sports and politics. We fondly remember events like Jesse Owens winning Gold and upsetting Hitler's vision of a Berlin Nazi Olympics in 1936, and generally share a distaste for multi-millionaire athletes and multi-billionaire team owners who want to strike or lockout every season because rich isn't rich enough for them. Fresh off the opening ceremony is as good a time as any to discuss the always controversial but ever present marriage of sports and politics, and how the Catalina Invitational Racquetball Tour happened in 1981 and how it changed the sport.

I have heard stories from countless players over the last thirty years that had it not been for the Catalina Tour they would have made it big in racquetball. Their careers were ruined, they protest, forehanding parts along assembly lines and backhanding pencils across desks. Some of their stories ring true but the numbers don't add up.

At no time since I was the first player to have a professional racquetball contract with Leach Industries and The National Racquetball Club seconds before my arch nemesis on court and respected friend off court, Charlie Brumfield, signed second, have more than twenty players in one season made a decent living playing pro racquetball. This didn't change appreciably between 1981 and 1983, but what did change was that the limited players who did make it big for the first time were hand selected as part of a political process and didn't just earn their status on the hardwood of the racquetball courts.

Who was in and who was out on the new 1981 invitational tour? The top three players on tour in the early and mid-seventies, Charlie Brumfield, Steve Serot and I, had all just retired from the game, so a changing of the guard was inevitable. Unlike you may have read, we weren't thrown out, we left on our own. Serot went back to St. Louis to pursue a successful insurance career, Brumfield settled permanently in San Diego and argued his points in a court of a different sort, and I went traveling through Mexico and South America taking in sites and seeding racquetball in one of my early pursuits of travel and adventure.

The high profile Catalina tour was to originally consist of four-time defending National Champion, Marty Hogan, along with nine of the top players on tour, Mike Yellen, Dave Peck, Rich Wagner, Steve Strandemo, Craig McCoy, Donny Thomas, Dave Fleetwood, Doug Cohen, John Eggerman and two young, hard hitting teen phenoms, Bret Harnett and Gregg Peck, with the very capable Scott Hawkins and Ed Andrews as alternate players. At first glance it's a murderer's row of proven champions and talented young guns that would make a heck of a tour.

What you'd be missing in that glance was the players who were omitted like former NRC and IPRO National Champions, Davey Bledsoe and Jerry HI lecher, Pro Racquetball Rookie of the Year and top five player Benny Koltun, and the best Canadian players, Lindsay Myers, Ross Harvey and Brad Kruger. Additionally, new players who wanted to give the tour a go would have very limited opportunities to quality. The new tour also came with a novel scoring format that's stuck to this day. The twenty-one point games were gone and replaced by three-out-of-five games to eleven to make the matches quicker and more fan friendly.

The souvenir photo from the 1981 CBC International Classic tournament in Winnipeg, Canada. It was a challenge event between Americans and Canadians, and the first of its class. It was more prestigious than an official pro tour event, and it was taped for broadcast on CBC in Canada and ESPN in the USA. (US RB Museum)

Front row (left to right) Sherman Greenfeld, Linda Forcade, Shannon Wright, Heather McKay, Heather Stupp, Susie Dugan, Karen Walton-Trent, and commissioner Dan Bertolucci.

Back row: Davey Bledsoe, Dwayne Kohuch, Wes Hadikin, Wendell Talaber, Dave Peck, Brad Kruger, Marty Hogan, Wayne Bowes, Ben Koltun, Don Thomas, Jerry Hilecher, Bob Daku, Lindsay Myers, and Craig McCoy.

By rule, there would be only four qualifying spots per regular season event, and no not-invited player could qualify in more than two Catalina Tour events per season. By qualifying at least once you were eligible to try to qualify and play in the three supplemental yearend events: The Catalina Finals, the Ektelon Nationals, and the Granddaddy of them all the Leach Pro Nationals. With these rules even if they were willing to play in the qualifying rounds, Hilecher, Bledsoe, Koltun, Myers and the rest could play a maximum of five tournaments on an eleven stop tour.

Now that you know the on court players and understand the official rules, the big question remaining is why? Was Catalina Tour Executive Director and my housemate of three years Charley Drake crazy? Were Hogan and the other top players whom I roomed with afraid of competition? What was driving this change? The answers are as simple as the questions.

My old friend from Michigan and sometimes doubles partner, Drake wasn't crazy. He was an astute businessman, master of manipulating circumstance and a Doctor of Sociology. No, Hogan and the guys weren't afraid of playing the best players, for the most part, since they were the best and enjoyed tough competition. The new tour was driven by two things that ultimately corrupt all pro sports: power and money.

By 1981, NRC founder Bob Kendler was on his last legs physically and no longer in a position to lead. He passed away a year later quietly in church just after the eighth and final NRC/Leach Pro Nationals in 1982. Leach was now owned by DP who thought the big money they invested annually on the pro tour wasn't really necessary. Seamco was gone as a viable company and certainly as a viable sponsor. IPRO founder Bill Tanner had dropped out of pro racquetball and sponsored his last event. Ektelon had been sold to Browning who thought sponsoring one pro tournament a year was plenty. The upshot is Charley Drake was left with all the power but none of the usual sources of money. He was clearly in control of the tour but without a major sponsor there would be no tour.

Ed Murphy, President of Catalina, liked racquetball. He already sponsored Hogan and a couple of events and thought that it would be a good vehicle to stretch his successful swimwear line in to an even broader sports appeal. Catalina was a division of the major conglomerate Golf Western, so a few hundred grand here or there was nothing to them. Drake approached Murphy who liked the idea of doing an invitational racquetball exhibition tour with Hogan and a few other players who would wear Catalina at all times. When it became apparent to Drake that none of the other logical sponsors were stepping up, the Catalina Tour became the only tour. What started as a fashion exhibition circuit of racquetball players had become an ill-conceived invitational pro tour.

Catalina had no problem forking over enough cash to make the events worthwhile, but oddly the high cost of the Catalina clothing helped do in the tour. Each player was to wear Catalina apparel on and off the court during events. Unlike normal racquetball attire, a full Catalina wardrobe cost $5,000 per player. The bill to outfit the twelve full-time and two alternates was a whopping $70,000, and adding additional outfits would have cut the prize money and Drake's profit. In order to work within the Catalina parameters and still make a buck, Drake's new invitational tour was limited to a dozen players of his choosing.

As mentioned, top players like Bledsoe, Hilecher and Koltun were left off, and that didn't sit well with Jerry Hilecher. A competitor to the end on and off the court, Jerry filed suit and took Drake and Catalina to court. At the same time, Jerry proved his case on the racquetball court, winning the first two events beating Hogan, Yellen and the rest all the way and showing everyone that he was too good to be left off the tour. A key to his quick success was the new shorter 11-point games and three-out-of-fire match that favored the streak players of which Jerry was the most explosive in history with aces and booming forehands.

Court coverage: 6-time World Champion Marty Hogan faced little competition in his prime until Leach Industries launched Smarty, a robot programed to cover, hit, and vacuum the court. (US RB Museum)

After a couple of events the first season, Dave Fleetwood put down his racquet and went to work with Memphis media mogul and former IRA president, Bill Tanner. After the court case was settled, Jerry took Fleetwood's spot and was one of the top players during two Catalina seasons. Dave Peck and Mike Yellen enjoyed tremendous success on the

490

Catalina tour, and both captured the #1 ranking for the first time, Peck in 1982 and Yellen in 1983. Though Marty Hogan won his fifth consecutive Pro Nationals and more prize money and more events than any other player over the two Catalina years, he lost his #1 ranking on tour and it took him a half dozen years after Catalina left the sport to officially regain it. I was worst dressed of the early champs in dual colored Converse Chucks and stenciled shirts 'Refuse Sucrose', so besides traveling in the autumn of my career would have been the last Catalina offered a contract.

What made Marty lose his edge? The answer to that lies with the tour's official ball, the Voit Rollout Blue. Several months before Catalina, I had given Hogan a drubbing in the Voit Championship finals 21-5, 21-6 with the same ball. Some of it might have been attributed to Marty body surfing in the waves, red eyes and clogged ears that made the dead ball sound deader than it was, but the main reason that day is he simply wasn't the same dominant player with the slow Voit Blue as with the superfast Seamco. As much as Marty could dominate them with the fast ball, Peck, Yellen and Hilecher were all basically on par with him using the much slower one. The only thing Marty hated more than that slow Voit ball was having his Doberman Maxwell fetch it back to him.

Drake, Hogan and all the top players on tour did well financially and while it wasn't the evil plot that some make it out to be, the closed tour stunted the growth of the sport. The bottom line is always simply, and the bottom line when sport, money and politics collide is it's usually the fans who lose.

Open Letter to Young Players – How to Get a Racquetball Sponsorship

from Brett Elkins

Tell them to write the large national racquetball companies for racquet sponsorship. Go to the major manufacturers' websites for their addresses to mail a request-to-sponsor letter along with a resume. The National bodies have buy-in programs. It's doable.

Or, even better, go up to any great sponsored player who is decked out in that racquetball company gear which means they are probably sponsored.

Companies give top players racquets and clothes for free but in most cases if you're a rising 'stat' you can start out getting new equipment and gear worth about $800 for just $199 a year- basically the price of a new racquet and a discount of 40% of everything. Top players have top equipment!

It's getting tougher than ever to get sponsored and it's who you know, most importantly. So become friendly with everyone and ask to be sponsored. Generally they don't come up to you; you need to approach them!!

It helps being in this select fraternity because you'll definitely win matches when say an Ektelon player who watches gives you advice on how to win the match as it unfolds.

For getting money to play at events, you basically have to win prize money yourself and play a lot and/or work at a large corporation that will help with tournament expenses.

Google companies that sponsor Olympic athletes and apply. You had better get good quick and win lots of big money tournaments to cover your expenses too. Ask the tournament directors to help get local housing!

Other avenues are rich benefactors. Get an instructor or top flight player to mentor you. When already traveling, write letters to airlines requesting discounts for travel.

If you live way out there, go to local companies, and wear t-shirts just ugly with ads for companies. Promote the shirts like you're racing for NASCAR. Start w/ sports clubs, sports stores, health and fitness shops, and restaurants. Expand to plumbing, hardware stores, whatever. Make a video to show them of how you won wearing their logo.

Mexico, Central and South American countries have very strong sports federations for national teams including support for racquetball and RB players. So, in Latin America start there.

If you're top 20 Usar ranked, you may get your travel or tournaments paid for, and you may not. Top 10 and you will! Rollout will give you free clothes if top 50 usually.

And you can try to get local companies to sponsor you and put their logo on your clothes. You may get some local patron or company to help partially fund your endeavor or tournament fees. The top two players in the world make under $300k a year and most of the top players struggle to make say 50k by also giving lessons clinics, etc.

This is not a lucrative career you want to go into. A former #1 star whom you all know makes approximately $60k a year through sponsorship, senior tour events, prize money, and lots of lessons, and is still top 20! My suggestion is get a PhD instead and use your head-no not the brand!

Thank you.

Brett Elkins
Chairman WOR - World Outdoor Racquetball Hall of Fame
Nov. 2, 2014

Today's Juniors may play in tomorrow's championships via university scholarships. 2014 Pro Kennex Tournament of Champions. (Mike Augustin)

Ruben Gonzalez and Rocky Carson embrace at the 2005 Virginia pro stop. (Ken Fife)

Best Original & Moderns
Keeley Awards

This introduction to the pioneer and modern Champions breaks down their serves, strokes, strategies and more to clue you which early pro pictures to view and which living pros to watch for tips to improve your own game. The cut-off date between the two eras is 1990.

Best Forehand Original - Bill Schmidtke

Best Forehand Modern - Kane Waselenchuk

Best Backhand Original - Steve Serot

Best Backhand Modern - Sudsy Monchik

Best Pinch Shot Original - Davey Bledsoe

Best Pinch Shot Modern - Alvaro Beltran

Best Splat Shot Original - Marty Hogan

Best Splat Shot Modern - Kane Waselenchuk

Best Killshot Original – Steve Keeley

Best Killshot Modern – Sudsy Monchik

Best Serve Original - Jerry Hilecher

Best Serve Modern - Cliff Swain

Best Strategist Original – Carl Loveday

Best Strategist Modern - Jason Mannino

Best Competitor Original - Charlie Brumfield

Best Competitor Modern - Cliff Swain

Best Outdoor Player Original - Charlie Brumfield

Best Outdoor Modern - Brian Hawkes

Best Doubles Player Original - Charlie Brumfield

Best Doubles Modern - Ruben Gonzalez

Best Diver Original - Steve Serot

Best Diver Modern - Jason Mannino

Best Hands Original - Bud Muelheisen

Best Hands Modern - Kane Waselenchuk

Most Power Original - Marty Hogan

Most Power Modern - Chris Crowther

Fastest Player Original - Davey Bledsoe

Fastest Player Modern - Jason Mannino

Best Lefty Original - Bud Muelheisen

Best Lefty Modern - Cliff Swain

Best Winning Streak Original - Marty Hogan

Best Streak Modern – Kane Waselenchuk

Best Sportsman Original - Bill Schmidtke

Best Sportsman Modern – Mike Ray

Best Gamesman Original - Charlie Brumfield

Best Gamesman Modern – King Kane

Best Pass Shot Original - Mike Yellen

Best Pass Shot Modern – Jack Huczek

Best Serve Return Original - Charlie Brumfield

Best Return Modern - Rocky Carson

Best Coach Original - Carl Loveday

Best Coach Modern - Jim Winterton

Best Author Original – Steve Keeley

Best Author Modern – Steve Keeley

'MY NAME IS CLIFF SWAIN, and you will hear more of me!' In this 1984 Montreal Open Cliff defeated Lindsey Myers in the finals and Ruben Gonzalez in the semis and Bruce Christensen in the quarters. He beat Bruce 21-2, 21-1 in the quarters. When asked how he beat him by those scores which nobody did in those days, he said, 'Christensen served well.' Ruben who was a top ten pro didn't score twenty points in the match, and Lindsay Canada's best managed to play great and lose 21-19, 21-5. No one could believe their eyes or ears, except Scott Hirsch, Cliff's roommate and practice partner on the Providence College team, who said, 'It was at that time I realized what I already suspected, that I was practicing with the best player in the world. Three months later, Hilecher, Harnett and the rest of the draw were shocked by Cliff winning his first official pro stop in Tulsa, and the next month Hogan and Peck suffered the same fate when Cliff won the Ektelon Nationals. Everyone knows the rest of the story, but Montreal is where it became a matter of when not if Cliff would be #1. *(Murray Diner)*

Pros Speak from the Box
Psyche the Opponent

My consistent racquet has always done the talking.   *- Mike Ray*

The best way to insert your will on the other player is by controlling the tempo of play, hence funneling him away from his game style into yours.   *- Corey Brysman*

There's no need for your mouth on the court if f you've got heart, guts and endurance.
                                                                          - Ruben Gonzalez

Charlie Brumfield, Chuck Leve and Marty Hogan at a 1970s awards ceremony. (US RB Museum)

The strong game is the most potent psych, and I like to punctuate it with exclamations.
                                                                          - Marty Hogan

In emergencies, employ various rhythm breaking techniques to slow or quicken the pace against a power or control player, respectively. Motive plays a part: I was the last guy picked on the baseball team, and so far there hasn't been a sportsmanship trophy.

- Charlie Brumfield

Who needs it when you've got the shots? The other guy.   *- Jim Spittle*

Outthinking comes with preparation, and as long as you believe you're outthinking the other guy then you probably are.   *- Sudsy*

Psyching out the other guy isn't an active goal, but sometimes occurs in the normal course of play due to my physical size, aggressive manner and execution.

- Derek Robinson

Focusing on the moment is key.   *- Brian Hawkes*

One way to 'out-think' an opponent is to reduce him physically so he can no longer react mentally. A famous squash coach once told me, 'Go into the match and don't worry about winning the first points. Volley, volley and just get him tired so that if it goes to the third game he'll be dead tired.' This delayed gratification allows you to exploit his weakness as he tires in the second game, working him over until I can 'out-think' him in the rubber game to win the match.   *- Jeff Leon*

I always liked my opponent to play his best, and I didn't want to try and beat anybody by getting the psychological edge on him. I didn't need the money or recognition and, after all, you're truly playing solitaire out there for a feeling of personal achievement.

- Victor Niederhoffer

My way is to 'walk softly and carry a big stick', and when only when the opponent brings it on himself do I not mind getting physical and active out there.   *- Cliff Swain*

The Proven Recipe to Beat Kane

Everybody and nobody likes an undefeated champion and clearly Kane Waselenchuck has earned this status. The upcomers love him as a model for their strokes, strategies and in some cases careers, while the has been champs as well as challengers on the pro tour want to see him toppled just once.

Why only once?

Cliff Swain laid out the recipe to beating Kane and did so seven times in a row. He put more pressure on him with his big serve than Kane could put on him.

- Attacked at all times putting Kane on the defensive.
- Rarely skipped the ball or left the ball up.
- Kept the pressure on relentlessly.

You need only possess the following seven ingredients and put them all together:

1) A serve as big or bigger than Kane's
2) Ability to hit the ball as hard as he can
3) Great court coverage
4) Ability to hit all shots off both wings
5) Nerves of steel
6) Constant aggression
7) A lot of confidence

You should be able simply to follow Cliff Swain's special recipe. The only problem is we're looking for one player today who has all the ingredients. Cliff beat Kane the first seven in a row when Cliff was between the ages of 33-36 and Kane was between 20-23. Kane won ten out of eleven after Swain's 37th birthday. Is there a young cook in the racquetball kitchen to manage this recipe? Then Kane will go down.

Rookie to Pro

with Dave Peck

I want to show you a path from amateur to pro. Like any other path, you may pick and choose what suits you, as well as from other pros who know the agony and persistence of reaching for the top. This reflects how it happened to me.

Young Players

First, learn your good stroke mechanics for the forehand and backhand. This will be the foundation for the rest of your time on the court since everything else - serve, return and shot selection - is derived from proper stroke mechanics. Second, then gradually come to understand all the aspects of the game including the serve, return, offensive and defensive play, positioning, and so on. Third, there's a thing called 'muscle memory' where if you practice alone the strokes that you've learned, then when you get in a game those muscles will automatically react as you've trained them to hit the shots well.

Aspiring Pros

Find someone who can help you get to the next level. Perhaps you've surpassed the local competition, and that's where you'll stagnate (unless you're a tenacious solo practitioner) unless you can find a mentor or brain trust to help you leap to the next level. Once you've found that help - a person, camp, or the right book or video - commit. Commit to reach the stars. What I say comes from personal experience.

Grip Forehand

The forehand grip I used is revolved around the handle to close the face of the racquet before the swing starts. This for me causes when the extension of the arm is full at the point of contact the racquet to be square and come through flat on the ball. When the frame is flat to the front wall through the contact zone, the ball goes straight and true without skips and risers. I'll repeat to avoid confusion: The handle revolves within the palm for a grip that closes the face more than the traditional grip did. Actually, at the moment of contact with my arm fully extended, the frame is square or parallel with the front wall.

Grip Backhand

I use the more revolved backhand grip to close the racquet face before the swing starts.

The closed face that begins the swing squares to parallel to the front wall with full arm extension. At the instant of contact the strings are parallel to the front wall to cause the ball to fly solid and straight. Once more for clarity: The more closed face actually becomes flat to the front wall due to the full extension of the hitting arm at the point of contact.

Dave Peck leaps from a rookie to World Champion vs. Rich Wagner. (Art Shay)

Full Extension of the Arm

I emphasize extending the arm as the swing approaches the ball contact so that at the hit the arm is fully extended. The full length gives a longer radius of torque for greater head speed hence faster ball velocity. In this sense, the full extended arm is like using a longer

501

hammer handle. The other plus is as the arm fully extends n the hit zone, the extension of the elbow causes the wrist joint to supinate (lay back) to slightly open the face of the racquet. This makes the frame flat to the front wall at the point of contact for a straight shot.

Equipment and Strokes

Lighter racquet and faster ball obliterated the old swing long ago. There simply isn't time to take the controlled swing of yore. The focus now has to be simple: Racquet back and up early in a Bow, elbow extends, follow through to the front wall. This levels the ball flat and hard. Go with a traditional quadriform head, and try a racquet that fits your swing speed. A fast swing uses a heavier racquet to avoid over-hitting and hurting the arm, and a slower swing a lighter racquet.

Strokes

Let's talk about body rotation, the power source. The hips coil and uncoil is this source, rather than shoulder rotation. That is, the hips rotate on the backswing, as a golfer, toward the back wall, then twist back forcefully with the swing. This rotation accelerates all the stroke mechanics. The moving hips envelop the leverage of the elbow and wrist going on during the swing and contact.

If you find yourself bending overly at the waist, it's a poor excuse for hip rotation. It encourages shoulder rotation which are weaker than the hips. Some players think to get lower on the ball by bending at the waist, which is possible, but it also discourages hip rotation.

I don't use premeditated spin, except on certain shots, such as sidespin on pinch shots. Spin for me is a natural side and topspin due to the Bow strokes.

Forehand

First, for advanced players I recommend you use a more closed face, like a few other pros. Second, at your ball contact make sure your racquet is square, meaning the top of the racquet frame (and the handle) point directly at the side wall to ensure a stroke that comes through straight rather than vertically. The frame is also parallel to the front wall at the hit.

Backhand

For advanced players, first the grip. Have it rotated so that when the arm extends at ball contact, the face is square. Second, racquet prep. I teach the elbow and racquet are like drawing a bow. The elbow is up and crooked at about 120 degrees and raised up and back across the body in the racquet prep upswing. This bow isolates the stronger lats for the swing motion, rather than the weaker deltoids. Then, when you step into the ball, there's a tightness in the right lats for right handers that 'releases' the bow of the elbow and arm, giving awesome power.

Center court battle: Dave Peck beats Mike Yellen for the 1982 World Championship. (Legends)

503

Stroke Power

The power I play with and teach comes from first bowing the arm in early racquet preparation. Next, the hips rotate on the setup to uncoil forcefully on the swing. The goal of bowing and coiling is to uncork at once with full elbow extension on the ball. There it goes. Understand that you don't have to work hard to achieve maximum power, just get all the leverages working together.

Practice Solo

I solo practiced a lot. The early goal was to get proper stroke mechanics. The continuing goal is to ingrain those mechanics into muscle memory. In a tournament they come without the interruption of thought.

I use X-Marks-the-Spot in a progression of practice shots around the court. Start on the backhand side behind the service box and drop-and-hit or set-and-hit; then go to the center court a little deeper for backhand pinches; then go to the backcourt backhand side for deep shots; and then for the forehand duplicate these X's on the forehand side of the court.

Conditioning

Weight loss coupled with conditioning. It's a simple formula derived to keep me from getting winded that had caused me to miss some shots. Second, and for everyone, I'm looking for tougher competition locally to hone my game and steel my mind. At a tournament I'm ready from the get-go. For off court conditioning, I lift weights, life cycle, run, bicycle, and other exercises for a diverse program.

Before a Match

I stretch out in the Jacuzzi or sauna to loosen the muscles and alert the mind of an upcoming shift into high gear. The second part of the preparation is coming up with a game plan that maximizes my strengths, avoids my weaker areas, while doing just the opposite to the opponent's strengths and weaknesses. When I come out of the whirlpool or sauna I'm relaxed and the only thing that need be done in the next hour is execution.

Concentration

This is from the heart of experience. While playing if you have to go through the analytical process – how to move the feet, backswing, which serve, what shot to hit, what's happening in this match – then you're doomed to mediocrity. If you're caught up in this process then your attention is peripherally on the match rather than properly central on execution. The biggest mistake advanced players make is starting to think result oriented thoughts instead of staying in the mode of direct performance. Concentration is keeping the mind in the now of execution.

Rhonda Rajsich World Champion 2 times, US Open 4 times, National Singles Champion 3 times, and WPRO #1 4 times. Her power source is similar to Dave Peck's with a bow backswing and rotated hips to which Rhonda adds a shoulder roll. (2006 Ken Fife)

Dominate

Everything in my personal success has stemmed from being competitive. Couple that with not giving up. And third with practice to make everything automatic. Those three reasons take anyone far in anything.

Vs. a power player

Start by defining the opponent's strengths and weaknesses. If the other guy has more power, pick the shots and returns where he has less. He will probably hate slow serves, the ceiling, and a slower pace of game, or anything that breaks game rhythm.

Control momentum

Pace of game is controlled through a variety of legal tricks such as raising the arm on the service return, hurrying or delaying your serve, shot selection designed to press or not the rally, little comments, and bumping bodies in some cases. I was known for intimidation on the court because I was dealing with psych artists. It the opponent is a gentleman, I tone down my tactics.

Handle Psych

There are simple ways to handle the psych artist. You can throw the same psych techniques back in his face, you can remain stoic and wait for him to wither, and if need be a forearm shiver delivers a point. I've a reputation for tirades on the court, but the revelation is that only 10% were out-of-control and the other 90% intricately designed to take advantage. It's inferred that the intelligent opponent is left to figure out which was which.

Comparing Champs

There is tremendous athleticism in the modern game! However, with the exception of Swain and maybe one other player, their understanding is diminished compared to yesteryear. So, where early pros were cerebrally dependent, the present ones are body dependent. The pros now can learn the game, but they lack the performing mentors to teach them.

Coaches, Camps, Lessons

Ruben Gonzalez's classic bow and body coil for power at the 2005 Virginia pro stop. (Ken Fife)

507

Do It Your Own Way

Not Taking Lessons May Be The Best Thing For Your Game

by Brad Kruger

Carl Loveday, racquetball's most prominent coach, peered through the haze of his own cigar smoke as he piloted his '69 Cadillac westbound on San Diego Interstate 8 toward a lesson scheduled at a popular beach club.

As the applauded mentor of Charley Brumfield, Rich Wagner and countless others, Loveday's expertise is attested to by a fee that would cause many attorneys to blush ($100 per hour). I reclined in the passenger seat and let the tape recorder roll.

"Let's face it," Loveday mumbled, his lips wrestling between words and the smoldering, soggy butt of his trademark, a Beaconsfield cigar, "Anyone looking for a competent racquetball instructor is going to be hurting. He's better off leaving his money at home and shooting the locker room breeze with better players until he learns the ropes. Like the old saying goes, 'a fool and his money are soon parted'."

From the fat executive in his gray cotton sweat suit to the slender fashion model in her vogue Fila outfit, everyone wielding a racquet has a common goal: consistent optimal performance by the most expedient learning process. Now we have one of racquetball's top coaches revealing that conventionally accepted paths- the advice of teaching pros; the commands of coaches- are bogus to the average player.

"Here's how it is," Loveday said. "Most players don't need coaches. Only those ranked in the top 50 or so who have a decent shot at climbing higher." Loveday added a touch of mysticism, vanishing behind a cloud of smoke as he exhaled.

"And because racquetball is so young, I just don't think there are that many qualified instructors. Their advice could be more detrimental than helpful." An individual, according to Loveday, would be better off on his own, following a specific plan of improvement.

"Sure, babe," Loveday said, "Of course I'll tell you the plan ... but first let me explain what I said. I don't want to step on anyone's toes.

"It seems pretty obvious to me that the relationship between the coach and player is far too specialized for the average player. Besides being an expert in athletics, the coach has to be a public relations man, an agenda setter, a guidance counselor and a motivator. Plus, he has to know strategy, psychology, personal relations, neuro-muscular coordination, reaction time, fatigue and conditioning. It doesn't take a complete genius to realize that there's only a handful of players who need this kind of attention; even fewer who can afford it."

Loveday was painting, of course, the picture of the mountaintop guru and the kid who hikes up daily for insight into the hows and whatfors, growing stronger with each climb. Together they grow into a special unit, a team to be dealt with. It is a marriage of productivity- commitment must be absolute.

Marty Hogan was ridiculed early on for the power strokes that eventually all the pros used. (Shay)

Preparation is the coach's major concern. "In pretty much all the individual sports, what a coach can do for the player has to be done on the practice court. The coach tries to prime the player for optimal performance when it counts - in the contest.

"At game time, there are really only two ways a coach can help. First, he has to set a game plan. Second, as a security blanket. Brumfield once said he wanted a coach because it took the pressure of decision-making off his shoulders and put it onto the coach's, so he was free to concentrate on shot execution."

Loveday flicked some ashes into the car ashtray. "If you analyzed the psyche of the game's top players, you'd understand the major reason why the average player doesn't want or need a coach. Most players have one motivation: They play individual sports because they're loners - if they lose, they take all the blame; but if they win, they get all the glory. And glory is what it's all about. They don't want to share."

Concentrating on the road, his cigar, trying to tune the radio and then rolling down the window, Loveday reached to the back seat and produced a copy of *Sports Illustrated*. It was folded open to an article about Wayne Gretzky. Loveday read out loud, "'What I do is instinctive. I feel my way down the ice. I see where I want to go, and I go there. How could I teach that?'

"You listening? The greatest ever hockey player said that. I think racquetball's moved in the same direction- instinctive play- you know? When the ball was made quicker and the ceiling shot was all but eliminated, the great players began to play strictly on instinct. There is not a great deal of conscious thought involved.

"The jargon changed. 'When in doubt, go to the ceiling' was replaced by 'When in doubt, shoot it out.' But racquetball's wham-bam-slam-it-where-you-can-and-hope-it-wins game style can't be blamed for the lack of qualified instructors. There aren't many qualified instructors in racquetball because there isn't any way for a beginning instructor to train someone with experience."

Loveday smirked as he explained how some clubs recruit teaching pros. "Club managers turn to their own membership roster for an instructor. First, they'll ask the best player to try and employ him. If he doesn't accept, they'll simply move down the line until they find somebody else.

"Remember that racquetball is a young sport; it's still growing. What this means is that most of today's instructors were self-taught. They didn't have anyone to teach them when they began playing.

510

"The teaching pro is supposed to make on-the-spot corrections, suggestions for improvement within the very short time of a lesson period. That's all. He's concerned with obtaining short-term results.

"More often than not, the teaching pro treats the symptom and ignores the cause. A quick fix is prescribed. The stroke improves on the surface for a short time. But the core mechanics are still lacking. When something goes wrong, nobody knows why. They look for deviations from the instructor's swing and they attempt to make the student's swing a copy. But they never really understand the basic principles of physiological movement. The relationship becomes parasitic: Not teacher and student, but pusher and junkie. The player lacks the self-learning process. He's trying things he doesn't understand.

"You've read all the answers, the differing answers: the texts of Strandemo, Keeley and Brumfield, the pamphlets of lesser knowns. Each month you rush to the mailbox for the latest update in *National Racquetball*. You've questioned your local teaching pro and all you get is, 'Hey, you want to play well, ya gotta pay well.' So you fork out a few more bucks ... and still, that forehand remains the same.

"One of the problems in racquetball today is misinformation," Loveday said. "So many people saying so much. I guess it's expected in a growing sport because the sport has got to change, but it is hardly attractive.

"The answer is simple. It's hard to function unless you have a strong, rudimentary foundation, and this is tough to develop with the overabundance of differing advice. The player has to be able to judge the good from the bad. With Charley [Brumfield], all we did was identify the correct physical principles of hitting the ball. Then we incorporated them into his body. We decided where the ball should be hit, relative to his body, to develop maximum power.

"Ten years ago," Loveday said, "The self-taught pros reigned. The same is true today. They still do it alone. The game has changed, but the process of learning hasn't.

"Above all else, the player must first gain a sound knowledge about the principles of physiological movement in sports. This can be done by reading a couple of textbooks and theorizing with buddies. The movements in other sports should be analyzed too, until you compile a mental rule book for sports movement. Hey, films and video ain't bad either.

"Then, the player should practice what he has learned with strict adherence to the law of specificity." (George B. Dintiment: 'Exercise programs should simulate movements of the activity for which training is designed whenever possible.')

In the Golden Era 1970s, steely eyed, tanned with pigtails at rest, Karen exploded on the ball with both wings – forehand and backhand. Here she blasts pro Janelle Marriott. Karen was the 1977 IRA Women's Open National Champion, and 1978 NRC Women's Pro Racquetball National Champ. (Art Shay)

"The quickest way to learn is to buy a ticket, fly down to San Diego and pay me for a lesson," Loveday laughed, "Second to that, the best way to learn would be to come to San Diego and do nothing else other than analyze and try to learn how Marty Hogan hits the ball. In most cases, the better the skills analyzed, the better the skills that will develop.

"Obviously, most players can't do this, so the student should watch the best players in his area. But watch the player, not the game. He should define the player's individual strengths, and then analyze the physiological foundations, eliminating the weaknesses in the process.

"When this is done, he should jot his discoveries down in a notebook- for comparative reference later- and then move on to another player with a different set of strengths and weaknesses.

"If you run into a problem, ask a better player for his advice," Loveday said. "Remember, he got to where he is by the same process. Very few players will give you a bum steer. They have too much respect for the game.

"'Know something of everything and everything of something,'" Loveday quoted, cautioning players to sift through the vast bulk of misinformation before they form their own individual doctrines. "It takes a lot of work all right. There's no free ride.

"Just consider the non-effects of forking out the dough to a pro, and besides the attractiveness of developing a genuine rapport with the better players. There is a larger plus: when something goes wrong, you can turn to yourself for the answer. You analyze the situation on the spot and, because you were instrumental in the building process, you can come up with your own solution. Who better to fix the broken plumbing than the plumber who designed it? A player's confidence develops. And this can't be bought, stolen or rented."

Loveday extinguished his cigar, leaned into a hard left turn and docked his car in a vacant spot in the parking lot. As we walked through the club's entrance, we were greeted by the stale odor of damp locker rooms and a cacophony of exploding racquetballs against concrete.

"Hey, but listen," I said, "What about conflicts of interest? I mean, it looks like your fate is about the same as last decade's pinkie black ball. If it's true, you're going to be out of a job. Don't you think --"

"C'mon, let's get going," yelled a balding man of about 40 to Loveday, "I've been waiting here over 15 minutes!"

Loveday got dressed in an aura of confidence. "People," he said, "don't always want to hear the truth. I can't remember who, but someone said, 'There is no darkness but ignorance.' Well, you sure don't need any sunglasses around here."

'Do It Your Own Way' first appeared in National Racquetball *(Jan. 1986, Vol. 15 #1) as the cover feature on Carl Loveday and counter-argument on an interior facing page to, 'The Benefit of Lessons'. Brad Kruger is a former Canadian racquetball and handball singles, and swim, champion who trained and lived with Loveday while attending San Diego State University in journalism and political science, and teaming in doubles and doing due diligence for Charley Brumfield. Loveday, who coached Bud Muehleisen who taught Brumfield, is frequently called the Father of Racquetball, while Joe Sobek is the Grandfather of Racquetball.*

How to Choose a Coach
12 Tips

Coach Jim Winterton

Now just how do you find a good coach? This is hard to do because there are hundreds of racquetball coaches but few good ones. Here is one thing to look for: How many students have they taken from beginner to top level-nationally ranked or professional? And how many students have they coached from beginner to pro? A great coach will have many. A good talker will not. I am not talking about sliding in when the player is an A player and working with him, but walking into the coach's club, a true beginner, and winning a national championship with him or at least putting him in position to win that national or pro title. That takes hard work, dedication to the athlete, research of the game and its rudiments, and support of the player's family. Now on to the coaching keys!

One question that players have is... How in the world do you pick a coach? Everyone wants to help you. You get done with a match and everyone has advice. I have been there. Who do you listen to? Here are 12 considerations to help you. Tip # 12 is the most important!

1. Do they need you or do you need them?

I see coaches openly campaigning for students. Why? They don't have any-that's why! My advice... Be careful! Look for coaches who have built kids from beginners to the top.

2. Do you like them?

Have they ever gone back on their word? Have they ever short-changed someone on money or commitment? Ask around. You really need someone who is honest.

3. Are they loyal?

Have they ever dumped a student to take a higher ranked student? Will they give more time to the perceived better player and thus short change to the lower-ranked athlete?

4. Does the coach change from year to year?

A good coach is always learning and changing. Beware of the 80s coach who has not changed. The game has.

5. Does the coach treat everyone the same?

514

Mountaintop photo with an early prototype Pro Kennex racquet at Machu Picchu in the Peruvian Andes during 1984, and the first ever clinic tour of South America. Travel throughout South America was by bus, train, thumb, and three days earlier in this photo by hiking. There were no guides and no marked Inca Trail up to the famed archeological site at 8000 feet. Besides the racquet the gear was a blanket, dozen oranges, and sheepskin coat. The trek took two days through frozen streams to be greeted by overwhelming silence and a few llamas at the top for this cover photo of *National Racquetball* magazine. (1984 Chelsea George)

This sounds right...but it isn't. Not everyone is the same so a good coach changes technique based upon a person's body type and mental attributes. The 'one way or the highway' system cannot work.

6. What are billboard players?

A billboard player is someone who has worked with the coach from beginner to top level. A billboard player would be someone you could observe and you could see the techniques the coach will teach being implemented at a higher level.

You can also watch your prospective coach work with an athlete during matches.

7. How high are the players ranked that the coach works with?

High ranking does not happen unless the athlete has a high level of ability, a great work ethic, the proper training, and the best coaching.

8. How does a coach react to a win or a loss?

This tells quite a bit about a coach. A professional stays detached, and does not make it personal.

9. Does this coach understand priorities?

A good coach understands the importance of religion, family, work, as well as racquetball and will never mess with that hierarchy.

10. Have you interviewed your coach?

Ask the prospective coaches what they think of your game. Ask them how they would attack your shortcomings. Ask them what your strength are. They will work for you so don't be afraid to ask these questions.

11. Is your coach USA Racquetball Instructor certified, CPR certified, first aid certified, or have a degree in Physical Education?

A true professional will have at least a CPR certification and an USAR-IP certification.

12. Interest in your game or in you as well as your game?

Most importantly- a good coach tries to develop people more than winning. The last thing to remember here; A good coach cares about your game, and a great coach cares about your character and your life more than racquetball development. Remember, good coaches coach, great coaches inspire!

516

Coaching and Teaching

Bo Champagne

Let's begin by agreeing that there are some distinct differences between teaching and coaching.

Coaching is what takes place before, during, and after a match between the player and one or more people watching the match. They are trying to help that player to play as well as possible during that match.

Teaching is what takes place between the student and one or more people who are trying to show the student how to learn and improve, with the goal of helping the student to be able to play better in the future. Some coaches are good teachers, and some are not; and vice versa. There is plenty written about coaching racquetball, so I'll limit myself to teaching here.

It's kind of hard to get started writing this. You see, I've never had a specific system to put each student through, nor a mold to shape each prospective player into. If I teach a thousand people (which I imagine I have), I teach a thousand different ways. I've yet to meet two people who are exactly alike. So I start from the foundation by asking myself, "What is the best thing to teach this person right now, and what is the best way to go about it?" Then there's constant revaluation as he progresses.

Everyone brings to the court a different set of physical and mental skills. He steps on with different reasons for playing, and for wanting to learn more, a unique set of expectations, and a varying amount of time and effort to spend learning. My goal as a teacher to react to all these variables; and to provide each person with what I can best determine is needed at that moment. The better any teacher gets at this, the more rewarding the teaching experience - for both the teacher and student.

There are many avenues to explore in the new teacher–student relationship, so let's talk as an example about teaching and learning the strokes. The more you watch racquetball - and especially, the pros - the more you will come to realize that no two players strike the ball exactly alike. So, your conclusion should be that there is no universal racquetball stroke. If you are trying to learn to hit the ball exactly like someone else, you are probably limiting yourself to some degree; and if you're trying to teach all your students to swing the exactly same way, then you are limiting quite a few of them!

The question each player (no matter what level) should be asking is, "What is the best, most natural, most effective way for *me* to strike the ball, and to have it go where I want, at the speed I want, and at the angle I want?" The best answer is to observe the field of the best players you can, draw what you want from each, and quickly progress to your perfect stroke. And, by all means, try out different teachers.

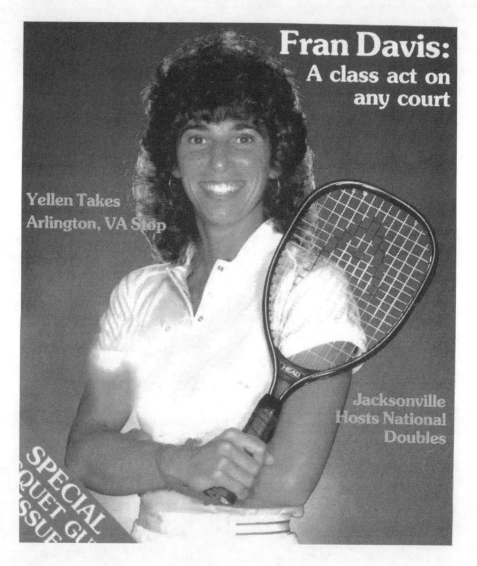

Fran Davis is the most successful pro turned racquetball businesswoman in converting a strong all-around game into a modern instruction empire. Her career has spanned 30 years as a competitor and coach.

518

New Tricks for Sports

From a lifetime in various sports, there have always been four stages to test any new act for the proven repertoire.

1. Does the new thing work in solo drill?

2. Does it weather practice games?

3. Does it withstand great fatigue?

4. Does it carry through tournament stress?

Thus, any new thing to be added to your sports show is not proven until it wins a tournament. At that point, you may relax and continue to use it to success.

Only about 1 in 10 of my early new tricks withstood the rigors to become a sweet spot of my game. Sweet, because any simple new thing added to a standard act usually makes a dramatic change in performance.

The first racquetball camp ever. The top 13 pros of the Golden Era met in Steamboat Springs at Steve Keeley's annual camp for this historic photo. (Left to right, top to bottom) Charley Drake (President Leach Industries), Jay Jones, Ben Koltun, Ron Strom, John Lynch, Steve Chase, Mark Morrow, Ro Rubenstein, John Weaver (Road Manager), Steve Keeley, Rich Wagner, Charlie Brumfield, Marty Hogan, Steve Serot, Craig McCoy, and Barkie the author's Mascot. (1977 Art Shay)

Drills

Jose Rojas drives at the 2014 Pro Kennex Tournament of Champions. (Mike Augustin)

The Slick Six Practice Tricks

Coach Jim Winterton

Let's talk about preparing for tournament nerves. Here are a few practice tricks that veterans of the racquetball wars know how to do. I call it the Slick six practice tricks!

1. Pick practice opponents to prepare for tournaments- seek out folks who emulate the game styles of players you will match up with. For example, if a lefty is who you have to beat, you have to scrimmage a lefty and if it is a slugger, practice with Sluggo!

2. Here is an unusual tip. Play the cheater. Every club has that unsavory competitor that people avoid, I advise you embrace that social outcast and play him! That's right...the character everyone avoids in practice- the cheater. I suggest you find one and play because he puts you under more pressure in practice and it is just like a tournament. If you play them in a tournament that is even better because a ref gives you points you didn't get because the cheater stole them from you during the week!

3. Play tournament situations in your mind. For example, finish your practice match with your weak side swing aiming for the perfect shot and visualize this shot as the game winner.

4. Play the five points in a row game. In the old days, back in Rochester, NY, a player named Mike Levine, a 15-year-old junior player, was a quarterfinalist in the men's pros. He invented this game and the rules are simple. The server has to score five points in a row. If they do not, they lose the serve and the receiver comes in to serve. The first player to win five points in a row wins a game. The game is played to three wins of five in a row. That can take a long time and it makes the server think sequentially on the serve.

5. Play your opponent's strength in practice. This one is crucial. You are young, mobile, hostile, agile and you are playing someone old and senile! Why drive serve them off the court? If you meet them in a tournament, go for it, but in practice? Play them at their strength, a control game. That gives you a better workout and gives them a workout also. If they beat you and get the 'all that' attitude, just smoke them a game with drive serves and go back to work on your game.

6. Last tip...do the chameleon trick. Take on different identities each game. Be Paula power in game one and work on the drive and jam serves. In game two be

Zelda Z-serve, and in game three be Constance control. In game four put all of the identities together and work on all of your serves mixing them up within one game.

These are six simple tips to more productive practice and tournament preparation. Happy killshots!

Coach Winterton awaits students at the ladder of success. (Mike Augustin)

Worst Case Scenario Practice

The most important thing a starting practitioner can do is to experiment with the full range of possibilities on every aspect of the stroke: Early racquet preparation, backswing, feet placement, weight transfer, zone of contact, concentration, length of time the ball's on strings, follow through, and so on. Sooner or later, he learns he can hit a strong return off the worst possible combination of these variables. A worst case scenario may be standing on one foot on a sweat spot, falling backward, reaching, twisting, and hardly looking at the ball. If he can do that - hit the ball well with the worst situations - he may walk confidently into the court that he may hit anything. It is the fire walking experience, and after that on the court he is Superman.

Rocky Carson front cross-over to a backhand at the 2014 WOR Nationals. (Stephen Fitzsimons)

Pros Speak from the Box

Practice

My solo practice sessions are fairly regimented. I start on one side of the court and hit down-line kills, then down-line passes, and cross-court with each shot too, followed by ceiling shots. Then I switch to the other side of the court. I know to move on to the next shot when I've hit about twenty good ones – that may be in the first twenty, or forty. I spend additional minutes drilling the pinch kills since they're so much a part of my game. I practice only when I get the urge that it will be enjoyable or useful, which is about 2-3 times a week. I cross the border twice a week to play some strong San Diego, CA players. When I play practice games, each narrows in on a topic of the day. One day I'll hit mainly drives against the opponent, without any ceiling balls. The next day all my kills might be straight-in as opposed to pinches.   *- Alvaro Beltran*

Fifteen percent of my time is spent in solo practice. I also do much off-court conditioning, play matches, and devote an enormous amount of time to teaching clinics. I have racquetball days, off-court training days, and teaching days. If it's an on-court day, I stretch for fifteen minutes, do 30 minutes of drills, then set up a match. The practice match resembles tournament conditions with the same goals.   *- Derek Robinson*

Advanced players should break their routines into about thirds: Practice play, solo drills, and off-court conditioning. Lower level players want to put more time into solo practice, and mature pros more into play practice. Every pro was a beginner once. No pro got great without a lot of time alone with a ball and his racquet in a court. He experimented, drilled what he knew, and invented.   *- Jim Spittle*

With a purpose! 100 reps of everything. Simulate set ups you'll see in the game, and practice all shots off of those set ups.   *– Cheryl Gudinas*

I practice based on the things I need to work on. This is called practice with purpose.
                                                                   - Charlie Pratt

I like to put some music on and hit several shots from all over the court. I will set myself up and simulate a shot I am struggling with it in play. I will practice returning it until I get it down.   *– Jackie Paraiso*

I practice two to three times a week, armed with these: A plan, a backup plan, a goal, just

524

a couple skills to drill, a measuring metric like a % good out of 5, and always one part of practice is for serving and another to keep a rally going with myself to train for endurance, and to better simulate live play and improvised shot making creativity, and because it's fun.   – *Ken Woodfin*

Mechanics and drive serve are the focus of both my solo drills and practice games.
                                                                                                                         – *Jose Rojas*

I both drill by myself and hard practice games.   - *Cristina Amaya Cassino*

Short focused practice sessions with breaks in the middle.   – *Andy Hawthorne*

For long hours of practice alone play mental games or you will go nuts: Attempt to hit 10 perfect DTW kill/pass, and if I skip start over. This helps to endure in practice but don't reach a point of diminishing returns.   – *Dave Fleetwood*

You would cross-train with running, sprinting, nautilus, and repetitive drills on the court.
                                                                                                                     – *Davey Bledsoe*

I play other players and work on certain skills during our games, rather than drill alone.
                                                                                                     - *Kerri Stoffregen Wachtel*

These days I host practices for the main pros out of Stockton, California so I'm actually practicing more than I used to as a pro. We have a bunch of active drills that we do and we're constantly trying to create new ones. We play a lot of "situational games," which are fun to work on specifics. I'm lucky I have 6 of the top 40 pros in the same city as me.
                                                                                                                          – *John Ellis*

I approach practice like actual play – focused and enthusiastically. I break the drilling up to stationary, moving, and also to alone and with partner drills. My practices cover all the aspects of the game.   – *Fran Davis*

As many practice matches as possible, so I could practice mainly my serves and returns. Afterwards with a partner we would just practice serves. We would set a minimum number of good serves to hit in a row and would stay until we met our goal. Sometimes it took hours.   – *Brian Hawkes*

Drills, drills, drills. With the right regimen of drills from a coach and the will to practice, you may make dreams come true.   – *Susy Acosta*

"Enjoy the game, Practice makes perfect!" - *Paola Longoria.* WPRO #1 2008-2009 season, US Open winner 2008, 2011, Gold Medal World Games, 8 times consecutive, Jr. World Championship 2000-2008, National Singles 2006, 2008, 2009, Gold Medal Central-American Games, Gold Medal Pan-American Games, 2006, 2008, 2011. (Mike Augustin)

526

Prevalence of Front and Back Cross Over and Open Stance
- *Definitions*

Ken Woodfin

Question: "I've been watching videos and shadow rehearsing in a tiny office the back crossover vs. the front crossover for covering shots. The videos go so fast, even in slow mo, that often I can't tell if it's a back or front crossover. In old school, and with slow balls, there was only front crossover. I'm guessing that now it's more back crossover and hitting shots off both wings in an open stance... Will you educate me?"

Cooperative Educational Offering on Modern Racquetball's Movement Changes and New Directions

• **Feet-work training**, how novel - I hope there's a change afoot. Although players may not yet focus on it specifically in drilling or as a point of emphasis in their technique enhancement - as they do their strokes and serves - players constantly move with more improvised, creative day to day footwork than even their coaches may realize or encourage. And hopefully drilling their feet-work is beginning to happen, in addition to time spent running ladders, working with resistance like bands and medicine balls, and ideally plyometrics training.

• **Why change** - Sure it's the speed of game, the agility of players, and the crushing blow mentality. And it's also the whatever is available effort to shorten the rally or make a get that calls upon all of the resources at the player's disposal to respond in real-time, in the mere blink of an eye.

• **More front or back crossovers and open stance hitting?** To your point..,

Whether players back crossover more than front crossover and whether they open stance stroke more in the modern game is a living example of innovation being the very mother of invention. The back or *behind* or accurately retreating crossover and crisscross (cross step behind with trail foot) would both logically be the extension of the premise that the game is fast, hitting on the run is a given, and hitting off the back foot by just stepping over and lunging back with the trail foot is just bad, inefficient form. Using a hastily established open stance off a diagonal drop either at the end of (a) the behind crossover and then lunge with the posting foot, or (b) the behind crisscross and then lunge would both seem to be better than just a long, desperate lunge with the closest leg

527

and a squash-like reach to flick or maybe a worse case layout into a full out dive and whack to the back-wall.

• After crossover best case

If time allows, either the back cross or back crisscross may be followed up with the feet-work move to get behind and beside the ball to then drive back into the ball with the stroking stance the player does best. That's Plan A to step in and stroke. Plan B is the Open stance.

Open stance lunge bow forehand by Brandon Davis at 2014 WOR Nationals. (Stephen Fitzsimons)

• Plan A Stroke to fool um

In Plan A, an advanced stance should be a deceptive one that disguises the shot or leaves the cover player to guess at the intended target. Pointing with your feet or even locating the ball in your stance would both raise a warning flag to the alert cover allowing her or him to recognize and cover that shot or angle and thus augment their anticipation, revealing their coverage run plan right-as-you-stroke forward or right after they see your racquet butt commit to move forward. The partially closed stance is both deceptive and ergonomically sound. Half a tennis shoe closer to the sidewall opens up all angles and allows for knee drive, hip pop, and upper body triangle flow (triangle = formed by shoulders and waist).

• Full lateral move risk

Slight desperation may elicit a direct lateral crossover to gain space fast, but odds are against the cover player having much offensive success because of multiple challenges of poor visual perception of a ball being intercepted as it hurtles by in front of your face, prep time is squeezed down, and the wall is both a physical and mental barrier.

• Plan A and the "L" to stroke

In less pressured moments, players do execute little *"L" shaped maneuvers and the front crossover finalizes their stroke stance.

*Consider this: the "L" is backwards on the floor at your feet. *_|*. The back foot steps on the bottom of the "L" closest to you and front foot steps up to the top of the "L".

• Plan D emergency turned into routine put-away

In exigent circumstances players also use the front cross to lunge diagonally forward for gets. Or, like the Kane bump, it's used to lunge and flick a put-away into a low target. An example is Kane's routinely selected corner pinch put-away.

• What's best, crisscross or crossover forward? It depends...

In my postage stamp floorspace, from a standstill start about two steps behind the ball, the crisscross forward seems to provide the *banana stem in* I enjoy for its increased inwards pulling force. I choose it over the crossover forward, which appears to send my weight laterally away from my center. So that's perhaps why it seems more instinctively and intuitively attractive to me to use and endorse the behind crisscross. However, over the long haul, the forward crossover is a major space gobbler. For a long dash forward, I'd suggest the forward crossover anytime as the igniter for your run. The forward crossover is especially effective from a balanced, more upright cover position than say at

Kerri Wachtel hits from closed stance defeating Angela Guiser in an open stance in a 2006 WPRO final. Kerri was the 2001 US Open Champion and Top Ten for all of the past ten years. (Ken Fife)

the end of a low, knees scraping the floor stroke where a push off to regain balance is step one. To recover from a low body angle stroke, a crisscross might get you going best because it can be incorporated into the rebalancing move. Study this and let me know.

• Plan B, the Open stance

The open stance is such an integral part of the game why it's practiced or emphasized so little just amazes me. Forms of it are used a substantial percentage of the time in rallies and ROS situations. Although granted tennis players do use it also as an aid to clear the net, with its upwards momentum ingredient, they also do it to add disguise, spin, and of course body rotationally generated force. They leave the ground to swing up and over, but they also do it to take the torque off their legs, hips, back and shoulders. I think that's the next step in elevating the movement of players, jumping and shooting, even from the back court in what used to be ceiling ball rallies or in bang-bang mid court rallies to attack belly to eye high balls with leaping swing volley, high-to-low strokes.

I hope I answered your question and raised a few more. It'd be a blast to study tape with you.

• **Plan C plyometrics,** and in case you forget…

The only way to get there in Feet-work is to train, and pylometrically speaking. It is "jump training", or "pylos" exercises based around having muscles exert maximum force in as short a time as possible. The goal is to increase speed and power. The focus is leg movement as to move from a muscle extension to a contraction in a rapid or "explosive" way, as with repeated jumping. Plyometrics are used by high jumpers and discus throwers to improve performance, and to a lesser degree in the fitness field. The explosive bursts define racquetball with all forms of jumps in the shortest execution time. Jump training gets you there quicker than you used to.

Airborne open stance by Rhonda Rajsich at the 2014 WOR Nationals. (Stephen Fitzsimons)

531

Weighted Timing

with Mike Wisniewski

With fourteen amassed National Singles titles in racquet sports between the authors, this weighted timing drill will benefit players in any sport using a hitting implement. Arguably, the most crucial skill one acquires when attempting to play a sport well with hand/eye coordination is timing. It cannot be overplayed how significant timing is and will be to your enjoyment and success. In this article we will begin to discuss the best way to improve your timing.

Timing is a multifaceted skill that is important in all movements on and off the court. First, to explain what timing is in relation to striking of the ball. A couple seconds here, a couple nano-seconds there, and Bang you're in a different country.

Timing has always fascinated me; it has been the driving skill set that has allowed me to achieve great things on and off the court. Excellent timing is the basis for all the good accomplishments in the racquet sports.

There are a couple of terms to define.

A.   Stroke Mechanics – with or without timing: The awkward flailing motion without timing that some players exhibit on the court when attempting to hit the ball. However, with timing, stroke mechanics become smooth, graceful and as consistent as water. pouring from a glass.

B.   Muscle Memory: The test of one's ability to connect brain waves to muscle groups in order to repeat a series of motions to form a more perfect union of the racquet face to the ball. In other words, the ability to repeat muscle motions exactly the same way over and over again.

One may think timing is pretty simple and that with practice he or she can figure it out. However, unlike baseball or golf where the striker of the ball is stationary, the variables of motion in a court while trying to strike the ball make it very challenging. To get it right, one needs stroke mechanics, muscle memory and knowledge of the planets … What? That's right, just as the planets revolve around the sun in our solar system, so shall the striker of a ball while in motion revolve around the ball and position himself perfectly to strike with accurate timing. Therefore, the ball becomes the center of the racquetball universe and the player gets in unison with it.

For now, we will focus on static timing (no movement of the ball), and the best drill for timing done off the court while waiting for lunch to heat up or watching a racquetball

532

video. Generally, five minutes of timing drill once a day will produce big benefits on the court in about one month. Developing the correct arm and hand muscles is key to having great racquet timing, racquet head control, consistent arm speed, and the unmistakable whip sssound when the head follows through the contact zone with perfect timing.

This drill is done with a top weighted racquet of approximately 16 to 20 ounces, and it is done with care as not to hit walls, wife, kids or pets…Yikes! Note: Do NOT do the whip stroke with a weighted-up racquet to avoid the weight flying off or an arm strain. Instead, use a smooth, flowing stroke. Practicing your form with a top weighted racquet is guaranteed to build a better grip, better racquet control, more acceleration, quicker hand speed and sharper punch, and faster pass-and-reload reflexes with an overall strength enhancement. The benefits match those of a weighted baseball bat.

Keeley for a season used weighted racquets in practice games, and even in minor tournaments, with speaker wire wrapped around the top rim or throat that adversaries suspected was picking up signals from a remote coach, and the hippies of the era believed were from outer space! Wiz, a professional mechanical engineer, has toyed with the thought of a lead filled racquet a la the baseball bat for the purpose of weight training.

Good form will naturally begin to fall into place due to the effect of the extra weight trying to follow a natural arc, similar to a pendulum. Relax, as you swing over and over from a stationary stance without a ball. It may be done in full concentration in a court without a ball, or in the living room. Allow nature to take its course and the racquet will rise and fall naturally as your timing improves. .

Things to consider while doing this drill:

1. Your swing will start to smooth out in short order, so *do not force or over accelerate while doing this exercise.*

2. Make sure the weight is securely attached to end of racquet.

3. Do not over-swing and do not snap through, hold and swing racquet at a fixed slow controlled rate of speed.

4. Use smooth controlled acceleration and deceleration within a full range of motion. Start high on the backhand and finish high on the forehand while rotating through your torso but in the stance of a static leg position.

5. Do not over-do it. This is a short 3 to 5 minute drill, done two or three times a week, maximum. In the second week, you may increase to a one session a day, and after one month to two a day, as long as the arm doesn't complain.

6.   Always finish by swinging your game racquet at half speed after using the weighted one to cool down.

The comedic joke, 'What's the secret of my comic succes...''Timing!' is the rapid response before the adversary knows what happened. With enhanced timing you enter a quick zone that the opponent may not read. Everything in the game sharpens- the stroke, serve, return and coverage. You will have increased endurance and be less prone to

Timing a shot at the 2014 3-wall World Outdoor Championships. (Mike Augustin)

injury. If your opponent blinks at the wrong moment he will miss your swing, like the gunslinger who drew and shot and holstered, as the dying challenger boasts, 'Go ahead and draw!'

The bottom line of training in a racquet sport, or any sport at all, is summed in the Golden Three Training Effects. There are three ways to make gains in training. You may:

A)   Increase speed

B)   Increase the number of reps

C)   Increase resistance (weight)

Racquetball, like bicycling, running, boxing, swimming, tennis and many other sport, involving a high number of high speed reps benefits five times as much as the other two factors combined by increasing the weight during the motion. This is the principal of the Weight Training Drill.

Mike 'The Wiz' Wisniewski's unorthodox in most things that always work out. The result is an unprecedented nine National Singles Championships. Here at the 2012 3-WallBall World Championships in Las Vegas in September in long sleeves, cooler than anyone. (Mike Augustin)

Intense vs Pleasure Workouts

With a background in physical fitness for fifty years, as a professional athlete and now amateur athletic nut, the bottom line of training always reaches for one question. Should my workout be for pain or pleasure?

The stock answer is that a workout should be accepted with suffering.

The exception is when there is stress at home, or job, or from the workout itself.

As a racquetball player who ran marathons and biked across America, my daily training for one decade without ever missing a day except for tournaments was:

- Bicycle one hour into the wind

- Run seven miles

- Racquetball match for one hour

- Weights for 30 minutes

- Practice for one hour

- Bicycle into the wind for one hour to hone

- Wind down jog for 30 minutes

It is seen from this regimen that there was a combination of intense, painful exercises alternating with moderate ones. The menu was devised to keep the appetite up each morning on rising from and each evening on going to bed.

A purely intense routine is superior for any serious athlete or as a life experiment for the amateur, but in my case there were the stresses of writing articles and books, and a loud household. Also, I discovered over the years, training itself becomes a mental strain from which a break to fun workouts should be added.

Training for fun or profit begins with a choice in location. The advantage of being able to step out the door of home or office at any time of day or night to train cannot be overemphasized. A workout begins with the first step, and if it is directly into the workout there is the advantage of inertia. And there is less time lost from life; Otherwise, why live.

The first step can be onto a bicycle of the neighborhood, jog in the park, or hike along a mountain trail. Virtually every place I ever chose to live was with location for training in mind. If you are, or are planning to become, a pro at a sport, then take root near other pros or a mecca of the activity.

When physical fitness becomes a lifestyle rather than a hobby or job, the highest peaks are reached.

The harder you practice the better you perform. There are some remarkable hard hitting specimens outdoors like Ben Croft at the 3-WallBall Championships in Las Vegas. (Mike Augustin)

Three Easy Steps to Walk All Over Your Opponents

To hang my credential on your court door: I have spent hundreds and hundreds of hours teaching private and group racquetball lessons, ran many instructional camps that lasted a month and have written a 288 page best-selling book to help players improve their racquetball play. That is past, and today I can condense over forty years of play, instruction and observation into three easy steps to walk all over your opponents.

1.   Spend twenty minutes every time before you play practicing your serve. The serve is the major common denominator that gave the most dominant players in modern racquetball the edge over all others. Marty Hogan, Cliff Swain, Sudsy Monchik and Kane Waselenchuk all control the game with the big serve and you can too. When you think about it, the serve is the one time in the game when you are in total control of the action. You decide how low to drop it, how hard to hit it and what serve to hit. It's your chance to take control of the point as soon as it starts.

Practice your drive serve from the left side of the court, the right side of the court, and center court. It's important to be able to hit at least three serves from each position with nearly identical motions. From each location on the court practice your drive serve to the left and to the right as well as the Z and jam serves until you find at least three serves you are really comfortable hitting from each spot. In total you should have at least ten power serves in your rotation. Just like a top pitcher in the majors, top players have a variety of serves to keep the opposition off balance.

In addition to variety, work on keeping your serves as low as possible. Practice dropping the ball lower and contacting it lower in the bounce. Ideally you'd like the served ball to bounce twice before hitting the back. But if you can keep a variety of serves low enough that your opponent fears might bounce twice you've done your job and will often solicit weak returns. Remember you drop the ball, don't bounce it unless you are hitting an overhead serve outdoors. Drop it low and contact it low, it's that simple.

It is also important when serving the ball down the line and cross court drive to avoid hitting the side wall. Years ago champs like Charlie Brumfield made a living hitting crack drive serves into the side wall. You too might catch some cracks when hitting a low jam serve, but as fast as today's game is you don't want to give your opponent more time to set up by catching the side wall on your straight drives. Save the side wall for your jams and Z serves. If you find your drives are hitting the side wall, adjust your point of contact in the motion. In other words, if your cross court drive is going into the side wall, drop the ball a little less in front of you until you find the contact point that takes it

538

straight into the rear corner. If your down the line drive is catching the side wall drop it a little more in front of you until you find that perfect contact spot.

You may not see immediate results until you improve and eventually perfect your new serves, but stick to them and keep a variety of serves coming low from multiple angles and the free points are sure to come your way.

Tip #1 – Practice the drive serve. Eric Harper drives at the 2013 3-WallBall Nationals. (Mike Augustin)

2.   Work on your swing preparation. Practice during drills, warms ups and matches getting your racquet up as early as possible and ready for the next shot. You may have to exaggerate ESP at first running from shot to shot with your racquet high in the air. That's OK, Swain did it for years. When the ball is traveling 130 to 170 MPH you have little time to think and even less to prepare. The entire game including focus gets easier when you prepare to swing earlier. By getting your racquet up early and prepared to swing you'll be able to contact most shots with maximum power and save you the step of having to bring your racquet up when you arrive to the ball. Early swing prep also gives you that split second more to see what your opponent is doing before you strike the ball and that in itself is a big advantage. In a game decided by inches and milliseconds when two players with similar skills vie, the player with ESP wins almost every time. Get your racquet up early and give yourself the winning edge.

Tip`#2 – ESP on the run like De La Rosa in the 2014 Pro Kennex Champions. (Mike Augustin)

3.   Everyone knows racquets have a sweet spot but you might not have known until now that the court has a sweet spot too. Step three is the simplest and the easiest to engineer into your game. After you hit a shot immediately return to the five foot line. Let the five

foot line be your magnet that pulls you to return after each ball is struck. With today's big racquets and fast game playing in front of the five foot line limits your ability to react to balls hit in excess of 130 MPH and leaves you in position to be passed easily. You don't want to be back too far either, so plant yourself just behind the five foot line. You are close enough to get anything but a perfect kill that you wouldn't have reached anyway, but deep enough to handle the pace and avoid getting passed. It's the ideal spot to combat the power game, so always return to your sweet spot after each stroke.

No camps, no books, no private lessons necessary to follow this simple three step plan that I guarantee will improve your game a full level from where you are now with just a

Tip #3 – Let the 5′ dashed line be a magnet like Rhonda at the 2010 US Open. (Mike Augustin)

few months practice. It's a cakewalk, it´s free, and if you're a C player you'll soon be a B, if you're a B player you'll become an A, and if you are an A player you'll soon join the big boys in the Open division as easily as one, two, three!

541

Cross-train for Racquetball with Racquetball

We invented all kinds of games to cross-train for pure racquetball. Some were as banal as two-on one, like cut-throat except two players vs. a stronger one for an entire match. There were ceiling games where after the serve only that shot was allowed, and the same for kill shot games. One of the best control tools is marking a ´squash ´tin´ with masking tape 3´ high across the front wall and all shots must hit above it without using the ceiling. Another is one wall four-wall racquetball in which if the ball touches the side walls it´s an out. There were three doubles teams on the court simultaneously that got dangerous with the arrival of the superball. A great conditioner is touching the short line after each shot and trying with a partner just to keep the ball in play. How about ´Chinese racquetball´ in which the ball strikes the floor twice before the return. Serve and Kill games improve the drive serve and kill return- the Big Game- in which only the serve and return is allowed, and if the receiver doesn't put the first shot away it´s a point. One of the best conditioners is Moving racquetball in which the players must keep in motion even if it´s just a shuffle at all times in the service box, waiting to receive, and between points. You may play singles or doubles with two or more balls at once making it possible to score more than one point per rally. If ambidextrous you may play yourself, and once at an Open tournament I made lefty to the semi´s and righty to the finals hoping to meet myself in the finals, but lost lefty before it happened.

Not to sound ridiculous but the early pros also played boxcar racquetball in which a ball and racquets were taken into the moving boxcar of a freight- half the size of a regular court- and hit until the ball flew out the door. We played scuba racquetball in which the ball was injected with a correct amount of water as ballast, and knocked it about underwater with scuba gear in a swimming pool. There were all sorts of handicaps in the early days that still may be used today to even out games. I played with swim flippers, or more difficult with three gallons of water sloshing in a jug in a backpack. Backward running during rallies by one opponent evens out games with kids. Ankle weights limits the faster competitor, or shortening the court with a taped rectangle for just one hitter. One player can hit with a wood paddle or squash racquet as a handicap against the big head racquet. Kids can use a sawed-off tennis racquet. We played soccer racquetball in which a soccer ball was used striking with the feet and hands using racquetball rules, which may have been the predecessor of indoor 4-wall volleyball. Alaska doubles is each team has one player mounted on his partner's shoulders, so the teams run around like totem poles with both the tops and bottoms swinging but only the lower half running. You can also put on cardboard blinders like a horse to limit peripheral vision to increase focus, or invent other ways to play and handicap the regular old game.

22-Time National Champion and Holder of All Titles Brumfield cross trains for racquetball with San Diego Charger tackle Bob Petrich. Brumfield has flat feet, strong legs, and a straight backbone against intimidation by anyone. (US RB Museum)

Specificity of Training in Racquetball

Specificity of training is hard to beat in any sport. Yet, there are countless variations to beat the boredom of endless racquetball…

- A great conditioner is **TOUCH AND GO** played by touching the short line after each hit with a partner trying just to keep the ball in play.

- How about a little **CHINESE RACQUETBALL** where the ball may strike the floor twice before a return.

- **SIDE WALLS OUT** is the best training for straight-in kills, a la outdoor one-wall.

- **SERVE AND SHOOT** games generate the Big Game of drive serve and kill return, over and over.

- The best conditioner is **MOVING RACQUETBALL** in which the players must stay in motion even if it's just a shuffle awaiting the service.

- You may play **SINGLES DOUBLES** with two balls at once, making it possible to score more than one point per rally.

- If **AMBIDEXTROUS** you may play with yourself, and try to win in the finals.

At the end of the day, the best training for racquetball is racquetball.

Cast into a Championship Mold

How low do you bend to contact the ball? I have a history behind it.

Before there were coaches, before there were professionals, I observed that many of the strongest killers of the sports contacted the paddleball or racquetball as low as possible, often scraping their paddle or racquet on the floor. The stroke is easy for stout players, but becomes problematic as you get taller because the hitting implement doesn't get any longer.

One day my game shifted higher that became the key to winning multiple titles in both sports. In the crack of an instant, I raised my strike on the ball to the knees or higher, and often above the waist. Why?

A leg injury put me on crutches for a month. I left those crutches outside the court and used a hobble cast to practice, and won a doubles tournament. I couldn't bend at all, and learned to kill the ball from an upright stance, cast into a championship mold.

Later, after the cast was removed, I found I could kill 90% as well contacting the ball high. I retained the upright stroke because, despite the 10% disadvantage in rolloffs, it provided three advantages.

- The setup was faster.
- Fly kills were easier.
- Deception – when I killed upright the opponent assumed it was a pass.

The net gain from these was about double the points per game. Now you know the strange secret behind many championships.

Another eccentricity I tacked onto the stroke got a few laughs and points per game. It was to always look and step the opposite direction that the ball was going off the strings. For example, when I stood upright for a forehand but stepped crosscourt, looking left, and contacted the ball at the waist, the opposition leaned back and left on his heels anticipating a pass shot… even as the ball rolled out the front corner. Coverage against me was a difficult study.

The moral is to think outside the box: Every problem comes with a solution if you look long enough.

Able to leap tall walls for balls at the WOR Outdoor Championship 2012. (Mike Augustin)

See Yourself - Video Tip

A tip for anyone who cannot travel to pro tournaments but wants to hit, think and play like the pros is the free YouTube videos of pro tournaments. Model your strokes and strategies after the theirs.

You can also video *yourself* with a digital camera to really improve your game. Just have a friend video your practice or tournament session, and then and evaluate your progress over time. You may accumulate an historic tape of yourself from beginner to open to pros. Review your strokes, variety of serves, watch to see that you are getting your swing prepared early, and be sure you are consistently returning to optimal court position.

One day, your home video may fast forward to seeing yourself fly in a pro tournament on YouTube!

Manny Gregorio. (Murray Diner)

547

Historic Video Analysis Aids your Game
Two Champs of Two Eras Strike: Hogan vs. Brumfield

The online video is of Hogan defeating Brumfield in the finals of the 1977 Tanner ProAm when Hogan was getting just good enough to beat Charlie and Brum was still great enough to defeat Marty. It is extremely revealing for three reasons.

· The historic content of what happens in the cusp of two racquetball legends from two sharply distinct eras when the two meet and it´s anybody's ball game.

· The behind the scenes strategies of the two champions are dissected in a way most fans miss.

· The video explains the strengths and weaknesses of your game by comparison.

The two eras in transition were Slow Ball with the control game where Brumfield had dominated for the seven years (1971-78), and Power Racquetball that Hogan had just invented and was about to publish a book by the same name (January 1, 1978). Note the video is labeled ´78 but the match took place in December of ´77.

Many questioned after watching the video why Charlie Brumfield didn't seem to make a backhand kill shot behind the short line, and how he could have been tired in finals. They didn't understand what Marty Hogan was doing (hitting it 140MPH+ with that little Bandido) was otherworldly this year!. Playing him with a small racquet and fast ball in ´77 was like racing Usain Bolt in the London Olympics that just ended. If you came close you should consider it a victory.

They gallery and video viewers probably also didn't understand the Brumfield Sword and Shield game, and that using his backhand as defensive shield and only attacking with it in front of the short line was his tried and proven strategy.

They also didn't get how deep the tournament draws were. Brumfield was tired after beating Steve Strandemo and Rich Wagner in the 16's and quarters, and beating you in a 15-13 tiebreaker after two long 21-point games in the semis. ´You´ was *me*, but imagine beating young Mike Yellen in the first round, Steve Serot in the 16´s, and Davey Bledsoe who was defending national champ in the quarters, before getting to play Brumfield in a tough semis.

What a blast in the Golden Decade 1970´s! You may follow the sport's evolution, and your own, with online videos up to this day.

De la Rosa swoops in at the 2014 3-wall World Outdoor Championships. (Mike Augustin)

5 More Novel Ideas to Improve Your Game

1. The first rule is always practice against someone your equal or better. Try never to break it.
2. The second rule is to handicap yourself if there is no equal. Some methods are:
   a) A point spot, or the opponent having to reach 15 before you get 100 points.
   b) Time odds, as in chess, where you may never stop moving even between points and receiving service.
   c) An implement disadvantage such as using a wood paddle against the racquet which automatically lowers the player one division.
3. For stamina, play simultaneous where one of a string of players enters the court after each point. If there are five players on the opposing 'team' you will get one-fifth their rest.
4. Play opposite handed - It's surprising what you'll learn about your correct hand game, and the handicap opens a new league of competitor until you are their champion.
5. Resistance training is the best method for any racquet, where resistance is weight. Add a few ounces of speaker wire braided around the frame, or wear ankle weights, or a weight vest with increasing increments of 5-40 pounds.

Not a novel but the only racquetball cartoon book created from the author's imagination. (1978)

Conditioning

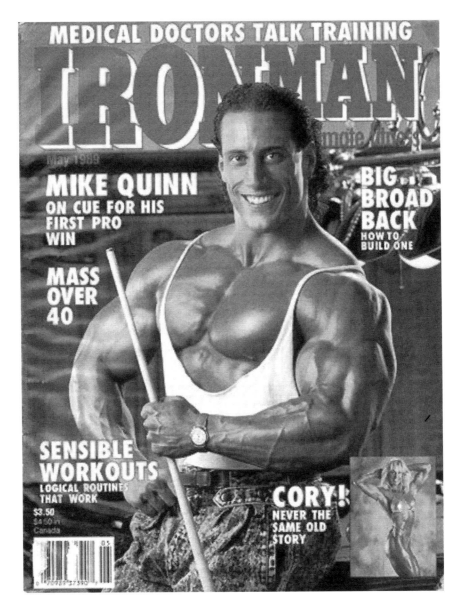

Mr. Universe Mike 'The Mighty' Quinn trained some of the Legends including Cliff Swain.

Mr. Universe Offers Racquetball Conditioning Tips

with Mike Quinn

Mr. Universe and some of the top racquet players heft the common goals of individualism and personal perfection. A few years back, I dug into a 'Gold's Mine' of training tips from Mike 'The Mighty' Quinn. Make that mighty, as in savvy and gracious.

'You can make a chorus line of doctors and psychologists who disagree, but serious sports competitors need conditioning and nutritional advice to progress. Athletes discovered twenty years ago that the ones coming out on top had personal trainers and nutritionists.'

We met in 2003 in the Coral Gables Racquet Club boiler room as I strained to shove a 600 lb. extinct water heater out the door to make room for a bed. I was the new club pro. He heard the scrapping through the ceiling pumping iron, and descended to help. I tipped the heater on edge, he squatted beneath, lifted, and hauled it out the door.

'I held the same cup as Arnold Schwarzenegger,' he cracked, loosening the weight belt, and returned upstairs to pump iron.

Seven years before this 2010 WOR Outdoor Championship overhead,
Cliff Swain trained for one summer under Mike Quinn. (Mike Augustin)

That afternoon he offered training tips to me on an adjacent treadmill. 'Let's start nutrition with an analogy. There are Lamborghinis and Volkswagens, and owners who care for them in different ways. You can put high or low quality fuel, oil and so forth into

552

each. At the same time, there's a genetic predisposition to everything. My father is a butcher, as big as the beef he carves, but I don't eat beef. Are you with me so far?

'The intense athlete must train himself to eat every three hours. The intake should be high protein because that's the building block of muscle. I eat chicken, protein shakes, salads, fruit and no red meat.'

He asserts the most important eating spurts are 90 minutes before, and 90 minutes after working out. 'Build and recover,' he keeps repeating. Interestingly, he takes some sugar with meals 'to pull the other nutrients into the muscle cells'.

How about a training regimen for the devoted wannabe?

'Young athletes get on the tournament court, field or mat and run out of steam before the finals. Their coaches berate them for not trying hard enough; however, in most cases, they peter out because they've been working too hard up to the tournament date.'

'Here's a training regimen for very serious players who have a low (non-playing) and high (tournament) season. In the first month of the low season, don't play much of the prime sport at all. Train at weights and machines intensely, and for short amounts of time, with short rest periods.'

'If your workouts in the first month are twice daily for an hour each, follow these principles: In the month's course, gradually increase the intensity, decrease the rest time between exercises, and maintain the duration of the overall workout.'

He grins broadly, 'It makes you puke'.

'In the second month of training during the low season, cut back half the weight training, while spending most the hours on the court, field or gym practicing and playing.'

'In the third month of low season, don't weight train at all, and don't play hard. Eat wisely throughout the three months, and go gentle on the ladies…

'You're a Lamborghini in the season opener!'

Quinn's analysis of over-training supports a personal belief that I over-trained throughout a fifteen year pro racquetball career, rarely taking a day off from hours of practice (one hour), playing (two), running (one), biking (two) and lifting weights (one hour). Tournaments were breathers.

'You never peaked!' assays Quinn.

'Right, but my priority was working out rather than winning tournaments. I loved it,' I asserted.

'Most players want to win more than that, don't they?' he countered.

'Yes,' I agreed, recollecting six national championships.

In a challenging silence, I asked to grab collars to test my better sport, judo.

He grasped my lapels at arm's length, lifted me a foot off the ground, and whisked his sneaker under mine, exclaiming, 'This is a foot sweep!', and gently lowered me to the floor.

Quinn put me on a 3-month regimen of weights with a high-protein diet to gain slight weight and much strength, while increasing speed and stamina- can you beat that?.

'There's an ancient controversy of muscle vs. sport, that should be muscle *and* sport. The stronger the player of any sport, the greater the edge- period! However, don't think muscle equals bulk. Think of tiny individual muscle fibers growing thicker, and stronger end attachments to the bones. This increased density is a strong muscle, not a huge muscle.'

Huge muscles are for bodybuilding, Quinn's profession.

'Arnold Schwarzenegger, Lou Ferrigno (The Incredible Hulk) and I hold the same trophy for Mr. Universe. We just held it in different years (1984 for Quinn). Arnold is a smart, hard worker who likes to 'bust your balls'. He and I had words once, that fortunately for each of us, didn't go any farther. Lou, on the other hand, demands everyone's regard for achieving greatness through deafness. He's a friend who would have worn the green skin, even with good ears.'

Mike Quinn set the world pumping iron aflame by winning Mr. America at 18-years old. 'It was too early to peak into fame, but I plowed on as best I could.' Title after title, in country after country, followed. In the early 90s, he opened two Gold's Gyms in southern Florida, then exited business to train professional football, baseball, racket and other players. There was a two-year stint with Tae-Bo boxing guru Billy Blanks trading daily lessons- weights for martial arts.

To look at Quinn is to behold a bull with a quick glint behind the eyes. 'I rose out of a dysfunctional family, neighborhood rubble, and attention deficit, and it's the best inspiration I can offer whiners.' He's extremely graceful, honestly sociable, and highly self-educated on health, nutrition, exercise physiology and psychology. He likes to stick you between a dumbbell and a hard place with mental puzzles, and watch the workout.

Jose Rojas is a strikingly conditioned figure at the 2013 3-WallBall World Outdoor Championships in Las Vegas. (Mike Augustin)

As I listened to the gentle giant speak, it dawned on me that despite my life-long study of unorthodox pet and human training methods, there was not a thing to disagree with. His hair-brained theories fit my hair-brained theories to weave Sampson a wig.

Thanks to Mr. Universe Mike Quinn for the conditioning tips of a lifetime.

Physical Training for Advanced Players

by Corey Brysman

Corey Brysman just out of the Juniors beat Mike Yellen twice in 1984-5 for what is called the 9th greatest upset in the history of racquetball. He became a consistent fourth ranked pro, Legend player, and now is a Miami certified personal trainer. This article was written expressly for the serious conditioner.

I want to outline a conditioning program targeted at the racquetball player who either wants to get better fit to play harder, or simply to get healthier. Racquetball demands greater physical strength while not limiting flexibility. This is different from body building where one makes the muscles bigger, so as you progress through the weeks with the program, don't worry so much if the muscles don't get bigger, but enjoy more power and endurance without losing range of motion.

Conditioning can be fun if you keep these goals in mind. And remember: The harder you work the more gains come. If you're presently out of shape, start slowly, and build gradually because you have a life ahead of you, and if you're older or infirm in some way then first seek the counsel of a physician.

The general description of the program is a moderately high rep with lower weight resistance. If you're lifting weights, then I advise 12-15 reps per set with low to moderate weight for each body part. This provides 'racquetball conditioning' for sustained strength through the match.

The body parts can be divided generally into the upper and lower body, though as you get into weight lifting you'll begin to isolate the feet, front and back of calves, and of thighs, the hips, the abdominals, parts of the back, arms and hands, and the neck and head. The number of sets you perform depends on your time and seriosity. My suggestion is to consider three sets for each body part an average. Don't forget to play racquetball.

Start your program simply, and develop complexity as you gain confidence, knowledge and power. Think about hiring a personal trainer for the first lesson, and tell him that you want to learn how to use the program I'm suggesting by yourself after that initial lesson. Then there's no reason why you can't proceed alone. Or, you can watch others train, or eavesdrop on someone else's session to learn. There are also good books and videos.

Here's a day-to-day program for the player that can be customized as desired. Pick three days a week to lift weights, three days to play racquetball, and one to warm down or rest.

The best conditioned athlete of the Golden Era 1970s was Steve Strandemo. (John Foust)

Stagger these days for a balanced schedule, for example, Monday racquetball, Tuesday lower body weights, Wednesday racquetball doubles, Thursday upper body weights, Friday league racquetball, Saturday biking or running outside, and Sunday is up to you.

When you lift weights for each body part, remember to use full range of motion and not so much an explosive motion as a strongly sustained movement, sort of like a controlled power stroke that builds strength and endurance without bulk. Big muscles in racquetball don't necessarily mean more power on the stroke, coverage and so forth, because they weigh more and can infringe on the movement hence leverage of the swing. Right now I'm as strong as I've ever been as a professional player, yet you couldn't decipher this by 'then and now' photos. I like the deception of that, to watch the opponent wilt in the third game while I'm, or one of my students, is relatively fresh. Their shots and strategies fall apart due to exhaustion, while ours hold to the last point.

My thought is that week-to-week you should change the routine so that you stay fresh, and pop out of bed in the morning ready to have at something new. Also, your body won't adapt muscularly to any training regimen but works toward an overall conditioning effect. You'll be ready for about anything within four months.

If you play tournaments and there's a season, this is a nice break in the long-term routine. You should build strength off-court during the off-season to peak just before the season begins, then transition into playing more in the month before the season starts. You can continue to lift and train outside the court during the season given time, but it will be less arduous.

If I were to pick one specific activity to train for racquetball... well, let's see. There are stairs, running, sprints, treadmill, Stairmaster, cross-training sports like squash and basketball, and my personal favorite is cycling. This can be done inside or out, and

Marty Hogan vs. World Arm Wrestling Champion in *National Racquetball* magazine February, 1979.

558

like indoor bikes with tension adjusters that function as varying resistance which is sometimes easier than finding a hill to ride up outdoors. I do two types of intervals, mixing them during one workout, or from day to day. The first is intervals while varying the RPM or cadence, and you can think of about 80 rpm being the average. So, you can do a minute at 130 rpm with a low tension, then 'rest' with a minute at 80 rpm with a low tension. You repeat these intervals, say ten times, for a workout. The other kind of interval is changing the tension. You cycle for a minute at a high tension with a cadence of about 80 rpm, and follow with a lower tension for a minute. Again, ten is a good number of intervals to shoot for.

Interval sprinting is another top tool for conditioning though a bit more rigorous. It gives speed, enhances endurance, builds strength, and - importantly - trains recovery. Of all aspects of conditioning for racquetball, the most significant is recovery, where you're ready after an exertion, ready after another. Isn't that racquetball itself? A good interval sprint workout, and again this can be augmented to personal taste, is ten 200-yard sprints each separated by 30-60 seconds of walking for rest. As your fitness improves, reduce the period of rest.

Another schedule has the appeal of an athletic smorgasbord. You mix say 20 minutes of running, 30 minutes of cycling, 10 minutes of stairs, then play racquetball. So you use different muscles and movements to get your heart rate to a training level. You'll stay fresh mentally, quick and strong muscularly, and ultimately perform better on the court and in other walks of life.

Fast flying action as Ben Croft reaches for the Championship at the 2010 US Open. (Mike Augustin)

Conditioning

Through the Agony of Da Feet

Brad Kruger with Keeley

'Exercise programs should simulate movements of the activity for which training is designed, wherever possible,' wrote Gerge B. Dintiman in Sprinting Speed, *about 'specificity'. In other words, a conditioning program must have actions closely related to those in an actual game situation. For example, in training for racquetball, running windsprints is better than, say, striking a punching bag. The drills of this article are the conditioning ones that follow the movements of racquetball closely, the 'specificity designed' exercise routines used by the game's top speed demons. And if motivation is slightly lacking, repeat aloud these words of Nietzsche, 'That which does not kill me makes me stronger.' The words don't make your workout any easier, but it's a great deal more impressive than stringing together obscenities. And, the drills improve your game tremendously.*

Scurrying

The most specific drill, the Scurry, is reserved for those who wake up to read signs taped to the bathroom mirror that say, "His physical presence intimidated his foes, his raw talent bedazzled them.' A favorite drill of the five-time National Champion Charley Brumfield, arguably the best court coverer through King Kane, scurrying is done on the court with a playing partner and a stopwatch. Essentially, you play a frantic game of multi-bounce racquetball (i.e. no limit on ball bounces) for five minutes, or until one of you drops. Then take a breather and do it again.

The objective is to return the ball to the front was as soon as you can, and hit some good shots in the process while literally working your butt off.

Pan Drills

Anyone who has trained under the watchful eye of pro coach Carl Loveday has been subjected to the teeth-clenching Pan Drills And undoubtedly they also have reaped the rewards.

Taking less than 20 minutes, on average, the Pan Drills will show an improvement in footwork within two weeks. On the physically conditioning side, the drills improve agility, strength and endurance. On the mental side, they develop a great inner toughness.

To begin, place six small objects about five feet apart down the center (from front to back wall) of the racquetball court. Players weave in and out of the stationary objects.

560

Loveday says to struggle through each drill until you feel a slight burning sensation in the thigh muscles- then attempt one last rep. If you don't collapse on the

floor from exhaustion- or even if you do- take a short breather, congratulate yourself, and move on to the next drill.

Pan Drills can be done in the following variations:

2) **Quick, quiet, short steps.** Imagine you are at a football training camp, at the obstacle course, and you are running through 10 or 12 lined-up tires. You probably feel like a barefoot gorilla on scorching hot pavement. Well, believe it or not, you have just mastered the Pan Drill.

Staying up on the toes, knees slightly bent, step as quickly as possible in weaving the pans. Not the crunch of the heel on the floor, but the squeaking noise caused by friction between your shoes' rubber and the court floor.

3) **Shoulder-width Hop.** With feet spread shoulder-width apart, hop up and down the court, one foot on each side of the pans. This strengthens the groin and stomach muscles.

4) **High knee-ups-** Lift your knobbies as high as you can, weaving through the objects at a snail's pace. If your knees don't go as high as you thought they would, lean back a little, or tilt your pelvis upward. Once again, stay on your toes. This drill is only recommended if you have strong knees. If you even fear knee problems, sit this drill out.

5) **Four-step shuffle.** The weaving changes slightly for this drill. Facing close to the front wall, begin by shuffling four steps diagonally to the left, then to the right, and so on slaloming the objects in large swings like a waterskier. Turn around at the back wall and shuffle back in the same manner.

6) **Number one done backwards.** There are a few other notes. When working your way through the pans, try to raise your racquet hand high in the air. This helps recreate a game situation, and trains your arm for racquet preparation.

Line Drills

Loveday jammed grit down your throat, whether you're hungry or not, until the only way to get rid of the bad taste is to sweat it out... here's another drill. The Line Drill, originally

561

developed in football and basketball training camps, improves your forward and backward mobility.

Working with another person, player A begins with his back against the back wall. He sprints to the short line, returns to the back wall, then sprints to the front wall and again to the back wall. In relay fashion, player B then sprints the same pattern, while player A

Tri-sport Canadian National Champion in racquetball, handball, and swimming Brad Kruger hustles at the Canadian Klondike Open final against Linsey Myers. (Brad Kruger)

catches his breath. When player B returns, player A is off again. How many? Clench your teeth and aim for 10 minutes. This drill improves your endurance, mobility and agility on the racquetball court.

Kangaroo Hops

Crouch on your haunches at the back wall and thrust upward and forward more like a kangaroo than a frog. Hop to the front wall, and return. Repeat the court lengths for three minutes.

Monster Walks

Start at the back wall and take a giant step forward bending at the knee as the lead foot posts. The thigh bone should be parallel to the floor, and then thrust up, take a similar step with the other leg continuing to the front wall. Turn around, and do laps for three minutes. This and the previous drill provide propulsion in coverage.

Perpetual Rally

Alone on the court, with ten minutes to spare, drive the ball into the front wall and kill the return. This is a no-bounce routine where the ball may bounce many times during a rally that never stops, as long as you keep hitting drives and kills.

Motion Game

Play a regular game except the players must stay in motion at all times. During the service and return, and between shots in a rally, each must walk rather than stand. It is never allowed to be still for more than a split-second.

Another name for this is 'anaerobic racquetball' and it will make your regular game seem like a cake walk.

Important

In conclusion, try not to kill yourself with these drills. Not that there's anything wrong with fitness fanatics, but remember that quasi-masochists have a habit of gracing the sidelines with injuries.

Start your conditioning program slowly, and add drills and time in daily increments. Remember the backpacker who put one small stone in his knapsack each day and walked 100 meters farther, until at the end of six months he could carry the earth on his shoulders.

Alternate the drills on different days; three on day 1, three on day 2, and the Motion Game on day 3.

And only use these drills for *advanced* conditioning. If you are totally out of shape, check with a doctor for any problems that might develop before starting a more gradual activity to get your body ready for these hard conditioning drills. You want to be in action, not the sidelines.

Paddleball and Racquetball National Champion Bill Schultz was a circus performer and Big Time Wrestler. Here he flips John 'The Duke' Wayne in Hollywood. (Bill Schultz Jr.)

564

Burst Conditioning

Top level racquetball is a sequence of little explosions through a match. Hundreds. This is how you practice to reach the top.

Each burst lasts eight seconds. On average. Each at about 70% maximum effort.

There's a short break, and then the next burst. The cycle repeats for an hour match.

Specificity of cardiovascular training is required to compete at this pro level. The off-court exercises elicit specific adaptations, creating specific training effects. The effects are due to improvements in the specific muscles and energy systems involved. Specificity of training is a hard, fast rule. As you train, so shall you play.

I disagree with coaches who preach aerobic training for pro racquetball. It is an anaerobic sport all the way. Besides, as you train anaerobically, you gain aerobic effects. However, the reverse is false. Anaerobic means literally 'without oxygen' whereas aerobic is 'with' it. The reason is anaerobic training induces fast twitch, or 'white muscle'. Fast twitch fibers contract quickly and powerfully, but fatigue very rapidly, sustaining only short, anaerobic bursts of activity before muscle contraction becomes painful. Slow twitch, or 'red muscle', is dense with capillaries giving the muscle tissue its characteristic red color. It carries more oxygen and sustains aerobic activity using fats or carbohydrates as fuel, as the muscle fibers contract for long periods of time but with little force.

2014 3-WallBall Outdoor Championship dive in a burst by Jessica Parrilla. (Mike Augustin)

565

In veterinary school we learned that anaerobic white muscle that is least dense in mitochondria and myoglobin is characteristic of rodents. This is the fast muscle type, explaining the plate color of their flesh.

So, there you are off the court burst training for racquetball and trying to prove me wrong. You don't need fancy equipment to condition for racquetball. You do need to remember that any conditioning should closely resemble the activity of racquetball. Bicycle sprints with short rests between, stairs, wind sprints, chopping wood, anaerobic love, shoveling snow, swimming lap sprints, or anything you can think of.

Once you've selected the activities ponder the effort-rest intervals. You should go gang-buster at about 70% effort for eight seconds, rest for eight second walking around, and repeat for an hour. DECREASE THE REST BREAK TO IMPROVE DRAMATICALLY, RATHER THAN INCREASE THE DURATION OF WORKOUT.

Besides specific training, there is one other principal called training effect. You improve, which is to say get a training effect, by one of three methods: 1. Decrease rest break, or 2. Increase resistance, or 3. Increase speed. For racquetball and off court training for racquetball, the best is to decrease the rest. Next best is increase resistance, which means adding weight to the exercise. And it's worthless to increase speed which comes naturally with the former two methods of training effect.

Vary your off court conditioning activities to stay fresh.

If you choose weights, the general program I've designed could be called lift and puke. Start a specific exercise with a safe weight and do six reps with full extension for eight seconds. Take a break of equal time. Repeat the exercise for six sets. Then go to the next exercise or machine that uses a different body part; usually you alternate upper and lower body. Do another six reps, rest, and on for six sets. The duration of the workout is about 30 minutes. Over time, decrease each rest break by one second per week, and gradually increase the weight by 10% per week, but keep the speed (intensity) of 70% the same.

Here are some tips for off court conditioning:

- Alternate upper and lower body.

- Once a month take a week off and do something else.

- Utilize burst training mostly in the low season, usually the summer when there are fewer tournaments.

- Remember there are a thousand ways to condition off-court for racquetball.

Repeat this mantra, 'As I work harder I will want to drink more, eat more, and sleep more.' So, your conditioning brings you to the cross-roads of deprivation. Attend these requests.

You're on the Spartan path.

Brian Pineda, Pro Paddleball Doubles Champion in 2012, smashes a forehand. (Mike Augustin)

Hybrid Racquetball

Shotgun Marriage of Racquetball to Paddleball

Hybrid Racquetball is racquetball using wood paddles. The action is faster than original paddleball with more control than traditional racquetball. The game should be popular among beginners, women and juniors because of a short learning curve and quick workout. At higher skill levels, the surgical control in longer rallies replaces racquetball's vexing big serve and short rally. The new wood/graphite paddles are lighter, springier and more durable, and game balls are never be a problem. Any racquetball is used, though the green Penn ball is official for the Legends Pro-Paddleball (Hybrid) tour that was born last weekend (2003) at the Multnomah Athletic Club.

Racquetball history started with paddleball a half-century ago when players carved wood paddles plywood and skinned tennis balls to gain the rubber playing core. The new sport of Hybrid ball is the marriage of processor paddleball with offspring racquetball with the advantages of both. The hybrid game is more control than power, like sweaty chess. The. recent Portland event proved that top racquetball players adapt quickly to the game using their familiar power strokes. Among beginners to open players, the first practice session

A vertical bow about to pop at the 2014 Paddleball Nationals in Riverside, CA. (Mike Augustin)

568

typically begins with a few minutes of frustration, but he light paddle and lively make it end with solid hits and hunger for more.

Paddleball horizontal bow backhand with Emmett Coe vs. Brian Pineda in the 2013 Pro Paddleball final at the 3-WalBall World Outdoor Championships in Las Vegas. (Mike Augustin)

Racquetball and paddleball purists alike may find the new game great for cross-training. Strong advice to beginners is to learn a soft, lob serve, and a down-line service return. Rally aggressively with kills and passes, and volley when possible. As in other sports, conservative play wins initially, however offensive shots take one up the club ranks. Above all, play hard and have fun.

Cross-Train for Racquetball with Squash, Handball

Jerry Hilecher

Along a slightly different line, the best training for racquetball comes from my personal philosophy and the practices and of the St. Louis Power Hitters who became national racquetball champions.

We believe that the best training for racquetball is racquetball AND Squash and Handball.

For me, squash was similar to racquetball in basic movements but added the aspects of a deeper thinking. Squash for us was primarily for endurance and the capacity to think when dog tired as the rallies were much longer. In regards to movement, squash added a focus on maintaining center court position, cutting the ball off, and for hitting defensive control shots down the line. Center Court was a priority as you would often hit the ball and re-direct yourself back to center court in the same motion. All of the St. Louis Power generation - Marty Hogan, Steve Serot, Andy Gross, David Gross, Doug Cohen, and myself were accomplished squash players.

Handball is the equal to squash in cross training for racquetball. Even when I gave up handball for pro racquetball, I would go back to the game now and then. It adds two key components that are needed for racquetball but absolutely required for handball: Focus on footwork, and ball contact point. Handball requires good footwork on the chase because the ball is farther away to reach, and on the stroke because the feet and legs must participate for the ball to reach the front wall. Every St. Louis Power Hitter had exquisite counter-rotation and then rotation into ball which is called body torque.

As well, handball has an extremely small contact point - your hand - so you have to focus on making not only contact on your hand but just an inch or so of your hand. Add the fact that you lose the reach with an extended racquet makes you move quicker to the ball. This helped my racquetball quickness and reaction to the ball, and focus on hitting the ball properly. Hogan, Serot, and myself were accomplished handball players with Serot winning the 16-and-under Junior Handball Nationals, while I finished 3rd in the 18-and-under Junior Handball Nationals.

Try squash AND handball to boost your racquetball game.

'The greatest shot in outdoor handball history ' was in Las Vegas on September 30, 2010. (WOR)

World Squash Champion Victor Niederhoffer was one of racquetball's great retrievers. (Art Shay)

571

Many pros cross-train indoor and outdoor. 2014 World Outdoor Championship. (Mike Augustin)

Racquetball and Paddleball hold side-by-side Outdoor Nationals in Las Vegas. (Mike Augustin)

Pros Speak from the Box

Conditioning

I have a treadmill and use it every other day for forward, backward and lateral footwork. I lift weights for an hour three-times a week, and mountain bike, run hills and play squash. I have a series of on-court conditioning games, including 'squash racquetball' where the rallies are five times as long on your lungs as regular play. *- Derek Robinson*

I live in Tijuana, Mexico where there are 30 courts spread among six clubs, mostly private and country clubs. It's too bad, but right now (2003) it's difficult for an upcoming young player to get into one of these clubs without sponsorship. I start every day at 7am with running and a lot of sprints. Then I work my upper body with the medicine ball. In the afternoons, I go to the courts to practice and play. *- Alvaro Beltran*

A mature pro has no flaws so his practice is for maintenance. His racquetball time breaks down approximately: Practice play about 40%, solo drills 15%, and off-court conditioning 35%. Off court condition is anaerobic and resembles the game as closely as possible whether it's on a treadmill, bicycle, swimming pool or weight room. –Jim Spittle

Conditioning is actually my favorite part of the sport. I do anything and everything. Biking, running, stair climbs, sprints, weights, calisthenics, etc. Also on court speed drills. *- Charlie Pratt*

I like to work on all aspects of my game when conditioning. Cardio, speed/foot drills, strength training, stretching, mental drills, and resistance training are all important for my racquetball conditioning. *– Jackie Paraiso*

The same way LeBron James or any top athlete train or condition: Weights, interval training, plyometrics. *– Jose Rojas*

I do a lot of spin classes, a bit of speed workouts and a lot of RB. I'm terrible at stretching as I do not like it much, but I still get it done most days. *– John Ellis*

I fuel, hydrate, resistance train, bomb the core, run stairs, run in the shallow end if the pool, do racquet leaning against the wall, and feet-work drills. I rest when I'm not conditioning and I sleep as hard as I play, while sometimes dreaming about RB. *– Ken Woodfin*

2013 WOR Summer Legend Ben Croft. (Mike Augustin)

I work out about 2 hours/day, 6 days/week. Sometimes, I will do doubles if I need to get more racquetball in that day.   - *Kerri Stoffregen Wachtel*

When I was winning no one was working harder than me in the gym. I train specifically for movements I need on the court. Specificity of training is key. I've never lost a match because I was tired.   – *Cheryl Gudinas*

Weights, spinning, running, and playing way too much.   – *Andy Hawthorne*

An all-around routine of gym, run, footwork exercises, drills, games, and diet.
                                                                   - *Cristina Amaya Cassinot*

The National Portrait Gallery in Washington, D.C. offers the first known racquetball photo. Babe Ruth took this bat to a local YMCA and started hitting baseballs against the wall. The YMCA general manager then kicked him out for "making such a racket." The next day the general manager did the same thing himself and called the game "Racket-Ball."

(Top) The first known 'racquetball photo' of Babe Ruth. (Below) The 'racquetball strokes resemble a baseball swing, with permission of Mihael Williams for his daughter the batter.

Author pedals up to the St. Louis JCCA from San Diego for the 1975 Nationals. (Mike Zeitman)

Scuba paddleball at Michigan State when the courts flooded. (NPA)

Equipment

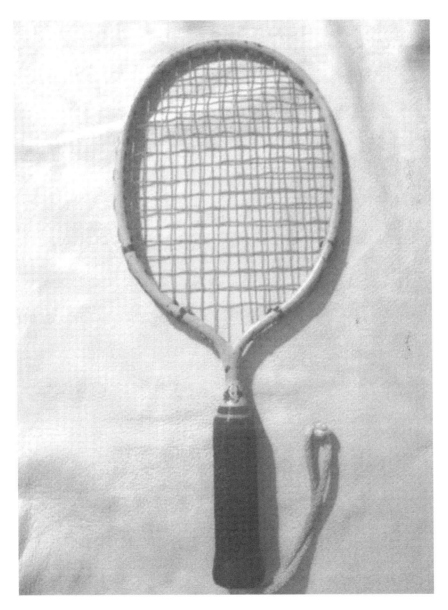

The Dayton Steel Racket was double strung that won the 1969 ´First´ racquetball Nationals.

Dr. Bud & the First Metal Racket

Dr. Bud Muehleisen

For the record, for my match with Charley Brumfield in the 1969 Nationals in St. Louis, I used a Dayton Steel Racket which was double strung with a corrugated smooth wire. The racket was very light in the head but would wear out quickly, because at the throat of the racket the single-tube steel would bend (back and forth) and finally give way and break.

Charley used a wooden racket made by Sportcraft which we called a 'Wooden Clunker'. I tried playing with the Dayton and had very little success getting it to do what I wanted it to do. I think that I went broke three Dayton rackets in our finals.

When I called the Racket Company after winning, and I think that they were in Dayton, Ohio (Da), I spoke with the President who seemed like Connie Mack to me. I offered that as a truly special racquet just brought out, they would endorse me in any way since I had now put their Racket on the map, and he replied......'Oh no, their company doesn't do anything like that, but they would sell me rackets at a somewhat reduced rate'.

Well, that was the end of the Dayton connection, and right away Bud Held came up with the Ektelon Bud Muehleisen aluminum extrusion model, and away we went.

Charley used the 'Bud' for quite a while until I got Bud Leach started in the Industry by designing his early racquets, for which he never even bought me a cup of coffee. He then signed on Brum and others to carry on his banner. He had about $1.50 in his original fiberglass racquets with a markup to $19.50. With great marketing they were up and running fast, especially with Keeley, Serot, and anyone else who would play with it. Then over to Taiwan where Keeley demonstrated with a 4-foot model and they made even more money. Charley Drake came on board and disallowed Brumfield and me from playing doubles together anymore. However, we had a great run though the 70s playing 7 ½ years without ever losing a game! The most points ever scored on us was 13 in one game by Serot and Valier in a St. Louis National Finals.

I also happily report that Brum and I are the closest of friends to this day and it has been a 'fun' relationship, despite starting with the Dayton steel and Spalding Clunker.

Pros Speak from the Box

Racquet

I like a light racquet that's slightly head-heavy for enhanced feel. *- Corey Brysman*

Go with a traditional quadriform head, and try a racquet that fits your swing speed.
– Dave Peck

I like wide body racquets, and don't think there are enough of them around. The big advantage is in power, which has been demonstrated in tennis and has even more bearing in racquetball. The wider throat and face, and especially thicker frame gives greater stability. *- Mike Ray*

Look past lightness for other qualities in modern racquets like frame thickness, balance and string tension. The big head racquets have gotten so light that to go any further exceeds diminishing returns. This is how to select a racquet: Lay out some without knowing their weights, and hit a few for feel. Pick the one that feels most like an extension of your arm. *- Marty Hogan*

Pick up the racquet, put it in your hand and hit a couple. Next racquet, same thing. Finally, decide on the straightest shooter. *- Sudsy*

Hit 'em all. *- Derek Robinson*

Take a personal knowledge of game style into to the shop and select a suitable racquet. Is your style control or power, and which racquet provides it? *- Ruben Gonzalez*

Think about what kind of ball you want to play. If it's recreational then pick an economical one and have fun. If you want to spend more money for a better racquet, try out a few and buy the one that feels best. *- Alvaro Beltran*

Most amateur players should test a slightly heavier modern racquet because the very light racquets are used by the pros who have pro quality swings with great acceleration that's lacking in the lower ranks. Force equals mass times velocity squared, and when there's not enough velocity you need more mass. This should prevent the amateurs from over-swinging to correct their biggest problem, hitting the ball off the back wall.
- Charlie Brumfield

I string my racquet at slightly less than the manufacturer suggests. My swing has ample natural power, but can use a little extra control by the lower tension. The ball stays on the strings a fraction longer. I think the effect of tension and gauge on the game outcome is generally underrated.   *- Jim Spittle*

I've tinkered with string tension over the years and conclude that it depends on the type of shots you want to hit. I try to get players to go to a lower string tension and higher gauge (about 19 gauge) for about 6 mph more speed and 15% more control due to the 'trampoline effect'. Yet it's a subject of long controversy.   *- Jeff Leon*

The ball on strings tells its direction and spin at the 2014 WOR Nationals. (Stephen Fitzsimons)

Jennifer   Harding

The poster that launched a thousand smiles in court clubs across America belongs to pro champion Jennifer Harding. The Ektelon poster shows her swinging the Ektelon Jennifer Harding signature racquet. The Jennifer racquet was designed for women with a new I-beam extrusion for increased flexibility, and a special modified head shape with a larger hitting area. This was the first and only racquet named for a woman player, and Jennifer requested an extra small grip. With it she became the number-two professional player in the heart of the Golden Era.

The First Oversized Racquetball Racquet

A Slice of History

Randy Stafford

I had no money to pay for my time with Dr. Bud Muehleisen, so I brought two ice chests on the plane with me full of bear meat that I just shot in Alberta. It was the summer of '72 and having just graduated from high school and moved there, I lost in the second round of the Klondike Open to Dr. Bud.

'Come to San Diego and spend the rest of the summer at my home and playing racquetball,' he urged.

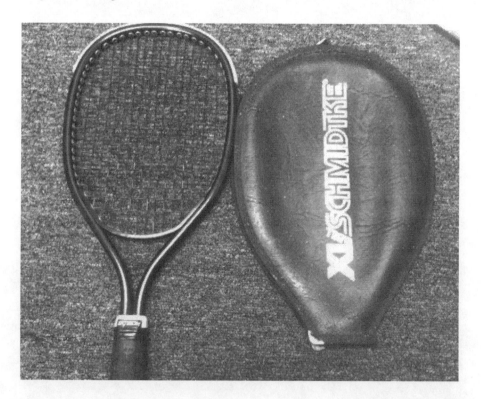

'Wow!' I said, and showed up with the bear meat. I thought if I could not pay him at least I could cook for him.

My life changed forever that summer, but what does this have to do with the first oversized racquet?

After my arrival in San Diego, Dr. Bud hooked me up with a great southpaw named DC Charleston. DC was going to college and he picked me up in an old Volkswagen daily and we played at Mel Gorham's and at the beach in La Jolla. DC was a top national doubles player with Charley Brumfield, the county's smoothest beach runner, and could 'Name that Tune' of any rock-and-roll song after hearing two notes,

Racquetball was in its infancy and especially with equipment. I had just changed over from the Dayton Steele to the Muehleisen Ektelon racquet. Leach was also coming on as a popular racquet brand. So, basically there were two companies making racquets and both located in San Diego.

Mel Gorham, owner of his namesake Sprots Center, the San Diego racquetball mecca of the Golden Era 70s. (US RB Museum)

Both DC and I were playing with Ektelon's at the time, and we would sit around after our matches talking about the sport and invariable it wound around to every detail of the racquets. A racquet could make or break a player.

583

One afternoon DC said, 'Let's go over to the Ektelon plant and look around.' We arrived at a small metal building with a stringer machine being rolled outside so the stringer could enjoy the sunshine as he worked. Inside the door was a modest machine shop and we zeroed in on one guy bending aluminum frames for the Dr. Bud racquet. Overhead a dozen frames hung at the mid-point of fabrication, ready for the wood handles to be installed.

We fingered the metal frames looking at the throat where the metal extended into the wood grip. One of us exclaimed, 'We can make this throat an inch longer and install the wood grip leaving the racquet an inch longer.' Our thought was to get more power out of the racquet.

We walked out of Ektelon with one slightly longer racquet and off to the beach court to give it a try. It worked! It did allow us to hit the ball harder, so we made up a few more and used them through the summer. A few months later, a black Ektelon racquet came on the market called the Schmidtke XL.

The first oversized racquet was born and with it power racquetball.

Early balls broke under pounding by the XL racquets.

The Racquetball's Colorful History
Is it a racquetball or a racquetball ball?

Call it what you will, the racquetball's evolution would entice Charles Darwin to the game. In 1971, my first tournament year, the balls were slow and mushy. Of course, we didn't call them 'dead' because there was no standard at the time. 'Dead' and 'live' were not in our ball vocabularies.

Still, there was selective pressure among the players for a faster ball. Tournament committees would designate a 'ball person' to be responsible for keeping the tourney balls pepped up. He accomplished this by piling boxes of balls (no cans then) onto hot sauna benches to roast for at least thirty minutes before game time. The ref plucked a game ball from the oven, the players fondled it and hit a ceiling shot to ensure the heated sphere would carry to within ten feet of the back wall, and then the service. Once the match was underway the sauna air cooled but was compensated by the heat of the rally.

If no sauna was available, the ball person knew a doctor, dentist or veterinarian who provided a syringe and small-gauge needle to pump a few CC's of air into each ball making them custom pressurized. It was time-consuming by the gross but the balls retained the internal pressure for nearly a half-game before the air pounded out them and the ball person was called again to pump up.

Clearly, something had to be done about the miserable balls in the burgeoning sport.

A Colorful Past

The racquetball started out as the 'pinkie'. This ball of the late 1960's was actually the inner core of a tennis ball without the fuzz jacket. It got its name from its color- a gaudy pink which camouflaged itself well against the hardwood floor. After pink came black, then green, followed by blue. Funny enough, studies showed that blue is the hardest color to see in our sport.

In the early 1970's, racquetballs were pressurized but bounced like fat maggots unless doctored by a ball person. I played Charlie Brumfield with a maggot ball in the 1971 National Singles Invitational in San Diego, his hometown with a Brum's Bums fan club hogging the front row and waving signs 'Brumfield #1, God #2, Keeley #3'. We injected the ball in a privacy before the match with a mutually agreeable number of CC's that pounded out by game two, and I declined an invitation to a livelier second ball that would enhance his ceiling rally. Just how dead was the ball? I hit a drive to Brumfield's famous forehand that flailed and the ball vaporized from the court- it disappeared. The gallery

Cans Collection of Kevin Deighan.

hushed as we discussed a second ball until I pointed to his racquet where the ball wedged in the throat! His great shot to bring in the second ball had failed.

Broken Balls and Superballs

The year 1973 was the pivot in the racquetball's lively evolution. In this season, manufacturers heeded countless pleas and began producing a ball that was acceptable by the common standard that a well-struck ceiling shot would bounce to reach the bottom of the back wall.

The shortcoming was these faster balls due to increased internal pressure broke rather easily. In 1973, the first year of the pro tour, three to five balls broke per match. At a Detroit match Mike Zeitman and Steve Serot broke a record 10 balls in their three-game contest! Thousands of balls across the nation in '73 bit the dust and Seamco was obliged to replace them if the logo was intact- the balls were mint yet split- and a better solution had to be found or the company would go broke along with the NRC pro tour.

I saw the most perfect killshot ever hit that year at the San Diego PPA court when Muehleisen wound up in deep court for a booming lefty forehand, struck and the ball

586

split in half over the service box and each half rolled off in the respective front corners. Dr. Bud blew on his autograph racquet and proclaimed, 'Two points, babe.'

Another ball era ripened in 1974 and lasted all season. The breakage problem was brought under control and players fell to their knees in thanks in service boxes that the big bust was over, and who cared if the new batch was as out of round as the planet earth? A warped ball bounces untoward because of a bulge somewhere that makes one cockeyed like trying to roll a strike with a wad of gum stuck to the bowling ball.

The lopped ball was blinked off that season for the real cause- superballs! Not every ball of '74 was out-of-round but they all raced faster than speeding bullets. Every top player of the early 70s pushed the ball around the court like a chess piece contacting it off the lead foot, but the superball was no controllable chess piece. The tournament balls were soaked in ice water and deflated with needles to no avail. Then Marty Hogan's scorching kills with the 18'' small head racquet in vogue was clocked at 142 MPH, and his 1975 Burlington first pro win ushered in Power Racquetball.

Now the pioneer players were out-of-round chasing aces and ceiling shots flying over the back wall until they too were blasted off the courts into evermore. The old warhorse Charley Brumfield adapted one more season with pass jams, but likewise bowed out. The sport named racquetball in 1969 by Bob MacInerney lost its early definition; however millions of new players took up the new fast game as the manufacturers kept pumping out the rubber hummingbirds that made the game easier to play by youth, females, and the masses.

The Heyday

By 1975 the balls were molded and pressurized with stronger quality control, and came up simply round and fast. The standard to judge a game ball was a ceiling shot that rebounded off the back wall between 2-6 ft. high, and they stopped going over the back wall.

The Big Game, though the term and 'serve and shoot' didn't re become part of the vocabulary for a decade, was the *only* winning strategy. Drive serves right and left went for aces or weak answers that were killed. If a drive came off the back wall it was RIP. Jerry Hilecher introduced camouflage on the drive serves left, right and Z with the walking screen motion, and Carl Loveday tutored the first consistent crack ace serves, Hogan was the first and only for one decade to master the R-A-W (run along wall) backhand return, while every other returner sought to neutralize the rally. The ceiling as defense was abandoned forever.

The years 1976 and 1977 were the heyday for both manufacturers and players. The sport exploded across the country with thousands of new courts and newcomers demanding a rational, less lively ball. The result was the ball stabilization at somewhere between lively and super-lively that caused a more controlled serve-and-shoot game. In addition, the rash of ball busts and bubble gum bulges disappeared for good. AMF Voit commissioned a full-color sound film with superstar action and stumbled lines by Brumfield, Serot, Steve Strandemo and Keeley.

Early pro and artist Campbell. (US RB Museum)

Then 1978 to 1982 was the age of ball zaniness. A dozen manufacturers showered the courts with an astonishing array of racquetballs . It was a far cry from 1972 when a single black balls, striped balls, pro balls, hack balls... there was a ball you could inflate like a basketball, and another dimpled like a golf ball to (theoretically) increase spin.

In fact, the only constant among racquetballs in this era was inconsistency... with the exception that they almost all came packed two to a can so they wouldn't get lonely. My joy one full year was saving an unopened can of balls the manufacturer had neglected to include a mate in the container for the other to rub against.

What is Lively?

The sport of racquetball had progressed since 1969 in just over a decade from a YMCA and University monopoly to a commercial Court Club free-for-all. The reason was the racquetball, and the shortening learning curve from a mush ball to a superball until it equalized at a 'lively' ball that could quickly be hit by nearly everyone. That's the game story in a can.

But what is 'lively'? The rules now stated that the racquetball should be 21'4' in diameter and weigh 1.40 ounces, and should rebound 68"-72" when dropped to the floor from a height of 100" at a temperature of 76F. It was impractical to test each ball at a tournament where the draw sheets covered one hall cruised by up to 500 participants, and so the quality control was assigned to the singles or doubles contestants before their handshakes by one of two rough methods.

The first technique was for the tallest player to lift on tiptoes and drop balls from overhead one-at-time until two were selected that bounced to about nose height of his flatfoot opponent. The goal was two game balls and sometimes a dozen were required to meet the limitations. The second method that also took into account the ball hardness was for everyone on the court to hit ceiling shot with force until two balls carried 2-6 ft. high off the back wall. Anything less than these two measurements was rejected 'as dead' and anything beyond was refused as 'superball, and one just right in between was the game 'lively' ball.

The Ball Ceremony

Spectators lined the glass throughout the 70s and early 80s to watch the ball ceremony that began with a rain of four or more from the ref with the players' pockets already bulged with their personal choices. I initialed mine with a magic marker to avoid mix-ups during the ceiling shot test to the left rear corner. There was still time to excuse oneself to the bathroom to heat a ball in hot water or with a hair drier and return to pass muster. There was sleight of hand during the bounce tests, and barter to 'throw' the first three points if it's with 'my' ball. Eventually the two players faced off with a ball in each hand and a duty of picking two as the #1 and #2 game balls. 'Yeah, this one is ok,' or, 'Nah, I reject that one,'… the banter continued until the ref descended from the gallery perch for the final test and say.

One could sit back in the bleacher, watch the test results, and then handicap the players since the range of acceptability was wide. The ceremony determined the outcomes between finesse and shooters as much as the sum of their strokes and strategies before the first serve was even hit!

Once a ball was mutually acceptable and the game bust open with the first serve, you watched it like a hawk, and between rallies and time outs. It wasn't uncommon for a shyster to leave the court with the game ball to upgrade with another from his gym bag. Long serves sailed over the back wall into the waiting hands of a comrade who threw back a different one. Razor blades were secreted in shoe tongues to slit balls while tying the shoelaces, and the ball broke on the next rally.

'Ball change!' was the inevitable cry late in the first game by the losing player as a psychological ploy or because the air had been pounded out the rubber. A savvy opponent never agreed to the request and let him stew. However, it was an early gray rule area where if one player vetoed the change it wasn't allowed unless the ref judged the ball was 'unplayable'. The ball and referee determined many championships.

External Factors

Tournament directors became the prime human influence on the winners of their tournaments by providing the refs with unopened cans from the sauna or refrigerator or hoarded for months from a slow or fast batch to jumpstart different players' modes. He could switch on the heater or AC of the exhibition court before the big match.

A ball dropped from 100" to bounce to 72" height in the Michigan summer sweatboxes was like playing with photons, whereas one that rebound to 68" on the refrigerated Houston court was a marshmallow. In the rarified air of Steamboat Springs the less ambient pressure inflated the ball about 10%. Winter tournaments on unheated courts of a Chicago club had the participants wearing sweats, but it would have been smarter to put little jackets on the balls.

The court floor, wall and ceiling also affected the ball play. On entering a tourney club lobby the grapevine quickly shook loose the ball facts with questions like, 'How do the

20th Anniversary.

1969

Paddlerackets became "racquetball." The International Racquetball Association was formed (later to become the American Amateur Racquetball Association or AARA). A set of national rules was standardized. And the first international racquetball tournament was held in St. Louis.

The tournament was won by San Diego's Dr. Bud Muehleisen, who later became known as the father of racquetball. He was the first to play with an aluminum racquet, manufactured by an upstart company called Ektelon.

The racquetball has gone through some colorful variations over the years. Early paddlerackets players tried the Pinky, the core of a tennis ball, but found it too lively. A black, less bouncy ball was an improvement. Switching to the current color, blue, made it easier to see the ball. The pros tried a green ball briefly in the 70s. And some players experimented with a pressurized, plum-colored ball in 1973.

1973

Racquetball went professional. And as with most sports, it was a modest beginning. The Leach-sponsored pro tour visited six cities. The first tournament's $1,500 top money was snatched by 17-year old Steve Serot when he upset Charlie Brumfield.

A colorful but historically incorrect ad. Serot beat Schmidtke in the first NRC event final after Strandemo upset a cramping Brumfield in the round of 16. (US RB Museum)

courts play?- Oh, the ceiling is a sponge, but the floor is a trampoline.' And then the players walked the halls to view their draws, and then into the courts to jump up and down on the floors to determine if they were the 'floating style', rapped on walls to know if they were paneled, and inspected the glass..

Even color affected a ball's playability. The rash of breakage when the first green balls arrived to replace the black ones in 1973, the year of the inaugural pro tour, was caused by the dye that weakened the rubber during the molding process. Kelly green was the official NRC tour color for balls, logos, and the magazine. I wore one Kelly Converse Chuck and one Forest green in accord with my apparel contract, but tired of running around like St. Patrick's and returned to the black and white ones. The green ball didn't show up at all against the first glass back and side walls that were starting to be installed at classier clubs around the country, but NRC wanted its own ball color whether or not the players could see it.

Manufacturers vie to sponsor tournaments and draw name players who 'play by the brand' in attending events with the ball that suits their games. The traditional brands were Seamco, Voit, then Penn, and that was their general order of liveliness. I would not travel a long distance to a Seamco tournament, but would hitchhike to a Penn event with slower balls that helped my control play. Charley Brumfield preferred a Voit for his patented ceiling game and once grumbled to a ref at a northwestern tournament, 'I can't believe that you guys play with this brand of ball up here. A broken ball of my brand is more lively than an unbroken one of yours.'

When all is said and done in the racquetball's curious history, the ball manufactures champions.

Ball History Affects Play Today

Racquetball has evolved from a thinking game into *a* reaction game. Players of the early 1970's recall a game called racquetball which featured 10 to 15 shot rallies, great reaching gets, long ceiling rallies, variety in shot selection, controlled swing, and a smooth flow of somewhat predictable play ending with a 90 MPH killshot. Then, in the mid-1970's, the noble slow game was torn apart by the fast ball.

In the blink of a few tournaments manufacturers flooded the demand market with lively balls, and the best example of two top players coping with it and each other was the classic mid-70s matchups between the game's premiere controller Charley Brumfield and the top shooter Marty Hogan. Brumfield had dominated Hogan during the slow ball era. He handcuffed the kid with drives into the body that stifled all that power, and he lulled him into a ceiling game that sent Marty up a wall. But when the first lively ball was tossed into the court the Old Man was no match. Thinking time was reduced to a fraction and Charley admitted. 'My analytical prowess and the ability to pinpoint my opponent's weaknesses have been neutralized by the raw power to hit the ball 125 mph.'

592

Point of contact is a few 'frames' long as the ball mashes, the strings give, and the frame flexes. 2013 Outdoor Doubles Champion Almee Ruiz in Las Vegas. (Mike Augustin)

The 80s ball was more consistent in both liveliness and endurance and in professional matches rarely became a focus of controversy. The USRA had an official ball tester who got them in his mailbox from the manufactures as the tallest person in the office. Over the years he tested hundreds in a closet set up with a chair on a hardwood pad with the proper height lines marked on the walls. He climbed up, released and marked the drop line at

100 inches and the bounce lines at 72 and 68 inches for the different brands. His thumbnail was the durometer to test the hardness of the rubber. If the official ball tester did not approve a ball, he could expect a call or visit from the company CEO to find out if other arrangements could be made to get it approved. Nobody knows what happened in the closet after that, but the balls were homogenous throughout tournaments.

In 1983 Ektelon introduced the first graphite CBK which was lighter, stiffer and hit the consistently fast ball better. In '85 players grabbed the first oversized racquets and began to swing like carnival hammers with as much force and, as technology advanced into the new century, the big racquets got so light, long, wide and balanced that there is no turning back from the Big Game.

Consequently, today's players know a game called racquetball with rallies on the professional level that last an average of three explosive shots between serves, the ceiling ball with the IRT ball bounces eight feet high off the back wall, and killshots go180 MPH!

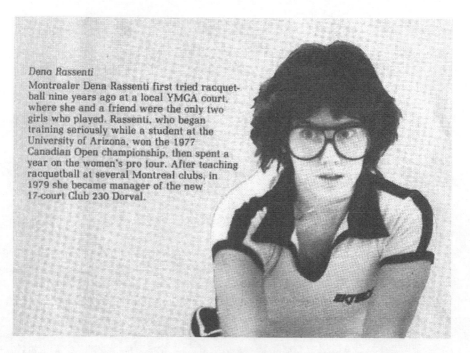

Dena Rassenti
Montrealer Dena Rassenti first tried racquetball nine years ago at a local YMCA court, where she and a friend were the only two girls who played. Rassenti, who began training seriously while a student at the University of Arizona, won the 1977 Canadian Open championship, then spent a year on the women's pro tour. After teaching racquetball at several Montreal clubs, in 1979 she became manager of the new 17-court Club 230 Dorval.

This famous shot taken at a pro stop of the late 1970's appeared in *Canadian Racquetball* magazine and boosted eye-guard use during a rash of eye injuries. (Dena Rassenti)

594

Racquet Grip Glue and the One-Grip System

The bent handle racquetball racquet of the early 1980's reminds me of a one month experiment with every type of adhesive on the market, about thirty in all from Elmer's to Superglue, using various styles of gloves and racquet grips to stop grip slippage.

I recognized with the onslaught of the fast ball and tightly strung racquets of the early 80s that the primary problem of most players in their entire games was ball deflection on contact due to grip slip. It started moments after the coin toss in tournaments when the glove, hand and handle got sweaty. Everything in the strokes and strategies of millions of advanced players across the nation was right except the angle the ball came off the strings. Given a good eye or fast camera, the handle rolled about two degrees within the strongest palm. Even power racquetball's inventor Marty Hogan screamed at the injustice. I needed a glue to stop it.

Over the course of a month, in my secret 'laboratory' of a Michigan garage via tedious daily hours of applying adhesives to gloves, my palm and handle, I gripped and formed opinions of the best glues... and went to the courts to test them. The best was Barge Cement and to this day I keep a quart on my desert property for all purpose contact. The result of the glue experiment was conclusive for cement type, but over a period of ten minutes of hard play, though the grip didn't slip twixt the glove and handle, it started to rotate between the hand and glove for the same misdirection. Gluing the hand to the racquet was the logical next step which I did for a new one grip system for forehand and backhand. Yet I couldn't let go during timeouts, plus the heating glue felt unhealthy climbing my circulation from palm to armpit, so I abandoned the idea of gluing the hand to handle.

The nationwide grip slippage of the early 80s due to the advent of superballs, tight strings, Tarzans hands, and double ball speeds, I believe to this day, is the prime reason for the concurrent historic introduction of the one-grip system that previously was all but unknown in racquetball.

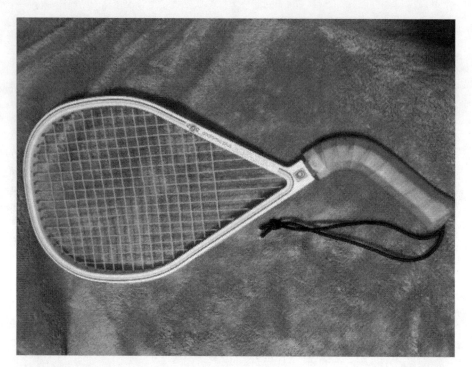

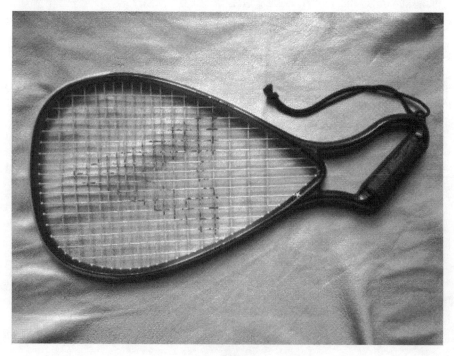

Inside Story of the Inflatable Z-Ball

by Bill Stevens

I was involved in several aspects of racquetball in the mid-70s golden era when Charlie Brumfield and Steve Keeley were just bowing out as the world's best to St. Louis whipper snappers like Marty Hogan and Steve Serot. Dr. Bud Muehleisen was beginning to accumulate a handful of what would accrue a record 70 national and international titles.

I was an open tournament player, daily fodder for the superstars, strung racquets, and worked for Trenway Racquets as their in-house player and product tester. Trenway was essentially the goliath Leach Industries predecessor, and early players like Keeley before pro tourneys were offered started to take money under the table from Trenway to be able to travel to the annual and only Big Four tournaments: National Singles and Doubles, and National Singles and Doubles Invitationals.

The question on every players' lips was fast or slow? The sport pivot in the '70's was either to a slow, sweaty chess game of control, or a fast big serve game in the footsteps of tennis. The entrepreneur gods Charley Drake who became president of Leach, and Bob Kendler who ramrod the racquetball magazine and tour, didn't scratch their heads long in figuring that if you maintained or slowed the ball the game got intellectual and better, but would die for lack of participants, whereas if you speeded it up the kids and their grandparents could play and shout, and moreover females who drew the males would flock into the burgeoning courts across America.

We at Trenway blindsided everybody with the first inflatable ball, called the Z-Ball. I did not invent the pump-up ball, but was involved in ongoing secret discussions of a solution to there being so many balls on the market, all with different speeds. The actual idea came from a Dr. Parnell who made heart valves. He was a racquetball aficionado who made the first Z-Ball for my boss Jim Wilson and us. It had a hardened nipple on the sphere that accepted a pump needle.

Dr. Bud and I did all the testing of the pump-up ball, and thought it had merit. Control players could decrease internal pressure for a slow game, or hard ball hitters, kids, and ladies could increase the pressure for longer rallies. I blew one up like a pumpkin until it exploded in testing the limits. It was consistent on the strings and court surfaces except when pumped to a higher pressure the nipple caused a slight deviation of bounce that maybe foretold the future of the ball.

597

The ball went into production and for a few months was the hottest experiment across the nation. The unpressurized can came with a needle and little pump, and the yellow can with the original Z-Ball has my likeness on it.

The upshot is that the fast ball won the race for racquetball on the day the notion of the inflatable Z-Ball died, and that is an inside story of the history of the game.

The Inflatable Z-Ball kit.

598

The Name Game...The Best and Worst of Racquet Names of All Time

by Tim Deighan

Have you ever heard of the Xenon? What about the Aris? I didn't think so. Well, these are racquet names. Bad racquet names. Some people might say that a racquet's name is as important as the strings or the grip. While that's debatable, it's safe to say that a good racquet name contributes significantly to a racquet's success. Give a stick a bad name and chances are it was a dud of a racquet. The Air Hammer. That was a Wilson racquet. One of the first ultra light racquets, it was given a great name and became a big seller. The Strobe. An Ektelon racquet and one that everyone remembers. The Polaris? A snowmobile right? Yes, and a racquet.....that nobody used.

Since the game of racquetball was invented in 1949, hundreds of racquets have been produced by dozens of manufacturers. The names attached to these racquets run the gamut from the bland and laughable to the inspired and ingenious. Keep in mind while reading – this isn't about identifying the greatest, best looking or most influential racquets of all time. This is about beautiful names and names that make you go "doh".

Daniel De La Rosa advertises at the 2014 Pro Kennex Tournament of Champions. (Mike Augustin)

One of the earliest racquets was called Paddle Racquets. Honest – that's what was affixed to this hunk of wood. And a hunk of wood it was; the earliest wooden racquets weighed around 400 grams. Later, while Americans were getting fatter, racquets by 1978 had done the complete opposite dropping in weight to a standard 250 G for this graphite composite and yes if you can believe that was a racquet name created in the 1978 by a great guy no one has ever heard of named Jack Sisson. Today, racquets have shed even more poundage and "done a complete 180 g"-get it and we expect to see that name soon too. Ok sorry for the digression so back to our story of "It's a racquet!" Their grips (the old wooden clunker paddle rackets that) were made for the likes of Dr. J. Other racquets from the early days went by simple names like Match Play, Varsity, Ace, Falcon, Charger, Champ and one of my favorites, The Killer. I get it... you would die from holding it? Another wooden beauty was the Autograph Model. Whose autograph you ask? Who knows. It went only by Autograph Model. In any event, these names should be classified as "Classics".....simple and elegant.

#1 name – The Rogue.

Speaking of autograph models, signature sticks have been in play since the beginning. In fact, one of the earliest autograph models belongs to the inventor of racquetball, Joe Sobek. He never played in a tournament but had a huge ego (maybe?) plastering his name on this clunker for reasons you and I will never know. No racquet collection is complete without one. Bud Muehleisen had his own model as did another of the early greats, Bill Schmidtke. The XL Schmidtke was an all-black billy topped by a white bumper and had a star wars planetary like cover- the coolest cover ever. This club was probably one of the best sellers ever (and one of the worst racquets ever designed). I can also blame the Bill for my bad backhand. As a 13-year-old, I needed two hands to swing this sledge hammer and never developed the proper form from the weak side.

600

Over the years, many great players have been honored with signature sticks, though they were certainly more popular in the 70s and 80s. Serot and Wagner had their own and so did Bledsoe, Hilecher, Brumfield and Marty Hogan of course. Shute, Marty had a whole fleet of racquets from a who's who of racquet companies) bearing his name when he teamed up with Pro Kennex years and years ago. Girls got game too. Peggy Steding, Shannon Wright and Jennifer Harding all their own autograph models. Even Marty Hogan's wife Linda (don't know if he had one named Linda but yes that was a racquet too).

From the more recent era - Swain, Inoue, and Obremski all had their own signature racquets. And our favorite signature model is one from Sportcraft from a guy no one has ever heard of except his father and mother. Its name...you guessed it was the infamous Art Diemar...a yellow clunker that no one has ever played with except for one of the authors here (out of curiosity). We researched this guy and luckily discovered that he was a "rising star" rising to the almighty number 8 (at his club-no on the pro circuit) but it sounded like a great idea for Sportcraft to make a racquet named after someone (ok anyone)...After all, companies figure if you name it after someone like Linda or Art people will buy it. Does anyone in the country know who is number 8 player today. Ok don't ask because he actually does deserve a racquet since he had been hurt (Beltran).

Weather-related names have been used up over the years. We've had a Thunder and a Lightning, a Tornado, Cyclone and a Tsunami. NASA helped name a few racquets. Just kidding. But we did have a Launch Pad, a Big Bang and various forms of Blast, Ignite and Fire.

Weaponry and police terminology have been worn out. Spaulding offered the Assault and Felon in the 90s. We've had the Pistol, the Nightstick, the .357, the Bullet, the Machete and the Saber. And Dirty Harry would have been especially proud of the Enforcer and Magnum. Both of those were popular many years ago.

With racquet names, one thing is for certain; there have been a lot of bad racquet names over the years. Try these on: Boomer, Spoiler, Zinger 500, Wrangler, Baron, Lexis, Aris, Phycon, Dynax and Futura. I could go on and on but you get the picture.

While we've noted that hitting on a successful name is every company's goal and doing so may lead to increased sales, successful racquets and good names don't always go hand-in-hand. The Magnum, Master, 250-G and CBK were huge sellers. The names, while not bad, were not Hall of Famers. What about the Toron? A gasoline or maybe a motorcycle or lawnmower, right? No, it was a racquet from the late 70s. A pretty successful racquet, as I recall. So good in fact that Ektelon brought it back in 2012 for a cameo. Apparently, sometimes we don't care what they're called.

In the 90s E-Force took the name game to a new level with "in your face" monikers like the Terminator, Real Deal, Chaos, Anarchy, and Bedlam. At times, the game does have a certain chaotic feel to it, especially if its B doubles.

Fernando Ríos draws the bow vs. David Horn at the 2014 Juarez Open. (Ken Fife)

Perhaps the funniest racquet name ever was Cliff Swain's Bad Influence by Transition in the early 90s. OK, maybe it wasn't the name necessarily, but the marketing piece behind it. Who could forget the picture of Cliff straddling a motorcycle, sporting shorts and a jean jacket with cut off sleeves. Pure cheese wiz. Cliff also beat the drum for a fledgling company called Burt in the late 80s. They may have had the longest name ever given a racquet – the Comp III Power Handle Dry Grip "Cliff Swain" Signature. Did I mention they went out of business after just a few years?

Ok let's toss out the Top 10 and Bottom 10 Racquet Names of All Time.

Top Ten Best Names of All Time ("the hits")

10. Colossus (Head) – You don't hit it you ride it (Six flags Magic Mountain)

9. Zorro (Trenway) – We unmasked it

602

8. Sidewinder (Aldila)

7. Eminence (Ektelon)

6. Untouchable (Point West) - How do you play with it if its untouchable

5. Borealis (DP)

4. Beaumark (Ektelon)

3. Spitfire (Vittert) I guess this model was never "shot down"

2. Bandido (Leach) – Yes it was little

1. Rogue (Ektelon)

Honorable Mention: Goliath (Spaulding); Deliverance (Ektelon); Mean Streak (Spaulding); Trinity (Ektelon); Ripstick (Ektelon); Sharp Shooter (Wilson); Graphite Boss (Wilson); Scorpion (Seamco); Vendetta (Ajay); The Answer (E-Force); Big Bang (Head)-we have a "theory on this racquet".

It's back to the drawing board with this group below:

Bottom 10 Worst Names Of All Time (the ones that should have been "skipped" long ago)

10. Whisper Damp (Ektelon)

9. Thrust (E-Force)- Guys PG please

8. Mad Raq (Omega)

7. Phycon (Ektelon)

6. Swinger (Leach) –Only for doubles

5. Espirit (Omega)

4. Xiter (Ektelon)

3. Explo (Sportcraft) Do you exploit, explore it or explode it. I don't get it

2. Digger (Ajay) –The company was "gold-digging" here but it never "panned" out

1. Xenon (Spaulding)

Dishonorable Mention: Innerbeam (Pro-Kennex); Elantra (Ektelon); Strion (Ektelon); Rollers 195 (Wilson); Radial (Head); Micro-Ceramic (Pro-Kennex); Nightstalker III (Sentra); Ice (Transition); System 10 (Richcraft); Jazz (Head); Genius (Fin)-it didn't take a genius to name that racquet.

(Thanks to the 'History of Racquetball' magazine series, Racquetball Museum, and Tim Deighan)

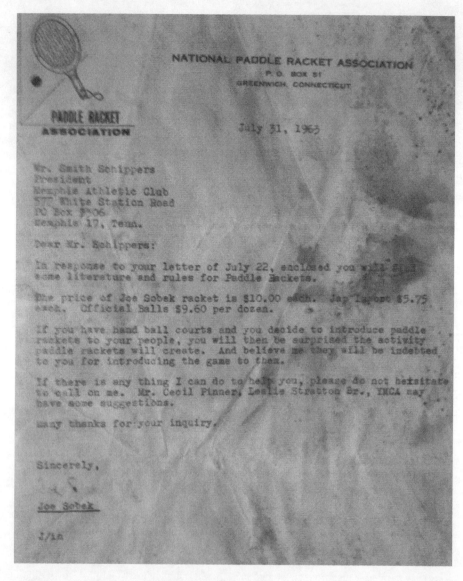

1963 letter from Joe Sobek: 'The price of the Joe Sobek Racket is $10 each. The Jap import $3.75 each...' (US RB Museum)

Pros Speak from the Box

Sponsors

Wilson is solid.
- Corey Brysman

Head and Spalding makes quality racquets and have been good to me. *- Mike Ray*

I'm grateful to every company and person who's helped me, and I remember my family.
- Marty Hogan

Head Penn, Head Penn.
- Sudsy

Ektelon is a great sponsor, and Jack Scott and my New York friends are great supporters.
- Ruben Gonzalez

Wilson got me on tour my first year, and I've been well sponsored by Ektelon since.
- Dave Peck

E-Force is my sponsor, and they also make the best high-end racquet for advanced players. The reason is early technology that surpassed the other companies, and their research and development department still takes the time to explore what's best for the player.
- Alvaro Beltran

Ashaway Strings has made a tremendous improvement in my game. HEAD Racquets have also made a significant difference in my game. They are a great company to represent.
– Jackie Paraiso

Wilson sporting goods has made my career, and they're caring for racquetball. I do a 80-stop 'Big D's Road Show' tour each year that consists of two-hour clinics for which there's no charge. My mom and dad are great to me too.
- Derek Robinson

E-Force, and these days Gear Box. The Legends should never be forgotten. *- Jim Spittle*

My favorite relationship was with Leach Industries, the kernel of Pro-Kennex, at the time when they were in the forefront of creating racquets and helping racquetball.
- Charlie Brumfield

Boxes Casino, One-Route, Crew West, Wilson and Scott Hirsch.　　　*- Cliff Swain*

I've only had two RB companies as sponsors over the past 24 years, so I enjoy the loyalty of being a part of one company. Ektelon picked me up when I was almost done with the sport, thanks to the former sponsor. I owe Ektelon all the loyalty I've given over the past 13 years.　　　*– John Ellis*

The first racquetball sponsor to pay players cash was Bud Leach, founder of Leach Industries, who flew his plane and star players to tournaments. (US RB Museum)

Ektelon is a great company to play for, and Formula Flow.　　　*– Jose Rojas*

There are two categories of sponsors and they are: (1) Those entities that offer goods and services which you promote that may not be racquetball related and simply put your image as theirs; and (2) The second type of sponsor is your equipment sponsor or sponsors and they both outfit you and together you both promote your sport, its growth, the junior programs, and the recreational player. By this sponsor's equipment quality, innovation and utility, you both promote the product line in demonstrations, print ads, personal appearances, and at competitive events where your performance, behavior and personality play a role in yours and your sponsor's combined success.   *– Ken Woodfin*

Wilson has been family.   *- Kerri Stoffregen Wachtel*

EFORCE has been awesome to me for 14 years. Without them, I could not have done all the traveling and competing. Forever grateful to them.   *– Cheryl Gudinas*

Ektelon has always provided great product for me to compete with and have also helped me out financially. American Metal Recycling is a local company in Cleveland that has also helped me through the years. If it wasn't for those two companies I wouldn't have been able to compete on the pro tour as long as I did.   *– Andy Hawthorne*

I am proud to say that Ektelon was my sponsor, and I appreciated their continued support throughout my career. Ektelon represents excellence in the racquetball industry.
– Brian Hawkes

Huge thanks to Ektelon, Rollout, Racquetball Warehouse, Advocare, and Restrung Magazine for all of the support and top-shelf products/coverage every season, every event!   *- Rhonda Rajsich*

I've been with HEAD for close to 30 years, and working with Doug Ganim and Ben Simons has been awesome. We all started just as a sponsored player so we know what is needed now as administrators at HEAD.   *– Fran Davis*

Wilson was good to me but Leach placed the bounty on my head after I beat their #1 horse. Players walked away with more money for beating me in the first round than they would have for winning the whole tournament.   *– Davey Bledsoe*

Steve Keeley was my first behind the scene sponsor who got me to my first tournament, I found out ten years later. I played well, and he got me my first real racquetball sponsor, Leach Industries. I am forever grateful to him and Leach, and I am proud to have been part of the sport in its pioneer days.   *– Rich Wagner*

607

First sponsor, Goldie Hogan, with 7 National titles, kisses her son Marty, with 6 World titles. (Shay)

De La Rosa's dives showered by s logos at the 2014 Tournament of Champions. (Mike Augustin)

608

Voit Video
First Racquetball Promo Movie

The 1970's Rollout Voit Advertisement- and the Vintage Racquetball Play video (Watch the video at US Racquetball Museum http://racquetballmuseum.com/videos.html)

ʹThis is different from any racquetball video you've ever seen. Charlie Brumfield, Steve Serot, Steve Strandemo and I acted in it, had lines, with a full Hollywood crew and even a shower scene. It took three days to make the six minute film in different spots around Los Angeles with the director shouting, ʹGet the talent on the ball before we lose the light!ʹ The full story of the first racquetball promotional video was written the anecdote book ʹIt´s a Racquet!ʹ. Now you can see the film.ʹ   - Steve Bo Keeley

"This video was produced in the early 7's by Voit to advertise their racquetball product line. It has to be the most iconic six minutes of vintage racquetball play that exists. Four very famous players (Charlie Brumfield, Steve Keeley, Steve Strandemo, and Steve Serot) are featured in this film actually playing doubles. All of these players were pro champions during the 70s, and it is great to see them play doubles. It is further interesting to see the smaller racquets, slower balls, and 70s clothing. The dashed receiving line and doubles lines were not a part of the court during this time. Eyeglasses were not required during this era and normally not used. Watch the entire clip, as near the end of the video, they are walking past outdoor racquetball which was just starting to become popular. I believe this is the only early vintage footage that exists of the three Steve's playing racquetball and certainly the only footage of them on the court all at the same time. Check other vintage matches here in the museum of Brumfield playing."
- Randy Stafford

Go see the movie at http://racquetballmuseum.com/videos.html.

Randy Stafford created The Racquetball Museum so that racquetball fans could go and explore all the memorable and historical items of racquetball. Visit http://www.racquetballmuseum.com/ and take a tour of the various museum rooms which include racquets, balls, documents, magazine covers, clothing, videos, and more!

"Rollout"

It takes a camera crew like this . . .

Brumfield, Keeley,
Serot and Strandemo
they're
now
in
movies!

By Robert H. Black, Jr.

To help popularize the sport of racquetball by exposing it to more people, AMF Voit recently commissioned a new, full-color sound film named "Rollout." Aimed at making more men and women interested in playing the game, it has enough superstar action to hold anyone's interest. The cast consists of four top touring pros—Charlie Brumfield, Steve Keeley, Steve Serot and Steve Strandemo.

These four were turned loose on the courts and were captured in some great action during a three-day filming session. The result is exciting, non-commercial drama that should go a long way towards interesting people in playing racquetball.

Seeing the pros at their indoor game is enough of a challenge to interest any athlete in racquetball and the outdoor court scenes in the film will convince sun loving athletes that all they need in order to play the game is an outdoor court, a racquet, and a ball.

The non-commercial nature of "Rollout" provides some unsung heroes who deserve recognition from racquetball fans. Along with Voit, the cooperation of Brumstar Corporation, Ektelon and Leach Industries in making the film is indeed gratifying.

The overall concept was created by the Cochrane Chase & Company advertising agency of Newport Beach, California. The creative team of Gary Cunningham and Ken Sakoda set out to make this film different from the normal sports film, where "we all bid fond farewell to the scenic slopes." Instead of a lot of glamorous footage, "Rollout" has a story line, with a Mission Impossible theme. Those who seen it agree that it captures the sounds, strategies, skills and emotions experienced on the court.

Locations included three super Southern California settings—Long Beach Athletic Club, Orange Coast College, and Del Webb's Newporter Inn. It was produced by The Moving Pitches Company and directed by Harvey Stewart, an avid racquetball player. (Stewart has produced and directed commercials for Honda, U.S. Forest Association and First Federal Savings, California.)

46

The film begins with a black screen and court sounds, familiar to the racquetballer, but a real mystery to the uninitiated. It then cuts to an office where a young executive (yes, that *is* Charlie Brumfield) receives a confidential phone call and signs off by saying "Don't worry, I'll be there." Now the four stars go into action, leaving their businesses and heading off to an important yet undisclosed rendezvous. The viewer still has no idea where they're headed or what they're about to do.

Suddenly, as the ball smacks into the center of the screen at about a hundred miles per hour, it's obviously racquetball. But the viewer is not on the court or over it; he is getting an eye-level look at the game. The action is filmed from a vantage point never seen before, by a camera behind the front wall. Viewers are able to catch expressions and the players they've never had time to observe when following the ball in a game.

Next comes a ballet-like sequence combining slow motion photography and music. Technique is very easy to observe at this point. Steve Strandemo was particularly interested in analyzing his performance as he viewed each day's slow-motion footage. As the tempo picks up once again, the action builds to a climax and the game is won.

Following the game and a brief outdoor sequence, the four sit down to lunch at the Newporter. The com-

. . . to capture action like this.

eraderie of the players comes out loud and clear as they relive the game and lightly poke fun at each other's techniques. As the film draws to a close, Steve Serot is seen in a series of flash backs. These scenes reinforce the fact that the strategy of racquetball demands as much of the mind as it does of the body.

If the action looks real, that's because it was. The four pros were playing an actual game. In most Hollywood productions, the good guys in the white shirts naturally win. But in fact, the blue team of Charlie Brumfield and Steve Strandemo takes the white team of Steve Keeley and Steve Serot by the score of 21 to 19.

The premier showing of "Rollout" was at the posh Century West Club in Los Angeles, attended by such dignitaries as Carl Reiner, who personally congratulated Harvey Stewart on the film. In late January, the movie was shown to sporting goods dealers, mass merchandisers, and equipment manufacturers at the National Sporting Goods Show in the Houston Astrodome. A similar group was treated to a showing in Montreal at the Canadian Sporting Goods Show and the movie is now circulating among sporting goods dealers. "Rollout" has been shown at I.R.A. regional tournaments in California, Washington, Minnesota, Indiana, Oklahoma, New York, Virginia, and Tennessee.

Since its introduction in January, the "Rollout" film has already captured the CINE Golden Eagle award presented by the Council on International Nontheatrical Events. The CINE award is recognized as a high honor by the film industry here and abroad. With the award to its credit, "Rollout" can now be officially entered in more than 100 international film festivals.

Individual dealers plan to show the film to prospective players, or any group that expresses an interest. Also, AMF Voit is planning to use it on the airlines for in-flight showings.

The film is available on a rental or purchase basis by contacting Richard G. Smith, AMF Voit, Inc., 3801 South Harbor Boulevard, Santa Ana, California 92704.

RACQUETBALL

Aw Chucks

I had the first racquetball apparel contract for all clothes with Converse for the old 'Chucks'. They were ugly, high tops to protect against sprained ankles, and lightweight to move quickly, plus a thin insole so cornering was as if barefoot. They carried me through five national paddleball singles championships and on to become what others say a legend in racquetball in Christmas shoes. However, it was as much the shoes as shots.

I remember in 1972 sitting in a Michigan cafe on the Red Cedar River waiting for the Converse representative to sign the contract. He was genial, invited me to tour the Converse factory in Malden, Mass., and printed $2000 per year for the money and, after I explained my style, put an addendum for all the shoes I wanted in mix-and-match colors. I wore different colored sneakers depending on the tournament season, for example, red and blue for the Fourth of July Open, red and green for Christmas, and orange and black for the Halloween Tournament.

Someone has said, 'When you're #1 you can do anything you want, and people will imitate' Other players soon sported mismatch Chucks including Bo Champagne, Steve Mondry and a few other pros. My contact with Converse ran for three years, and then they cancelled when the feet got slower but the shoes moved as rapidly.

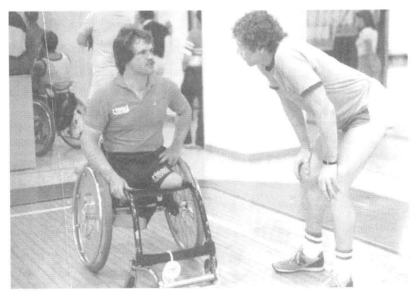

The first shoe sponsored racquetball player Steve Bo Keeley tries to talk Three-Time (1982, 83, 85) National Singles Wheelchair Champion Jim Leatherman into a sponsorship. Leatherman declined and talked Keeley into a wheelchair match that Keeley lost. (US RB Museum)

611

Ball Speed

The dividing eras in racquetball are not by players or styles but by ball speed. That's really all that matters. It dictates the players and styles that won out. Here are the eras:

1968-1974 Typical balls travel 70-90 MPH (The Pioneer Era) Top Players: Schultz, Muehleisen, Brumfield, Schmidtke, Keeley, Serot, Finger, Lawrence

1975-1977 Faster Seamco balls travel 90 to 130MPH (The Original Pro Era) Top Players: Brumfield, Hogan, Serot, Keeley, Bledsoe, Strandemo, Hilecher, Wagner

Rocky Carson...the swifter the head speed the faster the ball. (2005 Ken Fife)

1978-1981 Even faster Seamco balls and early graphite racquets increase speed to 100 - 145MPH (The Power Racquetball Era) Hogan, Yellen, Peck, Hilecher, Wagner, Brumfield, McCoy

1982-1984 Balls are slowed down Voit official tour ball, Penn is popular playing ball 95-135MPH (The Catalina Era) Yellen, Hogan, Peck, Hilecher, Wagner, Harnett, G. Peck, Gonzalez

1985-1989 Big Racquets and Penn Balls replace Voit on Tour 115-155MPH (Post Catalina Big Racquet Era) Hogan, Harnett, Yellen, Gonzalez, Swain, G. Peck, Andrews

1990-2002 Big racquets get better, Pro Renn ball faster 135-185MPH (Big Game Super Power Racquetball Era) Swain, Monchik, Ray, Kachtik, Roberts, Mannino, Ellis

2003 to Current Racquet technology breakthroughs slow to incremental improvements. Pro's switch to slower Pro Penn HD balls but continue to get stronger/faster/more fit. 120-170MPH (Super Power Era continues plus increased player court speed) Kane Waselenchuk dominates everyone. Carson, Huczek, Croft, Beltran, Vanderson, Rojas and De La Rosa

Go for broke!

Faster than a speeding bullet...De La Rosa at the 2014 Tournament of Champions. (Mike Augustin)

613

Personality

Freddy Ramirez and his signature two-handed return in 2012. (Mike Augustin)

Elvis and the Memphis Racquetball Mafia

Steve Bo Keeley

Elvis walloped the ball around the court like he was strumming a guitar for the fun of it. He looked like he was on stage except with the racquet, the moves in the court comparable to his moves on stage, and to work the audience with his physical performance. His guitar became more of a prop, and so did his racquet.

Elvis Presley and his Memphis Racquetball Mafia loved the sport. E's main contenders at Graceland were touring pros Davey Bledsoe (National Champion 1977), Randy Stafford (Intercollegiate Champion and touring pro), Steve Smith (Intercollegiate and Tennessee State Champion 1975), Mike Zeitman (Three-times National Doubles Champion with three different partners), David Fleetwood (National Collegiate Doubles Champion and never ranked out of the top 16), and Dr. Fred Lewerenz (Elvis' sport physician and Michigan Racquetball Hall of Fame with two years on the pro Tour). Other members of the racquetball group were the bodyguards Red and Sonny West, actor Dave Hebler, harmony singer Charlie Hodge, and road manager Joe Esposito. Linda Thompson also played.

Elvis was introduced to racquetball in 1968 by his physician, Dr. George Nichopoulos, who told me, 'I started playing racquetball in 1955 at the Nashville JCC by sawing off the handle of a tennis racquet. That is just five years after Joe Sobek is credited with inventing racquetball in Connecticut. I showed Paddle Rackets, as we called it, to young players with ambition and talent, and then in the mid-60s moved the game with my medical practice to Memphis, and was still looking for young talent to coach.' Dr. Nick also taught his son Dean to play, who soon teamed with a young Marty Hogan in a Junior National Doubles. Dr. Nick began treating Presley in 1967 for 'saddle pain', and a year later prescribed racquetball. That blossomed into a lifelong friendship lasting thousands of racquetball games.

Elvis wore white tennis shoes, shorts, and his safety goggles which were huge because Dr. Nick didn't want anything to happen to his eyes. His headband was white and he always wore a glove. He played daily, or nightly before heading out into the darkened Memphis streets on motorcycles with the bodyguards and the Racquetball Mafia in sidecars to movies and nightclubs. 'The week before going on music tour, E wore a tight rubber suit with tight wrists to sweat off five pounds per racquetball session to look good to the fans on tour,' describes Bledsoe. 'He thought a quick weight loss would make him look better.'

He had a strong forehand as an extension of karate, a standard club backhand, and hit the gamut of serves. The sport was a workout and a release from the pressures of being the

615

King of Rock and Roll. 'To be honest, Elvis wasn't much of an athlete,' Bledsoe recalls. 'He was very rigid. He just wanted to move around, get him some exercise. He'd get in the court and bang the ball around. I'd try to teach him the rules or orchestrate a formal match, but he wasn't much interested in that. He did like the game though, and wound up building a $250,000 racquetball court in back of Graceland.' David Fleetwood compares Elvis' game to his own singing voice. 'It was horrible! He was a pro singer and I was a pro player. But E loved the sport and that's what muttered.' 'He got a couple points most of the time,' hints Bledsoe, 'And once he got eight on me to 21.' Fleetwood says, 'I tried to give E the Donut (zero points), and sometimes did, but against Linda Thompson, who cares?' Steve Smith chimes, Elvis loved the game like he loved gospel, just belted it out.'

Elvis and the RB Mafia traveled to learn the court club business at Ray Stern's Dallas club.

Dr. Fred Lewerenz of Michigan concurs. 'Elvis loved to play the sport. He was a club player, a C with a higher level of pleasure. We played a lot on the Graceland court. Elvis loved the game but not for the same reasons as others. He just liked to hit the ball. He was competitive and emotional. His forehand was good, and his backhand was sufficient to just hit the ball around and have a good time in a workout.' Lewerenz had become Elvis's sport physician by a quirk. 'There was a racquetball tournament in Memphis that Dr. Nick played in before we got to know each other. During a match he injured his back and the back of his leg, and the call went out, 'Is there a doctor in the courthouse?' It was the kind of injury that was difficult to self-treat. I worked on Dr. Nick's back and leg in the training room for forty-five minutes, and he seemed pleased. Two weeks later, I got a call asking if I wanted to be Elvis's sport physician.' Dr. Lewerenz won 140 tournaments overall, and played on the IPRO tour as did the rest of the pro Racquetball Mafia I from 1975 to 1976

Elvis didn't attend any tournaments outside Graceland. 'It would have been mayhem with the fans, tells Smith. 'We didn't throw any tournaments at Graceland either, just fierce competition among the entourage and visiting pros. The best player at Graceland after the pros went home was bodyguard Red West who fell just short of Open play. Dr. Lewerenz describes Red as a 'great athlete who brought those talents to the court.' Yet, if they wanted to, the pros could hold any Graceland bodyguard or musician to under five points, but didn't because the purposes were exercise, coaching and fun. 'I once challenged seven of E's bodyguards to one game to 21 for $100 per man,' relates Bledsoe. 'It was against Red, Sonny, Dave Hebler, and others. I played with an antifreeze bottle and they used their racquets. I went home that morning with $700.'

Racquetball boomed across the nation from 1975-6 as Bledsoe and the others 'ran' with Elvis at Graceland, and riding the night streets of Memphis on motorcycles with sidecars. Memphis was the second racquetball capital (after San Diego) of America. Dr. Nick knew Jerry Lee Lewis and got his DC-3 14-seat plane to fly the Racquetball Mafia to the Atlanta Southern Regional. The group included Nick and his son Dean, Stafford, Bledsoe, Zeitman, Smith, Steve's brother Stuart, Jack Fulton, Gary Stevens, Larry Lyles, IRA President Bill Tanner, and pros Sarah Green and Steve Strandemo. 'Elvis didn't go because he was mobbed wherever he went outside Graceland, and besides, the tough old geezer Colonel Parker wouldn't let him out to play in tournaments,' amends Fleetwood. Randy Stafford remembers, 'Our plane was an old DC-3 with twin engines, and the interior had captain's chairs and couches around. It sat about 14. Under the center table used for drinks was an 8-track tape player that was huge, and next to it a file of 8-track tapes. All of them were Jerry Lee Lewis tapes, and we partied to his songs all the way to Atlanta.' Zeitman agrees that it was a unique way to travel to a Regional, and that the old DC-3 could have been the same Jerry Lee Lewis 14-seat DC-3 that, in 1985, Ricky Nelson's pilot radioed again, 'Smoke in the cockpit!' Then the plane disappeared from radar. The DC-3, previously owned by notorious widow-maker, Jerry Lee Lewis, crashed, killing Nelson and the entire band.

The 'star' pro with the most access to Elvis Presley was his wardrobe manager and Tennessee State racquetball champion Steve Smith. Steve had grown up best friends and playing racquetball with Dr. Nick's son Dean. Steve had seen me pull up to a Tanner IPro Memphis stop in 1975. 'You were in an old van with a beat up bicycle strapped to the back that you rode to the tournament instead of driving like everyone else'. I recall Steve as slight and as quick as a deer, always a threat to upset me by his pure athleticism. Brumfield too had played the smooth Southern mover 'without a backhand.' Following one of their matches, Brum quickly corrected the backhand, if not by Christian charity then by rubbing salt in the wound. 'After the match,' continues Smith, 'Outside the court we made up and were surprised to find that each of us professed to be a golfer. 'I don't believe it,' we said at nearly the same time. Then Brumfield told me, 'Steve, all your backhand needs is to swing like it's a golf club. Keep your elbow close to your body, and you'll get control. When the elbow is tight to the body the forearm and wrist don't waver, and your control increases substantially.' It worked, and later in the year he took #3 Steve Serot down the wire before losing by four in a 21-point tiebreaker.

The author rides a Peugeot bicycle 2400 miles from San Diego to Michigan, and stops to play at the 1975 St. Louis Nationals, finishing third. (Jan Campbell)

Charlie Brumfield in 1975, on the dual pro circuits, picked up multiple national titles including the NRC Pro Singles, IRA/IPRO Singles, IRA Doubles with Craig McCoy, National Outdoor Racquetball Singles, and Outdoor Doubles with Steve Serot. He toured with a dedicated contingent of shouting, drinking Brum's Bums, even as Elvis maintained the equally rowdy Memphis Mafia of bodyguards, musicians, girlfriends, and pros. The associates were there for camaraderie and also filled practical roles. Brumfield had a designer of signs and monogrammed shirts, plus a wine fetcher, and E had his bodyguards, road and stage managers, and 'floaters' like Steve Smith who produced whatever was needed on the spot. In each case, after the tournaments and music gigs ended there were enough people to party deep into the night. Brumfield, the King of Racquetball, and Elvis, the King of Rock, surrounded themselves by these supporters who truly cared for them, and the Kings cared back.

I was Brumfield's popular nemesis and complimented him that his Bums looked like the stinking winos I saw on skid rows. Colonel Parker said the members of the Memphis Mafia (excluding the pros) looked 'like a bunch of old men.' The Colonel wouldn't let the pros take pictures of Elvis, and tried to pen him up in six-star Graceland whenever there wasn't a music tour. 'Colonel Parker was sharp, shrewd, and merciless" accuses Smith. 'No, he didn't play racquetball. If it didn't pay, he didn't play. Yet, Elvis owned Parker, not the opposite.' In one deal reported by Bledsoe, 'Dr. Nick, Elvis, his guitarist

Joe Esposito and I were breaking ground on Presley Center Courts with plans to build an American chain of clubs starting in the Southeast. There were already a few clubs in Nashville and Memphis when Colonel Parker made us take E's name off of it. He had all rights to Elvis' name. Parker was a greedy old bastard!'

'Yes,' agrees Steve Smith. 'The Colonel was selfish and took half of everything Elvis had. Ultimately, I hold him responsible for E's death. My roots with Elvis run pretty deep. I grew up best friends with Dean Nichopoulos who was Dr. Nick' son. Dean and I were like brothers. Dr. Nick taught all of us to play racquetball: Dean, Elvis, me, the bodyguards, and he coached many of the Memphis to-be pros. Dr. Nick became E's personal physician in 1968, and two years later Dean and I moved to Graceland and lived there full time with a group of about six others that were the core of what the press smiled when they called us the Memphis Mafia. I was a 'floater' at Graceland, helping Elvis with whatever he needed, and playing racquetball with him and the group of bodyguards, musicians and actors. I was with Elvis from 1970 until three months before his death in 1977.'

Memphis and San Diego were the two warring racquetball capitals during the Golden Decade, clear across a country of crazed Elvis, Disco, and racquetball fanatics. Racquetball was the fastest growing sport in the world. Before the Graceland court opened in 1975, the Memphis Racquetball Mafia worked out at Memphis State, the Memphis Athletic Club, and a single court facility that may have been the model, as well as the impetus, for the eventual construction of Elvis' private court at Graceland. For there was another man about town who was as moneyed as Elvis, with nearly as much clout, and adored the sport of racquetball just as much. Bill Tanner in 1975 was called 'the most prestigious man in Tennessee' by the press that he controlled. He was one of Memphis' most prominent businessmen and racquetball promoters who had a court on top of his 7th story office building on Union Avenue Extended. Elvis and his group played there often because it was private, and Tanner would open up at night. I was up there once on the outside running (18-laps to a mile) track around the outer perimeter of the top floor where the sliding glass doors of Tanner's office opened to a panoramic view of Memphis, as joggers swept by. We had climbed, each by habit, the couple hundred stairs to the top track, and then Tanner swept his hand down across the city offering, 'The key to the city is yours, Keeley, if you play ball with the Tanner team.'

William B.Tanner was the President of the International Racquetball Association (IRA), and had just started a competing IPro Tour that was taking the whack out of the National Racquetball Club (NRC) monopoly. Tanner brought me up here to play a game, and of racquetball, and then to make the proposition. I jumped out of the way of a jogger, returned to face Bill, and told him point blank that I was die-hard Leach, the opposing tour's sponsor. 'Come move to Memphis,' he cajoled. 'Play with Randy Stafford, Bledsoe, Zeitman, Fleetwood, and see the girls. There is nothing San Diego has that Memphis does not except an ocean, but San Diego doesn't have Elvis Presley.' That wasn't true; Marty Hogan was my present roommate in San Diego, and on seeing that I was squared away, Tanner went for Hogan. 'Well, tell your boy Hogan that the same offer is open to him.' So, I missed a chance to play Elvis, but between 1974-77 I visited Memphis five times to compete against members of the Memphis Racquetball Mafia in the Tanner ProAm, and to visit the Memphis media mogul Bill Tanner.

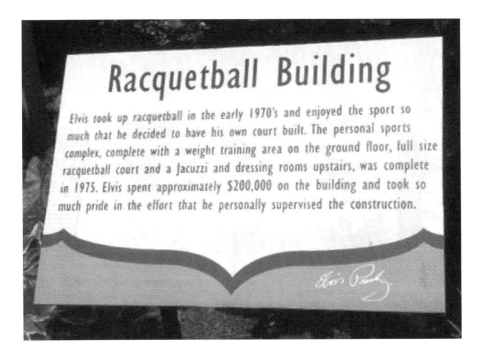

You will never, as far as I know, see another story about Elvis in racquetball, or about the Memphis Racquetball Mafia. This is because, although it was the time of glitz racquetball, when other Hollywood, rock, and political stars made the monthly covers of the only publication, *National Racquetball,* in the chess game for political control of the burgeoning players, the Chicago based NRC (and close tie with San Diego Leach) put an embargo on Elvis. NRC Executive Director Chuck Leve explains, 'Elvis was Memphis and Memphis was Tanner and IRA, and well, you know the story...So we chose to pretty much ignore Elvis, although I thought whoever did the 'damage control' when he died on the court was brilliant. Elvis never was covered in the NRC magazine because the time when racquetball 'went Hollywood' Elvis would have been prime material for our magazine, however the National Racquetball Club owner Bob Kendler sensed Elvis was in the Tanner Memphis camp which was opposing our NRC pro tour with a tour of their own, so while Batman, Lana Wood, and Governor Thompson of Illinois got coverage, Elvis in racquetball remains a secret.'

Tanner, as IRA President, was every bit as tough and ruthless as boss Kendler in Chicago and Charley Drake in San Diego. 'Tanner can't be compared to either of them,' clarifies Randy Stafford. 'He was one of a kind.' Mike Zeitman worked for Tanner from 1975 to 1978 as a media placement buyer, racquetball instructor, interim executive director of the IRA, editor of the magazine, and director of the IRA's IPRO Tour. All the dozen of top players in the city came to play on the Tanner rooftop court including Elvis and his group. Under Dr. Nick's and the pros' tutelage Tanner became what was known as a strong player without a backhand that was forgivable among open players at the time, but he was no match for Intercollegiate Doubles Champion David Fleetwood. David informs, 'I played him once and it was no fun. I was fresh out of college and had no concept at

The Graceland court where Elvis and the Memphis Racquetball Mafia played. (US RB Museum)

that time of how huge he was. Thus I didn't really understand the significance that everybody deferred to this guy who couldn't play. His forehand was very good, and he loved to go down the line. Considering his backhand grip, his backhand was passable. He made up for it by doing whatever it took to win. He as much as any player knew how to legally cheat. I made up for it after the match by going out to the track and shooting water balloons and racquetballs with surgical tubing made into a giant slingshot at cars below. He was sort of an A player, better than Elvis but not as good as Nick. He won when racquetball was at its pinnacle when winning was war. He would win at all costs, as an expression of his business acumen. He was a master bridge player, which is the highest category in cards, and he was out for the trump regardless of the activity… That was his DNA.'

The Graceland racquetball court now houses the Elvis Presley museum. (US RB Museum)

Tanner never went half-way on a project. He owned a chain of Holiday Inns and the world's largest radio and television time-buying and placement services. In 1974 he bought the newly named Tanner Building to house the broadcasting company, and it just happened to have a racquetball court on the top floor. So, Tanner determined to learn the game and to be the best he could. Full steam ahead, he hired Bledsoe, and later Zeitman, as staff members of his company to give racquetball instruction. The fruit of it would come to bear long after Fleetwood's display of water balloons across Memphis when, in 1980, Tanner would win that year the Tennessee state racquetball titles in masters singles, the Tennessee State Doubles Championship, the Masters Singles Championship and Seniors Singles Championship in the USRA Regional Tournament, the Veterans Masters Racquetball Championship, the Masters singles title at the Fulton Open in Memphis, and was inducted into the Tennessee Sports Hall of Fame.

Kicking back late one night after the matches at the Tanner Penthouse Suite, Elvis and the Racquetball Mafia sank into a circle of cushion chairs like tennis shoed capitalists in the large boardroom, and the King put his feet up on the boardroom table. Steve Smith who was there describes, 'Elvis put his legs and tennis shoes up on the ornate table, and someone in the group mentioned that Tanner would not like that, and he'd better put them down. Elvis didn't like rules, so he cursed a streak, and word got back to Tanner about this.' E hadn't been kicked out yet. 'But then,' rejoins Bledsoe, 'Elvis had this three-foot flashlight that he used to flash at everybody…which actually blinded you where you stood. A few nights after the boardroom incident, Tanner was in his private shower when E walked in and started shining his 3' light into everyone's face. When he shined it into Tanner's face, that was it. The irrepressible force of Elvis Presley met the irresistible object of William Tanner, and they glowered at each other. Bill's face turned purple, and he kicked Elvis the hell out.' Presley was banned from the building, and the Mafia loyally stayed away with him.'

Short one court, Nick persuaded Elvis to build one behind his house. Now, in 1975, when a cry went up in the middle of the night, 'Everybody up! Let's play racquetball!' everyone just walked out the back door and to the Graceland court. Dr. Fred Lewerenz describes, 'The racquetball building was posh. There was a viewing lounge behind the back wall glass, weightlifting gym on the same ground floor, and a dressing room and Jacuzzi upstairs. Elvis liked gold, and while the players' dressing room had standard stainless steel showerheads, the one in the King's private stall was with solid gold 360-degree swivel showerhead.' The only one he would allow in his private dressing area was Linda Thompson. The pros admired that the facility cost $250,000 to build, and for the times, it was a premier court. Mike Zeitman describes, 'Behind the glass wall was a sunken area with a monster curved leather couch at the wall where you could sit back and watch the games. Also in the viewing area was the biggest, most expensive stereo outfit money could buy. I'd never seen anything so cool.' The action inside the four-walls was like any other club, with a lounge with a bar outside where people sat and drank, watched and kibitzed, until their turn to play came up. Some of them drank beers, but the focus was on racquetball. It was just a small club with a select group of some of the best players and musicians in the country who all happened to know the owner, Elvis Presley.'

'When E went out in the daytime, he was touched by a thousand people,' relates Dave Fleetwood. Dr. Lewerenz started with Presley for two years at Memphis State before moving to Graceland. 'He played at Memphis State for a few years before building the court at Graceland. Most of his games were after midnight to 3am at Memphis state to avoid the mad rush of people. No one was there at night except him and whatever part of the Memphis Mafia and racquetball group that he brought. Finally, he and Dr. Nick thought it would be better to build a court on Graceland. After it was constructed he played there daily. I visited Dr. Nick often on my medical or racquetball swings through

Memphis, and when the game moved to Graceland so did I on the visits. The most astounding thing about the place to me was when you walked in the front door there was an aquarium in the living room half the size of a racquetball court. It was 12' high and could have been emptied and used for squash. When we played at Graceland it still often was at night because he had become nocturnal for privacy.'

Dr. Fred Lewerenz describes, 'The racquetball building was posh. There was a viewing lounge behind the back wall glass, weightlifting gym on the same ground floor, and a dressing room and Jacuzzi upstairs. Elvis liked gold, and while the players' dressing room had standard stainless steel showerheads, the one in the King's private stall was with solid gold 360-degree swivel showerhead.' The only one he would allow in his private dressing area was Linda Thompson. The pros admired that the facility cost $250,000 to build, and for the times it was a premier court facility. Mike Zeitman describes, 'Behind the glass wall was a sunken area with a monster curved leather couch at the wall where you could sit back and watch the games. Also in the viewing area was the biggest, most expensive stereo outfit money could buy. I'd never seen anything so cool.' The action inside the four-walls was like any other club with a lounge with a bar outside where people sat and drank, watched and kibitzed, until their turn to play came up. Some of them drank beers, but the focus was on racquetball. It was just a small club with a select group of some of the best players and musicians in the country who all happened to know the owner, Elvis Presley.

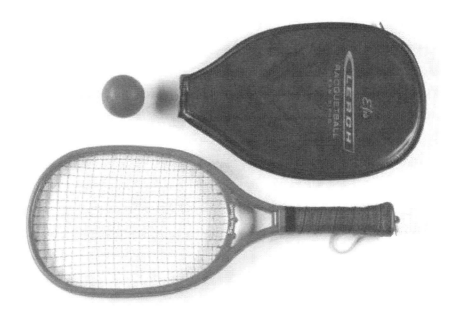

Elvis' gold embossed Steve Serot racquet cover, autograph racquet, and Voit ball.

'A typical afternoon at Graceland went like this,' takes up Steve Smith. 'Everyone would be sitting around the house, and one of the group would want to motivate the rest to action, to get off our asses. Elvis or I would jump up and shout, 'Everybody out here! We're playing racquetball.' We'd play and play. We'd play for two, three hours. Elvis would laugh while he played and have a good time just blasting the ball. Then we'd shower up, and someone would yell, 'Hey, let's go to the movies. We'd get on the motorcycles and six or eight of us would ride downtown to the Memphian or two other theaters that Elvis liked. It was crazy, night after night. One evening I sat between Eric Clapton and the King who he'd come to pay his respects to. That's when the movies were still reel-to-reel.'

'The next day it was the same, but always a bit different. There would be a new rock star visiting the House. Different doubles teams. Elvis played racquetball when it struck him, which was usually a daily dose when we weren't on tour. The road trips were two weeks on, and two weeks back at Graceland. On the road, Dr. Nick sometimes found a private court for us and the bodyguards to play on, but not Elvis. Each concert was like a championship performance. Elvis the same energy into performing that he did racquetball. It was all out, and he'd come off exhausted. On tour he loved his fans and

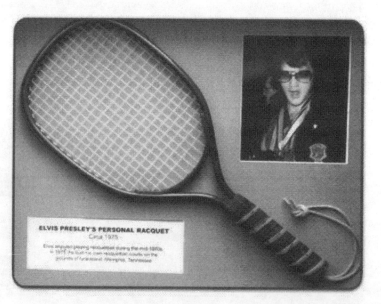

E's personal racquet made for him by Bill Stevens at Trenway in San Diego.

never wanted to disappoint them. You are guaranteed the last drop of sweat from Elvis Presley will be on the stage by the end of the concert, and the same when he jammed on the racquetball court. After the concert he'd go back to the hotel suite and just sit down in a cushion chair and pass out, he'd worked so hard. At Graceland, after a racquetball session it was the same thing. We'd leave the court and go to the lounge in the racquetball building, and relax. Relaxing there means that half of the group was 'old school' that didn't understand the 'new school', but we all sat together for an hour and a half, two hours... then someone would leap up and call out like a coyote to energize everyone, 'Let's go!' Usually it was dark by then, and we'd go out.

'How he played! He had a mind of his own. He had a big forehand and moved around the ball to hit with it. He liked the intensity of being in four walls for sport. He let go, and could have a blast,' observes Smith. In the early 70s, Elvis used the Ektelon Muehleisen racquet because it was the best at the time, and the connection was that Dr. Muehleisen had given Dean Nichopoulos racquetball lessons. Elvis could hit with the Muehleisen model. It wasn't until about 1974 that Charley Drake at Leach sent him a green Leach Serot and a pair of sweats with Elvis' name embroidered across

the back, and from then on, he used the Serot model. He was in good shape, but got on the court in the Leach sweats or a rubber suit to sweat off about five pounds a workout for his fans on tour. Davey Bledsoe was the player rep for Leach at the time, and Drake had told him, 'Anything Elvis wants, he gets.' Elvis was playing his best racquetball from 1974-6 when the pros were stopping by, and he was enjoying the game nearly daily when we didn't leave for two week music tours.'

By 1976, physician and friend Dr. Nichopoulos had been living part-time at Graceland for over a year since the court construction. Out of the blue, Elvis suggested, 'It's time to build your 'dream house'. Construction got underway immediately at another location by Steve Smith's father who owned a construction company, and, of course, the building plan included a racquetball court in the back yard. Dave Fleetwood evokes, 'Elvis and the Memphis Mafia would drive up on motorcycles to the site while the house was being framed to make sure all the nails were straight. Once we were playing a flag or touch football game in the front yard when the King and a dozen others drove up on big Harleys. They took off the helmets, all their hair flew out, and suddenly they became recognizable as the Memphis Mafia. Steve Smith adds proudly, 'You know who played quarterback? – Elvis. You know who he threw to? – Me.' Dr. Lewerenz reminisces, Elvis helped Nick financially to build the dream house. One day Presley arrived during the laying of the racquetball court foundation with fists full of gold coins. I was there. They put a few dozens of gold coins into the foundation of the court!'

The pros, like Presley, pour out accolades for Dr. Nick as a player, doctor and friend. I personally knew when we met at a Tanner IPRO stop in Memphis that he was the Johnny Racquetball Seed of the South, and he knew my reputation from *The Complete Book of Racquetball* as the game's unofficial laureate. He was an A player of the time, an even better coach, and a hands-on promoter of the spot. The group called their patron the Silver Fox, due to the silver- not gray- hair, and because he hit shots like a fox. 'The Silver Fox was shifty, and you never knew where his shots would go until after they were hit,' guesses Stafford. Dave Fleetwood comes from a family of medical practitioners,

and testifies, 'I thought it was cooler knowing Nick than even E. He was a great doctor for me. Everywhere he went he got attention. He signed menus, paper napkins, patient charts, everything, and even in hospitals. You ask any resident that did a six- week tour at a hospital with Dr. Nick, and every single one would stand up in court and tell you how good of a physician he was...every one.'

Nick saw subtle changes in Elvis in late 1976, and so did E's sports physician Dr. Lewerenz, but neither was particularly alarmed at the weight gain. Still E toured, hit racquetballs, played his mamma's gospel on the lounge piano, and did favors for his friends. Bledsoe describes, 'A week before a music tour was to begin E put on his rubber suit each day on the court to sweat off five pounds of water weight because he thought it made him look good for the fans.' Fleetwood chimes,' By 1976, E was still the King and I called him that but he was morbidly fat, and jiggled when he ran around the court. Hell, the Beatles recorded an album here, and from what I heard they could not wait to get an audience with the King just to meet and hang. The Led Zeppelin wanted to know what went on past the Graceland gate, and the band respectively submitted permission to enter. I was young, a wet behind the ears college pup and only saw fetching the ball. I had no freaking idea he was a superstars' superstar. All I knew he was Elvis, with the enormous hind end that was difficult to get around to shots.'

On April 24, 1976 I saw Elvis in concert at the San Diego sports arena while sitting next to Charley Drake of Leach industries and his wife Patty. Before the final number, Charlie urged her to the stage, saying, 'Maybe Elvis will blow you a kiss!' She pshawed but Charlie prevailed, and his wife waded through the fans and, surprisingly, a way cleared

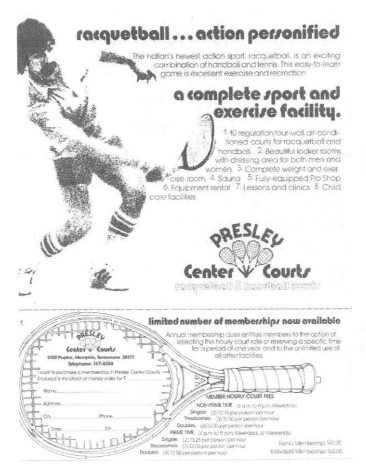

for her to rest her elbows on the music platform. Elvis began to sing, 'Can't Help Falling in Love, and during a protracted instrumental, he walked over to her, removed a royal purple scarf from his shoulders, and it wafted in the hot arena air into her outstretched hands. Six months later, on October 31st, 1976, Elvis made his last recording with a vocal overdub on 'He'll have to Go' done in the Jungle Room at his home in Graceland.

On June 11, Davey Bledsoe shocked the racquetball world and especially Marty Hogan by defeating him in the final of the Leach/Seamco National Championship in San Diego by scores of 21-20, and 21-19. The day before he had edged by me in the quarters, and

629

afterwards in the locker room, came over to console me, putting his thumb on my temple and uttering, 'My Daddy did this when I was a young man, and he spoke, 'One day you're going to be a champion.' The Bledsoe victory is recognized as one of the most unexpected results in racquetball history. Two weeks later, on June 26, 1977, Elvis gave his last concert at Market Square in Indianapolis, IN for a crowd of 18,000. Back on the Graceland racquetball court, Elvis appeared pale, weak and overweight, but there was nothing to suggest impending death. Indeed, there was nothing unusual in his verve once he took to the stage or court. 'He looked gray in 1976,' is all,' portrays Dave Fleetwood.

In May that year the three bodyguards Bledsoe had beaten with an anti-freeze bottle –Red and Sonny West, together with Dave Hebler- released *Elvis: What Happened* in UK serials that was later published in August, 1977. The three had been fired by Presley's father, Vernon, from their jobs as bodyguards for the singer. Bledsoe says 'Elvis was pissed!' This was the first book that focused on Elvis's addiction to prescription drugs, but E loved those boys, according to the pros, and whatever was said in the book, Elvis forgave and wanted them back. 'The book devastated Elvis,' insists Bledsoe,' but Smith is a greater authority in a parallel experience in the same month that the book was released in UK serials. Smith accused Parker of being an accomplice in making life so miserable for Elvis that it hurt his health. However, 'The public misconception is that in his last few months Elvis was off, and lethargic, not like his earlier wild self. That's the toilet paper account and it's not true. Up to the end E had good days and bad days, and on any given day we could get him excited to like play racquetball, go to the theater, or head for the open road. He still had life in him, and for many years.'

The same May as the UK book release, and three months before Elvis's untimely death on August 16, 1977, a few hours after leaving the racquetball court, Steve Smith hung up the phone and went to his boss in tears. 'Sir, I've worked for you loyally for seven years, but now my daddy is sick and there's no one to take over the construction. I don't want to leave…' 'Boy,' boomed Elvis. There's one thing you must never forget. That's the bottom line. And the bottom line is your daddy.' He hugged me by the neck. Then he said, 'Hey, why don't we bring your father out here and he'll get better.' But he was too ill for that. We hugged again, and I cried all the way to the gate. The next thing I heard, 'Elvis is dead!' But I know where my boss is, and so does anyone else who knew him. E is in heaven singin' gospel.'

What follows is the untold story of the death of Elvis Presley… and of the Racquetball Mafia. Graceland was shut down very quickly. The court wasn't used again after the Mafia left, and it was converted to a trophy room. Hundreds of thousands of tourists per year travel to stand in the last place Elvis Presley stood in the Graceland court that is now the trophy room, with the walls of the court covered with platinum and gold records, and with the Steve Serot racquet on display under glass next to an old blue ball. Elvis died in the racquetball building, not the mansion upstairs bathroom. You probably know that

630

Elvis loved gospel music, peanut butter and banana sandwiches and karate, but did you know The King loved racquetball to death!

Davey Bledsoe defeats Marty Hogan in the final of the 1977 NRC Pro Nationals that is considered the greatest upset of all time. Bledsoe parlayed the World Championship to become Elvis Presley's racquetball coach. (Art Shay)

631

Pros Speak from the Box

My On Court Alter Ego

Always a joy to play, but extremely boring to watch. I won the sportsmanship trophy ten years in succession, and will be remembered for dry execution.   *- Mike Ray*

Determined, explosive and constant high energy.   *- Marty Hogan*

I'm a thug: physical, vicious and in your face.   *- Sudsy*

Pissed. That's right, I find something to artificially elevate myself to higher arousal. There's always something to get mentally aggressive about: The opponent, the ref, the state of the human condition. If I can't find anything to get pissed about, there's always myself.   *- Derek Robinson*

Execution.   *- Ruben Gonzalez*

I attempted to make myself the center of attention on the court, not to gratify my ego but to take the life out of the opponent who himself is used to being the focus.
     - Charlie Brumfield

Patience.   *- Alvaro Beltran*

I am confident on the court. I would hope to be perceived as someone who is a fierce competitor with integrity.   *– Jackie Paraiso*

I found it energizing to be in a mass game among screaming spectators after coming from the elite sport of squash from which I brought a stogy efficiency of execution plus quiet personality that a few of the crowd intellectuals appreciated. You recall we (the author and he) initially met at one of my baptismal national tournament, each of us in different colored sneakers representing a mutual individuality, and that's personally one of the best things to come from the sport.   *- Victor Niederhoffer*

Absolute Warrior.   *- Rhonda Rajsich*

Focused, determined, No-nonsense.   *– Cheryl Gudinas*

632

I like to be the calm collected player that does not get to upset or too excited.

– Andy Hawthorne

I was very competitive and fierce on the court. Didn't give an inch.   *- Fran Davis*

My on court personality others see as intense is alert and it may not seem it at times, but it's fun-based; but I'm trying either to change that persona or others' perspectives of it.

– Ken Woodfin

'Absolute Warrior' Rhonda Rajsich. (Mike Augustin)

I'm pretty relaxed as a player, and happy. I do have a unique ability to disturb my opponent with comments, but I wouldn't call it "sh_t talking," just comments that can force my opponent to pay attention to me a little more than what they're trying to accomplish.   *– John Ellis*

Calmed and serious.   *- Cristina Amaya Cassino*

Personality? That depends - In my early days I was as much of a jerk as one could be on the court. I tried to intimidate my opponents and argued with anyone who would argue with me. Late in my career, I had found God and played with a higher purpose - to glorify Him by treating others with respect even when things didn't go my way.

– Brian Hawkes

Calm, collected, intense.   *– Jose Rojas*

My on court personality is usually pretty grouchy.   *- Charlie Pratt*

A cross between Mr. Intensity and an occasional Mr. Smiles.   – *Davey Bledsoe*

Good sportsmanship and feisty.   *- Kerri Stoffregen Wachtel*

The great unsung Paul Lawrence. National Paddleball Singles Champion and National Paddleball Doubles Champion with Craig Finger. Semi-Finalist in 1970, 71, 72 in IRA National Racquetball Tournaments. Played on first ever NRC Pro Tour 1973. Wrote early racquetball instructional manual 1973. First ever Ektelon Rep. If I ever had a hero it was Paul Lawrence. He was tall and as graceful as a gazelle and, unbelievably, had the best

strokes in the Golden Eras of paddleball (1960s) and racquetball (1970s). I modeled my thinking after his. He was just out of U of Michigan dental school, one of the toughest, and i out of MSU vet school, the toughest, and yet when we walked the streets he knew things. i learned his thought process was to go from the particular to the general, and back again, very quickly, like looking at one tooth and knowing the set, and then looking at the set and knowing any one. He also never got lost in life. In 1973 he came to me in the height of my career and sponsorship with Leach and said he was leaving competitor Ektelon as their first player rep, and wanted me to replace him. He promised i would be treated princely. Yet, I was faithful to the brand and stayed with Leach. Paul just got tired of the racquetball shenanigans that hadn't existed in paddleball. Charlie Brumfield had beaten him for the paddleball National Singles Title by pounding him repeatedly in the ear with the ball after California coach Carl Loveday put on the 'hit sign', and Paul saw more coming around the bend in racquetball. He just wanted to go back to Michigan and start a practice. Lawrence was huge, maybe 6'5, but he was a nice guy who disappeared into the mouth of dentistry. – *Steve Keeley*

Willing and Able
Inside John Foust

"I had a foot in two racquetball worlds, so to speak. One was able-bodied that you're used to playing, and the other in a wheelchair. In the early 80s, the wheelchair game was coming on and though I was legally handicapped from polio in youth, I never dreamed of myself as that. I managed the Denver Sporting Club (known in the early years as the Denver Sporting House) and was a consistent able-bodied winner in A division, and once won the 25+ Open regionals. Luke St. Onge, the USRA executive director, asked me to play in the wheelchair division alongside my normal event, and I replied, 'I spent time in a wheel chair when young, and may again when I'm old, but I don't want to in-between.' However, Luke persevered.'"

"It was bizarre going from the regular events where I was perceived as the ';good guy' with the game leg who beat most the field, to the wheelchair division where I was truly the 'villain'' because after the match I could rise and walk with a limp from the chair. Before each match, I grimaced at having to approach another player to beg his chair. I was third and fourth ranked in the world from about '85-87 by virtue of my able-bodied racquet skills, but always lost in the finals to one of the top two wheelchair champs (Chip Parmelly or Jim Leatherman) because of their familiarity with the chair. Understand that the chair is equipment, just like the glove, racquet and shoe."
— John Foust

I first met John Foust at the Denver Sporting Club, home to many pro and amateur national tournaments, as I cruised the courts observing the Open division matches. One player on a somewhat withered leg used a devastating strategy, shooting everything from all over the court to shorten the rally. After he won, I yoked him back into the court for tips on spin in keeping the ball along the sidewall so he wouldn't have to run and dive so much, and that sealed a relationship. "I learned racquetball from Myron Roderick and Steve Strandemo, but sort of put Steve Keeley on a pedestal. He was a role model, offered help when it wasn't asked, and at the tournament hotels collected all the brochures of local interest places, and then visited them between matches."

"My able-bodied style is to shoot the ball from everywhere, because the longer the rally the less chance I have to get to the opponent's shot because of my game leg. I practiced hundreds of hours shooting from every conceivable court position, and to drive serve to earn weak returns."

Foust was an outstanding high school wrestler known for strength and single-leg takedowns. "The opposition licked their lips at seeing my little leg during weigh-in, but then shrank on discovering it weighed ten pounds less that put me into a lower weight

Chip Parmelly, John Foust, and Jim Leatherman. Chip and Jim were the top players, and James E. Golden was in the hunt. All were outstanding athletes. Their wheelchair and athletic skills overshadowed every able challenging pro's racquet skills and determination. They beat Brumfield in a wheelchair too. On some courts the doors were so small they had to get out of the chair, fold it up, and then get back in on the court. (US RB Museum)

class." He tried wrestling at Oklahoma State and decided to forego for journalism studies on discovering he was out-classed by the then NCAA championship team. However, he was introduced to racquetball there when wrestling legend and racquetball Seniors national champ Myron Roderick forced the grapplers onto the courts in rubber suits and played them one-against-two while riding them to play harder.

Foust trained hard at those killshots, and after graduation moved to Denver, where he stepped into racquetball full-time at the Denver Sporting House. Now he plays able-bodied only, manages the hottest racquetball retail and Internet store, *Racquetball Catalogue Company*, and is a moving inspiration..

Racquetball Marathon Record
Jim Easterling Sets Early Mark to Beat
61 Hours of Racquetball!

Jim Easterling is a slight, polite man who always seems on the verge of some flurry. In 1977, when we were tourney traveling companions, the Michigan Department of Transportation 26-year-old set his sight on the world's record of 60 hours of continuous racquetball. It was a crazy era for the sport with a fledgling pro tour, the ball changing speeds every month, manufacturer and sponsor competition, the blossoming of state and national organizations, participant numbers skyrocketing, and characters like Easterling who jumped onto the hardwood all over the country. I knew him as an open player with big feet who could run all day and out-eat anyone in the banquet room, but no one suspected his secret desire to break the record.

The Grand Rapids, Michigan Racquet Club has a glass-back exhibition court that Easterling called home for 61 hours and 10 minutes in breaking the old record. Earlier marks had been smashed sequentially about once a year during that decade of racquetball rage across the nation, and Jim's record would be but another in the progression. The rules were that continual games were to be played, with two-minutes breathers between each, and a five-minute rest (that could be deferred and accumulated) every hour. Contestants queued outside the court during daylight as Jim closed on 50 hours, and word spread via the local media. In the wee hours, the timekeeper shagged the pizza deliveryman to play. Most contestant were B, C and D skills against Easterling's Open level. Each paid $5 to charity for a chance to beat him, and one B player returned every 12 hours throughout the marathon promising each time, 'I'm going to keep coming back until I beat you', but neither he nor the majority of comers won a game.

'I was OK up to 55 hours, and then the body began to go,' describes Jim. My right knee gave out so I used the rest period to bandage it, then at 57 hours the other knee went and I wrapped it also, and began looking like the Mummy.' He felt strong and determined, however, in closing on the record. 'I have to admit that at 60 hours the mind began to go too. Once, the ball suddenly wound up behind me as if materializing out of thin air, and I didn't know how but I swung behind my back and hit a roll-out. A bit later, I went for a

637

ball off the glass-back wall and there was a little boy standing inside the court corner who I had to jump around, and it was only after the rally that I realized he was really outside the court.'

The smiling Michigander stepped out of the court with the new record. He went home to watch himself on the 10 o'clock news, then fell asleep. 'I yawned about a hundred times daily for a month before fully recovering'. Sleep deprivation hadn't bothered him so much during play because he'd been so psyched. He had sustained the marathon with Burger King Yumbos and Gatorade, and encouragement from fans.

'I sent the account with timekeeper's, contestants' and witnesses' reports to the *Guinness Book of Record* headquarters in England, and they returned a letter of commendation with an explanation that they'd put me into their records but not into the actual book because the sport wasn't yet an international competition.'

Easterling now ramrods the National Racquetball Hall of Fame and encourages, 'Records are made to be broken. Go for it!'

Feet-work Head over heels. (2012 Mike Augustin)

Myron Roderick, One Tough Racquetball Player

Myron Roderick was fun loving with no backhand, and at 5'5, the last man in the world I'd cross. I ran late onto the Orange Outdoor Nationals court as he served, and returned for sideout. He picked me up over his head into an airplane spin laughing and so was only a few feet off the ground. He tackled Dave Messer in Dr. Bud's living room thinking he was Don Craig and rubbed his ear in the rug to say howdy. At the '80 Houston stop he greeted Randy Stafford by picking him up by the heels and dangling him over the court back wall before they descended to play.

I knew, feared and respected three-time national wrestling champ Roderick before I picked up my first racquet and beat him. He was the youngest college wrestling coach in history and moreover won the first of many national championships for Oklahoma State that year. Roderick was the single wrestler my MSU coach Grady Penninger, also a multi-national champ and paddles/racquet player, commented, 'that's one tough character'. MSU wrestling was second in the nation that year and when Oklahoma State came to Lansing, Mich. There was electricity in the first-ever jammed fieldhouse. I saw

Penninger shake his head, look at his wristwatch, bang both, and asked him after Okla State defeated MSU, "coach what happened with the watch?". He replied, "I hardly want to say but every time Roderick and his team come to town I get so wound up that my watch stops."

Myron Roderick | Stillwater, Oklahoma   (Hall of Fame 2009 Inductee)

Many GREATS in our sport consider Myron Roderick as one of the "Founding Stalwarts of Racquetball." Myron was an accomplished Racquetball player in the 1970s, garnering 7 National Open Titles: however, he is best remembered for his many contributions to the sport of Racquetball during the International Racquetball Association's formative years. After serving on the Board of Directors for over 6 years, Myron bravely stepped up to the plate BIG TIME during the early to mid-

639

1970's when Racquetball had NO monies, funding, or direction. Myron's experience, hard-work ethic, and ability to get along with all kinds of people allowed him to almost single-handedly take over the reins as Executive Director and put the Association back on its feet financially and to get it headed in a positive direction. Myron conducted the Association's business out of his hometown of Stillwater, OK, where he also devotedly oversaw the monthly publication of the Association's Magazine. During the 1970s, Myron formed a company called Sports Unlimited that primarily built racquetball courts, including the one for Elvis Presley at Graceland in Memphis, TN. Myron is also a member of the USA Wrestling Hall of fame. He was a National Wrestling Champion numerous times and later served as its Executive Director for a number of years.

"Let him up, Myron, his dues are paid!"

"But if you are one of the five or six who haven't renewed....Wow!"

☐ 1 YEAR $6.00   ☐ 2 YEARS $10.00

NAME ....

ADDRESS ....

CITY/STATE/ZIP ....

Make checks payable to I.R.A.; add $1.00 per year outside U.S., Canada & Mexico

☐ HERE IS MY PAYMENT   ☐ NEW
                              ☐ RENEWAL

PLEASE RENEW (OR START) MY MEMBERSHIP NOW.

Mail to: IRA — P. O. Box 1016 — Stillwater, Oklahoma 74074

Racquetball Magazine subscription drive July/August 1975

Key Racquetball People: Results of Poll

Former top pro Mike Zeitman wrote me yesterday, March 19, 2013, asking, ´I was thinking about the men who most contributed to the growth of our sport in its pubescent, the 60s and 70s. Not the great athletes at play, but the men and women who started it, nurtured it, and helped to spread it across the US and the world. Who are your picks for the top 5? Push it out to your list of contributors so the selection has a large enough pool of people to make the list creditable.´

´Great idea!´ I wrote back, and dashed off a request to about fifty players, movers and shakers of the Pioneer era. The Pioneers competed from the first Nationals event in 1968 to the mid-seventies when the fast ball altered the sport and cast forever.

The purposes of this article and poll are to inform the more modern gallery of just whose shoulders they are standing on. There has been a strong push in the past five years to usher many of the unknown but deserving key figures of early racquetball into the Hall of Fame. It has been successful in promoting Steve Serot and Art Shay into the Hall, and more should follow them.

The Pioneer era in which I lived was the wild, wild west of sport with all the top guns in San Diego, and the rest of the country was boot hill.

> The pioneers of championship racquetball were more often described as Docs than Jocks! We played sweaty chess, a slow strategic contests won by the smarter player and not the best athlete. We played with an extremely slow ball with wood frame and new-fangled medal racquets strung at less than fifteen pounds tension in two out of three games to twenty-one point marathons. The ball only moved 90mph and typical rallies went six or eight shots before a point ended. How accurate was the Doc moniker? Well, five of the top ten of the era and numerous contenders just off the list had Doctoral level degrees in medicine, dentistry, law, psychology, and in my case veterinary medicine. — from The Mythical Racquetball G.O.A.T.

And now these are my picks for the Top 5 Most Influential People in the growth and character of Pioneer Racquetball.

#3 **Charley Drake**, President of Leach Industries

#2 Bob **Kendler**, founder of NRC and the first pro tour

#1 **Bud Muehleisen**, the seed of pioneer racquetball

Charley Drake and Kunan sign first racquetball international contract in Taiwan in 1974 to form Kunan-Leach Racquet Company. (US RB Museum)

Let us remember Joe Sobek, without whom one contributor wrote, 'Nobody plays.' This isn't entirely true but Sobek and guys like Carl Loveday who taught Mule and Brum who taught the rest fell in the selection process into a satellite list of influential people but obvious not close to the Big Three. More on the satellite list include Art Shay in photography, me in instruction, Marty Hogan in stroke, Charles Brimfield in charisma, Bill Schmidtke, Phil Smith, Larry Lederman, Bob Seamco Coates , Kunan of Taiwan, Bill Tanner, Ken Porko, Myron Roderick, Jim Hiser, Hank Marcus, Randy Stafford, Mike Zeitman and the lesser political forces, and so on.

It´s not anyone´s fault that some of those early key characters aren't seen in the Hall of Fame, on shoes shoulders their successors deservedly strolled into the Hall. The jinx is in the lag between the early sport developers who should be in H. of F. and the modern organizers and volunteer staff of Hall of Fame. If any one of them had been inside the factories of the first racquet manufacturers- a garage for Bud Leach running his pickup tires to press the first composite racquets, and in a hot steel hut for Bud Ektelon Held bending the first steel on homemade machines, to place a fiberglass or metal racquet in the hand of nearly every amateur and pro of the 70´s Pioneer era- the two Buds would be shoe-ins.

Bob Kendler at podium at San Diego Fiesta Inn before a 1970's Nationals. (US RB Museum)

Following the Pioneers through racquetball expansion came the other three eras outlined in The Mythical Racquetball G.O.A.T.:

> We can divide racquetball in to four distinct eras since the first national tournament in 1968. Each with its own version of the game, personalities, strategies, equipment, rules, and one great champion. The Pioneers competed from the first National event until the mid-seventies. The players of the Golden Era vied from the mid-seventies through the eighties. The Modern Era of the sport consisted of the nineties to the mid-two thousands. The Current Era is the last five years through the present 2013.

What about today, who are the keys to the future of racquetball after this Current Era? IRT Director Jason Mannino wrote:

> Some of the key figures today:

643

Doug Ganim - Director, US OPEN; product development for Head/Penn

Steve Harper - Military Racquetball Federation

Peggine Tellez - Military Racquetball Federation, President California State Racquetball Association (largest in the world)

Hank Marcus - World Outdoor Racquetball, former IRT Commissioner, Classic Professional Racquetball Tour, Director of the IRT Tournament of Champions

Jennifer Johnson - IRT Director of Communications (responsible for a large portion of our sports current media)

Kim Roy - Event Director who runs more than 10 high quality tournaments per year, a junior sleepover camp, junior program, and one of the largest events in the country "IRT Florida Spring Break ProAm" (7 years running)

Leo Klamiatas - Philanthropist who built the clear court, countless dollars spent supporting the sport

Pat Taylor - same as above

Dan Whitley - Programmer Veta Sports, runs Missouri Junior Racquetball Association (largest junior program in the country)

Fran Davis - #1 instructor in the game, 15 camps per year for 20+ years, author of #1 selling book today, #1 DVD series, programmer, event director, etc.

Yours Truly - player, teacher, promoter, administrator.

There are many more....but these are some of the top people that keep our sport going.

And Racquetball keeps rolling through the dust of time. Thanks to the pioneer contributors Dave Fleetwood, Marty Hogan, Jim Hiser, Bud Muehleisen, Jerry Hilecher, Brett Elkins, Randy Stafford, Mike Zeitman, John Foust, Bill Stevens, Ron Starkman, Jim Schatz, Hank Markus, Dena Rassenti, Charles Brumfield, Davey Bledsoe, Bo Champagne, Donna Noguchi, Judy Turlington, Eric Campbell, Art Shay, Jim Easterling and Chuck Leve for naming some of the key characters in this poll.

John Wayne receives American Heart Association check for $6,000 from Ektelon Director of Marketing Ron Grimes and Natural Light representative Kevin Forth at culmination of 30 tournament series.

World Champion and IRT president Jason Mannino. (IRT)

St. Louis Power Hitters

While most racquetball players with a little knowledge of sports history know that power racquetball was forged in St. Louis, they don't usually know when and who really started the fire. Most answer that power racquetball was invented by Marty Hogan in 1979 when he released the book and video of the same name with help from Charlie Brumfield and Art Shay. I sat on the pool edge cooling my heels beside the trio at the Steamboat Springs Athletic Club.

Shay is a world famous author/photographer with over 1000 *Look, Life, Sports Illustrated, Time,* etc. cover shots, and more importantly the first professional racquetball photographer who developed early techniques such as shading the glass and the front wall portal that are responsible for the shots that grace today's magazines and websites. Charlie Brumfield was legend in his own time and words with three national singles titles (1972, 1973, 1975) and perhaps the greatest analyst ever. Hogan that year was cultivating a head of golden curls for the newfound winner's circles after recent blitzkriegs into the pro top seeds with a new-fangled power stroke. And, I ramrodded the annual Steamboat Springs racquetball camp observing sports evolution.

To correct history from this edge, Shay snapped shots of Hogan tanning and strong as Atlas for the *Power Racquetball* book. He also recorded eloquent Brumfield's dissection of Hogan coiling like an anaconda, wrist cocked holding a swim flipper, and bashing water droplets. Hogan swung repeatedly forehand and backhand and taking dips when Shay changed batteries in the tape recorder, while over the hours mighty Brumfield finally lost his voice, and that is how the book was written that changed our sport's history.

The bible *Power Racquetball* authored by Hogan, Shay and Brumfield in Steamboat Springs was etched eight years earlier in 1970 inside Hogan's hometown St. Louis JCC courts alongside other budding power hitters... Steve Serot, Jerry Hilecher, Benny Koltun, Jerry Zuckerman and lesser players hitting the model, as if patented, St Louis power stroke.

At that time, our old winning strokes coast to coast were tennis with a wrist snap on the ball. In contrast, the St. Louis boys- each about a decade younger than the incumbent champs Muehleisen, Brumfield and Keeley- shown high on the backswing an exaggerated body torque and wrist cock, ball contact as far back as the rear heel, and a sweeping follow through with most important, as Brumfield pointed out at poolside, in the split-second frame of strings on rubber the St. Louis hitters cracked a bullwhip to generate about double the racquet head speed.

646

To approximate the ball speed using 90mph as the base for the top players Brumfield, Keeley and Steve Strandemo in 73-.74, Serot estimates at 115mph, Hilecher at 105mph, and Hogan at 130mph before hitting 142mph with a super ball in 1978.

Hogan won his first pro stop in 1975 at Burlington, VT beating me in the finals and screaming at the fans through the aquarium glass, 'Get my mother on the phone!' I won!' Power racquetball won that day and seeded across the nation and world. Back in St. Louis, by his example, the power machine revved up to produce more hard hitters, but none matched the original forgers of the early 70's.

Serot and Hilecher were great athletes who became great racquetball players. They were the first Jocks to invade a sport ruled by Docs. Both were strong baseball players with very supportive fathers, both ranked among the top world junior handball players, and each learned to play power racquetball at the St. Louis JCC. As much as they had in common their games were totally different.

Steve Serot, a natural righty who converted to lefty after an early injury, owned the first and best real power backhand in the sport. At the unbelievable age of fifteen he was a semifinalist at the first 1971 IRA National Invitational Tournament in San Diego. Two years later at seventeen he teamed with Brumfield to win the IRA National Doubles becoming the youngest player at the time to win an 'Open' level National Championship. Months after his first National Title, Steve made racquetball history at only seventeen by winning the first ever Professional Racquetball tournament in Houston, Texas defeating me in the semis and multiple National Champion, Bill Schmidtke in the finals. Steve would go on to reach the finals of the IRA National Singles in 1974 and 75. Steve not only holds the permanent record as first ever professional champion but thirty nine years later Serot is still the youngest player to ever win a pro event. At his best, there may have been no better player and certainly no better power player in Serot's best days. He was one of the top five players in the world for eight consecutive years from 1971 to 1978, genuflecting out at last to the faster ball even as we were recording the book in Steamboat. He was finally inducted into the Hall of Fame in a steamroll I started in 2012… because he was my toughest opponent over the years.

Jerry Hilecher ignored the strategy of all the top players of the 60s and 70s from the Michigan and San Diego schools of racquetball, and brought to tournaments a power style all his own. Jerry was the first true serve-and-shoot big game player. He was the first to rely on aces, and on the ensuing setup of near-aces. He was murder to play. While most players needed six or eight strokes to win a rally, Hilecher's unmatched drive serves and power forehands gave him more quick points than any top player before him. He was the first of the streak players, knocking off five points unless you took a timeout to cool his jets. I first noted Jerry's booming big game in the round of sixteen 1973 Nationals in St. Louis. I was one of the favorites along with 1971 and 1972 National Champions Bill

Hall of Fame indoor and outdoor singles and doubles champion Steve Serot (Art Shay)

Schmidtke and Charlie Brumfield, but this young hometown favorite almost kept me out of the quarters. In the second game I made the mistake of instructing him how to hit a better backhand ceiling ball by aiming toward center court to keep it off the left side wall that developed the toughest match I had that year 27-17 in the tiebreaker, besides a memorable finals against Brumfield. Jerry won the first ever Intercollegiate National

Racquetball tournament that year before joining the fledgling pro tour. He was one of the most consistent players in pro racquetball history retaining a top six ranking every year from '73 to '86. Jerry played his best against the best. It was Jerry who stopped the streak of five-time national singles champion, Brumfield by winning the 1976 IPRO Nationals, and then upsetting the same 'Holder' in the quarters of the '77 National Championship on his way to a semi-final run that year. 1978-79 was Jerry best season of all, finishing #2 only behind fellow St. Louis star, Marty Hogan. He continued beating the other legends in winning the first two Catalina events in 1981, even though in a strange political move he had to qualify after not being one of the twelve invited Catalina players. To qualify, Hilecher beat the top three players in the world, Hogan, Mike Yellen and Dave Peck to win consecutive events and briefly hold the world number one ranking. Jerry's long and successful career also landed him a place in the Racquetball Hall of Fame in 2005.

Serot and Hilecher preceded Hogan as power hitters!

While Steve and Jerry deserve credit as the innovators, the St. Louis power racquetball story is deeper than just two Hall of Fame players from one club. Charlie Brumfield said 'We polish the diamonds in San Diego but they mine them in St. Louis.'

Jerry Zuckerman of the St. Louis 'J' won the first ever Junior National Championship in 1974 beating Marty Hogan and Rich Wagner along the way. The young lefty power player also won both the USRA and IRA Open Nationals in 1977 and was a top sixteen professional player. I had the shave of my career ouching him in a St. Louis pro stop with a 20-20 third game backhand reverse overhead from the left rear corner.

Benny Koltun came from the same courts and won the USRA Junior and Open National Tournaments in 1976 before being named the 1977 Pro Racquetball Rookie of the Year. Benny spent five consecutive seasons in the top ten including twice finishing top five in the pro rankings. He scared me, so turbulent and then so cool, and once in a close match as I wound up to push a ball off the back wall, he dropped his racquet by the thong to his side and watched me roll it off, quipping, 'I just wanted to study your stroke.'

The accomplishments of Marty Hogan, the most famous St. Louis power player, are well documented. He won the second ever Junior National Championship in 1975 and months later became the second youngest player to win a pro event behind Serot. Marty did it by beating Brumfield, Serot and me consecutively on his way to his first victory in an incredible racquetball career. Prior to that breakthrough 1975 Burlington event, Hogan had never even won a single game from Serot or Hilecher, and I was beating him with a wood paddle. Marty finished #2 behind Brumfield and ahead of me at #3 on the 1975-76

St. Louis power hitters Ben Koltun serves to Jerry Hilecher in 1974 at the Denver Sporting Club. (John Foust)

tour but that was only a start. He went on to win more total pro racquetball titles every year for ten consecutive years from '77 to '86, a record that I doubt will ever be broken. He is also the only player in history to win the Pro Nationals, Outdoor Nationals and Paddleball Nationals in the same year in 1979, and the only player awarded eight Pro Racquetball Player of the Year Awards, one of only two players along with Kane

650

Waselenchuk to go over a calendar year without losing a match on tour, and one of only two players along with Cliff Swain to have been ranked in the top two for ten or more seasons..

Though Marty's accomplishments are unrivaled, he is only part of the story, and had it not been for the power backhand of Serot and the power serve and forehand of Hilecher before him, the world might never been handed Marty Hogan.

How dominating was the St. Louis power game at its best? In the final 1976-77 NRC Pro Tour ranking four of the top seven players in the world came out of the St. Louis JCC: Hogan, Serot, Hilecher and Koltun, all playing the new brand of power racquetball. That same year the finals of the 1977 IPRO Pro National Doubles consisted of Charlie Brumfield and three St. Louis 'J' players, as Brum and Serot defeated Hilecher and Zuckerman for their third national doubles title.

With faster balls and bigger and better racquets the power game has totally eclipsed the strategy and control game that Muehleisen, Brumfield and I played. The power backhand of Serot has been slightly adjusted to less wrist snap and more body torque by today's pros, and the players now use the top third of the racquet instead of the dead center sweet spot that Hilecher hit his forehand serve and kills, but there is no mistake that Steve Serot and Jerry Hilecher pioneered power racquetball and the game has forever changed.

The new 2015 power hitters are Latin like Daniel De La Rosa. (Mike Augustin)

651

Peggy Steding: The Hottest Stick

When all is said and done in women's racquetball... there stands Peggy. There is never a more deserving champion, and forever more as mysterious and beloved on the pro circuit

Except for one flaw when *Sports Illustrated* Curry Kirkpatrick, covering the 1974 Nationals in 'The Game Plan is to Avoid Getting Waffle-Faced' tagged Peggy as, 'She looks like the substitute waitress at a truck stop.' The same article extols Peggy's speed and endurance. After being taken apart by her explosive serves in the semifinals of the '74 Nationals, Jan Campbell admitted, 'Not only does she kill us, she doesn't even sweat. I tried to aim for her stomach, but I was so nervous. The humiliating thing is she's old enough to be my mother.' That was before Peggy got hot in the late 70s!

The first great woman player in the game was Peggy Steding. In the 1970s, as racquetball exploded across the land and strong women stormed the courts to play for blood money, little Peggy beat everyone and then took a step back as she accepted the first place trophies.

She was grudgingly succeeded in the early 80s, by the speedier ball and Shannon Wright, who was then rivaled by Heather McKay throughout the mid-80s. Then history records the great dual against Lynn Adams through the end of the decade. The 1990s belonged to Michelle Gould and, as the game sped along into the early 2000s, Jackie Paraiso and then Cheryl Gudinas were the dominant players. Then in the mid-2000s Christie Van Hees and Rhonda Rajsich took over, but near the end Paola Longoria finished #1.

Steding, unlike the rest, was stung often by the press favoring a local girl with color pictures in the press. She seemed resigned after each victory, and didn't give a guffaw. 'I can't piddle around,' she said. 'These girlies are settin' down there around 20 years old. I wish I could go back to 30.'

Her 1998 Hall of Fame Entry reads: Peggy Steding – Odessa, Texas. Born 4-17-36. Deceased 11-17-91. *Professional Athlete, Inducted 1988.* Peggy started playing racquetball in 1971. She had always been athletic and was attending Odessa College on a tennis scholarship. She had also competed in basketball, volleyball, and fast-pitch softball before discovering racquetball. Peggy dominated women's play in the early 70s continued playing in the senior divisions prior to her death in 1991. In 1992 the USRA Female Age Division Athlete of the Year award was renamed the Peggy Steding Award in her honor. It is said that Peggy elevated the game of racquetball for women during her reign as champion...Without ever calling a time-out in her life!

652

Everybody loved steady Peggy when *Sports Illustrated* called her 'A look-alike for a substitute waitress at a truck stop.' (US RB Museum)

653

Pros Speak from the Box

Concentration

One of racquetball's and life's ultimate challenges is to stay right in the moment when the chips are down. The adrenalin hits and all the better to try harder to try less. It's a balance of intensity and relaxation most suited for a given situation. I try to enter a match right on that exact line between the two, and maintain it throughout, with a little fine-tuning as I go.
- Cliff Swain

Concentration comes naturally to the intense competitor. My focus in play is on myself rather than anyone else who's around.
- Marty Hogan

Keep your thoughts simple during play. For example, when going to serve, consider just it. One thought at a time.
- Corey Brysman

One point at a time. Playing for the moment, in the now, helps me concentrate. My mind wanders less when I do that.
– Jackie Paraiso

Get your mind off tournament jitters by watching the ball. Watching the ball is 90% of concentration. I used to carry a ball around at school or during travel to look at and toss from hand to hand. Get your eyes to go automatically to the ball on the court. Then I play each shot and let the ref keep the score. Half the time the games over and I'm the last to know when it's announced.
- Mike Ray

I see only white and the blue ball on the court (even when the ball's green, because that's what I practice with).
- Alvaro Beltran

These poor young guys out here have to think when they play, where we vets just react. That's something to look forward to on concentration.
- Ruben Gonzalez

All your preparation should have taken place before you walk into the tournament court, because once there things move so fast as to be instinctual. If you're not ready, you know the right thing to do.
- Sudsy

Concentration isn't my asset at the moment, so what I'm hearing in the question is 'What tip should someone give to me to improve my concentration?' I need to develop better game plans. When you have plans and backup plans, the focus can be on playing the individual shots rather than the flow of the game and match.   *- Derek Robinson*

You have to do in a tournament what you've practiced, so relax if you've done your homework. It's difficult to make changes after the game ball's been thrown out, so be prepared with the fundamental strokes and shot selection.   *– Jim Spittle*

Know the percentages of every situation before going on the court, then play them. Remember how badly it feels to lose when you didn't observe the percentages, and if it continues then re-examine the premises.   *- Charlie Brumfield*

Ronda Rajsich concentrates on the varnish. (2006 Ken Fife)

Focus is being here and now in front of the ball, not outside the court thinking of something else. It's an earned trait through practice. If something's awry in a game, then I concentrate on the basics of getting into position quickly, picking the right serve and taking the correct shot. But if a match flows well with shots and strategies on line, then I only adjust my rheostat focuser to lower or higher intensity as needed. You can focus hard and have fun, in fact that *is* fun.   *- Jeff Leon*

I always thought my own game was more important than my opponent's, so I didn't try to suit my game to his. So I played a generic game against X as I would against Y, and concentration came easily because this is how I've played racquet sports since a youth.

- Victor Niederhoffer

I have always tried to focus on one point at a time.   *— Andy Hawthorne*

I imagine there's a wall in the glass and it's only me, the opponent and the ref.

- Cristina Amaya Cassino

I tend to play with my strings in between points. That helps me settle down. I also will focus on a family member or friend to get encouragement.   *- Kerri Stoffregen Wachtel*

Visualizing.   *— Susy Acosta*

My main goal is to focus on the moment. When I was at my best mentally I would focus on each point separately, never getting angry at what just happened or anxious about what may or may not happen. Sometimes I would be so focused on the moment that I wouldn't realize the game was over.   *— Brian Hawkes*

Take your time before you serve or raise your racquet until you are ready to receive the serve. In this moment replay the patterns of the game.   *— Davey Bledsoe*

I take long, deep breaths. And just focus on the ball.   *— Jose Rojas*

I took TM, and read Timothy Gallwey's *Inner Game of Tennis.* If you practice with strong players that also becomes a source of concentration.   *— Dena Rassenti*

Concentration: Before a match I like to listen to music and not talk to anyone. I repeat positive things to myself if I feel anxious or nervous.   *- Charlie Pratt*

I studied Zen Philosophy over the years. Key words and phrases, and positive thoughts in notecards courtside. No one liked when I pulled out the cards - They usually worked!

— Cheryl Gudinas

Lots of mantras on and off the court.   *— Fran Davis*

I had rituals before a match: I would take a short whirlpool, shave before most matches, and warm up until I broke a good sweat. These rituals became a habit that created concentration. I entered the court with my eyes and brain focused, knowing I was going to play well. That didn't always compute to winning, but I would know I gave it my best.

— Rich Wagner

Concentration is easy. I just focus on winning the point. There is nothing else.

– Jerry Hilecher

I focus on the very next thing on the horizon, the task at hand, the next rally, the next corner, the next rep, the next sentence, the next day, the next hour, the next half hour, the next 5 points, the next minute, and I always think the challenge surmountable, the goal attainable, the hurdle passable, the struggle worth it, the timing right and the day all mine to be seized.

– Ken Woodfin

Marty Hogan never drank, smoked, did drugs or had trouble concentrating. (Art Shay)

This part is easy. I've found as I age, it's easier to stay mentally focused on the moment. Thanks to knowing the RB court so well, I enjoy this aspect more than ever.

– John Ellis

Ode to a White Knight: Dr. Bud Muehleisen

After starting vet school and paddleball in 1967 before racquetball had come to Michigan State, three years flew swiftly and I was Intramural handball and paddleball champ while hardly losing a game. I had learned to serve and shoot the ball, get on and off the court quickly, because it was still an attrition sport of best two of three games to twenty-one, singles and doubles crammed into a three day weekend, and like other sports such as wrestling and tennis you had to adopt an offensive style of play or wilt in the finals.

I was a big hayseed in a small stack and thought I was ready for a big time tournament. I traveled jacketless by thumb in six rides from Lansing, Michigan to Fargo, North Dakota in the winter of 1970 to take on the best at the paddleball Nationals. I was disappointed to learn that top seed and multiple national champion Bud Muehleisen wouldn't be playing the event due to a broken metatarsal in his foot. Being the good sport he was, Dr. Bud as he was fondly known, would be still making an appearance to shake hands.

He must have seen my first warm up game and decided to enter. Suddenly his name appeared in a blank space on the draw sheet. He would be playing with his foot broken against doctor's orders. I noticed he was on my side of the draw and thought I wouldn't get an opportunity in the semi's to play the legend... There was no way a 42-year old mild mannered dentist from San Diego was going to plow through this tough field of mid-western champions to the semi's with only one good foot.

Come Sunday finals, I had managed to make the semi's in spite of my lack of experience, and broken foot and all, Dr. Bud was there waiting for me. I figured with his injury it would be an unfair mismatch and it was... just not the way I figured. Turns out Bud Muehleisen the player is even better than Bud the legend. He used his experience, intellect and strategy to run me crazy. My cross country background only made me more susceptible to a longer tour of the court, rally after rally. I learned that day the Muhl, the legend, had forgotten more about paddleball than Keeley the kid had learned, and Bud didn't forget much!

The education from that loss was greater than from any win I'd ever had, and with it didn't lose another paddleball tournament match for the next eight years collecting five national singles championships and two national doubles titles along the way. I stopped entering tournaments to let my friends have a chance, as Bud had made me look good in '70.

As the years went by and I started to become an elder statesman in the new sport of racquetball, I passed on the lessons I'd learned that day Muhl kicked my ass with a broken foot to in matches against future national champions like the young Marty Hogan and Mike Yellen.

The only time I learned a greater racquetball or paddleball lesson was two years after the Fargo nationals after I had graduated from vet school in 1972 and moved to racquetball mecca San Diego. One night in the comfortable confines of Dr. Bud's living room, he drew the curtains and cleared the living room furniture. We each took a racquet in hand and 'shadow boxed' me mirroring his left hand moves like a kid learns to play the guitar watching Elvis on TV. Though I had moved to San Diego as the national paddleball champion and one of the top three racquetball players in the world, I'd never given a lesson to a newbie player in my life. He instructed me step by step how to be a good instructor. After the tour of the living room I was ready, and was given the job as the first full-time club pro at George Brown's 70th Street Racquet Club.

Thousands of lessons, hundreds of published articles, six racquetball books, and hundreds of clinics and camps later, I still draw on those important lessons I learned from Dr. Bud Muehleisen.

Charlie Brumfield: King of Racquetball

The son of a US Marine Corps officer and a former chemistry teacher, Charlie Brumfield's first home was on base at Camp Pendleton in Oceanside, CA. There are threads to support his rise to Racquetball King during this period. His sister reports he 'drove' a TV antenna around the hours at night sleepwalking in search of something.

His father put young Charles on a raft in the middle of a lake and told him to swim for shore. On jumping in, Charlie decided he couldn't make shore until dad stepped on his fingers to prevent him from clawing onto the raft. At high school recess, he remembers, 'I was the last picked for every sports team, and it hurt. I was determined to be the best at some given game.'

Hence, the Holder of All Titles was born to racquetball in 1962 on a Mar Vista Junior High School outdoor court. He hit the cement court hard, daily, at lunch, PE, and before and after school. The sport was pink ball handball, the painful predecessor to pink ball paddleball that gave rise to pink to black ball racquetball, which is where I stepped into Charlie's life.

'I started playing pink ball in 7th grade while in junior high at Mar Vista in 1960. We moved to San Carlos, in the south of the county in 1963, and I played my first paddles after dislocating my finger in early '64. Then, in 1965 in the eleventh grade, I won the San Diego City Schools pink ball doubles championship with DC Charleston.'

The next threads of championship came quickly in graduating magna cum laude from the University of San Diego (USD) with degrees in economics and business administration. He then went on to earn a degree in law from USD, all during the period he was playing championship amateur, and thereafter professional racquetball. Unfortunately for his opponents in both courts, sport and law, he has by his own admission a photographic memory to catalog everyone's moves.

This, however, does not make a world champion. It's said dragons lurked in the dungeon courts at the San Carlos Racquet Club just down the street where Charlie teethed and lived on black ball racquetball. A single bulb hung from a ceiling cord illuminated the action. Charlie Brumfield, 6', 175 lb. and built like Jim Thorpe with a ducktail haircut slayed everyone in sight. When the ball rattled around the in-court pipes and returned, it was playable. The Donkey Kick of lunging for shots while kicking the rival out of center court was born. There was no such thing as an avoidable hinder; you risked getting hit with the ball or paddle. Late in the day, as the hours of games wound down, someone flipped the High Sign – a signal to warn by raising the hand to the chin and wiggling the fingers at the opponent. The loser of the final match, after the high sign, would bend over, grab his ankles, and his victor would line up behind him and blast a point blank kill shot.

Many years later, 1977 NRC National Champion, Davey Bledsoe, recalled playing doubles against Charlie on those San Carlos courts in a close match. 'The courts were dungeons with concrete back walls and 'California Cut-Outs' meaning an open area on the side walls of two adjacent courts.' Bledsoe and partner Randy Stafford (curator of the US Racquetball Museum) took it to a third game and went to the wire. Randy takes up, 'Davey hit a rollout and we were to serve for the game, but right as the ref was calling the point, Charlie pointed on the floor to a ball that magically appeared, yelling, 'Ball Hinder!' We had to replay the point and lost the next point and game. After the match, we found out there was no one playing next to us. I am not saying that ball came out of Charlie's pocket, but from then on we always checked to make sure Charlie did not have any balls in his pocket. I put Davey in charge of that.'

In 1964, his play came to the attention of Bud Muehleisen who would become a lifelong friend. Dr. Bud had been a Navy badminton champion where he was tagged 'Birdy Basher Bud Muehleisen,' and later was a college tennis star at Berkeley, participating in that school's national tennis title in 1953. Muehleisen dominated paddleball when Charlie, overwhelmed at 15, first met him at the Kona Kai Club in San Diego. The hotshot kid was a handful, and in two years they adjourned up to the real competition in San Diego at the Pacific Paddleball Association (PPA). The one-court facility was built in 1966 on private land of sport aficionado, Jim Skidmore, on a hill overlooking present day Charger Qualcomm Stadium. It's a shrine, as the first court club in the US for paddleball, and soon racquetball. Paddleball is the beautiful older sister of racquetball, and some of the best players in each sport graduated from the court of hard knocks on this hill. Brumfield, Muehleisen, Carl Loveday, and Dr. Chuck Hannah played daily doubles in paddles, and later racquets, for wagered steak dinners and beers in the balcony lounge next to the well-stocked trophy case.

The gate to championships via Brumfield, Muehleisen and Loveday in the early 1970's was out of the PPA. It became a racquetball mecca in attracting the future world champs Jerry Hilecher, Steve Serot, Dave Peck, myself, and Marty Hogan blasted a few there. At the PPA these young gentlemen were tactfully taken apart and put back together in losing to Muehleisen who gave each player about 20 years, whereas Loveday gave 30 to each of them. Brumfield's uncanny ability to move forward to the ball came from outdoors, and his coverage was honed in these daily doubles matches. Brum and Muhl became the best-record paddleball and racquetball doubles team of the 20th century, and both won dual sport National Singles titles multiple times. Carl Loveday, a former world badminton champion, was about to become another key figure in Charlie's life of racquetball. Now, Brumfield had all the traits to become #1 *and* the coaches.

(From *Charlie Brumfield: King of Racquetball*, Chapter 1 'Born on an Outdoor Court').

Forty three years ago, I met my career long nemesis, Charlie Brumfield, in the final of the first ever Mel Gorham's Christmas Classic. Brum had just won the 1971 IRA National Invitational, where he bested me in the semis. I had just captured my first National Paddleball Championship defeating Craig Finger in the final after he took out Brumfield in the semis. The San Diego draws were deep in those early days and legendary racquetball pioneers including Bud Muehleisen, Chuck Hannah and Paul Lawrence had all competed for a trophy and a chance to win the last event of the year. After a shaky start I edged the Bearded Wonder 6 - 21, 21-15, 21-16 to win the tournament. Charlie would go on to win twenty tournaments in a row including the 1972 and 1973 IRA Nationals. The next time I beat Chas was in 1973 in the final of the second ever Pro Racquetball Tournament in Long Beach, California. It wasn't easy to beat Brum in a final in those days, and you had to consider it a Christmas present when you did any time of year! (US RB Museum)

1980s Racquetball
Marty Hogan Interview

The eighties were not quite as exciting as the seventies. Steve Keeley was out in 80 and Brumfield was out after the 82 season, Serot and Schmidtke were long gone. The fast game was introduced in 76 and I won my first events that year. It got faster in 77 and I won over 300 matches and lost four from 1977-1979. So, 1980 and 1981 went pretty much the same. I made the final of every tournament and won over 80% of them. I had dominated the tour for six years in a row.

In 1982 they threw in a curve. The equipment makers introduced graphite racquets and Dave Peck, who joined the tour and was rookie of the year in 1979, makes a charge with his Ektelon 250 G. The equipment took away some of my sting and money, since it was superior to what DP Leach was producing.

The Hogan-Peck rivalry started. We each won win the same number of events but I won more prize money and the DP Pro Nationals. Nonetheless, by the point system, Dave won his first tour title on points 1020 to 960, and it couldn't have happened to a nicer guy.

That year was also memorable because I also got all the players on tour clothing deals from Catalina. It was known as the Catalina Tour and the guys seemed to play better in them. In 1983-1988, Instead of getting fired up, I got complacent after 82. DP still paid me the #1 bonus for winning the Pro Nationals and the money title, and it was like gold. I started to do more lucrative exhibitions and travel. I stopped practicing and had to squeeze in family time. I was a millionaire due to money-spinning deals with Catalina, Nike, DP and others. I did constant media and even skipped events if a bigger payday was elsewhere. I just didn't feel challenged. I had beaten Yellen, Peck, Harnett, Hilecher, G. Peck at least 5 to 1 at this point, and had never lost a match to Ruben, Ray, Corey or any of these guys.

Do you want to know the upshot? I found out, that if I didn't practice and used inferior equipment, my talent would keep me near the top, but I'd drop matches. In 1983, Mike Yellen edges me by a few points even though I beat him head to head. He was more consistent. Dave Peck finishes third. They are both using the new Ektelon CBK. It's a lighter, more powerful graphite composite, even better than the 250 G.

1984 - Yellen is one again, I'm a close second, Dave is third.

1985 - It's a three man race. They have to figure the points of a new complicated system in a photo finish after the Nationals. I won the most events and was #2, Gregg Peck won

663

a few big events and The DP Pro Nationals and was #3, and Yellen was number one by points by a tiny hair. In a rare move the players voted Gregg Peck the Player of the Year, and he deserved it. But the biggest thing in 85 came out of the blue. Cliff Swain came to qualifying at our Tulsa event, where it had front and side walls glass. Nobody could see his serve. He was the only qualifier ever to win a Pro event. He did it in his first try. He went on to show up at the Ektelon Championships that were on ESPN at season's end in

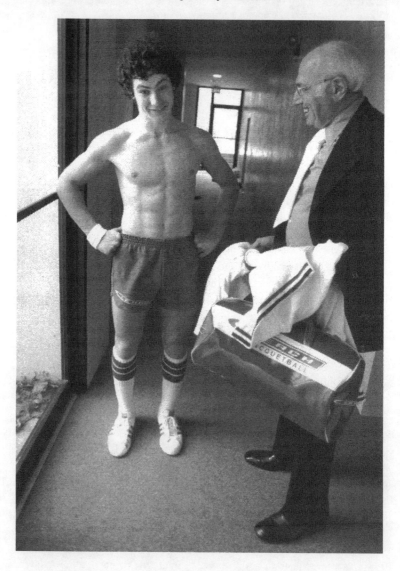

A young, conditioned Marty Hogan with NRC commissioner Joe Ardito. (Art Shay)

California. He somehow slew me, Dave Peck, and Gregg Peck consecutively to win his second event. More in 85 - Yellen is using the new Ektelon Toron oversized racquet, and so is Ruben. Everyone else is playing with the small or mid racquets.

1986 - A three man race again: Bret Harnett wins more tournaments than anyone. Yellen and his big racquet are most consistent. I play pretty well for not practicing. Yellen finishes #1, Harnett #2, Hogan #3 and Swain #4. Brett is voted Player of the Year.

1987 - Identical top four and order to 1986. Bret Harnett is voted Player of the Year again

1988 - I miss several events and can't find motivation. Ruben Gonzalez is #1, Bret Harnett is #2, Mike Yellen is #3, and Cliff Swain is #4

1989 - In the off-season between 1988 and 1989 they had ten unsanctioned tournaments around the country. This wasn't uncommon. Most players would play the events in their area and maybe go to a few others, so it wasn't unusual to have ten different winners. Top prize was $2,000 to $4,000 at these tournaments and Yellen, Peck, Harnett, Gonzalez, G. Peck, and others would play in them. Swain won all ten events. He didn't just win, he dominated. He killed Ruben, Yellen, Ray, Peck and Harnett.

I had been thinking of retiring, but a real challenge had got my juices flowing. Just like earlier I had wanted to beat Keeley and Brumfield, just to prove to everyone and myself I could do it! This wasn't about money; this was about my primal competitive instinct. I finally had a worthy challenger. I practiced and trained like I hadn't in years and left my smile outside the club. My game had risen to a level where I easily beat Yellen, Peck, Harnett, Ray and Gonzalez all over again, but that wasn't the point. The point was Cliff. I had five events left to decide an extremely close battle between Swain and myself. We met in four consecutive finals: I won two and Swain won two. All other matches were warm ups for a finale - The last tournament of the year was the IRT Nationals. Swain and I made it to the finals again. He fought like hell and served the lights out. I fought back even harder and beat him in a five game war. I think it was 11-9 in the fifth.

That was the end of my 1980s. I knew that was it, I had done what I set out to do. 1975-1976 were about *becoming* a champion. 1977-1981 were about *being* a champion. 1982-1988 were about making *money*. 1989 was again about becoming a *champion*.

Transition from Tennis to Racquetball in the Golden Era

by Jim ´Make Every´ Schatz

I first became aware of racquetball in 1976. At the time I was 29 years old and teaching and playing open tennis in Los Angeles. A tennis student of mine introduced me to racquetball. He took me to a health club in Century City called the Century City Health Club.

After learning the basic rules and beating my tennis student pretty easily, I could see this sport was fun, easy to learn, and that I could get good very quickly. I thought I was a lifer in tennis, and had no idea a racquetball boom was coming or that I was going to switch sports.

A few months passed and I was invited again by a friend to play who told me he was very proficient. I wanted to make a good showing so first I went to another racquetball club called Center Courts in West Los Angeles to play a little, to get a lesson, and hang out watching the best players. Jay Jones was the teaching pro and was ranked in the top ten in the pro division. Jones also won the USRA National Amateur Racquetball Singles Championship the year before so he was considered by far the best player in Los Angeles at that time.

Center Courts had no shortage of great players and pros. Mark Morrow was there who was also ranked in the top 20, and eventually top ten. There were many more tough guys and players to practice and train with. Every day there was ´Captain Kirk´ - Kirk Williams, Ian Flashman and the older pros: Bruce Radford, Joel Scheimbaum, Jay Streim and Lee Pretner, to name a few.

Jay Jones gave me my first lesson on the racquetball forehand kill at Center Courts. Several weeks later Jay got a better offer and moved his practice and teaching to the Century Racquet Club. I followed him there and joined. Through Jay I learned about the pro tour and watched him practice practically every day for it. I followed him to all his exhibition and tournament matches.

Jay and I played only a few times. He didn't like to practice with good players- It always seemed to turn into a fight or war for him. The first time we played, believe it or not, I was ahead 18-17. At that point he deliberately hit me with the ball. I didn't score another point from there on, not knowing how to react. After that experience he wouldn't practice with me ever. I wasn't the first player who idolized Hollywood stuntman Jay who grabbed and raised me off the hardwood against the wall for talking too much. I guess I had Jay's number as I must have watched him hit the racquetball over 10,000 hours. I knew no one's game better. Not until he was retired would Jay play me, but somehow he and I managed to remain friendly during those experiences.

My game style was not stellar, nor was I an easy opponent to beat. My philosophy was to let you beat yourself so I would talk a lot to distract and try to control the speed and the pace of the game. I was impossible to cheat as the cheaters eventually would walk off the court in mental agony. I had learned how to defend myself from the best cheaters in the game.

Charlie Brumfield was also a very big influence on me in those psychological wars. He influenced everybody…quite the showman. Even he didn't enjoy playing me. I eventually became Charlie's assistant coach while working with his mentor Carl Loveday Sr. We had a similar 18-17 practice battle in San Diego when I first moved there. Instead of hitting me with the ball as Jones had, he just quit playing. He never practiced with me again. Power players and sadists, with quick tempers or big egos, were my bread and butter.

My favorite pro player was Steve Keeley. He was neither my bread and butter nor anything else like anyone, and in those days the mop topped Keeley was nearly everyone's favorite pro. We traveled in his '74 Chevy van that had an invisible fishline attached to the hand of Fillmore Hare, a 7' stuffed rabbit who would ride shotgun when I wasn't in the passenger seat, waving down interesting characters to take to the tournaments to cheer us on. Today Keeley and I are still close friends. He was so accessible and so friendly, and still is.

Keeley had the biggest following in racquetball after he wrote *The Complete Book of Racquetball* in 1976. He invented 'Keeleyisms' and he also published the racquetball comic book *The Kill and Re Kill Gang* based on some of our mutual players and experiences. He and I, I thought, were on the same page on the court in many ways. We both had strong backhands, defensives, and ceiling games. We were both considered strange and interesting characters, but the big difference was that I liked to talk and he enjoyed silence. On a 1979 van ride from San Diego to the Houston Pro stop somewhere over the Texas desert at the tick after midnight into February 8, I broke into 'Happy Birthday'. He told me to shut up. I did, but turned on a recording of the first round and played it over and over for a few miles until, like Jones and Brumfield, he wouldn't talk to me for quite a while.

What attracted me to the game at first was the characters and then the way the pro tour was run. I was not a traveling pro in tennis, never winning any money on tour, so racquetball was a fresh opportunity, looked much easier, to make a little money, play pro, and after all I had strong role models. You could qualify for a spot in the 32 pro draw, and then by beating some of them you could eventually earn a pro ranking. It wasn't a cakewalk but it was every young players dream as the sport blossomed across the nation.

I knew I was too old to really compete on the tour but tried hard and at age 32 climbed to rank in the top 50. They say that those who can do, and those who can't teach. My real motivation for playing was not for money but to be able to coach at the pro level. I played for the pro sport's playing experience to be able to pass it on. I traveled to practically every pro stop around the country from 1977 to 1981. To coach at the pro level you have to know the pro game and I was observing it from everyone everywhere..

In 1979 I moved to San Diego which was the racquetball mecca and lived with my coach, mentor, best friend and surrogate father Carl Loveday Sr. Carl had coached the great Dr. Bud Muehleisen, was tutoring Charlie Brumfield, Richie Wagner, Marcie Greer and an assortment of other top 24 pros including Brad Kruger, Bruce Christenson, Linsey Myers, Donnie Thomas, Ward Leiber, etc. Carl helped almost every top player at one

Top 8 pro and Hollywood stuntman of the 1970's Jay Jones played in *Star Trek* and *Poseidon Adventure,* and in the life of Jim 'Make Every' Schatz. (US RB Museum)

time or another and if Joe Sobek is the Father of Racquetball then Carl Loveday is the Grandfather and deserves to be in the Hall of Fame.

When I moved to San Diego Carl installed me as the teaching pro at George Brown's Racquetball Club where all the Leach and Ektelon pro players practiced. So, through Carl, I was able to achieve my goal of becoming a pro coach on the racquetball pro tour. I also became the editor of the racquetball section in a newspaper called 'Tennis Talk and Racquetball Report of Southern California'. But I admit the crowning glory after coaching, after helping young players into the pro ranks, and after teaching the pros to get more competitive against each other, was being put on the cover of the March 1982 coaching issue of *National Racquetball* magazine titled 'Planting Seeds for the Future'.

Carl Loveday analyzed and defined the power swing of Marty Hogan who had also moved from St. Louis to San Diego, and the power swing is what I taught my players. Carl explained the swing and I developed the teaching system for it. I taught the legendary coach Jim Winterton the power swing about thirty years ago at a junior regional in Redding, California.

A few years later Gary Mazaroff requested I write the racquetball fundamentals for the Racquetball Teachers Association. Later I founded the Southern California Racquetball Association. Then I set up and directed the Southern California Junior Pro Tour from 1982-1984. I coached practically every top southern California junior during that time. Brett Elkins, who now directs the LA juniors was one of my early best students.

Out of that program came many junior national champions: Corey Brysman, Jeff Conine, Ward Leiber, Billy Gamble, Jimmie Flannery, Kelly Gelhouse, etc.

I retired from racquetball in 1985. My last racquetball job was at the Family Fitness Center in Beverly Hills. It was a seven court facility then where I had a pro shop called 'Professor' Schatz's Coaches Corner. I had over 400 players on my make-a- date ladder board, and ran a full 12-month program for members with a tournament of some kind every month.

Why would I retire after reaching my dream and accomplishing my goals? The truth is I had a drug problem. I was addicted to pot, alcohol and finally cocaine and ended up losing the pro shop. I owed a ton of money to many of my suppliers and sponsors. I was sponsored by both Head and Foot-Joy at the time, and both companies let me off the hook for over $40,000.

So for whatever I gave to the game I ended up taking it back, plus. I'm not proud that my drug problems didn't stop after racquetball. I had a few more episodes, being addicted to crack from age 52 - 55 and meth from 55 -59. I'm 65 now and no longer a drug addict although I still have a beer occasionally.

Today I'm still in sports and known in basketball as a Free Throw master. My sport's goal is to become the world champion of free throw at some point. I had to create the event to have a chance to make that happen. I founded the National Basketball Shooters Association in 2009 with a group of shooting masters who have mentored me, just like in racquetball, and I also created a single elimination format for creating a champion. I can put a hundred shots through the hoop at the drop of the hat, and do each morning.

I will compete and direct the World Senior Free Throw Championship in October in Las Vegas this year. Last year I finished 4th ranked in the world at the free throw line. Think you can shoot- see you there.

But fondly my personal transition was from tennis to racquetball when the sport boomed in the big game.

Scrappy Alvaro Beltran wins his first career IRT Tier 1 pro Stop in Davison, MI in 2010. He has finished in the Top 6 in eleven of the past thirteen seasons. (Mike Augustin)

My Losses

I can't believe I have amnesia of a mononucleosis loss against the two-time national racquetball champion Bill Schmidtke. He swung a merciless forehand and impotent backhand that given a stronger backhand and patience was licked in every previous and subsequent match. I could scrape a (slow ball) ceiling shot along the left wall all day to his backhand until he miss-hit to yield a plum setup. I could hit a baseball cap in the left front corner 50% of the time from deep court, and went to a cigarette pack as a target. I had learned to 'float' the ball along the air mass hugging the floor depending on the court temperature so it virtually could not skip into the floor.

The mono month was nutty. It started when I fell on my face running on the Pacific beach one day, got up and went to the racquetball Doc Hannah. He returned the next day with a lab report, 'You have the 2nd worst case of mono in the history of San Diego County. I writhed in a bed kindly provided by multiple-national champ Bud Muehleisen's mother for one month listening to the top song 'There's got to be a morning after', till one morning I felt well and got up.

Doc Hannah prescribed one month of ceiling balls hit to myself to prevent a relapse, that I did daily in increasing blocks of half-hour sessions until I owned the second best ceiling game in the world, behind Charlie Brumfield. I entered the first tournament with muscle memory for no more than the ceiling stroke, as spectators' heads bobbed up and down counting upwards of 40-shot streaks against lefty Dave Charleston. I won in three, but lost the tournament famished from the exercise.

It must have been after that that I dropped the match to Schmidtke; I don't remember. He never beat me again, though others did.

The practical game strategy with the slow ball of the early 70s was to soft serve to initiate a ceiling rally followed by an error that the rival killed. This was the tedious method of the sport's early greats- Muehleisen, Charlie Brumfield, Steve Serot and less so Jerry Hilecher, Rich Wagner, Steve Strandemo, Benny Colton, a young Marty Hogan, Steve Mondry, Trey Sayes and the rest of the top 32 in the nation who sooner or later travelled to San Diego to graduate with the best. It's a rare person who climbs ranks without personal exposure via viewing or playing against the experts.

Victor Niederhoffer was an exception in taking his first racquetball into the court after winning a world squash championship, bouncing the ball once for study, and proclaimed to a witness, 'Now I'm the national racquetball champ.' He nearly was, soon beating Hogan in a Las Vegas thriller, and most of the field, before losing to Harlem Globetrotter Ron Rubenstein.

When the ball speeded up in the mid-70s, so did the players' mentalities. They became squat and groveling close to the hardwood for repeated passes and killshots, and new champions like Hogan, Peck and Yellen emerged. The big sponsors- Leach and Ektelon - deftly grasped that a livelier ball meant females, grandpas and youngsters could play making it a sport for the masses, but it ruined it at the pro level.

The athletes got meatier and meaner in a competitive way, and racquetball evolved into what you see today: blazing serves, driving returns, average 2-shot rallies, and you could put a table across the court 4'off the floor that the ball rarely rises above.

We lanky, meditative champs nonetheless passed the trophies and money purses with tooth and claw defeats. When the fast ball guys with big serves and shoots that required a fast game to win soaked the tournament balls in hot water before entering the court, or enticed the tournament director to store the whole batch in the sauna until plucking one-at-time for each match... we slow gamers retaliated in ingenious ways. Strandemo switched balls during timeouts with a molasses batch in his gym bag. Steve Mondry secreted a razor blade in the tongue of his hi-cuts and bent over to tie his shoe in the service box, and sliced the ball. And I used a hypodermic needle from vet school to deflate to even things out.

Losses with determination are the stepping stones to victory.

Early champions Mike Zeitman (defending) vs. Ken Porco and describes, 'We ran around and always bumped into each other. There were no avoidable hinders except among gentlemen, and there were few gentlemen in the sport on close calls.' (US RB Museum)

673

The Search for Bobby Fischer Ends
on a Racquetball Court
Bobby Fischer and Bud Muehleisen

by Dr. Bud Muehleisen

Here now is my true story regarding Chess in Racquets that I experienced.

Setting: There was a Religious College affiliated with the World Church of God, which was headed at the time by a guy whose last name was Armstrong. They even had a weekly radio show from there. It was a beautiful campus tucked in a three-block square of very expensive property in the wealthiest of districts in Pasadena. It was located between Orange and Colorado Avenues which are the two streets that the Tournament of Roses Parade is held on.

Time: Probably, the late 1970's.

Occasion: They had a beautiful very private Racquetball complex of about three courts and a plush upstairs lounge. I was asked to come up, give a little clinic with their two coaches, play a little doubles with them, and then go to dinner.

Trivia: At the time Bobby Fischer was World Champion and had 'disappeared' (presence unknown) in the World.

Okay, I do my thing and then it is time to play some doubles racquetball. Here's comes the 4th player and they introduce me to Fischer as my partner. He was a total recluse at the time and holed up secretly at the college and had taken up racquetball. He hardly even spoke a word for about three hours and was a C- player.

Anyway, we finish, all go upstairs to the lounge and start drinking tap beer (yes, at the Religious College) and munching on pretzels while watching the Laker playoff game on TV. I noticed two things. There was a gorgeous chess set on the table with the pretzels in between us, and Fischer has a little tiny portable chess set in the front lapel pocket of his coat jacket.

It was quite obvious that he was not there to take part in the conversation, be it racquetball or the Laker game on TV. I ask, 'What's that little portable chess set in your lapel pocket?' He took the time to take the chess set out and matter of factly explain how it was played and utilized. He was reserved, but responded factually and looked me in the

674

eye. Timid is accurate, never bragging while exuding an air of genius. His general continence was what I would imagine sitting across from Albert Einstein who wouldn't need to speak a word for his brilliance to be known.

After a while and idle chatter, there is a knock at the lounge door and it opens,... There stands the LA weatherman with the crazy helicopter swing in Open tournaments. In the those days he did a lot of racquetball promoting in the LA area. In any event, he had arrived late, of course, and missed everything.

So, he sits down and before long he remarks and marvels at the gorgeous chess set between us all on the table. So, I started my 'hustle' conversation with... "Do you play chess, Paul?"... And he replies, "Oh yes, I not only play, but I'm currently the faculty champion at UCLA." I quickly rejoined, "C'mon Paul, I'll bet anyone in this room could beat you... (pause-pause, and then pointing across to Fischer)..... I'll bet that guy right there could beat you, in fact, I'll bet you $50 that he can beat you!"

Bobby Fischer serves during a celebrity tennis game in California in June 1972.

At the point, Paul looks across at the guy and says in reply..."Dr. Bud, that wouldn't even be fair.... I'm really good!"... I then said..."Well do you want the bet or not?"... He replies.... "O.K., if he doesn't mind?" I look at Fischer and he calmly nods his head in an affirmative gesture. So then I said, slowly and calmly...."O.K. then, (and) Paul let me introduce you to Bobby Fischer."

Now here comes a real classic moment in a confrontation! As Paul stands up and extends his hand across the table to reach for Bobby Fischer's extended hand, who has also stood up by this time... he realizes who he is and before he can utta a word he starts stammering with an "UGGHHH"

Sound drooling out the side of his mouth. He literally could not get out a coherent word from his mouth. It was one of the 'all-time' Hustle's and the rest of us could not stop laughing. Paul slithered back into his seat and was virtually speechless from then on. As he sat there, over the next twenty minutes, he would sneak a peek at Fischer out of the corner of his eye if Fischer was not looking at him. What a moment in time that was.

Of course, Fischer being the non-personality that he was, never said a word the rest of the time either.

After about a 20-minute period of time passed, Paul excused himself to the group saying that he had another appointment. I walked Paul out the door shutting it behind me and when I did... Paul instantly jumped up on my back yelling.... 'How could you do that to me?!!!!'

I don't think I've seen Paul since then and I don't even know of his whereabouts or if he is even alive. I am sure though that he has never forgiven me. True Story.

Moral of the story, and there are possibly many...'Don't ever proclaim any EGO that you might have.....in public'.

So, there is MY story.

Pros Speak from the Box

Color of Success

I'm more outgoing and confident with success. I don't mind playing to the crowd with the 'Hollywood Hulk Hogan' image. Sometimes an inhibited gallery can be energized with the hero-villains, and I can do either. . *- Marty Hogan*

People like me now. I grew up at playing at the Spanish Harlem outdoor courts.
- Ruben Gonzalez

My desire to win has become stronger, and this is generalized to a greater competitiveness in life. *- Corey Brysman*

I deeply appreciate all the sport has given me. *- Mike Ray*

A little disappointment after being #1 in the world five times. I'll be back. *- Sudsy*

I've become more comfortable with myself so I don't need outward shows of confidence to become confident. Hunker down. It's a phrase you understand only if you've been there. I learned to hunker down anywhere no matter what it took. *- Charlie Brumfield*

The self-confidence I've gain through racquetball has absolutely carried into other areas of life. *- Cliff Swain*

I still try to improve and prove myself every day, but I've come to realize I have the greatest job in the world, traveling to play and teach racquetball. *- Derek Robinson*

My English is getting better. I won the 2003 Pan American Games in racquetball. Only twenty medals went to Mexico overall, and I took back the gold one to Tijuana. It put me in the magazines, newspapers, on television and radio. But every morning at 7am I head for the morning workout. *- Alvaro Beltran*

It may fall strange on some ears, but players in other countries where I coach are afraid of the United States. This is because they know the experience and advantages they have. So, when a star shines from another nation by toppling an American, it's a big deal for him and his peers, and they gain an observable confidence in their games and lives. Suddenly it's a different ball game! For me, the change over the years has been

677

humility. Each player has his own way of grabbing a racquet and discovering his own knacks for hitting and excelling with what he does best.   *- Jeff Leon*

My advance began when I became the 1982 #1 player in the world. It was a just reward for a lot of practice, conditioning and thinking. I haven't changed, just grateful.

— Dave Peck

Passing the winner's cup back and forth on the Legends 2003 Tour, Swain and Hogan. (Legends)

A loss used to mean the end of the world had occurred, but later on I calculated I'd played 10,000 competitive refereed racquet matches. I learned from these to bounce back to the top from the bottom. Now when I'm beset by the aggravations and competitions when all the things that happen to you in the hurly-burly and nitty-gritty of life come to bear, I can circle the wagons of sports experience and sorta chuckle at it all.

- Victor Niederhoffer

It made me become grateful and appreciative of my accomplishments.   *— Jose Rojas*

Racquetball has made me a more responsible and disciplined person.

- Cristina Amaya Cassino

I don't think it really has except for me having to make more advanced goals for myself.
– Andy Hawthorne

It hasn't, except my time with racquetball brought me a LOT of friends and eliminated my shyness.
– Cheryl Gudinas

Success hasn't changed me. It has just given me more opportunities.
- Kerri Stoffregen Wachtel

When I was ranked #1 I never looked at myself differently, and felt that I had to prove my abilities every day. To this day I still set my bar high as a businessman, husband, and father wanting to be better every day.
– Jerry Hilecher

Whatever success I've achieved has made me know how much more I have to see, learn, do, create, and help.
– Ken Woodfin

I'm way more confident in myself. I love the feeling of knowing that I know this game of racquetball well.
– John Ellis

It has made me more confident in terms of seeing that hard work, dedication, and sacrifice really do pay off - something I try to convey to my children as well as the students I teach.
– Brian Hawkes

I wouldn't say success has changed me. I believe I'm the same person with or without it. And that is the way I want it to be. It feels good to be recognized, but I cherish friendship based on who I am as a person and not a player.
– Jackie Paraiso

I don't feel i have succeeded. But the few big wins i have, i believe i haven't changed.
– Susy Acosta

It has made me a humble person in the world. People are amazed when they find out things about my life.
– Davey Bledsoe

It hasn't. I still work as hard and dedicated as I always have, striving for success.
- Rhonda Rajsich

History

Brian Pineda overhead for the 2012 WOR Championship. (Mike Augustin)

How 'Racquetball' Got Its Name
Eyewitness Account From

Dr. Bud Muehleisen

It was in early 1969, that the Jewish Community Center in St. Louis had the foresight and hutzpah to mail to virtually every facility in the United States, who might have a 4-walled indoor court, where they might be playing with a small strung racket, to a National Tournament.

The 'game' was invented by a tennis pro named Joe Sobek, who resided in Greenwich Village. The story goes that one winter, when the snow outside prevented Joe from teaching tennis, he thought of the idea of cutting down a tennis racket, and moving indoors to a 4-walled handball court in order to be able to get a workout while at the same

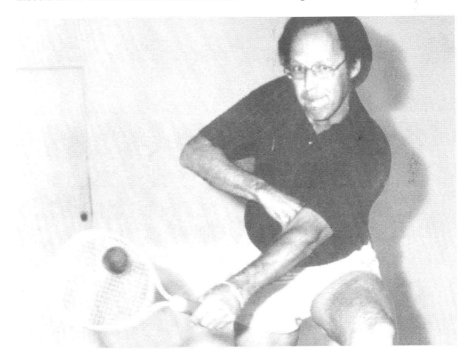

Dr. Bud Muehleisen was a champion player and promoter of early racquetball. (US RB Museum)

time practice his tennis strokes. He used the inside of a tennis ball which, at that time was called a Pensie Pinkie (made by Pennsylvania Tire & Rubber). The ball having a rubberized surface gave itself traction on the polished wooden floors, used by the

681

handball players. Soon a 'game' was started which patterned itself after handball. A Paddle Rackets Association was formed in the New England area and the game slowly spread to various hotbeds throughout the United States.

Now the game had a founder, equipment and association, but not a *name*.

St. Louis heralded its event as the 'The First National Tournament for Paddle Rackets'. Entries were mailed out, and at tournament time, lo and behold, upwards of 250 participants showed up from all corners of the USA.

Divisions were made up for both men and women in singles, and doubles as well as Senior age groups for both.

Early on in the tournament, time was set aside for a big 'Organizational Meeting' of the players at the tournament. The room was packed with the participants. The meeting was chaired by Mr. Robert (Bob) Kendler from Lake Forest, Illinois, the President of the National Handball Association at that time. A Board of Directors of seven was elected representing the different sections of the country, and each more or less headed a committee to further develop the 'new' sport. Bob Kendler was installed as Honorary President of the Association with the National Office being set up at his Lake Forest headquarters. He also used his handball staff there to start things underway, including the handling of the dues and communications with its new members.

Soon, that procedure was completed and it was announced that we needed to give a new name to our new sport and organization. A hum swept the room. The problem arose because the many paddleball players voiced the opinion that the racket was NOT a paddle. That opinion was unanimous.

A chalk board at the front was filled with 6-8 potential names, and then each was put up for nomination. After scrutinizing the names for a few minutes, and bantering their possibilities about, the room buzzed in confusion. The reason is each and every name seemed to conflict with other sports such as tennis, paddleball, paddle tennis, paddle rackets, etc…

In a lull in the action, a tall man in the back of the room stood up, and introduced himself as Robert (Bob) MacInerney from Coronado, California with the contingent from San Diego. He proceeded to offer the thought that…'Since the sport uses a Racket and a Ball… why not call it… (Racket)ball?' Well, it was like a light from above went off in the room. The name was quickly put in motion, seconded, and won by acclamation!

Then started a 25 minute debate as to the spelling of the sport. This was because of the connotation of 'Racket,' lending association with the Underworld of Rackets', and likewise reputed mafia members might object to their suspicions. Finally, Bob

MacInerney stood up again and suggested the French spelling of 'Racquet'… and once again, it was quickly adopted by acclamation.

As the meeting adjourned and the players filtered back to their matches, a pride began to permeate throughout the building that OUR SPORT, which was so much fun to play, was called.......RACQUETBAll!

How Organized Racquetball Started. When our sport was called Racket Ball or Paddle Rackets this tournament committee of the 'first' 1968 Racket Ball Nationals at the Milwaukee Jewish Community Center organized the next year's 1969 'first' Racquetball Nationals in St. Louis won by Bud Muehleisen over Charlie Brumfield in the final. The yellowed caption with this photo is torn leaving only the name of Larry Lederman (first Hall of Fame entrant 1975, Olympic Champion wrestler, with glasses) of the committee. However, three players at the 1968 event describe how organized racquetball came to be.

'This holy grail of racquetball pictures is of the **1968** committee that was the group that put together the first so-called "National" tournament, held at the Milwaukee JCC, won by Bill Schultz over Bill Schmidtke. At the invitation of Lederman, my dad, Mort Leve, director of handball's *Ace Magazine*, Bob, Kendler, who was our boss, and an attorney Ken Schneider all attended the Milwaukee event. Lederman was on the Board of the US Handball Association, run by Kendler, and he convinced the above mentioned USHA execs to take a look at this "paddle rackets" phenomenon that was pushing handballers out of the courts. That was the impetus to create the International Racquetball Association (IRA), and a year later, to hold the first "real" racquetball Nationals at the St. Louis JCCA in 1969 with the infamous Dr. Bud over Brumfield final.'   *– Chuck Leve, Executive Director of early IRA and NRC*

'I was in the locker room at that first National tournament in 1968 and heard Bob Kendler tell the assembled how he was going to make racquetball as popular as handball. He stood in front of a gathering of top players and told them what he'd done for handball and could do that for racquetball. He sure did get racquetball off the ground.' *- Bill Schultz Jr., son of the first 1968 National Racket Ball Champion Bill Schultz*

'I did attend the 1968 tourney and Bob Kendler's meeting. Kendler was charismatic and had chutzpah, charm, money, and presence. He looked and acted like a benign, indulgent grandfather who was going to open doors we didn't even know existed. He also came with all the accessories: an entourage, right-speak, a slick magazine, advertisers, national sponsors, and an organization. All of those were things racquetball wanted to legitimize our Olympics-bound sport. He was going to provide the jump start our sport needed into the Olympics and as a national recreation. Most important, he had connections: Seamco, and Avery Bundage, the Grand Poohbah of the Olympics. Kendler was the right man at the right time and our sport jumped on the bandwagon with willing eagerness. The timing was perfect. We were on our way! ' *- Mike Zeitman, early pro, 3-time National Doubles Champion with three different partners.*

(Photo courtesy of US RB Museum)

San Diego: Racquetball's Mecca

California Dreaming

Brad Kruger

In the early '80s, if you wanted to go pro there was only one place to go: Racquetball's Mecca ... San Diego.

"Ho hum... Another day in Paradise."

-- San Diego bumper sticker

In the early '80s, it was called "the fastest growing sport in history" and much ink has been spilled debating the cause of racquetball's decline. Yet virtually none has been spent identifying the cause of the game's skyrocketing popularity. Was it solely the game itself? You might be surprised.

Concealed in the shadow of Los Angeles, about two hours south, where America's Southwest dips its toe in the Pacific Ocean, San Diego in the early '80s was known far and wide as racquetball's Mecca - a place so enchanted, legend had it, your game would improve by five or 10 points OVERNIGHT... SIMPLY BY OSMOSIS.

And for a kid with great expectations from the frozen prairies of Northern Canada, San Diego wasn't the road, it wasn't even the gate- it was Paradise itself! San Diego was racquetball's equivalent of baseball's "Field of Dreams" only for real, AND EVEN BETTER because it was home to not only the game's past legends, but also its current greats AND its fastest rising stars... the best of the best drawn together not only to a single city, but often to a single club.

Not that my home town was anything to laugh at. Cabin fever has its advantages, and with Edmonton winters sliding below minus-40 - well, what better way to maintain one's sanity than to lock oneself in an unpadded concrete room and desperately chase a sub-sonic superball on a 3-dimensional flight pattern?

My earliest racquetball years were spent in Edmonton's infamous Court Club, home to the one-of-a-kind Klondike Canadian Open, populated by the likes of IRA champ Wayne Bowes to current six-time World Champ Kane Waselenchuk, Edmonton's "move it or lose it to frostbite" winters produced more than its share of racquetball's top dogs and a racquetball hub as competitive as any on the planet.

But nothing could fully prepare you for San Diego. It was just after the legendary PPB days, just as the game was truly kindling in '80, and Gorham's Sport's Center on Balboa

Ave was the only place to be. On any given weekday (weekends were for tournaments), at any given time, you could bump into any and often all of the following:

Charlie Brumfield, (aka "The Vision" self-proclaimed), who looked like the Prince of Darkness, moved like Groucho Marx and had the flawless arsenal of a platypus on steroids.

Carl Loveday, (aka "The Old Man"): racquetball's grandfather and greatest strategist who so loved the game, his body evolved into the shape of the ball.

Bud Muelheisen: (Dr. Bud "The Dissector"), even as he approached 50 could beat virtually any pro in a single match.

Steve "Bo" Keeley, (rarely sighted by this time), California surfer good looks, who played like the veterinarian he was, a remedy for every animal.

Marty Hogan, no weaknesses, a living nightmare, only one assured way to win- kick him in the groin (when he wasn't looking) and run like hell.

...AND the superstars who were yet to become legends like Dave Peck, Mike Yellen, Steve Serot, Jerry Hilecher, Davey Bledsoe, Mike Zeitman, Craig McCoy, Randy Stafford, David Fleetwood, Jerry Zuckerman, Ben Koltun, Jay Jones, Linsey Myers, Steve Mondry, Trey Sayes, Rich Wagner, Donny Thomas... and Ed Andrews, Bret Harnett Gregg Peck, Corey Brysman, Mark Morrow, Paul Lawrence, Len Baldori, Dan alder, Ray Bayer, Charley Drake, Egan Inoue, Ross Harvey, Professor Schatz, Craig Davison, Steve Lerner, Dan Factor, Beaver Wickham, Dave Doehr, Bruce Christianson...

It was a walk into Racquetball's Hall of Fame, not after the fact, but in its infancy, and instead of two-dimensional photographs looking down on you in their Sunday best, they were all here in the living, breathing flesh without a thought about their legacy, or on winning a tournament, a match or even a rally, but solely and simply and desperately focused on mastering a *single shot*... the rest would take care of itself.

My own pilgrimage to San Diego began a few years earlier when the Pro Tour rolled through my hometown in '76/'77 and we learned that the game we played up north was a universe removed from San Diego's evolving pro game. The Frisbee backhand, we discovered, had been replaced by Hogan's "reach for the stars" wind-up. The avoidable hinder had been knocked out by Brumfield's "tuck and butt" positioning. And the grace of Keeley's down-the-wall pass shot (a shot so slow it was said Hogan could autograph it mid-flight) was being evicted by the savage brutality of Hogan's 142 mph forehand- and every name, every player, straight off the pages of *National Racquetball*.

686

It was as good as it gets, and the only thing better would seem to most a mere side-note. A few of the pros took the time to "enlighten" the locals (and possibly their wallets), taking on all comers with large points spreads and/or using frying pans, bleach bottles and boxing gloves for racquets. Even better, for "only 500 pennies" (as the Keeley sign read) YOU could take part in a half-hour clinic followed by a shot at the pros for two points, and one-on-one analysis taught by the very same players who had just shattered all our illusions about the game.

As luck would have it, I got Brumfield, who changed my frying pan grip in the backswing, and then watched me focus harder than any time in my life only to drive my first kill shot deep into orbit over the back wall. Looking back, Charlie's self-control was beyond me. (Keep in mind, I was 14 years old at the time, and another 30 adult players were waiting in line: waiting and watching.) But after a few Hail Mary's and a hyperventilation, I gathered my courage and nailed my second shot for a straight killshot that prompted Brumfield to invite me down to San Diego to learn from the very best.

Vietnam veteran Trey Says returned stateside with a classic stroke and broke into the Top 8 in the Golden Era, while sleeping happily in a VW van outside Mel Gorham's Center. (Trey Sayes)

687

Years passed before I learned that this was not as exceptional as I'd thought; rather, it was commonplace... that as great the game of racquetball was, its wild popularity was due to its top players who literally "grew" the sport- spreading the word, and creating new disciples and followers wherever they went, and most went to San Diego.

The pros spread the gospel, and the masses came in droves: the driven and the delusional; the desperate and the depraved; the gifted and Gimped; the Fools; the Sinners and the Saints. From every corner of the continent, they came for their shot at the big time, they were seen and, for the most part, they were spit out.

Some lasted a month. Some lasted a year or two. And a very select few became legends.

It was minus-26 Celsius when I left Canada and plus-26 Celsius when I landed in San Diego with a student visa (the only way I could stay in the country), two gym bags, and a bicycle in a box, and within an hour of phoning from my hotel, Steve Strandemo picked me up and dropped me off at a nearby club for a midnight winner-take-all round robin among local players. Three hours (and two narrowly avoided fistfights) later, I emerged $200 richer. Word spread.

Within the next few days, my new racquetball buddies arranged a beachfront rental and free membership at Gorham's, and tours of the two manufacturers at the time, Leach and Ektelon.

It seems there were also two "camps"- the *innovators* and the *executors*. The innovators were Loveday, Brum, Keeley... in fact, most of the Leach group, who challenged every rule, examined and modified every approach and changed the game radically- these were the OUTLAWS, imaginative and inventive, whose reward came not only with winning, but with creating. They were the lions of the sport, its captains of industry focused as much on the game's progress as on their own career. They were unpredictable... the wild cards (gleam in Brumfield's eye when he unveiled the crack ace, the joy of the shocked crowd after one of Keeley's patented cartwheel "dives," after it. And because they thought for themselves, they were unmanageable... the mavericks of the sport. And in a game that required both athletic and intellectual brilliance, they were the giants of the sport.

The executors were Peck, Strandemo, Yellen, Hilecher... essentially the Ektelon camp, were their alter-egos, unimaginative but calculating, literally reducing, concentrating and optimizing what had come before not to expand into new, complex and fascinating territories of discovery, but working the odds, working them over and over and reducing the fields of error until each developed a relatively simple and exceedingly effective game. These were the yuppies of the sport, who took what they could from what had been and developed an approach that rewarded reaction. They were the scavengers but nobody could tell because they looked the part, they wore the right clothes, lathered on the cologne and joined the right groups. They were predictable, absolutely... and whereas in earlier days the sport, with its long rallies and exhausting strategic requirements, originally rewarded the innovators, now with increased ball speed, improved equipment and decreased length of rallies... The sport evolved to the point where imagination and thinking was not only triumphed by reaction and instinct... but thinking on the court was becoming a detriment to the game.

At the time, the Ektelon group, with equipment changes and perhaps the inevitable evolution of the sport, with a little political dancing thrown in, seemed to be advancing to dominate the sport: in fact, they were rendering the Leach group obsolete.

Which way was better? In the end, I guess it depends upon which history book you read- but at the time, both groups were battling for supremacy just as within each, they battled with each other.

A typical day at Gorham's began like Darwin's "Origin of Species," moved through Nietzsche's "That which does not kill me makes me stronger," and ended with us so exhausted, we moved like extras in George Romero's "Night of the Living Dead." But it was OK because we were practicing in the Hall of Fame. Loveday and Brumfield would stun a guy like Eric Campbell, and a hundred others over time, with shots and then back him into the hall and go through each point stroke by stroke that at first the young players thought was a ploy designed to awe them into submission of their intellectual skills, but soon realized they were really doing a point by point analysis. As time went by, the disciples began to do the same on a new level of focus, to move up, and add to the growing Leach camp.

It was Darwin's "Survival of the fittest" in a 20 X 40 concrete jungle- a symbiotic relationship: the pros fed us, AND FED UPON US. But there was very little that was "natural" about it. No strength was taken for granted. No weakness was tolerated. Flashback: match after match covered in plastic bags for weight loss, SCUBA weight belts to add spring, and masking-tape goggles with only pin-pricks to see through to heighten focus. Then, repeat the analysis with sit-ups and deep-knee bends in a steam room until you vomit or collapse (but try not to collapse into your vomit).

Nothing was taboo. Flashback: Brumfield, fetal, against the front wall, looking chubby in three gray cotton sweat suits- his anti-killshot armor- but in anguish, screaming at us again and again to hit him harder! Having been repeatedly pelted in an earlier tournament, Brumfield endured 15 minutes of high-velocity torture- whatever it took to exorcise the fear of ever being hit by Canadian pro Lindsay Myers again. Brumfield, fetal again, unable to crawl, looks up and screams obscenities at me before demanding, "What are you doing this afternoon? Let's do it again."

689

Rich Wagner and Charlie Brumfield beseech the referee at a mid-1970s NRC event. (Legends)

At night nothing was sacred. Flashback: Brumfield's place six months after arriving in town. Loveday's there, Muelheisen too, and the Super-8 projector's flashing images of Hogan's brutalizing forehand. Fast rewind and analyze. Fast rewind and analyze. Twenty times at least. For a laugh, we rewind the film through the projector to watch Marty hitting in reverse... just for a laugh. But the jokes on us: Hogan hitting his forehand in reverse was *a mirror image of his backhand in full form*. Hogan gets the last laugh. And we call it day.

It was exhausting, but you got up early the next morning because you WERE DOING IT WITH THE GREATEST.

It was exhilarating. Every day it was like stepping into iconic photographer Art's Shay's entire black-and-white photo album... only in living technicolor.

It was all-consuming. We survived on hustle matches and Happy Hours where for the price of a Happy Hour drink, you could eat like a king, and thrived on the repeating cycle

690

of deconstructing the game and then recreating it over and over again. Learning ... Discovery ... Invention ... until for many of us the means to the end was fast eclipsing the end itself- that is, given the exponential learning curve, practice was becoming even more intoxicating than the weekend tournaments.

Knowledge is power, or so it's been said, and power is the ultimate aphrodisiac. Imagine the game's greatest players not only competing against, BUT COLLABORATING WITH EACH OTHER- every technique, shot, rally and outcome was challenged, analyzed, improved- an ongoing cycle of destruction and creation. And of learning- well, not only learning, but discovering; not only discovering, but inventing. And there's nothing more all-consuming than that.

Of course, we knew it couldn't last. No affair this torrid ever could. Yet somehow, that only intensified the experience.

But in the end, racquetball's great decline came not from equipment improvements, faster ball speeds or decreased strategy and player/spectator appeal... but from a direction nobody could have foreseen- well, nobody except the small cabal of players and administrators that replaced the existing Pro Tour- with literally hundreds of contenders competing for 16 or 32 spots at each event to qualify, with an "Invitational" Pro Tour featuring only the top 10 or 12 in the game... except they weren't necessarily the top players, and contenders now fought for four qualifying spots that then eliminated each other before ever playing a marquee player. I'll never forget Brumfield's expression when he heard the news, and he struggled from disappointment through disgust and finally arrived at revulsion: "This makes me ill," is all he said.

The future had flashed before Brumfield' eyes. When you take a highly competitive sport, I recently wrote Keeley, cut out all but ten players for two years (and have any contenders eliminate each other), tell them they're the best and let them circle jerk to that vision for a while... after a while anything that challenges that order must be ignored, discredited or destroyed. Only conformists allowed. Lacking Darwinian fresh blood, and with its gene pool shrinking- the sport could only decline.

My timing couldn't have been worse- the two years with the stars I'd spent relearning the game with my left hand after shattering my playing elbow had cost me dearly. I had arrived just as the sport was vanishing.

For the chosen few, the "Invitational" was a two-year gig: Ten or 12 top players, and four contenders reduced physically to the power of nothing by the time they qualified. For the rest of us, a two-year wait-and-see with no guarantees, and a single dictum: conform or be cast out.

It was the perfect bloodless coup. And it drained racquetball's spirit dry.

"Life's a beach, and then you die."

-- San Diego bumper sticker

There is nothing emptier than a racquetball club the morning after a tournament: the competition, the crowds, the energy- ALL GONE... replaced by something less than zero. A void. THE ABYSS.

I spent the next two years on the outside looking in, an outcast from my own sport. Having just launched his legal practice, Brumfield, who always saw more in me than I saw in myself, graciously hired me on. Charlie's approach to the legal courts was parallel to his performance on the four-walled court- in a word, dominating. But amidst the madness and mayhem, we managed to squeeze in a match here and there. But with nowhere to apply, to truly test our discoveries- well, the magic was gone.

I drifted. I drifted north to Canada, Vancouver this time, convinced nothing like racquetball's golden era could ever happen again, and found myself living in an abandoned office building... but it isn't what you think. The building was on Georgia St. and bumped up against the legendary Elbow Room Cafe. The top floor had been commandeered by Steampunk artist Jim Cummins. The second floor housed Cattle Prod. the Vancouver booking agent for punk rock and alternative band in the Pacific Northwest, and at one time or another, virtually every alternative act from Cape Disappointment to Cape Hope came through that building, usually looking for a place to crash. It was seedy. It was gritty. It was grungy. But the power and water hadn't been cut off yet... And for a kid who'd just picked up the local rock column for one of the world's largest music magazines- well, my timing couldn't have been better. Mainstream music had gone corporate and, corrupted by the bookkeepers, had been declared D.O.A. But here in our virtual Sound Garden, something new was taking place, something very different. We didn't know it at the time, but we were playing a pivotal role in the genesis of something about to sweep the planet- a thing they called Grunge. And though I don't recall a single person ever calling our squatter's paradise the Mecca of modern-day music (I mean, lightning doesn't strike twice, does it?), in the mid-'80s, if you were into the music scene in the Pacific Northwest, they were all talking about Nirvana.

"Lately, it's occurred to me,

What a long, strange trip it's been."

-- The Grateful Dead

Freak Balls!

Takes One to Know One

Cliff Swain behind the back to Marty Hogan at a 2003 Legends event. (Legends)

There is no greater thrill than hitting a *freak ball*, the shot that has no precedent, and defies repetition. I've struck four in as many decades.

The first was in a national paddleball tournament at Flint, Mi. against the remarkable Paul Lawrence. We were neck-and-neck in the second game when I hit the ball, and was

693

surprised when the wooden face flew off the handle into the right front corner for a rollout. Lawrence ducked, returned my shot, and I stood waiting with an eight-inch handle in my fist. I choked down, and the astonished opponent banged back my return. I struck again, as did he. My third shot reflected awkwardly off the 6" handle for a skip ball, but it got me thinking after the national title that anything can happen on the court.

The second decade was at another paddleball nationals witnessed by Jim Easterling among the gallery. An opponent's shot reflected hard off my paddle that set the paddle into a helicopter spin on a 4-foot shoelace for a thong. Hinders were nonexistent those days, so play continued as the paddle whirled. The ball came back, and I hit it squarely with the whirligig. 'I wiped my eyes,' says Easterling, 'And nudged the guy next to me,' as the rally advanced.

Still later, I played in a pro racquetball nationals at the Las Vegas Tropicana with a glass exhibition court and gallery of sports gamblers. I arrived from desert camping with a Chevy van full of tarantulas, ready to play. That was the year dark horse Davey Bledsoe raked the field to take his sole national title, and I was one of the clods.

In that Bledsoe match, the ball flew over the court into the gallery behind the glass back wall. The ball struck the head of someone in the hung over audience, who bounced it into the court as I walked obliquely within the service box. The ball arched high over the back wall where I glimpsed it's reflection in the dark glass... without glancing thrust my hand behind my back and caught it as neatly as a catcher. No one blinked, except Bledsoe.

The fourth decade saw the best crack ace in history. Whereas the previous three freak balls spawned from skill, this was luck. It was a Michigan finals in 40s Ann Arbor courts with hanging chandelier lights and barnwood walls. I tapped a lob serve that arced high into a chandelier to upset a rain of earlier lobs stuck atop onto the court, giving the receiver a choice of which to return. 'Court hinder!'; yelled the ref, so I served another lob just below the blinking chandelier that dropped swiftly to the left rear corner. The ball split the crack between the floor and sidewall... and stuck.

'Ace!' yelled the referee, as I ran to the crack where my rival on hands on knees was trying to pry it out with his handle. A fair player, I screamed, 'It hasn't bounced twice, play it!' and kicked the ball out that my startled foe chased lest it bounce again He failed, and I won the tournament.

There's no way to practice a freak ball in a trillion years; don't be an oxymoron. However, there is way to call yourself lucky. Practice being alert on the court always, don't give up on shots, and put in long hours. Every few years you too will know a rare freak when someone shouts, 'Lucky shot!' After four of these, you amble off asserting, 'It happens all the time,' which it does.

Rocky Carson helicopter volley at the 2005 Virginia pro stop. (Ken Fife)

Pros Speak from the Box

My One Secret

Attack! I go at the ball every shot like I'm mad at it.

- *Sudsy*

Play offensively as often as possible. Thing in priority sequence for each shot: Kill, pass, ceiling.

- *Corey Brysman*

The secret is in the first ten years, when every little thing and think I did was for racquetball. My advantages through a long ongoing career are physical power and a strong backhand. I used to never get tired; in fact, I got stronger as the tournament matches progressed. Think of the court as having different levels to the floor, and that most players can kill the ball when the level is waist high. I got strong, and developed a swing that allows me to bring down nearly any ball within vertical reach. It's the result of training to be strong and learning smooth stroke mechanics. My backhand was fairly unmatchable because it took a couple years for others to emulate what I'd practiced as a kid.

- *Marty Hogan*

Start young and play lots of sports for good times. I brought speed and court sense from 1-wall and 3-wall handball, paddleball, and racquetball to my present 4-wall game, so all I had to learn along the way was the ceiling ball and pinches.

- *Ruben Gonzalez*

There's nothing like rubbing elbows with better players to boost your game. Not everyone can live with a Legend, but in my case an odd mutualism with many of them. They didn't say much but I learned and applied so much by observing while I was verbal and offered them advice.

– *Jim Spittle*

Motion is key, always moving forward to take the ball at earliest opportunity and catch the opponent with his shorts down.

- *Victor Niederhoffer*

The two most important parts of the game are the serve and backhand. The serve is the repeating 'assist' because it earns weak returns for your put-aways. The backhand is significant because 90% of the shots come here, so you've got to defend as well as score with it. Have you ever met a player possessing these two who wasn't tough to play? What do you want to practice?

- *Jeff Leon*

Shorten rallies, there is no good rally.

– *Andy Hawthorne*

There are no secrets in my game. There's just hard work and mental toughness, which comes from the hard work.   *– Cheryl Gudinas*

To keep a journal of your matches and your opponent's. What worked for you and what didn't. That way, the next time you play that person, you know what worked and what didn't right away.   *- Kerri Stoffregen Wachtel*

My strength was that I didn't really have a weakness, and my backhand was about the best amongst the gals in Canada in the day.   *– Dena Rassenti*

Since most of the players of the time were not as fit, I chose to play a more passing game to cause them to tire and make mistakes.   *– Jennifer Harding*

I was a well-rounded and ranked pro but never beat any of the #1 players in the day. The reason that I've resolved through years of coaching is I know now about mental toughness to the end of the day.   *- Fran Davis*

I still don't have any secrets.   *– Susy Acosta*

My secret of play is pace; I control when the serve happens and the pace of game, either fast or slow for game tempo and rally speed, as well; and no, I'm not a control freak.
                                                                               – Ken Woodfin

Repetition was the secret to perfecting the game.   *– Davey Bledsoe*

Have a good time and play the best I can.   *- Cristina Amaya Cassino*

Doing my best to not make excuses and continue to push myself in life on and off the court.   *- Charlie Pratt*

A true passion for the sport of racquetball and a desire to get better and learn the game thoroughly from the age of 3.   *– John Ellis*

I really enjoy playing and watching myself getting better. I also feel that I give as much effort as I can in reaching my goals.   *– Andy Hawthorne*

Joy - I play for the love of the game.   *– Rhonda Rajsich*

A great support system, headed up by friend and coach, Kelley Beane, and the best strength conditioning coach in the world, Tim Lang.   *– Cheryl Gudinas*

Hard work, sacrifice, but the most important thing is I enjoy what I do. - *Cristina Cassino*

"Life was like the country in which he lived … everything came too easily." The cross-training was key.   *– Davey Bledsoe*

Any minor success I enjoy I attribute to my parents and how they taught me so well how to think and then do everything I do do well.   *– Ken Woodfin*

Productive practice session.   *– Dave Fleetwood*

My life-long determination and persistence to the sport.   *– Jose Rojas*

The volley is the secret of many pros' games like David Horn at the 2014 Juarez Open. (Ken Fife)

The True History of Racquetball Declassified

The true history of racquetball was declassified in early 2013 during a two-month long Email round-table discussion by most of the fifty living professionals and movers and shakers of the industry.

Muted, dirty secrets as well as the genius decisions were presented that have contributed to the development of the game since it was named Racquetball at the 1969 National, and even before that at the 'first' 1968 Paddle-Racket National. One of the most interesting findings was the underlying reason for the most pivotal time in the sport from 1980-81 when the game went from boom to bust 'overnight'.

1979 was the best year racquetball ever had, and it had been a great decade. During that year, it was the fastest growing sport in the US and the world. A top USRA/NRC official recalls, 'By now Nielsen and other big-name research companies were agreeing, spouting 10 million players. 'Court clubs' were growing like crazy, with amazing 12-court, 16-court, even 32-court complexes. We had a few, mostly positive, television experiences. A portable glass court was a reality (if not financially feasible). It was a beautiful world.' And then the recession of '81-82 hit and unless you're 50 years or older, you don't know what it was like. Out of control inflation, prime interest rates at 22%, unemployment abounding.

'People did what people always do when they're scared—they hunkered down. They cut out unnecessary spending. Racquetball, like so many other industries, was hit hard. That would have been reboundable, except panic set in. The central figure in racquetball, Bob Kendler was in poor health (he died in December '82), and even worse financial straits as most of his wealth was tied up in real estate, highly mortgaged. He couldn't pay. The mafia bombed his house because he owed them. Seamco, which had been playing both political sides for a decade, had lost the market share battle to Penn, so NRC/USRA and Kendler was bankrupt. Several other racquetball associations went bankrupt, and many racquetball courts were forced to close, with the racquet companies headed in the same direction. The Kendler top staff for ten solid years from 1970-1979 left the Chicago office, and on return in 1982 for a quick two years last line defense, found the racquetball world had changed drastically in the two years while they were gone.

'So two decisions were made in the corporate board room that sealed racquetball's fate: 1) speed up the ball; 2) make larger racquets. Both were made as a means of generating new revenue to replace lost revenue. The competing organization IRA that in 1979 had changed its name to American Amateur Racquetball Association (AARA) did not have the old 'balls' sponsor to stand up to the sport's major funders, so they went along with the plan, rewriting the rules that had to be re-written in order to make these two decisions legal. Essentially, the governing AARA nailed the committed players with the have-to-purchase-new-equipment-or-you-won't-be-able-to-compete policy. Overnight, the game became faster and more dangerous—appealing to elite male athletes and that was about it. Quick profits almost never play well over the long haul. Good bye easy-to-learn. Good

Rhonda Rajsich behind the back at a 2006 WPRO stop. (Ken Fife)

bye to anybody-can-play. Good bye skill, finesse, and strategy. Good bye any semblance of looking to the sport's future. Hello, mine's bigger and faster.

'We had our decade in the sun and then the fickle American sporting public moved on to the next thing. In 1979 the USRA/NRC ran 128-page magazines with nearly 50 pages of ads in each. In 1982 it barely could publish a 32-page magazine with 10 pages of ads, and half of them were fitness companies. Agree or disagree. It doesn't matter because we'll never know the roads not taken. Unless the ball is slowed, and small head racquets come back. I think common sense tells us the sport could not have remained on the growth train that we all experienced especially, after all the horrible economic problems passed, it's simply not possible to have a club and make money. Club owners realized that they were not in the racquetball industry but in the fitness industry and had to provide as wide an array of fitness activities as possible to maintain their membership base even if it meant converting racquetball courts to new fitness areas. It's now an amenity for clubs, and it will be difficult to make it more.'

(Excerpt from *Charlie Brumfield: King of Racquetball*, Chapter 8' The True History')

Outdoors offers a fresh option to players. Rob Mijares unwinds at the annual 2014 WOR World Championships in Las Vegas. (Mike Augustin)

The Dirtiest Secret: Big Head

The 1980's brims with racquetball facts, however the most interesting one is rarely disclosed. I have no regret in revealing it here after witnessing all the shenanigans between the two racquet manufacture giants – Leach and Ektelon – through the golden era 70s. It is fitting that one really screw the other in the 80s.

Andy Hawthorne between the legs at a 2014 IRT pro stop. (IRT)

What was the dirtiest secret - the stunt that changed the game and you hold in your hand today? In 1984, the AARA conspired in a back room deal with Ektelon to change the rules to allow a big head racquet for which Ektelon had already designed the manufacturing equipment. The new oversize took the country by storm. It took competitor Leach about a year to dye the tools to make the big head to get back the 5 point spot per game their players were giving up, while losing championships to the oversize. A big head racquet, the second you take off the cover, having experimented with cross-sports and with sawed off racquets, is worth at least 5 points in a game to 15.

The greatest match of the decade has been called the battle of the Titans between Marty Hogan and Mike Yellen in the 1986 Ektelon National Final. Actually, it was a battle of small vs. big head. Marty using the smaller Leach-Kennex stock took on Yellen with the oversize Ektelon. Yellen had gained a few pounds by that time and Marty's conditioning carried him to an 11-2 win in the 5th of what had been a dead even match for the first four games. It was the last event of the 80s televised on ESPN.

That's the dirtiest secret of the 1980's among other advances in Racquetball: In 1980, the Women's Professional Racquetball Association formed; in 1981, the World Games I and the first Racquetball World Championships was held in Santa Clara, California, and Penn introduced the 'Ultra Blue' racquetball; in 1982, AARA was accepted as a member of the U.S. Olympic Committee; in 1984, the first National Elite Training Camp was held at the U.S. Olympic Training Center in Colorado Springs, the USA won the World Championships over 13 countries in Sacramento, CA, match rules changed from 21 points to 15 per game, with 11 point tiebreaker; and Ektelon introduced the oversize racquet frame…

That changed the face of the game.

The Roots of Pro Racquetball
Fortieth Year Anniversary

Racquetball for me started in 1971 at the most pivotal National Singles tournament that transformed the sport from amateur to professional.

I was a relative unknown, as was racquetball that year, never having paid it attention except for a few hits against the coming king of the decade, my nemesis Charlie Brumfield. Brumfield had moved from San Diego to become housemates at Michigan State University for the prior summer after I had beaten him in the finals of the '71 paddleball nationals where he screamed at the Flint, Michigan gallery before losing, 'Stick a fork in him, you farmers...he's done!' It was my first championship and when Brum returned to San Diego his mentor, Dr. Bud Muehleisen (present holder of 69 national and international titles) counseled, 'Keeley's your only threat, babe. Go back to Michigan and live and learn from him.' He did, and he did.

Later that year, the '71 national racquetball singles invitational rolled around in Mule and Brum's hometown San Diego. Indeed, they called me a hayseed despite beating in succession the incumbent national champion Bill Schmidtke and New York state champ Charlie Garfinkle, before taking on Brumfield in the quarters.

The tournament is memorable for a couple scenarios. At the time I was collecting $50/mo. under the table from Trenway Sports to use their wooden clunker racquet. Then lo, Bud Leach stood in the doorway of the Invitational host Gorham's Sports Center greeting each of the 16 invitees with a green Swinger racquet newly molded in his garage and a $20 bill wrapped around the handle. I struck a deal with him for equipment and plane tickets to each of the two National tournaments and two Invitationals for singles and doubles. My genius doubles partner Charley Drake, also soon to graduate from MSU with a PhD in sociology, hustled Bud at the tournament, and soon owned 51% of the company.

The craziest instant was losing to Brumfield in the quarterfinals. I took the first game with a serve right to surprise him, he flailed a famous forehand and the ball disappeared. He, the ref and gallery searched but could not find it. We adjourned to the drinking fountain where his Swinger racquet dangled by the thong... with the ball stuck between the handle and frame. He screamed to let the gallery know, 'When's Leach going to string the crotch!'

Bikinied girls handed out awards at the '71 Invitational, the Pacific lapped five blocks away, and a year later this hayseed vet school graduate took the sheepskin to California where a snafu in the vet licensing thrust me into the burgeoning sport pro racquetball.

Fists! Two of the greatest in 2013: Charlie Brumfield and Cliff Swain. (Roby Partovich)

Champs! Two of the greatest in 2013: Sudsy Monchik and Jason Mannino. (Roby Partovich)

'71 National Singles Invitational Tournament
The Opening Invitational

The San Diego National Singles Invitational is the first tournament in racquetball history where all the stars arrived from across the nation. Before this, there really were only regional champs. The reason is that for the first time the participants received plane fare to and from the tourney - I was taking money under the table from Trenway while in vet school at the time.

The first thing you notice on walking into the Mel Gorham's Sports Club is Miss San Diego in a bikini, the largest endowed behind the smallest material standing at the door.

Next in line is Bud Leach, fresh out of his old jalopy, with the new Swinger racquet recently forged in his garage, the first fiberglass prototype- with a $20 bill wrapped around the handle. At least mine had a Jackson.

Then my attention was taken to the glass left side wall of the exhibition court that I wondered if it would help my backhand against the best in the nation. I was erroneously worried only about Paul Lawrence of Michigan, rather than any of the San Diego or St. Louis stars.

Then you shook hands with smiling Mel Gorham, the proprietor, and were pointed to the French fry Men's locker room where the girls were led like the blind with towels wrapped around their heads as the only way to the far courts #4 and 5.

There was a soda machine that sold cold 7ups on that hot day for 25cents.

The first Singles Invitational was a success in every way including my second game point against Charlie Brumfield in the semi's. His winning game point shot lodged in his racquet throat, and he screamed to the gallery, 'Bud Leach, string this crotch!.'

Leach did insert a throat piece into later models, however it didn't help me then. The hometown referee declared the ball in play since it didn't touch the floor twice, and so Brumfield walked to the front wall and tapped the ball low on the wall for the winning rollout.

Charlie went on to win the tourney in a storm of shouts from Brum's Bums, his newly formed fan club at the first National Singles Invitational.

International Pro-Singles Championships

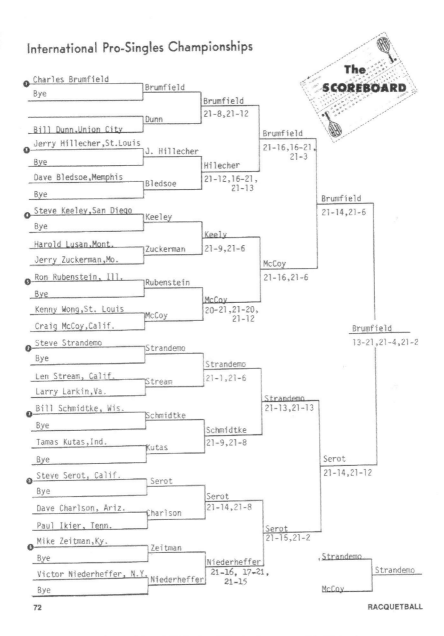

Drawsheet of the 1975 National Singles tournament in St. Louis.

Bud Leach, founder of Leach Racquets, was a three-time World Trick Ski Champion.

EKTELON   BUD HELD Circa 1953, World Record Holder — Javelin

Ektelon – Leach: The Pioneer Racquet Companies

From 1971 to 1986 virtually every top player in the sport was sponsored by one of two San Diego based racquet manufacturers, Ektelon and Leach Industries. Both companies were the brainchild of retired elite athletes. With the help of racquetball pioneer Dr. Bud Muehleisen, Ektelon was founded by Bud Held an Olympic Javelin Thrower and Pan Am Games, Gold Medalist. Leach was started by its namesake, Bud Leach, a multiple National Water Ski Champion. Others manufacturers tried to break in in the traditional manner of signing national champions to no avail*. The two companies had similar roots but very different cultures and both inspired fierce loyalty from their players. The most well-known from the Ektelon and Leach camps in the 70s and 80s are below:

Ektelon: Bud Muehleisen, Bill Schmidtke, Steve Strandemo, Jerry Hilecher, Mike Yellen, Dave Peck, Ed Andrews, Ruben Gonzalez, Cliff Swain

Leach: Charlie Brumfield, Steve Keeley, Steve Serot, Rich Wagner, Davey Bledsoe, Craig McCoy, Marty Hogan, Benny Koltun, Bret Harnett , Gregg Peck.

*Wilson signed 1977 National Champions Davey Bledsoe and Shannon Wright and pro racquetball rookie Dave Peck in 1978.

*Vittert signed multiple National Champions, Bud Muehleisen and Peggy Steding

*Brumstar was started by Multiple National Champion, Charlie Brumfield and his pal, Ron Starkman

* Head signed Canadian National Champion and top pro Steve Strandemo and Junior National Champion, Doug Cohen

My little place in the pioneer companies began at Ektelon with a nervous walk as a fresh Michigan State grad who despite multiple Paddleball championships had played racquetball for less than a year. Ektelon was little more than a machine shop with metal bending machines, however Bud Held greeted me with a warm smile and handshake. I admitted fishing for a new Muehleisen metal racquet at cost that gave the hitter a 10 point advantage per 21-point game. He told me as an athlete he understood, and I walked out with a free new racquet to test, and if I liked it the hint of a contract. In a matter of months the ´71 first Singles National Invitational was thrown just down the road at Mel Gorham´s Sports Center where I walked in as one of the sixteen participants and Bud Leach, whom I had never met, put a new fiberglass racquet in my hand with a $20 wrapped around the grip. After I won my first match he treated me to a steak dinner and for dessert offered an equipment contract for all the free racquets I wanted plus travel expenses to the Big Four (and only) annual tournaments: National Singles Open and Invitational, and National Doubles Open and Invitational. I had the first verbal equipment contract in the sport, and later the first apparel contract with Converse tennis shoes. It was an honor getting to know the Buds Leach and Held over the years, and I lived first with the Ektelon and later Leach general managers Doug Burns and Charley Drake respectively, as well as many of the players on both sides including Muehleisen, Brumfield, and Hogan. I played with a Leach Bandido 321 gram racquet throughout my ten year career.

The two pioneer racquet companies. (US RB Museum)

A Brief History of Racquetball

The game of racquetball was invented by Joseph Sobek. Sobek was a resident of Greenwich, Connecticut, where he was also a professional tennis and handball player. Growing tired of the indoor sports that were available, he sought a fast-paced sport that was easy to learn and play. After he and his partner began using paddles to play handball, he created a set of rules based on those of squash and handball, and in 1949 he named his game "paddle rackets."

In 1950, Sobek, using the tennis racket as a pattern, developed plans for a new, short strung racket. He had 25 prototypes made and started selling them to other members of the Greenwich YMCA to promote his new sport. The new game was catching on fast, but when players started to complain about the performance of the ball, Sobek decided to find something better. He came across a Spalding rubber ball that was luckily inexpensive, so he bought as many as he could to make his new sport a hit. Later on he founded his own company where he was able to craft balls to his exact specification.

In February 1952, Sobek founded the National Paddle Rackets Association. He codified a set of rules and printed them out into booklets and sent them out to continue the promotion. In 1969, Robert Kendler, head of US Handball Association, founded the International Racquetball Association (IRA). The sport officially had its new name, coined by San Diego tennis pro, Bob MacInerney.

The IRA took over the National Championship in 1969, holding their first tournament in St. Louis. In 1973, after a dispute with the board of directors, Kendler parted ways with the IRA and formed two new, short-lived organizations: the US Racquetball Association and the National Racquetball Club. Despite Kendler's departure, the IRA continued to grow while changing its name to the American Amateur Racquetball Association.

In the 1980's, racquetball became one of the fastest growing sports in the US. The Women's Professional Racquetball Association was founded in 1980. The United States hosted the first Racquetball World Championship in 1981, and just a year later, the US Olympic Committee recognized racquetball as a developing Olympic sport.

In 1995, racquetball achieved full medal status in the Pan-American games. During the period of the late 1970s to the early 90s, racquetball popularity exploded. There were approximately 10 million US players and 14 million players in over 90 countries. In 1997, the IRA took the name United States Racquetball Association (USRA) before changing their name for the final time in 2003 to USA Racquetball (USAR).

(US RB Museum and USRF)

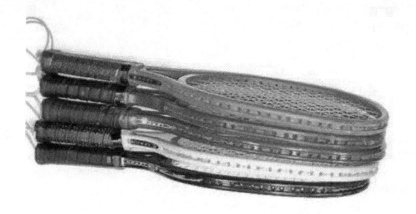

The first Leach racquets of the 1970's. The author used the 312 gram orange Bandido on top.

Along the Racquetball Boom Trail

In the beginning, there was Joe Sobek, Earl Riskey, Larry Leaderman, and Bud Muehleisen whose lineage led to San Diego becoming the racquetball mecca in the early 70s. One overseer, the International Racquetball Association (IRA), ran it from Chicago ramrod by handball aficionado Bob Kendler.

Kendler resigned before the embroiled IRA board in 1973 and formed the National Racquetball Club (NRC), still in Chicago. Meanwhile, Bill Tanner, a wealthy Memphis businessman and racquet enthusiast, became IRA president and moved headquarters to his Memphis office. There were two organizations, two presidents, and friction along the racquetball trails.

Kendler launched the first pro tour in 1973, and Tanner's new IRA countered with another, as the players were thrust into duel hog heavens. Kendler responded by founding an amateur branch of the NRC called the United States Racquetball Association (USRA), and took the lead in the race to control racquetball. The sport was skyrocketing in American. The Chicago organization secured exclusive contracts with the top racquet, Leach, and main ball, Seamco, manufacturers. The NRC promoted Leach and Seamco who financed the tour, and they ushered in the Golden Era.

From '73–'78, the NRC and USRA strengthened, while the Memphis IRA grew shakier. Always change a losing game is the strategy. The IRA abandoned its tour after the first season, but entrenched in 1978 with fresh aims at the sport grassroots: women and amateurs.

In a broader arena, the U.S. Congress in '78 passed the Amateur Sports Act to stop feuding between the Amateur Athletic Union (AAU) and the National Collegiate Athletic Association (NCAA). All amateur sports were placed under one hat of the United States Olympic Committee (USOC). Subsequently, in 1979, the IRA in an effect to comply with the ruling changed its name to the American Amateur Racquetball Association (AARA), and was accepted as the national governing body for all amateur racquetball.

At the moment, NRC and USRA gripped the sport at the pro and business levels. However, financial support from Leach and Seamco wavered in marketplace competition, so the NRC and USRA went bankrupt in the summer of 1982. The AARA assumed full function as the controlling organization of amateur racquetball, and in the same year became a member of the United States Olympic committee.

The pro players were thrown into a series of no-money tournaments including state, regional, national, inter-collegiate, and Olympics events. After the NRC pro tour folded in 1982, Marty Hogan, riding high the power and rank of the highest paid athlete in racquetball, formed the next and current professional International Racquetball Tour (IRT). The Legends Pro Tour followed up in '00 featuring the top 35-and-older early world champs, and racquetball came full circle.

The 'best shot in racquetball history' by Art Shay. The athlete suspended in mid-air in this famous poster is Jerry Hilecher at the apex of a diving kill against Ben Koltun. At this instant the score was deadlocked 8-8 in a tiebreaker game. The shot was a winner, and Hilecher won the match 11-8 and played Hogan the next day at the 1977 National Singles Championships. (Nikon FM, 3 frames a second, Tri-x film at 1600ASA, 1/250th, 58mm F 1:4 lens wide open. Through the glass back wall. (Art Shay)

Pacific Paddleball Association
The First Racquetball Mecca

This is the PPA Pacific Paddleball Association in San Diego above Charger football stadium. It was a racquetball mecca, a San Diego sports drawing card before Charger Stadium was built, for every 70s to early 80s racquetball champion. They arrived at the PPA doorstep, got trimmed one by one by these gents, and went on to use the lessons to become national champs. Over the years Steve Keeley, Jerry Hilecher, Steve Serot, Hogan, Dave Peck... in singles racquetball at the PPA they were given a tour of the court often on the heavenly donut truck by Charlie Brumfield, and then they were tactically taken apart and put back together in losing to their 20-year senior Dr. Bud Muehleisen.

Young Charlie Brumfield in center of the original PPA members (left to right): World badminton champion Carl Loveday; Chuck Hannah, racquetball physician to the early pros; Brumfield in center; Bud Muehleisen; 'racquetball aficionado' Al Chamberlin.

Brumfield is the best ever slow ball player because he started in paddles and graduated to racquetball with the best in the nation. He played the right side with Dr. Bud (left-handed despite the paddle in his right) who are probably the best doubles team ever. It is not questionable that Brumfield is the best court coverer from the right side at the time of this

715

photo in the late 1960′s. He also arguably has the best forehand, along with Dr. Bud, in the history of the game through 2012. If you don't believe it, a few months ago I heard they went on the road to teach clinics and you may see or play against them. Each hits shots under pressure in deep tournament fields as well as they did in the PPA. Each won National Paddleball and Racquetball Singles Titles, and each won them with the worst backhands relative to their forehands because of their doubles passion.

In this historic photo the player on the left with the large grin is everyone's mentor, world badminton champion Carl Loveday. Next is Doc Chuck Hannah the racquetball physician to all the early pros,, then Brumfield in the center, Muehleisen, and an 'A' badminton and racquet player named Al Chamberlin. These are the five founding members of the single court PPA that was the midwife of racquetball.

Addendum from Dr. Bud Muehleisen:

The Building was built in 1966 on the property owned by Dr. Jim Skidmore and was constructed on a plateau of land on the side of a hill below the home which overlooked Qualcomm Stadium, where the San Diego Chargers and the San Diego State University Aztecs play their home games.

The facility carried a 'rent free' lease from the owner of the property for 19 years. As agreed, when the Lease was up in 1986, the Building and its contents reverted back to the full ownership of the owner of the property. The PPA closed, to the best of my recollection in 2002. The lease was not allowed to be renewed and the facility still stands there today, intact, on what is now private property.

Three of the original members, (Loveday, Kobernick, and Hill) are now deceased and dearly missed.

For those who were fortunate enough to have played there, it was truly a memorable experience and one that they will not soon forget.

Just ask them!

Respectfully rendered,

"Dr. Bud" Muehleisen

The Blast Rule

by Otto Dietrich

Otto Dietrich has been a member of USA Racquetball's National Rules Committee continuously for more than 30 years - since 1982. Six years after first being appointed to the committee, he became the sport's National Rules Commissioner, a title that he has held ever since, except for the 5 years (1998 - 2003), when he stepped aside to serve as the USAR's National President. There is probably no one in the world who knows more or has thought more about the rules of the game.

Here's my story of how I got involved with reffing racquetball. I use to love reading articles on the rules/reffing in both the racquetball and handball publications. I actually started playing racquetball as a handball convert in St. Louis in about 1972. I moved to Indianapolis in 1973 and in 1974 entered my very first racquetball tournament – an IRA Regional event played at the University of Indiana in Bloomington, Indiana. The venue was in the Natatorium Building with many racquetball courts lining one side of the pool area. They were all in a row – side by side for as far as the eye could see. That was also the first event in our area where the new Seamco "pressurized" balls (the 558 and 559) were used. As you know, prior to that, racquetballs were generally to be found lying on a sporting goods store shelf in an open box and covered with dust!

It was also hot and very humid in the natatorium building. Everyone – from the best open players to the true hackers like me – had trouble controlling the ball. As a result, if you stood at one end of the upstairs court viewing area and looked down the hallway you would see ceiling shots flying out of one court, then another, and, soon, yet another - like a popcorn machine.

During one rally, my opponent hit the ball so hard that it flew from the front wall all the way to the back wall, then touched the floor once, and then traveled all the way to the front wall *before* I could hit it. I was confused. Everyone was confused. Was it still my turn to hit the ball, or was it my opponent's since the ball had hit the front wall once again; or had he just won that rally?

The referee told me that what I should have done was to have run up to the front wall and hit the ball as it was coming off and before it bounced a second time. Seemed very logical after he described it. His name was Earl Dixon – a top level Masters player at the time. Based on what he told me, I developed a simple statement.

There are only 3 basic rules to the game of racquetball:
  (1) When you hit the ball, it must go all the way to the front wall. It can touch any

717

number of walls or the ceiling any number of times as long as it doesn't touch the floor before it touches the front wall, and

(2) Once the ball reaches the front wall, it then becomes and remains the other player's turn to hit the ball, and finally

(3) That player must hit the ball before it touches the floor twice. Play then goes back to Rule (1) again.

Ask Otto! Two appealing prose at the 2010 WPRO stop in Arlington, VA. (Mike Augustin)

Afterwards, Earl and I were drinking a few beers, and I asked him how he knew things like that. He replied that the present rulebook was very small and easily learned. I think there were only eight pages of text back then. I then sought his sage advice on how to get a better view of the top level tournament matches, since there was only overhead viewing at the U of I. He suggested that I look at the draw sheets – as you may recall back then, the court number and match times were usually listed thereon - and get there early since a lot of people did the same thing.

But then he added that there was an assured way to get myself a good view of those matches – offer to ref them! He noted that I could wait until the designated match time, walk up to the crowded back wall, and ask people to stand aside for me, the REF. If the crowd was thick, I added pleasantly that the players would not drop the first ball until I told them I was ready. The best of all worlds!

Moving on, in 1975, I moved to South Korea. In 1980, I changed to Atlanta and got involved in organized racquetball once again. By 1982, I was appointed to the National Rules Committee by Jim Austin and have been on the Rules Committee ever since. Four years later, in 1986, I was named the National Rules Commissioner and have served in that position ever since, except for the five years (1989–1993) when I stepped aside to serve as the National President of the USAR.

One final note – this" **blast rule**" is far and away the most common rule question that I have been asked (and answered) over the many years that I have been doing that for racquetball.

At your service,

Otto

The Story of the 3 Foot Service Line

by Jim Hiser

It all originated during a highly debated event at Davison Racquet Club. Jerry Hilecher, in his normal modest but secretive style continued to stand on the far right side of the service line to hide his already deceptive drive serve. Although a reasonable spectator could say that every serve was a screen, Jerry understood that most officials would eventually tire, and many if not all his serves would eventually be allowed. This is exactly what happened but not without violent protest from many of his opponents.

After the event Steve Strandemo came to me (as I was the rules commish) and wanted a solution. As we discussed the issue the proposal of a drive service line surfaced. We then went onto the court, measured off different distances, and discussed various rules that may limit the screen. To test the line on the pro tour seemed too radical for most players, so I went ahead and tested it at the 1979 Michigan Super Seven Series.

To cut the explanation short, we used 5 ft. from the side wall to start, and eventually ended up with the 3 ft. line. I soon convinced the guys to use the rule on the tour and it was eventually adopted for the amateur game.

That's one small step for shooters, and one giant step for returners with Fernando Ríos and David Horn at the 2014 Juarez Open (Ken Fife)

History of Major Tour Rule Changes

Some of the dates for these changes are the best estimates

- Oct 2010: the US Open gives the top 16 players protected byes into the round of 32. Heretofore, the main draw started at the round of 64.

- June 2010: new commissioner Jason Mannino implements several rule changes to the tour to address various issues and complaints about the game (announced in the IRT Newsletter 2010).

  - I. **Two Serve Rule** - Player has two (2) chances to get the serve in play. *IRT has been one serve since August 1990; the belief is that this will lead to more drive serving among players who now rely fully on lob serves and will add more excitement to the game.*

  - II. **Ten Second rule** - Player has (10) seconds to put the ball in play after the referee calls the score. Referee is to call the score at the end of the last rally. If the court is wet, referee to call the score immediately following the court being in safe condition. *This rule is directly in response to "pace of play" complaints from sponsors and fans.*

  - III. **Arguing Skips, Double Bounce, Short or Foot Faults** - At no time may a player question or argue skips, double bounce, short or foot fault calls. *This rule is in direct response to repeated complaints from sponsors and fans about the incessant and continuous conversations that some players keep against the referees.*

  - IV. **Hitting after the Rally** - No player shall hit the ball after the rally has ended.

- Fall 2009 (for the 2009-10 season): Implementation of the use of side judges in tournaments that make use of the portable court (or in other words, for the Majors). For years the IRT has resisted calls to make use of the appeals judges as are available in amateur competitions. Reasons mentioned included costs, lack of enough qualified judges and the lack of empowerment of the primary referee.

- Fall 2002: IRT introduces tournament "dropping" scheme, resulting from a loophole in the rankings system that existed prior to the Fall of 2002. Players are now allowed to drop their worst tournament points from 1 or more tournaments based on the

number of events in the season. The number of results allowed to drop is as follows:
- 15 events or fewer: players can drop two (2) lowest results
- 16-18 events: players can drop three (3) lowest results
- 19 events: players can drop four (4) lowest results
- 20 or more events: players can drop five (5) lowest results

This decision was made in part to allow for players to be able to overcome injuries mid-season and not have any chances for a high ranking be automatically dashed. Previously, players who missed events were given "divider" points, which were defined as the average round position attained that season.

• Aug 1999: New tourney format announced: top 8 players get byes into round of 16 (except for the US Open and Pro Nationals, and other major tourneys as determined by prize $). Also, prize money distribution changes announced, paying to the round of 16.

722

Men's Doubles Final with Mejía-Gutiérrez over Cardona-X at the 2014 Juarez Open. (Ken Fife)

- Date (mid-90s): Seeds 5-8 are randomly generated each tournament, to eliminate the same matchups occurring at each tournament. Per Mannino, the rule was officially changed in 2005 but I thought it was done far before that (in the mid-90s). Official rules define the "Seedings Flip" as follows (text Mannino's from a meetandplay.com post 11/4/10): The tour will use "Flip" seedings, which randomizes the 5-8 players in order to prevent repeated matchups in the 16s and quarter finals. All Grand Slam events are a straight draw, as are the first and last events of the season. Otherwise, one of three seeding randomizations is used.
  - 1-6 2-5 3-8 4-7
  - 1-7 2-6 3-5 4-8

- 1-5 2-8 3-7 4-6

The rotation is said to go Straight draw, then two "flips" then another straight draw, excepting for any GS events.

- Aug 1991: Win by 2 implemented in in all games, not just in 5th super-tiebreaker. Qualifying protects the top 16 players into the round of 32.

- Aug 1990: Change to one-serve.

- Date unsure: Quadrant serving used in experimentation, as reaction to dominant drive serving from Swain, Inoue, others.

- Aug 1989: Mandatory eye guards, new ranking system, 5th game win by 2 (super-tiebreaker rule).

- Aug 1988: Some Finals were played USRA rules (2 games to 15, tiebreaker to 11, win by one) for TV length purposes.

- Oct 1981: scoring goes to 3/5 games to 11, win-by-one

- Summer 1981: 1981-2 season the first where the "Season ending Champ" is determined by season ending points, not just who won Nationals.

- Pro tournament entry open to all: top 24 given byes to round of 32, all others qualify.

- Aug 1974: NRC starts first real tour (IRA also holds pro events). The "Season Ending Champ" was determined from the year end nationals tournament, not from points accumulated during the year. Rankings were really just used as tools for seeding during tournaments. Thus the winner of the NRC Nationals/DP/Leach was the winner each year, until 1981-2 season. IRA also had Nationals in 1975, resulting in two "Season Ending Championships" for that year.

- 1973-4 Season had no Nationals and thus no real "Pro Winner."

- Aug 1973: First "Pro" event occurs.

- Aug 73: Original Pro tour Scoring was the best 2/3 games to 21, tiebreaker also to 21, win by one. Qualifying protects the top 16 players into the round of 32.

(IRT Historical Data Archive and Todd Boss)

Early Racquetball Pioneers in Ink

by Jan Campbell Mathews

Jan Campbell Mathews was a Top-Four player in the Golden Era of racquetball who designed the first Leach racquet Bandido logo and illustrated many instructional articles. The signature logo on her shirt underneath became the trademark of Leach Industries, the first manufacturers of the fiberglass racquets. Jan was the earliest equipment-sponsored female player on the day the first racquets rolled out the backyard operation of Bud Leach in San Diego. The company with this logo grew into the largest manufacturer in the world. Jan was an outdoor pink ball paddleball champion in the late 60s when our indoor game rolled around at the turn of the decade. She won numerous indoor local and state events, and placed in the semi-finals of the National Open Singles twice. Here, for the first time, is a medley of her ink drawings.

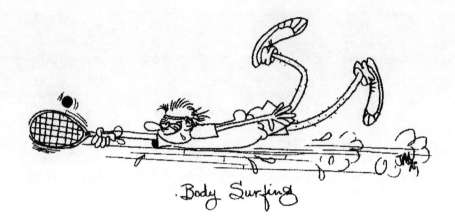

Body Surfing

Waffle face

726

Mickey Mouse theory

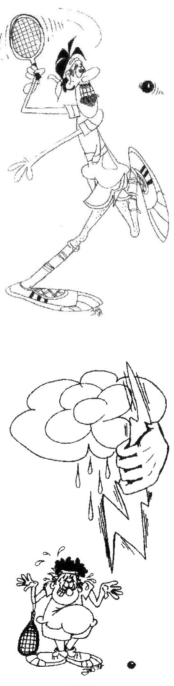

Carl Loveday Crack

"Patience"

Pros Speak from the Box

Game Changes

The pace of the game will continue to increase because of better racquet technology and a bigger pool of stronger players.

- Corey Brysman

Don't regulate or standardize racquets. Let innovations take the game to new levels. In general, the game is too fast because of the ball. Keep the one-serve rule to start rallies to keep spectators and entice television. It also takes a lot of pressure off the referee in calling faults at 170 mph a hair from the short line. The change to the one-serve rule has been at a sacrifice to my own game, but It's for the better of the sport. Professionalism by

2013 3-Wall World Championship Racquetball-Paddleball-Handball. (Mike Augustin)

each player, ref, and director should be raised to a level comparable to tennis and golf. Sportsmanship will trickle by example from the Pros and Legends down to the youth and body of players. We need heroes, not villains.

- Mike Ray

Ultimately, it will be the same as golf where they have to put restrictions on the equipment that over time has created an imbalance in the offense and defense of the players on the court causing the core of the game to suffer.   *- Charlie Brumfield*

Get the game on TV and bring in more money. Which comes first, the chicken or the egg? Also, what happens if you take a 2"x8" lumber in standard 10' lengths, and put two together horizontally across the front wall to form a $20 collapsible, squash-like tin that's installed or removed in a minute? The game changes to hard hits without kills for longer sweating rallies and greater spectator appeal. We're missing the boat, and I say this as the self-proclaimed all-time best at a sport I'm trying to demolish for the good of the future game. Now we're trying to appeal to the limited racquetball population, but should aim for the ignorant millions who don't give a ding-bang if there's a tin but will watch and play more once they feel the excitement.   *- Sudsy*

The older game with smaller racquets and slower balls demanded better stroke mechanics, execution and strategies. The modern game with hi-tech equipment brings up the level of the general play. So, today's more powerful players should remember their source, and I've seen both sides. The future? We'll never go back to the small racquets, but we should think about a slower or larger ball to regain the old game virtues.

- Marty Hogan

I see more youth and power down the line.   *- Ruben Gonzalez*

The Louisiana Racquetball Association has some creative works that I hope other states have or will launch as grassroots racquetball programs. The first is a beginning racquetball program at schools and colleges. We started from scratch in intramural programs at high schools, including one at a catholic high school. The catholic schools are big, connected and competitive and we hope the recent program will branch. I simply approach the athletic departments at the schools or colleges and they point me to the right person in the intramural department. The reception has been good, and the programs successful. The biggest selling point is to get kids onto the court, like putting food in front of hungry people. Then I line up free clinics to really introduce them to the sport. These can be done by local players, though Wilson graciously sends Derek Robinson on a nationwide 80-stops per year 'Big D Road Show' of free 2-hour clinics. Another grassroots approach is into the boy scouts and girl scouts. We just presented racquetball alongside other activities like volleyball and kayaking into the Louisiana girl scout camps, and our sport was voted the number one pick by the girls. So, you see, with strong beginnings by state organizations made up of dedicated individuals, racquetball can spread like wildfire.   - Charles Lee, President of the Louisiana Racquetball Association

Two things can improve the general sport: More grassroots Juniors development as the crop of the future, and more state organizations that along with the various associations and tours may come under one umbrella. In my ideal world of professional racquetball, the ball or racquet is slowed a bit a la car racing and baseball where there's enforcement of rules to keep the sport where they want it. Electronics may invade the game with big scoreboards, 'tattle' tape' foot fault and short lines, a sensor band for skips, in-court GPS and speed gun, with front wall camera portals and instant replays flashed on a wall. It's a great game that's had success, and can move along with the care of enough people.

- Jim Spittle

Samantha Salas with a bow forehand encourages 'more females and Junior players'. She won the IRF Junior Worlds (2004), eleven gold medals, Top 4 woman pro singles since 2010. (Ken Fife)

The Japanese have an innovative an abbreviated round robin method of tournament draw where each entrant is placed in two draws of 32, or two draws of 64, and the winners of each play in the finals.   *- Jeff Leon*

I would like to see the game grow south of the American border, and north as well, of course. But I'm a proud representative of the Latin American racquetball players, and want more people to love the game as I do. Racquetball is played throughout Mexico, with pockets in Chihuahua, Mexico City... and I hope more spring up. The main change should be in how we promote the sport in where it's played and who the sponsors are. Large sponsors like Coca-Cola, Corona Beer or Marriott Hotels should put up about a million dollars a year to have their name advertised in a 20-stop season tour for 50 grand per tournament in expenses and prize money, and played at sites other than court clubs such as the malls.   *- Alvaro Beltran*

I would like to see, at the pro level at least, the game taken out of the court clubs and into the beach, malls, fantasy parks for the masses. This would evoke the most dramatic shift in the history of the sport. On the court, I predict it will become more of a contact game. You're going to have to create space because guys are so fast these days. You'll have to physically post and block to create an open court for the kill that can't be reached.

- Derek Robinson

I'd like to see a portable court suitable for television, and the game taken out of the health clubs and into malls, theaters, Disneyland and Grand Central Station. These are places where there are already lots of people, and you get the 'billboard effect' of being witnessed by many passersby. I disagree that a squash-type tin should be installed and, in fact, think the ceiling should be taken out so there's constantly exciting rallies. There could be fans up there to catch the out-of-park balls and not feel so isolated from the people.   *- Cliff Swain*

The good of the game depends much on a correct, standardized teaching format, because as the new players learn, so will they teach the future generations. As this skill rises among the playing population, the interest in the sport will escalate, more facilities will arise, and all that goes with it.   – Dave Peck

It started with the "pro" ball made by Seamco that was green and identified the pro circuit. There were many other reasons however, why the ball got faster and faster. The major reason started on the court before every game because, you'll remember, there were so many different kinds of balls that players getting together to play would hold two balls head high and drop them... They always took the ball that bounced the highest. Also, the balls were pressurized and began to go flat after opening. You'll recall we used to keep flat balls soaked in hot water to exchange every few points to keep the pressure up. The underlying problem was that everybody wanted to hit it harder and faster, and people begin to forget what bounce actually produced the best rally for the good of the game. The ball got livelier and the rallies shorter. Later, the bigger racquets were introduced but the ball really didn't change, and the pace of the ball got faster and faster. It's called progress?

- Dr. Bud Muehleisen

Step over to an open stance by André Parrilla as Latins start to dominate racquetball. (Ken Fife)

There will be good changes in the coming decade in the game's organization and actual play. I think the various present organizations (men's pro, women's pro, amateur sector, intercollegiate, etc. should be brought under one umbrella for the purpose of smooth, synergistic progress. Once everyone's on a single ball, television has to be brought into the sport to turn around a losing battle. On the court, we'll see more superior athletes, and I would like to see the equipment change to slow the rallies back so the intellectuals and control players have an equal hand to compete. I don't think the racquets are going to get smaller or less powerful, but there can and should be ball slowing via internal pressure, size or thickness. The one-serve rule returns a pleasant control element from older days that I suspect will enter all divisions except the youngest who need two serves.

- Jim Hiser

A re-examination of what works and what needs to change, and ACTION. There is too much talk, too many great ideas, but not enough follow through. This sport is great, and it

should be shared with the masses, not just continue to be confined to our little racquetball family.
- Rhonda Rajsich

I have always thought that a 4-wall racquetball court should be similar in size to a Jai - alai fronton court or Irish hardball handball alley. The racquets can become weapons in the untrained player's hand.
- Andrew Hollan

Get a consistent and widely accepted ball and stay with it. The game needs to go back to the rally with 8-12 exchanges at least. Then the chess-like dimension will return. Serve and shot is not fun to watch.
– Davey Bledsoe

Better IRF. Exposure, take the portable courts to the streets. Very few people (outside racquetball) are going to know that the "best" tournament is going on underground at an LA Fitness, for example.
– Susy Acosta

Get people who have more interest in growing up the sport instead of growing themselves financially.
- Cristina Amaya Cassino

I'll say this, I love indoor much more than outdoor, but I believe in the outdoor game as a spectator sport more than indoor. I believe in outdoors sustainability so much more than indoor because you're outdoor and that's all that needs to be said of that!
– John Ellis

Racquetball will find growth in outdoor. We also need to get more juniors involved. The racquetball heyday is this new generation, and their children and growth. It's time to wake up and introduce the game to youth.
- Charlie Pratt

For racquetball to succeed the game must slow down to allow the masses to once again be able to pick up the game quickly and enjoy. Plus, it will actually be exercise.
– Dave Fleetwood

Tell you what... I recently watched a short YouTube clip of a match between two top pros. I watched and I was bored. I became less of a racquetball fan after seeing that the game was going too fast, especially after I started playing squash which is almost nonstop action! Drives me nuts to watch these guys bouncing the ball all over the court, extending the downtime, with too much time between rallies and not enough time during the rallies. Racquetball should take a lesson from squash.
- Brian Hawkes

It is a little paradoxical, but slowing the ball down would actually make the players move more and more quickly. What was exciting in the slow ball era was watching the pros give each other tours of the court with fantastic acrobatics. I will leave that up to the future of racquetball to decide.
– Rich Wagner

We have to popularize it with the youth. We need a lot of help there.   *– Cheryl Gudinas*

I teach junior tennis as well. When juniors start out in tennis, they go through 4 balls that bounce differently until they get to the "real" ball. I think racquetball needs to think like tennis. Kids are physically and mentally challenged to keep up with the pace of the ball. If racquetball should get a slower bouncing ball and maybe a larger, slower bouncing ball, it might be easier to teach Juniors.   *- Kerri Stoffregen Wachtel*

There are too many different entities. We need one solid umbrella to be able to plan for the future. Mexico and South America are the future. They are breeding racquetball players.   *– Jose Rojas*

Racquetball still acts like a sport in its infancy, with rival factions, politics, cliques, and most seriously the exchange of ideas. Today the exchange of knowledge isn't about full and open disclosure where secrets about technique are shared, innovative methods are welcomed, and a realization most of all that the sport is still evolving. Blow it wide open to a wider audience by sharing. We needn't dummy it down for the masses who actually can understand more than chop sticks on a baby grand, and the complexities of the biomechanics of movement need to be better understood and granted simply explained, but completely revealed, because whoever plays racquetball can understand actually what they're doing. For examples, impart topspin, crossover to return serve or to escape the box, jam serve and out the way, step into the ball vs. jump stop into a closed stance, roll their wrist and close their racquet face and still hit the planet, and use the sidewalls like handball and pro RB players. On the business angle, we need to worry less on squeezing the small market for all it's got, or more accurate doesn't want to part with, and worry more about getting every tennis player playing RB when it's cold, like Joe Sobek did. Every Pro athlete or gym rat using RB to anaerobic cross train, and every church, school, rec center or YMCA court could fill every Saturday morning, 2-3 nights a week, as well as at the crack of dawn, and with the working stiffs at lunch time and those retirees and lucky stiffs with flex schedules, too.   *– Ken Woodfin*

A lot. There needs to be more people involved with the sport on many levels: Juniors, high schoolers, college kids, adults, and pro players all need to grow. There needs to be a way to increase the value in advertising for other companies so there can be more money come into the sport.   *– Andy Hawthorne*

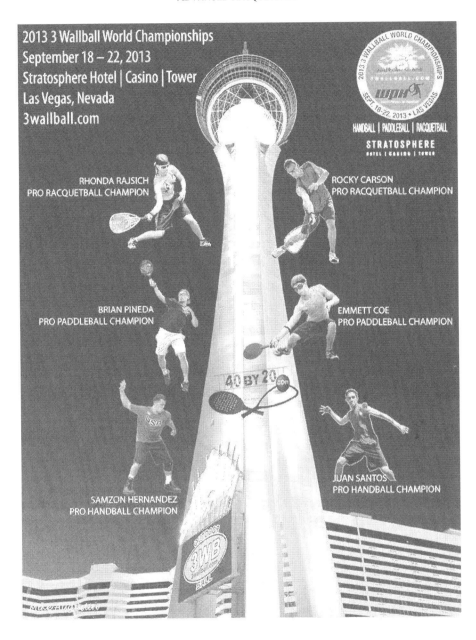

World Outdoor Racquetball-Paddleball-Handball 2013 World Championship poster in Las Vegas.
(Mike Augustin)

The Only
Charley Drake Interview

Charley Drake is the dark horse of racquetball business who no one saw cross the finish line first. He moved so quickly though his Sociology PhD, in the shortest time in Michigan State history, that I hardly had time to play him on the intramural courts. He was a Golden Gloves boxer, high school football star, and fond of saying, 'There's a lot about me you don't know.'

He then preceded me from Michigan to San Diego in 1970 when the first racquetballs were being hit around the country. I followed after a DVM at MSU and we lived together off and on for five years even as the game weaned off the old Pink Ball and Joe Sobek into what the modern sport became. I stepped off the

plane I had boarded in a snowstorm, and a San Diego blonde appeared at the end of the runway and threw a lei around my neck, kissed me hard, ran off, and behind her was Charley. 'I can't buy you for a million dollars,' he quipped, 'but no one is immune to manipulation.'

He was driving a flashy red MG and teaching statistics at San Diego State University, as we became housemates and racquetball partners, all the way to the National Doubles Semi's one year in Salt Lake, his Mormon roots. We lived in a series of houses from La Mesa to La Jolla as the sport grew from a handful Leach and Ektelon racquets produced respectively in a garage and hut and into the mid-70s Golden Era when giants roamed the court.

Charley told me early on, 'I'm going to be a millionaire one day from racquetball, 'and the next day in 1974 quit the university to become general manager of Leach Industries with an eventual holding of a third of the stock. He then hooked up with the NRC Tour and soon Leach had a deep stable of the finest players in the country, with more arriving daily at the San Diego racquetball mecca.

He called us the Odd Couple *from the TV show, and patiently taught me business acumen as I responded stubbornly with natural eccentricities. When I boiled a dead dog to construct a skeleton and the 'soup' odor permeated the house, he handed me a towel to stuff the crack under my door. When Marty Hogan moved in across the hall, he advised, 'He doesn't drink, smoke, and loves his grandmother. He'll be the next world champion; see if you can teach him something.' When I brought home tarantulas and let them roam the living room he finally put his foot*

Charlie Drake (left) and Bud Held, the Big Two leaders of Leach and Ektelon of racquet manufactures, hobnob at a mid-1970's tournament. (US RB Museum)

down. So, I moved out, but we remained cordial.

When I was on my hands and knees one day looking for a tarantula, I noticed a note taped under Charley's busy wooden desk where no one would ever see it, he thought. It read, 'Strong winds create stout trees.' Charley Drake was the prime mover and shaker of racquetball in the Golden Era and the biggest recluse until he granted this interview in 2003 with permission to publish.

History depends on whom you ask. It's the old story of the elephant described by the three blind men, one starting at the trunk, the other the tail, and the other the middle. If you ask me, the history of racquetball began in San Diego in the early 1970s when we moved there from Michigan. I quit teaching to work full time for Leach Industries in 1974 when I saw where the game was going and the money that would roll in.

741

In 1971, Bud Leach's sales manager Jim Wilson left Leach Industries and started Trenway Racquetball. Jim had set up a telephone marketing system for Leach and when he left Bud had no way to generate sells. I took over that responsibility and spent my morning working at Leach, and afternoon teaching sociology at San Diego State. Bud Leach was a self-made man, a champion athlete, and had a strong product in a too-boom market, but needed someone for marketing. Bud offered me equity instead of salary for my efforts on behalf of Leach Industries. I never owned more than 33% of Leach industries.

At the first IRA pro tour in 1974 Leach and Seamco provided almost all the prize money, and then for the NRC pro tour after 1974 the same. I was deeply involved with Bob Kendler in that, and consider him a capitalist and fair man who never welched on a deal. In 1974, the top 16 players were sponsored by Leach. And with that, between 1975 and 1982, we raised and contributed millions to promote professional racquetball worldwide. In 1979, I was able to secure Catalina Clothing Companies as a co-sponsor.

The conflict between the personalities within the NRC and IRA wasn't what the history books encourage. Tanner took up racquetball in 1974-75, and was taught by Mike Zeitman and Bledsoe. He liked the game. He secured Coca Cola as a sponsor for the NRC pro tour in 1979, and brought the tour to Memphis. By 1979, Bill and Bob Kendler were working together, and Tanner is on the cover that year of the November *National Racquetball* magazine. Go back and get the issue where Bill Tanner describes in his own words his personality and character. Despite their differences, he and Kendler worked together until Kendler's death in 1982.

Tanner went after Hogan, because where the top star is, the rest follow, and the dollars roll. He offered Marty a lot of money to manage his career. Marty turned him down about the time we were all living in La Jolla.

One of my brighter moves to make racquetball big time was to bring in Dave Armstrong of IMG (International Management Group) who managed Born Borg. Armstrong is brilliant, and was perfect for Leach Industries. His experience in sports management of players and events complimented our management talents at Leach, and filled a void in racquetball. Kendler had initially asked IMG to help secure sponsors for pro racquetball, and IMG sent Armstrong. Dave and I agreed about what racquetball needed. I was extremely lucky that Dave accepted a position at Leach, which led to a business relationship that lasted over 20 years. I will always be grateful to him.

Business is always about profit. That didn't take away from the fact that for many of us racquetball created a community we cared about and wanted to see grow and survive. I

742

1977 IRA Women's Open National Champion and 1978 NRC Women's Pro Racquetball National Champion Karen Walton watches the ball closely. (Art Shay)

743

didn't want to sell Leach Industries - that was Bud Leach's decision. He hired a broker to secure a buyer, and Colgate was in the market.

But Leach Industries was the champion innovator. We introduced the first composite racquet. Whether you use fiberglass, nylon, Graphite, or some other composite material, Leach was the first company to bring this technology to racquet sports. Today, nearly every tennis, squash, or racquetball frame is made from composites. I had brought Ray Bayer, our MSU racquet partner, to San Diego by that time (1974) to be plant foreman. You remember our trip to Taiwan with my missionary brother Bob as translator to secure the first international contract and form Kunnan-Leach.

We at Leach Industries made many inroads into racquet design, production and distribution. We were the first ones to import quality racquetball racquets from Taiwan. We shared our expertise with other manufactures in making racquets for Saranac, Seamco, Champion, AMF Voit, and others. We were the first company to offer special 'makeup's' to mass merchants, and the first to sell racquets to Kmart, Sears, Pennies, Wal-Mart, Target, etc. Our relationship with Kunnan Industries allowed us to remain competitive with product, both in price and quality, for the next two decades. Kunnan is a man of vision. Who cares a great deal about his country. Who is always trying to do his best. He is a person I will always be grateful to and trust.

In 1979, the first non-industry company put serious dollars behind professional racquetball. I secured Catalina Sportswear to sponsor racquetball. Catalina signed a three-year contract to spend hundreds of thousands of dollars on men's professional racquetball, with an option to extend another two years.

Everything in racquetball in the early 70s was influenced by Bob Kendler. His position with the US Handball Association (USHA) made him an important ally to racquetball. Bob Kendler was very good at consulting with others, particularly people giving him money before making final decisions. I often went to Chicago and met with Kendler and others to make plans that hopefully would benefit everyone associated with racquetball.

Kendler sold endorsements to equipment manufactures for the pro racquetball tour. In 1973, Leach, Seamco, Champion and others paid for those endorsements and were recognized as sponsors of the tour. The money from the endorsements and NRC magazine were the soul source of funds for the amateur and professional programs he offered. Leach and Seamco remained co-sponsors of racquetball until Kendler's death. He had a strong ego, successful, loyal to his friends, a very hard worker, and was a product of his time.

Jessica Parrilla's sswing sweeps flat with the handle parallel to the ground at the 3-Wall World Outdoor Championships womens pro singles final. (Mike Augustin)

Chuck Leve and his father Mort worked side by side for Kendler, his dad in handball and Chuck in racquetball. They were well known workhorses because of the magazines and their presents at most tournaments and other functions sponsored by the National Racquetball and Handball associations. Ball speed was an important factor in the development of the sport. Racquetball speed was influenced by better quality production. The problem in the early 70s was that the durability and consistency between balls was poor. Then, primarily because of AMF Voit entering the racquetball market, these qualities improved. I also had a good personal and business relationship with Al Mackie, president of Seamco. The balls got more durable and faster as the production quality improved, but they still had to fall within the equipment specs in the rule book. In 1982, Kendler died, and with his death, racquetball lost its best friend. Soon after, we lost the magazine, the NRC, and there was no organized group for the promotion of professional racquetball. The tour was aborted.

Ektelon's introducing the oversize racquet in 1984 changed the game forever. They applied for and received a patent for an oversize racquet. This in itself was a non-issue because the rules prohibited racquets in competition to be more than 27" combined length plus width. In 1984, they asked for a rule change allowing players to use oversize racquets in competition. Ever since Bill Schmidtke won the 1974 National Racquetball Championship with the first XL, we all knew that if we could make the racquets longer and wider, we could hit the ball harder giving the player with the bigger racquet a huge advantage. When the governing body of racquetball granted the rule they changed the sport and cut the financial resources from racquet manufacturers to only those available from Ektelon. If you own a patent on oversize racquets and they can be used in tournaments, not only do the players have an advantage on the court but the manufacture has an advantage in the marketplace.

I have always set goals for myself. I made the statement that one day I was going to be a millionaire, and it was one of my goals to be a millionaire by the age of 35. It was unrelated to racquetball at the time, but racquetball became the vehicle. I left racquetball in 1995 when I completed my tenure at Pro Kennex.

Sarah Green was the 1976 IRA Women's Open National Champion, and remained active through the 1980s. She was the most non-controversial player until 1980 when the women tour members were required to tithe 15% of their winnings to the WPRO, until Green led a protest. She wrote the unique 1970 *USA Racquetball* article 'Battle of the Sexes: How to Take a Man to Court.' (US RB Museum)

Women Professionals

The history of women's racquetball moves like the Pacific from a bashful lap on the shore to a tempest against sea walls. The initial 60s decade was a doldrums on back courts, when a few frustrated college coeds and girlfriends or wives tagged along to practice and tournaments.

This was the 1960's, before women's lib freed blindfolded ladies passing surreptitiously through the men's locker rooms onto the back courts of YMCAs and JCCs and onto the 'Women's court'. Private racquet clubs were yet a gleam in some man's eye, and a handful of the largest biceped women vied with men in the Big Four annual tournaments across the nation: National Singles and Doubles, and National Invitational Singles and Doubles.

In the 1970s, females burst upon the racquetball scene and, indeed, were the primary factor in the sport's meteoric rise. Where the gals went, the guys followed. The first women's tournament divisions were held early in the decade, as draw sheets spread on the walls from the lobby to the first women's locker rooms. Heads turned and many young champions were produced. In mid-decade, the first sponsored player, Kathy Williams, finally raked in the cash. Janelle Marriott started the first women's pro tour.

They were hard hitting stops. The January, 1980 Women's Professional Racquetball Association stop in Long Island, NY, is cherished for this first group photo of the elite. Women's professional racquetball has existed since the early 1970s, but did not organize until 1979 when Janelle Marriott, the tallest, intense and most beloved, was elected the group's first president. Most of the women of the time preferred to split from the men's tour, although a handful sensed a loss of harmony at the stops. The majority insisted that a properly showcased female pro tour would make its own mark in history.

Initially, the WPRA tour was run by International Management Group, and did well in the early 1980s, in part due to the great rivalry between Lynn Adams and Heather McKay. Also there was no period in history of greater depth of talent. The WPRA lasted until 1994 when the Women's International Racquetball Tour (WIRT) was created. In 2000, the United States Racquetball Association (USRA) took over administration of the WIRT, and renamed it the Ladies Professional Racquetball Association (LPRA). The tour flourished for a few years under the supervision of the USRA. In 2005, the players took over control and ownership of their tour, and again it was rebranded as the Women's Professional Racquetball Organization. Currently the tour is run by a seven-member board with the WPRO Commissioner, top two players, and four positions—one player and three non-WPRO players—elected by the WPRO membership.

The best identification of names is (from right to left): *bottom row*: Club manager Ellen Schurger, WPRA Executive Director Dan Seaton/ ? *1st row*: Lynne Adams/ Cheryl Ambler/ Elaine Lee/ Shannon Wright/ ? / ?/ Peggy Steding/ Martha MacDonald/ Pat Schmidt/ Patsy Ingle/ Alicia Moore. *2nd row*: ?/ Vicki Penzerri/ Judy Thompson/ ?/ Joyce Jackson/ Sue Carow/ ?/ ?/ Carol Chaufauros/ Fran Davis. *3rd row*: ?/ Janelle Marriott/ Jean Sauser/ Kippi Bishop/ Becky Callaghan/ Dena Rassenti/ Bonnie Stoll/ Mary Dee/ Melanie Taylor. *4th row*: Rita Hoff/ Lea Martini/ Jennifer Harding/ ?/ Sarah Green/ Hope Wisebach/ Marci Greer. *5th row*: ?/ ?/

(Excerpt from *Women Racquetball Pioneers*)

Janelle Marriott was a power player with a devastating drive serve and forehand as one of the first Big Game women players. Janelle was most liked by the players to become the prime organizer and started the first WPRO tour. She named her first son Keeley. (Art Shay)

Pros Speak from the Box

Tips to Females

Play men. It gives a better feel for the ball coming back hard and right back at you. It's a non-chauvinistic fact that females advance faster and farther by playing males.

- Mike Ray

Take all the advice aimed at male players and utilize it aggressively on the court. Forget femininity and masculinity on the court and hit, understand, and compete at your best.

– Dave Peck

Use a light racquet.

- Derek Robinson

Play hard and have fun!

- Sudsy

Utilize racquetball as a main fitness exercise.

- Marty Hogan

Build leg and arm strength. A strong person plays a full-blown version of the full-court game, and anything else isn't appropriate.

- Charlie Brumfield

Take early lessons, get into club leagues, and play tournaments later.

- Ruben Gonzalez

Each aspect of success for females at the early stages seems to come more slowly but sticks longer, so be patient and expect lasting rewards. Build physical strength with off-court conditioning and get some lessons to learn to swing, not derogatorily, like a guy.

- Jeff Leon

Sorry, but play like a man in a sports brassier.

- Jim Spittle

Develop power to have a tremendous advantage.

- Victor Niederhoffer

Love it! The more athletic a woman is the more she'll dominate, more so than within the male ranks.

- Cliff Swain

Don't let playing guys intimidate you.

- Kerri Stoffregen Wachtel

When starting off don't be afraid to play with the guys.

– Andy Hawthorne

Get used to playing men. There's not enough women in the sport, but playing men is the only way to get better.
– Jose Rojas

Make sure to find male partners/opponents that will let you take responsibility for your side in doubles and want to really play you hard in singles. You'll become better quicker for that, plus it's more fun to play with a partner that expects you to handle your shots.
– John Ellis

I just watched a special on the Ironman in Hawaii, and I was as excited for the women competing as I was for the men. There is no tip I would give to a woman that I wouldn't give to a man. If you are a competitor and want to exceed take it seriously, but at the same time have fun.
– Rich Wagner

First, decide with whom to compete. I recommend that women compete with men of equal playing ability; otherwise, neither player will benefit from the experience. To give you an idea of which levels of players are compatible, I'd suggest the following types of pairing (based on competitive levels of Open, A, B, C, and D/Novice). The Open female can play against some male A's and most B's; Women's A with some male B's and most C's; Women's B with Men's D/Novice. I suggest C and D/Novice level women continue to compete with women until the level of their playing ability improves. Of course, there are always exceptions, but I think you'll generally find the competition fairly equal if you stick to this system.' - *Sarah Green* in 'Battle of the Sexes: How to Take a Man to Court' in 1970 *USA Racquetball*.

The first thought for female players is to make the game attractive to young girls. I have a daughter, and I don't hear about any events for the youngsters. The advanced female should focus more on being able to kill the ball. Lynn Adams and then Michelle Gould were number one for a long time because of their ability to kill the ball. Perhaps too much focus is placed on fitness and not enough on ending the rally.
- Brian Hawkes

Stay strong, stay tough.
– Susy Acosta

Heather Stupp's Fearsome Forehand. Heather Stupp is the winningest woman racquetball player in Canadian history. She holds the most women's and the second most non-gender titles in Canadian history with a total of 15: seven National Singles and eight National Doubles championships. Heather's playing career spanned the late 70s into the early 90s, and she was the seven-times Canadian National Champion in 1981 and from 1987-92. (Murray Diner)

753

Compare - While Heather Stupp's bow prep in the facing photo places the racquet in the same horizontal plane as the arm and elbow, Rhonda Rajsich occasionally salutes the ball with a bow prep having the racquet, arm and elbow on the vertical as if it were a military tournament. (Janel Tisinger)

Indoor goes Outdoor

The invasion of the indoor pros to outdoor started in 1974. The Nationals the first two years were at the Orange Coast College outdoor three-wall courts a lob north from the San Diego home of the indoor champions. A couple weeks prior to the tournaments the four-wall pros typically left indoor practices for a couple weeks tune up outside before the opening day of the outdoor contest. They arrived with visors and sunburns and the fans pressing question was, who would win: Indoor Shirts or Outdoor Skins?

The top phantoms in outdoor history: Jim Carson (back right, long hair and beard) and his partner Rick Kosler (left side) vs. Bob Wetzel (middle front making the shot) and Barry Wallace (left back behind Rick). Bob and Barry were the early perennial Outdoor National Doubles Champions. (US RB Museum)

Top indoor pro Steve Keeley arrived on a local bus late to his match at Orange Coast and stepped onto the court against his first-round opponent and the three-time national wrestling champ Myron Roderick. Roderick was already serving 3-0, and Keeley asked for a warm up having never played the sport. Roderick lifted him over his head like a propeller on a beanie in a dizzying airplane spin, and served him on the court to make the point,´ Get to the court on time!'

The southern California fans began lining the sidelines. The other problems in adapting to the outdoor game included no side walls to reflect passes in deep court, no ceiling, and sunshine instead of fluorescent lights. During the age of small racquets and slower balls, outdoors was truly a specialty talent. The court In those days was huge by indoor standards, there were no side service lines and the slower ball invited the three-wall players to torment the pros with lobs into the sun, Z-serves off the court, and three wall ball 'out the door' shots onto a side court.

At the first 1974 Outdoor Nationals Charlie beat Steve Serot in the Open Division Finals. He teamed with Muehleisen to win the doubles that year. 'As you know my Brumfield is one of a kind. I went into every match with complete confidence we were going to win.

Ty Kelley and doubles partner Grrr at the 2010 WOR Nationals. (WOR)

Most teams including the top pros at the time were intimidated when we stepped on the court, which accounts for my satisfactory performance.' –Bud Muehleisen. The next year he beat Barry Wallace in the singles final, and teamed with Serot to win the Doubles. 'I knew exactly where he was at all times and when to shift. We had an unspoken language. It was a true honor to play with the People's Champion and never losing a match was icing on the cake.' – Steve Serot.

Indoors went outdoors, and though Charlie was no virgin outdoors he surprised everyone. Brumfield won the outdoor racquetball National Singles Championships in 1974 and 1975 in his only attempts at that title. Many were shocked to remembering that he had been born to the sport on the Helix Junior High outdoor court. In addition, there was only the sword and no shield required. You can step over the side line and hit a forehand at any time. Remember no side walls deep in court to stop a righty with a strong forehand to step to his left and put it away. When the opponent tries to play the weakness they are playing right in to the sweet spot.

The 1974 Outdoor for Charlie was rough after so long indoors. He says, 'The first national in '74 at Orange Coast was an unbelievable test. A large percentage of the pros lost in the first round, playing 3-wall players who looked like C-players but took most of us down to Chinatown. I and Serot were the best indoor-go-outdoor pros at the sport, for different reasons. He was extremely mobile and could shot from sixty feet, where the four wall player habitually found himself. I was able to survive the draw because I made few errors (i.e. kept the ball in the court), and stopped the Z-serve from getting wide when possible. The three wall god was Barry Wallace. He was kind enough to schedule the pros when the sun was cresting the cement front wall. They came the blizzard of lobs and three-wall up and outs- Three blind mice.'

Indoor pro Rich Wagner competed and was in awe of Brumfield's outdoor prowess. 'Charlie crossed over to outdoor very well because he started in diapers on outdoor and knew how to analyze the differences in outdoor versus indoor racquetball. He followed the angles and was able to hit the shots that would move his opponents 'out the door'. He also had the ability to hit amazing overhead corner kills from deep court, and he could hit the ball on the fly, and even developed a front court dump shot. In essence, Brum was able to implement the 'Tour of the Court' four wall strategy into the outdoor game.'

The next year 1975 National was a similar performance on wide, hot courts except Charlie defeated Steve Serot in the final. 'My opponents often played without shirts to try to stay cool. I was accurate and willing enough to take advantage of that fault.'

Veteran player Jim Spittle who watched him in 1975 observes, 'He ran his challengers from side to side and somehow hit inches from the sideline without hitting the ball out.

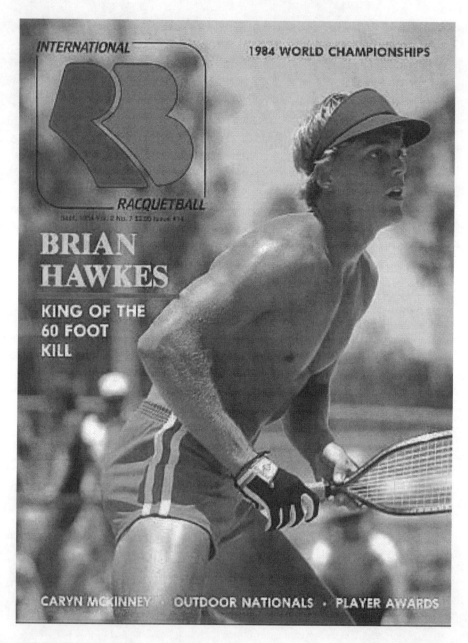

INTERNATIONAL

1984 WORLD CHAMPIONSHIPS

RACQUETBALL

BRIAN
HAWKES

KING OF THE
60 FOOT
KILL

CARYN McKINNEY · OUTDOOR NATIONALS · PLAYER AWARDS

Brian Hawkes, Outdoor Hall of Fame 2012, won 20 National and World singles titles spanning three decades. Hawkes won the National Pro Outdoor Singles title twenty times. 'I laugh when I hear people say I won 20 consecutive times. My first win was in 1981 and my 20th win was in 2005!' – Brian Hawkes.

When the opponent was in the front court he punished them with nearly perfect lobs into the sun. With the small fiberglass racquets and slow balls he couldn't rely on tricky serves like today's outdoor players. He didn't get free points on cheap aces on a wide court, but he gave free points to an exhausted opponent at the right moment by hitting it out.'

Earlier this year in 2013 the racquetball community was embarrassed and confused that Charlie Brumfield was not in the Outdoor Hall of Fame. He was quickly nominated by the World Outdoor Racquetball (WOR) H of F, and Brimfield responded typically as the only player in outdoor history with double inductions into the Hall. 'On the issue on dates of induction into the HOF, a review of the old magazines should disclose that I was inducted in 1974. The policies changed later so that applicants could not be considered so early in their careers. I like the 'new' rule, and will bring myself to be inducted a 'second time'.' That by virtue of winning both singles and doubles championships at the first outdoor national championship, his place in the not yet conceived Hall was assured in 1974. In other words he earned it on the over-sized concrete courts that weekend thirty nine years ago, and the rest is a formality.

At 3am on May 7, 2013 this flash arrived in the racquetball community inboxes. 'None will be surprised to learn that the Holder has been inducted by unanimous fiat into the fledgling Outdoor Racquetball Hall of Fame. The joyous confirmatory ceremony itself is to be held at the outdoor nationals in Huntington Beach on July 13th at 1:30. Out of respect, all tournament play stops during the fateful proceeding. The Holder should be introduced to the throng by a dignitary of equal standing in the sport. Mega-Shoes to fill. A coherent three-minute speech of introduction would also be required. That latter requirement may be too high a hurdle.'

Marty Hogan has described Brumfield as 'The best outdoor player ever to play the game.' Charlie won both the singles and doubles titles at the 1974 and 1975 Outdoor Racquetball Nationals teaming with trusted partners Muehleisen in 1974 and Serot in 1975. Brumfield would never again play the outdoor events leaving him unbeaten outdoors. Brumfield and Hogan are the only players to ever win the Triple Crown of singles championships in indoor racquetball, outdoor racquetball, and paddleball. Brumfield also won the triple crown of doubles championships, a feat unlikely to be repeated.

759

The author instructing the first Panama outdoor clinic in Latin America in 1984. (Chelsea George)

#1 Pros

Year End #1 Male Player

- 1981-82:   Dave Peck
- 1982-83:   Mike Yellen
- 1983-84:   Mike Yellen (2)
- 1984-85:   Mike Yellen (3)
- 1985-86:   Mike Yellen (4)
- 1986-87:   Mike Yellen (5)
- 1987-88:   Ruben Gonzalez
- 1988-89:   Marty Hogan
- 1989-90:   Cliff Swain
- 1990-91:   Mike Ray
- 1991-92:   Drew Katchtik
- 1992-93:   Cliff Swain (2)
- 1993-94:   Cliff Swain (3)
- 1994-95:   Cliff Swain (4)
- 1995-96:   Sudsy Monchik
- 1996-97:   Sudsy Monchik (2)
- 1997-98:   Cliff Swain (5)
- 1998-99:   Sudsy Monchik (3)
- 1999-00:   Sudsy Monchik (4)
- 2000-01:   Sudsy Monchik (5)
- 2001-02:   Cliff Swain (6)
- 2002-03:   Jason Mannino
- 2003-04:   Kane Waselenchuk
- 2004-05:   Kane Waselenchuk (2)
- 2005-06:   Kane Waselenchuk (3)
- 2006-07:   Jack Huczek
- 2007-08:   Rocky Carson
- 2008-09:   Kane Waselenchuk (4)
- 2009-10:   Kane Waselenchuk (5)
- 2010-11:   Kane Waselenchuk (6)
- 2011-12:   Kane Waselenchuk (7)
- 2012-13:   Kane Waselenchuk (8)
- 2013-14:   Kane Waselenchuk (9)

Years ended No. 1

1.	Kane Waselenchuk	9
2.	Cliff Swain	6
3.	Sudsy Monchik	5
3.	Mike Yellen	5
5.	Rocky Carson	1
5.	Ruben Gonzalez	1
5.	Marty Hogan	1
5.	Jack Huczek	1
5.	Drew Katchtik	1
5.	Dave Peck	1
5.	Mike Ray	1

(Source IRT)

Year End #1 Female Player

2014: Paola Longoria
2013: Paola Longoria
2012: Paola Longoria
2011: Rhonda Rajsich
2010: Paola Longoria
2009: Paola Longoria
2008: Rhonda Rajsich
2007: Rhonda Rajsich
2006: Rhonda Rajsich
2005: Christie Van Hees
2004: Cheryl Gudinas
2003: Cheryl Gudinas
2002: Cheryl Gudinas
2001: Cheryl Gudinas
2000: Jackie Paraiso
1999: Jackie Paraiso
1998: Michelle Gould
1997: Michelle Gould
1996: Michelle Gould

1995: Michelle Gould
1994: Michelle Gould
1993: Michelle Gilman Gould
1992: Jackie Paraiso Gibson
1991: Michelle Gilman
1990: Lynn Adams
1989: Caryn McKinney
1988: Lynn Adams
1987: Lynn Adams
1986: Lynn Adams
1985: Lynn Adams
1984: Heather McKay
1983: Heather McKay
1982: Lynn Adams
1981: Heather McKay
1980: Heather McKay
1979: Shannon Wright
1978: Shannon Wright
1977: Shannon Wright
1976: Peggy Steding

Years ended No. 1

7 times:	Michelle (Gilman) Gould
6 times:	Lynn Adams
5 times:	Paola Longoria
4 times:	Rhonda Rajsich, Cheryl Gudinas (Holmes), Heather McKay
3 times:	Jackie Paraiso (Gibson), Shannon Wright
1 time:	Christie Van Hees, Caryn McKinney, Peggy Steding

(Source: Todd Boss)

Debbie Tisinger-Moore Accomplishments

11 National Singles Championships

21 National Doubles Championships

25 US Open Championships

23 World Seniors Championships

11 Women's Senior National Championships

12 National Masters Championships

5-time winner of Peggy Steding Female Age Group
Athlete of the Year: 1999, 2004, 2005, 2008, 2010, 2012

USAR Hall of Fame – 2013

Hall of Fame

1	Acuff	Earl	VA	1999
2	Acuff	Mary Low	NC	1996
3	Adams	Lynn	IL	1997
4	Andrews	Ed	CA	2009
5	Austin	Jim	TX	1992
6	Baxter	Cindy	PA	1991
7	Bledsoe	Davey	GA	2010
8	Brumfield	Charlie	CA	1988
9	Calkins	Keith	CA	1996
10	Davis	Fran	WA	2004
11	Dubolsky	Van	FL	2000
12	Garfinkel	Charlie	NY	1989
13	Gonzalez	Ruben	NY	2000
14	Gould	Michelle	ID	2012
15	Grapes	Gene	PA	1982
16	Gumer	I. R.	KY	1982
17	Harnett	Bret	NV	2010
18	Hawkes	Brian	CA	2014
19	Hennen	Johnny	TN	1996
20	Hilecher	Jerry	CA	2005
21	Hogan	Marty	MO	1997
22	Kendler	Robert	IL	1988
23	Kenyon	Joanna	FL	1994
24	Layton	William (Mitt)	FL	2013
25	Lederman	Larry	WI	1975
26	Leve	Chuck	IL	1997
27	Liles	Larry	TN	2010
28	Lowe	Jimmy	HI	2014
29	Lyons	Mary	FL	2006
30	Martin	Connie	OR	2006
31	Mazaroff	Gary	NM	1996
32	McKay	Heather	AU	1997
33	McKinney	Caryn	GA	2001
34	Muehleisen	Dr. Bud	CA	1974
35	Obremski	Dan	PA	2005
36	Paraiso	Jacqueline	CA	2009
37	Peck	Dave	TX	1997

38	Pfahler	Susan	FL	2006
39	Ray	Michael	SC	2009
40	Remen	Ed	NC	1991
41	Roberts	Andy	TN	2002
42	Roderick	Myron	OK	2009
43	Schmidtke	William	WI	1989
44	Serot	Steve	MO	2012
45	Shay	Art	IL	2012
46	Sobek	Joe	CT	1974
47	Stafford	Randy	TN	2013
48	Steding	Peggy	TX	1988
49	Strandemo	Steve	CA	2005
50	Swain	Cliff	MI	2003
51	Tisiner-Moore	Debbie	CA	2013
52	Wilde	Luzell	UT	1989
53	Winterton	James	NY	2000
54	Wright	Shannon	MN	2004
55	Yellen	Mike	MI	1997
56	Zeitman	Mike	KY	2014

(Source: USAR. Editor's note: The author has refused induction for twenty consecutive years.)

Peggy Steding through the peephole of time. (US RB Museum)

Craig McCoy was the 1975 IRA National Doubles Champion with Charlie Brumfield, and Top 8 Singles pro throughout the 1970s, fondly nicknamed Howdy Doody. (John Foust)

Outdoor Hall of Fame

2012 Inductee
Brian Hawkes

2013 Inductees
Charlie Brumfield
Greg and Martha McDonald

2014 Inductees
Barry Wallace and Bob Wetzel
Robert Sostre

(Source WOR)

WOR Hall of Fame inductee in 2012 Brian Hawkes now teaches analytical calculus (Mike Augustin)

The McDonalds Outdoor Reign

Greg and Martha McDonald

Martha Byrd married into the most successful doubles team in history with Greg McDonald. Their perfect record of wins would strike Jonathan Livingston Seagull out of the sky:

Martha Byrd McDonald's Titles

6-time National Outdoor Women's Singles Champion (1976, 1985-87, 1991)

7-time National Outdoor Women's Singles Finalist (1977, 1980, 1982-84, 1988, 1990)

4-time National Outdoor Women's Pro Doubles Champion (2005-6, 2009, 2011)

2-time National Outdoor Women's Pro Doubles Finalist (2010, 2012)

3-time National Outdoor Pro/Open Mixed Doubles Champion (1991 in AARA w/ Waggoner); 2008 (Pro Kennex) & 2010 (WOR) w/ son Chris McDonald

National Intercollegiate Women's Singles Champion, University of Florida (1976)

Florida State Outdoor Women's Singles Champion (1977)

3-time Florida State Indoor Women's Singles Champion (1976 Open, 1987 Open & 30+)

Greg McDonald's Titles

3-time National Outdoor Men's Senior Singles Champion (1989-90, 1992)

National Outdoor Men's 50+ Doubles Champion (2009)

2-time National Outdoor Men's 100 Combined Doubles Finalist (2010, 2012)

National Outdoor Men's Pro/Open Doubles Finalist (1985)

AARA Southeastern Regional Indoor Doubles Champion (1984 30+)

Florida State Outdoor Men's Singles Champion (1977)

AARA Florida State Indoor Men's Doubles Champion (1984 30+)

Greg & and Martha McDonald's Titles (as a team)

2-time AARA National Indoor Doubles Champion (1988 – Mixed 25+ and Mixed 30+)

3-time Men's National Outdoor Men's Senior Doubles Champion (1991-92 in 35+, 2007 in 50+)

2-time Men's National Outdoor Men's Senior Doubles Finalist (1990, 2002)

9-time National Outdoor Mixed Doubles Pro/Open Champion (1984-87, 1992, 1995, 1997-98, 2000)

2-time National Outdoor Mixed Doubles Pro/Open Finalist (1983, 2002)

2-time National Outdoor Mixed Elite Doubles Champion (2010, 2012)

2009 – Finalist AARA Southeastern Regional Indoor Doubles Champion (1986 Men's 30+ finalist and Mixed Open finalist)

4-time AARA Florida State Indoor Doubles Champion (1986: Men's 30+ & Mixed Open finalist. 1985: Men's 25+ and Men's 30+ champions. 1984: Mixed Open-finalist and Men's 25+ and Mixed Open Champions)

(*WOR,* Photo by Mike Augustin)

Brian Hawkes Soars

BriBrian Hawkes is considered by most to be the Greatest Outdoor Racquetball player of all time. His Record of 20 National Outdoor Singles Titles may never be broken. Brian began playing racquetball in 1976. He won his first National outdoor Men's Open title in 1981. He went on to Dominate Outdoor Racquetball wining the event 16 years in a row (1981-1996). Brian won the event six (6) more times. Four in a row (1998-2001), 1998, 1999, 2000, 2001, 2003 and 2005.

Racquetball Accomplishments

USRA Hall of Fame Lifetime Achievement Award 2009

20 – Time World and/or National Open/Pro Outdoor Singles Champion: 1981 – 1984, 1986 – 1989, 1991 – 1994, 1996 – 2000, 2002, 2003, 2005

National Outdoor Doubles Champion: 8 times from 1982 – 1997

Toronto Pro-Am Singles 1992

Olympic Festival Doubles 1991

Member of the US Team 1989, 1991

Tournament of the Americas, Singles 1989

Tournament of the Americas, Doubles 1989

Indoor National Amateur Doubles - Baltimore, MD: 1988

Indoor National Amateur Singles - Atlanta, GA: 1984

Junior National Outdoor Singles - 1979

Junior National Outdoor Singles - 1980

Indoor National Amateur Singles - Atlanta, GA: 1984

IRT Professional: Highest Ranking: #7

Coach for Team Argentina (Bronze Medalists - Doubles) at the Pan-Am Games 2002

(World Wide Racquetball Academy)

Paddleball Hall of Fame

2013
  Andy Kasalo
  Andy Mitchell

2014
  Mike Wisniewski
  Steve Keeley
  Lou Giampetroni
  Charlie Brumfield

Source: NPA

Gale Mikles was the best right side doubles player I ever saw. He was a 2-time national wrestling champ at Oklahoma before taking over the Intramural department at Michigan State. When he competed against Charlie Brumfield on the MSU intramural courts in '71 he ended up chasing Charlie around the court like a boxed chicken for blocking shots, calling him 'Rooster'. Mikles and Herb Olson on the right, were the perennial MSU doubles champs until the team of Keeley-Andy Homa dethroned tem in '68. That's Lou Giampetroni, ref and the Spirit of Paddleball, in front and center. (*NPA*).

Top Ten

There are two lists: The first is based on the historical record. These are the top ten greatest players according to who would have beaten whom if a computer analyzed their performances based only on the historical records.

The second list of Top Tens, and the more accurate for a historic 'perfect round robin', goes beyond a computer's logic in requiring the eyes of some top players who saw everyone play through all the decades – 60s to 10s.

The two lists vary greatly. The Top Ten former based on historical records is pretty accurate, but the second Top Tens is exacting too on who would have beaten whom in a historic round robin given a level playing field (of racquets, balls and rules).

In a sentence, list #1 is based on historic records, and list #2 is based on actual talent.

The differences in the two lists are interesting and may be explained by at least two big reasons: One strong player eclipses another in an era, and the second list also takes into account the depth of the pros/champs over time that the historic records ignore, which is termed 'cloud eclipsing'.

So, have at it.

Top Ten based on historic record

1. **Cliff Swain**   Simply won more matches and tournaments than anyone, #1 six times, in the top five from 1985-2006.
2. **Marty Hogan**   #1 six times, #2 five times, #3 three times, had head to head edge over every rival including Swain, Brumfield, Yellen, and Peck, undefeated for over a year including while playing four versions of the game from Oct 78 - Dec 79 in Singles, Doubles, Outdoor and Paddleball holding all four national titles simultaneously.
3. **Kane Waselenchuk**   He is unbeatable right now but couldn't beat Swain in first seven matches and didn't beat him until Cliff was 35 years old, #1 nine times.
4. **Charlie Brumfield**
5. **Sudsy Monchik**
6. **Mike Yellen** and #6 **Bud Muehleisen**
7. **Jason Mannino** and #7 **Mike Yellen**
8. **Dave Peck**
9. **Steve Keeley**   Having defeated everyone in the first decade of the sport through 1980.

10. **Bill Schmidtke** and #10 **Mike Ray**

Top Ten based on actual talent

1. **Cliff Swain**
2. **Marty Hogan**
3. **Kane Waselenchuk**
4. **Sudsy Monchik**
5. **Jason Mannino**
6. **Steve Keeley**
8. **Mike Yellen**
9. **Steve Serot**
10. **Dave Peck**

Charlie Brumfield leaps with glasses in hand to better look over his dynasty...

Charlie Brumfield Dynasty

1968	National Paddleball Doubles Champion w/ Bud Muehleisen
1969	National Paddleball Singles Champion
1969	National Paddleball Doubles Champion w/ Bud Muehleisen
1970	National Paddleball Singles Champion
1971	Winner of IRA National Invitational Singles Championship (First time in history top sixteen players in one event)
1972	IRA National Singles Champion
1972	IRA National Invitational Doubles Champ w/ Bud Muehleisen
1973	IRA National Singles Champion
1973	IRA National Doubles Champion with Steve Serot
1973	IRA National Invitational Doubles Champion w/ Bud Muehleisen
1974	National Outdoor Racquetball Singles Champion
1974	National Outdoor Racquetball Doubles Champion w/ Bud Muehleisen
1974	IRA National Invitational Doubles Champion with Steve Serot
1974	Inducted into Racquetball Hall of Fame, youngest inductee ever
1975	NRC Pro National Singles Champion
1975	IRA/IPRO National Singles Champion
1975	IRA National Doubles Champion with Craig McCoy
1975	National Outdoor Racquetball Singles Champion
1976	NRC Pro National Singles Champion
1976	NRC Pro National Doubles Champion with Steve Serot
1977	IRA/IPRO National Doubles Champion with Steve Serot
1978	IRA/IPRO National Doubles Champion with Steve Serot
2004	Awarded Early Riskey Trophy for Lifetime Achievement in Paddleball
2013	Inducted into World Outdoor Racquetball Hall of Fame

(From *Charlie Brumfield: King of Racquetball*)

Greatest Upsets in Racquetball History

Initial List by Marty Hogan, Updated by Todd Boss
These also include great runs by unseeded/unheralded players

#1 Davey Bledsoe over Marty Hogan in the finals of the 77 NRC Pro Nationals. Considered the greatest upset of all time. Marty absolutely dominated the 76-77 season. He entered the National Championships with a record of 47-1 for the season. His lone loss on the entire season was in the final of the first tourney of the year. He had defeated Bledsoe four times over the course of that season. Both players breezed into the finals, where Bledsoe played the match of his life, beating Hogan 21-20, 21-19 in what most players of the era considered the greatest Racquetball match of all time (past or present).

#2 Marty Hogan's run at the 1975 Burlington Pro stop. Hogan was a brash up and comer on the tour, playing in just his 8th tour event. Hogan defeated Kruger and Bowman to make the quarter finals. Hogan had made two quarter finals before then, never advancing further. Not in Burlington. He defeated the defending season's champ (and eventual 75-76 champ as well) Brumfield in the quarters, squeaked out a tremendous win over Serot in the semis 18-21,21-16,21-20, and defeated Keeley in the final 13 and 17. Unseeded at the start of the tournament, Hogan's victories in the quarters, semis and finals were over the top three players in the world at the time.

#3 Cliff Swain winning the 1985 Tulsa Open as a qualifier. The only player to ever win a Pro stop as a qualifier (* this result is now asterisked with Waselenchuk's victory upon returning from suspension), Swain was playing in just his 7th pro event. Swain beat Steve Lerner in the 32s in a 5-game thriller, then rebounded to beat Bret Harnett (a top 5 player at that time) in the 16s. In the quarterfinals, Swain took on and beat Jerry Hilecher, who was on the downside of a stellar career, before taking out Gerry Price and Scott Oliver in the semis and finals, both in 5 games, both with a super-tie breaker of 11-10 in the fifth. Two interesting notes about Tulsa 85: current tour commish Dave Negrete made the main draw, losing in the 32s to David Gross; and Marty Hogan was not in the draw, one of the few tourneys he missed in his career.

#4 Sudsy Monchik's first win. CFC Pro Nationals, June 1994. Sudsy had just started playing the tour, with a string of early round losses to his name. While not quite unknown because of a semis appearance earlier in the year, Pro Nationals was only his 7th pro tourney, and only the second time he'd advanced past the round of 16. A quality 5-game win over #6 seed Mike Ray in the 16s setup a quarterfinal against hard hitting Egan

Inoue. After dispatching Egan in 4, Sudsy got his second win of the season over #2 Tim Doyle, and then beat #4 Drew Kachtik in the final 4,6,(8),0.

#5 Kane Waselenchuk winning the 2001 Chicago Pro Stop. Kane's first appearance on tour was a shot across the bow of the racquetball elite; an impressive showing at Pro Nationals in Las Vegas. However, his first tournament win was still impressive for its timing; coming in only his 6th pro event, the fastest win ever. He upset Mannino in the 16s, handled fellow Canadian Mike Green easily in the quarters, then swept through Monchik in the semis. In the final, he survived a 5-game thriller against Ellis for the victory. Mannino, Monchik and Ellis were 3 of the top four players of the day, an impressive run that helped spark Kane to a 4th place 2001-2 tour finish in his first pro season.

The most basic court coverage is a quick step into a wide open stance to kill the ball, as demonstrated by Greg Silos at the 2014 WOR Championships. (Mike Augustin)

#6 Mike Locker's run at the 2000 US Open. Mike was better known as a top-notch Open player from the great frozen north of Minnesota with a very unusual and frustrating style, but his play at US Opens past opened some eyes. He took out North Carolinian

777

Brent Walters in the opening round, and then frequent playing partner Jim Frautschi in the 32s. He then beat #6 seed Guidry in an epic 5-game round of 16 match, 12-10 in the fifth. He had to turn right around and play #3 seed Ellis in the Quarterfinals, and overcame a 2 game deficit to win the 5th game 11-9. At the end of the evening, Mike was so dehydrated he had to be taken to the hospital to receive IV fluids. This did not stop him from junk-ball serving his way through his semifinal match with Sudsy, eventually losing 9,(10),10,3. After the match, Sudsy had nothing but praise for Mike's effort and game.

#7 Eric Muller's run to the semifinals at the 1998 US Open. Racquetball's marquee event is known for drawing the best players from around the country, but rarely do non-tour players make the semis at the biggest stage. Muller was an off and on tourney player, always talented but never a regular. He was actually IN graduate school at Harvard, and took time off to play the event. His appearance paid off; He survived the early rounds to face fellow upset-minded Mike Locker (who had knocked off Andy Roberts in the 32s). After downing Locker in a 5-game round-of-16 match, Muller faced Ray in the quarters, beating him for the second time in as many tries in Memphis. His run ended in the semis, losing to training partner and fellow Bostonian Cliff Swain.

#8 Kane Waselenchuk's victory over Mannino at the 2000 US Open. Though not really an upset by the time the season was over, it was still a tremendous blow to the defending champion's season to go out in the round of 32 at Racquetball's premiere event. It was a terrible draw for Jason, and Kane triumphed (3),4,8,8. He didn't last much further, losing in the quarterfinals to Beltran, but it also wasn't long before Kane was playing, and winning, with regularity on tour.

#9 Corey Brysman just out of the juniors beating Mike Yellen twice in 1984-5. Corey doesn't have the greatest credentials on tour; his career record stands below .500 and his career best showing on tour were two separate semifinals appearances (a loss to Inoue in June of 87 and a loss to Harnett in October of the same year). But he can always hang his hat on two big wins over Mike Yellen. In Sept 84 he beat Yellen in a grueling 5-game match in Davison and then again later in the 84-85 season in Baltimore. These were shocking wins for a player who had difficulties getting past the round of 32, and who only made it past the 16s 6 times in his career. Despite the two early round losses for Yellen, he managed to win the season-ending title by Hogan's loss in the semis of the DP National tournament in June 1985.

#10 Tim Sweeney win over Swain in 32s in Chicago 95. Sweeney was a good tour player for many years in the late 80s and early 90s, and by 1994 had stopped playing tour events that were not within easy driving distance to his home town of Chicago. In October 1995, the tour rolled into Chicago, with three-time defending tour champ Cliff Swain fresh of a win in Montreal. Swain's dominance on tour was coming into question

One of the biggest upsetters of all time was when Australian World Squash Champion Heather McKay destroyed the women's pro racquetball field throughout the 1980s. (US RB Museum)

though; he had only won one of the four events thus far, with newcomer Sudsy Monchik playing better every week. A horrible draw puts #1 Swain against a fired-up Sweeney on his home court, and Sweeney did not disappoint, beating Swain in 4. The round of 32 loss, the only such loss in Cliff's professional career, eventually cost him dearly; not only did he lose the #1 ranking because of it, he lost the 95-96 tour title race by TEN POINTS (to put this in perspective, you got 20 points just for making the round of 32, which the top 8 pros got byes into anyway).

#11 Bill Schmidtke over Charlie Brumfield in the 71 Nationals. 1971 pre-dated the pro racquetball tour, and a host of Legends were pioneering tournament play. For several years, the US National champion was the equivalent of today's IRT Tour champion. Charlie Brumfield quickly came to dominate the early days, and for a period of time from 1971 to 1975 was as dominating as Swain or Monchik was in their prime. However, that did not stop Brumfield from losing the national title game to fellow racquetball pioneer Bill Schmidtke, in what was considered a very surprising result at the time. Schmidtke went on to gather another amateur title in 1974, by which time Brumfield had moved on to the fledgling pro tours.

#12 Rise of the Mexicans 2007 Motorola World Championships. Starting with the 2007-8 pro season, commissioner Dave Negrete unveiled a season-opening grand slam championship with major sponsors in Motorola and Verizon. Many questioned the presence of a major so early in the season, but tennis has had this situation with the Australian Open's timing or years. Sure enough, whether it be the altitude or early season rustiness, the #1 and #2 players at the time were both defeated in the round of 16. Youngster Polo Gutierrez beat 3 players just to qualify for the round of 16 main draw, then outlasted then #1 Jason Mannino in a 5-game thriller. Similarly, tour journeyman player Javier Moreno, who had only made one quarterfinal in a 10-year career, faced up then #2 Jack Huczek and handled him in 4 games. Both players continued their runs into the semis before losing to the #3 and #4 players at the time. The early season loss enabled Rocky Carson to win the season's first major and put some points-distance between himself and his rivals, helping him to eventually take the 2007-8 season ending title. This also marked the first time both top seeds had ever lost so early in a pro tournament.

#13 Rojas over Kane in Kansas City 2013. At the point in which Kane Waselenchuk met Jose Rojas in the 2013-14 IRT season opener, there was little question who was the favorite. Waselenchuk and Rojas had met 17 times previously, and Kane was 17-0 against Jose. Not only that, but Jose had managed just one GAME win in those 17 matches. When Kane won the first game of their Kansas City semi-final 11-2, no one would have been surprised to predict yet another quick 3-game set back. But Rojas fought back, took the second game 11-9, the third 11-8 before cruising to take the fourth game and the match 11-4. Is this a signaling of the changing of the guard in Pro Racquetball after years and years of complete Waselenchuk dominance, or a fluke victory by a possibly distracted Kane?

Honorable Mentions:

• Scott Reiff makes semis as a #14 seed in New Orleans 1995
• Sherman Greenfield run to quarters as qualifier, Chicago 1995 (beats Ray, Fowler)
• Brian Simpson's win over #5 Ellis as a #28 seed in Atlanta 1996
• Eric Muller's win over #7 Ray as a qualifier, US Open 1997
• Rocky Carson's two straight wins over #5 Mannino as a qualifier, Sept 1997 and Jan 98
• San Diego 1997: Paraiso, Gonzalez and Eagle all beat two seeds each to make quarters. Paraiso does the same thing later in the season, beating Ray and Karp in succession as a #23 seed.
• Derek Robinson's run to the finals as a #15 seed, Columbus 1998 (defeats Monchik, Guidry, Fowler)
• Steve Lerner (CA) Taking out #8 Ray as a mid-40s seed, Pro Nat'l 1998
• Jeff Bell over #5 Jason Mannino, Pro Nat'l 1998
• Tim Doyle's last gasp run to semis in Pro Nationals 1998 as a #23 seed; beats Karp,

Fowler, Robinson.

• Mike Guidry's first pro stop win, Jan 2003 in Long Island, after not having event made a final since 1996.

• Shane Vanderson's run to the semis of the 2003 US Open as an #11 seed.

• Derek Robinson's run to the finals of the 2003 US Open, despite making only 1 final previously

• Kyle Veenstra's two straight Quarter Finals appearances, after never having qualified for the 16s before, in mid 2 004-5. Wins over Mannino and Beltran.

• Jose Rojas's run to the semis in only his third pro event Jan2009; could this be a precursor to another Sudsy-esque junior becoming a force on tour?

• Alex Ackermann's upsets of #3 Croft and #12 Anthony Herrera at the 2012 US Open, reaching the quarters as a qualifier and the #28 seed. Almost as significant, #19 Daniel De La Rosa's upsets of Ruben Gonzalez (eliminating him from his last Pro tournament) and then #3 Jose Rojas to make the quarters as well.

#13 Greatest Upseter Jose Rojas at the 2014 3-WallBall Outdoor Championships. (Mike Augustin)

Top 10 Streaks

by Brett Elkins and Jim Spittle

They call them the Streaks!

These are the ten players with the Greatest Streaks in Racquetball History.

#10   Robert Sostre and partner Freddy Ramirez team up for 12 consecutive undefeated years in all Pro/Open 1-Wall New York tournaments from 1997-2009 which includes the events that are considered by most to be the Pro Championships of One-Wall.

#9   Lynn Adams ranks the World #1 or #2 every pro season between 1980 and 1991. With six women's Pro National Singles titles (1982, 1983, 1985-1988) and Player of the Year eight times (1982–88, 1990).

#8   Paola Longoria whose consecutive LPRT pro tour win streak ended after 142 consecutive pro singles LPRT match wins over 3 and 1/2 years. During this time, she lost only 18 games in those matches (best of five games). And her international streak still remains intact where she hasn't lost in any major world competition since the 2011 Pan American Games in Guadalajara, Mexico.

#7   Peggy Steding goes undefeated for almost two years in 1973 and 1974 winning the IRA National Singles and Doubles Championships both years, as well as every other tournament she entered. Rarely did an opponent score ten points in a twenty-one point games against this enduring Texan Racquetball Pioneer.

#6   Charlie Brumfield and Steve Serot go undefeated in doubles from 1973 to 1978. Brum and Serot won the 1973 IRA National Doubles, the 1974 National Invitational Doubles, the 1976 NRC Pro National Doubles, the 1977 IRA/IPRO National Doubles, and the 1978 IRA/IPRO National Doubles titles without dropping a match.

#5   Charlie Brumfield wins twenty consecutive tournaments in 1972 and 1973 including the 1972 IRA National Singles, the 1972 National Invitational Doubles with Dr. Bud Muehleisen, the 1973 IRA Nationals Singles, the 1973 IRA National Doubles with Steve Serot, and the 1973 National Invitational Doubles with Dr. Bud Muehleisen.

#4   Cliff Swain is at the top echelon of the pro game for twenty years … winning his first two pro stops in 1985 and his last two in 2004. In between, Swain won another seventy events and finished six seasons ranked #1 in the World, and five seasons at #2.

#3   Brian Hawkes rules the Outdoor courts winning twenty National Singles Titles over three decades in truly dominant fashion.

#2   Marty Hogan goes undefeated for over a year from October 1978 to December

1979 while playing three versions of the game. Hogan wins the Pro Nationals, The Outdoor Nationals, and The Paddleball Nationals in one year for the sports only Triple Crown during the most competitive and deepest draws in pro racquetball history.

#1   Kane goes undefeated for almost three years winning 137 consecutive matches and rarely losing a game. King Kane dominated the sport at the highest level like no other.

A wreath of photos going into 2015 and may your streak be the hottest! (Mike Augustin)

Paddleball National Champions

Open Singles

Year	Location	NPA Open Singles Champion	Hometown
1962	Madison, WI	Paul Nelson	Madison, WI
1962	Madison, WI	Paul Nelson	Madison, WI
1963	Madison, WI	Bill Schultz	Madison, WI
1964	Flint, MI	Paul Nelson	Madison, WI
1965	Ann Arbor, MI	Moby Benedict	Ann Arbor, MI
1966	E. Lansing, MI	Bud Muehleisen	San Diego, CA
1967	Bloomington, IN	Paul Lawrence	Ann Arbor, MI
1968	Mpls, MN	Bud Muehleisen	San Diego, CA
1969	Ames, IA	Charlie Brumfield	San Diego, CA
1970	Fargo, ND	Charlie Brumfield	San Diego, CA
1971	Flint, MI	Steve Keeley	E. Lansing, MI
1972	Knoxville, TN	Dan McLaughlin	Ann Arbor, MI
1973	Eau Claire, WI	Steve Keeley	E. Lansing, MI
1974	Ann Arbor, MI	Steve Keeley	E. Lansing, MI
1975	Livonia, MI	Dan McLaughlin	Ann Arbor, MI
1976	Adrian, MI	Steve Keeley	San Diego, CA
1977	E. Lansing, MI	Steve Keeley	San Diego, CA
1978	Ann Arbor, MI	R. P. Valenciano	Flint, MI
1979	Ann Arbor, MI	Marty Hogan	San Diego, CA
1980	Lansing, MI	Dick Jury	Haslett, MI
1981	Ann Arbor, MI	Steve Wilson	Flint, MI
1982	Lansing, MI	Larry Fox	Ann Arbor, MI
1983	Ypsilanti, MI	Steve Wilson	Flint, MI
1984	Lansing, MI	Steve Wilson	Flint, MI
1985	Saginaw, MI	Steve Wilson	Flint, MI
1986	Davison, MI	Mark Kozub	Livonia, MI
1987	Ann Arbor, MI	Marty Hogan	St. Louis, MO
1988	Davison, MI	Andy Kasalo	Calumet City, IL
1989	Ann Arbor, MI	Mike Wisniewski	Bay City, MI
1990	Davison, MI	Mark Kozub	Livonia, MI

1991 Saginaw, MI	Mike Wisniewski	Bay City, MI
1992 Midland, MI	Andy Kasalo	Kalamazoo, MI
1993 E. Lansing, MI	Mike Wisniewski	Bay City, MI
1994 Pontiac, MI	Mike Wisniewski	Bay City, MI
1995 Eau Claire, WI	Mark Piechowiak	Bay City, MI
1996 Midland, MI	Mike Wisniewski	Bay City, MI
1997 Midland, MI	Bob Groya	Bay City, MI
1998 Midland, MI	Mike Wisniewski	Bay City, MI
1999 Pontiac, MI	Andy Mitchell	Kalamazoo, MI
2000 Ann Arbor, MI	Andy Mitchell	Kalamazoo, MI
2001 Kalamazoo, MI	Andy Mitchell	Kalamazoo, MI
2002 Livonia, MI	Mike Wisniewski	Bay City, MI
2003 Midland, MI	Mike Wisniewski	Bay City, MI
2004 Ann Arbor, MI	Kelly Gelhaus	Riverside, CA
2005 Ann Arbor, MI	Kelly Gelhaus	Riverside, CA
2006 San Diego, CA	Chris Crowther	Riverside, CA
2007 E. Lansing, MI	Kelly Gelhaus	Riverside, CA
2008 San Diego, CA	Aaron Embry	San Diego, CA
2009 Ann Arbor, MI	Cesar Carrillo	Memphis, TN
2010 San Diego, CA	Mike Wisniewski	Bay City, MI
2011 Arlington Ht, IL	Cesar Carrilo,	Memphis, TN
2012 San Diego, CA	Cesar Carrilo,	Memphis, TN
2013 Riverside, CA	Todd Entrikin	Riverside, CA
2014 Riverside, CA	Todd Entrikin	Riverside, CA

3-time National Singles Champion and 18-time National Doubles Champion Andy Mitchel and some of his fans flock to another paddleball Nationals. (NPA)

Open Doubles

Year	Location	NPA Open Doubles Champions	Hometowns
1962	Madison, WI	John Blanchieu, Detroit, MI and Maurice Rubin, Detroit, MI	
1963	Madison, WI	Bob McNamara, Minneapolis, MN and Dick McNamara, Mls, MN	
1964	Flint, MI	Bob McNamara, Mpls, MN and Dick McNamara, Mpls, MN	
1965	A. Arbor, MI	Harold Kronenberg and Galen Johnson, Eau Claire, WI	
1966	E.Lansing, MI	Harold Kronenberg and Galen Johnson, Eau Claire, WI	
1967	Bl'ington, IN.	Harold Kronenberg and Galen Johnson, Eau Claire, WI	
1968	Mpls, MN	Bud Muehleisen and Charlie Brumfield, San Diego, CA	
1969	Ames, IA	Bud Muehleisen and Charlie Brumfield, San Diego, CA	
1970	Fargo, ND	Bob McNamara, Mpls,, MN and Bernie McNamara, Mpls, MN	
1971	Flint,MI	Craig Finger, Ann Arbor, MI and Paul Lawrence, Ann Arbor, MI	
1972	Knoxville, TN	Evans Wright, E.Lansing, MI and Dan Alder, E.Lansing, MI	
1973	Eau Claire, WI	Evans Wright, E. Lansing, MI and Dan Alder, E. Lansing, MI	
1974	A. Arbor, MI	Steve Keeley, San Diego, CA and Len Baldori, E. Lansing, MI	
1975	Livonia, MI	Dick Jury, E.Lansing, MI and R.P. Valenciano, Flint, MI	
1976	Flint, MI	Steve Keeley, San Diego, CA and Andy Homa, Williamston, MI	
1977	A. Arbor, MI	Dick Jury, Williamston, MI and R.P. Valenciano, Flint, MI	
1978	Portage, MI	Dick Jury, Williamston, MI and R.P. Valenciano, Flint, MI	
1979	E.Lansing, MI	Dick Jury, Haslett, MI and R.P. Valenciano, Flint, MI	
1980	A. Arbor, MI	Bob Sterken, Ann Arbor, MI and Greg Grambeau, Ann Arbor, MI	
1981	Flint, MI	Andy Kasalo, Kalamazoo, MI and Andy Mitchell, Kalamazoo, MI	
1982	Ka'zoo, MI	Steve Wilson, Flint, MI and Kevin McCully, Ann Arbor, MI	
1983.	Midland, MI	Andy Kasalo, Kalamazoo, MI and Andy Mitchell, Kalamazoo, MI	
1984	Dearborn, MI	Andy Kasalo, Kalamazoo, MI and Andy Mitchell, Kalamazoo, MI	
1985	Pontiac, MI	Andy Kasalo, Calumet City, IL and Andy Mitchell, Ft. Wayne, IN	
1986	Dearborn, MI	Andy Kasalo, Calumet City, IL and Andy Mitchell, Ft. Wayne, IN	
1987	Dearborn, MI	Andy Kasalo, Calumet City, IL and Andy Mitchell, Ka'zoo, MI	
1988	Portage, MI	Andy Kasalo, Calumet City, IL and Andy Mitchell, Ka'zoo, MI	
1989	Southgate, MI	Andy Kasalo, Kalamazoo, MI and Andy Mitchell, Kalamazoo, MI	
1990	Canton, MI	Andy Kasalo, Kalamazoo, MI and Andy Mitchell, Kalamazoo, MI	
1991	Taylor, MI	Andy Kasalo, Kalamazoo, MI and Andy Mitchell, Kalamazoo, MI	
1992	Lansing, MI	Andy Kasalo, Kalamazoo, MI and Andy Mitchell, Kalamazoo, MI	
1993	EauClaire, WI	Andy Kasalo, Kalamazoo, MI and Andy Mitchell, Kalamazoo, MI	
1994	Midland, MI	Andy Kasalo, Kalamazoo, MI and Andy Mitchell, Kalamazoo, MI	
1995	Ka'zoo, MI	Andy Kasalo, Kalamazoo, MI and Andy Mitchell, Ka'zoo, MI	
1996	Davison, MI	Andy Kasalo, Kalamazoo, MI and Andy Mitchell, Kalamazoo, MI	

1997 EauClaire, WI   Andy Kasalo, Kalamazoo, MI and Andy Mitchell, Kalamazoo, MI
1998 Davison, MI   Mike 'Wiz', Bay City, MI and Mike Czabala, Ann Arbor, MI
1999 EauClaire, WI   Andy Mitchell, Kalamazoo, MI and Andy Kasalo, Kalamazoo, MI
2000 Ka'zoo, MI   Andy Mitchell, Kalamazoo, MI and Andy Kasalo, Ka'zoo, MI
2001 Midland, MI   Andy Mitchell, Kalamazoo, MI and Andy Kasalo, Kalamazoo, MI
2002 Bl'ington, IN   Mike Czabala, Los Angeles, CA and Mike 'Wiz',, Bay City, MI
2003 EauClaire, WI   Andy Mitchell, Kalamazoo, MI and Andy Kasalo, Kalamazoo, MI
2004 Bl'ington, IN   Kelly Gelhaus, Riverside, CA and Steve Lerner, Riverside, CA
2005 Riverside, CA   Kelly Gelhaus, Riverside, CA and Steve Lerner, Riverside, CA
2006 Ann Arbor, MI   Kelly Gelhaus, Riverside, CA and Todd Entriken, Riverside, CA
2007 Riverside, CA   Kelly Gelhaus, Riverside, CA and Todd Entriken, Riverside, CA
2008 E. Lansing, MI Mike Wisniewski, Bay City, MI and Chad Krager, Bay City, MI
2009 San Diego, CA   Mike Orr, San Diego, CA and Todd Entriken, Riverside, CA
2010 Arlington Hts, IL, Dennis Negrete, Schaumburg, IL, and Chad Krager Bay City MI
2011 San Diego, CA, Mike Wisniewski, Bay City, MI, and Todd Entrikin Riverside, CA
2012 E. Lansing, MI, Emmet Coe, San Diego, and Brian Pineda Fountain Valley, CA
2013 Riverside, CA, Todd Entrikin, Riverside, CA, and Kelly Gelhaus Bakersville, CA
2014 E. Lansing, MI, Todd Entrikin, Riverside, CA, and Emmett Coe San Diego, CA

The earliest and the latest indoor paddleball paddles. The square paddle on the left is one of the earliest designed by Earl Riskey, the 'founder of paddleball', and the oval one appears to be a homemade job. The modern one on the right is a west coast favorite. (NPA)

Paddleball overhead at the 3-WallBall World Championships of three sports. (Mike Augustin)

Photo Credits

I am deeply grateful to the racquetball community for responding to my call for photos for this book over the past five years, and in appreciation have donated 1500 copies to the 2015 US Open, WOR Nationals, and Intercollegiate Nationals tournaments. Each photo has a credit, and the major donors are listed below. The book cover photo is of Smokin' Marty Hogan at the 1979 Outdoor Nationals at Orange Coast College with permission and courtesy of the Marty Hogan collection.

The author and Art Shay, official racquetball photographer, USAR Hall of Fame, and photographer of the US Presidents, weigh the racquetball grip in Burlington, VT 1975.

John Foust

Suzanne Gale

Chelsea George

USA Racquetball

Murray Diner and Racquetball Canada

Janel Tisinger

Michael F. Williams

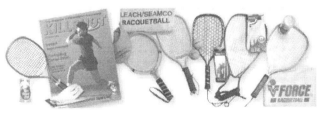

USA Racquetball Museum

Mike Zeitman

Ed Arias, PhD

US Open

RacquetBall Facebook

Stephen Fitzsimons

World Outdoor Racquetball

Steve Serot

Mike Augustin

National Paddleball Association

International Racquetball Tour

Ken Fife

Jan Campbell Mathews

Roby Partovich

World Wide Racquetball Academy

Freddy Ramirez

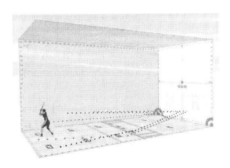

Xia Yang Virtual Graphics

Contributors

Top of the World Stratosphere at the 2013 World 3-WallBall Nationals. (WOR, Patty Leibofsky)

Marty Hogan: Developer of the power stroke, 6-time World Champion 1977, 78, 79, 80, 81, 89, Paddleball National 1979, Champion, one of two winners of the Triple Crown, Hall of Fame 1997.

Cliff Swain: 6-time World Champion 1990, 93, 94, 95, 98, 02, multiple titles in indoor, outdoor, singles and doubles.

Susy Acosta: Current high rank WRRO.

Kerri Stoffregen Wachtel: US Open Champion 2001, #2 WPRO 2006, 07.

Jose Rojas: Top 4 IRT pro for the past three years, five Times on Team USA, gold in singles at 2013 Pan American Games, National Doubles Champion 2014.

Andy Hawthorne: Current IRT high rank pro, winner of multiple events.

Jim Winterton: Coached the most top names For forty years, Team USA coach, head instructor US Elite Racquetball,, Hall of Fame 2000.

Bud Muehleisen: Holder of 100 National and International titles, 'First' National Singles Champion 1969, National Paddleball Champion 1966, 67, 68, dentist never missing a day of practice in 50 years, Hall of Fame 1974.

Alvaro Beltran: A top ranked IRT player, only player to win World Championships in both singles and doubles 2000.

Derek Robinson: Current high ranked pro and touring clinician.

Rhonda Rajsich :#1 WPRO player 2005, 06, 07, 10, Four US Open Titles, IRF World Champion 2008, 10, multiple gold and silver in Pan American Games.

Dave Peck: 1982 World Champion, Ektelon National Champion 1981, 82, innovator of the Bow stroke, Hall of Fame 1997.

Charlie Pratt: Current high ranked Pro on IRT tour.

Randy Stafford: Pioneer pro, President USA Racquetball, curator US Racquetball Museum, coach, author, Hall of Fame 2013.

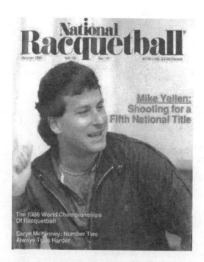

Mike Yellen: #1 ranked player 1983-87, winner of Ektelon, Catalina and DP Nationals in 1983, won DP Nationals in1984, Hall of Fame 1997.

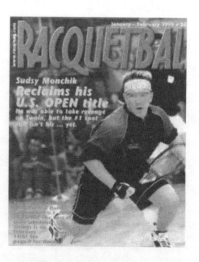

Sudsy Monchik: #1 Player in the World 1996, 97, 99, 00, 01, Four time US Open Champion.

Mike Ray: #1 ranked Player in the World 1992, Winner of Pro Nationals 1989, 92, 93, Hall of Fame 2009.

Ruben Gonzalez: 1988 Pro Nationals and World Champion, Hall of Fame 2000.

Cheryl Gudinas: 3-time World Champion 2000, 02, 04, #1 women's pro 2000-2004,US National Champion 1999, 2000, 01, 02, 03.

Cristina Amaya Cassino: Current high ranked pro.

Jerry Hilecher: Top 4 pro Tour for 10 years, #1 in 1981, coach and author. Hall of Fame 2005.

John Ellis: Ten years in the Top Ten pros, and instructor.

Davey Bledsoe: 1977 Pro National Champion, Hall of Fame 2010, Elvis Presley's racquetball coach.

Jackie Paraiso: #1 WPRO player 1991, 98, 99, 7-time World Champion in women doubles.

Charlie Brumfield: PhD law, 5-time National Singles Champion in 1970s,, one of two players to win the Triple Crown, Paddleball National Champion 1964, Hall of Fame 1988, Outdoor Hall of Fame 2013.

Mike Wisniewski: Nine-time National Paddleball Singles Champion, two-time National Doubles Champion, Paddleball Hall of Fame 2014, Instructor, author.

Ken Woodfin: 1990s pro, multi-sports, author, Houston trainer and coach.

Corey Brysman: 1982 USRA Junior National Champion. Top 8 pro 1980s.

Brad Kruger: Three sport Canadian National Champion (racquetball, handball, swimming), multiple singles and doubles titles in Golden Era with both hands, author.

Bo Champagne: 'Spirit of Racquetball', champion of six States during the Golden Era, coach.

'International Man' Jeff Leon, Father of Latin racquetball and Singles Champion in multiple age divisions.

Otto Dietrich: USAR National Rules Commissioner since 1982, except for six years as USAR National President 1998 – 2003.

Dena Rassenti: Canada's #2 or #3 woman player from 1975 to 1981, current coach.

Todd Boss, the 'Racquetball Statistician', webmaster of IRT Historical Data Archive.

Hank Markus: WOR director, the 'Benjamin Franklin' of racquetball.

Chuck Leve: Executive Secretary of IRA and NRC in 1970s, Director IHRSA, wrote the first serious racquetball book *Inside Racquetball*

Jason Mannino: IRT director, #1 Player in the World in 2003, winner of 1999 US Open, winner of 2001 IRT Pro Nationals, 2006 US Open Champion.

Jim Hiser: CEO and past Executive director of USA Racquetball, PhD mycology.

Brett Elkins: chairman LA Juniors, WOR Hall of Fame director, curates of the West Coast Racquetball Museum.

Doug Ganim: US Open event director, MBA, 3-time IRF World Doubles Champ

Other contributors

Lori Bingham, Greg Childs, Fran Davis, Charley Drake, Brian Hawkes, Jim Easterling, Dave Fleetwood, Lou Giampetroni, Jennifer Harding, Dean Kachel at the Coral Springs Quadrangle Athletic Club, Jamie Lawson, Patty Leibofsky, Chuck Leve, Greg Lewerenz, Heather McKay, Dr. George and Dean Nichopoulos, Victor Niederhoffer, The Ghost of Elvis Presley, Mike 'The Mighty' Quinn, Bonnie Rejaei, Ken Ruth, Trey Sayes, Jim 'Make Every' Schatz, Bill Schultz Jr., Steve and Stuart Smith, Jim Spittle (pseudonym), Bill Stevens, Debby Tisinger-Moore, Rich Wagner.

Alejandro Cardona eyeballs it at the 2013 Grand Slam Juarez Open. (Ken Fife)

Historic Timeline

1949

... Joe Sobek invents racquetball in Greenwich, Connecticut. He designs a "strung paddle racket," combines the rules of handball and squash and calls his variation "paddle rackets."

1950

... The sport gains a following among cross-over handball enthusiasts .... Robert Kendler, president of the U.S. Handball Association (USHA), takes an interest in the game, both as a player and a promoter.

the sixties

1960 ... Increasing popularity of the game attracts new players in all age groups .... Administrative structure begins to evolve.

1968 ... The First Gut-Strung Paddle Rackets National Championships held in Milwaukee, Wisconsin .... Joe Sobek turns sport over to Robert Kendler .... Bill Schultz wins first Men's Open national title.

1969 ... Paddle rackets renamed RACQUETBALL .... International Racquetball Association (IRA) incorporated .... Ken Porco named IRA Executive Secretary .... First IRA National Singles held in St. Louis, Missouri.

1930's paddle with instructions for wearing the thong. (Brett Elkins)

the seventies

1970 ... First metal racquet introduced by Bud Held and Ektelon .... Robert Kendler elected President of IRA .... 50,000 amateur players estimated in the U.S. .... National Singles held in St. Louis, Missouri.

1971 ... National Singles Championships held in Salt Lake City .... Aluminum alloy frames introduced.

1972 ... Inaugural issue of RACQUETBALL Magazine published in November .... First Pro Tour formed .... Chuck Leve named IRA Executive Secretary .... Fiberglass frames introduced .... National Singles held in Memphis, Tennessee.

1973 ... Robert Kendler leaves IRA to form National Racquetball Club pro group .... DeWitt Shy named IRA President .... Myron Roderick named Executive Director of IRA .... New age groups established in Juniors, Masters and Golden Masters .... National Singles held in St. Louis, MO.

1974 ... Membership requirement established for all sanctioned tournaments .... IRA holds first pro tournament .... IRA membership cost was $3.00 per year .... Number of amateur players in the U.S. jumps to 3 million .... National Singles held in San Diego, California.

1975 ... Tom McKie named IRA Executive Director .... IRA offices move to Memphis, Tennessee .... Official IRA patch issued .... Muehleisen, Porco and Sellers leave IRA board after five years .... Canadian Wayne Bowes wins Men's International Open Singles.

1976 ... U.S. Racquetball Association (USRA) founded as rival amateur organization .... William Tanner takes over as IRA President .... IRA headquarters move to Dallas, Texas .... IRA membership fees double to $6.00 per year .... Seamco 444 becomes the official racquetball of the IRA .... National Singles held in Chattanooga, Tennessee.

1977 ... Racquetball becomes an American fitness rage .... Tom McKie resigns as IRA Executive Director .... IRA headquarters move back to Memphis, TN .... National Singles in Southfield, MI.

1978 ... IRA re-organized in Denver .... Luke St. Onge takes over as IRA Executive Director .... Bob Folsom named as President .... National Singles held in Denver, Colorado.

The first and only gathering of the racquetball Pioneers and Legends at the 2013 US Open. Count the World Titles and Hall of Famers! Front row kneeling (left to right): Polo Gutierrez – Jason Mannino – Sudsy Monchik –Shannon Wright – Cliff Swain – Sarah Green – Dave Fleetwood – Eric Mueller. Front row standing: holding mic Steve Strandemo - Chuck Leve - Rich Wagner – Randy Stafford - Ed Andrews - Dr Bud - Kane Walenchuk – Kim Russell (Kane's wife)- glasses Andy Hawthorne - Mike Ray (in back of female). Next row: black shirt Anthony Herrera – black pants Álvaro Beltran next to Jose Rojas - Jerry Hilecher - Charlie Brumfield - Ron Strom - Mike Zeitman. Back row: black shirt Chris Crowther – drink in air Charlie Pratt – Davey Bledsoe – Marty Hogan – Charlie Garfinkel - with Rhonda Rajsich. (Roby Partovich)

the eighties

1980 ... Keith Calkins becomes Board President .... Han van der Hiejden of Holland becomes IARF President .... Boron and graphic frames introduced .... Women's Professional Racquetball Association (WPRA) and pro tour founded .... National Singles held in Miami, Florida.

1981 ... World Games I and First Racquetball World Championships held in Santa Clara, California .... U.S.A. wins first World Cup title over six other countries ....Penn introduces the "Ultra Blue" racquetball.

1982 ... AARA accepted as member of the U.S. Olympic Committee .... USRA organization folds .... RACQUETBALL Magazine sold .... AARA signs racquet sponsorship with Diversified Products .... Penn named official ball .... Paul Henrickson elected Board President .... National Singles held in Buffalo, New York.

1983 ... AARA headquarters relocate to Colorado Springs .... U.S.A. dominates first IARF Regional Games .... Downtown YMCA in Houston, Texas established as long-term National Singles site.

1984 ... First National Elite Training Camp held at the U.S. Olympic Training Center in Colorado Springs .... U.S.A. wins World Championships over 13 countries in Sacramento, California .... Ektelon introduces and test markets the oversize racquet frame .... Match rules changed from 21 points to 15 per game, with 11 point tiebreaker.

1985 ... Racquetball is recognized by the International Olympic Committee (IOC) .... World Junior Racquetball Championships added to Junior Orange Bowl in Miami, Florida.

1986 ... Mandatory eyeguard rule passed .... Twenty countries compete at III World Championships in Orlando, Florida .... U.S.A. ties with Canada to share World Cup .... Pan American Racquetball Confederation (PARC) formed .... AARA membership dues increase to $10.00 per year .... Van Dubolsky named Board President.

1987 ... U.S.A. wins Pan American Championships at U.S. Olympic Training Center in Colorado Springs .... First AARA National Leadership Conference held at the U.S. Olympic Training Center.

1988 ... U.S. National Team wins IV World Cup over 22 countries .... AARA televises its National Championships for the first time .... IARF drops the word "amateur" from its title and logo .... SGMA releases study setting the number of U.S. amateur players at 10 million.

1989 ... Racquetball granted full member status within USOC .... As 38th sport, racquetball makes premiere U.S. Olympic Festival appearance in Oklahoma City .... Random drug-testing of athletes instituted .... First World Seniors/Masters Championships held in Albuquerque, New Mexico .... First AARA instructional video produced .... AARA membership fees increase to $15.00 per year.

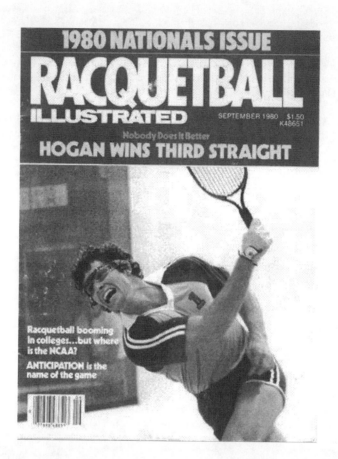

the nineties

1990 ... U.S.A. wins V World Cup in Caracas, Venezuela, over 28 countries .... AARA produces and telecasts five national championships on cable television .... Keith Calkins named Board President .... AARA resumes publication of *RACQUETBALL* Magazine after 12 years.

1991 ... AARA telecasts ten national events on cable sports channels .... U.S. Team Alumni Association is formed .... Junior Team USA takes its first international title at the Junior World Championships .... Racquetball placed on the schedule for the Pan American Games in 1995.

1992 ... U.S.A. wins VI World Cup in Montreal over 33 countries .... National Singles celebrates 10th year at the Downtown YMCA in Houston .

1993 ... AARA celebrates its 25th Silver Anniversary .... National offices move to new building in Colorado Springs.

1994 ... U.S.A. wins VII World Cup in San Luis Potosi over 27 countries .... New Skill Level National Championship introduced .... Competitive license fees increase to $20.00 per year ....IRF adopts "one serve" rule in international competition ... Van Dubolsky elected Board President.

1995 ... Racquetball makes its debut in the Pan American Games in Buenos Aires, Argentina – U.S. National Team "sweeps" medal count .... Instructor certification program renamed the American Professional Racquetball Organization [AmPRO].

1996 ... Promus Hotel Corporation U.S. OPEN Racquetball Championships debut in Memphis with pros and amateurs in a single event, played on a specially-constructed "made for TV" glass court .... First live coverage of racquetball finals broadcast at World Championships in Phoenix .... U.S. wins VIII World Cup team title .... Nationwide regional weekend established .... AARA debuts two websites on the internet ....

1997 ... The AARA changes its name to the United States Racquetball Association, adopts new logo .... National Singles and Doubles Championships celebrate 30th anniversaries .... USRA rule change allows oversized frames 22" in length.

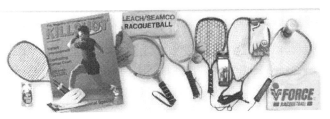

United States
Racquetball
Museum

1998 ... U.S. wins IX World Cup team title, over 32 opponent countries in Bolivia .... Otto Dietrich elected Board President .... Skill Level competition added to National Singles & Doubles Championships ....

1999 ... Racquetball in 13th Pan American Games in Winnipeg ... U.S. Team sweeps medal platforms ... All five major manufacturers take part in title sponsorship of national event series ... *RACQUETBALL* magazine named official publication of the professional tours ...

a new century

2000 ... Canada wins X World Cup team title for first time over the United States, and 30+ other countries, in San Luis Potosi, Mexico ... Ladies Professional Racquetball Association formed, under the guidance of USRA ... One-serve rule in Open divisions adopted after multi-year trial ...

(USA Racquetball from the USRA Historical Timeline)

813

Links

Facebook:

Racquet Ball
World Outdoor Racquetball (WOR)
International Racquetball Tour (IRT)
USA Racquetball

Fast paced racquetball with more athleticism. De La Rosa vs. Rocky Carson. (Freddy Ramirez)

US Open
Racquetball Museum US
The Racquetball Museum

Bo Keeley
Marty Hogan is the Greatest of All Time
Charlie Brumfield King of Racquetball
40BY20.com Racquetball & Paddleball Forum

Websites:

World Outdoor Racquetball (WOR)
International Racquetball Tour (IRT)
USA Racquetball
USA Racquetball Hall of Fame
US Racquetball Museum
Women's Professional Racquetball (WPRO)
Military Racquetball Federation (MRF)
International Racquetball Federation (IRF)
National Masters Racquetball Association (NMRA)
Ladies Pro Racquetball Association (LPRT)
Association of Fitness Studios (ASF)
IRT Network – Watch pro racquetball live
ProRacquetball.Net – Where the pros play live
Ask Otto – Team USA
Pro Racquetball Academy
Big 'D' Road Show
National Paddleball Association (NPA)
Pacific Paddleball Association (PPA)
The Court Company of construction
Boss Consulting IRT Historical Data
Wikipedia   Steven Bo Keeley
'He Found his Racquet' (*Sports Illustrated Vault*)
Legends Racquetball Tour (LRT)
Dailyspeculations.com
Fife Photography
The Art of Racquetball
The Chicagoist: Art Shay Vault

Contact:

bokeely@hotmail.com

About the Author

Steve Bo Keeley is the author of the best-selling *Complete Book of Racquetball, It's a Racquet, The Kill & Rekill Gang, Women Racquetball Pioneers, Racquetball's Best: Pros Speak from the Box,* and hundreds of articles from the sport's inception to the present. He was Charlie Brumfield's and Marty Hogan's primary nemesis throughout the Golden Era of the game in the 70s. He has won five National paddleball singles titles, one US National Racquetball runner-up, Canadian National Champ, three Pro titles, and was ranked 2nd or 3rd throughout the sport's heyday. He was the first equipment-sponsored player, the first apparel sponsored, the first club pro, ran the first clinics and camps, and was the sport's foremost early instructor. Keeley opened up Central and South America to racquetball, and the rest of his adventures in Wikipedia read like Indiana Jones.

A study of the Golden Era 70s racquetball equipment, pro Steve Bo Keeley focuses through lensless frames with a handwipe tucked in shorts, 3xl jock, and wired Bandido frame for balance at the Kings Court International Invitational. (US RB Museum)

Author Timeline

1968

- · Introduced to paddleball at Michigan State University
- · MSU Intramural singles champion in paddleball and handball.
- · Paddleball Intramural B doubles champ playing on crutches.

1969

- · Organize the first MSU Paddleball Club.
- · Intramural champion in paddleball singles and doubles.

1970

- · Intramural paddleball, handball and badminton champion.
- · Walk 45-miles from Jackson, MI to MSU for a Christmas tournament.
- · Develop the Look-the-Other-Way Stroke disguise of always looking the opposite direction of the target.

1971

- · First Paddleball National Singles title in Flint, MI. beating Lawrence, Brumfield & Finger.
- · Introduced to Racquetball by Charlie Brumfield as summer housemates in Lansing, MI.
- · Provided the first Ektelon Muehleisen Signature racquet by Bud Muehleisen.
- · Third-place in inaugural National Racquetball Singles Invitational in San Diego.
- · First unofficial sponsored racquetball player with $50/monthly under-the-table from Trend Way.
- · Second equipment sponsored player after Bud Muehleisen by Ektelon.
- · First official sponsored racquetball player by Bud Leach of Leach Industries.
- · First racquetball instructional article in history in *Ace Magazine* 'The Service and How to Return It' co- authored by Keeley and Brumfield.
- · Win 1st Gorham's Christmas Classic defeat Charlie Brumfield in final.

1972

- · 'Invent' the Z-ball and Around-the-World with Charlie Brumfield at MSU.
- · Create the 'Offensive Theory of Play, always taking the most attacking shot.
- · Develop the idea of 'Positional Shots' repeating the same shots form invisible X's on the court.
- · Over 100 written tutorials and 'Keeleyisms' as racquetball's first freelance author in *Racquetball*, *International Racquetball* and other magazines.
- · Semi-finals finish in the National Singles in Memphis, TN defeating two former champions.

1973

- Graduate from MSU veterinary school and move to San Diego to train for racquetball.
- Daily six hour regimen for seven years of bicycling, running, weights, practice and playing racquetball.
- Housemate and instructed to teach by Bud Muehleisen.
- The nation's first paid racquetball club pro at George Brown's Racquet Club in San Diego.
- Introduce the volley as a serve return.
- National Racquetball Singles Runner-up.
- Second paddleball National Singles title.
- National Paddleball Doubles Champion with Len Baldori.
- Win second ever pro racquetball event at NRC Long Beach ProAm def Charlie Brumfield in Final.
- Win NRC Oceanside ProAm defeat Steve Strandemo in Final
- 2nd place at the inaugural NRC Pro stop.
- Team with 15 year old Marty Hogan to defeat Charlie Brumfield and Carl Loveday in Open Doubles Final.
- Live with Charley Drake, head of Leach Industries, and young Marty Hogan in La Jolla.
- Use the 312-gram Bandido exclusively for a 10 year Leach career.

1974

- Racquetball becomes the national fitness craze with 3 million players.
- Visit Taiwan with Charley Drake and Ray Bayer to form Kunnan-Leach, which becomes Pro-Kennex
- Third paddleball National Singles title.
- Canadian Racquetball Singles Champion.
- California State Handball B singles champ, and second in B doubles.
- 3rd at San Diego National Singles tournament.
- First shoe contract in racquetball with Converse to set a trend in two different colored sneakers.
- Help organize and part-owner of National Racquetball Clinics (NRC).
- Hundreds of clinics, camps, grand openings and exhibitions across the country.
- Trade instruction for medical, dental, ophthalmic, accounting, drum lessons, company tours, 100 lbs. of granola, and 500 lbs. of Purina Dog Chow.
- Canadian National Doubles Champion with Bud Muehleisen
- Win NRC Livonia ProAm defeat Steve Serot in Final.

- Win NRC Oceanside ProAm defeat Steve Serot in Final.
- Use prize earnings to buy a '74 Chevy team van to drive to events throughout the west.
- #3 ranked player on 73-74 NRC Pro Tour behind Brumfield and Serot.

1975

- Bicycle 2400 miles from San Diego for 3rd place in the St. Louis National Singles Tournament.
- First and second place finishes in about 50 pro satellite racquet tournaments.
- First recipient of the 'Most Christian Player of the Year' award presented by Bobby Bible.
- Bicycle 1800 miles from Vancouver to San Diego for a racquetball tournament.
- Walk 40 miles from San Diego Gorham's Sports Center to Gorham's Oceanside to teach a lesson.
- Train non-stop 7-minute miles on Pacific Beach, Ca. working up to 2½ hours of beach running.
- Drive a '58 Caddie cross-country with Marty Hogan and the Michigan racquetball crew to San Diego.
- Lose Burlington Pro Final to Marty Hogan in his first ever pro win.
- Win IPRO Dallas Pro Stop defeat Steve Serot in Final first event with $2,500 1st Prize.
- #2 ranked player on 74-75 NRC Pro Tour behind Brumfield.

1976

- Fourth paddleball National Singles title.
- Win National Paddleball Doubles Tournament with Andy Homa.
- Enter tournaments righty, and lefty under an alias, to try to meet self in the finals.
- Hustle games left and right handed with racquet, paddle, book, bleach bottle, mini-racquet, or shoe.
- First player to defeat handball legend Paul Haber *mano* vs. racquet and *mano* vs. paddle.
- Defeat handball champs Gordy Pfier and Fred Lewis in hands vs. racquet exhibitions.
- Fashion the Physical vs. Mental error ratio.
- Run 26-mile San Diego Mission Bay Marathon wearing high-top Converse Chucks in 3:42.
- Author of the 'sport bible' *The Complete Book of Racquetball* (DBI Books, 200,000 sold).
- Peak money year total of $20,000 includes $5k prize money, equal in per diem, $3k endorsements, $6k book royalties, $10k clinics, and $1k betting.
- Win IPRO Tucson Pro Stop defeat Steve Serot in finals.
- #3 ranked player on 75-76 NRC Pro Tour behind Brumfield and Hogan.

1977

- Fifth paddleball National Singles title.
- Dallas NRC pro stop 1st place.
- NRC Houston Pro Stop defeat Serot, Strandemo and Hilecher final.
- 40-state tour by freight train, bus and thumb with clinics, tournaments and

exhibitions.
· Win a Chicago pro match after one eye after blindsided by a volley
· Vision experiments include blind spot, fovea, peripheral, blinders, B&W, and sight returns.
· Wear a clown suit and makeup on court to win the Davidson, MI satellite stop.
· Run without training the 26-mile Mission Bay Marathon in 3:49.
· Organize with Steve Serot the first San Diego racquetball camp in the country.
· Open the nation's premier one-month racquetball annual camp at Steamboat Springs.

1978
· 2500 hour study of ball spin.in a Michigan garage.
· Write and self-publish two racquetball books in one day: *It's a Racquet* and *The Kill & Rekill Gang* (Service Press).
· Win 1st Davidson ProAm.

1979
· *Sports Illustrated* November 19, 1979 feature 'Keeley Found his Racquet' by Tim Yost.
· Write and record the first audio-cassette course *Racquetball Lessons Made Easy*.
· Author of racquetball's only instructional flip-books *Strokeminder Racquetball 101, 102* and *103*.
· One week water fast to steel workouts.
· Win 2nd Davidson ProAm.

HOGAN.

1980
· The *SI* article triggers a year of *SI* Court Club openings.
· Beat Miss World Runner-up with a shoe in a *Sports Illustrated* exhibition.
· Partner chimpanzee in a coat-and-tie steals the show at Detroit Sportsmen's Press Club luncheon.
· Clinic tour and knowledge quest of America driving '74 van with a 7' stuffed rabbit riding shotgun.
· Organize with Rick Frey the first Salt Lake racquetball camp.
· *Women's Book of Racquetball* by Keeley & Shannon Wright (Contemporary Books).
· Win Voit Championship defeat Marty Hogan in Finals.

1981

- Win the last two minor racquet money tournaments played in at Detroit and Toledo.
- Quick lead in a Michigan Celebrity Decathlon loses in final rounds.
- Retire from professional racquetball having beaten every national champion to date.
- Experimental diet of 2000 calories/day to lose 25-lb during workouts.

1982

- *Racquetball Illustrated* cover (April) swinging a 4" miniature racquet.
- Executive Hobo Tours with racquetball players.
- Invent boxcar handball on moving freight until ball flies out the door.

1984

- First international racquetball clinic tour through Mexico, Central and South America seeds Latin racquetball.
- *National Racquetball Magazine* cover (August) on Machu Picchu with racquets and llamas.

1985

- Read the first of hundreds of books upside-down and writing in mirror-image to improve lefty sports.

1989

- Swap meet racquets mogul in Southern California.

1993

- Michigan Racquetball Hall of Fame

1995

- Sequester one year to write in Victor Niederhoffer's CT home with multi-courts to study ball spin.

2003

- Racquetball Legends Pro Tour consultant for one year.
- Organize and play left-handed in the first pro paddleball tour.
- Co-invent with Jim Spittle Hybrid Racquetball using a racquet and paddleball.
- Teach History of Racquetball Clinic at USA Racquetball National Summit, Colorado Springs.
- Meet look-alike Bo Champagne on tour in two-color Chucks.
- *Tips from Dr. K* column published.
- Begin the first *History of Racquetball* book.

- Donate the NRC racquetball photo archives to the US Racquetball Museum.
- Spirit of Racquetball Award for the 20th century.
- Decline nomination for the national Racquetball Hall of Fame.

2004

- Return to Sand Valley, Ca. to write sport and travel articles in a buried trailer.

2007

- Earl Riskey Trophy for contributions to paddleball.

2003- 2015

- Refuse induction into Racquetball Hall of Fame annually since 2003.

2012

- 30th Anniversary racquetball clinic in Panama City.

2913

- *Racquetball Pioneer Women* (Free Man Publisher)
- Facebook founder and webmaster of RacquetballMuesum US.
- Giving virtual/online racquetball and paddleball lessons/coaching via Facebook and email.
- *Charlie Brumfield: King of Racquetball* (Free Man Publisher)
- History of Racquetball Clinic with Marty Hogan in Davie, Florida to benefit JCC.

2015

- *Advanced Racquetball* (Service Press)
- *Bill Schultz: Ringmaster of Sport* (Service Press)
- *Racquetball's Best: Pros Speak from the Box* (Service Press)

The most popular Leach Racquets catalog cover in history circa 1973.

Other Books

Complete Book of Racquetball (1976, DBI Books)

Racquetball Made Easy (1977, Service Press)

It's a Racquet (1978, Service Press)

The Kill & Rekill Gang (1978, Service Press)

Racquetball Flipbook Series (1979, Strokeminder)

The Women's Book of Racquetball (1980, Contemporary Books)

Hobo Training Manual (1986)

Keeley's Kures (2011, Free Man Pub)

Executive Hobo: Riding the American Dream (2011, Free Man Pub)

Charlie Brumfield: King of Racquetball (2013, Free Man Pub)

Women Racquetball Pioneers (2013, Free Man Pub)

Basic English One Page (2013, Virtual Bookworm)

The Longest Walk (Third Edition, 2013, Free Man Pub)

The Longest Walk Companion (2013, Free Man Pub)

Stories from Iquitos (2014, Service Press)

Advanced Racquetball (2015, Service Press)

Greatest Photos Around the World (2014, Service Press)

Chess and Sport (2014, Service Press)

Elvis' Humor: Girls, Guns & Guitars (2015, Service Press)

Bill Schultz: Ringmaster of Sport (2015, Service Press)

Racquetball's Best: Pros Speak from the Box (2015, Service Press)

Book of Bo: Gems of My Life, Vol. 1 and 2 (2015, Service Press)

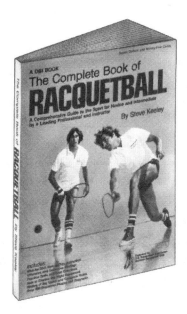

Forty Years Later the sequel....